BaT 29.95

W9-CKH-203

The Frontier Experience

Z
1251
W5
F76
1984

The Frontier Experience

A Reader's Guide to the Life and Literature of the American West

Edited by

Jon Tuska and Vicki Piekarski

with
Paul J. Blanding

McFarland & Company, Inc., Publishers
Jefferson, North Carolina, and London

Library of Congress Cataloging in Publication Data

Main entry under title:

The Frontier experience.

Includes indexes.
1. West (U.S.) — History — Bibliography.
2. West (U.S.) — History — Fiction — Bibliography.
3. West (U.S.) — History — Film catalogs.
4. Frontier and pioneer life — West (U.S.) — Bibliography.
5. Frontier and pioneer life — West (U.S.) — Fiction — Bibliography.
6. Frontier and pioneer life — West (U.S.) — Film catalogs.
I. Tuska, Jon. II. Piekarski, Vicki. III. Blanding, Paul J.
Z1251.W5F76 1984 [F591]   016.978   84-42611

ISBN 0-89950-118-4

© 1984 Jon Tuska, Vicki Piekarski, Paul J. Blanding
All rights reserved

Printed in the United States of America
McFarland Box 611 Jefferson NC 28640

Dedicated to J. Frank Dobie,
the "Cowboy Professor"

Table of Contents

Table of Contents

General Introduction

by Jon Tuska

From fruitful trees I gather
withered leaves
And glean the broken ears
with miser's hands.
—Ralegh

The initial impetus behind *The Frontier Experience: A Reader's Guide to the Life and Literature of the American West* grew out of our frustration at the lack of any reliable and comprehensive guide to the myriad nonfiction books on various aspects of the American West. Of course, there is J. Frank Dobie's *Guide to Life and Literature of the Southwest* (Southern Methodist University Press, 1952), but the scope of this book is very limited as to region, the annotations very brief and not uniformly enlightening, and vast areas such as the *"Literature"* in the title are dealt with too cursorily.

What, instead, Vicki Piekarski and I wanted to do was to put together a volume that would focus on the entire American frontier experience but with special emphasis on the American West; that would provide some discussion of such basic concepts as that of frontier and section; that would incorporate, albeit in a limited way, a literary history of the growth and development of Western American fiction while providing the reader with the necessary theoretical and critical sensitivity to understand the distinct varieties of narrative structures in the genre; that would address briefly the realm of Western films; and that would deal with a number of areas we feel are vital to the study of the American frontier experience, from the roles of women and the character of pioneer life to the U.S. Cavalry, frontier gunmen, Mexican-Americans, and the character of range life.

In writing the annotations for *The Frontier Experience*, Vicki and I have tried, as have the other contributors, to evaluate the books cited; yet, when there are a great many errors, or a questionable point of view, space is such that we have usually limited our critique to one or two illustrations. As a general rule we have not assumed that a secondary source is accurate about a primary source and, accordingly, in virtually every case we sought to make ourselves familiar with the primary source.

Because this is a book intended only as a reader's guide and because it is already very long, it has not been possible for me to append to the discussion of general history texts any theoretical discussion about the idea of history and the rules for writing it. However, since what is termed "historical reality" is used as the standard for evaluation of Western fiction and films and because the reader may be interested in pursuing this aspect of the subject, I should like to mention that I have titled the first study in my forthcoming book, *Four Studies in Western Fiction*, to be published by McFarland & Company, Inc., "The Concept of Historical Reality and Its Use as a Standard for Evaluation." In the course of this study I address the questions of the role of logic in historical inquiry, and of ethics, define what I regard as the basic concept of historical reality, and attempt to demonstrate how it must be applied to the study of narrative structures derived from the events of Western American history.

What can reasonably be expected from *The Frontier Experience* is that it will assist and guide a general reader through the vicissitudes of studying the American frontier and the Westward expansion. As was St. Joseph, Missouri, in the middle of the last century, this book is a "jumping off" spot, whence the reader can begin his own overland journey into the American past. While we have not intended *The Frontier Experience* to be read from beginning to end, it certainly can be. However, in subtitling it *A Reader's Guide*, we have designed it to be just that, and not a comprehensive bibliography, much less a chronological and historical bibliography. We have tried to confine ourselves to books which will be useful and, in a few cases, to those which may have been influential or popular but which are notwithstanding misleading, erroneous, or dubious. Because I firmly believe that historical reality has to be the basis on which all fictions about the American West are to be evaluated, we have appended to those sections where it has proven appropriate lists of relevant films and fiction that may be combined, or contrasted, with the study of history. Surely, the study of the actual history will open new dimensions in all of these fictional efforts and provide a challenging new perspective.

"I" and "my" occur often in these pages. The author is only being honest enough to admit that in history there is no *final* truth, only approximations to it, and that in taste there is only opinion; and that neither is ever free from subjectivity. Yet, for all this, should a reader feel that we have neglected one or another book, or even take exception with something that has been written, he or she should not hesitate for a moment to write to us in care of the publisher. We have tried to answer the questions that a reader might have regarding a particular book or a specific area, to suggest those books we feel are important or essential, and to take to task those books which we feel have somehow failed to accomplish what they set out to do. The world of the study of the American West is a volatile one and accounts for a substantial publishing activity in any given year and, therefore, it is our intention to revise periodically the contents of this book. In this, ideally, the dialogue we establish with its readers will prove beneficial.

Each book, film, and essay cited in the text of a section or subsection is dated. If a book was first published prior to the twentieth century, the year of publication only is given; if a book was published in this century, the publisher and year of publication are given, e.g., *The Virginian* (Macmillan, 1902). If the edition of a book cited is one published subsequently to the first edition, regardless of whether the book was first published in the previous century or this one, the original year of publication is followed by the publisher and date of the reissue, e.g., *The Vigilantes of Montana* (1866; University of Oklahoma Press, 1953). If the referent should be a film, the release year and the releasing company (which in most, but not in all, cases is the same as the producing company) are given, e.g., *The Virginian* (Paramount, 1929). If the referent is an essay not necessarily collected into a book, the year of first periodical publication is given in parentheses after the title of the essay. In the majority of cases we have avoided citing uncollected essays, since usually essays of merit have been gathered together for subsequent book publication. The same principle applies to short stories.

Generally only one word identifications are used for trade publishers, e.g., Harper's rather than Harper & Bros. or Harper & Row. The same practice is followed regarding film releasing companies, e.g., Warner's rather than Warner Bros. or Warner/Seven Arts. In the bibliographic checklist subsections, only nonfiction books are noted as being out of print, although we have tried, wherever possible, to refer a reader to a book that is in print. All references to fiction are to first editions unless a novel or story collection has been reissued by a university press or similar publisher, where it is likely to be kept in print for a long time. A film or book once dated in a subsection is not dated again if it is referred to again in that subsection and may not be dated again in another subsection of that same subject area, unless the date is of special significance.

We have divided this book into two major divisions, reflected in its subtitle, **The Life** and **The Literature.** "The Life," in turn, contains a general section on "Western History" and then is subdivided into "Part One: The People" and "Part Two: The Land." One section in "Part One: The People," namely "Native Americans," has been subjected to a condensation consistent with our present purpose. Culture areas which are traditionally kept separate have been combined: Northeastern with Southeastern, Arctic with sub-Arctic, Plateau with Pacific Northwest, and Great Basin with Southwest, so as to yield six, rather than ten, basic culture areas.

It probably goes without saying that almost any section in this book could be expanded to the point where by itself it could fill a volume of this size. However, because of the insistently general nature of this guide, it should be possible for an interested reader who knows nothing about a subject to begin reading the recommended books and emerge with a solid background of information, henceforth able to find his or her own way. Vicki and I live in Oregon and I am reminded that more than a century and a half ago, when the Oregon Territory was first being organized, the people came together to select a motto fitting for the new country in which they lived. They chose: *Alis Volat Propriis*. It is old Latin and it means: "Another Flies His Own Way." In that spirit, make use of *The Frontier Experience*.

The Life

Historia scribitur ad narrandum non ad probandum
[History is written for the purpose of narration and
not in order to give proof] — Quintilian.

Western History

by Jon Tuska

I

In James Warner Bellah's novel, *A Thunder of Drums* (Bantam, 1961), First Lieutenant Curtis McQuade finds himself transferred to Fort Canby in Arizona. The first night, during bachelor officer's mess, McQuade sees a fellow lieutenant named Petersborough reading the third volume of Gibbon's history. "'The history of the Roman Empire is the most pertinent reading an American of today can indulge himself in.'" Petersborough tells McQuade. "'It sets forth all the mistakes we will fall heir to ourselves in making this country ours.'"

I do not quite know what to think of this statement. The third volume of *The Decline and Fall of the Roman Empire* is concerned with the Middle Ages; and even the first volume begins with the Roman Empire already in the period of the Antonines. For the way the history being made on the frontier of the American West was conceived in the Nineteenth century, I would have thought that Lieutenant Petersborough would have been reading Julius Caesar's war commentaries. *"Veni, vidi, vici"* [I have come, I have seen, I have conquered] Caesar said after his victory at Zela in Asia Minor against Pharnaces. Well might the Anglo-Americans have said: *venimus, vidimus, vicimus* [we have come, we have seen, we have conquered].

"Yet, hear me, people," Tatanka Yotanka [Sitting Bull] said at a

3

Powder River council in 1875, "we have now to deal with another race — small and feeble when our fathers first met them but now great and overbearing. Strangely enough they have a mind to till the soil and the love of possession is a disease with them. These people have made many rules that the rich may break but the poor may not. They take tithes from the poor and weak to support the rich who rule. They claim this mother of ours, the earth, for their own and fence their neighbors away; they deface her with their buildings and their refuse. That nation is as a spring freshet that overruns its banks and destroys all who are in its path. We cannot dwell side by side. Only seven years ago we made a treaty by which we were assured that the buffalo country should be left to us forever. Now they threaten to take that away from us. My brothers, shall we submit or shall we say to them: 'First kill me before you take possession of my Fatherland....'"

"*Gallia est omnes divisa in partes tres...*" [Gaul is divided into three parts...] Caesar began *De Bello Gallico*, his memoir of the conquest of Gaul which, for centuries, was required reading for adolescents in the Western world — and was read in most American schools until after World War II when the "great forgetting" began, when grammar and logic and foreign languages and history and classical literature could no longer be taught because they were too difficult for American students to learn, when mathematics had to be translated into the "new math" so that tables need not be memorized and pocket calculators solved the necessity of having to "work" square and cube roots. "*Gallia est omnes divisa in partes tres...*" — but *who* divided Gaul so completely into three parts? Was it the Gauls? No, it was the Romans.

Frederick Jackson Turner, the historian whose "frontier thesis" so revolutionized the perspectives in the way American history was written and taught, wrote in "The Significance of History" (1891), citing E.A. Freeman, an historian he greatly admired, "Freeman's statement that into Rome flowed all the ancient world and out of Rome came the modern world is as true as it is impressive. In a strict sense imperial Rome never died. ...Even here in young America old Rome still lives. When the inaugural procession passes toward the Senate chamber, and the president's address outlines the policy he proposes to pursue, there is Rome!"

In "The Significance of the Frontier" (1893), the essay in which Turner first put forth his view of the American frontier, he declared that "this perennial rebirth, this fluidity of American life, this expansion Westward with its new opportunities, its continuous touch with the simplicity of primitive society, furnish the forces dominating American character. The true point of view in the history of this nation is not the Atlantic coast, it is the Great West. ...In this advance, the frontier is the outer edge of the wave — the meeting point between savagery and civilization." At this "meeting point" *who* was savage, who civilized?

Richard Drinnon answered that question in his book, *Facing West: The Metaphysics of Indian-Hating and Empire-Building* (New American Library, 1980). "In truth, Turner's 'meeting point between savagery and civilization' ... was the supreme expression by an historian of all the other expressions before and since by novelists, poets, playwrights, pulp writers, painters, sculptors, and film directors. It separated the cowboys from the Indians by making the latter easily recognizable dark targets, especially if they had war paint on to boot. It unmistakably shaped national patterns of violence by establishing *whom* one could kill under propitious circumstances and thereby represented a prime source of the American way of inflicting death."

To coin a term, for me a "popular culture fadist" is an academic who tries to elevate popular culture to the status of a subject (or subjects) worthy of serious intellectual attention. One of the leaders in the popular culture movement is John G. Cawelti who in his book *The Six-Gun Mystique* (Bowling Green University Popular Press, 1975) had this to say about fiction and films set in the American West. "The Western story is set at a certain moment in the development of American civilization, namely at that point when savagery and lawlessness are in decline before the advancing wave of law and order, but are still strong enough to pose a local and momentarily significant challenge. *In the actual history of the West, this moment was probably a relatively brief one in any particular area.*" I have italicized this last sentence because it only points up, and rather neatly, how thoroughly Turner's racist ideology came to be posited as an historical fact! Cawelti's whole approach to Western fiction and Western films was based on this perspective, what he called the "epic moment."

More bluntly, and without resorting to Cawelti's brand of what in *1984* (Harcourt, Brace, 1949) George Orwell termed "newspeak," this "epic moment" is merely occasion for "Two Minutes Hate." In *Green Berets* (Crown, 1965) Robin Moore described the reaction of a South Vietnamese strike force during the showing of a Western at Nam Luong. It did not matter that the film was projected against the side of a building and probably was a cinemascope print so that the figures appeared elongated. "...The strikers loved the action and identified themselves with it. When the Indians appeared the strikers screamed '*VC*,' and when the soldiers or cowboys came to the rescue the Nam Luong irregulars vied with each other in shouting out the number of their own strike-force companies."

"We must act with vindictive earnestness against the Sioux, even to their extermination, men, women, and children," General Sherman wrote to U.S. Grant after the Fetterman massacre in 1866. "Nothing else will reach the root of the case." One of the most persistent *idées fixes* in the foreign policy of the United States was born as a result of the Indian wars, the "domino" theory. To justify General Sherman's genocidal call to arms, Anglo-American war propaganda had to project the genocidal impulse into the Native Americans. In his memoir *Three Years Among the Comanches* (1859; University of Oklahoma Press, 1957) Nelson Lee charged, supposedly as a result of his Indian captivity, that all the Indians were about "to enter into an alliance with the view of waging an exterminating and implacable war upon every train of emigrants or other party moving towards California, Oregon, the Great Salt Lake, or other points in either of those directions." Lee's book is a fantasy and it is analyzed as such in the section on first-hand accounts below; but the most interesting aspect of its reissue by the University of Oklahoma Press is the Introduction Walter Prescott Webb wrote for it, in which he accepted the fantasy as authentic and termed it "invaluable." This was the same Walter Prescott Webb who wrote *The Great Plains* (Ginn, 1931), *The Texas Rangers* (Houghton Mifflin, 1935), and *The Great Frontier* (Houghton Mifflin, 1952).

"Webb, like Turner, never clearly or precisely explained how the individual forces which comprised American history came together...," Jerome O. Steffen wrote about Webb's thesis in *The Great Frontier* in his *Comparative Frontiers: A Proposal for Studying the American West* (University of Oklahoma Press, 1980); "but like Turner, Webb, too, was instinctively getting at some very important matters. He sensed that, in addition to specific frontier experiences, America was part of an international frontier process." In his Foreword to *The Great Frontier*, Webb felt two terms in particular needed to be defined. "The Great Frontier is one and the Metropolis is the other. The first term is applied to all the new lands discovered at the opening of the Sixteenth century; the second refers to the community of Western Europe without regard to the community of Western Europe, without regard to political divisions. The Great Frontier and the Metropolis, when used in reference to the whole frontier and the whole of Europe, are capitalized, but the unmodified frontier as adjective or noun is not."

Webb's perspective, in short, toward the whole world other than Europe was no different in spirit than Julius Caesar's perspective toward Gaul. The main drawback of such a perspective is that it encourages the historian to be excessively one-sided. A reader is well advised, therefore, in approaching any history of the American West, or any aspect of that history, to inquire first: what is the historian's point of view?

The American historian, John Carl Parish, was the first, to my knowledge, in criticizing Turner's rather simplistic generality about the American frontier to suggest, instead, that there were multiple frontiers. This was in 1926 and, since then, a number of other historians, including Jerome O. Steffen cited above, have put forward some variation of this idea. I am no exception.

I have found in my own reading about the history of the American West that it is most helpful to break down perspectives on that history into eight distinct frontiers. I make mention of them here because they might prove to be equally useful to the reader. They are The Natural Frontier, The Fur-Trading Frontier, The Military Frontier, The Agricultural Frontier, The Mining Frontier, The Ranching Frontier, The Technological Frontier, and The Apocryphal Frontier.

To take The Natural Frontier first, this might be perceived as identical to what Webb termed the "unmodified frontier," except for the fact that, insofar as Native Americans occupied the American frontier prior to the arrival of the Europeans, I am not completely certain that "unmodified" is the proper adjective. For me, The Natural Frontier is the perspective toward Nature and man's relationship with Nature true, albeit with many subtle variations, of Native Americans. I choose to discuss this frontier perspective first not only because, chronologically, it was first, but also because I feel it needs to be engaged first by anyone who wishes to read about the American frontier. From this point of view, the New World is not new, and was not new; it was not a wilderness. Above all, it was *not* savage. There are simply too many ethical questions, from slavery, the Inquisition, and the rights of the state in preference to the individual to class society, concentration camps, and the arms race to term the invading technological culture as more "civilized" or "superior" to the culture of Native Americans. Much of what I object to in the way the history of the American West has been written has to do with the failure of many historians to acknowledge the existence and significance of Native American cultures.

Once The Natural Frontier has been conceived and defined, it must be kept firmly in mind when dealing with any of the remaining seven frontier perspectives since they are all, save possibly The Apocryphal Frontier, characterized by an *attack* on The Natural Frontier. Now, in each case, there is a rationale behind the attack. This is not the place to argue the justification for these various rationales. That is for the individual historian. In dealing with The Fur-Trading Frontier, for example, great wealth was accumulated by systematically exploiting and, in many cases, exhausting the supply of fur-bearing animals. It can be argued, when it comes to the buffalo, that without their removal The Agricultural Frontier, i.e., farming, would not have been possible, nor would The Ranching Frontier, i.e., substituting cattle for buffalo as a source of meat for human consumption, nor The Technological Frontier, from the telegraph and the railroad through to modern industrial settlements. The Mining Frontier, also, played a role in the pattern of settlement of The Natural Frontier; it made a few men rich and created a great many rich corporations; while today, with strip-mining, The Mining Frontier allied with The Technological Frontier threatens to destroy the last vestiges of life on those areas where such mining is done. The Military Frontier is concerned with the warfare between the invaders' armies and those who sought to defend The Natural Frontier. The impulse for expansion did not stop, of course, at the edge of the Pacific Ocean but, allied with The Technological Frontier, became the force behind world-wide economic "development" and expansion of American industry and commerce. I emphasize The Natural Frontier in all of this because too often in the past it has been overlooked when the histories of these various other frontiers have been written; and it is especially poignant now during the time of the great forgetting because the combination of government and capital remain implacable enemies of The Natural Frontier and I, for one, remain convinced that before any allegiance to government — any government — or to the profit motive — personal profit — comes our allegiance to the natural order. I realize that there are many who would argue that *Homo sapiens* are not a part of Nature and that it is their destiny to dominate and control Nature. For me, such arrogance is a dangerous delusion.

"*Dulce et decorum est pro patria mori*" [sweet and delightful is it to die for your country] Horace has been quoted over twenty centuries; it is, I believe, far better to live for the betterment of your species and of all species. In "The Problem of the West" (1896) Turner declared that "the West, at bottom, is a form of society, rather than an area." In the minds of those who believe in the notion of one-settlement culture this was a dangerous, even a lethal, idea. But there is no question, however inadequate Turner may have been as a spokesperson, that The Natural Frontier in what the Europeans regarded as the New World gave a profound incentive to the idea that the individual *has the right* to follow his own vision, a belief so completely at odds with the contrary impulse toward totalitarianism.

In his Introduction to the first volume of his *Histoire des Institutions Politiques de l'Ancienne France [History of Political Institutions of Ancient France]* (1875) Fustel de Coulanges reflected on how he "had often heard the liberty of ancient cities talked of, and I saw that the Athenian citizen, for instance, was neither master of his fortune which he had to be ready to sacrifice unconditionally as soon as the lot had designated him to supply a ship by himself or support a choir in the theatre, nor of his body, since he owed military service to the state for thirty-three years; nor of his speech or beliefs, since he could at any moment be arraigned in court on the charge of disloyalty to the state; nor of his conscience, for he had to believe in and worship the deities of the state and he was not allowed to think that there was only one God. And I began to wonder where was that liberty I had heard spoken of so often." It is only now, as the Twentieth century draws to a close, that in spite of the great forgetting there are some historians who are addressing themselves to the contributions of The Natural Frontier to all existing American institutions. In the stress The Natural Frontier places on the importance of the individual and on the relationship the individual has with the natural order — a natural order differently conceived than that of the Europeans — is embodied a new image of the human being. To return to Fustel de Coulanges' Introduction, "I thought it obvious that the opinion that man forms of human nature must in every society have a great influence on the manner in which he lives and governs himself."

Chief Joseph of the Nez Percé in his address in Washington, D.C., on 14 January 1879 said: "We ask to be recognized as men. We ask that the same law shall work alike on all men. If the Indian breaks the law, punish him by the law. If the white man breaks the law, punish him also. Let me be a free man — free to travel, free to stop, free to work, free to trade where I choose, free to choose my own teachers, free to follow the religion of my fathers, free to think and talk and act for myself — and I will obey every law, or submit to the penalty." I am not about to say that Joseph's appeal has been fulfilled, but there is some satisfaction to be drawn from the fact that it is still an ideal among Americans and, beyond this, that it implies an opinion of human nature that I should not want to see vanish from the world.

There have been pernicious ideas incorporated into traditional views of the meaning of the American frontier. Foremost among them is the European notion of empire which has no place set alongside Chief Joseph's vision of human nature. The imperialism of political pioneering early allied itself with spiritual pioneering, the imposition on Native Americans of Christianity and its white god. Yet the Native American, from the beginning, argued on behalf of religious tolerance and, fortunately for us all, because many Europeans came here to escape religious persecution in Europe, this became part of the American Constitution. This is not to say that religious freedom, as every other form of freedom, is not being perpetually threatened, only that it may be hoped that the impulse to preserve it will prove the stronger.

In retrograde motion to those who would find individual liberty a product of the frontier experience, there are those, such as Harold P. Simonson in *The Closed Frontier: Studies in American Literary Tragedy* (Holt, Rinehart, 1970), who assert that, in light of the Turner thesis, and Turner's declaration in 1893 that the frontier was closed, that "in the sense of tragedy, this is what it means to 'know thyself.' It is a self-sought knowledge that one's existence has meaning only within the symbolic walls of a closed frontier." Simonson, it seems to me, was only grafting onto his reading of Turner the ideas rampant in post-war European Existentialism. It is possible to accept as true Ray Allen Billington's conclusion in *America's Frontier Heritage* (1963; University of New Mexico Press, 1974) that the legend of frontier individualism was based more on what people wanted to be true than on what was true and yet not despair entirely in the power of that desire. Indeed, in the aggregate, the American frontier experience may well have emphasized equally the need for social cooperation as well as the right to individual liberty and on that balance our national destiny might be said to depend.

A second pernicious idea is the tendency to conform to the dictates of a one-settlement culture, a tendency that is intolerant of social deviation and which would impose the values of that one-settlement culture on other societies, not only on the North American continent but all over the world. When the period of what I have called the great forgetting was just beginning, Thomas Mann was conducting classes at Princeton University. "*Lieber Gott*," he wrote to Karl Kerényi in a letter contained in the collection of their correspondence published as *Gespräch in Briefen* [*Conversation in Letters*] (Zürich, 1960), "*meine* Faust-lectures *waren recht harmloser Art, für* boys *bestimmt, und höchstens war das 'inkommensurable' Werk mit leidlich frischem Auge gesehen, was man das Amerikanische daran nennen kann*" [Dear God, my Faust-lectures were truly harmless material, intended for boys, and in the extreme the 'incommensurable' work was regarded with passably naive eyes — what one might call the American point of view]. In bitter irony Mann parodied in his short novel, *Die Betrogene [The Deceived Woman]* (Fischer Verlag, 1953), the American posture toward Europe, so cocksure, so "innocent," so optimistic, and so seductively exploitive. The United States, in the iconography of this fiction, would impose the great forgetting onto Europe, to simplify, to reduce, to commercialize, to materialize Europe into the one-settlement culture of an American suburb. Secretary of State John Hay commented on his Open Door policy toward China in 1903 that "we have done the Chinks a great service which they don't seem inclined to recognize." During the period of which Mann wrote, the salvation being offered to Europe under another plan was named not by, but for, a Secretary of State — the Marshall Plan.

In an essay, "Recent Trends and New Directions in Native American History," included in *The American West: New Perspectives, New Dimensions* (University of Oklahoma Press, 1979), edited by Jerome O. Steffen, Reginald Horsman observed that "much of the best work by [American] historians is on the shaping of white attitudes and policies toward the Indians. Here the [American] historian is on familiar ground." But he also remarked that "the parochial assumptions of white progress and Indian savagery inherent in the whole Turner tradition are now no longer the norm." This is because there is an increasing awareness of what I call The Natural Frontier. It is to be hoped that in the future this awareness of cultural divergence in narrating the history of the American frontier experience will also come to influence the way in which historians view the inter-relationship between the United States and other societies and peoples. Ethnocentricity is still too commonplace and, in reading or writing history, one must ever be on guard.

I have found it convenient to divide historians into four distinct categories. These categories are not mutually exclusive; there is much overlap; but the distinctions in themselves are useful. The most prevalent of the four categories is that of the *rerum scriptor*, the historian who collects facts and publishes brief essays now and then containing assemblages of these facts. Little or no effort is made to interpret these data. That province is usually reserved for the *colligator*, the historian who organizes groups of facts collected from the assemblages prepared by the *rerum scriptores*. For example, a *rerum scriptor* might compile data of frontier populations and publish the results. The *colligator* would write an essay comparing the findings of a number of studies of frontier populations and make tentative surmises as to possible correlations and meanings of these figures.

The *historicus contemplativus* is one who devises broad, generalized theories, even before he has accumulated any facts or investigated fully the research done by others. Frederick Jackson Turner was definitely an *historicus contemplativus*. He published very little, but he did devise a number of generalities. One of them was the frontier thesis; another was his concept of the section. For Turner in his essay, "Sections and Nation" (1922), "the various sections of which this country is composed are thus seen as potential nations. We are led to wonder why the United States did not in fact become another Europe, by what processes we retain our national unity. The imagination stirs at the possibilities of the future, when these sections shall be fully matured and populated to the extent of the nations of the Old World. We must also remember that each of the sections of this continental nation — New England, the Middle States, the Southeast, the Southwest, the Middle West, the Great Plains, the Mountain States, the

Pacific Coast — has its own special geographical qualities, its own resources and economic capacities, and its own rival interests, partly determined in the days when the geological foundations were laid down."

Turner, having devised this concept, then left it for the *rerum scriptor* and the *colligator* to research its significance, to refine the concept into a subsidiary number of concepts, and to come up with a few hesitant theories. However, it is up to the *historicus magnus* — and there have been few enough of them — to review all of these rampant theories in terms of the factual evidence and arrive as a result of this process at a series of general interpretations. Of course, there are historians who would have us believe that they are among the *historici magni*, but who give us a thesis instead of multiple interpretations. This group are at best a perversion of the bonafide *historicus magnus*. They violate Quintilian's principle that history is to narrate and not to prove. The *historicus magnus* narrates events, but he does so from a position of multiple perspectives which would make monocausationist thinking prohibitive and ethnocentricity impossible.

All too many people approach history the way students in the United States are encouraged to approach their teachers: tell us what to think and keep the focus directly on what it is we are to think; above all, do not confuse us with conflicting evidence or unsettling perspectives. Yet to do these things, to encourage the reader to see levels of meanings and alternate perspectives is precisely the function of the *historicus magnus*. As Socrates in philosophy, the *historicus magnus* dealing with history embraces a number of seemingly viable interpretations because history in terms of its historical constructions can only approximate a past reality.

I have left to last The Apocryphal Frontier. The sections devoted to Western fiction and Western films concern themselves with this "frontier." Because of the historical content in these artifacts, they, too, frequently embody historical interpretations. Historians have only recently become aware of this dimension of human activity and, as yet, the study of it remains in its infancy as a discipline. As in the dark world of Orwell's *1984*, The Apocryphal Frontier has become in our time a strong ally of the great forgetting. However, it is entirely possible that if historians become increasingly vigilant in their aspirations and achievements toward the goal of the *historicus magnus*, they will be of invaluable assistance to those among us who still want very much to remember and to know.

II

A Chronology

by Vicki Piekarski

1800 — Census of 1800 shows the U.S. population to be 5,300,000.

1801 — Thomas Jefferson is elected President.

1803 — The Louisiana Purchase doubles the territory of the United States at a cost of $11,250,000.

— Lewis and Clark expedition head West and winter near St. Louis, Missouri.

1804 — Lewis and Clark expedition crew start up the Missouri River.

1805 — Zebulon Pike is ordered to lead an expedition to explore the headwaters of the Mississippi River.

— Lewis and Clark sight the Pacific Ocean, "the object of all our labours, the reward of all our anxieties."

1806 — Lewis and Clark expedition begin return trip and arrive in St. Louis.

— Zebulon Pike heads a second expedition to explore the country between the Arkansas and Red Rivers.

1808 — John Jacob Astor organizes the American Fur Company.

1809 — Manuel Lisa and associates organize the St. Louis Missouri Fur Company.

1810 — John Jacob Astor forms the Pacific Fur Company, a subsidiary company to take charge of the Columbia River post.

1811 — Astoria is founded by Anglo-Americans.

1812 — War of 1812 with Great Britain.

1813 — Astoria is sold to the British North West Company.

1817 — Major Stephen H. Long is sent to the upper Mississippi by the Topographical Corps of the Army for exploration purposes.

1818 — Treaty of Joint Occupation is signed which allows both British and American nationals freely to enter Oregon.

1819 — Major Stephen Long and Colonel Henry Atkinson begin Yellowstone expedition using steamboats.

— Adams-Onis Treaty with Spain which cedes Florida to the United States and establishes the Western boundary of the Louisiana Purchase.

1820 — Census of 1820 shows the U.S. population to be 9,600,000.

— Death of frontiersman, Daniel Boone.

— Moses Austin visits Texas and discusses with the governor his wish to settle three hundred colonists.

1821 — Death of Moses Austin.

— Hudson's Bay Company and North West Company merge.

— Independent Republic of Mexico established under Agustín de Iturbide.

— William Becknell (Father of the Santa Fe Trail) organizes a trading expedition to Santa Fe, New Mexico.

— Stephen Austin, son of Moses, settles first group of colonists in Texas.

— Missouri enters the Union.

1822 — Stephen Austin travels to Mexico City to have his land grant confirmed.

— William Becknell organizes a second expedition to Santa Fe, New Mexico, including the use of three wagons.

— Lexington and Liberty, Missouri, founded.

— Reversing traditional Spanish policy, Mexico throws open the door of New Mexico to American trade.

— Major Andrew Henry and General William R. Ashley organize what would become the Rocky Mountain Fur Company.

1823 — Mexican government confirms land grant to Stephen Austin to settle three hundred colonists in Texas.

— Jedediah Strong Smith and a small party are the first to cross the Rocky Mountains in a Westerly direction through South Pass.

— James Fenimore Cooper's *The Pioneers* is published.

1824 — Fort Vancouver is founded by Hudson's Bay Company.

— Mexican Congress enacts the National Colonization Law.

1825 — William Henry Ashley devises the "rendezvous" system.

— A regular trade pattern is fairly well established with Santa Fe.

— President James Monroe requests Congress to set aside Oklahoma as permanent Indian territory.

1826 — Jedediah Strong Smith leads the first American party to California overland through the Southwest.

— J. Stephen Abbot builds the first Concord wagon.

— James Fenimore Copper's *The Last of the Mohicans* is published.

— John James Audubon's *Birds of America* is published.

1827 — Independence, Missouri, is founded.

— Treaty of Joint Occupation in Oregon renewed indefinitely.

— John Jacob Astor buys out the Columbia Fur Company.

— James Fenimore Cooper's *The Prairie* is published.

1829 — Led by Antonio Armijo, thirty-one men pioneer the Old Spanish Trail from Santa Fe to Los Angeles.

— Fort Union is established at the mouth of the Yellowstone by the American Fur Company.

— Andrew Jackson is elected president.

1830 — *Book of Mormon* is published.

— Indian Removal Act is adopted by the U.S. Congress.

— Mexican Congress passes the Colonization Act.

— Jim Bridger, Thomas Fitzpatrick, Jedediah Strong Smith, *et al.*, buy out interest in the Rocky Mountain Fur Company.

1831 — Led by Joseph Smith, the Mormons begin their Westward trek from New York.

— Josiah Gregg starts with a caravan to Santa Fe.

1832 — Black Hawk War.

— A corps of mounted troops are enlisted for use on the Western plains.

1833 — Mexican Congress enacts the Secularization Act.

— Bent's Fort built by Charles Bent and Ceran St. Vrain on the North bank of the Arkansas River.

1834 — Methodist missionary, Jason Lee, travels to Oregon with Andrew Wyeth.

— Rocky Mountain Fur Company is bought out by the American Fur Company.

— Indian Intercourse Act is passed.

1835 — Presbyterians send Reverend Samuel Parker and Dr. Marcus Whitman to Oregon.

1836 — Arkansas enters the Union.

— Narcissa Whitman is the first white woman to cross the Rocky Mountains.

— Marcus and Narcissa Whitman set up a mission near the junction of the Columbia and Snake Rivers.

— Battle at the Alamo — 187 Texans dead, 1,544 Mexicans dead.

— Massacre at Goliad — 350 Texas army men surrender and are killed eight days later.

— Battle of San Jacinto led by Sam Houston — 630 Mexicans dead, 730 Mexicans captured (including Santa Anna), 9 Texans dead.

— William Holmes McGuffey, a Presbyterian minister, writes his first "reader" textbook.

1837 — United States recognizes Texas as a republic.

1838 — Jesuits send missionaries to the Far West.

— Territory of Iowa is formed.

— By Act of Congress, the Topographical Corps now reports directly to the Secretary of War.

1839 — Led by Thomas J. Farnham, thirteen men make their way West to Oregon from Peoria, Illinois.

— Mormons settle in Illinois to form the colony of Nauvoo.

1840 — Census of 1840 shows the population of the United States to be in excess of 17,000,000.

— The "rendezvous" era of the fur trade business ends.

1841 — The Bidwell-Bartleson party — first substantial-sized immigrant party — make their trip overland to California.

— Distribution-Preemption Act is passed by Congress.

1842 — John Charles Frémont leads a small surveying party for the Topographical Corps up the Platte-Sweetwater Rivers route to South Pass.

— Commodore Thomas Ap Cateby Jones, believing war had begun with Mexico, sails the *United States* to Monterey, California, where he takes the fort and runs up the American flag.

1843 — Fort Sutter completed by John Augustus Sutter in Sacramento.

— John Charles Frémont begins his second expedition, traveling over what would become the Oregon Trail.

1844 — U.S. Congress passes legislation providing the setting aside of 320 acres for town sites.

— Joseph Smith and his brother, Hyrum, shot by vigilantes.

1845 — Texas enters the Union.

— Newspaperman John O'Sullivan writes of "manifest destiny" in a New York paper and use of the term sweeps the country.

— Catherine Beecher's *The Duty of American Women to Their Country* is published.

1846 — Brigham Young and his group of "pioneers" consisting of 143 men, 3 women, and 2 children set up Winter Quarters along the banks of the Missouri.

— Chief Yellow Wolf of the Cheyennes predicts the end of the buffalo at the hands of the whites.

— Invasion of Mexico by Anglo-Americans at Rio Grande boundary led by General Zachary Taylor.

— Bear Flag Revolt in California led by John Charles Frémont.

— Stephen Kearny and his army reach Santa Fe.

— Francis Parkman travels to the West.

— By treaty Oregon country is given to the United States.

— Legislation is passed to establish fixed American posts in the West.

— Smithsonian Institution is founded.

1847 — Brigham Young and his "pioneer" band begin Westward trip to find their Mormon desert Zion.

1848 — Contracts awarded for semi-monthly mail service by sea between New York and San Francisco.

— Treaty of Guadalupe Hidalgo — Mexico surrenders New Mexico and California to the United States and the Rio Grande is accepted as the boundary of Texas.

— Gold is discovered at Sutter's Mill in California.

— Under newly appointed governor, Joseph Lane, Oregon is made a territory.

1849 — William Bent blows up Bent's Fort.

— Mormons organize the "provisional government of the State of Deseret."

— Gold rush to California.

1850 — Mail service is established to Santa Fe from Independence.

— California enters the Union.

1851 — The lynching of Juanita in Downieville, California.

1852 — Harriet Beecher Stowe's *Uncle Tom's Cabin* is published.

1853 — Gadsden Purchase in which the United States acquires for $10,000,000 the land South of the Gila River in New Mexico and Arizona.

— Congress divides up the Oregon country and creates Washington territory.

— Congress authorizes the Army to survey all feasible routes between the Mississippi Valley and the Pacific Ocean for a transcontinental railroad.

1854 — Kansas-Nebraska Bill is passed.

— Cholera epidemic.

— Gold is discovered at Fort Colville in Washington.

— Alexander Majors forms a partnership with William H. Russell and W.B. Waddell to found a freighting company.

1855 — Rock Island Railroad opens the first bridge across the Mississippi River.

— Blizzard conditions hit the plains region.

1856 — Mormon handcart brigades begin across the plains to Salt Lake City.

1857 — Post Office Appropriation Act authorizes the postmaster general to call for bids on a semi-monthly, semi-weekly, or weekly mail service from some point on the Mississippi River (selected by the contractor) to San Francisco.

— Mountain Meadows Massacre.

— John Butterfield receives the government contract to organize a stage-line between Missouri and California for $600,000.

— President James Buchanan orders a force of 2,500 men under Colonel Albert Sidney Johnston to march against Utah.

1858 — Russell, Majors, and Waddell freighting company has in operation 3,500 wagons and employs 4,000 men.

— President Buchanan offers a full pardon to all Mormons who will submit to the authority of the United States.

— Large scale use of the Concord wagon begins in the West.

— Gold is discovered in Colorado.

1859 — Horace Greeley makes an overland journey to California.

— Gold rush to Pike's Peak, Colorado.

— Oregon enters the Union.

— Discovery of the Comstock Lode in Nevada.

1860 — Census of 1860 shows the population of the United States to be 31,400,000.

— Republican National Convention nominates Abraham Lincoln for President.

— Spencer repeating rifle is invented.

— Congress passes the Pacific Telegraph Act to facilitate communication between the Atlantic and Pacific states by telegraph.

— There are 7,090 men and officers stationed in the West to handle the "Indian problem."

— Pony Express service inaugurated leaving from St. Joseph, Missouri, on 3 April.

1861 — Kansas enters the Union.

— Territory of Nevada is organized.

— Territory of Colorado is organized.

— North Dakota is organized as part of the original Dakota territory.

— Great transcontinental telegraph line is begun in July and is completed in October of the same year.

— Confederate soldiers open fire on Fort Sumter.

— Shoot-out between McCanles and "Wild Bill" Hickok.

— Gatling gun is patented.

— Pony Express service comes to an end in October.

1862 — Homestead Act is passed on 20 May and will go into effect 1 January 1863.

— Gold is discovered near Bannack, Montana.

— Ben Holladay purchases the assets of the Central Overland, California, and Pike's Peak Express.

1863 — While on furlough Daniel Freeman takes the first homestead claim in Beatrice, Nebraska.

— Territory of Arizona is organized.

— Territory of Idaho is organized which includes all of Montana and much of Wyoming.

— Atchison, Topeka, and Santa Fe Railroad receives 3,000,000 acres

1864 — Hanging of Jack Slade.
  — Hanging of Henry Plummer and other Montana outlaws.
  — Discovery of gold at Last Chance Gulch (Helena), Montana.
  — Congress separates Montana from Idaho territory and creates Montana territory.
  — Nevada enters the Union.
  — Archduke Maximilian becomes Emperor of Mexico.
  — Sand Creek Massacre.
  — American Fur Company sells out its holdings to the Northwest Fur Company.

1865 — General Robert E. Lee surrenders to Ulysses S. Grant at Appomattox and the Civil War ends.
  — John Wilkes Booth assassinates President Abraham Lincoln.
  — Slavery is abolished by the Thirteenth Amendment to the Constitution.
  — 10,000 immigrants arrive from Norway, Sweden, and Denmark.

1866 — First "long drive" of cattle North from Texas.
  — Ben Holladay sells out to Wells, Fargo Company.
  — Goodnight-Loving Trail is laid out.
  — Congress authorizes the enlistment of two regiments of black Cavalry and two regiments of black Infantry to aid in the "pacification" of the West.

1867 — Nebraska enters the Union.
  — United States purchases Alaska from Russia for $7,000,000.
  — Emperor Maximilian is executed.
  — The National Grange of the Patrons of Husbandry is formed by Oliver Hudson Kelley.

1868 — The cattle industry moves into Wyoming.
  — Territory of Wyoming is organized.
  — Ulysses S. Grant is elected President.

1869 — Union Pacific railroad meets Central Pacific railroad at Promontory Point, Utah, on 10 May.
  — Woman suffrage is adopted in Wyoming.

1870 — Three out of every four teachers in the United States are women.
  — Fight between "Wild Bill" Hickok and Fort Hays Cavalry men.

1871 — Blizzard conditions hit the Plains region for three days.
  — Shooting between "Wild Bill" Hickok and Phil Coe.
  — Extensive cattle raising begins in Montana.

1872 — Duke Alexis of Russia arrives in Nebraska to hunt buffalo.
  — Buffalo "boom" begins and hide hunters flock to the plains.
  — Yellowstone is created as the nation's first national park preserve.
  — Mark Twain's *Roughing It* is published.

1873 — Horrell War in Lincoln County, New Mexico.
  — Timber-Culture Act is passed.
  — Easter blizzard hits the plains.
  — Hide trade flourishes amid a financial panic.

1874 — Grasshopper plague hits from Oregon to the Dakotas, South to Texas and into Missouri.

—Joseph F. Glidden secures a patent for his barbed wire fencing.

1875 —Silo is invented for storing corn.

—15,000 people enter the Black Hills of South Dakota in search of gold.

1876 —Colorado enters the Union.

—Deadwood, South Dakota, is founded.

—Murder of "Wild Bill" Hickok.

—James-Younger gang raid on Northfield, Minnesota.

—Battle at the Little Big Horn.

1877 —Desert Land Act is passed.

—Grasshopper Act is passed in which grasshoppers are put in the category of "public enemy."

—Flight of the Nez Percé Indians.

1878 —Lincoln County War begins in New Mexico and lasts for three years.

—Magazine repeating rifle is invented.

—Cheyenne trek led by Dull Knife and Little Wolf from Indian territory.

—Timber and Stone Act is passed.

—Corn-binder is perfected.

1879 —Carlisle Indian school is founded in Pennsylvania.

1880 —Census of 1880 shows the population of the United States to be 50,100,000.

—Cattle industry is firmly established throughout the Great Plains.

—Pat Garrett's manhunt for Billy the Kid and his gang.

1881 —Sarah Bernhardt plays *Camille* in Tootle's Opera House in St. Joseph, Missouri.

—Billy the Kid shoots his way out of jail in Lincoln, New Mexico.

—James Brisbin's *Beef Bonanza, or How to Get Rich on the Plains* is published.

—Murder of Billy the Kid.

—Gunfight near the *OK* corral in Tombstone, Arizona.

—Helen Hunt Jackson's *A Century of Dishonor* is published.

1882 —Murder of Jesse James.

—Chinese Exclusion Act is passed.

—105,000 immigrants arrive from Norway, Sweden, and Denmark.

1883 —Theodore Roosevelt invests one-fifth of his fortune in a cattle ranch in the Dakota Badlands.

1885 —Union Pacific posts special rates of $45 from Missouri to Portland.

1886 —Harsh winter into 1887 disastrously damages the cattle industry, bankrupting many cattlemen.

1887 —Doc Holliday dies in Glenwood Springs, Colorado.

—General Allotment Act is passed.

1889 —Ella "Cattle Kate" Watson is hanged by a vigilante gang.

—Oklahoma land rush.

—North Dakota, South Dakota, Montana and Washington enter the Union.

1890 —Idaho and Wyoming enter the Union.

—Territory of Oklahoma is organized.

— Massacre at Wounded Knee.

— Gold is discovered at Cripple Creek, Colorado.

1991 — Forest Reserve Act is passed.

1892 — Dalton Gang raid on Coffeyville, Kansas.

— Practical corn-husker is patented.

— Populist Party drafts first platform and nominates James B. Weaver for President.

— Johnson County War in Wyoming.

1893 — Shoot-out between lawmen and the Doolin gang in Oklahoma.

— Woman suffrage is adopted in Colorado.

— According to Frederick Jackson Turner, the frontier is officially closed.

— Representatives from fifteen mining unions meet at Butte, Montana, to form the Western Federation of Miners.

1894 — Oil is struck in Corsicana, Texas.

1895 — Murder of John Wesley Hardin by John Selman.

1896 — Utah enters the Union.

— Gold is discovered in Bonanza Creek, a tributary of the Klondike River in Alaska.

— Death of Bill Doolin, shot by a posse.

— Woman suffrage is adopted in Utah.

— Woman suffrage is adopted in Idaho.

1898 — Gold is discovered in Nome, Alaska.

— Heyday of Butch Cassidy and his Wild Bunch.

1900 — Census of 1900 shows the population of the United States to be in excess of 76,300,000.

1901 — Oil gusher "Spindletop" is struck in Beaumont, Texas.

1902 — Owen Wister's *The Virginian* is published.

1907 — Oil is struck near Tulsey Town, Oklahoma, changing it to Tulsa, the Oil Capital of the world.

— Both parts of Oklahoma enter the Union as a single state.

1908 — Murder of Pat Garrett.

1912 — New Mexico and Arizona enter the Union.

1914 — Last carrier pigeon known to exist dies in the Cincinnati Zoo on 1 September.

III

i

In the course of his essay, *"Ein Moderner Mythus von Dingen die am Himmel Gesehen Werden"* [A Modern Myth of Things Seen in the Sky], contained in *Zivilisation im Übergang/[Civilization in Transition]* (Walter-Verlag, 1974), the tenth volume in his collected works, C.G. Jung remarked that "it cannot be the task of education to promote rationalists, materialists, specialists, technicians, limited beings who, unconscious of their origin, find themselves thrust into the present and toward the fragmentation and splintering of society, and neither can a psychotherapy lead to satisfactory results by limiting its field of vision...." The same must be said for history and, unfortunately, as yet, Western history has not been dealt with in a truly comprehensive fashion either in a single book or in a series of books.

Despite the emphasis given above to The Natural Frontier, so far in historiography this perspective has been invoked only charily. I am in the process of editing an anthology, to be titled *The American West in History*, a companion volume to *The American West in Fiction* (New American Library, 1982), which will incorporate first-hand accounts focusing consecutively and respectively on seven of the eight frontiers; The Apocryphal Frontier is dealt with in *The American West in Fiction* and, my third book in this mini-series, *The American West in Film* (see the annotations for these books elsewhere in the present volume). In the interim, while it is confined to Anglo-American viewpoints, *The Wilderness Reader* (New American Library, 1980) edited by Frank Bergon, composed entirely of excerpts from first-hand accounts, does give some notion of The Natural Frontier.

Some years ago Holt, Rinehart began publishing the Histories of the American Frontier series under the general editorship of the late Ray Allen Billington. Not all of the books announced for inclusion in this series were published. Many of the more notable entries, however, are now being reissued by the University of New Mexico Press. While books in this series refine the frontier experience into a great many more categories than I have above, some deserve to be cited as authoritative, or at least valuable, in studying the special subjects to which they pertain. Foremost among these are Ray Allen Billington's *America's Frontier Heritage* (Holt, Rinehart, 1963) and Gilbert C. Fite's *The Farmers' Frontier 1865-1900* (Holt, Rinehart, 1966), both of which are annotated below. Other entries worth citing, which are annotated elsewhere in this book, are Rodman Wilson Paul's *Mining Frontiers of the Far West* 1848-1880 (Holt, Rinehart, 1963) and Oscar Osburn Winther's *The Transportation Frontier: The Trans-Mississippi West* 1865-1890 (Holt, Rinehart, 1964). Finally, an extremely worthwhile entry, although somewhat outside the perimeters of the study of the Westward expansion *per se*, is Reginald Horsman's *The Frontier in the Formative Years* 1783-1815 (Holt, Rinehart, 1970).

The Bancroft Library, under the general editorship of Hubert Howe Bancroft, constitutes a thirty-nine volume work. Organized chronologically, the volumes in this series can be cited for their inclusion of original documents but ought to be avoided in terms of their historical narratives. This means that Bancroft's series is of more interest to the professional historian than to the reader of history interested in an overview.

The histories annotated below have been divided into two categories, Interpretive Studies and General Histories. The latter category consists, for the most part, of narrative histories. Among the historians cited in both categories perhaps Robert V. Hine ought to be distinguished as approaching most nearly what above was defined as the *historicus magnus*.

Lastly, while there is really no proper place to include mention of this book elsewhere and while it does not really fit into the subject of Western history, Ramon F. Adams' *Western Words:A Dictionary of the American West* (University of Oklahoma Press, 1968) is particularly recommended because it includes myriad words, slang, and special terms especially relevant to the American West which cannot readily be found in other sources and which, for the most part, are excluded from *Webster's New International Unabridged Dictionary*, Second Edition, and *The Oxford English Dictionary*.

ii

Interpretive Studies

Billington, Ray Allen, *America's Frontier Heritage* (Holt, Rinehart, 1963) O.P.; reprinted by the University of New Mexico Press; *Land of Savagery Land of Promise: The European Image of the American Frontier* (W.W. Norton, 1981).

Professor Billington's career as an historian proceeded in a sense under the shadow of Frederick Jackson Turner. His purpose in *America's Frontier Heritage* was to reappraise the entire Turner frontier hypothesis in the light of modern research. In addressing Turner's speculations as to the effect of the frontier on the American national character Billington relied largely on the first-hand accounts of foreign visitors to the frontier. He broke down Turner's idea of the frontier into two aspects, the frontier as a place and the frontier as a process. Among the ideas Turner propounded that Billington had to reject was that of the frontier as a classless society. He found on the frontier that "class divisions occurred in the most primitive communities, and deepened as the social order matured." Americans, Billington concluded, prefer the term "status" to the idea of class and tend to believe that there is superior vertical mobility in the United States than in Europe. Billington objected to the latter and felt that while Americans want to believe this and, because of the frontier experience, that America remains the land of unusual opportunity, in actual practice these things are not altogether true; just as the legend of frontier individualism was (and is) based mostly on what people wanted to believe (including Turner) and not on historical reality. There was, in fact, a tremendous dependence on social cooperation even among cattlemen and law enforcement. The abundance of the frontier did for a time promote a sense of social and economic equality, but this sense was confined to the white population.

Based on his research for *America's Frontier Heritage*, Billington found that Sir Walter Scott and Oliver Goldsmith were more widely read on the frontier than James Fenimore Cooper, precisely because of Cooper's unrealistic view of frontier life; while in *Land of Savagery Land of Promise* he sought to address in a topical fashion many of the European fantasies about the American frontier. "Ideological and political preconceptions were as destructive of accuracy as personal prejudices," he wrote in the chapter, "The Image-Makers: Land of Promise." Fortunately, Billington did not subscribe to what is called the Henry Nash Smith thesis — see the entry for Smith's *Virgin Land: The American West as Symbol and Myth* (Harvard University Press, 1950) elsewhere — and his viewpoint cannot be criticized on this score. Yet, he was a *colligator*; he relied too often on others second hand. His facts, especially in *Land of Savagery Land of Promise*, are only as trustworthy as his sometimes untrustworthy sources. He penetrated no subject very deeply. He was most comfortable as a collector of opinions and perspectives to be found in the secondary literature. To have been more than this he would have had to have delved more extensively than he did into primary sources.

Drinnon, Richard, *Facing West: The Metaphysics of Indian-Hating and Empire-Building* (New American Library, 1980).
      This is one of the most significant books yet to appear on the dynamic role racism and racial attitudes played in the history of the United States, beginning in the Colonial period, extending through the frontier experience, and persisting in the American global adventurism of this century. Drinnon defined racism as the "habitual practice by a people of treating, feeling, and viewing physically dissimilar peoples — identified as such by skin color and other shared hereditary characteristics — as less than persons." When viewing American political expansion in these terms, Drinnon found that he had to re-explore cultural artifacts and historical events, and re-examine roles traditionally assigned to Jefferson, Monroe, Lincoln and others. Every American should read this book.

Hine, Robert V., *The American West: An Interpretive History* (Little, Brown, 1973).
      There are some errors of fact in this book. Some chapters, such as "The Cowboy and the Cult of Masculinity" and "The Western Hero," are inadequate and lacking in depth. This is unfortunate because so many of what Hine drew by way of conclusions were in large measure dependent on concepts such as the "cult of masculinity" and "the code of the Western hero." Yet, the book is extraordinarily valuable for many of the insights and viewpoints it does incorporate. To illustrate both the strength and weakness of Hine's approach, in addressing the issue of frontier violence, Hine was at his best in detailing the fundamental causes, in his words, "fears of anarchy and ... the struggle for economic and political power. The state instigated its own violence — Indian wars, the forced removal of Indians to reservations, the vaunted brutality of groups like the Texas Rangers, and the dispatch of federal troops to battle labor unions." He was at his weakest in concluding that "all forms of violence ... were supported by myth and opinion, the cult of masculinity and the code of the Western hero." These generalities are insufficiently conceptualized to function as

meaningful interpretive principles. Yet, while Hine's book is not a place at which to begin studying frontier history, it must be stressed that it is an important landmark and he was conscious of The Natural Frontier.

Klose, Nelson, *A Concise Study Guide to the American Frontier* (University of Nebraska Press, 1964).

The major problem with this study guide would be determining to whom it would be useful. About a third of it is devoted to a series of bibliographical sections, but none of the books included are annotated. The four major sections of the book deal, first, with historians' theories about the frontier, and then with regional frontiers, problems and features of the frontier, and leading types of frontiers. In this last section Klose sub-divided "Early Agricultural Frontiers" from "The Farmers' Frontier in the Far West." His study guide, in fact, is overall the work of a *colligator*, but without Billington's sureness of grasp and willingness to admit underlying assumptions. For example, dealing with the rise of big business and multinational corporations, Klose observed that "the old freedoms sometimes ring hollow as compared with the economic and social benefits of more organized society." Most of the sections and sub-sections of his study guide offer vignettes in chronological sequence of major events or movements, but invariably with this kind of superficial insensitivity to social, economic, and psychological issues. Ultimately, since the historical sections are inadequate and the bibliographies nothing more than book lists, the term "study guide" would seem somewhat inflated.

Lamar, Howard R., (ed), *The Reader's Encyclopedia of the American West* (Crowell, 1977).

Here, again, on a small scale is one of the vast compendium volumes devoted to entries written by a colloquium of scholars on many of the more familiar people and places and events of Western American history. My problem with it is that there is at least one small error of fact in quite a few entries and some entries are altogether unreliable. I would recommend it only if the reader has no intention of reading further on the general history of the American West in all of its aspects and would like a reference which might serve as a sometimes accurate overview of the whole area, since its chief virtues are obviously its convenience and portability.

Steffen, Jerome O., (ed.), *The American West: New Perspectives, New Dimensions* (University of Oklahoma Press, 1979); *Comparative Frontiers: A Proposal for Studying the American West* (University of Oklahoma Press, 1980).

Steffen's contribution to *The American West* was an essay, "Insular v. Cosmopolitan Frontiers: A Proposal for Comparative American Frontier Studies," which he expanded to book-length proportions for *Comparative Frontiers*. Two of the essays by other historians in *The American West* are particularly worth reading: John Opie's "Frontier History in Environmental Perspective," since it is definitely a statement in favor of The

Natural Frontier, and I could not agree more with Opie's conclusion "that there is no next step in human history unless it is the creation of an ecologically responsible humanity"; and Reginald Horsman's survey, "Recent Trends and New Directions in Native American History," which is extremely interesting as far as it goes. Of more specialized interest are John C. Hudson's "The Study of Western Frontier Populations" and Roger G. Barker's "The Influence of Frontier Environments on Behavior." These essays were written in the style *rerum scriptorum*, but they have their value. The most disappointing essay is Richard W. Etulain's "Western Fiction and History: A Reconsideration" which consists of one-half superficial opinions about authors such as A.B. Guthrie, Jr., and Vardis Fisher and one-half a rehash of the plot of Wallace Stegner's *Angle of Repose* (Doubleday, 1971).

Steffen's thesis in *Comparative Frontiers* is that "American frontier experiences fell into two broad categories, cosmopolitan and insular. Cosmopolitan frontiers were associated only with modal change or change caused by factors not found exclusively within the confines of the frontier. Insular frontiers were associated with fundamental change caused primarily by factors exclusive to the frontier experience." According to this thesis, the "trans-Appalachian agricultural settlement was the only insular frontier in American historical development, because the number of interacting links between it and the main body of American civilization were few in number." The remainder of Steffen's book is devoted to demonstrating the accuracy of this thesis through an examination of four frontiers, the trans-Appalachian frontier which Steffen preferred to term the "Cis-Mississippi Pioneer Agricultural Settlement," the "American Fur-Trading Frontier," "The Ranching Frontier," and "The Mining Frontier." Unfortunately, the Cosmopolitan/Insular thesis was not wholly derived from the facts, but rather had to be imposed by Steffen onto these last three frontiers. In the "American Fur-Trading Frontier," Steffen was unaware of Thomas Jefferson's ambivalent attitude toward the Native American, an attitude Drinnon explored in detail (see above). In fact, what is wrong with Steffen's thesis is his failure to recognize the decisive contribution of The Natural Frontier to the Anglo-American character. To state concisely Steffen's view of The Fur-Trading Frontier: continuity between the mountain men and fur traders with European and East Coast influences militated against what Steffen viewed as "fundamental change." He did not research the characters of mountain men sufficiently. Had he done so, he might well have perceived how profoundly they were influenced — and in fundamental ways — by the Native Americans with whom they came into contact. This influence can be seen in a number of first-hand accounts.

In dealing with The Ranching Frontier, Steffen would have histories of ranching rewritten from the perspective of big business and industrial trends in the East. As for The Mining Frontier, it was, in Steffen's words, "in some cases, perhaps most, reinforced [by] prefrontier attitudes." In his Epilogue, Steffen questioned Walter Prescott Webb's claim for uniqueness of the Great Plains (see below) and would instead seek continuity. Yet, most of these assertions are based on untenable, or at the very least vague, assumptions. For example, with reference to the buffalo, Steffen wrote concerning Native Americans and the buffalo that "adaptation to this buffalo migration pattern resulted in profound changes in long-standing institutions and beliefs." The truth of the matter is that the buffalo did not have a "migration pattern." Had they, it would have encouraged Native Americans, dependent on them, to camp in a certain pattern. In his footnote, Steffen cited William T. Hornaday's *The Extermination of the American Bison with a Sketch of its Discovery and Life History* (1889), which book has been superseded, and Tom McHugh's *The Time of the Buffalo* (Knopf, 1972) — albeit McHugh made a specific point to stress the fact that the buffalo "wandered" and did not follow a "migration pattern." Why did Steffen cite a book in support of his thesis when it does not support his thesis? It is enough to make me wonder how familiar he could have been with the many sources he cited, especially when, as in the case of "cowboy mythology," another instance, he declared "the best works on this subject" to be an essay and two books which are not even adequate!

A better approach, I would suggest, would be to contrast European attitudes and values and beliefs and customs with those of The Natural Frontier and in this fashion arrive at just what changes were indeed fundamental and what changes were not. Steffen was, it seems to me, still too much under the influence of Turner's specious contrast between "civilization" and "savagery."

Turner, Frederick Jackson, *Frontier and Section: Selected Essays* with an Introduction and Notes by Ray Allen Billington (Prentice-Hall, 1961); *Frederick Jackson Turner* (Twayne Publishers, 1975) by James D. Bennett; *Frederick Jackson Turner: Historian, Scholar, Teacher* (Oxford University Press, 1973) by Ray Allen Billington.

There is perhaps no sound reason for reading the nine essays selected and introduced by Billington in *Frontier and Section* except that Turner has been so extraordinarily influential among American and European historians. On the other hand, being a *historicus contemplativus*, Turner's writings are often filled with occasional intuitions which might inspire research to arrive at a viable historical construction. Yet, he could as easily come up with curious notions. In "The Contributions of the West" (1903) Turner would have his reader believe that the captains of American industry were a product of the American West; probably for this reason he closed his eyes to the economic disenfranchisement of the pioneer by capital interests.

Bennett's entry on Turner in the Twayne United States Authors Series is more concerned with responses to Turner's theories than with Turner as a human being. Bennett pointed out that historian William F. Allen, a general historian whose specialty was Rome, was Turner's mentor and that Allen's methods, including the use of maps, to show the expansion of Roman civilization influenced Turner's methods for studying American history. "Allen," Turner said, "taught me all the history I know." Very much a Turner advocate, Bennett's conclusion, predictably, is that while there may be some serious reservations about Turner's theories there is much of value in them.

Billington, too, was very much a Turner partisan, but in his case this / proclivity enabled him to bring Turner alive as a human being and to permit the reader to admire what Turner in general terms symbolized as an historian — a man who felt history encompassed all of the social sciences, indeed all the humanities and the sciences — and that this quality may be more important than any of Turner's individual contributions. As Turner, Billington retired to work as a senior research associate at the Huntington Library. My sympathies are with Billington's appraisal of Turner's spirit, that "it has been his misfortune to be labeled by later generations as a monocausationist, riding his hobby-horses of frontier and section, and ignoring the broader historical currents that emerged from the industrial-urban world of the Twentieth century. No judgment could be more false. Turner, more than any scholar of his generation, recognized the complexity of the historical process and the need of employing every tool available to understand its every facet." This perspective is not derived from what he wrote; it is clear thanks to Billington's fine biography.

Webb, Walter Prescott, *The Great Frontier* (Houghton Mifflin, 1952) O.P.; reprinted by the University of Texas Press with an Introduction by Arnold J. Toynbee.

In his *Civilization on Trial & The World and the West* (Meridian Books, 1964), Arnold Toynbee made the point that there were only two attitudes toward Westernization: Zealotism and Herodianism, or fanatic resistance and abject accomodation. Toynbee felt that European expansionism (or, variously, Westward expansion) was the single most important historical force over the last five centuries and hence he was naturally inclined to celebrate Webb's view of the "frontier" as global in its implications. Webb's approach to the American frontier experience was well advised insofar as he was concerned with viewing the phenomenon in global terms and as part of global process; while the debilitating weakness of his book derives from the innumerable assumptions which Webb was inclined to make and on which he based the most sweeping generalities. "Though in American life it has been every man for himself," he wrote, "there has been a deep harmony in the confusion among men who made no assumption about class, who were practical, who were willing to work, to accept whatever would work in their interest. ...And the measure of the influence the frontier had in leveling artificial distinctions, in making men practical, in turning them toward work, is the measure of the effect of the frontier on American art in its broadest sense." To address only one of Webb's assumptions, the frontier population he was extolling was white; and this premise overlooks Billington's finding (see above) that "class divisions occurred in the most primitive communities, and deepened as the social order matured." In the final analysis, Webb concocted a flattering fantasy, but his book is of limited utility.

iii

General Histories

Athearn, Robert G., *High Country Empire* (McGraw-Hill, 1960) O.P.

Athearn confined himself to the areas adjacent to the Missouri River — the mountain states of Montana, Wyoming, Colorado, and the plains states of the Dakotas, Nebraska, and Kansas. Although Native Americans are treated with some impartiality, there is no real awareness of The Natural Frontier as is evident in the title of Chapter 5, "Picket Line of Civilization." However, Athearn did provide a reliable portrait of the Fur-Trading Frontier, The Military Frontier, The Agricultural Frontier, The Mining Frontier, The Ranching Frontier, and, to a lesser degree, The Technological Frontier (particularly as concerns petroleum) as these frontiers were involved in the history of the region he selected. Athearn was influenced to an extent by Turner's conceptual framework, but not in such a way as to compromise seriously the integrity of his historical narrative which, consequently, may be regarded as a solid introduction to the early white history of these areas.

Billington, Ray Allen, *The Far Western Frontier: 1830–1860* (Harper's, 1956); *Westward Expansion: A History of the American Frontier* (Macmillan, 1974 expanded Fourth Edition).

Billington was, as noted above, a *colligator* on a grand scale. Of his historical works, *The Far Western Frontier* is perhaps his finest attempt at narrative history. There is no awareness of The Natural Frontier; Billington was too profoundly moved by the dynamics of the Westward expansion for that. Yet, he was able to record the effects of successive waves of migration so destructive to varying life-styles. The combination of integrating the perspectives of social and economic history with individual experiences and events was masterfully done and his history grips the reader's attention throughout. Read in conjunction with Athearn above and Gibson below, one might be in possession of the best introduction so far to the general history of the American West in the Nineteenth century.

Westward Expansion is somewhat different. Too often, it is regarded as a textbook, in which case it is inadequate because of its neglect of The Natural Frontier. In his "Preface to the Fourth Edition," Billington observed that "I have, with considerable reluctance, identified the heroes or villains of expansion as Negroes or Mexican-Americans when those designations applied. ...The understandable need of minority groups for a prideful association with a cultural heritage has outmoded these beliefs of a generation ago, and today authors are obligated to let Negroes or Mexican-Americans or Indians speak loudly from their pages. Yet I cannot resist a lingering hope that the tide will turn again, and that all men will be recognized as part of the family of mankind, all equal, all deserving of recognition for their exploits or ideas, rather than because of race, color, creed, or nationality." On the surface this might appear to be a praiseworthy sentiment. However, what is behind it, first of all, is the assumption that history is peopled by heroes and villains, a specious notion at best; and, more importantly, that "the family of mankind," as Billington meant the term, seems to be another way of saying "one-settlement" culture. Richard Drinnon's book was recommended above for precisely this reason, as a counter-action or antidote to the idea of one-settlement culture. As the matter stands, *Westward Expansion*, ideally, can be read only after so much preparation that much of its content will be already familiar. The same applies to Billington's extensive bibliography. Billington's critical comments are informed by his prejudices regarding Westward expansion and must be approached with caution. Also, Billington was too inclined to accept the figure 90,000,000 for the number of Native Americans living in North and South America at the time of Columbus' arrival; this figure seems rather exaggerated. *Westward Expansion* is an amalgamation of the findings of legion *rerum scriptores* unified by the bias of a one-settlement culture. The book is in fact a *collegium* of sources rather than a narrative history.

Dick, Everett, *The Sod-House Frontier*: 1854–1890 (D. Appleton-Century, 1937); *Vanguards of the Frontier* (D. Appleton-Century, 1937); both O.P. and both reprinted by the University of Nebraska Press.

    The Sod-House Frontier is a fine book to be read in conjunction with Athearn (see above) in view of the fact that Dick concentrated on the social, economic, and cultural history of Nebraska, Kansas, and the Dakotas during this given time-span. Among its drawbacks is the fact that Dick dealt only generically with whole groups of individuals, e.g., women and Native Americans; yet, in its favor, he did manage to recreate vividly patterns of culture and ways of living.

    Vanguards of the Frontier is, if anything, even better as narrative history, an excellent introduction to the social history of the Northern Plains and Rocky Mountains. Dick's portrait of the way mountain men dressed and behaved is particularly fascinating as is his coverage of the riverboat industry. Perhaps the weakest aspect of this book is the final chapter in which Dick attempted to abstract the general characteristics of the frontier.

Gibson, Arrell Morgan, *The American Indian: Prehistory of the Present* (D.C. Heath, 1980).

    This is the best one-volume treatment yet to appear on Native American history. No general, balanced understanding of American affairs is possible without taking The Natural Frontier and Native American history fully into account. Gibson noted that in 1500 A.D., "the time of European exploration and settlement, Indians numbered an estimated 1,500,000." Gibson's text is generally reliable even if space considerations dictated that some of his sections be superficial. Perhaps the most serious shortcoming is the totally inadequate index, something of a surprise in a professional work.

Fite, Gilbert C., *The Farmers' Frontier*: 1865–1900 (Holt, Rinehart, 1966) O.P.; reprinted by the University of New Mexico Press.

Despite its immense economic, and for a time social and political, importance in the history of the American West, The Agricultural Frontier usually is dealt with cursorily in general histories and, as a setting, has contributed very little to The Apocryphal Frontier; nor has it been any less neglected by strictly specialist historians. We are therefore most fortunate to have Fite's fine introduction to the subject, a reliable narrative history that will do much to dispel many of the illusions associated with the subject. Fite presented a graphic picture of the hardships, both natural and economic, with which the frontier farmer had to contend. Because of his broader scope and his avoidance of delimiting assumptions, Fite's is definitely recommended above Webb's study (see below).

Hafen, LeRoy R., and Carl Coke Rister, *Western America: The Exploration, Settlement, and Development of the Region Beyond the Mississippi* (Prentice-Hall, 1941) O.P.

Although this general history is more difficult to find than Billington's *Westward Expansion*, it is superior in a number of ways. It is a factual history presenting dates and events in rigid sequence and focusing on the American West from the Spanish period until the beginning of the Twentieth century. It is the history of the *rerum scriptor* at its most articulate. It remains a volume of solid reference which can be consistently consulted on a number of varied topics without too much caution about perspective — albeit The Natural Frontier is ignored — and without reservation because of the existence of some thesis or other. It should be revised and reissued.

Hawgood, John A., *America's Western Frontier: The Exploration and Settlement of the Trans-Mississippi West* (Knopf, 1967) O.P.

This is decidedly not a book with which to begin a study of the Westward expansion, but it is a fine supplement because of its many graphic illustrations, line drawings, reproductions of paintings, maps, etc., and because of the number of interesting documents which are reproduced in its pages. Hawgood's approach was topical, rather than strictly linear, and he made an effort, when he could, to engage a vertical perspective. The Natural Frontier is neglected and the treatment of Native Americans — primarily the Plains tribes — may be less than adequate but, at least, it is not openly hostile.

Keleher, William A., *The Fabulous Frontier: Twelve New Mexico Items* (University of New Mexico Press, 1945; revised edition, 1962) O.P.; reprinted by the University of New Mexico Press.

This book is included precisely because it is an anomaly. If one subscribes to the notion that even blackguards and corrupt politicians deserve an advocate, Keleher, who was a practicing New Mexico attorney, performed this function for men important — usually infamously — in New Mexico history, above all Thomas B. Catron, Albert B. Fall, Oliver Milton

Lee, and James R. Gililland. Most of what Keleher wrote about these individuals, and some of the others, must be regarded with extreme caution. Beyond this, Keleher fell victim to the most flagrant kinds of errors. "Reports," he wrote, "came to Silver City that Geronimo and his Apaches were on the warpath near Pinos Altos, nine miles from Silver City, riding up the hills and down the valleys, scalping men, carrying off women and children, burning and plundering." As Angie Debo documented in *Geronimo: The Man, His Time, His Place* (University of Oklahoma Press, 1976), it was indeed rare for the Apaches to scalp, although they readily burned and plundered. Because Keleher was wont to this kind of exaggeration, his book is not trustworthy even in a general sense. Most of the time when Keleher is cited it is in order to secure support for one or another prejudice. Yet, his chapter, "Writing Men," is a pleasure to read and many would agree with George W.P. Hunt, President of the Arizona Legislative Council in 1909, in a message opposing New Mexico's "Hawkins Act" which clearly made the vested interests of railroads and other corporations sacrosanct against prosecution from American citizens. "The Arizona law," Hunt wrote, "will know neither rich nor poor, king nor peasant, and those who have or may hereafter invest their millions here will have to content themselves, as well as they can afford to, with statutes moulded with an eye single to the welfare of the whole people." No state in the Union can boast of an unblemished history, but Keleher tried his best to "rewrite" New Mexican history in such a way that a reader, knowing no better, might believe New Mexico to have been an exception.

Sale, Randall D., and Edwin D. Karn, *American Expansion: A Book of Maps* (1962; University of Nebraska Press, 1979).

The excellence of this brief book is in the *number* of maps showing the patterns of Westward emigration and the changes in population densities throughout the Western states. The locations of United States Land Offices are also shown in the series of maps, organized chronologically. I am a firm believer in maps in the study of history and therefore find a volume such as this truly indispensable.

Webb, Walter Prescott, *The Great Plains* (Ginn, 1931) O.P.; reprinted by the University of Nebraska Press.

An excellent critique on the inadequacy of Webb's perspective and his ways of treating his subject is to be found in Fred A. Shannon's "An Appraisal of Walter Prescott Webb's *The Great Plains*: A Study of Institutions and Environment" in *Critiques of Research in the Social Sciences* (Social Science Research Council, 1939). Webb's prejudices compelled him to ignore The Natural Frontier and much of what he had to say has been proven insupportable by later research. However, his book does contain a wealth of factual information, charts, and maps which are still valuable in attempting to form an historical construction of this area during the last century.

Part I

The People

Women

by Vicki Piekarski

I

When this book was merely a two-page outline, the chapter on "Women" arbitrarily followed the chapter on "Mormons" and preceded the "Mountain Man" chapter. However, in my own research about frontier women and the history of women, I discovered the writings of feminist historian and President-Elect of the Organization of American Historians 1981–1982, Gerda Lerner. In "The Challenge of Women's History" (1977), an essay contained in her collection *The Majority Finds Its Past: Placing Women in History* (Oxford University Press, 1979), Lerner stated that "women are not a minority in any sense. Women are a sex. They have experienced educational, legal, and economic discrimination, as have members of minority groups, but they, unlike marginal groups, are distributed through every group and class in society." In this part of *The Frontier Experience*, concerned with the people of the American West, the focus is variously on ethnic groups, religious groups, and professional groups. Women, while they may be in the minority in most of these divisions, are nonetheless, only if peripherally, dispersed throughout. Therefore, without any further comment, explanation, or apology, Part One begins with "Women," one of the two sexes, one half of the human experience who have shared equally, but too often without recognition, in the making of history.

The American West, almost from the beginning of white settlement, was defined as a masculine experience and this androcentric perspective has been very much maintained in the retelling of white America's movement West. It has, in fact, been maintained despite the great number of letters, journals, and books of reminiscences left by women who shared in the trans-Mississippi immigration. In even the most comprehensive "standard" works about the West, women are virtually excluded. Ray Allen Billington's *Westward Expansion: A History of the American Frontier* (Macmillan, 1949), for example, is an all-inclusive seven-hundred-plus-page volume which, as of 1974, had gone through four revisions. This history, deemed by Southwestern historian J. Frank Dobie as the "Alpha to Omega treatise" on the Eastern and Western frontiers, lists only two white women in its thirty-seven page index: Helen Hunt Jackson, author of *Ramona* (1884), and Mary Elizabeth Lease. The slogan advising farmers to "raise less corn and more hell" was attributed to Lease. She was an avid spokesperson for the Farmers' Alliance and later for the People's (Populist) Party. Lease was a colorful and visible character in agrarian history, but surely she and Jackson were not the only women worthy of recognition by Billington! Narcissa Whitman—who in 1836 was the first white woman to cross the Rocky Mountains; who helped run the mission at Waiilatpu with her husband, Marcus Whitman; and who was killed in 1847 along with her husband and other mission occupants by Cayuse Indians whom the Whitmans were trying to convert to Christianity—is not mentioned by name in *Westward Expansion*, but characterized merely as Whitman's "wife." It is not my intention to chastize the late Professor Billington nor to deny him his stature as an authority on Western history; however, I feel his neglect of women is all too typical of the "masculine" approach to history.

Without question, the American West lends itself to this kind of limited interpretation due in large measure to the popular images about it. Those images suggest a vast arena in which lone male figures battle odds, Nature, and fellow males heroically. If we succumb to such false representations of the American frontier, to which films and fiction for the most part subscribe, then we are only learning half of our history.

The "taming" of the West was essentially an exercise in greed for many of the men who people the histories concerned with Nineteenth-century Manifest Destiny. For a great number of women, I think, it was something else, something perhaps more akin to the Native American way of looking at life as a continuous cycle. "We wanted to come to a new country," Susan Frances Lomax, an early settler explained, "so that our children could grow up with the country." Unfortunately, the family—the bearing and nurturing of human life—in which women play such a central role, has long been considered inconsequential in the history of humankind. Instead the preoccupation of historians has been with the "contributions" of men—politics, war, and the altering of land through conquest, building, or razing. This is no less true of the American West in which the destruction of the buffalo has merited more attention by historians than has the study of frontier women.

It is the preponderance of myths and stereotypes surrounding women who participated in the movement to and settlement of the West that makes it a formidable task to assess their actual roles and any such assessment may be premature since the study of women's history is relatively so new a perspective.

The very period with which we are dealing was a transitional and turbulent time for America and American women. The industrial revolution was rapidly changing the economy and mode of life in the Northeastern states. The home-centered economy in which women had shared an equally significant part was then shifting to a world outside the home. Women were losing their status in a society where class distinctions were sharpening; the importance of labor was measured by the amount of cash it could generate; the professionalization of occupations was excluding women; and the separation of the sexes was widening through a redefining of roles and spheres of the two sexes. In order to combat the problem a new definition of womanhood emerged from the pulpit and the publishers. In their view, women were superior to men in that they held the destiny of America in their hands since it was their responsibility to communicate cultural, moral, and civic values to children. Petty rules and restrictive codes concerning behavior, manners, and dress informed this new prescriptive ideology redefining women's sphere. Its objective was to provide an exemplary framework according to which women could model their expectations and goals. It was, however, despite women's public endorsement, an unworkable, impractical doctrine on a day-to-day basis for the majority of women.

As migration to the Far West became a viable opportunity for middle-class families, particularly those in the Mississippi Valley whose burden became even greater with the Panic of 1837, adherents of the genteel philsophy became greatly concerned. A land totally cut off from the East, as the West was, afforded an occasion for people to cast off the repressive social attitudes of "civilization." Perhaps women would fall victim to the free, unstructured life-style of the Western wilderness and neglect their obligations to society as "agents of civilization." These fears were instrumental, I think, in creating and popularizing two of the most prominent stereotypes of Western women.

When *The Soveraignty and Goodness of God, Together, with the Faithfulness of His Promises Displayed: Being a Narrative of the Captivity and Restauration of Mrs. Mary Rowlandson* was published in 1682, it was widely read for it reinforced the prejudices already held by the Eastern settlers toward the Native American. Rowlandson's account, and others like it, provided Nineteenth-century dime novel publishers with a ready-made, high-tension format with which to captivate their Eastern audiences. These captivity stories featured frail, defenseless women threatened with violent and inhuman aggression by fiendish, tomahawk-brandishing "redskins." Thus one of the first enduring images of women in the West was popularized: woman as helpless victim. At the opposite end of the spectrum was the cowgirl-queen. This breed of women were no helpless victims.

They had such colorful and descriptive sobriquets as Hurricane Nell, Arkansas Sal, Wild Edna, and Calamity Jane. These women were not equal to men; they were *superior*, and could out-shoot, out-ride, out-cuss, and out-spit any gent West of the Mississippi River. There was, however, one drawback. They were women without men or children and thus they would remain — for what man would have a frontier Amazon? Escapist and sensationalistic fiction though it may have been, it clearly contained a reinforcing message for those men and women who feared that frontier life had a disintegrating effect on women.

The advent of Twentieth-century formulary Western fiction diminished the status of fictional frontier women even more in that they were further relegated to the role of "romantic interest." These heroines were the incarnation of every man's dream of what a woman should be: they were virginal, beautiful, dependent, non-assertive, and not unlike the women of captivity stories in that fundamentally they were helpless when it came to taking care of themselves in the strange and violent world of the American West. These cardboard saint-goddesses, who also peopled the majority of Western films before 1950 and many after, fit into another category of stereotype — the "girl" — and they remain a popular image in the minds of millions of men and, to a lesser extent, women who grew up watching and reading good-guy-versus-bad-guy scenarios. They certainly reinforce the idea of the West being predominantly a masculine domain.

There are a number of "'bad woman" stereotypes that recur in Western fiction in both the Nineteenth and Twentieth centuries and in the Western films. The first is the "promiscuous" mixed-blood who frequently must sacrifice her life before the fade of the story for no other reason than her out-of-wedlock dehymenization. Another minority stereotype is the hot-blooded Mexican (minority women are almost without exception highly sexual) who has many problems adjusting to the Anglo-American world but whose main problem is keeping her peasant-style blouse from slipping off one of her shoulders. A somewhat more ambiguous bad woman emerges in the image of a prostitute with a heart of gold who commands great loyalty from the men of the community for whom she becomes a sort of mascot, while other members of her own sex view her with contempt and scorn.

If, and when, the historian decides to include women in his study of the frontier his approach is, of course, different from that of the Western fabulist. There is a peculiarly strong attachment on the part of historians to a most enduring stereotype: the pale, sunbonneted pioneer wife, a "poor haggard drudge," in the words of D.H. Lawrence. She made her appearance early in *De La Democratie en Amerique* (1835–1840) by Alexis de Tocqueville, nobleman and author, whose description of a "frail creature" with "pale face and shrunken limbs" who must endure "austere duties," "unbelievable miseries," and "privations which were unknown to her" previously was indeed a dismal portrait of American womanhood, but, for all that, heartily embraced by the French of the period. Emerson Hough, who was more of a romanticist than an historical novelist, popularized the image in his book *The Passing of the Frontier* (Yale University Press, 1921) when he had this to say: "The chief figure of the American West, the figure of the ages, is not the long-haired, fringed-legging man riding a raw-boned pony, but the gaunt and sad-faced woman sitting on the front seat of the wagon following her lord where he might lead, her face hidden in the same ragged sunbonnet which had crossed the Appalachians and the Missouri long before.... There was the great romance of all America—the woman in the sunbonnet; and not, after all, the hero with the rifle across his saddle horn." Scholars and popular historians alike continue to stress this image of the pioneer helpmate victimized by the harsh environment. Although it is certainly a truthful depiction of a particular type of frontier woman, it is too limited in its scope. It does not take into account such women as Elinore Pruitt Stewart, or the four Chrisman sisters (who homesteaded *sans* husbands in Nebraska), or even Mary Lease who for ten years farmed with her husband in Kansas and Texas before stepping into the political limelight.

On the other hand, the West is singled out as the birthplace of the "new democratic woman." This assertion is supported, say historians, by Wyoming's early adoption of women's suffrage in 1869. "The women of Colorado, Idaho, and Utah were voting before 1900," wrote Dee Brown in *The Gentle Tamers* (Putnam's, 1958), "indeed, the first dozen states to pass women's suffrage acts were all Western states.... The pioneers in petticoats were casting off their shackles in preparation for a final taming of the masculine frontier." The politicians of Wyoming, as those in California in 1849 who instituted legislation that would allow married women property rights, had an ulterior motive in advancing women's rights to include enfranchisement. Behind it all was the desire to attract families to the region to supplant the largely transient population which was considered unstable. Along with suffrage, the high percentage of co-educational institutions in the West is pointed out as reflecting a new attitude toward women, when in reality it was strictly an economic consideration to allow women to matriculate at the universities. The curriculum of the female student is conveniently excluded by these authors and understandably so with its emphasis on domestic "science"—cooking, etiquette, needlework, etc.

Diametrically opposed as the passive, sunbonneted helpmate and the autonomous, democratic woman are, they share as their basis the deep-seated idea the women, being both eternal and ahistorical, can be studied (and readily dismissed) as a unified group having identical experiences, attitudes, and interests. Common sense is too often suspended in the methods of historical inquiry when the subject of women is broached. The self-serving interests of men are protected through written history which maintains male-defined standards in both classification and periodization. Defining the entire American West as a masculine experience also negates by definition experiences and achievements of frontier women. Women can have no place in a wilderness characterized by violence and conquest. They can function merely as a looming symbol of sacrifice or civilization. But was the West predominantly a man's land? Uninhabitable by the "weaker sex?" Or has a myth spilled over into history?

Before the arrival of European explorers and conquerers untold numbers of Native American women lived in the Western regions of the North American continent. In what is now called the Southwest section of the United States, obtained through the Treaty of Guadalupe Hildago in 1848, lived some of the descendents of the Spanish invaders and the native inhabitants known variously as mestizos, Hispanics, and Mexicans. Mountain men, whose fur trade business flourished between the mid 1820s and the early 1840s, used the skills and bodies of these now minority women for their various business and pleasure needs. These "services" of Spanish-speaking women and Native American women are rarely mentioned in the books that examine the contributions of the mountain man era to American history.

As Anglo-Americans extended their frontier borderlands further West in the Nineteenth century, women (as wives, daughters, and servants/domestics) followed to the new settlements, be they open land, a small town, or a fort. When Protestant missionaries took it upon themselves to convert the "heathen" Indians of the Far West, they were often accompanied by their wives who shared in the running of the mission and teaching of children. Migration to the riches of the lands of Oregon and California in the 1840s and in the post-gold rush years was made up largely of families. When the cry of gold in 1849 reverberated throughout the land, some women, fearing the "unhingement" of their husbands, left everything behind to set up housekeeping on the ever-shifting mining frontier. On the Great American Desert, where it was thought nothing could grow or prosper, women joined the men in homesteading efforts to make the plains abound with life. Daughters were born to couples who settled the various frontiers West of the Mississippi.

The experiences confined in our minds to the male sex were just as commonly the experience of women. Women traveled to the West by covered wagon, boat, stagecoach, train, mule, and foot. They did not wait for the coming of "civilization" to the West, but brought it with them and shared in the development of community life. Single women came by the hundreds to teach school. Others came to practice a trade dominated by the male sex with the rise to professional standards of occupations in the East such as medicine and law. Women helped open such new territories as Oklahoma. They stepped outside the defined "women's sphere" and took part in farming, ranching, and politics. They drove stagecoaches, started businesses, and peddled their bodies, foodstuffs, or whatever they had to sell, and thus made important contributions to the economy of the West. They fought freezing cold, stifling heat, endless droughts, insect plagues, raging prairie fires, and starvation with the best and the worst of men. They defended their homes and protected their children. They joined organizations and started their own to fight for causes they believed in.

Frontier women came from different ethnic backgrounds, different classes of society, had different educational training, came from different religious affiliations, and from different regions East of the Mississippi River and from lands across the Pacific and Atlantic Oceans. But for all this women are excluded more often than not from the annals of frontier American history or summed up in a chapter, a page, or a paragraph in a stereotypical or patronizing fashion. It is as if the West had represented for the American male in both the Nineteenth and Twentieth centuries a total repudiation of American women. Yet, as generally outlined above, women participated in almost every aspect of the Westering process. They made contributions to those historical events cited as epic moments in Western American history by historians harboring androcentric concerns and standards.

Where then does one begin in an attempt to restore to frontier women their rightful place in history in reconstructing their past? The answer is with the women themselves. Contrary to the words of one immigrant woman who said, "pioneer women were quite too busy in making history to write it," a great many women did leave records. There are an immense number of primary sources, both published and archival, recounting women's experiences and feelings about traveling to and living in the West. There exist letters to loved ones back home. And there are books of reminiscences left by women who realized in their later years that they had contributed to a significant part of history and who wanted to put down on paper what they had done, seen, and heard in the West. In the words of one such memoirist: "It is my desire that these memoirs may help preserve to posterity the truth and the warmth of an unforgettable period in American history...."

Along with primary sources, the records kept by groups and organizations which included women, as well as those kept by churches and schools, can shed light on women's social roles. There is probably no other area in which women wielded as much power and influence as they did in the organization and development of frontier communities and in the educational system. Unfortunately, frontier communities and the history of American education in the West have remained generally outside the ken of Western frontier historians.

The first-hand accounts written by women and material containing any mention of women can provide us with factual information that can ascertain, finally, both women's historical and social roles in the settlement of the West. These published and archival research sources must, however, be approached with the right questions and a fresh perspective with the interest of women's history in mind. Women's history is different than men's because their concerns were different. Mostly they worked together, although sometimes they were at odds with each other. Women's contributions and achievements cannot be evaluated by the same methods nor measured by male-defined standards. But this does not mean women were of any less significance to history. It merely broadens the framework of history. And surely an expanded view of humankind, into which women are integrated, cannot be harmful or in any way debilitating to a country that claims to have been founded on the principle of equality for all.

II

i

Since references to women are few and far between in almost all the books considered to be standard works on the American West, one must necessarily rely on those books that fall under the category now called "women's studies": in this case, general histories about frontier women, anthologies of autobiographical writings or biographical sketches about women, and, most importantly, first-hand accounts written by women who lived in the West. The recurring problem in the general histories about frontier women, with the exception of Julie Roy Jeffrey's *Frontier Women: The Trans-Mississippi West* 1840–1880 (Hill and Wang, 1979), is that they are basically descriptive of what a handful of women did and how.

Fustel de Coulanges once wrote: "no documents, no history." Because the selection of books about frontier women is disappointingly and maddeningly limited in both quantity and quality and because I find Coulanges' statement profoundly truthful, this bibliography is made up largely of first-hand documents. In the course of my six-year study of frontier women I have found primary sources the most helpful in forming in my mind clearly defined images of Western women and their life experiences. First-hand accounts describe the experiences and feelings of the mass of women, the ordinary women who have been lost to history with the emphasis by historians on such atypical and deviant women as Calamity Jane, Belle Starr, and Carrie Nation.

There are unfortunately very few primary or secondary source-books concerned specifically with minority women. Native American women are the best represented in this bibliography for no other reason than that there is more material available about them. Black, Chinese, and Spanish-speaking women rarely left first-hand accounts and they are cursorily covered in minority studies which stress the achievements and hardships of men. However, two useful books are available: Delilah L. Beasley's *The Negro Trail Blazers of California* (R & E Research Associates, 1969) contains some material on black women and the roles of Chinese women are in Stephen Longstreet's *The Wilder Shore* (Doubleday, 1968).

The frontier woman is an area of Western American history still very much unexplored. Special topical issues of quarterlies about the West focusing on women — *Journal of the West* (XII, April, 1973) and *Pacific Historical Review* (XLIX, May, 1980) — however, might be helpful.

II

ii

Aikman, Duncan, *Calamity Jane and the Lady Wildcats* (Henry Holt, 1927) O.P.

Among the "lady wildcats" discussed in this collection of biographical sketches are Calamity Jane, Ella "Cattle Kate" Watson, Lola Montez, Belle Starr, Pearl Hart, and Carrie Nation. Almost one third of the book is devoted to the life of Calamity Jane whose autobiography Aikman accepted as being factual whereas most historicans believe it to be sheer hyperbole. This volume eschews some legends about infamous frontier women while indiscriminantly retaining others. Perhaps what is most misleading and disheartening about such books as Aikman's is that they perpetuate the enduring myth that the American West was populated with gun-toting, hardened adventuresses and bawds, or eccentric reformers.

Alderson, Nannie T., and Helena Huntington Smith, *A Bride Goes West* (Farrar & Rinehart, 1942) O.P.; reprinted by the University of Nebraska Press.

In spite of the setbacks and hardships experienced by Alderson, there is a humorous anecdotal quality to her story about cattle ranching in Montana in the last two decades of the Nineteenth century as told to Smith, who wrote and arranged this book of reminiscences.

Arnold, Mary Ellicott, and Mabel Reed, *In the Land of the Grasshopper Song* (Vantage Press, 1957) O.P.; reprinted by the University of Nebraska Press.

In this fascinating book Reed and Arnold recount their experiences in the Klamath River region of Northern California in 1908–1909 where they were sent by the Department of the Interior as field matrons to the Karok Indians. Being the only white women in "the Rivers" region, as it was called, Arnold and Reed were to act as a "civilizing influence" on the Karok enclave. What makes their story such a pleasure to read is their honesty and integrity as human beings. They recorded Karok customs and culture as well as their own everyday reactions, reflections, and adjustments to the Indian way of life, which to a certain extent they came to prefer to the white man's way.

Ball, Eve, *Ma'am Jones of the Pecos* (University of Arizona Press, 1969).

Southwestern historian Eve Ball set out in this book to tell the history of Lincoln County, New Mexico, through the eyes of the Heiskell and Barbara Jones family—the first Anglo-American family to establish a permanent residence in the Pecos Valley. However, as indicated by the title, the focus of the story is Barbara (Ma'am)Jones, homemaker, pioneer, doctor, teacher, storekeeper, and mother of nine sons and one daughter whose efforts to raise her children to be good citizens during the turbulent times of the Lincoln County War was no easy job. This biography, written with the intimacy of a novel and based on research into available records, historical materials, and personal interviews, contains a wealth of information on pioneer life in the Southwest as well as portraits of some of the more notorious people of that region such as Billy the Kid.

Bird, Isabella, *A Lady's Life in the Rocky Mountains* (1879) O.P.; various subsequent editions.

Bird was an unusual, educated, cultured British woman who wrote a number of books about her world-wide travels in the latter half of the Nineteenth century. This book, a collection of letters written to her sister, tells of her three-month expedition through the Rocky Mountains in 1873 covering over 1,800 miles. She had a keen eye for both Nature and people. This is a good example of a tourist's view of the West.

Bourne, Eulalia, *Woman in Levis* (University of Arizona Press, 1967); *Nine Months Is a Year* (University of Arizona Press, 1969); *Ranch Schoolteacher* (University of Arizona Press, 1974).

In this entertainingly written trilogy Bourne discussed her years in Southern Arizona juggling her dual career as a country schoolteacher and a rancher. Her love of bovines, and Nature in general, is the concern of her first book, *Woman in Levis*. The children whom she taught (most of them Mexican-Americans) in the San Pedro Valley are the focus of her two subsequent books. Her methods both as a schoolteacher and as a woman rancher were creative and often iconoclastic. This Twentieth-century Western "woman in Levis" had pluck, wisdom, common sense, and humanity — all of which are to be found in her writings.

Brown, Dee, *The Gentle Tamers* (Putnam's, 1958) O.P.; reprinted by the University of Nebraska Press.

This book is the best known of the handful of studies attempting an overview and analysis of the role of white women in the American West. With a vast collection of facts and trivia and a limited exposure to women's history and frontier first-hand accounts, considering the extensive scope of the subject, Brown essayed a topical approach; and it would seem he bit off more than he could chew. The reader is presented merely with the external world of Brown's chosen exemplary frontier women. Many of his conclusions — i.e., women, by virtue of their femininity, tamed the frontier and the men who settled on it; or women in the West were more independent and enjoyed greater freedom as is demonstrated by such women as Calamity Jane, Ann Eliza Young, and Mary Lease and by Wyoming's early adoption of women's suffrage — are whimsical and certainly not based on solid historical research. Brown viewed the Western frontier as primarily masculine turf which is not in itself uncommon but it did color his interpretation of the way women experienced the West. Ultimately, *The Gentle Tamers* fails in that it is not synecdochical, that is, it does not come to any far-reaching generalized conclusions in terms of the relationships between frontier women, the region in which they lived, and the ideologies in which they thought or which influenced the way they thought. The book is, however, well written and can be enjoyed for its richly anecdotal style.

Cabeza de Baca, Fabiola, *We Fed Them Cactus* (University of New Mexico Press, 1954).

The author's childhood was filled with stories of the *ciboleros*, the Comancheros, the rodeos, and the fiestas of the early Hispanic settlers of the Staked Plains (the Llano Estacado) of New Mexico. These tales and others are retold in this book which is a history of the Llano from the Spanish-American point of view, as seen through the eyes of four generations of the Cabeza de Baca family. If it is flawed at all, it is by the fact that, as her female ancestors before her, Fabiola Cabeza de Baca remained too much in the background, although she did point out that women "played a great part in the history of the land."

Clappe, Louise A.K.S., *The Shirley Letters*, various editions with the best being reprinted by Knopf (1949), edited by Carl I. Wheat.
          These twenty-three letters written from Rich Bar and Indian Bar on the Feather River in California between September, 1851 and November, 1852 have become a classic in gold rush literature. They were originally published in *The Pioneer*, a short-lived San Francisco magazine, in 1854–1855 and were then forgotten about for nearly seventy years. Written by Clappe, a sickly, frail, Victorian gentlewoman (affectionately known as Dame Shirley) to her sister, they faithfully record life in a California mining camp. In addition to describing all that her eye took in from the Empire Hotel to the interior of a small cabin to the natural scenery, Clappe's letters reveal a human side of a frontier mining settlement, rarely found in other personal accounts on the subject. Incidents contained in these letters are said to have served as the inspiration for a number of Bret Harte's short stories.

Cleaveland, Agnes Morley, *No Life for a Lady* (Houghton Mifflin, 1941) O.P.; reprinted by the University of Nebraska Press.
          Along with Nannie Alderson's book (see above) Southwestern historian J. Frank Dobie considered Cleaveland's account the "best book on range life from a woman's point of view ever published." It still stands as one of the finest personal documents about ranching and cowboying in late Nineteenth, early Twentieth-century New Mexico. Cleaveland, a Westerner by birth and a gentlewoman, could track grizzlies, ride horses, and round up cattle with the best men in the region. She possessed an extraordinary sense of humor and her prose glitters with anecdotes drawn from the daily occurrences in her life. This is an exceptional volume combining history and personal reminiscences, and is insightful in its portrayal of two generations of women — Cleaveland's and her mother's — coping with the rigors of Western life.

Coleman, Ann Raney, *Victorian Lady on the Texas Frontier: The Journal of Ann Raney Coleman* (University of Oklahoma Press, 1971), edited by C. Richard King.
          Coleman was a young British lady of refinement when she arrived in Texas in 1832. Her upbringing and expectations for the future had little prepared her for the misfortunes that would plague her during her subsequent

years in Texas and Louisiana. The tone of this book is exceedingly sober, the story of a woman struggling for a living against overwhelming odds to protect her interests and those of her offspring that unfolds amidst Texas' fight for independence and later the Civil War. The men in Ann's life, as well as her sister's and her daughter's, were unreliable wasters and by the end of her life Ann came to view women's lot as being terribly inequitable, compared to that of men. King in editing this book supplied copious footnotes.

Custer, Elizabeth Bacon, *Boots and Saddles* (1885); *Tenting on the Plains* (1887); *Following the Guidon* (1890), all three reprinted by the University of Oklahoma Press.

Elizabeth Custer's trilogy is so well known and so often cited because of its portrait of George Armstrong Custer — *his* picture is reprinted on the title page of *Tenting on the Plains* and not the author's. These three books are also historically important for their depiction of fort life as seen through the eyes of a woman. *Boots and Saddles*, the first to be published, is actually the last book chronologically, and tells about the Custers' last years together. *Tenting on the Plains*, the first book chronologically, is about their trip West after the Civil War and their experiences in Texas and Kansas. Lastly, *Following the Guidon* deals with Custer's most active years fighting Indians — 1867–1869. If the reader can get past the white-washing of her husband in these books, Elizabeth's reminiscences are well worth the reading.

Drago, Harry Sinclair, *Notorious Ladies of the Frontier* (Dodd, Mead, 1969) O.P.

As Duncan Aikman (see above), Drago, fabulist and popular historian, found the "notorious" women of the West the most interesting. However, his is the more reliable book on prostitutes, brothel madams, gamblers, adventuresses, and "women whose morals were a departure from the norm." Drago claimed that there were 50,000 bawds — "and very likely more" — between Kansas City, Missouri, and the Pacific Coast. He might have been right, but he did not give any evidence as to how he came up with the figure, so at best it is an estimate based on undocumented sources since the book contains no bibliography. Each chapter is devoted to a "notorious" woman or women and includes biographical material when available, as well as pertinent historical information. The chapters about Calamity Jane and Belle Starr are fairly reliable although there are some errors — e.g., Calamity Jane married Clinton Burk in El Paso, not Deadwood, as Drago contended. Until a better documented in-depth study on the infamous women of the West is produced, this volume will remain a good general reference.

Earp, Josephine Sarah Marcus, *I Married Wyatt Earp: The Recollections of Josephine Sarah Marcus Earp* (University of Arizona Press, 1976), edited by Glenn G. Boyer.

Just as one reads Elizabeth Custer's books (see above) for their portrait of George Armstrong Custer, one reads this autobiography for its portrait of Wyatt Earp. And this is one of the best books on Wyatt Earp, the man, and most particularly his later, post-Tombstone years. A fiercely independent and somewhat eccentric woman, Josephine's life story is just as fascinating as Wyatt's since she was forced to make various adjustments as they traveled throughout the West and to the gold fields of Alaska. In much of this book, which was written as a tender love story, Josephine is unfortunately only a minor character. Glenn G. Boyer provided excellent footnotes correcting Josephine's obvious omissions — it is generally believed that she and Wyatt were never, in fact, married — as well as an Afterword discussing the literary legend of Wyatt Earp.

Ellis, Anne, *The Life of an Ordinary Woman* (Houghton Mifflin, 1929) O.P.; reprinted by the University of Nebraska Press.

This first-hand narrative richly details the day-to-day experiences of two generations of a poor mining family, beginning in the 1880s. Ellis' recollections about her family and her childhood, young womanhood, and own motherhood in Colorado, Utah, and Nevada illustrate the precarious nature of life shared by women and children on the mining frontier. The book presents an invaluable portrait of lower-class women's roles as wives, mothers, and workers.

Faunce, Hilda, *Desert Wife* (Little, Brown, 1928) O.P.; reprinted by the University of Nebraska Press with an Introduction by Frank Waters.

Transplanted from the rain forests of Oregon to the desert land of Covered Water, Arizona, Faunce lived for four years (1914–1918) on the Navajo reservation where her husband ran a trading post. The daily occurrences in their lives are straight-forwardly described in this book as are their relationships with the Navajo people. What is most interesting about this narrative is the author's changing attitude toward the Navajos and the bonds of friendship she formed with a number of Navajo women.

Fischer, Christiane, (ed.), *Let Them Speak for Themselves: Women in the American West* 1849–1900 (The Shoe String Press, 1977) O.P.; reprinted by E.P. Dutton.

This is an anthology containing twenty-five excerpts from journals, autobiographies, and letters written by women living in California, Nevada, or Arizona in the second half of the Nineteenth century. It is strictly a collection of resurrected women's writings accompanied by brief biographical and stylistic comments, and not an interpretive book about the mass of frontier women. The excerpts themselves, however, illustrate both the unity and diversity of women and women's experience in the American West.

Foote, Mary Hallock, *A Victorian Gentlewoman in the Far West: The Reminiscences of Mary Hallock Foote* (The Huntington Library, 1972), edited and introduced by Rodman W. Paul.

Foote, an educated New York Quaker who gained national recognition as an illustrator and an author, felt ambivalent about the West although she lived in it for half a century, beginning in 1876. This book, primarily about her years in California, Colorado, and Idaho is noteworthy for both its telling portrait of a class-conscious Victorian woman living a "protected" life in the West as a wife, mother, and professional artist and for its depiction of the engineering community's early efforts in the West in which her husband had a large, although financially unsuccessful, part.

Gray, Dorothy, *Women of the West* (Les Femmes, 1976).

Gray attained in this relatively short volume a marvelous blend of biography, character interpretation, and history. Following a loosely structured chronological order, Gray recounted the lives of twenty women from the more familiar—Sacajawea, Narcissa Whitman, Esther Morris, Carrie Chapman Catt, Ella "Cattle Kate" Watson, Mary Elizabeth Lease, and Willa Cather—to the lesser known—Juliet Brier, Juanita, Biddy Mason, Ann Eliza Young, and Miriam Davis Colt. More importantly, however, Gray analysed how each of these women fit into her respective social environment. The book may appear to be a hodge-podge, but, reminiscent in form of Plutarch's *Lives*, Gray's treatment of the material is marked by both originality and perception. Gray's chapter on minority women is particularly good in its examination of the oppression of black and Mexican women whose racial victimization became even more intense with the arrival of white women. This book is well worth reading for its intelligent treatment of women as participants in history and for its analysis of their roles as wives, mothers, homemakers, laborers, professionals, political activists, and spokespersons. It also contains a useful bibliography.

Guerin, Mrs. E.J., *Mountain Charley* (University of Oklahoma Press, 1968).

Although a number of women are known to have lived as men in the West, this is a rare account of one such successful attempt. Mrs. Guerin donned male attire for thirteen years while searching for the slayer of her husband. Her brief autobiography describes her experiences as a riverboat cabin boy, a railroad brakeman, a miner, an entrepreneur, a trader, and a rancher in the 1850s. She was the mother of two children. Appended to this edition—originally privately published in 1861 by the author—is another woman's version who claimed to be Mountain Charley which culminates in her achieving the rank of lieutenant in the Union Army during the Civil War.

Howard, Harold P., *Sacajawea* (University of Oklahoma Press, 1971).

Based on the Lewis and Clark *Journals* and other available materials, Howard, a newspaperman, reconstructed in this book the life of Sacajawea. A well researched book containing an extensive bibliography, it concludes with an examination of the controversial issue of the death of Sacajawea and weighs the evidence. To date, this is the best book about her.

Ise, John, *Sod and Stubble* (Wilson-Erickson, 1936) O.P.; reprinted by the University of Nebraska Press.

The author, one of twelve children of Henry and Rosie Ise, recounted simply and gracefully the struggles of his homesteading family in Western Kansas where they settled in 1873 and in which his mother comes to occupy the central role.

Jeffrey, Julie Roy, *Frontier Women: The Trans-Mississippi West* 1840–1880 (Hill and Wang, 1979).

This insightful interpretive study of white frontier women is not merely a descriptive history of women's external world, but, also, an examination of the ideologies which influenced women who participated in the movement West between 1840–1880. Originally, Jeffrey viewed the pioneer woman from a feminist perspective; however, in researching the subject, she found that the ordinary frontier woman was not liberated, nor interested in becoming liberated, but was, in reality, highly influenced by the prescriptive domestic ideology of the first half of the Nineteenth century which stated that woman, as a genteel lady of fashion, was to function as an agent of civilization and a keeper of morals. Focusing on the agricultural, the mining, the urban, and the Mormon frontiers through their various stages of development, Jeffrey explored the familial and social roles of women. Having made use of more than 200 diaries, books of memoirs, collections of letters, along with numerous secondary resource books, *Frontier Women* not only adds to our understanding of pioneer women but also to our comprehension of Western American history through its firm grasp of the milieu of the Nineteenth century.

Jeffrey devoted a portion of the book to women's organizations, reform movements, and educational opportunities — as both teacher and student — in the West in which she assessed what these groups and institutions actually meant to and did for women. Her conclusions contradict those of other historians as Dee Brown (see above). Concerning the myth that women in the West had a more egalitarian status Jeffrey wrote, "Certainly, frontier social and sometimes political arrangements stood in contrast to those in the East. But this was hardly because men appreciated the 'unalienable rights of women.' Women valued themselves and were valued for their traditional qualities." This is a ground-breaking work and it contains a valuable bibliography.

Jones, David E., *Sanapia: Comanche Medicine Woman* (Holt, Rinehart, 1972) O.P.

As the author stated in his Introduction, this is an "ethnographic portrait" of Sanapia, a Comanche medicine woman. Based on three years of field research, Jones was an eyewitness to Sanapia's doctoring practice. This study details the role and methods of a Comanche Eagle doctor and records Sanapia's view of herself as a doctor and as a member of Comanche society.

Klasner, Lily, *My Girlhood Among Outlaws* (University of Arizona Press, 1972), edited by Eve Ball.

Lost until 1966, this first-hand narrative will probably become an important primary sourcebook because of its account of the Lincoln County War and for its portrait of John Chisum, whom the author knew intimately. Born in Texas, Klasner, who moved with her family to New Mexico in 1867, was called upon throughout her girlhood to help the family out by performing what would be considered generally "unfeminine" chores and jobs. She heard about and in some cases witnessed the hardships and violence of the Texan and New Mexican frontiers which she recounted in this book along with her experiences, when a young woman, as a telegrapher, teacher, and rancher.

Linderman, Frank B., *Pretty-Shield, Medicine Woman of the Crows* [alternate title: *Red Mother*] (John Day, 1932) O.P.; reprinted by the University of Nebraska Press.

According to agency records, Pretty-Shield was seventy-four when Linderman (who spent forty years studying the Western Plains Indians) recorded the story of her life. She was the mother of five children and a highly respected woman among her people, the Crows. This book gives a portrait of the life ways of the Crows with special emphasis on the roles and lives of women.

Ross, Nancy Wilson, *Westward the Women* (Knopf, 1944) O.P.

This book explores the role of women in the settling and civilizing of the Pacific Northwest region — Washington, Oregon — and Idaho. Six of the eleven chapters are devoted to the lives of individual women who rose to the challenges of frontier life in the Far West under diverse circumstances, among them Sacajawea, Narcissa Whitman, Eliza Spalding, Abigail Scott Duniway, and Bethenia Owens-Adair. On the subject of Northwestern frontier women generally, Ross devoted chapters to the rigors of overland travel, the efforts of men to attract women to the area, the roles of prostitutes and adventuresses, and the vicissitudes of pioneer life from the female point of view. Although a very brief study, this book is a good regional study of frontier women which contains some portraits not to be found elsewhere.

Royce, Sarah, *A Frontier Lady: Recollections of the Gold Rush and Early California* (Yale University Press, 1932) O.P.; reprinted by the University of Nebraska Press, edited by Ralph Henry Gabriel.

Over thirty years after she had made the 1849 overland journey with her husband and two-year-old daughter, Sarah Royce at the request of her son, philosopher Josiah Royce, committed her memories to paper. The covered wagon trip to California as well as the Royces' early years spent in California moving from one mining camp to another are vividly recalled by this Victorian woman raised in New York. This book is often singled out as one of the more important first-hand accounts of the gold rush period.

Sanford, Mollie Dorsey, *Mollie: The Journal of Mollie Dorsey Sanford in Nebraska and Colorado Territories* 1857–1866 (University of Nebraska Press, 1959).

This diary was begun when the Dorsey family moved to Nebraska Territory in 1857. For nine years, Mollie, who worked briefly as a teacher and a dressmaker, recorded her reflections and observations about frontier life and people in Nebraska and in Colorado where she moved in 1860 shortly after her marriage to By Sanford. Although the diary entries are often erratic and lack a narrative structure, the book presents a simple and honestly written account of the early community settlements of Nebraska and Colorado.

Sekaquaptewa, Helen, *Me and Mine: The Life Story of Helen Sekaquaptewa as Told to Louise Udall* (University of Arizona Press, 1969).

This is a beautifully written autobiography in which the history of the Hopi people is interwoven with the personal reminiscences of Sekaquaptewa. Especially moving and interesting is her account of the period she spent in government schools, beginning in 1906.

Shaw, Anna Moore, *A Pima Past* (University of Arizona Press, 1974).

A civic- and religious-minded Presbyterian Pima, Shaw described in her autobiography her efforts to combine and harmonize the old Pima ways with the ways of the whites in Twentieth-century Arizona. She was extremely optimistic about the cultural adjustments made and to be made by the Indians of the Southwest. As is true with most Native American autobiographies, a great deal of space is devoted by Shaw to her ancestors. Brief biographical sketches of what Shaw called her "Indian Hall of Fame" are appended to the book.

Stewart, Elinore Pruitt, *Letters of a Woman Homesteader* (Houghton Mifflin, 1914) O.P.; *Letters on an Elk Hunt* (Houghton Mifflin, 1915) O.P.; both reprinted by the University of Nebraska Press.

Stewart, an autodidact, was a natural born storyteller. These two volumes contain letters written between 1909–1914 to her former employer about her adventures and the people she knew in Wyoming as a woman homesteader. *Letters on an Elk Hunt* includes a Foreword by Elizabeth Fuller Ferris which includes biographical background on Stewart, a truly extraordinary woman.

Terrell, John Upton, and Donna M. Terrell, *Indian Women of the Western Morning: Their Life in Early America* (Dial, 1974) O.P.; reprinted by Doubleday Anchor Books.

Historian John Terrell was joined by his wife Donna in the writing of this book which somewhat fills the gap created by the dearth of material in Indian and women's history about Indian women. A fairly general yet useful anthropological work, it eschews the misconceptions about Indian women as abject drudges or chattel of a male-dominated culture by showing

Indian women as contributing members of families and tribes and as economic producers. Because the Terrells wanted to demonstrate that women were in fact highly regarded among many tribes and often held positions of honor, the matrilineal tribes (where descent is traced through the female line) are emphasized more than non-sedentary, non-agricultural tribes where women are "relegated to the status of second class citizens." The Terrells' book is predominantly descriptive in approach. They studied ten areas in the lives of Indian women — mythology, status, duty, crafts, adornment, food, sex, life cycle, children, and health/and physique — outlining what women did and how they did it. However, unfortunately, the authors are not above this kind of sexist generalization: "Costume was important to Indian women. They were self-conscious. ...Vanity was not an invention of women of another race." Yet, despite such short-comings, this is an important work which seriously attempts an overview.

Western Writers of America, The, *The Women Who Made the West* (Doubleday, 1980); reprinted by Avon Books.
   This is a fairly consistent collection of vignettes of the lives of eighteen frontier women. It is the thirty-sixth volume put together by the Western Writers of America and it is their first "all-woman" book — women writing about women. The women presented are well chosen, displaying a diversity of character and experience, and include women in the roles of wives and mothers as well as unskilled workers and professionals. Each chapter is supplemented with a list of sources that can be used for further research on the subject.

Williams, Brad, *Legendary Women of the West* (David McKay, 1978) O.P.
   This book contains nine biographical sketches of women who lived in the West — Juana Maria (an Indian "princess"), Dona Tula, Julia Bulette, Eilley Orrum Bowers, Pearl Hart, Ella "Cattle Kate" Watson, Mammy Pleasant, Baby Doe Tabor, and Aimee Semple McPherson. It is both uninspired and ahistorical. The author's *modus operandi* seems to have been to find and then emphasize the most shocking and sensational aspects of his subject. The basis for much of the information given here will remain a mystery since the book does not contain a bibilography.

Suggested Fiction

Bower, B.M., *Lonesome Land* (Little, Brown, 1912)
Capps, Benjamin, *A Woman of the People* (Duell, Sloan, 1966)
Cather, Willa, *My Ántonia* (Houghton Mifflin, 1918)
Cook, Will, *Elizabeth, By Name* (Dodd, Mead, 1958)
Ferber, Edna, *Cimarron* (Doubleday, 1930)
Gardiner, Dorothy, *The Golden Lady* (Doubleday, 1936)
Hum-Ishu-Mu (Mourning Dove), *Cogewea, The Half Blood* (1927; University of Nebraska Press, 1981)

Jackson, Helen Hunt, *Ramona* (1884)

Laughlin, Ruth, *The Wind Leaves No Shadow* (1948; Caxton Printers, 1951)

McCunn, Ruthanne Lum, *Thousand Pieces of Gold* (Design Enterprises, 1981)

Manfred, Frederick, *The Manly-Hearted Woman* (Crown, 1975)

Richter, Conrad, *The Lady* (Knopf, 1957)

Sandoz, Mari, *Miss Morissa, Doctor of the Gold Trail* (1955; University of Nebraska Press, 1981)

Scarborough, Dorothy, *The Wind* (Harper's, 1925)

Stewart, George R., *East of the Giants* (Henry Holt, 1938)

Suggested Films

Annie Oakley (RKO, 1935) directed by George Stevens.

Calamity Jane (Warner's, 1953) directed by David Butler.

Destry Rides Again (Universal, 1939) directed by George Marshall.

Duel in the Sun (Selznick Releasing, 1946) directed by King Vidor.

The First Traveling Saleslady (RKO, 1956) directed by Arthur Lubin.

The Guns of Fort Petticoat (Columbia, 1957) directed by George Marshall.

The Hired Hand (Universal, 1971) directed by Peter Fonda.

Johnny Guitar (Republic, 1954) directed by Nicholas Ray.

McCabe and Mrs. Miller (Warner's, 1971) directed by Robert Altman.

True Grit (Paramount, 1969) directed by Henry Hathaway.

Westward the Women (M-G-M, 1952) directed by William Wellman.

Wings of the Hawk (Universal, 1953) directed by Budd Boetticher.

Native Americans

by Jon Tuska

I

Unfortunately, even at this relatively late date, the field of Native American historiography is an ideological battleground for rival *idées fixes* and intrepid scholarship.

There are principally two kinds of partisanship. In the broadest terms, there have always been white historians who have felt that Native Americans are inferior, albeit this inferiority might be racial or it might be cultural; and, more recently, there have been those who have viewed Native Americans as the helpless victims of a holocaust. One might think that the former group has become less commonplace than it once was, but, actually, in the wake of the reaction to Dee Brown's *Bury My Heart at Wounded Knee* (Holt, Rinehart, 1971) — the keystone of the books typical of the latter group — it has found a new lease on life.

One example must suffice. T.R. Fehrenbach in *Comanches: The Destruction of a People* (Knopf, 1979) made the point, central to his thesis, that "the Amerindian was not inferior to his enemies in brain or physique. He was desperately inferior in culture, the acquired culture of thousands of years of experience." For Fehrenbach, Native Americans fell into new classes at the time of European contact, "predatory savages" and "high barbarians." He adopted social Darwinism as his metaphor for what happened after first contact. "...From the viewpoint of the rest of the world,

51

everything they [Native Americans] had achieved had already been achieved before." He dismissed Native American religion as "soul-satisfying superstition" and wrote that the "cosmic vision of the world, which they brought out of Asia, did not seek to connect cause with effect, made magic a surrogate for science, and substituted subjective experience for empirical observation." In Fehrenbach's opinion religion was only a primitive, inferior forerunner of technological science, indeed "the basis for all human religion" was men's will to "understand the cosmic forces that ruled the physical world so that they might bend them to their needs and wishes...." He also asserted that "many of the hunting bands certainly practiced cannibalism," that "North America was a world of constant, brutal change long before Europeans impinged on it," that "the torture of captives was as universal among Amerindians in North America as the custom of taking scalps," and that the Nermernuh (Comanches) "did not understand Nature, or man in Nature, or even man against Nature, any more than animals did." "...The diffusion of the horse across the Great Plains actually may have worked a cultural regression" because "it halted any normal progress toward agriculture, organization, and diversification." As for the destruction of the buffalo, "the bison ... was a beast unfitted by Nature to survive. A sluggish, mild-tempered, and unintelligent herbivore, it was obstinate and even stupid compared to other animals." As bad as the Comanches may have been, the Athapaskans were identified by the Zunis as "*Apaches* or enemies, and the Spanish, with some justice, recorded them for posterity as enemies of mankind." With so little going for them, one can only record the passing of the Native Americans as one can that of the buffalo. "The Nermernuh," Fehrenbach summed up the Comanches, "would also vanish like the rest, but not before they rode into history like a whirlwind."

The amazing thing about Fehrenbach's book is not that its author was possessed of all these *idées fixes* about Native Americans, or even that he had such a smug attitude about the supposedly unquestionable superiority of Anglo-American materialistic, technological culture (to the extent that the Native American achieved *nothing* that had not been first acheived by the Anglo-Americans, or the Europeans); no, the amazing thing is that Fehrenbach's book was published by a reputable New York publisher in 1979!

Nor need social Darwinism, that is, applying a biological scheme to the study of cultures, result in a tragic ending. Peter Farb in *Man's Rise to Civilization as Shown by the Indians of North America from Primeval Times to the Coming of the Industrial State* (Dutton, 1968) arrived at a less bleak conclusion. Vine Deloria, Jr., a Sioux, in reviewing Farb's book remarked ironically that it was a good thing to know that the Indians finally made it. "The key to modern evolutionary theory," Professor Elman R. Service wrote in his Introduction to *Man's Rise to Civilization* etc., "lies in the concept of adaptation: every society has a culture that adapts, more or less successfully, to an environment. Some of the Indian societies reached a dead end of adaptation, while others continued adapting in ways that made for (or allowed) the rise of greater complexity." The underlying value here is that complex is better. According to Farb, "the answer to why certain societies survived while others became culturally extinct will be found, in many cases, in the varying levels of cultural evolution they had attained." In Farb's account Native Americans did not, collectively, so much "vanish" as they adapted or did not adapt to the superior white culture.

It is possible to be critical of James L. Haley's prefatory remarks to *Apaches: A History and Culture Portrait* (Doubleday, 1981), but at least Haley was willing to admit his partisanship, something many historians are disinclined to do. "To those who meant the Apaches well," Haley wrote, "the ignorance and suffering and violence of their life-style were plain to see; if it was wrong to exercise coercion to assimilate them into a more advanced state, would it not have been more wrong to have left them entirely alone?" Here, once more, is the Anglo-American claim to cultural superiority. Yet, on Haley's behalf I will grant that while there is nothing really new in his culture portrait — if you are familiar with his sources, you know where every fact and perspective came from — his bias did not permeate his text to the degree that Fehrenbach's did his text so that the reader must needs be reminded on virtually every page just how inferior the Apaches were when compared to the invaders. Yet, when it came to disputed matters and Haley had to make a choice, somewhat predictably the choice usually ran against the Apaches. For example, on page five of her book, *Geronimo: The Man, His Time, His Place* (University of Oklahoma Press, 1976) Angie Debo wrote: "Scalping, however, did occur on rare occasions." Haley, in approaching this issue, commented that "some scholars insist rather highly that Apaches never scalped and that accounts of it are the result of 'imaginative editing.'[5]" The "5" is a footnote citation: "5. Debo, *Geronimo*, p. 5." Did Haley mean to imply that Debo claimed the Apaches never scalped? "However," Haley continued, "it seems certain that it was practiced to a limited extent." Notwithstanding, there is a subtle, but real, difference between "rarely" and "limited."

Space does not permit me to persist in cataloguing the problems rampant in white men's scholarship about Native Americans. Let me only say this: while a great many books have been published about Native Americans, their history and cultures, and even more fictional and cinematic works have used them in varying and erroneous contexts, it is unfortunate that so few of these images are wholly reliable and that so much of what has been written has been guided and influenced by white men's stereotypes.

II

i

In the first part of this bibliographic essay, I have included books of a general nature. The second part is devoted to books on specific tribes or culture areas outlined in the General Introduction. The only exception to this bifurcation is individual autobiographies and biographies which have been subsumed under this heading in the first part.

General Histories

Perhaps the best place to begin is in terms of a general overview of Native American history from prehistoric times through the present. The single finest book of this kind which I found is Arrell Morgan Gibson's *The American Indian: Prehistory to the Present* (D.C. Heath, 1980). It is an extremely well researched, well documented, balanced survey written from the perspective of an *historicus magnus*. Because it is general, however, Gibson's history has to be supported by various specific studies in terms of individual culture areas and it is also best supplemented by three additional general books, Ruth M. Underhill's revised edition of *Red Man's America* (University of Chicago Press, 1971) and Angie Debo's revised edition of *A History of the Indians of the United States* (University of Oklahoma Press, 1979) along with the illustrated anthology, *Forked Tongues and Broken Treaties* (Caxton Printers, 1975) edited by Donald E. Worcester.

Two general books with a somewhat narrower focus which can also be recommended are Edward H. Spicer's *A Short History of the Indians of the United States* (Van Nostrand, 1969) and the revised edition of D'Arcy McNickle's *They Came Here First: The Epic of the American Indian* (Harper's, 1975). McNickle questioned the division into ten culture areas usually used by anthropologists in classifying the multitude of Indian nations; and in this context, it should be noted that Ruth M. Underhill managed to introduce a higher degree of accuracy and clarity in her methods of classification in *Red Man's America*. Spicer's book is especially notable for the number of original documents which are reproduced and McNickle's history is concerned principally with Indian treaties and, hence, is a good companion volume to Worcester's collection.

Indian Wars

The most popular book on this subject has been Dee Brown's *Bury My Heart at Wounded Knee*. In its way it continued a trend begun by Paul I. Wellman in *Death on Horseback* (Lippincott, 1947). What it comes to — as of the time of this writing — is that a general history on this specific subject that is at once factually reliable and balanced in perspective has yet to be written. There is, however, Mari Sandoz' *Cheyenne Autumn* (Hastings House, 1953) which is devoted to an aspect of the Indian wars that might readily serve as a paradigm for such a general history.

Somewhat related to the Indian wars is the reservation system which was the Anglo-American alternative to extermination and both interesting factual studies, such as Clark Wissler's reissued *Red Man Reservations* (Macmillan, 1971), and stirring fictional treatments, such as D'Arcy McNickle's *The Surrounded* (1936; University of New Mexico Press, 1978) and Benjamin Capps' *The White Man's Road* (Harper's, 1969), have appeared.

Although confined to specific tribes, two extremely moving accounts of reservation life are also worth reading, John Joseph Mathews' *Wah'Kon-Tah: The Osage and the White Man's Road* (1932; University of Oklahoma Press, 1981) and Donald J. Berthrong's *The Cheyenne and Arapahoe Ordeal: Reservation and Agency Life in the Indian Territory*, 1875-1907 (University of Oklahoma Press, 1976).

Religion

Ruth M. Underhill's *Red Man's Religion: Beliefs and Practices of the Indians North of Mexico* (University of Chicago Press, 1965) is an excellent book with which to begin studying a very complex subject. Underhill described Indian religious behavior, belief, and ceremonies in understandable, non-technical, and quietly respectful terms. Frank Waters' two studies of specialized aspects of this subject are also to be recommended, *Masked Gods: Navajo and Pueblo Ceremonialism* (University of New Mexico Press, 1950) and *Book of the Hopi* (Viking, 1969). The metaphysics of the Navajo and Pueblo systems are as complicated as anything in Plotinus or Hegel or Heidegger, a circumstance which may well come as something of a surprise to those exposed only to the "complex is better" school and to those who dismiss Native American religion as pre-technological superstition.

Members of the many Christian sects generally do not appreciate having Biblical narratives reduced to comforting myths and legends, and perhaps this same courtesy should have been extended long ago to Native American peoples. However such was not the case and in view of the titles of most of the books mentioned below nothing can be done to correct this situation here. Therefore, collections of Indian "myths" and "legends" are usually subsumed by anthology editors and publishers under the heading of literature.

Literature

There are two general collections worthy of inclusion as valuable introductions to this subject, Frederick W. Turner's *The Viking Portable North American Indian Reader* (Viking, 1974), a fine sampling of myths, tales, poetry, oratory, and autobiography, and Alan R. Velies *American Indian Literature: An Anthology* (University of Oklahoma Press, 1979) which has a much wider selection of Indian poetry and — something Turner's collection does not have at all — a selection of Native American songs accompanied by piano scores. In classes I have conducted on images of Indians in the popular media, Native American students have usually presented a number of traditional songs and ballads and, if little known among Anglo-Americans, this is a particularly beautiful aspect of Native American cultures. Both of these collections have parts of the Winnebago trickster cycle, Velie's more of it than Turner's, and a good complement to reading this cycle is Paul Radin's *The Trickster: A Study in American Indian Mythology* (Philosophical Library, 1956) with additional commentaries by C.G. Jung and Karl Kerényi.

Theodora Kroeber rewrote nine California Indian stories for *The Inland Whale* (Indiana University Press, 1959), but despite the book's many virtues it does not have, of course, the cultural and spiritual depth — nor was this Kroeber's intention — of George Bird Grinnell's studies, *Pawnee Hero Stories and Folk-Tales* (1889; University of Nebraska Press, 1961) with notes on the origins, customs, and character of the Pawnee people, *Blackfoot Lodge Tales: The Story of a Prairie People* (1892; University of Nebraska Press, 1962), and *By Cheyenne Campfires* (1926; University of Nebraska Press, 1971). Of almost equal interest are Ruth Warner Giddings' *Yaqui Myths and Legends* (University of Arizona Press, 1959), Ella A. Clark's *Indian Legends from the Northern Rockies* (University of Oklahoma Press, 1966), and Eugene Lee Silliman's collection of Blackfoot tales by James Willard Schultz (Apikuni), *Why Gone Those Times?* (University of Oklahoma Press, 1974).

Not since the height of the Roman Republic has human oratory been the consummate art it was among the American Indians. *Indian Oratory: Famous Speeches by Noted Indian Chieftains* (University of Oklahoma Press, 1974) edited by W.C. Vanderwerth is perhaps the best over-all collection. Vine Deloria's *Custer Died for Your Sins* (Macmillan, 1969), on the other hand, presents a contemporary Sioux' view of the dominant Anglo-American culture and its misunderstandings about Native Americans.

Twentieth-century Native American authors are discussed in subsection I v of Western Fiction and Charles R. Larson's *American Indian Fiction* (University of New Mexico Press, 1978), a critical survey, is particularly recommended in III ii of that section.

Autobiographies and Biographies

A good place to begin is to read Lynne Woods O'Brien's *Plains Indian Autobiographies* (Idaho State University, 1973) which surveys the principal works written by Plains Indians with or without the assistance of a collaborator from an alien culture. One of the most interesting of the "as told to" autobiographies is *Plenty-Coups, Chief of the Crows* (University of Nebraska Press, 1962) by Frank B. Linderman, originally published as *American: The Life Story of a Great Indian, Plenty-Coups, Chief of the Crows* (John Day, 1930).

It was a practice among the Plains Indians for every young brave to go out into the wilderness and, through fasting, wait for a vision to come to him. The vision was to give shape to his entire life in the future and might be equally relevant to the life of his nation. Certainly the best known of these visions is that narrated in *Black Elk Speaks* (Morrow, 1932) "as told to" poet John G. Neihardt. Black Elk was a Sioux medicine man and a book more concerned with the metaphysics and rituals of the Sioux is *The Sacred Pipe: Black Elk's Account of the Seven Rites of the Oglala Sioux* (University of Oklahoma Press, 1953) edited and recorded by Joseph Epes Brown.

Because until recently no tradition of women's autobiography was encouraged among Native American women, only a few such accounts have appeared. One of the best is *Pretty-Shield, Medicine Woman of the Crows* (1932; University of Nebraska Press, 1974) "as told to" Frank B. Linderman. Another of the most searching "as told to" narratives, because of her intimate understanding of Native American cultures, is Ruth M. Underhill's *The Autobiography of a Papago Woman* (Kraus Reprint Co., 1974). Of related interest are *Karnee: A Paiute Narrative* (University of Nevada Press, 1966) by Lalla Scott and *Me and Mine: The Life Story of Helen Sekaquaptewa* "as told to" Louise Udall (University of Arizona Press, 1969). Finally there is the "biography" and culture record prepared by David E. Jones with the assistance of tape recordings, *Sanapia: Comanche Medicine Woman* (Holt, Rinehart, 1972). The best biography to appear so far on the most famous Native American woman — most famous among Anglo-Americans — is Harold P. Howard's *Sacajawea* (University of Oklahoma Press, 1971).

In those cases where Native Americans were removed from reservations and educated in white schools, those who chose to write autobiographies often did so with the intention of comparing Indian and white cultures. Almost invariably, Native American authors came to perceive that honesty and truthfulness, the concern for others and the instinctive generosity of Native Americans were qualities all too distinctly Indian whereas it was the lack of these very qualities — however much they might be praised by white man — which come to characterize the successful white man in white culture. Charles A. Eastman, a Sioux who became a physician, wrote *From the Deep Woods to Civilization, Chapters in the Autobiography of an Indian* (Little, Brown, 1931) in which he recorded his greatest shock as being the discovery, when he became a lobbyist for Indian treaty rights in Washington, D.C., that buying legislators' votes was part of the accepted white man's civilization. Luther Standing Bear's three-part autobiography is of enduring quality also, *My People, the Sioux* (1928; University of Nebraska Press, 1975), *My Indian Boyhood* (Houghton Mifflin, 1931), and *Land of the Spotted Eagle* (1933; University of Nebraska Press, 1978).

Among Southwestern Native American autobiographies, one of the very best is *Sun Chief: The Autobiography of a Hopi Indian* (Yale University Press, 1942) by Don C. Talayesva edited by Leo W. Simmons, an articulate account of the conflict between cultures. To this should be added *Geronimo: His Own Story* (Ballantine, 1971), originally edited by S.M.

Barrett but in this edition newly edited with an Introduction by Frederick
W. Turner III, augmented by Angie Debo's *Geronimo: The Man, His
Time, His Place*. Another excellent source is Eve Ball's transcription of
James Kaywaykla's oral history, *In the Days of Victorio: Recollections of a
Warm Springs Apache* (University of Arizona Press, 1970), supplemented
by Dan L. Thrapp's *Victorio and the Mimbres Apaches* (University of Oklahoma Press, 1974). Also, Dover Books has reissued a book which has
become a standard of its kind since it was first published by the University of California Publications in American Archaeology and Ethnology in
1920, Paul Radin's transcription of S.B.'s *The Autobiography of a Winnebago Indian*. Of almost equal substance is *Jim Whitewolf: The Life of a
Kiowa Apache Indian* (Dover Books, 1969), issued as an original publication edited with an Introduction and Epilogue by Charles S. Brant.

Without a doubt one of the finest Indian biographies is *Crazy
Horse: The Strange Man of the Oglalas* (Hastings House, 1942) by Mari
Sandoz who, many have said, was more Indian then Anglo-American,
although it was culture by adoption. Also highly recommended is John H.
Seger's first-hand account, *Early Days Among the Cheyenne and Arapahoe
Indians* (1924; University of Oklahoma Press, 1956).

II

ii

While it is never a good practice to generalize about a publisher,
one exception can perhaps be made for the University of Oklahoma Press
and its The Civilization of the American Indian Series which, as of 1980,
numbered some 146 titles, each on a specific tribe or aspect of Native American history or culture. Several books from this series are mentioned below,
but, with regard to those that are not, a reader can be assured, I believe,
that each entry tends to be factually reliable and does not argue on behalf
of some special interest group or cultural bias.

Northeastern and Southeastern

Although it is a very old book, still I rate it highly: Cadwallader
Colden's *The History of the Five Indian Nations Depending on the
Province of New York in America*, published in two parts, in 1727 and 1747
respectively, and reissued in one paperback volume by Cornell University
Press in 1964. But, once having read Colden's history, it must needs be
supplemented with Georgiana C. Nammack's *Fraud, Politics, and the Dis-
possession of the Indian: The Iroquois Land Frontier in the Colonial Period*
(University of Oklahoma Press, 1969). With these two books by way of
background, then the reader is prepared to tackle three important, even
vital, but not always reliable accounts, Lewis Henry Morgan's *League of*

the Ho-de-no-sau-nee, or Iroquois (1851; Citadel Press, 1972), Francis Parkman's *The Conspiracy of Pontiac* (1851) especially in the now out-of-print reissue edition published by Collier Books in 1962 with an Introduction by Samuel Eliot Morison, and George T. Hunt's *The Wars of the Iroquois: A Study in Intertribal Trade Relations* (University of Wisconsin Press, 1940). Finally, there is a particularly significant collection of primary sources edited by James Axtell, *The Indian Peoples of Eastern America: A Documentary History of the Sexes* (Oxford University Press, 1981).

The best general account of the cultural impact of removal on the Five Civilized Tribes — Cherokee, Chickasaw, Choctaw, Creek, and Seminole — is to be found in a brace of volumes, the texts of which incorporate amply original documents and primary sources, written by Grant Foreman, *The Five Civilized Tribes* (University of Oklahoma Press, 1934) and *Indian Removal* (1932; issued in a new edition by the University of Oklahoma Press, 1953). In addition, there are three excellent supplementary volumes on three of the five tribes, Angie Debo's *The Rise and Fall of the Choctaw Republic* (University of Oklahoma Press, 1934), Grace Steele Woodward's *The Cherokees* (University of Oklahoma Press, 1963), and Arrell Morgan Gibson's *The Chickasaws* (University of Oklahoma Press, 1971). For the Middle Border area I would also strongly recommend William T. Hagan's *The Sac and Fox Indians* (University of Oklahoma Press, 1958) and, of equal interest in itself and of special interest because of their decision to flee to Mexico during the period of Indian removal in the Eastern United States, Arrell Morgan Gibson's *The Kickapoos: Lords of the Middle Border* (University of Oklahoma Press, 1971).

Plains

As a consequence largely of their horse culture, Western fiction, wild West shows, and motion pictures, the Plains Indians are often incorrectly identified as American Indians *par excellence*. An ideal volume to read first, a work both of history and literature, a rare combination indeed, would be George Bird Grinnell's *The Fighting Cheyennes* (1915; University of Oklahoma Press, 1956), followed with Grinnell's two-volume *The Cheyenne Indians: Their History and Ways of Life* (1923; University of Nebraska Press, 1971).

The best volume on the history and culture of the Sioux which I found that might serve as an introduction is Royal B. Hassrick's *The Sioux* (University of Oklahoma Press, 1964). It is well complemented with Virginia Cole Trenholm's *The Arapahoes, Our People* (University of Oklahoma Press, 1970).

As in the case of Grinnell's *The Fighting Cheyennes*, John Joseph Mathews' *The Osages: Children of the Middle Waters* (University of Oklahoma Press, 1961) may be regarded as more than a history and culture study, something more akin to a spiritual journey. Of uniform quality and also to be recommended as introductory studies are George E. Hyde's *The*

Pawnee Indians (University of Oklahoma Press, 1951) and Donald J. Berthrong's *The Southern Cheyennes* (University of Oklahoma Press, 1963).

A good reading plan for beginning a study of the Indians of the Southwestern plains would be to start with *The Indians of Texas: From Prehistoric to Modern Times* (University of Texas Press, 1961) by W.W. Newcomb, Jr., and go on immediately to *The Comanches: Lords of the South Plains* (University of Oklahoma Press, 1952) by Ernest Wallace and E. Adamson Hoebel and *The Kiowas* (University of Oklahoma Press, 1962) by Mildred P. Mayhall.

Southwest and Great Basin

In addition to the land areas gained through the signing of the Treaty of Guadalupe Hidalgo between the United States and the Republic of Mexico in 1848, the United States also became responsible for the administration of some 125,000 Indians. The finest introduction to the Indians of these land areas is Edward Everett Dale's *The Indians of the Southwest: A Century of Development Under the United States* (University of Oklahoma Press, 1949). However, should the reader prefer a somewhat more extended temporal perspective than merely the period since 1848, two books in particular come to mind, Edward H. Spicer's truly impressive and exhaustive study of influences in *Cycles of Conquest: The Impact of Spain, Mexico, and the United States on the Indians of the Southwest, 1533–1960* (University of Arizona Press, 1962), and Jack D. Forbes' more circumscribed and less detailed *Apache, Navajo, and Spaniard* (1960; Greenwood Press, 1980).

However, neither Spicer nor Forbes dealt specifically with the cultures of the Indian nations in these land areas; for this, the reader will have to go to books which especially focus on these aspects. A good place to begin in studying the Athapaskans is Donald E. Worcester's *The Apaches: Eagles of the Southwest* (University of Oklahoma Press, 1979), augmented by C.L. Sonnichsen's *The Mescalero Apaches* (University of Oklahoma Press, 1958), Morris E. Opler's *An Apache Life-Way: The Economic, Social, and Religious Institutions of the Chiricahua Indians* (University of Chicago Press, 1941), and *Western Apache Raiding and Warfare* (University of Arizona Press, 1971) compiled from the notes of Grenville Goodwin and edited by Keith H. Basso. The authoritative book with which to begin studying the Navajo people, blood relatives to the Apaches, is Ruth M. Underhill's *The Navajos* (University of Oklahoma Press, 1956) and, because of the controversy with which this brief period is surrounded, supplemented by Gerald Thompson's *The Army and the Navajo: The Bosque Redondo Reservation Experiment, 1863–1868* (University of Arizona Press, 1976). To complement these books, I would also recommend *Pueblos, Gods, and Spaniards* (Dial, 1973) by John Upton Terrell, *Pages from Hopi History* (University of Arizona Press, 1974) by Harry C. James, and *The Yaquis: A Cultural History* (University of Arizona Press, 1980) by Edward H. Spicer, this last book being particularly well illustrated.

For the Bannocks and the Northern Shoshonis (a branch of the Snake Indians who, unlike the Comanches, did not venture onto the Plains), I would recommend two books, both by the same author: for a brief overview, Brigham D. Madsen's *The Lemhi: Sacajawea's People* (Caxton Printers, 1979), and Madsen's *The Northern Shoshoni* (Caxton Printers, 1980) for a more detailed chronology.

California

The Indians of this culture area present a unique problem for the historian due to their diversity. For an appropriate overview and exhaustive basic reference, I would suggest A.L. Kroeber's *Handbook of The Indians of California* (Dover Books, 1976) which is a reprint of *Bulletin* 78 of the Bureau of American Ethnology of the Smithsonian Institution, first published in 1925, with over 400 illustrations and some forty maps. Kroeber's handbook can be supplemented, ideally, by the revised and enlarged second edition of R.F. Heizer's and M.A. Whipple's *The California Indians: A Source Book* (University of California Press, 1971).

Pacific Northwest and Plateau

There are three books that stand out devoted to the Indians of the Pacific Northwest with which one ought to begin the study of the peoples of this region. They are Keith A. Murray's *The Modocs and Their War* (University of Oklahoma Press, 1959), Stephen Dow Beckham's *Requiem for a People: The Rogue Indians and the Frontiersmen* (University of Oklahoma Press, 1971), and Robert H. Ruby's and John A. Brown's magnificently mounted and illustrated, *Indians of the Pacific Northwest* (University of Oklahoma Press, 1981). This same pair also collaborated on the altogether remarkable *The Cayuse Indians: Imperial Tribesmen of Old Oregon* (University of Oklahoma Press, 1972).

When it comes to the Nez Percé, a good introduction is *The Nez Percés: Tribesmen of the Columbia Plateau* (University of Oklahoma Press, 1955) by Francis Haines. Should the reader desire a somewhat more thorough history, I would recommend the original edition of Alvin M. Josephy, Jr.'s *The Nez Percé and the Opening of the West* (Yale University Press, 1965) which was reissued in an abridged edition by the University of Nebraska Press in 1979. The best book I have found on Chief Joseph is the revised edition of Helen Addison Howard's biography, *Saga of Chief Joseph* (1971; University of Nebraska Press, 1978), and a book specifically on the Nez Percé War of 1877 and Chief Joseph's role in it (setting to one side many of the fantasies about Joseph's being supposedly an American version of Napoleon Buonaparte), Merrill D. Beal's *"I Will Fight No More Forever": Chief Joseph and the Nez Percé War* (University of Washington Press, 1963).

Finally, there is John Fahey's fine study, *The Flathead Indians* (University of Oklahoma Press, 1974).

(I cannot help remarking at this point, that not only is the term Indian a white man's mistaken fantasy, but so also are the notions of *nez percé* [pierced nose] and *tête plat* [flat head]: the peoples so referred to by the French did not have pierced noses or flat heads. Yet the descendants of these peoples, this notwithstanding, must continue to go through life being referred to by such meaningless verbiage as Flathead Indians!)

Arctic and Sub-Arctic

Technically speaking, a valid objection could be raised to making mention of these peoples in a reader's guide focused on the life and literature of the American West, although some would say that Alaska was the last frontier and it is in a Westerly direction from the East Coast. Rather than engage in a defense for so doing, for the interested reader I would recommend three books, Philip Drucker's *Indians of the Northwest Coast* (McGraw-Hill, 1955), the collection of essays in *Indians of the North Pacific Coast* (University of Washington Press, 1966) edited by Tom McFeat, and Robert F. Spencer's *The North Alaskan Eskimo: A Study in Ecology and Society* (Dover Books, 1976), a reprint of *Bulletin* 171 of the Smithsonian Institution's Bureau of American Ethnology.

Lastly, I should like to recommend a volume that remains a classic in its own right, now reissued in two volumes with more than three hundred illustrations, some of them in color, George Catlin's *Letters and Notes on the Manners, Customs, and Conditions of North American Indians* (1844; Dover Books, 1973). This book in this edition belongs in everyone's library.

Suggested Fiction

Braun, Matthew, *Black Fox* (Fawcett, 1972)
Brown, Dee, *Creek Mary's Blood* (Holt, Rinehart, 1980)
Capps, Benjamin, *A Woman of the People* (Duell, Sloan, 1966)
Comfort, Will Levington, *Apache* (1931; Gregg Press, 1980)
Culp, John, *Timothy Baines* (Holt, Rinehart, 1969)
Grey, Zane, *The Rainbow Trail* (Harper's, 1915)
Henry, Will, *From Where the Sun Now Stands* (1959; Gregg Press, 1978)
Kelton, Elmer, *The Wolf and the Buffalo* (Doubleday, 1980)
Kesey, Ken, *One Flew Over the Cuckoo's Nest* (Viking, 1962)
Manfred, Frederick, *Conquering Horse* (1959; Gregg Press, 1980)
Mathews, John Joseph, *Sundown* (1934; Gregg Press, 1979)
Mourning Dove, *Cogewea: The Half-Blood* (1927; Nebraska, 1981)
Neihardt, John G., *When the Tree Flowered: An Authentic Tale of the Old Sioux World* (Macmillan, 1951)

Silko, Leslie, *Ceremony* (Viking, 1977)
Waters, Frank, *The Man Who Killed the Deer* (Farrar and Rinehart, 1942)

Suggested Films

Aguirre, the Wrath of God (German, 1973) directed by Werner Herzog.
Apache (United Artists, 1954) directed by Robert Aldrich.
Arrowhead (Paramount, 1953) directed by Charles Marquis Warren.
Battle of Rogue River (Columbia, 1954) directed by William Castle.
Broken Arrow (20th-Fox, 1950) directed by Delmer Daves.
Daniel Boone (RKO, 1936) directed by David Howard.
Drums Along the Mohawk (20th-Fox, 1939) directed by John Ford.
Guns of Fort Petticoat (Columbia, 1957) directed by George Marshall.
Little Big Man (National General, 1970) directed by Arthur Penn.
One Flew Over the Cuckoo's Nest (United Artists, 1975) directed by Milos Foreman.
Run of the Arrow (RKO, 1957) directed by Samuel Fuller.
Winterhawk (Howco, 1975) directed by Charles B. Pierce.

Mexican-Americans

by Paul J. Blanding

I

The reader who wishes to know more about Mexican-Americans on the frontier must be forewarned immediately of the difficulties to be encountered. First is the problem of nomenclature. No fewer than five of the works cited below begin with discussions of what to call the people(s) who form the subject of their books. Each writer presented a brief listing of the names presently in use. Each writer argued cogently and convincingly for a different name. The reader will encounter Mexican-Americans referred to as Mexican-Americans (or Mexican Americans), Spanish-Americans (or Spanish Americans), Spanish-speaking Americans, hispanics, chicanos, Mexicanos, Californios, Tejanos, and, occasionally, as Latin Americans, Americans of Mexican (or Spanish) descent, or simply as Mexicans. "What's in a name?" Shakespeare asked. Power, should be the reply, for naming is the power to define, to exclude, to include, to ridicule, to extol. If this is so, then what does the proliferation of names used in connection with Mexican-Americans tell us about the state of their history? That it is a history in flux? Certainly. That there is an ongoing struggle to define it? Certainly. That there are disagreements as to interpretation and meaning? Certainly.

If matters of interpretation and meaning are still up in the air, a few facts are fairly set. The Mexican-American frontier was located in the states of the Southwest: Texas, New Mexico, Arizona, California, and Southern

Colorado. Three distinct political eras mark its chronological limits. The first was the Spanish colonial era (which actually could be divided into an era of exploration and a longer period of colonization) from the Sixteenth century to 1821. This is the period of the Spanish Borderlands (which are often defined to include Florida and the Louisiana territory). While this period is not unimportant in American history and certainly not unimportant to the overall history of the Southwest, its nature is that of a Spanish (colonial) frontier. Anglo-American penetration into the Southwest was negligible and commerical relations with Spanish colonies were prohibited (though some illegal trade existed). The second era, that from 1821 when Mexico gained independence from Spain to 1848 when the United States took control of the Northern half of Mexico, was the most significant in terms of impact on both nations (in relation to each other). This is the period in which the Santa Fe trade was begun, in which American fur trappers began penetrating Mexican territory, in which American colonists began settling in Texas, in which these Anglo-Texans revolted and formed the Texas Republic (1836), and finally in which the United States and Mexico went to war (the Mexican War, 1846–1848). The Treaty of Guadalupe Hidalgo in 1848 ended the Mexican War with the result that Mexico relinquished all claims to Texas and ceded the other Southwestern states to the United States. A strip of land along the border was later "sold" to the United States — the Gadsden Purchase of 1853.

The final era, from 1848 to the closing of the frontier (this is variously defined: some say in the 1890s, some would argue 1910 or 1914 in the Southwest), was one of conflict between Mexican-Americans and Anglo-Americans. The gold rush in California had the most immediate impact on Mexican-Americans after the war. It is perhaps ironic that the techniques of placer and quartz gold mining were taught to Anglo-Americans by Mexicans. The first large group of miners into California during the rush was made up of Sonorans who were practiced in the mining arts, but soon the "greasers" were pushed from the gold fields by their pupils and a period of banditry by some Mexican-Americans and random violence by Anglo-American mobs ensued. This is the period of Joaquín Murieta, Tiburico Vasquez, and the vigilantes. Simultaneously the ranchos of the Californios (native Mexican Californians) were overrun by Anglo-American squatters. In Northern California the takeover was relatively swift, whereas the larger Mexican-American population and the political influence of some wealthy Mexican-American landowners made the struggle for control of the land in Southern California more protracted.

New Mexico and Arizona were spared the worst of this violence immediately after their conquest. Isolated geographically, it was not till the 1880s that Mexican-Americans in these states began to feel the pressure of Anglo-American land grabbers. Resistance to this encroachment was organized in the early 1890s and several Mexican-American societies such as *Las Gorras Blancas* (The White Caps) fought a kind of guerrilla war against the large Anglo-American business interests. In Texas similar conflicts marked this last frontier era and repression of Mexican-Americans, often by police authorities such as the Texas Rangers, became a way of life in some areas of the state.

It would be correct to say that the Anglo-Americans borrowed wholesale large portions of Mexican-American frontier culture (especially the mining and ranching cultures, including the cowboy). Mexican-Americans were not immigrants into the United States during the frontier era; rather they were conquered and their lands were annexed (and often appropriated). It would be satisfying to say that the violent/clashes between Mexican-Americans and Anglo-Americans during the frontier period might result in a just and lasting peace between co-equal partners in the American experiment. It would be satisfying to say so, but this part of our history has not yet been written.

II

i

Until Carey McWilliams' book (see below), published in the late 1940s, a general survey of Mexican-American history could not be found. Sociologists had done work on/Mexican-American culture, immigration, and labor problems in the Twentieth century, but even the best of this material has only limited relevance to the earlier frontier period. Historians covered the important "events" of the Anglo-American Mexican clashes, the Texas Revolution and the Mexican War, and local conflicts were touched on in state histories and the like. However, most of this material was written from an Anglo-American perspective or lacked the systematic approach of the best historical writing.

Large gains have been made in the writing of Mexican-American frontier history since the 1960s. While the reader will not be overwhelmed with the amount of material available on the subject, one will certainly find introductory material on most of the sub-topics within the field.

Unlike the latter period of Anglo-American Mexican conflict, the Spanish colonial period in the Southwest has been extensively researched. A good book to begin with is John Francis Bannon's *The Spanish Borderlands Frontier, 1513–1821* (Holt, Rinehart, 1970) which supplies the reader with an extensive bibliography as well as a readable survey of the period. The works of Herbert Eugene Bolton shaped the contours of historical writing on the Borderlands. His *The Spanish Borderlands: A Chronicle of Old Florida and the Southwest* (Yale University Press, 1921) was the first attempt to define the Borderlands and to include their study in the mainstream of American historiography. The rest of his work ranges over the whole of the period, including early exploration as in *Spanish Explorations in the Southwest* (1916; Barnes and Noble, 1967) and in his last major work, *Coronado, Knight of Pueblos and Plains* (Whittlesey House, 1949) also published as *Coronado on the Turquoise Trail, Knight of Pueblos and*

Plains (University of New Mexico Press, 1949). A posthumous collection of Bolton's essays, *Bolton and the Spanish Borderlands* (University of Oklahoma Press, 1964) edited and with an Introduction by John Francis Bannon, is scholarly in tone and offers a serious look at the essentials of Bolton's thought. Another excellent collection of essays edited by David J. Weber is *New Spain's Far Northern Frontier: Essays on Spain in the American West* (University of New Mexico Press, 1979), a selection of eighteen essays by various scholars that bring the reader up to date on research in the area. Finally, a social history of the settlers of the Borderlands, Oakah L. Jones' *Los Paisanos: Spanish Settlers on the Northern Frontier of New Spain* (University of Oklahoma Press, 1979), goes a long way in correcting the impression that the Borderlands were colonized only by soldiers and missionaries. Jones proceeded, region by region, in demonstrating who colonized the Borderlands Frontier while describing the distinct physical culture that emerged in the area.

The period after Mexico's liberation from Spain (through to the end of the frontier in the Southwest) is a difficult one. There are hundreds of books on the Southwest, including state histories, regional histories, reminiscences, and collections of folk tales and fictional accounts of the frontier, and the material on Mexican-Americans is scattered, helter-skelter, throughout this literature. Until recently, little attempt was made to come to grips with the issues that stem from Anglo-American Mexican conflict on the frontier. It is perhaps indicative of this lack of attention that four of the seven books annotated below are general and social histories dealing with much broader periods of time (the Spanish colonial period and the Twentieth century) rather than just the era of frontier conflict. Still, background history is necessary for an intelligent examination of the issues and specifics of Mexican-American history. Lynn I. Perrigo's *The American Southwest: Its People and Cultures* (Holt, Rinehart, 1971) is a good overview of all the peoples and cultures that make up the Southwest, while Odie B. Faulk's *Land of Many Frontiers: A History of the American Southwest* (Oxford University Press, 1968) surveys the history of the region. D.W. Menig's *Three Peoples in Geographic Change, 1600–1970* (Oxford University Press, 1971) is an overview of three peoples (Anglo-Americans, Indians, and Mexican-Americans) and their changing relationships to the geography of the region. The reader will find listings of state histories with chapters or sections on Mexican-Americans in the bibliographies of both Meier's and Rivera's book and in Weber's (see below). Alvin R. Sunseri's *Seeds of Discord: New Mexico in the Aftermath of American Conquest, 1846–1861* (Nelson-Hall, 1979) covers the aftermath of the Mexican War in that state and the resultant conflicts between the Anglo-American conquerors and their new subjects. Texas has been the subject of a great deal of literature (too little of it portraying Mexican-Americans in a favorable light). William C. Binkley's *The Texas Revolution* (Louisiana State University Press, 1952) is a general history of the key events in the state's struggle with Mexico, while *The Mexican Side of the Texan Revolution* (P.L. Turner, 1928) edited and translated by Carlos E. Castañada is a collection of official Mexican documents relating to the conflict. Little other material has been published on the Mexican view of the revolt. Two recent surveys of the Mexican War, Otis A. Singletary's *The Mexican War* (University of Chicago Press, 1960) and Connor Seymour's and Odie B. Faulk's *North America Divided: The Mexican War, 1846–1848* (Oxford University Press, 1971) will give the reader a balanced view of that conflict, although one must really go directly to José M. Barcena's *Recuerdos de la Invasion Norteamericano, 1841–1848* (Editorial Porrúa, 1947) in Spanish for the Mexican side of the war.

A work which is not political or social history, but literary history, is Cecil Robinson's *With the Ears of Strangers: The Mexican in American Literature* (University of Arizona Press, 1963); revised as *Mexico and the Hispanic Southwest in American Literature* (University of Arizona Press, 1977). It is one of the most illuminating works on the ideological basis for Anglo-Mexican conflict on the frontier (and in the Twentieth century) and is highly recommended. Lastly, the Chicano Heritage Series, reprinted by Arno Press, includes many hard-to-find documents and previously out-of-print volumes.

II

ii

Acuña, Rodolfo, *Occupied America: The Chicano's Struggle Toward Liberation* (Harper's, 1972).

This general history of the Mexican-American (chicano) people is divided into two parts: the first part covers the Nineteenth century from first contact through conquest to "occupation" of Northern Mexico by Anglo-Americans, while the second part deals with the Twentieth century. In the beginning of this book Acuña stated both the background for his beliefs in the chicano struggle for liberation and his thesis that chicanos in the United States are a colonized people. What follows is an angry look at the history of the Southwest (state by state) from the point of view of a chicano activist and historian. Although Acuña's work is not fresh history (the first section at least is based largely on secondary sources), it is a fresh viewpoint on our history, a chicano response to the assertions of Anglo-American historians. I will leave to the reader how much of Acuña's argument to accept, but it is an argument worthy of a hearing.

Campa, Arthur L., *Hispanic Culture in the Southwest* (University of Oklahoma Press, 1979).

This book is a social history of the "hispanic" (Spanish, Mexican, hispanized Indian) Southwest from early Spanish colonial times to approximately the present day. The work, as too many others on the subject, lacks focus and good organization. Campa sometimes organized his chapters by region, sometimes by historical period, sometimes by subject area. This loose organization created a patchwork in which important themes (education, economic organization, agricultural and culinary practices, etc.) are dispersed between bits and pieces of political history. (In fairness, the later chapters on single subjects, e.g., witchcraft, folk singing, arts and crafts, etc., are more clearly focused than the early chapters.) Despite this drawback, the patient reader can learn a great deal about the frontier culture of the hispanic Southwest from this work. There are also numerous (black and white) photographs and clear maps.

McWilliams, Carey, *North from Mexico: The Spanish Speaking People of the United States* (Lippincott, 1949) O.P.; reprinted by the Greenwood Press.

This book was the first clear attempt to write a general history of the Mexican-Americans. McWilliams, a civil rights lawyer, argued that the Southwest was both a true borderland, isolated by deserts from central Mexico and thus difficult to defend against Anglo-American expansion, *and* a geographic and cultural extension of Mexico with many more common ties to that country than to its ultimate conqueror. His survey of Nineteenth-century Mexican-American history is especially strong on the Mexican-American contributions to the culture of the "conquerors," e.g., mining techniques, cattle ranching, irrigation farming, etc., contributions without which the conquerors would not have been able to exploit this arid region. McWilliams' later chapters on Twentieth-century Mexican-Americans are also well worth reading. Recent books include more up-to-date historical scholarship, yet this book is still one of the best introductions to Mexican-American history.

Meier, Matt S., and Feliciano Rivera, *The Chicanos: A History of Mexican-Americans* (Hill and Wang, 1972).

This work is a general survey of the history of Mexican-Americans. The strength of Meier's and Rivera's work is in the thorough and straightforward presentation of the many strands of Mexican-American history as compared to the fire of Acuña and the engaging style of McWilliams (see above). The first six chapters (those dealing with the era before the Twentieth century) form a good introduction to Mexican-American frontier history for those who know little about the subject.

Pitt, Leonard, *The Decline of the Californios: A Social History of the Spanish-Speaking Californians, 1846–1890* (University of California Press, 1968).

The word "conquest" takes on real meaning when we view the erosion of the political and economic position of the Californios (native Mexican-Californians) in the aftermath of the Mexican War. In Northern California, subjugation was rapid as a huge influx of Anglo-American miners and adventurers overran the ranchos (cattle ranches) of the conquered. Pitt's work focuses on Southern California (as surviving documents

are mainly from the South) where upper-class landowners were able to
wage a protracted struggle to maintain their political and property rights,
but Pitt also described the conditions faced by Mexicans in the mining
camps and the period of banditry that followed their exclusion from them.
If the work has a weakness, it is that surviving documents from the period
tend to reflect the viewpoints and concerns of the literate *ricos* (the rich)
rather than those of the illiterate poor.

Rosenbaum, Robert J., *Mexicano Resistance in the Southwest: "The Sacred
Right of Self Preservation"* (University of Texas Press, 1981).

This book is a major study of the violence that marred the Anglo-
Mexicano relationship in the latter half of the Nineteenth century. Covering the years between 1848 and 1914, Rosenbaum went beyond a mere recapitulation of the violent clashes that took so many forms (social banditry
in California, guerrilla warfare in New Mexico, etc.) as he recreated the
mind-set and value system of the Mexican-American who fought valiantly
but unsuccessfully to protect his traditional way of life. The reader, unfamiliar with the violent struggles between Anglo-Americans and Mexican-
Americans that took place after the Mexican War ended, will find this work
an illumination of a bloody, unsavory chapter of American history.

Weber, David J., (ed.), *Foreigners in Their Native Land: Historical Roots
of the Mexican Americans* (University of New Mexico Press, 1973), with a
Foreword by Ramón Eduardo Ruiz.

This book is a collection of essays and historical documents (originally in English or translated) organized chronologically to introduce the
reader to the various phases of Anglo-Mexican contact in the Southwest
(California, New Mexico, Arizona, and Texas). Except for the first chapter,
which deals with the Spanish colonial period, the emphasis is on the Nineteenth-century frontier: the book ends the frontier period with the Mexican
Revolution in 1910. Despite the textbook-like format, the work is quite
readable (due to the excellent selection and editing of the documents) and is
a particularly useful introduction to the subject.

III

Other Minorities

A fine introduction to the entire subject of the roles played by what
are now termed "racial minorities" is the chapter so titled in Robert V.
Hine's *The American West: An Interpretive History* (Little, Brown, 1973)
and it is well worth reading before approaching any of the specific books
mentioned below. One point is worth stressing: the histories of these
various groups and their contributions to the American frontier experience
is one of the most neglected areas. Moreover, what books there are tend all
too often to be linear and not vertical, descriptive rather than analytical.

Kenneth Wiggins Porter's *The Negro on the American Frontier* (Arno Press, 1971) comes closest to a definitive history of the blacks in the West. It is a collection of essays with a bibliography and of particular interest are the essays on "Negroes and the Fur Trade," "Negro Labor in the Western Cattle Industry, 1866–1900," and an excellent study on the Seminole-Negro Indian scouts. A good companion volume — because of its many rare photo illustrations and documents — is William Loren Katz' *The Black West: A Documentary and Pictorial History* (Doubleday, 1971). W. Sherman Savage's *Blacks in the West* (Greenwood Press, 1976) covers the period of 1830–1890 and is a well documented examination of why blacks moved West, where they settled, the jobs they took, as well as the political and social forces they faced. While there is little attempt at analysis, Savage did demonstrate that more opportunities — although this is wholly relative — existed for blacks in the West than in the East or South. Rudolph M. Lapp's *Blacks in Gold Rush California* (Yale University Press, 1977) covers the period from 1848 to 1861 and addresses the lives of blacks in mining camps, their relationships with other minorities, and contains some interesting information on the conventions they held to fight against discrimination. Philip Durham's and Everett L. Jones' *The Negro Cowboys* (Dodd, Mead, 1965) was an effort to set in more balanced perspective the roles of black cowboys during the post-Civil War era. Black cowboys, according to the authors, numbered over 5,000, a factor usually obscured by the concentration on white cowboys so characteristic of the entertainment media. Among first-hand accounts, three should be singled out: *The Life and Adventures of Nat Love, Better Known in the Cattle Industry as "Deadwood Dick"* (1907; Arno Press, 1968), a "highly exaggerated" narrative of a black frontier personality; *A Woman's Life Work* (1882; Arno Press, 1970) by Laura S. Haviland, an abolitionist who aided the Exodusters in Kansas in 1879 (a subject covered definitively in Nell Irvin Painter's *Exodusters: Black Migration to Kansas After Reconstruction* [Knopf, 1977]); and *Negro Frontiersman: The Western Memoirs of Henry O. Flipper, First Negro Graduate of West Point* (Texas Western College Press, 1963) edited by Theodore Harris. It might also be remarked upon in passing that the Arno Press has undertaken an aggressive policy of reissuing a series of "classic" works devoted to black history.

Although it is a laudatory and partisan account, I. Harold Sharfman's *Jews on the Frontier* (Regnery, 1977) broke new ground, with information on traveling peddlers and when and where synagogues were built.

Jack Chen's *The Chinese of America* (Harper's, 1980) can be taken as a standard work insofar as the first half of it deals with Chinese on the American frontier in the Nineteenth century. Chen narrated why Chinese left the mainland to come to the United States, how they came, their involvement with mining and in helping to build the transcontinental railroad, their work in agriculture, fisheries, and light manufacturing. A history that is more concerned with rioting and prejudice — although one would not know this from its title — is Gunther Barth's *Bitter Strength: A*

History of the Chinese in the United States, 1850–1870 (Harvard University Press, 1964). Two works which also address Anglo-American attitudes and prejudice are Stuart Creighton Miller's *The Unwelcome Immigrant: The American Image of the Chinese*, 1785–1882 (University of California Press, 1969) and *"Chink": A Documentary History of Anti-Chinese Prejudice in America* (World, 1972) edited by Cheng-Tsu Wu which contains many legislative documents and information on specific events such as the anti-Chinese riots in Seattle in 1885–1886.

The Japanese immigrants are even more poorly represented, with the inadequate coverage supplied by Yamato Ichihashi's *Japanese in the United States* (1932; Arno Press, 1969) being the best to be had so far in the field.

Lastly, although the book is a topical analysis of frontier violence in general, W. Eugene Hollon's *Frontier Violence: Another Look* (Oxford University Press, 1974) has a wealth of information on minorities, in particular Chinese, blacks, and Mexicans in Texas. While Hollon felt that violence is more characteristic of urban societies than on frontiers, he did demonstrate that much frontier violence was caused directly by bigotry and prejudice on the parts of white Anglo-Americans toward other racial groups. Interestingly, Jewish merchants in California escaped from a good deal of discrimination because they avoided mining or any other occupation in which they might successfully compete with Anglo-Americans.

Suggested Fiction

Austin, Mary, *Isidro* (Houghton Mifflin, 1905)
Braun, Matthew, *Black Fox* (Fawcett, 1972)
Eastlake, William, *The Bronc People* (1958; University of New Mexico Press, 1975)
Fergusson, Harvey, *The Conquest of Don Pedro* (1954; University of New Mexico Press, 1974)
Fisher, Clay, *Black Apache* (Bantam, 1976)
Gulick, Bill, *Treasure in Hell's Canyon* (Doubleday, 1979)
Kelton, Elmer, *Wagontongue* (Ballantine, 1972)
_____, *The Wolf and the Buffalo* (Doubleday, 1980)
Laughlin, Ruth, *The Wind Leaves No Shadow* (1948; Caxton Printers, 1951)
Lea, Tom, *The Wonderful Country* (Little, Brown, 1952)
McCunn, Ruthanne Lum, *Thousand Pieces of Gold* (Design Enterprises, 1981)

Suggested Films

Buck and the Preacher (Columbia, 1972) directed by Sidney Poitier.
Charley One-Eye (Paramount, 1973) directed by Don Chaffey.
The McMasters (Chevron, 1970) directed by Alf Kjellin.
Pancho Villa (Scotia, 1973) directed by Gene Martin.

The Scalphunters (United Artist, 1968) directed by Sydney Pollack.

The Soul of Nigger Charley (Paramount, 1973) directed by Larry G. Spangler.

Soul Soldier (Hirschman Northern, 1970) directed by John Cardos.

Valdez Is Coming (United Artists, 1971) directed by Edward Sherin.

Walk Like a Dragon (Paramount, 1960) directed by James Clavell.

Wings of the Hawk (Universal, 1953) directed by Budd Boetticher.

Religion:
From Missionaries
to Mormons

by Paul J. Blanding

I

Humankind's religions have been and are the source of both its greatest communion and its bloodiest conflicts. It is possible that the American frontier experience displays in high relief this communion/conflict dialectic, as the extremes of frontier life (the freedom and the chaos) seemed to bring to the front the extremes in religious behavior.

Robert V. Hine wrote in *The American West: An Interpretive History* (Little, Brown, 1973), "Exceptions abound, but none destroys the essential fact that the Nineteenth-century American frontier was fundamentally Protestant." Taken as a given, Hine's insight leaves us with the obvious question: what was the effect of Nineteenth-century Protestant ideology on the character of the frontier, its people, and institutions? Much of the most interesting historical work presently being done addresses this question in its myriad forms, and rightly so. Anglo-Protestant ideology was the dominant American ideology for the whole of the Nineteenth century and the first half of the Twentieth. However, pressure for its revision has been continuous (certainly throughout this century); and we seem to be

74

living in an era in which that ideology will become more accepting, expanding to include the diverse subcultures that make up the United States, or in which, as part of the last defense of parochial privilege, the ideology will be destroyed. The reader is free to agree or disagree with any of these particulars, but I think it is difficult to disagree that the basic theme of Protestant ideology's influence on American history is worthy of continued research, reflection, and argument.

Several writers have suggested that there are only a handful of truly "American" religions. Mormonism is almost universally accepted as one of them. Mormonism began in upstate New York in 1830. A spin-off of orthodox Protestant Christianity, it is based on the revelations of its founder, Joseph Smith, as revealed through the *Book of Mormon* (1830) and other works, plus the continuous prophecy of its leaders. Mormonism grew fast, and the community moved West almost as soon as it began, first to Kirtland, Ohio, then to Western Missouri. In each community where the Mormons settled, they came into conflict with the non-Mormon ("Gentile") population. The roots of these conflicts were not only religious, but involved disputes over land and local political control, the communally-living Mormons being perceived as a threat to locally entrenched interests. By 1838 a state of virtual civil war existed in Western Missouri. After a massacre of Mormons (at Haun's Mill, 30 October 1838) by a "Gentile" mob, the Mormons agreed to move. They founded the city of Nauvoo, Illinois, which was to become their new "Zion." After a short period of intense growth (Nauvoo was the largest city in Illinois for a brief time), conflict again erupted between the Mormons and their neighbors. Joseph Smith was assassinated in 1844 and the Mormons were again forced to agree to move West.

In 1846 the Mormon migration to the Great Basin area began under the leadership of Brigham Young. Much of what is now Utah and parts of Nevada and California were settled by Mormons who based their communities on irrigation farming and other industries. Mormon immigration (especially from Scandinavia and the British Isles) continued into Utah for several decades, and the "Mormon Trail" became one of the most used overland trails West.

Conflict between Mormon leaders and federal officials grew throughout the decade of the 1850s, culminating in the Mormon War (1857–1858) in which President Buchanan sent 2,500 federal troops to Utah to enforce the federal government's mandate. It was during this period of conflict that the Mountain Meadows Massacre occurred. This now infamous incident involved a wagon train of California-bound non-Mormons who were killed by a combined force of Mormon militia and Indians. After this bloodshed, the "war" ended quietly and an uneasy truce held sway throughout the rest of the territorial period. It was during this time that Mormon polygamy (practiced mostly by church leaders) became a public issue. Utah's statehood was held up over the issue, until, in the 1890s, the Mormon leadership agreed to give it up.

Who were the Mormons and what was their impact on America's

frontier? Why did this "American" religion suffer such brutal treatment at the hands of Americans? Some of the books cited below help answer those questions.

The question of Christianity's general impact on Native Americans is perhaps too broad to be addressed in this short section, but a narrower question can be posed: what was the impact of Christian missionaries on the people they sought to convert and on the frontier in general?

Spanish Roman Catholic missionaries ventured into what is now the American Southwest as early as the Sixteenth century. Their influence in the Southwest, especially New Mexico, was real, although secular colonization was at least equally as important. In 1769 the Franciscan order launched a missionizing effort into California. Missions were established from San Diego to North of San Francisco and the order virtually ruled California till the decades just before the American conquest.

Further North, in the Oregon territory, Protestant missionaries played a leading role in establishing American settlements and setting the tone of American relations with the Indians. In the 1830s Jason Lee, a Methodist missionary, established himself in the Willamette Valley in Oregon. Lee played a significant role in the subsequent land grab by American pioneers, if only a minor part in the spiritual lives of his Native converts. Farther to the East (in what is now Eastern Washington), the Congregationalist missionaries, Narcissa and Marcus Whitman, influenced white-Indian relations chiefly through their deaths at the hands of Cayuse Indians in 1847.

Not all the Christian missions to the Indians had results antithetical to their original purpose (the efforts of Father Pierre-Jean DeSmet come to mind), but the basic effect of the Christian missions on the Indians was one of tragic misunderstanding between two groups literally "worlds" apart. The many questions that arise concerning the missionaries and their influence continue to be the subject of historical scrutiny.

II

i

A complete bibliography of all the literature pertaining to religion on the American frontier might easily run to book-length proportions. Many of the major Christian denominations are affiliated with publishing concerns which have busily cranked out local church histories, biographies of church people, and tracts on political, historical, and spiritual questions for many decades. This large body of literature does not even include the anthropological studies of Native American religions, the books and pamphlets of small, defunct sects, the tracts of individual religious enthusiasts, or the works of the anti-church societies. Fortunately, the reader will lose little by concerning himself only with the more general historical works, for much of the above-mentioned church literature is either tainted by extreme partisanship, narrow in its focus, or so tediously written that only an academic, fanatic, or close relative of the author might find it worth reading. (To say this is not to denigrate the interest members of a denomination or sect might have in their own church, its practices, or history. Some fine histories, aimed at an audience of the faithful, have been written.)

Many of the works on American religion are sources of sources and can supply the reader with historical background that books specifically on the frontier tend to lack. Two such valuable histories are: Sydney D. Ahlstrom's *A Religious History of the American People* (Yale University Press, 1972) and Edwin Scott Gaustad's *A Religious History of America* (Harper's, 1966). A bibliography on American religion is Nelson R. Burr's *Religion in American Life* (Harlan Davidson, 1971). Another source on four of the major denominations is William W. Sweet's *Religion on the American Frontier* (University of Chicago Press, 1931–1946) in four volumes. Each of the four volumes is a collection of documents on one of the four major Protestant denominations: Baptists, Congregationalists, Presbyterians, and Methodists.

Readers interested in Roman Catholic influence on the Western frontier may want to supplement their general reading with some biographies. John Upton Terrell's *Black Robe: The Life of Pierre-Jean DeSmet, Missionary, Explorer, & Pioneer* (Doubleday, 1964) is a popular biography of one of the most fascinating of frontier missionaries. Readers with a deeper interest in DeSmet may also want to read his own works, published as *Life, Letters, and Travels of Father Pierre-Jean DeSmet, S.J., 1801–1873* (Francis P. Harper, 1905) in four volumes. Paul Horgan's *Lamy of Santa Fe: His Life and Times* (Farrar, Straus, & Giroux, 1975) is an excellent biography of the Archbishop of Santa Fe from 1851–1885.

Readers interested in the story of the Mormons will find Fawn Brodie's biography of Joseph Smith, *No Man Knows My History: The Life of Joseph Smith* (Knopf, 1945; revised edition Knopf, 1971), a must. Unfortunately, no such excellent biography of Brigham Young has yet been written. A recent biography, Stanley P. Hirshson's *The Lion of the Lord: A Biography of Brigham Young* (Knopf, 1969), though based on current scholarship, has a definite anti-Young bias. An interesting memoir by one of Young's many wives is *Wife No. 19* (1875; Arno Press, 1972) by Ann Eliza Young. It is in many ways typical of the anti-Mormon literature of the Nineteenth century while providing a first-hand glimpse into the world of the Mormon hierarchy. The Mormons were always good record keepers, hence there are a large number of first-hand accounts of Mormon frontier life. The bibliographies of most of the general works cited below can provide the reader with an entrance into this literature, although perhaps the best place to begin would be *Among the Mormons: Historic Accounts by Contemporary Observers* (Knopf, 1958) edited by William Mulder and Russell Mortensen. The Mormon point of view on their own history is covered in an extensive literature. The best introduction is a general history by James B. Allen and Glen M. Leonard, *The Story of the Latter-Day Saints* (Deseret Book Co., 1976). This official history also has an excellent bibliography.

For readers interested in Protestants on the frontier, the autobiography of a fire-breathing circuit rider, *Autobiography of Peter Cartwright, The Backwoods Preacher* (1856) makes good reading. For biographies of the Protestant missionaries in Oregon, the reader should turn to the works of Clifford M. Drury, especially his *Marcus and Narcissa Whitman and the Opening of Old Oregon* (Arthur H. Clark, 1973). Regrettably, no critical biography of Jason Lee (another important Oregon missionary) has been published so far. Cornelius Brosnan's *Jason Lee,The Prophet of the New Oregon* (Macmillan, 1932) does not take a sufficiently critical view of Lee's wheelings and dealings.

The reader will notice that there is no single comprehensive general survey of religious influence on the American frontier listed below. One has yet to be written.

II

ii

Roman Catholics

Berger, John A., *The Franciscan Missions of California* (Putnam's, 1941) O.P.

It is with some hesitation that I recommend this work as an introduction to the history of the California missions. However, the standard work on the missions, Reverend Zephyrin Engelhardt's *The Missions and Missionaries of California* (James H. Barry, 1908), is four volumes of detailed history, suited more for the scholar than the general reader, and other works treat of the "romance" of the missions or focus on their architecture. In his work, Berger reviewed the history of Franciscan California through the secularization of the missions (in the decades before the conquest of California by the United States) and described the history of each individual mission along the *Camino Real*. Unfortunately, his perspective is so biased toward the padres and against the Indians that the reader will not obtain a balanced picture from this work alone. Terrell's work (see below) is to some extent a correction of this (his bias having been just the opposite) and a recent work by Bruce Walter Barton, *The Tree at the Center of the World: A Story of the California Missions* (Ross-Erikson, 1980), is a better balanced, though less formal, history; it has many beautiful black and white photographic illustrations as well.

Burns, Robert I., S.J., *The Jesuits and the Indian Wars of the Northwest* (Yale University Press, 1966).

The Jesuit missionaries in the Northwest wielded influence among the Indians that far outweighed their numbers. Burns, a Jesuit himself, sketched the history of the Jesuit missions in the Northwest and discussed the events leading to and including the wars between whites (mostly Protestant) and the Yakimas, Cayuse, Coeur d'Alene-Spokane, and the Nez Percé, and the missionaries' involvement in them. Those interested in the Roman Catholic influence in the Pacific Northwest, the Indian wars, or the general history of the region, will find this a valuable work.

Shannon, James P., *Catholic Colonization on the Western Frontier* (Yale University Press, 1957) O.P.; reprinted by the Arno Press.

If the Western frontiers were, in Robert V. Hine's words, "essentially Protestant," there was notwithstanding, from the beginning of European activity in North America, an important Roman Catholic component. Although most will recognize the importance of Roman Catholic culture in the Spanish Southwest and, to a lesser degree, in the French-Canadian aspect of the fur trade, it is often assumed that pioneer farming was largely a Protestant (or Mormon) activity, the Roman Catholic immigrants remaining behind in urban areas. Shannon's book dispels this misconception by telling the story of Roman Catholic rural migration to the Western prairies of Minnesota as organized and encouraged by Bishop John Ireland of St. Paul. Shannon covered such issues as Roman Catholic recruitment of immigrants, the role of the railroads in opening the prairies to farming, and the daily life of the pioneers in the Roman Catholic settlements. Although Roman Catholic colonies on the prairies formed only a small part of the American conquest of the West, it was an interesting and largely successful constituent of that process.

Terrell, John Upton, *The Arrow and the Cross: A History of the American Indian and the Missionaries* (Capra Press, 1979).

This work is included in this sub-section because more than two-thirds of it is taken up with the Roman Catholic missionaries in New Mexico, Arizona, and California, and even the final third deals with both Roman Catholic and Protestant missionaries in the Pacific Northwest. Terrell stated his point of view at the beginning: "Lest it be assumed by some persons that this work is an anti-religious diatribe, let me forcefully state at the outset that it is, and, as the bibliography and notes confirm, a product of diligent research." There are no heroes among the missionaries Terrell portrayed (except, perhaps, Father Kino in Arizona), and he stood firmly against the cultural chauvinism which allowed "civilized" missionaries to subvert and in some cases brutally dismantle the cultures of Native Americans with the utmost self-righteousness. The reader, whether he agrees or disagrees, will find Terrell's arguments stimulating.

II

iii

Mormons

Anderson, Nels, *Desert Saints: The Mormon Frontier in Utah* (University of Chicago Press, 1942).

Anderson was a sociologist and his history of the Mormons on the Utah frontier blends a knowledge of the community structure of (Mormon) Southern Utah with a command of the political and economic issues that they confronted during the frontier era. His chapter on Mormon polygamy uses case histories and statistics to elucidate the human reality of that institution while placing it in perspective. (He contended that polygamy was not as important an institution within Mormon society as outsiders made it and that without the legal pressure applied by the federal government polygamy might have "withered away" on its own.) While Anderson focused on the "Dixie" Mormons of Southwestern Utah, his work serves as an introductory history to the entire Mormon frontier.

Arrington, Leonard J., *Great Basin Kingdom: An Economic History of the Latter-Day Saints*, 1830–1900 (Harvard University Press, 1958) O.P.; reprinted by the University of Nebraska Press.

Arrington, a Mormon, was (briefly) the official historian of the Mormon Church, but his prodigious scholarship was of the highest caliber and his point of view, while sympathetic to Mormonism, was seldom one-sided and never propagandistic. This work tracks the growth of Mormon economic policy throughout the Nineteenth century, covering such topics as the Mormon "anti-bank" in Kirtland, Ohio, Morman land policy in Utah, the planned growth of Mormon communities, Mormons and the transcontinental railroad, and Mormon cooperatives. If the subject of Mormon economic history does not sound compelling on its face, the reader might do well to remember that many of the themes of Mormon economic history are still central to present-day world economic realities: comprehensive planning versus individual economic freedom, the redistribution or fair distribution of wealth, and the organization and growth of economies with limited capital are all themes in current economic debate as well as the central problems of Mormon development. Arrington's book is recommended to those with even a slight interest in the subject.

Brooks, Juanita, *The Mountain Meadows Massacre* (Stanford University Press, 1950); revised edition published by the University of Oklahoma Press.

This is the best history of the tragic massacre by Mormons and Indians of a party of overland migrants in Southern Utah in 1857. Brooks, a Mormon, took great pains to bring to light the whole of this often misrepresented episode. Without covering up the guilt of Mormon military and church leaders, she recreated the wartime mentality of the Mormon community during the period and made understandable (if not justifiable) their vengeful feelings towards a group, some of whom may have been involved in previous atrocities perpetrated against Mormons in Missouri. This is a tragic story, well told, and it points out the bitter fruit of religious intolerance and unchecked civil violence.

Flanders, Robert Bruce, *Nauvoo: Kingdom on the Mississippi* (University of Illinois Press, 1965).
    The Mormons, after being driven from Missouri in the late 1830s, settled in Western Illinois and built the town of Nauvoo. By 1845 it was the largest city in Illinois, yet by the next year the Mormons were again headed West, hounded out by their "Gentile" enemies and forced to seek a new "Zion." Flanders' work covers the story of Nauvoo with the detail it deserves, dealing with the peculiar city charter which allowed the church leaders to control the civil government, the land deals of the church, the Nauvoo Legion (the Mormon militia), and the final explosion of violence between Mormons and their neighbors which led to Joseph Smith's death and the Mormon migration to Utah.

Furniss, Norman F., *The Mormon Conflict* 1850–1859 (Yale University Press, 1960) O.P.; reprinted by the Greenwood Press.
    The practice of polygamy is the first issue that comes up when the average (non-Mormon) reader looks back upon the early conflict between Mormons and "Gentile" society. However the root of the clashes was much more a conflict over political authority, especially a conflict over the civil authority of the hierarchy of the Mormon church, than over the relatively minor issue of plural marriages. Furniss' work covers the build up of tensions between Mormons in Utah and the federal officials sent to administer the territory and the Mormon War (1857–1858) to which they led. *The Mormon Conflict* is an excellent overview of the issues and events of the turmoil.

O'Dea, Thomas F., *The Mormons* (University of Chicago Press, 1957).
    This book is the single best introduction to Mormonism and Mormon history that the reader will find. It gives an overview of Mormon history, explores the intellectual and religious roots of the Latter-Day Saints movement, and describes the organization of the church and some of the political and intellectual issues confronting the modern church. O'Dea (a non-Mormon) was fair, neither glossing over the stormy history of the church and the controversies that have surrounded it, nor indulging in simplistic anti-Mormon rhetoric.

Stegner, Wallace, *The Gathering of Zion: The Story of the Mormon Trail* (McGraw-Hill, 1964).
    The Mormons fled Nauvoo, Illinois, in 1846, heading West across the plains to the "New Zion" in Utah. Although the first migration was

forced by violence, subsequent voluntary migrations (especially of European converts) continued overland through 1868. The Mormons were organized (planting crops and establishing way stations for those who followed) and inventive (witness the handcart experiments in the 1850s).This work covers the story of the overland migrations of Mormons to Utah from the abandoning of Nauvoo to the building of the transcontinental railroad. A specialized work on the handcart migrations is LeRoy R. and Ann W. Hafen's *Handcarts to Zion: The Story of a Unique Western Migration 1856–1860* (Arthur H. Clark, 1960) which is recommended for those interested in this aspect of the migrations.

II

iv

Protestants

Berkhofer, Robert F., Jr., *Salvation and the Savage: An Analysis of Protestant Missions and American Indian Response*, 1787–1862 (University of Kentucky Press, 1965) O.P.; reprinted by Atheneum.

The author of this work wished to "avoid moral judgments" by using recent anthropological work on acculturation as an organizational framework for his history of Protestant-Indian mission contact. I will leave to the reader whether the author proved his hypothesis (that "American civilization not only determined the white responses but also delimited the Indian responses" to white-Indian contact); but I must say that either because of or despite the social-scientific techniques he employed, the author wrote an admirable introduction to the subject. Covering such topics as missionary educational institutions, religious teaching, and attempts to introduce the "work ethic" into non-European native cultures, he explored the effects of missionary contact both on the tribes (factionalizing many of them) and on the missionary movement itself (it was seen as a failure by many missionaries and mission boards). This is certainly not the last word on missionary-Indian relations, but it is a beginning. The book has a good bibliographic essay at its conclusion.

Goodykoontz, Colin B., *Home Missions on the American Frontier* (Caxton Printers, 1939) O.P.; reprinted by Octagon.

Home missions were missions from Eastern (American) Protestant churches to their white neighbors living on the "seas of iniquity," i.e., the frontiers. Professor Goodykoontz' book is considered the standard work on the subject and, though somewhat detailed, it is a most readable history. Although he centered the work on the American Home Missionary Society (Congregationalist and Presbyterian), Goodykoontz also followed the efforts of the Baptists, Methodists, and Episcopalians (Protestant), analyzing the impact of the Home Missions on each frontier region as well as on such general national issues as education and slavery.

Jones, Nard, *The Great Command: The Story of Marcus and Narcissa Whitman and the Oregon Country Pioneers* (Little, Brown, 1959) O.P.; reprinted by Binford & Mort.
    Although this book focuses on the Whitmans and the events leading to their massacre by Cayuse Indians in 1847, it also serves as an introductory history of the early Methodist mission of Jason Lee and, to a lesser extent, the early Roman Catholic missionaries in the Oregon country. Jones did an admirable job in portraying the individuals whose characters were so bound up with the tragedy at Waiilatpu and of sketching the historical backdrop to this event. Unfortunately, the book is marred by its failure to realize the Indian perspective to the tragedy and by Jones' habit throughout the book of referring to Native Americans as "savages."

Miyakawa, T. Scott, *Protestants and Pioneers: Individualism and Conformity on the American Frontier* (University of Chicago Press, 1964).
    The first thesis of this book is that Protestants on the frontiers made up not an "atomistic society" of "lone individuals" but, on the contrary, "were members of disciplined groups and an increasingly organized society." The second thesis is that "deprecation of intellectual and cultural interests (by popular Protestant denominations) may have stimulated the later growth of the alleged materialism that those same denominations deplore today." As always, I shall leave it to the reader to decide whether Miyakawa proved his theses, but will say that his arguments were cogent and his writing style brisk and accessible (despite the sociological jargon in the Introduction). The work focuses on Baptists and Methodists as being the largest of the frontier denominations, and on the Presbyterians and Quakers as representing the extremes in formal and informal church structure (respectively). All in all, Miyakawa's work is stimulating, although the "West" it covers is only the Trans-Allegheny frontier (Kentucky, Ohio, Indiana, Illinois, Michigan, and Tennessee) between the years 1800 and 1836 and so it can not be considered comprehensive.

Suggested Fiction

Cather, Willa, *Death Comes for the Archbishop* (Knopf, 1927)
Ehrlich, Jack, *The Fastest Gun in the Pulpit* (Pocket Books, 1972)
Fisher, Clay, *Apache Ransom* (Bantam, 1975)
Fisher, Vardis, *Children of God: An American Epic* (Harper's, 1939)
Grey, Zane, *Riders of the Purple Sage* (Harper's, 1912)
McNickle, D'Arcy, *The Surrounded* (1936; Univ. of New Mexico Press, 1978)
Morrow, Honoré Willsie, *We Must March* (Stokes, 1925)
Reese, John, *Angel Range* (Doubleday, 1971)
Sorensen, Virginia, *A Little Lower than the Angels* (Knopf, 1942)

Suggested Films

The Ballad of Cable Hogue (Warner's, 1970) directed by Sam Peckinpah.
Brigham Young, Frontiersman (20th-Fox, 1940) directed by Henry Hathaway.
The Fighting Parson (Allied, 1933) directed by Harry Fraser.
Hell's Hinges (Triangle, 1916) directed by William S. Hart.
McCabe and Mrs. Miller (Warner's, 1971) directed by Robert Altman.
Wagonmaster (RKO, 1950) directed by John Ford.

Traders, Trappers, and Mountain Men

by Paul J. Blanding

I

In the film *Man in the Wilderness* (Warner's, 1971), mountain man "Zach Bass" (Richard Harris), left in the wilds to die, struggles against all the forces in the universe set to destroy him — wild beasts, cold, hunger, his wounds, his own despair — and he prevails. While *Man in the Wilderness* is not an historical film, the story of one man struggling alone against hostile elements parallels actual stories of historical mountain men (especially the lone trek of Hugh Glass). Because too much of our frontier history has been debased by myth-makers or outright liars, it is often difficult for skeptics as I am to believe in the traditions of the American hero, while others, of the opposite persuasion, will argue the veracity of some of the most outrageous tall tales and historical distortions. Perhaps the lives of the fur traders and the trappers form one of the best subject areas for both sides to examine their prejudices, for so many American themes stand displayed in high relief in the stories of these men. Trappers were intimately linked with Native Americans and their way of life (for both good and ill); and they were the first Euro-Americans to face the geographic, climatic, and biological realities of the Far West. Traders, on the other hand, were among the first of American businessmen to face the economic realities that shape our lives still: the hegemony of concentrated capital, the destruction of the natural resource base, and the moral dilemmas that face those who, for short-term gain, debased the lives of consumer-laborers.

It is not possible in a short introduction to outline the lives of even the most important traders and trappers. Some names may be already familiar to the reader—Kit Carson, Jim Bridger, John Jacob Astor—while many others have had little of the popular exposure of these, their more famous contemporaries. All, however, share the common ground of fur trade history (though several are famous for exploits outside the fur trade); and it is for this reason that I urge the reader with some interest in mountain men to start with at least one general history of the fur trade. Such a general history will put these individual lives into some historical perspective. Three ideas, surely, to keep in mind while reading on the subject are: first, only some of the many trappers that gathered beaver and other furs were Anglo-Americans; many were French-Canadians or French-Americans, and others were mixed-bloods and Native Americans (some from Eastern tribes such as the Delawares and the Iroquois). Few of these latter groups have been properly credited for their exploits or participation in the trade. Second, most trapping was done in brigades, either the formally engaged parties of the fur companies or the looser organizations of the free trappers. Only a few of the hardiest (or most foolhardy) trapped alone: efficiency and protection required a degree of communal cooperation not generally admitted to in the popular conception. Third, the personnel of the fur trade was a very mixed lot in terms of temperament, background, and motivation. Some of the trappers were rugged, hard-bitten misanthropes, but others were pious, hard working, even frugal, while the company clerks and bourgeois were simply businessmen, little different from their Eastern counterparts. In short, the traders and trappers of the American fur trade both embody the traditional view of them as American heroes and defy it with a variety and complexity that make their study both a challenge and a pleasure.

II

i

The personnel of the fur trade are the subject of an extensive literature, making a systematic approach to it almost mandatory. For ease of reference, I have divided the books below into three categories: (1) general works, that is works that cover many or all of the trappers and traders or some common aspect of their lives; (2) first-hand accounts; and (3) biographies. The first-hand accounts listed below barely scratch the surface of original source material available in the form of journals, diaries, memoirs, and even novels, but the reader who wishes to delve deeply into this specialized literature will find access to it through the bibliographies of many of the general works listed below. Of the biographies, I have attempted to recommend the best work on the most important or widely known of the traders and trappers. No claim is made that this list is either encyclopedic or "definitive," but the reader ought to find it a good point at which to begin. When I use the connotation "scholarly" for biographies, I refer not to advanced degrees earned nor impregnable tenured university positions held by the author, but to an adequate search for, and critical use of, source material and an honest approach to gaps or ambiguities in the historical record. As with lawmen and outlaws, certain mountain men have been the long-standing subjects of dime novels and popular fictional treatments out of which a legendary or heroic personality developed. Unfortunately this material sometimes creeps into biographies of the individual and is perpetuated as historically accurate. In my reading of the following, I seldom encountered works whose readability waned or whose color and drama flagged because the author took pains to be honest about the historical record.

II

ii

General Works

Hafen, Leroy R., (ed.), *The Mountain Men and the Fur Trade of the Far West* (Arthur H. Clark, 1965–1972), ten volumes, O.P.

This work is a biographic encyclopedia of the mountain men and other personnel of the Western fur trade. The first nine volumes contain biographic sketches of the mountain men, each done by a scholar in the field. The final volume contains an excellent bibliography, an index, and other materials on the fur trade. This is the best overall reference work on the subject.

Miller, Alfred Jacob, *The West of Alfred Jacob Miller* (University of Oklahoma Press, 1951); revised and enlarged edition published by the University of Oklahoma Press, both O.P.

Miller, an artist, went into the mountains with an expedition led by the Scottish adventurer, William Drummond Stewart, in 1837. His sketches from this expedition form the single largest graphic record of the mountain men and the mountain fur trade left by an eyewitness. Besides the large number of black and white reproductions (200), the revised edition also contains Miller's own notes on each picture as well as eight full-color reproductions. One can hope that someday technology will allow for the complete color reproduction of Miller's work at an affordable price.

O'Meara, Walter, *Daughters of the Country: The Women of the Fur Traders and Mountain Men* (Harcourt, Brace, 1968) O.P.

This book treats of a subject that, when not ignored by other historians, is often dismissed with a casual wink towards the "Indian tarts" who became the wives, mistresses, or prostitutes of the fur traders and mountain men. O'Meara took his subject seriously, believing, as he stated, that white men's relations with Indian women "... profoundly affected the character of frontier life." Never resorting to the romantic "noble savage" arguments of some Indian apologists, he gave a sympathetic view of Indian culture (especially sexual and feminine culture) and described the complex history of white-Indian relations without being either prudish or prurient. Although such a broad social history is bound to require revision over time, it is likely that this book will stand out as a pioneering effort not only in the field of fur trade social history but in the broader subject of white-Indian relations. A glossary and appendix on tribal distribution heighten the readability of the work.

Russell, Carl P., *Firearms, Traps, and Tools of the Mountain Men* (Knopf, 1967) O.P.; reprinted by the University of New Mexico Press.

The title describes the contents of this book, which is the standard work on the subject. Russell included an introductory chapter on "The Mountain Men in American History," a chapter on blacksmithing on the frontier, and a discussion of the techniques of beaver trapping, as well as his individual chapters on firearms, knives, axes, and miscellaneous tools. This profusely illustrated book supplies much detail on the tools and techniques of mountain life.

Vestal, Stanley, *Mountain Men* (Houghton Mifflin, 1937) O.P.

This is a collection of "heroic" tales about various mountain men. Although many of the stories are true, or are considered to be so, there are also many factual errors in the book and in Vestal's often dubious historical analysis. Had Vestal stuck to a re-telling of tales, he might have written an occasionally entertaining work, but he did not and his book, as a consequence, is not really worth reading.

II

iii

First-Hand Accounts

The reader who wishes to experience "first-hand" the world of the fur trapper will find no dearth of material. Many literate observers either plied the fur trade or visited the trappers in their mountain habitat. Of course some observers are more accurate than others; and, perhaps more to the point, some writers are more readable than others.

Among the first-hand accounts I would particularly recommend are

Zenas Leonard's *Narrative of the Adventures of Zenas Leonard* (Lakeside Press, 1934). Leonard was a free trapper, then worked for Captain Bonneville, accompanying Joseph Walker on his famous trip to California. His work, covering the years 1831–1835, touches on many important events in the mountains and California during these years. Warren A. Ferris' *Life in the Rocky Mountains* 1830–1835 (Rocky Mountain Bookshop, 1940) was arranged by Herbert Auerbach and annotated by J. Cecil Alter. Ferris was an employee of the American Fur Company and his brief account of mountain life covers the years 1830–1835. James Clyman's *James Clyman, Frontiersman* (California Historical Society, 1928) comprises the existent fragments of Clyman's reminiscences and diaries, and covers the period from 1823–1849. Osborne Russell's *Journal of a Trapper, or Nine Years in the Rocky Mountains*, 1834–1845 (1914; University of Nebraska Press, 1965) is the memoir of a man who came West with Nathaniel J. Wyeth, liked the mountain life, and stayed for nine years. This work, covering the years 1834–1843, is probably the most literate of the trappers' accounts.

II

iv

Autobiographies and Biographies

John "Grizzly" Adams (1812–1860)
    "Grizzly" Adams was not a mountain man during the heyday of the fur trade; he did not go West from Massachusetts until 1849, and even then he spent several years as a miner and rancher before retiring into the mountains. However, his name has become linked with the popular image of mountain men through his own self-promotion in the 1850s and through a television program, and his years spent in the Sierra Nevada and Rocky Mountains as a hunter probably entitle him to that appellation. Richard Dillon's popular biography, *The Legend of Grizzly Adams: California's Greatest Mountain Man* (Coward-McCann, 1966), is heretofore the only attempt to find the real John Adams behind the legends. The book maddeningly lacks systematic footnotes, a bibliography, or an index, making the identification of sources for much of the text difficult. Adams dictated his memoirs to Theodore Henry Hittle in *The Adventures of James Capen Adams, Mountaineer and Grizzly Bear Hunter of California* (1861). While this book is full of tall tales, it is entertaining reading if not reliable history. (N.B. For this book, Adams used his brother's name!)

General William H. Ashley (1778–1838)
    General Ashley has been credited with organizing the Rocky Mountain fur trade, but he did much more, being in his lifetime a soldier, politician, entrepreneur, and spokesman for Western interests in Congress. The best full-length biography of Ashley is by Richard M. Clokey, *William*

H. Ashley: Enterprise and Politics in the Trans-Mississippi West (University of Oklahoma Press, 1980). Clokey's scholarship is up to date, and his treatment is sympathetic. Another work on Ashley, Dale L. Morgan's *The West of William H. Ashley* (Old West Publishing, 1964), is a collection of documents, including the General's diaries and many letters from the period when he was a fur trader. The reader might well find Morgan's excellent introduction and notes of more interest than the documents themselves.

John Jacob Aster (1763–1848)

Astor was not only the founder and driving force behind the American Fur Company, but also America's leading business magnate in the early Nineteenth century. The standard biography of Astor, Kenneth Wiggins Porter's *John Jacob Astor Business Man* (Harvard University Press, 1931) in two volumes, is a "business" biography, one based on company records, deeds, business letters, and the like, and chronicles Astor's commercial life. The reader wishing an intimate glimpse into Astor's personality will be disappointed with the dry, removed tone of Porter's work. John Upton Terrell's *Furs by Astor* (Morrow, 1963) also deals exclusively with the fur trading aspect of Astor's life and has little to do with Astor's acquisitive personality or with his family life; yet it is probably a better introductory biography than Porter's massive work. Astor still awaits definitive biographical treatment.

Jim Beckwourth (1800?–1866)

Jim Beckwourth belongs in the first rank of mountain men along with Jim Bridger and Kit Carson. He was a trapper, trader with and member of the Crow tribe, explorer, road builder, Army scout, and tradesman. Unfortunately, the popular conception of Beckwourth is that he was a liar and, in the words of Francis Parkman, "a ruffian of the worst stamp, bloody, and treacherous, without honor or honesty." Why has he been smeared so viciously by writers and historians, few of whom actually knew him? Probably because Jim Beckwourth was black. Beckwourth's collaborative autobiography as told to Thomas D. Bonner, *The Life and Adventures of James P. Beckwourth* (1856; University of Nebraska Press, 1972) edited and with an Introduction by Delmont R. Oswald, is a prime document on the mountain fur trade. As other accounts by mountain men, it has its limitations (Beckwourth had a poor memory for dates, and he exaggerated statistics, especially when describing battles), but, overall, it is accurate. Many full and abridged editions of this work have been printed, but the University of Nebraska edition cited above is recommended for its textual accuracy and excellent notes. Elinor Wilson's biography, *Jim Beckwourth: Black Mountain Man and War Chief of the Crows* (University of Oklahoma Press, 1972), covers all of Beckwourth's adventurous life, filling in the family background and later years that are not covered by the autobiography, while corroborating and expanding upon the years that are.

Jim Bridger (1804–1881)

Jim Bridger went into the mountains as a teenager with the first Ashley expedition, became a leading trapper and eventually a partner in the Rocky Mountain Fur Company, ran a trading post on the immigrant route to Oregon, and acted as a scout for the Army in his later years. Cecil Alter's *James Bridger: A Historical Narrative* (Shepard Book Co., 1925) revised as *Jim Bridger* (University of Oklahoma Press, 1962) has long been considered the standard biography of Bridger. (The revised version is especially recommended as it contains much new material and some new interpretations based on recent scholarship.) Alter's fact-filled work is often dry, though it contains a spirited (if not downright contentious) chapter in which Alter discounted the Hugh Glass legend (and Bridger's role in it) as largely Glass' fabrication. Alter is probably wrong, but he argued a good case. An improvement in readability, though not necessarily in scholarship, is Gene Caesar's *King of the Mountain Men: The Life of Jim Bridger* (Dutton, 1961). Caesar did not doubt that it was young Bridger (with an older companion) who left Glass to die, but he made the event a plausible turning point in the molding of Bridger's otherwise unwavering character. Caesar's descriptive powers and unswerving focus on the character, Jim Bridger, make his work a welcome addition to Alter's. It is not so with Stanley Vestal's biography, *Jim Bridger: Mountain Man* (1946; University of Nebraska Press, 1970). Vestal's work is based largely on Alter's original biography and adds nothing but some fanciful dialogue to our knowledge of Bridger.

Christopher "Kit" Carson (1809–1868)

Kit Carson is the most remembered of the mountain men. Although he was never a fur company partner, or even a brigade leader, Carson caught the imagination of the American public as the prototype of the Western hero, largely through his efforts as a guide for John C. Frémont and later for the Army. There are more books about or mentioning Carson than any of the other mountain men, yet there is still no "definitive" biography of the man. Two recent biographies are fairly adequate, though, especially when read in concert. M. Morgan Estergreen's *Kit Carson: A Portrait in Courage* (University of Oklahoma Press, 1962) is especially good on Carson's fur trade days and the Frémont expeditions, while Bernice Blackwelder's *Great Westerner: The Story of Kit Carson* (Caxton Printers, 1962), though superficial on his early years, does well on his later years as a rancher and Indian agent. Both biographers (in fact, all recent biographers) owe much to the seminal work by Edwin L. Sabin, *Kit Carson Days* (A.C. McClurg, 1919). Sabin's work should still be consulted by those with a serious interest in Carson, although some of his material has been shown to be apocryphal. In fact, all of the above-mentioned biographies have some factual errors on such subjects as Carson's literacy or his participation in the building of Bent's Fort, but they also help to dispel much of the legendary and dime novel material that has clung to his image. The reader would do well to consult Carson's "autobiography." Two reliable versions of this work are widely available. Recommended is Harvey L. Carter's *"Dear Old Kit": The Historical Christopher Carson* (University of Oklahoma Press, 1968) which, in addition to Carson's memoirs, contains an excellent bibliographic essay, extensive annotations of the memoirs, and a chronology of Carson's life. The other reputable edition is Milo M. Quaife's *Kit Carson's Autobiography* (1935; University of Nebraska Press, 1966). Quaife's Introduction is not as good as Carter's nor are his notes as extensive. Finally, the reader should be warned that these works only touch the surface of the Carson books still available. Many other biographies, incorporating legendary or downright fictitious material, have been written, such as Stanley Vestal's *Kit Carson: The Happy Warrior of the Old West* (Houghton Mifflin, 1928), but the reader who wishes an accurate picture of Kit Carson's life is advised to steer clear of them.

John Colter (1770?–1813)

Colter, a member of the Lewis and Clark expedition, remained behind on the upper Missouri when the explorers returned to St. Louis, thus becoming one of the first Anglo-American trappers in the Trans-Mississippi region. He is best known, however, for his lone journey through rugged country undertaken at the behest of Manuel Lisa, a journey on which he explored what is now Yellowstone Park and much of the surrounding region. Colter's story, including his miraculous escapes from the Blackfeet, is told by Burton Harris in *John Colter: His Years in the Rockies* (Scribner's 1952), a book that largely supersedes the earlier work of Stallo Vinton, *John Colter Discoverer of Yellowstone Park* (Edward Eberstadt, 1926), because of Harris' detailed analysis of Colter's route on the epic journey.

Mike Fink (1770–1822)

Mike Fink, who was "half horse, half alligator" and more than half legendary, was a keelboat man and trapper, known largely for his exploits as a brawler, rifle shot, and drinker. The most reliable book on Fink's life is *Half Horse, Half Alligator: The Growth of the Mike Fink Legend* (University of Chicago Press, 1956) edited and introduced by Walter Blair and Franklin J. Meine. Fink's life is outlined in the Introduction, and the most important narratives about Fink are presented with annotations. It is doubtful, given the sources still existent, that we will ever get closer than this to a full biography of Mike Fink.

Thomas Fitzpatrick (1799–1854)

Called "Broken Hand" "White Hair," and "Three Fingers" by his Indian and white companions, Fitzpatrick was one of the most noted of the mountain men. Originally a trapper for General Ashley, he became the leading partner in the Rocky Mountain Fur Company and later acted as guide for immigrant trains and the Army. The last portion of his life was spent as a most effective Indian agent for plains tribes. Leroy R. Hafen and W.J. Ghent's *Broken Hand: The Life Story of Thomas Fitzpatrick, Chief of the Mountain Men* (1931; University of Nebraska Press, 1981) is the only full-length biography of Fitzpatrick. Hafen and Ghent covered the public image of Fitzpatrick thoroughly, although they delved little into the personality and familial background of their subject. An appendix contains the story of "Friday," the Arapaho boy Fitzpatrick found in the desert and befriended.

Hugh Glass (?-1833?)

Glass was a trapper and possibly a sea captain and unwilling pirate, and he was the principal in one of the most incredible "lone trek" tales told of the mountain men. John Myers Myers' *Pirate, Pawnee, and Mountain Man: The Saga of Hugh Glass* (1963; University of Nebraska Press, 1976) is the only full-length biography of Glass. Myers did a creditable job of sorting through the variants of the "left in the wilderness to die" tales and filled in other fascinating areas of Glass' life from the sketchy evidence left to us. Barring discovery of some new source, a "definitive" biography of Glass will always be out of reach, and the controversy surrounding the legend (especially Jim Bridger's part in abandoning Glass) will remain open to some debate; but Myers' book goes most of the way towards discovering the historical Hugh Glass.

Manuel Lisa (1772-1820)

The moving force behind the Missouri Fur Company, the shadowy, sometimes shady character, Manuel Lisa, is the central figure in the pre-Ashley Trans-Mississippi fur trade. Richard Oglesby's biography, *Manuel Lisa and the Opening of the Missouri Fur Trade* (University of Oklahoma Press, 1963), is the best biography of Lisa so far, largely supplanting the somewhat sketchy *Manuel Lisa* (Missouri Historical Society, 1911) by Walter B. Douglas.

Joe Meek (1810-1875)

Meek, one of the many children of a Virginia planter, went into the mountains in 1829 with William Sublette and became a leading partisan of "mountain" life. When the fur trade waned, Meek went to Oregon as an early pioneer, eventually becoming U.S. Marshal of the Oregon territory. Meek (and his daughter Olive) collaborated with Frances Fuller Victor on Meek's memoir, published as *The River of the West* (1870; Long's College Book Co., 1950). *The River of the West* ranks with *The Life and Adventures of Jim Beckwourth* (see above) as an early history of the Rocky Mountain fur trade, although, as with the latter work, some dates and chronology are inaccurate, and Meek, as Beckwourth, was prone at times to "exaggerate." The reader, armed with a little fur trade history, will find the book a pleasure to read. Of the two biographies of Meek, Harvey Elmer Tobie's *No Man Like Joe: The Life and Times of Joseph L. Meek* (Binford & Mort, 1949) is strongest, covering Meek's life thoroughly without losing the dash and color of the mountain man. The other, Stanley Vestal's *Joe Meek: The Merry Mountain Man* (1952; University of Nebraska Press,

1963), is far from Vestal's worst work. Although it does not add a great deal to Tobie's work on Meek, it avoids many of the pitfalls of Vestal's other books and is an adequate biography.

Jedediah Strong Smith (1799–1831)

Smith was one of the most notable men to ply the fur trade in the American West. Besides being a leading trapper and fur company partner, Smith was an important explorer and trailblazer. Dale L. Morgan's *Jedediah Smith and the Opening of the West* (1953; University of Nebraska Press, 1964) is recommended as Morgan's scholarship eclipses that of previous biographers. A small work by G.W. Garber, *Jedediah Strong Smith: Fur Trader from Ohio* (University of Pacific, 1973), fills in some of Smith's family background with material that has come to light since the publication of Morgan's biography. Three more specialized works contain Smith's journals and materials on his exploration: Harrison C. Dale's *The Ashley — Smith Explorations and the Discovery of the Central Route to the Pacific* (Arthur H. Clark, 1918), Maurice S. Sullivan's *The Travels of Jedediah Smith* (The Fine Arts Press, 1934), and George R. Brooks' *The Southwest Expedition of Jedediah Smith: His Personal Account of the Journey to California 1826–1827* (Arthur H. Clark, 1977).

William Sublette (1799–1845)

Sublette was the eldest of the Sublette brothers, several of whom figured prominently in the fur trade. He began his career with General Ashley whom, in partnership with Jedediah Smith and David Jackson, he bought out to form, Smith, Jackson, and Sublette, the forerunner of the Rocky Mountain Fur Company. John E. Sunder's *Bill Sublette, Mountain Man* (University of Oklahoma Press, 1959) gives thorough cradle-to-grave coverage of Sublette's life, as well as offering glimpses of the rest of the family and their dealings. No other full-length biographies of the other Sublettes has been published, although Doyce Blackman Nunis, Jr., wrote a "narrative outline" of Andrew Sublette's life, published as *Andrew Sublette, Rocky Mountain Prince* (Dawson's Book Shop, 1960). Unfortunately the limited printing of this work makes it difficult to come by.

Joseph Reddeford Walker (1798–1876)

Walker was a leading trapper and brigade commander, famous for his journey into California undertaken for Captain Bonneville and for his service as a guide (with Kit Carson) for John C. Frémont. Douglas S. Watson's *West Wind: The Life Story of Joseph Reddeford Walker* (Johnck and Seeger, 1934) is the only biography of Walker and suffers only a little from its early publication date. A more recently published work, Daniel Ellis Conner's *Joseph Reddeford Walker and the Arizona Adventure* (University of Oklahoma Press, 1956), is not a biography, but a first-hand account of a prospecting trip the author took with Walker in the 1860s. The book portrays Walker and some of his later adventures, but sheds little light on his early life in the fur trade.

"Old" Bill Williams (1787–1849)
    Williams was one of the most fascinating personalities among the mountain men (no mean feat in that collection of individualists). In early life an itinerant Baptist preacher, he lived with the Osage Indians, first as a missionary, and then in a kind of conversion married into the tribe. After the death of his wife, he drifted West, entering the mountains (via Santa Fe) where he became a fur trapper and Indian trader, occupations he pursued (along with horse stealing) till just before his death. He also acted as a guide for John C. Frémont. Several books and pamphlets (all out of print) contain legendary material about Williams, but the best work on his life is Alpheus H. Favour's *Old Bill Williams, Mountain Man* (1936; University of Oklahoma Press, 1981). Favour's research of Williams early life with the Osage and before is excellent, as is the final section on the Frément expedition and Williams' death; but by his own admission the middle portion of Williams' life is "sketchy" and the middle third of his biography is commensurately weak.

Ewing Young (1794?–1841)
    Young was a leader among the American trappers who worked out of Taos (where he was involved in several adventures). He later became an early pioneer in the Oregon country where his death led to the formation of a provisional government. His story is told in Kenneth L. Holmes' biography, *Ewing Young, Master Trapper* (Binford & Mort, 1967), a thorough and well illustrated work.

Suggested Fiction

Berry, Don, *Trask* (Viking, 1960)
————, *Moontrap* (Viking, 1962)
Blake, Forrester, *Johnny Christmas* (Morrow, 1948)
Brackett, Leigh, *Follow the Free Wind* (Ballantine, 1963)
Fergusson, Harvey, *Wolf Song* (Knopf, 1927)
Fisher, Vardis, *Mountain Man* (Morrow, 1965)
Grey, Zane, *Man of the Forest* (Harper's, 1920)
Guthrie, A.B., Jr., *The Big Sky* (Sloane, 1947)
Manfred, Frederick, *Lord Grizzly* (1954; Gregg Press, 1980)
Ruxton, George Frederick, *Life in the Far West* (1849)

Suggested Films

The Big Sky (RKO, 1952) directed by Howard Hawks.
Jeremiah Johnson (Warner's, 1972) directed by Sydney Pollack.
Man in the Wilderness (Warner's, 1971) directed by Richard Sarafian.
Man of the Forest (Paramount, 1933) directed by Henry Hathaway.
Wolf Song (Paramount, 1929) directed by Victor Fleming.

The Military Frontier

by John D. Flanagan

I

The Romans called the Carthaginians *Poeni*, or Phoenicians, and they fought three Punic wars with them consistent with the Latin verb *punio* which means to punish or to avenge. The third Punic war was fought from 149B.C. to 146B.C. It was begun by the Romans without provocation, it was pursued ruthlessly, and it resulted in the total destruction of Carthage and the extermination of most of the native population.

The adjective most often associated with the conduct of Anglo-American military operations on the frontier was punitive. Yet, unlike any of the Punic wars, it was informal and undeclared, however bloody it might have been. From the beginning the role of the Army was felt to be that of a "peace-keeping" mission. When Native Americans were decimated and their remnants herded onto small reservations, they were said to have been "pacified."

The United States Dragoons were first organized in 1833, but they were more a mounted Infantry unit than a bona-fide Cavalry. Congress, thanks to lobbying by then Secretary of War Jefferson Davis, authorized the formation of a horse regiment to battle Indians in 1855. It was organized in March of that year at Louisville, Kentucky, and titled the *Second* Cavalry. The enlisted men were issued breech-loading Springfield rifles and .36 caliber Navy Colts, primarily for service on the Texas frontier.

96

Although in earlier periods forts had been built by the British and then the Anglo-Americans to prohibit immigration beyond the Allegheny Mountains, they sprang up on the Texas frontier in the 1850s, looking more impressive on maps than they were militarily useful. Contrary to wild West shows and Hollywood films, Indians did not storm forts so they could be shot down in large numbers. However, the forts on the Texas frontier, whatever their intended function, were totally unlike Eastern models in previous decades. They were constructed of raw timber and the quarters, bakeries, and hospitals within the log walls were, as one inspection report put it, "unfit for human habitation." In later years General Sheridan, on an inspection tour, remarked that if he owned both Hell and Texas, he would rent out Texas and live in Hell. Supplies had to be transported many miles, in some cases even over water.

Before 1860 the Army was principally a mercenary force and was regarded with contempt by the civilian population — although the Anglo-American population at no time in the Nineteenth century could have been termed enthusiastic about the Army, including the decades after the Civil War when it achieved more of a professional status. The enlisted man's lot was a harsh one throughout the century. Army conditions amounted to almost penal servitude and often recruits were brought to a fort guarded by a military escort to discourage desertion. Pay in the 1850s was five dollars a month for privates; it went up to sixteen dollars a month during the Civil War, but afterwards it fell again to thirteen dollars a month. The rations were often inedible: bread baked and canned in 1861 was still being issued to troops in 1867! Punishments were harsh and frequent and on the average ten percent of the ranks were being disciplined. Lack of sanitation caused sickness and death; adultery and alcoholism caused more attrition than engagements with Indians. Officers were permitted to maintain wives, but that word "maintain" might best be interpreted as officers' wives were allowed to subsist. The wives and daughters of non-commissioned officers were permitted to work as "laundresses" and all other women, having no status and given no support, were declared to be "camp followers." Adultery became such a fearsome problem that at some posts men openly carried on multiple relations with a "wife" and in one recorded case a wife, married many times, upon her death turned out to be a male! Yet these unnatural conditions served the Army's purpose: they tended to make the men savage and this, in conflict with "savage" Indians, was considered a virtue.

Following the Civil War, the Army was reduced to 57,000 enlisted men. This figure was further reduced to 37,000 during the years 1869 and 1870 and during the period 1871 to 1890 there were only between 24,000 and 29,000 men under arms. These soldiers endured everything: hardship, physical suffering, exposure, malnutrition, stupidity, disease, and danger. Notwithstanding, when they were defeated in battle, it was nearly always because of the mistakes and miscalculations of their commanders, the most obviously irresponsible loss of enlisted lives being Custer's defeat at the Little Big Horn. This having been so, it is difficult, if not altogether incomprehensible, for a student of American military history to understand the persistent and intense interest which Custer's atypical career continues to excite.

The frontier Army succeeded in its mission. It did so, first of all, because of the constancy of the men and the determination — after the Civil War — to pursue a punitive operation against the free tribes of Indians; and it did so because of the quality of the officers — at least half of them were educated and graduated at West Point. This institution at the time was unique, and its graduate officers were imbued with an almost mystical professional pride found then in few standing armies. For the most part, these officers avoided blind passions and sought to skirt the political hypocrisy with which they had constantly to contend. As General Sherman once pointed out, the Army had much to lose and little to gain in fighting Indians, and most officers respected this principle, concerned more with minimizing their losses in terms of human lives and materiel than with pursuing glory.

II

i

Because of the complexity of The Military Frontier in the Nineteenth-century American West, I decided to divide it into four bibliographical sub-sections which, more or less, reflect both the interests of certain readers and the subject areas covered by a majority of the books. The four sub-sections are general books, first-hand accounts, Custerana, and books pertaining to some aspect of frontier forts.

II

ii

General Books

There are three general books which ought to be singled out since, taken as a unit, they provide an excellent overview of the history of the American military frontier in the Nineteenth century and, at least to a degree, treat all of the subjects covered by the books annotated below. They are Francis Paul Prucha's *The Sword of the Republic: The United States Army on the Frontier, 1783–1846* (Macmillan, 1969), Robert M. Utley's *Frontiersmen in Blue: The United States Army and the Indian, 1848–1865* (Macmillan, 1967), and Robert M. Utley's *Frontier Regulars: The United States Army and the Indian, 1866–1891* (Macmillan, 1973). These are chronological narratives that concentrate on subjective facts simulate impartiality. For example, in introducing Lieutenant Colonel George Armstrong Custer to his narrative, Utley wrote that "Custer had rocketed to fame as a hard-hitting—some said reckless—Cavalry leader in the Civil War. A major general with his own division at twenty-five, he now had to content himself with a regiment. Hancock's expedition gave Custer his first experience with Indians. By the time of his last, on the Little Big Horn nine years later, he would be, depending on one's point of view, either famous or infamous, idolized or abominated." In none of these books are the numerous Indian nations ever really characterized nor is there any sense of The Natural Frontier; they are narrative histories of American military activities and are confined to this narrow focus. However, this is not to say that a reader of their—when combined—more than 1,200 pages will not have a comprehensive linear outline of important events and individuals (characterized more among the Anglo-Americans than among the Native Americans), because one surely will. What ultimately is absent is a human and spiritual dimension, an inadequacy common for centuries in the writing of military history. However, this shortcoming can certainly be overcome through reading the first-hand accounts and some of the social histories annotated below and certain selected histories and first-hand accounts to be found in the section on Native Americans.

Fowler, Arlen L., *The Black Infantry in the West*, 1869–1891 (Greenwood Press, 1971).

Fowler's study of the Army's two black Infantry regiments was patterned after William Leckie's account of the black Cavalry regiments (see below). It traces the early history of the Twenty-Fourth and Twenty-Fifth Infantries. The book's chief merit is its casual exploration of prejudice against blacks within the white officer corps and the federal government, not to mention the Texas Rangers who rarely missed an opportunity to harass and malign them; but in other respects, despite its effort to fill an important gap in our understanding of the frontier Army, Fowler's study is inferior to Leckie's.

Leckie, William H., *The Buffalo Soldiers: A Narrative of the Negro Cavalry in the West* (University of Oklahoma Press, 1967).

In the wealth of material written about the Cavalry and the Indian wars, scant attention has been paid to the black Cavalry units that were as much a part of the military frontier experience as were the Second or Seventh Cavalry. Leckie followed the development of the Ninth and Tenth Cavalry from their experimental beginnings in 1866 to their last engagement with Indians at Drexel Mission in December, 1890. The so-called "buffalo" soldiers—called that because of their hair—readily became tough and disciplined troops with one of the lowest alcoholism and desertion rates in the frontier Army. For example, in 1877 General Mackenzie's Fourth Cavalry had 184 desertions, the Seventh 172, the Tenth 18, and the Ninth 6. Prejudice toward these units there certainly was, their record notwithstanding, and frequently they received the worst horses and the most inadequate equipment, although, for better or worse, Leckie did not deal with this issue to any great extent.

Lummis, Charles F., *Dateline Fort Bowie: Charles Fletcher Lummis Reports on an Apache War* (University of Oklahoma Press, 1979), edited by Dan L. Thrapp.

Lummis is not particularly known for having been a war correspondent. Nonetheless, this series of newspaper reports, written by Lummis from Arizona during an Indian campaign, provides a reader with a marvelous portrait of General Crook, of Frank Leslie, "the liar scout," and Frank Bennet, a "real scout," and a retrospective view of the fighting with the Apaches in 1883. Although Lummis was an admirer of General Crook and fell ultimately under his influence, it cannot be said that what he wrote ever descended to boosterism or sycophancy.

Rickey, Don, Jr., *Forty Miles a Day on Beans and Hay: The Enlisted Soldier Fighting the Indian Wars* (University of Oklahoma Press, 1963).

There is no lack of books by Army officers who fought in the Indian wars. Many officers kept detailed journals on their marches and campaigns and turned them into books at the first opportunity. This was not true for the enlisted man. As a result, the life of the enlisted man in the frontier Army remained somewhat obscure until the appearance of this book. The product of a massive amount of research and interviews with men who served on the frontier, Rickey's study is possessed of a mastery of detail and yet it remains withal eminently readable. Fortunately, Rickey was not intimidated by the prudery that characterizes most Nineteenth-century accounts of American military life in the field and this dimension is not overlooked.

Thrapp, Dan L, *The Conquest of Apacheria* (University of Oklahoma Press, 1967); *General Crook and the Sierra Madre Adventure* (University of Oklahoma Press, 1972).

Generals Crook, Custer, King, Captain J.G. Bourke, and even Martha Summerhayes (*et al.* see below) were of the opinion that many, if not all, of the Army's problems with the Indians were caused by corrupt Indian agents, greedy post traders, and intruding white squatters, rumrunners, robe buyers, etc., and that the frontier Army was as much a victim of this assorted viciousness as were the Indians. Based on Thrapp's research in both of these books, such an argument was erroneous and self-serving. The soldiers were as inclined as anyone else to regard Native Americans as a lower form of life, scarcely human. Quoting from a first-hand account in *The Conquest of Apacheria* describing the torture of Mangas Coloradas, Thrapp made the scene quite vivid. "'Watching them [the soldiers] from my beat in the outer darkness,'" Thrapp quoted, "'I discovered that they were heating their bayonets and burning Mangas' feet and legs. This they continued to do until Mangas rose upon his left elbow, angrily protesting that he was no child to be played with. Thereupon the two soldiers, without removing their bayonets from their Minie muskets, each quickly fired into the chief, following with two shots each from their Navy six-shooters. Mangas fell back into the same position ... and never moved.'" The impression gained from reading these two historical accounts is that the frontier Army was definitely not blameless when it came to savage conduct.

Whitman, S.E., *The Troopers: An Informal History of the Plains Cavalry*, 1865–1880 (Hastings House, 1962).

This book, written in a conversational style, is no substitute for Don Rickey's account (see above); although, as Rickey's, it is a topical study rather than a linear historical narrative. However, whatever its shortcomings, it is still a better introduction to the subject than Richard Wormser's *The Yellowlegs: The Story of the United States Cavalry* (Doubleday, 1966) which is informal to the point of absurdity, comparing Naval operations during the taking of California to "the script of an old Keystone Kops comedy."

II

iii

First-Hand Accounts

Bourke, Captain John G., *An Apache Campaign in the Sierra Madre: An Account of the Expedition in Pursuit of the Hostile Apaches in the Spring of 1883* (1886; Scribner's, 1958) O.P.; *On the Border with Crook* (1890) O.P.; reprinted by Time-Life Books.

Bourke was General Crook's adjutant and aide de camp, an inquisitive and observant man, witty, independent of mind, and possessed of a breadth of human sympathy not usually associated with the professional soldier. His accounts of the Apache wars, as a consequence, have become classics of frontier literature. *An Apache Campaign in the Sierra Madre* is a brief narrative of the pursuit of Geronimo, Chato, and Kantenne, filled with superb descriptions, caustic diatribes on Mexicans and Indian agents, and vivid portraits of the Third and Sixth Cavalry in the field. Yet, as fine as it is, it is not the equal of *On the Border with Crook*, one of the best first-hand accounts of Indian fighting on the post-Civil War frontier. This memoir is a clear window on a vanished era. It is particularly noteworthy for its picture of Tucson and Prescott during this era and of Apache life-ways. However, if Bourke did have a fault, it was his almost idolatrous view of Crook and Crook's policies.

Carr, Captain Camillus, *A Cavalryman in Indian Country* (Lewis Osborne, 1974), edited with an Introduction by Dan L. Thrapp.

Thrapp did a good job of editing Carr's memoir of his service in Arizona territory from 1866 to 1869, originally published in 1889 in the *Journal of the United States Cavalry Association*. Carr's account of his duty at Fort McDowell is a good companion volume to Bourke's chronicles and is especially valuable for its description of fort life and the Pima Indians.

Crook, General George, *General George Crook: His Autobiography* (University of Oklahoma Press, 1960), edited and annotated by Martin F. Schmitt, O.P.

Written between 1885 and 1890, Crook's autobiography was never completed or polished for publication. It breaks off abruptly on 18 June 1876. However, what there is of it, unlike General Miles' memoir (see below), is rough-hewn and straight-forward. Crook was not one to romanticize killing Indians. It was a nasty, shameful business and he knew it. There is so much sound sense and fine humor in what General Crook did write that we can forgive him his occasional impulse to look good and shift the blame, as in his account of the Battle of the Rosebud. Also recommended is James T. King's article, "Needed: A Re-Evaluation of General George Crook," in *Nebraska History* (September, 1964), for a somewhat negative view of Crook's stature.

Johnson, Hervey, *Tending the Talking Wire: A Buck Soldier's View of Indian Country*, 1863–1866 (University of Utah Press, 1979), edited by William E. Unrau.

This is a rare and splendid book. Hervey Johnson was a Quaker farmboy who joined the Eleventh Ohio Volunteer Cavalry in 1863 and spent his enlistment guarding the telegraph at the Deer Creek and Sweetwater stations in Wyoming. The book is comprised of Johnson's letters home, carefully written, unpretentious letters that provide an incomparable view of the enlisted man's experience on the frontier during the Civil War era. There are no "great events" recounted here, nor none of the consciously fabricated romance one finds, for example, in Captain Eugene F. Ware's account (see below), but instead the unmistakable texture of real life.

King, Captain Charles, *Campaigning with Crook* (1880) O.P.; reprinted by the University of Oklahoma Press with an Introduction by Don Russell.

King is primarily noted for having been an author of Western fiction, novels and stories set at military posts on the frontier. This was his first book, incorporating a series of newspaper sketches he had written about his participation with the Fifth Cavalry during the Sioux campaign of 1876. He had little use for Indians, was an ardent promoter of the image of the military, and had a great admiration for both Crook and Custer. This account of skirmishes, the discovery of the Custer massacre, the miserable "horse meat march" to Deadwood is remarkably well written in the fashion of a grand adventure. Some of what he wrote must be taken with a grain of salt, but this does not discount the importance of his memoir.

Marquis, Thomas, *Custer, Cavalry, and Crows: The Story of William White as Told to Thomas Marquis* (The Old Army Press, 1975).

As Hervey Johnson's letters (see above), this is a fine memoir and we owe a debt of gratitude to Thomas Marquis for having rescued it. White enlisted in the Second Cavalry at Louisville, Kentucky, in 1872 and served with the Second in the West, generally stationed at Fort Ellis, Montana. Most of the book is concerned with White's activities during the fateful year of the Centennial campaign, his memories of the Custer battlefield, and the pursuit of the Indians in 1876. White was with Lieutenant Doane in the summer of 1877 on his mission to the Crows and the exploration of the Snake River country. Discharged in 1877, White then served as a civilian wagoneer with Lieutenant Doane during the pursuit of the Nez Percé. In 1878 White married a Crow woman and settled down at a farm site near the Crow Agency in Montana. Whether recounting the massacre and axe-murdering of Piegan Indians by troops or the utter billboard sham of "Buffalo Bill" Cody as a scout, White's recollections are clear, distinct, and always fascinating.

Miles, Nelson A., *Serving the Republic: Personal Recollections and Observations of General Nelson A. Miles* (1896) O.P.; reprinted by DaCapo Press.

There is something unconvincing about General Miles as he comes through in this autobiography. Perhaps it is the hint of the *arriviste* in him — of a man on the make, smooth, glib, well oiled. His tone always has something of the booster about it. There are here no disturbing truths, no radical illuminations. Yet, Miles was an intelligent man and an efficient, ambitious, highly successful officer. His account of his experiences on the frontier tend to depict the imperial march of American empire, an historical process of which he was proud to have been a part.

Summerhayes, Martha, *Vanished Arizona: Recollections of the Army Life of a New England Woman* (1908) O.P.; reprinted by the University of Nebraska Press with an Introduction by Dan L. Thrapp.

Thrapp, based on his Introduction to this book, was not of the opinion that women who wrote memoirs about military life on the frontier had much to contribute that would be of interest to an historian. This is myopic. Summerhayes recounted her experiences on The Military Frontier, beginning at Cheyenne, Wyoming, but for the most part in the Southwest and her reflections *are* of tremendous interest. First of all, contrasted with the memoirs of Elizabeth Custer (see below), Summerhayes was not in Elizabeth's somewhat exalted status and so her record of the harshnesses of Army life for women is extremely relevant. Second, and perhaps of equal importance, she detailed the day-to-day life on the Southwestern military frontier, something that is significantly absent in accounts such as Bourke's or Carr's (see above), and yet an aspect of frontier life much in need of documentation.

Ware, Captain Eugene F., *The Indian War of 1864* (University of Nebraska Press, 1960), edited with an Introduction by Clyde C. Walton.

Ware served with the Seventh Iowa Cavalry at Fort Cottonwood, later Fort McPherson, near the junction of the North and South forks of the Platte River, and at Julesburg. His memoir was written many years later and so lacks the detail and substance of Hervey Johnson's letters home (see above) — in fact, Johnson's unit passed through Fort McPherson on its way to Fort Laramie, Wyoming. The ultimate value of Ware's account, given his many prejudices and his conviction that all Indians had to be exterminated, is the insight it gives us into the thinking of the times, how some officers on The Military Frontier felt about and responded to events during the parlous era.

II

iv

Custerana

Perhaps the best place to begin is with Custer's memoir on Indian fighting, published originally as a series of articles in *Galaxy* magazine, and afterward titled *My Life on the Plains* (1868; University of Nebraska Press, 1971), the reissue edition edited with an Introduction by Milo Milton Quaife. "Taking him as we find him," Custer wrote, "at peace or at war, at home or abroad, waiving all prejudices, and laying aside all partiality, we will discover in the Indian a subject for thoughtful study and investigation. In him we will find the representative of a race whose origin is, and promises to be, a subject forever wrapped in mystery; a race incapable of being judged by the rules or laws applicable to any other known race of men; one between which and civilization there seems to have existed from time immemorial a determined and unceasing warfare — a hostility so deep-seated and inbred with the Indian character that in the exceptional instances where the modes and habits of civilization have been reluctantly adopted, it has been at the sacrifice of power and influence as a tribe, and the more serious loss of health, vigor, and courage as individuals." Obviously, given this attitude, one could scarcely go to Custer to learn anything about Native Americans; but his reminiscences are filled with vivid, colorful, and entertaining anecdotes about himself and his life on the frontier and provide a degree of insight into the man and the image of himself put forward for the reading public of his day.

After Custer's death, his widow, Elizabeth, initially because her pension was inadequate and also because she wanted to control the way historians and others regarded her husband, wrote three books about her life with Custer and the Seventh Cavalry on the frontier: *Tenting on the Plains* (1887; University of Oklahoma Press, 1976) about their life in

Louisiana, Texas, and Kansas from the close of the Civil War to 1867; *Following the Guidon* (1890; University of Oklahoma Press, 1976) covering the period from the Battle of the Washita in 1868 to their posting in Kentucky in 1871; and *Boots and Saddles* (1885; University of Oklahoma Press, 1977) concerning their years at Fort Abraham Lincoln in the Dakota territory from 1873 to 1876. Although these books are favorable to Custer to the point of idolatry and offer no insights into the darker side of Custer's character, they are notwithstanding valuable sources for certain aspects of Custer's career and his private life and, along with Martha Summerhayes' first-hand account (see above), they do render a vivid portrait of Army life as it was for an officer's wife. Elizabeth Custer had the reputation on the frontier of having been a sparkling conversationalist and some of this quality, surely, was carried over into her narrative style.

For a fuller, albeit still favorable, view of Custer, one must turn to Jay Monaghan's *Custer: The Life of General George Armstrong Custer* (1959; University of Nebraska Press, 1971), a polished biography and, however cautiously and circumspectly written, probably still the best general survey of Custer's life. D.A. Kinsley's *Favor the Bold* (Holt, Rinehart, 1968) contains more specific details, but it is generally less reliable than Monaghan's biography. The best negative view of Custer remains Frederic Van de Water's *Glory Hunter: A Life of General Custer* (Bobbs-Merrill, 1934).

Stan Hoig's *The Battle of the Washita: The Sheridan-Custer Indian Campaign of 1867–1869* (Doubleday, 1976) is the only really good book on this important phase of Custer's career, whereas one of the more convincing negative views of Custer during this period is to be found in Robert M. Utley's *Life in Custer's Cavalry: Diaries and Letters of Albert and Jennie Barnitz, 1867–1868* (Yale University Press, 1977). Barnitz served as a captain with the Seventh Cavalry until being seriously wounded at the Battle of the Washita. He was a poet, somewhat fastidious in temperament, and given to narcissistic lamentations. Nevertheless, his picture of Custer as an overbearing martinet surrounded by a claque of crude sycophants was drawn from life and shows that Custer's problems with some of his officers did not first begin on the Washita.

Donald Jackson's *Custer's Gold: The United States Cavalry Expedition of 1874* (Yale University Press, 1966) is a small, enchanting investigation into the lives of the participants in the trek into the Black Hills. This elegant little book is almost required reading for students of the Cavalry on the plains. The best single volume on the Battle of the Little Big Horn, or for that matter on the military dimension of Custer's career, is Edgar I. Stewart's *Custer's Luck* (University of Oklahoma Press, 1955). After decades of seemingly endless controversy over Custer's last fight, Stewart provided what appears to be as final an answer as we are likely to get. Although his focus was on the expedition and the battle, Stewart ranged widely over Custer's career and the political background of this final campaign. If you were to read only one book on the Battle of the Little Big Horn, this should be it. However, should you be without much time and want a shorter, yet beautifully written, account, there is Mari Sandoz' *The Battle of the Little Big Horn* (1966; University of Nebraska Press, 1981). Although Sandoz was more sympathetic towards Benteen and Reno than Custer and portrayed Custer as an ambitious, arrogant ingrate, her narrative of the campaign is essentially sound. Thomas B. Marquis' *Keep the Last Bullet for Yourself: The True Story of Custer's Last Stand* (Two Continents, 1976) presents the intriguing thesis that many of Custer's soldiers shot themselves at the Little Big Horn. Marquis was at one time a physician at the Crow Agency, Montana, and was among the most knowledgeable to have written about the battle, so that his argument is worth reading even if it is ultimately incapable of demonstration. Colonel W.A. Graham's *The Custer Myth: A Source Book of Custeriana* (sic) (Stackpole, 1953) is a fine collection of eye-witness accounts of the Little Big Horn fight and the subsequent debate over exactly what happened and who was to blame. This book is indispensible reading in any effort to study the Custer controversy. Of almost equal interest is the material gathered by Walter Camp concerning the frontier Army and his many interviews with soldiers and Indians who participated in the final Custer battle, gathered together and edited by Kenneth Hammer in *Custer in '76: Walter Camp's Notes on the Custer Fight* (Brigham Young University Press, 1976).

Two books of more peripheral interest are Ernest L. Reedstrom's *Bugles, Banners, and Warbonnets: From Fort Riley to the Little Big Horn—A Study of Lt. Col. George A. Custer's Seventh Cavalry, the Soldiers, Their Weapons and Equipment* (Caxton Printers, 1977) and Marguerite Merington's *The Custer Story: The Life and Intimate Letters of General Custer and His Wife Elizabeth* (Devin-Adair, 1950). Reedstrom's book is an odd mixture of good material on Custer, including excellent photographs of Custer, his Cavalry companies, and their equipment, along with often superfluous details on the Second Reactivated Cavalry of which Reedstrom was a member. Merington's book ought to be especially engaging to anyone who has first read the personal reminiscences of the two principals and offers the most intimate glimpse we are ever likely to get of the relationship between them.

Two books have been written specifically on the growth of the Custer myth in the popular media. Robert M. Utley's *Custer and the Great Controversy: The Origin and Development of a Legend* (Westernlore, 1962) traces the debate about what happened at the Little Big Horn through newspapers and books and is essentially a good bibliographical essay while Brian Dippie's *Custer's Last Stand: The Anatomy of an American Myth* (University of Montana Press, 1976) is a far more sophisticated analysis of the evolution of Custer's popular image and of the battle in poetry, fiction, painting, and motion pictures.

II

v

Forts

The subject of frontier forts is perhaps ideally divided into three groups: (1) surveys of individual forts in terms of *locus* and the individual history of each; (2) forts as a part of a narrative history; and (3) narrative histories of individual forts.

Foremost in the first group are Henry M. Hart's *Old Forts of the Northwest* (Superior Publishing, 1963) and *Old Forts of the Southwest* (Superior Publishing, 1964). Hart was a retired colonel of the U.S. Marines and these books consist of one-or two-page accounts of each fort included along with directions on how to find where each of these forts was (or still is) located. An even more comprehensive survey is *Soldier and Brave: Historical Places Associated with Indian Affairs and the Indian Wars in the Trans-Mississippi West* (National Park Service of the U.S. Department of the Interior, 1971) edited by Robert G. Ferris. Both of Hart's volumes and Ferris' are amply illustrated. An absolutely indispensible reference is Robert W. Frazer's *Forts of the West: Military Forts and Presidios and Posts Commonly Called Forts West of the Mississippi River to 1898* (University of Oklahoma Press, 1965) because it includes not only every fort that existed in this area during this time-frame but notations are also included of the name changes many of these forts underwent. Kent Ruth's *Great Day in the West: Forts, Posts, Rendezvous Beyond the Mississippi* (University of Oklahoma Press, 1963) is a particularly well mounted and illustrated book, the one-page descriptions of which might—at least in those cases where it applies—be supplemented by then Lieutenant Colonel Phil Sheridan's *Outline Descriptions of the Posts in the Military Division of the Missouri* (1876; The Old Army Press, 1969) with its careful record of what was located within certain forts and what the surrounding areas were like at the time. Somewhat related are Colonel George Croghan's *Army Life on the Western Frontier: Selections from the Official Reports Made Between 1826 and 1845* (University of Oklahoma Press, 1958) edited by Francis Paul Prucha; and Colonel George Archibald McCall's *New Mexico in 1850: A Military View* (University of Oklahoma Press, 1968) edited by Robert W. Frazer, the latter consisting of reports during an inspection tour of Southwestern forts following the Mexican War.

Two excellent books in the second group are Robert G. Athearn's *Forts of the Upper Missouri* (1967; University of Nebraska Press, 1972), a well written and authoritative narrative history of the forts in this area from the 1820s through the 1890s; and Max L. Moorhead's *The Presidio: Bastion of the Spanish Borderlands* (University of Oklahoma Press, 1975), the only really thorough study of Spanish and Mexican forts in the Southwest from the Seventeenth century to the end of Mexican rule.

A pre-eminent book on an individual fort is *Fort Smith: Little*

Gibraltar on the Arkansas (University of Oklahoma Press, 1969) by Ed Bearss and Arrell Morgan Gibson. Of lesser interest are George Walton's *Sentinel of the Plains: Fort Leavenworth and the American West* (Prentice-Hall, 1973), which traces this fort's history from its origin to the present day, Chris Emmett's *Fort Union and the Winning of the Southwest* (University of Oklahoma Press, 1965), marred by an extremely dull style, and Dee Brown's *Fort Phil Kearny* (1962; University of Nebraska Press, 1971) which is sympathetic to Carrington, scathing in its treatment of Fetterman, and in which the Indians remain at best insubstantial shadows.

Suggested Fiction

Bellah, James Warner, *Sergeant Rutledge* (Bantam, 1960)
————, *A Thunder of Drums* (Bantam, 1961)
Cook, Will, *Two Rode Together* (Bantam, 1961)
Fisher, Clay, *Red Blizzard* (Simon & Schuster, 1951)
Gardiner, Dorothy, *The Great Betrayal* (Doubleday, 1949)
Haycox, Ernest, "Tactical Maneuver," "Scout Detail," "Weight of Command," and "Change of Station" from *By Rope and Lead* (Little, Brown, 1951) and "The Colonel's Daughter" and "Dispatch to the General" from *Murder on the Frontier* (Little, Brown, 1953) [short stories]
Horgan, Paul, *A Distant Trumpet* (Farrar, Straus, 1960)
Kelton, Elmer, *The Wolf and the Buffalo* (Doubleday, 1980)
King, General Charles, *Two Soldiers* (1888)
————, *Dunraven Ranch* (1890)
————, *An Army Portia* (1890)
Patten, Lewis B., *The Red Sabbath* (Doubleday, 1968)
Remington, Frederic, *John Ermine of the Yellowstone* (Macmillan, 1902)
Short, Luke, *Ambush* (Houghton Mifflin, 1950)
Wister, Owen, *Red Men and White* (1895) [short stories]

Suggested Films

A Distant Trumpet (Warner's, 1964) directed by Raoul Walsh.
Duel at Diablo (United Artists, 1966) directed by Ralph Nelson.
The Great Sioux Massacre (Columbia, 1965) directed by Sidney Salkow.
The Last Frontier (Columbia, 1955) directed by Anthony Mann.
Little Big Man (National General, 1970) directed by Arthur Penn.
Major Dundee (Columbia, 1964) directed by Sam Peckinpah.
Seminole (Universal, 1953) directed by Budd Boetticher.
She Wore a Yellow Ribbon (RKO, 1949) directed by John Ford.
Soldier Blue (Avco-Embassy, 1970) directed by Ralph Nelson.
Soul Soldier (Hirschman Northern, 1970) directed by John Cardos.

Gunfighters, Lawmen, and Outlaws

by Jon Tuska

I

Jack Schaefer in his *Heroes Without Glory: Some Goodmen of the Old West* (Houghton Mifflin, 1965) complained about what he felt was the undue, and even silly, emphasis accorded the study of the lives of Western "badmen." On the surface, the explanation is simple enough: there is, as for a long time there has been, a keen interest in them on the part of the reading public. This interest, however, as that commensurately in frontier gunfighters and lawmen, has never been solely the product of self-generation. Almost without exception, the names of outlaws, gunfighters, and lawmen familiar to the general public became so initially because, by one means or another, they were already being publicized while they were still alive, or just shortly after they died. Their subsequent fame, or notoriety, is the result of the images the media of their day and the media since created for them, or which they helped the media to create.

Their names are familiar, but rarely the events associated with their names. I was telephoned sometime ago by a producer of a special for the ABC network who wanted my suggestion as to an appropriate film clip showing Billy the Kid that he could feature in the program.

"How are you treating the Kid?" I asked the producer.

109

"Why, as a hero, of course," the producer replied. "How is it you ask?"

"For one thing, because it will tell me what kind of film clip to suggest."

"Are you implying that the Kid wasn't a hero?"

"No. I would state outright that the Kid wasn't a hero."

The producer assured that he would get a research expert on the matter right away, that the special was to deal with the legends and the realities of the old West and if the Kid was not a hero, he would be presented as he was. I should have known better. When the special was aired, the viewer was informed that Billy the Kid's real name was William S. Bonney, that he was a savage killer who had killed twenty-one men by the time Sheriff Pat Garrett gunned him down, and that he had killed his first man at the age of fourteen. There is not a single element of historical truth in this image.

Unfortunately, there continues to be no middle road in the way the media present frontier outlaws, gunfighters, and lawmen: they were either heroes or villains. Such a dichotomy, in an historical sense, is patently ridiculous. In *The Western Hero in History and Legend* (University of Oklahoma Press, 1965) Kent Ladd Steckmesser undertook to separate fact from fiction concerning at least four frontier legends, Kit Carson, Billy the Kid, "Wild Bill" Hickok, and General George Armstrong Custer. There is much of value in such an attempt; but in Steckmesser's case the attempt was less than successful. Too much fiction crept into his renderings of the "history," too many assumptions such as his lack of sympathy for the Native American point of view; but the most significant failing of the book came about through Steckmesser's uncritical acceptance of what can be termed the Henry Nash Smith thesis. Smith set forth this thesis in his book *Virgin Land: The American West as Symbol and Myth* (Harvard University Press, 1950). In treating Kit Carson, for example, Steckmesser appealed to the Smith thesis when he proposed that Nineteenth-century "mountain-man biographies ... reveal less about frontier life than they do about the literary techniques and moral ideas of the period in which they were written."

More to the point, the treatments of so-called frontier legends reveal very little about the "period" in which they were written but a great deal about the "moral ideas" of those who worked at manufacturing the legends. What was wrong, in my opinion, with the Smith thesis was the emphasis it mistakenly placed on the public receiving the media action. Presumably, so the implication went, the public get only what they want and what they want is to be reassured of what they already believe, that the most successful "popular" notions are always those which reflect and reinforce what the public want. This is too static a conception for an interchange as essentially dynamic and interactive as the relationship between media and public. A better concept, one that is more workable, is that the media, in the Nineteenth century as in the Twentieth, tend most of the time to be *prescriptive*, not reflective. The "moral ideas" embodied in media projections of frontier legends are moral ideas prescribed for the receiving public. Popular literature, newspaper accounts, and in this century radio, films, and television are all components of *emotional* media, that is, media seeking to persuade through the manipulation of the emotions. In these terms, Nineteenth-century mountain man biographies, while they may reveal little about actual frontier life, do act as indicators as to what certain individuals, namely their authors, wanted the public to believe concerning certain moral ideas.

Stephen Tatum in his book, *Inventing Billy the Kid* (University of New Mexico Press, 1982), would have the reader believe that *Dirty Little Billy* (Columbia, 1971) directed by Stan Dragoti and *Pat Garrett and Billy the Kid* (M-G-M, 1973) directed by Sam Peckinpah can somehow tell us something about what Americans were thinking and feeling during the Nixon years. Here again is the Smith thesis. What Professor Tatum did not record was that *Dirty Little Billy* did so poorly at the box office that it has never been sold to network television for domestic showing, was never put into syndication, and never made it to the foreign television market. *Pat Garrett and Billy the Kid* cost $4,345,000 to make and grossed $2,754,218. I question the premise that even a truly popular film — popular in terms of box-office receipts — can tell us anything about what those who paid to see it were thinking or feeling; but it is even more absurd to assert that these Billy the Kid pictures, both box-office failures, somehow provide an insight into the minds of people who did not see them.

The more intelligent approach in contrasting a legend with the historical reality, rather than what Professor Steckmesser and others have attempted, is to discern and isolate what were the individual distortions to which an historical reality was forced to submit and thus arrive at a distinct notion as to what its author hoped a reader or a viewer would think or feel after experiencing it. The question as to how effective was the distortion in producing the intended effect in the reader or viewer can only be discovered by empirical, and not by intuitive, means.

The producer of the ABC special had, he felt, two ways to go to achieve *his* desired effect, which was to demonstrate to the viewer that the image generally held about Billy the Kid was false. He could say that the Kid, branded as a villain, was actually a hero; or he could say that the Kid, often shown to be a hero, was actually a villain. In either case, the treatment was prescriptive: because he did such and such he was a hero; or because he did such and such he was a villain. What the media does reinforce is the reliance on such dichotomies. After all, without it, could politicians ever convince a voter that there are only two basic differences in a society because only two political parties are allowed to exist? The most amazing sleight-of-hand of which the media has been guilty consistently, both in the last century and now, is reducing human diversity to a dichotomy.

Nearly all the media legendry about frontier gunfighters, lawmen, and outlaws has supported the notion of one-settlement culture. One manifestation of this phenomenon is the color-line which Frederick Jackson Turner posited between civilization and savagery — albeit only *one* — and Richard Drinnon addressed it in *Facing West: The Metaphysics of Indian-*

Hating and Empire-Building (New American Library, 1980) when he wrote that "Turner's color-line was the supreme expression by an historian of all the other expressions before and since by novelists, poets, playwrights, pulp writers, painters, sculptors, and film directors. It separated the cowboys from the Indians by making the latter easily recognizable dark targets, especially if they had war paint on to boot. It unmistakably shaped national patterns of violence by establishing *whom* one could kill under propitious circumstances and thereby represented a prime source of the American way of inflicting death." Turner's racial dichotomy is absent in many familiar accounts of frontier legendry, but one thing has remained the same: *the author invariably prescribes who may be killed with impunity.*

II

i

The majority of books which have been selected for inclusion in this section have been chosen on the basis that either they have been particularly influential or they are generally reliable. Three reference books, however, can be cited as absolutely essential and, hence, they are listed first, out of sequence.

Adams, Ramon F., *Burs Under the Saddle: A Second Look at Books and Histories of the West* (University of Oklahoma Press, 1964) O.P.; *More Burs Under the Saddle: Books and Histories of the West* (University of Oklahoma Press, 1979) with a Foreword by Wayne Gard.

"Adams never took time to retire," Gard wrote in his Foreword to *More Burs Under the Saddle.* "Even in his last years, when he was in his eighties, he spent part of each day in research and writing, turning out new books and updating earlier ones. Yet he always had time to give a hand to another writer who might need help. Many will remember him as one who swept some of the cobwebs from the history of the American West and who set a fine example in telling the story of the frontier as it really happened." Frankly, I do not know whom we will find to replace Adams. In *Burs Under the Saddle* he set out to correct the numerous errors, oversights, and omissions in more than four hundred books; and in *More Burs Under the Saddle* he tackled another two hundred books. Adams' particular concerns were gunfighters, lawmen, and outlaws, and so his corrections are singularly focused on these areas. While this may be a source of frustration for some who would consult him for books in other areas or about other areas in the books he cited for critique, it does nonetheless constitute a boon for whoever is interested in the focus of his expertise. It is likely that *Burs Under the Saddle* will be reprinted before too long. In the meantime, anyone who wishes to read one of the more than six hundred books he did reference is strongly urged to consult Adams' entry on it; or, if a specific

book is selected which deals with a frontier gunfighter, lawman, or outlaw, that individual's name should be consulted in the comprehensive
indices to both of these books and the relevant entries read for a résumé of
common errors in histories or biographies dealing with that individual.

O'Neal, Bill, *Encyclopedia of Western Gunfighters* (University of Oklahoma Press, 1979).

Virtually every notable frontier outlaw and lawman was classified
as a gunfighter by O'Neal in preparing this consummate encyclopedia.
Each entry has a *terminus a quo* date where it is known, as well as a place
of birth, and a *terminus ad quem* date. This is followed by a brief biographical sketch in chronological order and then the gunfights in which the
entry was involved, indexed by date and place, also in chronological
sequence. Finally a list of sources and page citations conclude the entry.
There is a detailed bibliography at the rear of the book and a praiseworthy
Introduction with a number of statistical charts enumerating, among other
things, the number of killings and number of gunfights which can be documented for a select group of gunfighters, the occupations of gunfighters,
and a chronology of notable gunfights broken down by year and by state.
Jim Miller heads the list for number of killings with twelve men killed,
followed by John Wesley Hardin and Bill Longley, each with eleven.
Generally, the biographical sections are accurate; but in some cases,
O'Neal unfortunately did not pursue his research far enough. For example,
in describing the ambush of Frank Coe, Ab Sanders, and Frank McNab
during the Lincoln County War on the night of 4 April 1878, O'Neal had
Coe taken into custody by the ambushers "leaving behind both the
wounded Sanders and McNab's bullet-riddled body." Sanders was in fact
not left behind, but was instead cared for and ultimately taken to the Fort
Stanton hospital. A more serious, and less excusable, error occurred when
O'Neal attributed Pat Garrett's assassination to Jim Miller rather than to
Wayne Brazel who confessed to and was tried for the crime. O'Neal could
have had no evidence — or, if he had, he did not show its source — to vali-
date his statement that, after shooting Garrett, "Miller galloped away from
the scene to create an alibi." Among his references, O'Neal cited Glenn
Shirley's *Shotgun for Hire* (University of Oklahoma Press, 1970) which
bears the subtitle "The Story of 'Deacon' Jim Miller, Killer of Pat Garrett,"
and also Leon C. Metz' *Pat Garrett: The Story of a Western Lawman*
(University of Oklahoma Press, 1974) which source makes a very strong
case for Brazel's probable guilt. It is one thing to suggest the guilt of either
Miller or Brazel, another to state unequivocally that it was one or the
other. In all justice to his sources and the documents in the case, O'Neal
should not have been quite so positive in attributing guilt to Miller without
corroborating his assertion, or at least without somehow recognizing that
the attribution of guilt to Miller is disputed by other historians. Such instances notwithstanding, it can be said O'Neal's book is reliable in the main
and ought in any case to be consulted whenever reading about one of the
gunfighters whom he indexed.

ii

General Books

Cunningham, Eugene, *Triggernometry: A Gallery of Gunfighters* (Press of the Pioneers, 1934) O.P.; reprinted by Caxton Printers.

There is a good deal of misinformation in this book, and only some of it is corrected by Adams in the entry for it in *Burs Under the Saddle*. The chapter on Billy the Kid is so totally unreliable that it is not even worth reading. However, one of the virtues of this book is that Cunningham included certain gunfighters who have been more or less neglected in the compendium volumes to be found in the field, especially John Slaughter, Captain Bill McDonald, and General Lee Christmas. Cunningham did rally to the defense of Tom Horn and made a good case for him in view of the prejudice with which he was surrounded. Less admirable, Cunningham's sympathies were very much on the side of the cattlemen as opposed to the nesters and throughout he showed too much enthusiasm for killing, an element also typical of the *Blut und Boden* kind of Western fiction he pioneered. Another regrettable practice was the tendency toward racial stereotyping, with Cunningham characterizing blacks as "niggers" or Jim Smolly as "quarter-Mex', quarter nigger, half-white and all bad...." A bit of pure fantasy (in more ways than one) is the assertion that when one gunfighter "killed another, automatically he inherited the dead man's list of notches." Cunningham also defended Dallas Stoudenmire's accidental shooting of a Mexican in this way: "... his first shot missing [Johnnie] Hale and killing an over-curious Mexican gaping at the scene." Cunningham supported the notions of social Darwinism, as did William MacLeod Raine (see below), quoting Owen Wister and then lamenting that "weaklings have it easier out here, nowadays." However, Cunningham's familiarity — based on personal experience — with Central America added much to his account of the Bonilla revolution in Honduras and his indictment of the Taft administration for backing President Dávila because Dávila gave Wall Street the economic concessions it demanded. Although many of his facts must be approached with caution, Cunningham did write with a novelist's flair and he was particularly adept at characterizing individuals and re-creating scenes.

Gard, Wayne, *Frontier Justice* (University of Oklahoma Press, 1949).

If there is a single book that I would cite as the best introduction to the subject of frontier outlaws and lawmen, this would be it. Gard's subject is a broad one, since his intention was to outline and survey the development of "law and order" from 1836 until the turn of the century. His vignettes of virtually all of the more familiar frontier confrontations — and many not so familiar — are apt, balanced, and almost invariably reliable. He avoided controversy and error by confining himself to facts which have been documented or about which there is no dispute. His brief portraits of Henry Plummer and William Tilghman are particularly noteworthy. Some may regret that he did not pursue some episodes or individuals all the way: the narrative of Pat Garrett concludes with his shooting of the Kid and collecting the reward; that of John Wesley Hardin ends with his arrest, conviction, and imprisonment. But, perhaps, to have included so much additional information would have unwisely expanded the length, if not the scope, of the book. As it stands, it is a first-rate achievement of thorough historical research. One point certainly worth stressing is that Gard's approach is such that the reader becomes acutely aware of the *context* in which most frontier violence occurred and this context is, taken in the aggregate, totally different in terms of causes and character than the images so frequently put forth in the popular media. In connection with frontier feuds, Gard observed that "usually the feud died out when effective statutory law caught up with the frontier." The key word here is "effective." In the contemporary United States, with law and order firmly established, the justice system is nonetheless often ineffective. This phenomenon ought not to be considered separate from the historical growth of the justice system in the United States and Gard's book is a vital contribution to precisely such a linear attempt at understanding. Most of the issues related to the justice system, so pressing today, were no less pressing in the last century; and many of the so-called "solutions" now being offered as innovative or a return to "the good old days" can be seen to have been tried in the previous century. Gard's history allows us to study such "solutions" in terms of their human consequences.

Johnson, Dorothy M., *Famous Lawmen of the Old West* (Dodd, Mead, 1963) O.P.; *Western Badmen* (Dodd, Mead, 1970) O.P.

Johnson's reputation is that of a capital Western short story writer and, frankly, as in the case of William MacLeod Raine (see below), she should not have attempted to write Western history. There is nothing new in either of her two books — unlike Cunningham (see above) or Raine (see below) who did provide personal anecdotes based on their encounters with various eye-witnesses — and, what is worse, much of what is there is misleading, erroneous, or both. Adams made an effort in *More Burs Under the Saddle* to correct many of the errors in both of these books, but there are still errors which even he missed; and with so much misinformation and no virtue to act as a sufficient counterweight, both books are best left unopened.

Masterson, William Barclay ("Bat"), *Famous Gunfighters of the Western Frontier* (Frontier Press, 1957) O.P.

This book consists of a series of magazine articles by Bat Masterson which originally ran in *Human Life Magazine* in 1907. It has chapters on Luke Short, Bill Tilghman, Ben Thompson, Doc Holliday, and Wyatt Earp. The major errors occurring in the text were corrected by Adams in *Burs Under the Saddle*. The real advantage of the book is that Masterson was a competent author — he quit gunfighting to pursue a writing career — and he knew personally each of the men about whom he wrote. When he commented that Doc Holliday's "whole heart and soul were wrapped up in Wyatt Earp and he was always ready to stake his life in defense of any cause in which Wyatt was interested," he enabled the reader both to understand something of the close friendship which joined these two very different men as he depicted another instance of "siding" another, so dramatically widespread on the frontier and so rare among individuals in the more alienated atmosphere of the contemporary United States.

Raine, William MacLeod, *Famous Sheriffs and Western Outlaws* (Doubleday, 1929) O.P.

While many of the factual errors in Raine's text were corrected by Adams in *Burs Under the Saddle*, Adams did not comment on perhaps this book's most significant drawback: Raine's social Darwinism. Of filibusterer Henry A. Crabbe, the reader is told that "by natural fitness he was a born leader" and of Billy the Kid that "by grace of natural fitness he was to become chief, because he was the worst bad man that ever strapped on a six-shooter in the West"—definitely an exaggeration. Native Americans had no more motivation when Raine wrote history than when he wrote fiction. For example, "it became apparent early in 1868 that the frontier Indians were about to take the warpath"; and he wrote of the Cheyenne trek North that during "the campaign of 1878 ... Dull Knife set out from Fort Sill on the warpath with his band of plundering and murdering redskins." He used Apaches as a standard of evaluation, e.g., "a tribe notorious for diabolical outrage and unrestrained savagery," so that it could be written of a person that "he might be evil, callous, treacherous, revengeful as an Apache." For Raine "the Anglo-Saxon has a passion for law and order. It may come slowly, but come it does—the wiping out of the bad man." There are a few personal anecdotes which add some value to the book, but most of what is in the text must be approached cautiously.

Rosa, Joseph G., *The Gunfighter: Man or Myth?* (University of Oklahoma Press, 1969).

This is a fine general account contrasting the historical reality of gunfighters and gunfighting with the fantasy elements of films and fiction; and only occasionally is there a serious slip, such as Rosa's assessment of William S. Hart's screen work which could not possibly have been based on having seen Hart's films. Rosa found that at the bottom of most frontier killings were women, gambling, or revenge. There was no romance whatsoever about shoot-outs. The idea of a fast draw is a latter-day fantasy. "In the years 1870 to 1885," Rosa wrote, "forty-five men died by violence in Abilene, Ellsworth, Wichita, Dodge City, and Caldwell, most of them cowboys and gamblers shot by town marshals." As far as Rosa was concerned, the gunfighter mentality belonged to a breed of men indifferent to human life, although gunfighters historically did know some kind of emotional turmoil, in distinct contrast to the *Blut und Boden* sub-genre of Western fiction and the view Eugene Cunningham (see above) incorporated into his accounts of gunfighters. There are errors of historical fact, few in number but important, and they have been corrected by Adams in *More Burs Under the Saddle.*

Schoenberger, Dale T., *The Gunfighters* (Caxton Printers, 1976).

Ideally this book, which provides detailed biographical accounts of Clay Allison, Wyatt Earp, "Wild Bill" Hickok, Doc Holliday, Bat Masterson, Luke Short, and Ben Thompson, should be read in conjunction with Joseph G. Rosa's book (see above); together they provide a composite, and yet complementary, view. There are some errors of fact — and a few disputed items — which Adams pointed out in *More Burs Under the Saddle,* i.e., did Earp purchase a part interest in the gambling concession at the Oriental Saloon in Tombstone or was it given to him for protective services; did Wyatt pistol-whip "Curly Bill" Brocius after Fred White was accidentally killed? But for the most part the accounts are to be relied upon and some new material, based on archival research into letters and first-hand accounts, was incorporated into the narrative and the book is extremely well illustrated.

Steckmesser, Kent Ladd, *The Western Hero in History and Legend* (University of Oklahoma Press, 1965) O.P.

Above in I of this section I criticized Steckmesser for his reliance on the Henry Nash Smith thesis. His purpose was to provide accurate, albeit brief, historical accounts of four frontier personalities who subsequently were turned into legends — Kit Carson, Billy the Kid, "Wild Bill" Hickok, and General Custer — and then to trace the growth and diversification of their legends. Adams, unfortunately, did not address the many errors in the historical portions of Steckmesser's accounts, and that creates a problem, since there are many inaccuracies, e.g., there is no evidence that there ever was a William H. Bonney, Sr., and positing such a person creates a confusion when it comes to the fact that the Kid's real name was Henry McCarty. Therefore, this book is to be recommended *only* if the reader discounts, or at least holds in abeyance, the biographical sections. Its chief value is in its tracing of the growth of the legends and the various uses to which they were put by the various media over the years. However, Steckmesser's anti-Indian prejudice is another red flag. He praised Custer's "autobiography," *My Life on the Plains* (1874), for striking "a realistic note" in one respect, that being Custer's "views of Indians." Custer considered the Native American "a *savage* in every sense of the word; not worse, perhaps, than his white brother would be similarly born and bred, but one whose cruel and ferocious nature far exceeds that of any wild beast of the desert." There is more of this, much more. In what way can it be termed "a realistic note?" I do agree with Steckmesser that "people ... have a right to know whether they are reading fact or fiction, and the historian has a responsibility to draw the line which separates the two."

Sterling, William Warren, *Trails and Trials of a Texas Ranger* (1959; University of Oklahoma Press, 1969).

Sterling became commander of the Texas Rangers in the 1930s when he served as adjutant general of Texas. He wrote this book late in life. He did not intend it to be a history of the Texas Rangers; he left that for Walter Prescott Webb (see below). "My aim," he wrote in his Preface, "is to give a Ranger's eye view of the Service, and to deal with aspects that cannot be fathomed by hearsay or research." In a sense, it is a first-hand account; but it is also an effort to add biographical details and perspective to other written accounts, including that of Eugene Cunningham (see above) who dealt with some of these same men. Sterling was not above hero-worship in a few cases; but this can be forgiven in view of the attention he paid to the interrelationship, too little understood by most, between state and local politics and law enforcement. It is precisely this attention which imparts a unique value to the enterprise. Also, in his accounts of Captain John Hughes and Captain Bill McDonald, Sterling did provide viewpoints somewhat at variance with Cunningham's — an area that Adams in *Burs Under the Saddle* did not address at all in assessing Cunningham's book. There is, above all, an unmistakable humanity in Sterling's narrative, and this is a dimension not readily associated with accounts of law enforcement officers. Too often, in fiction and film, Texas Rangers are portrayed as hard, cold, mechanical fighting machines, and this is an image that many of them, as individualized by Sterling, do not deserve.

Webb, Walter Prescott, *The Texas Rangers* (Houghton Mifflin, 1935) O.P.; reprinted by the University of Texas Press with a Foreword by Lyndon B. Johnson.

In his *Guide to Life and Literature of the Southwest* (Southern Methodist University Press, 1952) J. Frank Dobie's annotation for Webb's history was brief and concise: "The beginning, middle, and end of the subject." That far I would not go. Professor Webb himself, had he lived, intended to make a number of corrections and additions to the text. What I would say is that if the reader is inclined to read further about the Texas Rangers than the biographical vignettes in either Cunningham or Sterling (see above), then this would be the best book one could consult. For example, in Cunningham's account of the Brownsville, Texas, riot by black soldiers on the night of 13 August 1906, Captain Bill McDonald emerges a hero, even though he was not on the scene when the riot occurred. Cunningham wrote much in the spirit of Captain McDonald himself who in Albert Bigelow Payne's biography, *Captain Bill McDonald, Texas Ranger* (Little and Ives, 1909), is quoted as having said to black soldiers at the gates of Fort Brown: "'You niggers hold up there! I'm Captain McDonald, ... and I'm down here to investigate a foul murder you scoundrels have committed.'" Sterling was more circumspect and reserved in his handling of the episode. Webb, striving for the impartial tone of the historian, was able to perceive the underlying racist current in the episode and he concluded, with some justification, that "the citizens of Brownsville do not accord to Captain McDonald much credit for his action in the negro riot. Their view of the affair is given in the words of Judge Harbert Davenport as follows: 'It so happened ... that the Rangers' part in this affair was wholly in the newspapers. The riot occurred between midnight and daybreak; and when the dawn came, it was all over. There was nothing for the Rangers, or anyone else, to do but allay the uneasiness of Brownsville inhabitants.... What remained to be done was for the Army and not the police—either state or local.'" In his Foreword, President Johnson cited Ranger Captain McNelly's definition that "courage is a man who keeps on coming on." He felt that "in the challenging and perilous times of this century, free men everywhere might profitably consider that motto." I am more inclined to lend a sympathetic ear to such a sentiment than I am to President Johnson's assertion that the "instinct to preserve the equality of opportunity, the dignity of the individual, the commitment to justice for all ... [derives] from the spirit of the Frontier era." No less than the U.S. Cavalry, the Texas Rangers were an extension of the white man's claim to suzerainty over other peoples—primarily Mexican- and Native Americans—who did not welcome it. Webb's sympathies were too much with this force for him to escape partisanship; but his history of a century of the Texas Rangers will remain an important source book for future studies.

iii

Autobiographies and Biographies

Sam Bass

Born 21 July 1851 at Mitchell, Indiana, Sam Bass died at Round Rock, Texas, on 21 July 1878 of a gunshot wound when his attempt to rob a Round Rock bank was foiled by Texas Rangers, alerted by a member of his own gang. Bass' life is particularly interesting because, while brief, he was involved in a number of diverse frontier activities from horse racing and gambling to freighting and mining, before turning to stage robbery and one lucrative train hold-up. Charles L. Martin's *A Sketch of Sam Bass, The Bandit*, published originally in 1880 and very difficult to find, was reissued by the University of Oklahoma Press in 1956 as part of its Western Frontier Library series. Ramon F. Adams wrote the Introduction to the reissue edition and I cannot but agree with him that the main advantage of Martin's book is the portraits he provided of members of the Bass gang and it is this perspective which gives the reader some understanding of the psychology operative in such a group. Also in his Introduction Adams lamented that Wayne Gard's *Sam Bass* (Houghton Mifflin, 1936), in his words "the most complete and accurate biography of Sam Bass yet published," had gone out of print. Fortunately this situation was remedied by the University of Nebraska Press which reprinted Gard's book in 1969 and has kept it available. For the reader interested in *the* book on Bass, Gard's is still the one.

Judge Roy Bean

Born sometime between 1825 and 1830 in a cabin in Mason County, Kentucky, Roy Bean died at the Jersey Lily, his saloon at Langtry, in Texas on 16 March 1903. He was a self-appointed justice of the peace, enamored of Lily Langtry, whom he never met, and tolerated by the Texas Rangers who seemed to endorse his common sense approach to justice. The only book written on him is *Roy Bean: Law West of the Pecos* (Macmillan, 1943) by C.L. Sonnichsen, later reissued by Devin-Adair Company in 1973. "I have heard only one Bean story since the book was written," Sonnichsen confided in his Preface to the reissue, "but it has the right flavor. It is about the time a lady of non-existent virtue came to Langtry and in due course shot and killed a man who aroused her indignation. Roy Bean was called in as coroner and held an inquest. After a very brief consideration, he rendered his verdict: 'This man committed suicide, and that's my rulin'.' A lawyer, who happened to be among the spectators, objected. 'Roy, you can't hand down such a verdict. This man has obviously been murdered. You can't do it.' 'Oh, yes, I can,' Roy replied. 'I told him if he played around with that chippy, he was committing suicide. And by God he did!' What can you do with a man like that but enjoy him?" Sonnichsen not only pointed out that Bean, tagged "the hanging judge" by Hollywood, never hanged anybody, but he also included a wide assortment of anecdotes about the kind of folk justice Bean dispensed.

Billy the Kid (Henry McCarty)

According to what the Kid told an 1880 Fort Sumner census taker, his birthplace was Missouri and his age twenty-five, which would have him born in 1865 or 1866; he died at Fort Sumner, New Mexico, on 14 July 1881 when he entered Peter Maxwell's bedroom, unarmed except for a butcher knife, and was shot from the darkness by Sheriff Pat Garrett who recognized his voice. Pat Garrett (see below) had M(arshall) Ashmun ("Ash") Upson ghost a book for him titled *The Authentic Life of Billy the Kid* (1882) which was a failure when first published but which, in the Twentieth century, has been more in print than out. Adams submitted this account to a close and detailed analysis, correcting its numerous errors, in *Burs Under the Saddle*, and, if any copy of it is consulted, it ought to be that edition annotated by Maurice Garland Fulton published by Macmillan in 1927, due to Fulton's many annotations and corrections (although Fulton by no means corrected *all* the errors). In my book, *Billy the Kid: A Bio/Bibliography* (Greenwood Press, 1983), I have narrated all that is factually known about the Kid and then traced the various manifestations of his legend among historians, in fiction, and in films, finally making some effort to explain all this fabrication. In addition, Ramon F. Adams' *A Fitting Death for Billy the Kid* (University of Oklahoma Press, 1960) is still in print and is extremely trustworthy, although it is devoted more to a critique of secondary materials about the Kid and has only a brief chapter on his life. On the strictly negative side, Walter Noble Burns' *The Saga of Billy the Kid* (Doubleday, 1926) should definitely be avoided; it is a mass of misinformation and yet, despite the fact that it has been out of print for years, for some reason otherwise reputable historians and biographers have an inexplicable temptation to believe what is in it — and this, despite efforts such as Adams' in *Burs Under the Saddle* to correct its many errors. Lily Klasner did not like the Kid, but she did provide an interesting first-hand portrait of him in *My Girlhood Among Outlaws* (University of Arizona Press, 1972) and there is a no less valid, if somewhat more generous, view of the Kid in *Ma'am Jones of the Pecos* (University of Arizona Press, 1969) by Eve Ball, an excellent example of oral history compounded with the most scrupulous efforts at corroboration, an area which has belatedly but deservedly won acceptance. For the record, Billy the Kid verifiably killed only four men. He was neither hero nor villain, but if anything a victim of an historical process the nature of which he only dimly grasped and consistently misjudged.

Butch Cassidy (Robert LeRoy Parker)

Born on 13 April 1866 at Beaver, Utah, Parker died, while living respectably under the alias William T. Phillips, on 20 July 1937 at Spangle, Washington. Larry Pointer is to be congratulated for the painstaking research that went into his book, *In Search of Butch Cassidy* (University of Oklahoma Press, 1977), unquestionably the most authoritative and reliable work to have appeared on Cassidy the bandit and his felonious activities as well as on Parker's life after he eluded the law and embarked on a wholly new career as a manufacturer of business equipment. Pointer made liberal use of Parker's own hitherto unpublished memoir and his account has all the excitement of investigative reporting and historical research at its finest.

Bill Doolin

Born in Johnson County, Arkansas, Doolin, for a time a member of the Dalton gang before their destruction and then a gang leader in his own right, was shotgunned to death by an Oklahoma posse at Lawson, Oklahoma, on 25 August 1896. Ramon F. Adams wrote an Introduction to the best book-length account, Colonel Bailey C. Hanes' *Bill Doolin Outlaw O.T.* (University of Oklahoma Press, 1968), a volume in the Western Frontier Library, and in it he gave a short résumé of the inaccuracies, errors, and idiocies that have been printed about Doolin's life in a number of other sources. Doolin was not a killer. He was very attached to his wife and family. It was his hope, when Heck Thomas and the posse caught up with him, to flee and start life over. Eugene Manlove Rhodes, the Western fabulist, knew Doolin, and he based his character William Hawkins in *The Trusty Knaves* (1933; University of Oklahoma Press, 1971) on Doolin.

Wyatt Earp

Born at Monmouth, Illinois, on 19 March 1848, Earp died at Los Angeles, California, on 13 January 1929. Although Earp lived a long and interesting life, he is remembered primarily for having been a participant in the shoot-out between himself, his brothers, Morgan and Virgil, and

Doc Holliday with Ike and Billy Clanton and Frank and Tom McLaury. Walter Noble Burns began the specious process of making Wyatt and the others into heroes in his book, *Tombstone: An Iliad of the Southwest* (Doubleday, 1927); novelist W.R. Burnett followed suit in his novel, *Saint Johnson* (Dial, 1930), based on the Earp legend; and the *pièce de résistance* was Stuart N. Lake's completely unreliable *Wyatt Earp: Frontier Marshal* (Houghton Mifflin, 1931). Motion pictures and television did the rest. Adams in *Burs Under the Saddle* did what he could to set the record straight with regard to both Burns' effort and Lake's. Lake's technique was to narrate Wyatt Earp's story as if it were all a first-person account, but he later confessed in a letter to Burton Rascoe on 9 January 1941 that Rascoe's "suspicions [had been] well founded.... As a matter of cold fact, Wyatt never 'dictated' a word to me.... He was delightfully laconic, or exasperatingly so." Frank Waters' *The Earp Brothers of Tombstone* (Clarkson Potter, 1960) has been reprinted by the University of Nebraska Press. "Although this book is valuable to the historian for showing the Earps in their true colors and for correcting some of the fiction of Walter Noble Burns and Stuart N. Lake," Adams wrote in *Burs Under the Saddle*, "the author makes a few mistakes himself." Actually, while its portrait is not all that it could be, the most reliable book to appear on Wyatt Earp remains *I Married Wyatt Earp: The Recollections of Josephine Sarah Marcus Earp* (University of Arizona Press, 1976) collected and edited by Glenn G. Boyer. Much of this book's value is derived from Boyer's footnotes and annotations. Although he made errors, e.g., the circumstances surrounding the second make of *Frontier Marshal* (20th-Fox, 1939) based on Lake's account, they are minimal compared to the overall accuracy. A combination of Waters' account, Adams' corrections, and the Earp/Boyer collaboration is the best to be had until a consummate biography is finally published. For the record, the Earp-Holliday faction in Tombstone had no more of truth and justice on its side than had the Clanton-McLaury faction.

Pat Garrett

Born 5 June 1850 in Chambers County, Alabama, Garrett, while micturating, was shot in the back, most probably by Wayne Brazel, near Las Cruces, New Mexico, on 29 February 1908. Leon C. Metz' *Pat Garrett: The Story of a Western Lawman* (University of Oklahoma Press, 1974) is the best book so far to appear on Garrett's life. This is not to say that there are not errors in it, the most serious of which being that Metz has the Kid armed with a sixgun the night he was killed; but most of the errors have been cited by Adams in *More Burs Under the Saddle*. I would prefer more of an attempt than Metz made to probe somewhat into Garrett's psychology. Metz, in a letter to me dated 1 April 1981, related that it is his intention to update his biography. He also drew attention to an unfortunate assumption he made. "I accepted Garrett's description of the landscape around the rock house where Bowdre was killed. Described was how the horses were hid behind a hill, etc. Well, a guy wrote me about a year ago saying he had visited the spot and there are no hills. The land is flat. Garrett and the others crawling up and down banks is not correct, if my informant is correct. ...I should have gone and looked the area over myself—and drawn my own conclusions." In view of the many excellences of Metz' biography, and the numerous careless and needless errors in Richard O'Connor's *Pat Garrett: A Biography of the Famous Marshal and the Killer of Billy the Kid* (Doubleday, 1960), the latter is best avoided. There is also much new material in Metz' book for which he is to be particularly commended.

John Wesley Hardin

Born on 26 May 1853 at Bonham, Texas, Hardin was shot in the back by John Selman on 19 August 1895 at El Paso, Texas. Hardin wrote an autobiography while he was in prison—*The Life of John Wesley Hardin as Written by Himself* (1896; University of Oklahoma Press, 1961)—but he was not altogether honest and lacked many documents he would have needed to have been more accurate. Therefore, it is best to begin with *John Wesley Hardin, Texas Gunfighter* (Morrow, 1957) by Lewis Nordyke, and to supplement this fine biography which definitely deserves to be reissued with the relevant section of Leon C. Metz' *John Selman: Texas Gunfighter* (Hastings House, 1966), also out of print, and the pages Walter Prescott Webb devoted to Hardin in *The Texas Rangers* (see above). In view of the customary exaggerations in so many accounts of Hardin's life, it is perhaps worth noting that he was involved in nineteen gunfights, verifiably killed eleven men with one possible additional killing, and that only Jim Miller, with twelve killings on his record, exceeded him. One thing is certain. Hardin was scarcely the hero that has been made of him.

James Butler ("Wild Bill") Hickok

Born 27 May 1837 at Troy Grove, Illinois, Hickok was shot in the back by Jack McCall at Deadwood, Dakota territory, on 2 August 1876. The most reliable brief account of Hickok's life is to be found in Dale T. Schoenberger's *The Gunfighters* (see above); and Mari Sandoz in *The Buffalo Hunters* (Hastings House, 1954) supplied the details with regard to Hickok's cold-blooded shooting of the Sioux peace chief Whistler, an episode most of his biographers tend to ignore. However, Adams in *More Burs Under the Saddle* should be consulted in connection with both. Adams did not have an entry in either of his books for *They Called Him Wild Bill: The Life and Adventures of James Butler Hickok* (University of Oklahoma Press, 1964) by Joseph G. Rosa and so there is no readily available source to correct many of the small errors to be found in Rosa's text. Perhaps the most contrived argument in his biography is the attempt he made to mitigate somehow the probable causes of Hickok's failing eyesight: it was more likely a side-effect of *Spirocheta pallida* than gonorrheal ophthalmia. But this is a debatable issue at best. More serious is the needless vagueness with which he surrounded the shooting of Mike Williams, depending too much on the account of Theophilus Little. Notwithstanding this and other quibbles, *They Called Him Wild Bill*, while not definitive, is the finest book-length biography available. It is to be hoped the future will produce a biographical study more probing into Hickok's blatantly homicidal personality. At any rate, other accounts, such as Richard O'Connor's *Wild Bill Hickok* (Doubleday, 1959), are to be consulted only after referring to the appropriate entry in Adams' *Burs Under the Saddle*, or avoided entirely.

John Henry ("Doc") Holliday

Born early in 1852 at Griffin, Georgia, Doc Holliday died of tuberculosis at a sanatorium at Glenwood Springs, Colorado, on 8 November 1887. Just about his last words were, "This is funny," an ironical reference to the fact that, given all the shooting scrapes he had been in, he had not expected to die in bed. Trained as a dentist, Holliday, once he went West for reasons of health in 1873, seldom practiced his profession, preferring instead to make a living, when the cards were with him, by gambling. There are currently available two book-length biographies in addition to the chapters devoted to him in both Masterson and Schoenberger (see above) which ought to be read. The least reliable is *Doc Holliday* (Little, Brown, 1955) by John Myers Myers, reprinted by the University of Nebraska Press; Adams corrected many of the errors in it in *Burs Under the Saddle*. More throughly researched and generally accurate in its treatment both of Holliday and of the Earps is Pat Jahns' *The Frontier World of Doc Holliday* (Hastings House, 1957), also reprinted by the University of Nebraska Press. Frankly, since we have Jahns' biography and can couple it with Masterson and Schoenberger, there is no good reason to go further unless it would be to learn many of the legends and fantasies with which Holliday's popular image is still surrounded. As a personality, he strikes me as one of the more interesting men on the frontier.

Tom Horn

Born on 21 November 1860 at Memphis, Missouri, Horn was executed by hanging on 20 November 1903 at Cheyenne, Wyoming. Perhaps no frontier gunfighter has inspired more controversy. Even Bill O'Neal in his usually reliable *Encyclopedia of Western Gunfighters* (see above) went out on a limb and stated baldly that Horn was determined to kill Kels P. Nickell but "mistakenly shot Nickell's fourteen-year-old son...." Among his references is Horn's own autobiography and other sources from which he could have derived the correct spelling of Joe LaFors' name, which he rendered as LeFors. Perhaps he depended too heavily on the acounts of Dane Coolidge in *Fighting Men of the West* (Dutton, 1932) and William MacLeod Raine in *Famous Sheriffs and Western Outlaws* (see above). The truth of the matter is that we do not know whether or not Horn shot young Willie Nickell and the best anyone can hope to do is to make an educated guess based on an historical construction of the event. My tendency is to give Horn the benefit of the doubt based on my reading of Horn's autobiography, the letters and documents assembled by James D. Horan with an Introduction for his facsimile edition published by Crown in 1977 of the original *Life of Tom Horn: A Vindication* (Louthan, 1904), and Lauran

Paine's not always reliable *Tom Horn, Man of the West* (Barre Publishing, 1963). It is just as possible — although it would make Horn more adept at the art of dissembling than he seems to have been — to assert that he did accidentally kill Willie Nickell and from some deep-seated motive felt compelled to deny it. Of one thing I am sure, we have yet to see a definitive biography of Horn and one is sorely needed.

Jesse James

Born 5 September 1847 in Clay County, Missouri, Jesse died as a result of being shot in the back by Robert Ford on 3 April 1882 at St. Joseph, Missouri. In the case of Jesse James, the amount of printed matter is staggering in its dimensions, riddled with factionalism, partisanship, and fantasy, with virtually the only reliable account being *Jesse James Was His Name* (University of Missouri Press, 1966) by William A. Settle, Jr., reprinted by the University of Nebraska Press, more a sourcebook than a definitive biography. This situation is indeed strange when one considers that Jesse James is in all likelihood an even more challenging study in psychopathology than "Wild Bill" Hickok and that, instead of addressing this aspect, most of his biographers have resorted to name-calling or apologetics as if his conduct, whatever its ostensible behavioral or environmental motives, is to be viewed as somehow readily comprehensible without need of further analysis. The James gang was able to operate successfully for nearly sixteen years at least in part because, in Settle's words, "the general public was not seriously aroused over the plundering of banks and trains ... since this was a period of protest against oppressive interest rates at the banks and questionable practices by the railroads." It perhaps goes without saying that Jesse James did *not* rob from the rich and give to the poor.

William Barclay ("Bat") Masterson

Born November 1853 in County Rouville, Quebec, Canada, Masterson died working at his desk at New York City on 25 October 1921. Although known as a gunfighter, throughout his career Masterson took part in only three gunfights and killed only one man. Until recently, little that was reliable could be found on him. The chapter Schoenberger (see above) devoted to him is the most accurate of any account in his book, but it is rather brief. Richard O'Connor's *Bat Masterson* (Doubleday, 1957) is rife with fantasies and inaccuracies and was rightly taken to task by Adams in *Burs Under the Saddle*. Fortunately, a definitive biography has now appeared, *Bat Masterson: The Man and the Legend* (University of Oklahoma Press, 1979) by Robert K. DeArment which dissects fact from fiction in its account of Masterson's life while demonstrating the sources from which much of the original fiction was derived. It is because of this dual purpose that DeArment's book is particularly fascinating, tracing the origins and the development of legends around Masterson and the embarrassingly dishonest scholarship practiced by a later generation of supposed historians as it presents the details of his career. It is a paradigm of its kind and should be so used by authors who in the future would address the lives of gunfighters even better known, and more obfuscated by fantasy, than has been the case with Masterson.

iv

There are of course numerous other gunfighters, lawmen, or outlaws whom I have failed to cite individually, because of lack of adequate biographical and historical material or simply because of my very limited space. As critical as I may have been at the beginning of this section, I am pleased to be able to conclude on a more positive note. The truth of the matter is that while numerous frontier personalities still stand in need of adequate biographical treatment, the trend among biographies that have been recently published is toward a degree of accuracy and truthfulness formerly significant by its absence. It is no longer the custom for an author simply to rewrite what previous authors have written without questioning the source, even if it were a first-hand account. On the whole this is a healthy sign of an increasing cultural maturity and a degree of intellectual integrity to be welcomed.

Suggested Fiction

Burchardt, Bill, *Black Marshal* (Doubleday, 1981)
Clark, Walter Van Tilburg, *The Ox-Bow Incident* (1940; Signet #CW1007)
Cunningham, Eugene, *Texas Sheriff* (Houghton Mifflin, 1934)
Guthrie, A.B., Jr., *Wild Pitch* (Houghton Mifflin, 1973)
Hall, Oakley, *Warlock* (1958; University of Nebraska Press, 1980)
Haycox, Ernest, *Trail Town* (Little, Brown, 1941)
Henry, Will, *I Tom Horn* (Lippincott, 1975)
Hogan, Ray, *The Doomsday Trail* (Doubleday, 1979)
Mulford, Clarence E., *Hopalong Cassidy Serves a Writ* (Doubleday, 1941)
Patten, Lewis B., *Death of a Gunfighter* (Doubleday, 1968)
Schaefer, Jack, *Shane* (Houghton Mifflin, 1947)

Suggested Films

Death of a Gunfighter (Universal, 1969) directed by Allen Smithee.
The Gunfighter (20th-Fox, 1950) directed by Henry King.
High Noon (United Artists, 1952) directed by Fred Zinnemann.
Hoppy Serves a Writ (United Artists, 1943) directed by George Archainbaud.
Lawman (United Artists, 1971) directed by Richard Winner.
The Ox-Box Incident (20th-Fox, 1943) directed by William Wellman.
Ride the High Country (M-G-M, 1962) directed by Sam Peckinpah.

Rio Bravo (Warner's, 1959) directed by Howard Hawks.
Shane (Paramount, 1953) directed by George Stevens.
Tom Horn (Warner's, 1980) directed by William Wiard.
Warlock (20th-Fox, 1959) directed by Edward Dmytryk.
Young Billy Young (United Artists, 1969) directed by Burt Kennedy.

Cowboys, Cattlemen, and the Cattle Industry

by Vicki Piekarski

I

It is curious that of all the possible occupational types to choose from that played a role in the white history of the West, it was the cowboy that emerged as the most romantic Western figure. Here was a man, quite often a boy, whose time was routinely spent on a horse—riding line, rounding up cattle, eating dust, and earning twenty-five to forty dollars a month which was usually spent in town carousing with prostitutes—a man who for a living castrated animals and placed red hot iron on the hind-quarters of cattle to sear into its flesh a brand used for identification. It is difficult to find any trace of the romantic in the actual work of the cowboy. But the realities of cowboying were early ignored and the mythological image of the cowboy as described by Owen Wister and others caught the imagination of the public. "Lounging there at ease against the wall was a slim young giant, more beautiful than pictures. His broad, soft hat was pushed back; a loose-knotted, dull-scarlet handkerchief sagged from his throat; and one casual thumb was hooked in the cartridge-belt that slanted across his hips. ...But no dinginess of travel or shabbiness of attire could tarnish the splendor that radiated from his youth and strength." The man was the Virginian, the twenty-four year old cowboy long remembered for his command, "when you call me that, *smile*," and brought to life on the silver screen by such Western favorites as Gary Cooper and Joel McCrea.

The Virginian (Macmillan, 1902) is a cowboy story which oddly enough finds the bread and butter of the hired man on horseback — cattle — *in absentia*. However, without cattle and the industry that developed out of the raising and marketing of cattle between 1865 and 1885, the romance of the lone, independent, soft-spoken cowboy might never have taken root.

Just about every book dealing with the Western cattle industry begins with Texas, the heartland of the industry, where the Spanish had introduced cattle along with horses and sheep. It was the Mexicans who developed the equipment and techniques — herding on horseback, branding, and the round-up (*el rodeo*) — used in the open range system which were adopted and later associated with the Anglo-American cowboy and cattleman. The cattle, progenitors of the Texas longhorn bred by Moorish herdsmen, roamed the lush feeding grounds of Southern Texas between the Nueces River and the Rio Grande. And they multiplied.

Although during the 1840s and 1850s small herds of cattle were sporadically driven East, North, and West, the story of the cattle industry of the West begins with the close of the Civil War. (The Union blockade of the Mississippi River had virtually stopped any marketing of the Texas cattle.) It is estimated that there were approximately five million cattle in Texas in 1865. Defeated Confederate soldiers returning to Texas had little hope for a bright, prosperous future. However, demands for beef in the East, where the supply of cattle had been fairly well depleted during the war and the arrival of the Missouri Pacific Railroad in Sedalia, Missouri, triggered an idea in the minds of a few astute men who saw money on the hoof littering the Texas plains.

In the spring of 1866 the first postbellum "long drive" of cattle guided by cowboys to a Northern railhead was attempted. Approximately 260,000 cattle reached Iowa, Missouri, or Kansas that year in spite of the problems encountered along the way. Those problems included excessive rainfall, swollen streams, cattle stampedes caused by Indians who hoped in turn to obtain a reward for rounding up cattle they had caused to stampede, nervous and unmanageable cattle in the timbered areas of the Ozarks, and last, but not least, enraged and armed Missouri and Kansas farmers bent on turning back the Texas herds which carried the dreaded splenic disease known as "Texas" or "Spanish" fever from which the Texas longhorn was immune. Nonetheless, incentive for further "long drives" was provided by potential profits — cattle priced at three to seven dollars per head in Texas could bring ten times as much outside the state — if a less problematic route to market could be found.

Joseph G. McCoy, an Illinois meat dealer, has been credited with establishing a market for Texas cattle West of the edge of settlement when he transformed the sleepy little hamlet of Abilene, Kansas, into the first of the infamous Kansas cattle towns which came to include Ellsworth, Newton, and Dodge City. Although Abilene was not ready in time to accomodate the early spring herds, 35,000 cattle reached its shipping facilities in 1867. Fictional and filmic cowtowns have come to be symbolic of the violent and sinful frontier towns of the West.

The railheads were attained by a number of trails such as the Chisholm Trail—an old trading trail laid out by mixed-blood Jesse Chisholm—and the Western Trail which provided the arteries of travel for the herds being driven overland. In 1884 an attempt was made to set up a national cattle trail that would be immune to state interference; however, legislation was rarely on the side of the cattleman, who represented big business in an agrarian society, and it never came to pass.

In the years of the "long drive," which lasted until 1884 (the year Kansas passed its strict quarantine act), at least four million cattle reached the Kansas railheads. The cattle were disposed of in one of three ways in the cowtowns: some were shipped to the East for market, others were sold to contractors as beef supplies for Indian reservations and the agencies and forts that were designated to watch over them, and others were used for the stocking of Northern territories where ranches were quickly springing up.

With the plains abounding with free grass such a potentially lucrative business, as the cattle industry was, could not be contained in the state of Texas for long. That cattle could survive on the Northern ranges had been demonstrated by road ranches in use during the mass migration years of the antebellum period. Widespread expansion of the industry was made possible and attractive in the 1870s by the steady push Westward of the railroads, the "pacification" and banishment to reserves of the Indians, the slaughter of the buffalo, and advances in beef breeding and handling. Already by the late 1860s ranches dotted the ranges of Kansas, Nebraska, and parts of Indian Territory. In the 1870s, the industry, in order to meet the local beef demands of the West, spread into Colorado, Wyoming, Montana, the Dakotas, and, by the turn of the decade, into the unlikely regions of Arizona and New Mexico.

By 1880 the cattle industry was firmly established in the Northern and Central plains of the United States and the first five years of the decade marked a boom period for the business as beef demands increased and capital poured in from Eastern and British investors. Full-scale speculation entered upon the scene and books as General James S. Brisbin's *The Beef Bonanza: or, How to Get Rich on the Plains* (1881) and in England J.S. Tait's pamphlet *The Cattlefields of the Far West* (1884) were extremely popular among those with savings to invest or the willingness to borrow money at outrageously high interest rates. The expansion of the industry was so mammoth, yet ill thought out, that between 1882–1884 the number of cattle reaching the West for range stocking purposes was equal to the number shipped East for marketing purposes. Prices were driven up at the selling block and at the Chicago stockyards—the major railhead distribution center of the East—while owners consolidated existing small ranches and purchased herds while in boardrooms in the East or in a manor in England.

By 1885 the industry had over-expanded. Experienced cattlemen knew the grazing areas of the plains could support the already existing herds only if weather conditions were favorable. That same year 200,000 head of cattle were in need of new pasturage when President Cleveland ordered all ranchers off the Cheyenne-Arapaho reserve. Mounting operational costs — for fencing, stock-breeders' association dues, and improved breeding methods — depleted much of the ranchers' profits.

The fate of the open range system was sealed when two consecutive bad winters hit the plains — the first in 1885–1886 which was followed by a drought in the summer months that withered grasses and dried up streams. Panicking cattlemen bailed out of the business or sent their herds North to Canada or East, causing prices to drop far below those of the previous year.

The winter of 1886–1887 was even worse. Already in late November the land was blanketed with snow making it difficult for the cattle to paw down to their feed. A series of blizzards came in December. The nervous cattlemen were relieved in early January when a Chinook wind swept across the plains. However, as the calm before the storm, the warming trend was followed by the worst blizzard in the history of ranching which hit the plains at the end of the month. The damage to the industry was made worse by the extensive number of fences put up earlier by the cattlemen in an effort to protect their pasture land and their hybrid cattle from interlopers. The fences acted as prisons against the cattle that normally drifted South ahead of a storm. Cattle piled up against fences and huddled in ravines and arroyos, dying by the thousands. In the spring the range was littered with carcasses and skeletal cattle stumbled blindly about on frozen feet. Trees off which the cattle had tried to feed were stripped of bark and the sky was filled with turkey buzzards. Losses were estimated at ninety percent over a large portion of the open range country. The luckier ranchers suffered a forty to sixty percent loss.

The winter was immortalized by artist Charles M. Russell in his postcard painting entitled "Waiting for a Chinook" changed to "The Last of the Five Thousand" in which was pictured a lone, gaunt, half-frozen cow, knee-deep in snow, encircled by wolves awaiting final death to set in.

The open range phase was finished. Very few cattlemen survived the overwhelming losses and for the next five years bankruptcies were common as creditors closed in. Some cattlemen drifted into Arizona and Oregon. Others switched to raising sheep — the dreaded enemy of the cattleman — which were easier to nurture and brought in higher profits. In the years ahead the cattle industry was forced to become a science: herds had to be limited in size, hay for winter feed had to be grown and stored, and leased or purchased land had to be fenced off.

The cattle industry did not follow the same deathwish course as had the beaver and buffalo hide industries. It survived and lived on. But its near destruction caused by over-expansion was fueled by the same human motive that had exploited the beaver and buffalo trade to extinction — unabating avarice. Notwithstanding, the ultimate success of the cattle industry may have destroyed something else, something perhaps more intrinsically important to the life of the land. The slaughter of the buffalo is usually accepted by historians of the cattle industry as a necessary step in opening up the plains to the rancher. The environmental upset created by the transition from buffalo to cattle is not generally part of the white man's historical baggage. In *The American West: An Interpretive History* (Little, Brown, 1973) Robert V. Hine described the ecological unbalancing. "The transition from buffalo to cattle had an unfortunate ecological effect that was not immediately apparent. In the natural cycle the buffalo ate the grasses, produced manure for new plant life, and in death returned nutrients to the earth. Because the Indian remained in the same general region, his inclusion in the cycle did not seriously disturb it. The cattle, however, after fattening on the plants of the plains, were at maturity transported long distances away for slaughter. Their blood and unused remains were dumped in rivers, and their flesh went even farther afield. The natural cycle of life on the plains was thus broken."

     Still, those individuals involved in the ranching industry did contribute significantly to the settling of the West even though they shared in its exploitation. Together, cattlemen and cowboys were the first to make use of the semi-arid plains region known as the Great American Desert. They built an empire on land that had been passed over for years by farmers and miners in search of one kind of pay dirt or another; and with that empire they attracted thousands of people, millions of dollars, and, most importantly, fed millions. To a large extent the presence of ranches throughout the plains spurred railroads into extended and accelerated building of transportation lines. The cattle kings and their hired men left an imprint on the land and on the minds of people throughout the world which has not faded with time. Although not in reality the romantic types we might believe them to have been, their actual achievements and conflicts provide a fascinating chapter in the history of the West. Cattlemen and their counterparts, cowboys, were dedicated men who knew as Dorothy Parker put it in her poem, "Coda," that "work is the province of cattle" — and of their guardians.

II

i

     The literature on the subject of the cattle industry is voluminous, especially on the topic of cowboys. It is a literature preoccupied with a mythology that emphasizes a rugged, masculine existence and environment. Cowboy reminiscenses, in particular, are largely descriptive and often tediously detailed in the art of cowboying. What follows includes books covering the various aspects of the cattle industry and its history, studies about cattlemen collectively, as well as books by and about cowboys. Studies limited to ranching in one state, area, or county and biographies and autobiographies of individual cattlemen, due to their great number, have been excluded. The reader interested in the lives of individual cattlemen is directed to bibliographies contained in any general cattle industry history or general work on cattlemen. Also recommended for further reading on the subject are Ramon F. Adams' *The Rampaging Herd: A Bibliography of Books and Pamphlets on Men and Events in the Cattle Industry* (University of Oklahoma Press, 1959) and the chapter entitled "Range Life: Cowboys, Cattle, Sheep" in J. Frank Dobie's *Guide to Life and Literature of the Southwest* (Southern Methodist University Press, 1952).

As a brief introduction to the subject of cowboying the chapters in Everett Dick's *Vanguards of the Frontier* (D. Appleton-Century, 1941) entitled "The Long Drive" and "Free Grass, Cattleman's Paradise" are useful while a more historical brief introduction to the entire cattle business can be found in Ray Allen Billington's *Westward Expansion* (Macmillan, 1974). To date a comprehensive survey of the cattle industry throughout the entire West has not been essayed.

The prospective reader will find a dearth of material on the subject of sheep and the industry that grew up around them West of the Mississippi. Although not very readable, the standard work on the subject is still Charles Wayland Towne's and Edward Norris Wentworth's *Shepherd's Empire* (University of Oklahoma Press, 1945) now out of print but available through Xerox University Microfilms. The distorted topic of cattlemen versus sheepmen wars is the focus of David H. Grover's biography *Diamondfield Jack: A Study in Frontier Justice* (University of Nevada, 1968) about a gunman hired by the cattlemen on the Idaho-Nevada frontier. The general reader would probably be best served by two beautifully written yet informative accounts — *The Flock* (1906; reprinted by William Gannon, 1973) by Mary Austin and Archer B. Gilfillan's *Sheep* (Little, Brown, 1929).

II

ii

Abbott, E.C. ("Teddy Blue"), and Helena Huntington Smith, *We Pointed Them North: Recollections of a Cowpuncher* (Farrar & Rinehart, 1939) O.P.; reprinted by the University of Oklahoma Press.

Smith, who wrote and arranged this book of cowboy reminiscenses spanning the years 1871–1889, met Abbott at his ranch near Lewiston, Montana, in 1937. Bits and pieces of Abbott's own writing were incorporated into his story as taken down by Smith in her many meetings with him in which they discussed cowboys, women both good and bad — Abbott was much more candid about prostitutes than were most cowboys who told their stories — , Indians, the winter of 1886–1887 in which Abbott claimed the big blizzard hit in early February, and the more illustrious people of the West whom he knew, such as Print Olive, Granville Stuart whose daughter he married, "Buffalo Bill" Cody, and Calamity Jane. Perhaps one of the better known of the first-hand accounts left by a cowboy, this book is made richer by the anecdotal style employed in relating Teddy Blue's experiences on and off the trail in Nebraska, Texas, and Montana.

Adams, Ramon F., *The Old-Time Cowhand* (Macmillan, 1961); reprinted by Collier Books, both O.P.

Those readers familiar with the work of Ramon F. Adams will find the prose of this book, written in the vernacular, an affectation unfitting to Adams' usual scholarly style. Similar to Philip Ashton Rollins' book (see below) in content but without the sweeping historical generalizations, Adams described in minute detail the experiences of the Nineteenth-century cowboy both on the job and off as well as his character, background, accouterments, and habits. Nonetheless, unless one is interested in taking a crash course in "Cowboyese," reading this book is a teeth-grinding experience even though Adams felt that "it seems more friendly, and it shore gives more flavor."

Atherton, Lewis, *The Cattle Kings* (Indiana University Press, 1961) O.P.; reprinted by the University of Nebraska Press.

This is a well organized study, topically arranged, in which the social, economic, and cultural significance of the Nineteenth-and early Twentieth-century "cattle kings" is assessed. With a firm grasp of the history of the cattle industry, an understanding of the vicissitudes of ranching, and a close familiarity with primary and secondary sourcebooks, Atherton described and analysed the achievements, life-styles, values, backgrounds, and philosophy of the cattlemen, both individually and as a group. Cattle kings are shown as having been highly capable managers, traders, and often trend-setters who "were far more important than cowboys in shaping cultural developments..."; and as men deserving of historical recognition for their attempt to dominate, or at least modify, their environment. Also examined are the roles of women, cowboys, and cow country fiction with especial attention paid to the veracity of Owen Wister's *The Virginian* (Macmillan, 1902). This is an invaluable study in that it refutes the romantic notion of the cowboy as the dominant cultural figure of The Ranching Frontier through a combination of solid information and sound critical analysis.

Branch, E. Douglas, *The Cowboy and His Interpreters* (Appleton, 1926); reprinted by Cooper Square Publishers, both O.P.

Approximately three quarters of this book is devoted to "the cowboy" and the remaining pages to "his interpreters" (see Western Fiction III ii). Branch cursorily discussed, by topic, the evolution, character, customs, and everyday experiences of the cowboy. Although written in fast-paced, flavorful prose, Branch fell victim to both his sources — in many cases they were such unreliable fabulists as Charles Siringo — and his structure, which is episodic and lacks any real chronological cohesion.

Blasingame, Ike, *Dakota Cowboy: My Life in the Old Days* (Putnam's, 1958) O.P.; reprinted by the University of Nebraska Press.

Blasingame, a Texas cowboy, was employed by the British-owned Matador Land and Cattle Company managed by Scotsman, Murdo Mackenzie. His first-hand account gives a good idea of the day-to-day difficulties of ranching on the Northern range (the Cheyenne River Reserve in South Dakota), particularly in the winter months, where the Matador had leased land beginning in 1904. This book, rich in character and anecdote, describes the people, the places, and the stock of the trade.

Dale, Edward Everett, *The Range Cattle Industry: Ranching on the Great Plains From 1865-1925* (University of Oklahoma Press, 1930) O.P.; revised edition, University of Oklahoma Press, 1960; *Cow Country* (University of Oklahoma Press, 1942).

The Range Cattle Industry is a scholarly, intensive, economic study of the cattle business which was originally written for the U.S. Department of Agriculture. Heavily documented, it is a chronological history in which is mapped the growth and subsequent decline of the range cattle industry of the Central and Northern plains — Kansas, Nebraska, Dakota, Montana, Wyoming, and Colorado — and of the Southwest — Texas, Indian territory, and New Mexico. An entire chapter is devoted to ranching in Oklahoma (Indian territory) which was the topic of Dale's Ph.D. thesis. The shortcomings of the book are its several obvious errors — John Chisum, the rancher, is credited with being the namesake of the Chisholm Trail — and its sketchy treatment on the topics of breeding, fencing, transportation, and range conservation, but this is a good general study containing an excellent series of informative maps.

No less enlightening is *Cow Country*, which is also a history of the cattle business. Written in a much freer and personalized style, this account is rich in human interest and includes anecdotes about the experiences of numerous colorful characters of the cow country era from the Civil War through its transition period. The songs and humor of the cowboy are treated in two highly entertaining chapters. This book would serve well as a general overview to those with a limited interest in the subject.

Dobie, J. Frank, *The Longhorns* (Little, Brown, 1941) O.P.; reprinted by the University of Texas Press.

This book concentrates on the source of the Western cattle industry — the Texas longhorn. Dobie, in his inimitable style, a combination of history and folklore, described the history, psychology, nature, habits, and instincts of the longhorn breed. It is not, however, a book of straight natural history since its narrative also tells the story of some of the men who encountered, guarded, and exploited one of the more neglected critters of Western American history; yet, it remains a sheer delight to read.

Dykstra, Robert R., *The Cattle Towns* (Knopf, 1968) O.P.; reprinted by Atheneum.

A reworking of Dykstra's doctoral thesis, this intelligent book presents the history of five Kansas cattle towns — Abilene, Ellsworth, Wichita, Dodge City, and Caldwell — between 1867–1885 in which the interaction of "impersonal" factors — economics, politics, and social circumstances — and human factors are examined, with particular attention paid to the decision-making process of town building. Cattle towns are shown to have been a complex combination of cooperation and conflict based on the author's research into community sociological studies, newspapers, and primary and secondary sourcebooks on the cattle industry and the cattle towns themselves. Of particular interest is Dykstra's chapter on violence in which his findings reveal that between 1870–1885 forty-five men (mostly cowboys and gamblers) died by homicide in the five cities, usually shot by town marshals. This is a well-laid-out social history and an important contribution to the study of town development in the West.

Ellison, (Glenn R.) "Slim", *Cowboys Under the Mogollon Rim* (University of Arizona Press, 1968); *More Tales from Slim Ellison* (University of Arizona Press, 1981).

Ideally these two books of reminiscenses about cowboying after the turn of the century in North Central Arizona written in the vernacular — " ... jist as we talked and thought in those days ..." — should be read aloud around a crackling campfire. With an education provided to him more by Nature than by books, Ellison, a cowboy, homestead rancher, and briefly a butcher, recalled his experiences from early childhood on while describing the old life ways of many a cowboy both at work and at play. With a keen eye and wit, the author in great detail distinguished the real cowboy from the mythical cowboy and recorded his observations of Nature and, "the worst predator and worst unbalancer of Nature thar is," man.

Frantz, Joe B., and Julian Ernest Choate, Jr., *The American Cowboy: The Myth and the Reality* (University of Oklahoma Press, 1955) O.P.

This book is much as E. Douglas Branch's (see above) in that it is devoted partly to the real cowboy and partly to the fictional cowboy (see Western Fiction III ii). The authors, who claimed there were forty thousand cowboys on the trail between 1870–1885 without giving any evidence as to how they arrived at this figure, attempted to show how the cowboy fit into the "whole Western panorama." They covered the usual ground in discussing the workaday life of the cowboy while relating general historical events that occurred in the West. Unfortunately, the lawless quality of the West is emphasized and all too much time is spent on familiar characters as "Wild Bill" Hickok and Billy the Kid. However, my biggest objection to the book, which has its share of factual errors, is that the authors, feeling embarrassed and perhaps a bit too defensive in having written yet another book on the subject of cowboys, assumed throughout a patronizing tone toward the reader.

Hale, Will, *Twenty-four Years a Cowboy and Ranchman in Southern*

Texas and Old Mexico (1905) O.P.; reprinted by the University of Oklahoma Press.

There is some confusion as to the real identity of Will Hale and Professor A.M. Gibson in an Introduction to this work, in which he explained his detective work into the matter, suggested that it may in fact be a biography. Spanning a period of time from the Mexican War through the 1880s, Hale's preoccupation was with thievery and killing, lending a dime novel quality to the entire book even the title of which is misleading. With what could be called sadistic glee, Hale described his version of fights with Indians and Mexicans, the hanging of a Pinkerton detective, the Lincoln County War, and the pursuit of Billy the Kid.

Hanes, Colonel Bailey C., *Bill Pickett, Bulldogger: The Biography of a Black Cowboy* (University of Oklahoma Press, 1977).

The first black cowboy to be named to the Cowboy Hall of Fame, Pickett was billed as the "Dusky Demon of Texas" in wild West and rodeo shows in which he performed his unique stunt of bulldogging—downing a steer by biting its lip! Unfortunately, little information could be ascertained on Pickett's personal life so this biography is primarily concerned with Pickett's professional feats and recounting background information on the Miller 101 Ranch and its traveling show for which Pickett worked.

McCoy, Joseph G., *Historic Sketches of the Cattle Trade of the West and Southwest* (1874) O.P.; various reprints with the most recent being a facsimile edition published by University Microfilms, Inc.

Joseph G. McCoy, the "Father of Abilene," provided Twentieth-century historians with a landmark sourcebook when he wrote this, the first of the range histories. As an eyewitness, he documented the story of the cattle industry from the early cattle drives and the birth of the Kansas cowtowns through the financial panic of 1873 and covered such diverse aspects as Texas fever, banking, railroad building, breeding improvements, the rise of meat packing industries, and the pros and cons of the open range system. Containing biographical sketches of everyone who was anyone in the industry's first two decades, McCoy was the first to propose that there were distinct types with common characteristics among ranchers, drovers, and cowboys. Although reflecting the open prejudices of his day, McCoy's often ungrammatical yet always candid account is a fascinating record of the first two decades of the old-time cattle business.

Osgood, Ernest Staples, *The Day of the Cattleman* (University of Minnesota Press, 1929); reprinted by the University of Chicago Press, both O.P.

This history is listed in every bibliography on the subject of the cattle industry as a thorough, general, prime work. However, its focus is specifically on cattle ranching on the High Plains (Montana and Wyoming) from 1845 through the turn of the century. Osgood attained his goal of demonstrating that cattlemen were significant achievers who opened up and utilized one of the last Western frontiers but he disappointingly presented cattlemen as a general type since individual cattlemen are rarely mentioned by name. Thus the narrative is devoted to detailing the events and various factors involved in establishing and developing High Plains ranching. A final chapter is concerned with the winter of 1886–1887 and its aftermath which marked a transitional period for cattle raising and, according to the author, the disappearance of the old-time cattleman. This is a concise treatment of the evolution of the Nineteenth-century plains cattle industry containing an extensive and useful bibliography.

Pelzer, Louis, *The Cattlemen's Frontier: A Record of the Trans-Mississippi Cattle Industry from Oxen Trains to Pooling Companies* 1850–1890 (Arthur H. Clark, 1936) O.P.

Generally cited as a standard work, this book is essentially an economic treatment of The Ranching Frontier. The history of the cattle industry from the cattle drives Northward out of Texas, through the boom period, to the decline of the open range system is outlined by Pelzer who was primarily concerned with presenting the economic and financial motives of occupying and stocking the Western range. A large portion of the text is devoted to documenting the business and financial dealings of cattle companies and stock breeders' associations. The serious student and scholar might find the book useful, but the general reader would be better served elsewhere. An appendix contains the Wyoming Stock Growers' Association's book of brands from 1882.

Randolph, Edmund, *Beef, Leather and Grass* (University of Oklahoma Press, 1981).

A partner for twelve years in the 385,000-acre Antler ranch on Crow reservation land in Eastern Montana, Randolph recorded his observations about the physical and financial aspects of large-scale ranching in the 1940s and 1950s. In a final chapter the author summed up all too briefly his anxiety about the recent desecration of wilderness land in Montana through strip-mining and along with it the destruction of a way of life.

Rollins, Philip Ashton, *The Cowboy: An Unconventional History of Civilization on the Old-Time Cattle Range* (Scribner's, 1922) O.P.; revised edition, 1936; reprinted by the University of New Mexico Press.

Rollins' narrative social history describes in great detail the every-day life and routine — character, costume, speech, customs, manners, equipment, and duties — of the Nineteenth-century cowboy embellished by illustrative anecdotes. An Easterner, by birth and habit, Rollins spent brief periods of time in the West in the 1880s and 1890s observing and collecting information about the range experience. Although there is contained in this book a wealth of material on the cowboy profession itself, many of the scattered statements made concerning its history, and of Western history in general particularly as it pertains to the cattle industry, are sweeping, simplistic, and basically insupportable opinions. This is not to say this book has no merit; it is very useful to anyone interested in a study taking in all that cowboying entailed. However, Rollins' depiction of cowboys as "virile, warm-hearted men of real idealism, of high courage and brave achievement, of maturest force and child-like simplicity, of broad tolerance if often of violent prejudices" and as great empire builders almost solely responsible for the shaping of American Western history is excessive, overstated, and, to the minds of men as historian Lewis Atherton (see above), unwarranted. The revised edition contains expanded information on branding, roping, trail driving, buck riding, social customs, technical terms, and slang.

Sandoz, Mari, *The Cattlemen, From the Rio Grande Across the Far Marias* (Hastings House, 1958); reprinted by the University of Nebraska Press.

In this book, the last in the author's six volume Trans-Missouri history series, Sandoz cursorily surveyed the history of the cattle industry of the Great Plains spanning a period of time from Coronado to the mid-Twentieth century. While the primary focus is the character and actions of the cattlemen themselves, the dramatic, evocative narrative encompasses the uses, nature, and varieties of cattle, the long drive, the cowtowns, the industry's expansion, the cattlemen's organizations, the economics of ranching, and the shift in cattle raising from an open range system to a "hard business profession." For Sandoz beef producers represented a "continuous and enduring symbol of modern man on the Great Plains," and in the course of the book she paid tribute to dedicated men as Charles Goodnight and condemned the actions of others as Print Olive.

To assess the historical technique of Sandoz is problematic. Her narrative structure was often confused, containing arbitrary jumps back and forth in chronology; she haphazardly introduced characters, many of whom were irrelevant; and she wove into her historical narrative undocumented, and some say undocumentable, incidents, conversations, and characters under the over-used aegis of "it was said" or "there were rumors." Factual errors are commonly found, especially when it comes to the subject of gunfighters—in this book, for example, about Wyatt Earp, John Wesley Hardin, Ben Thompson, and Clay Allison. Yet there is an unmistakeable quality of humanity in her work. Also, as even her harshest critics have pointed out, Sandoz could communicate the Indian life ways and world-view as few writers are able. Although not recommended as a single sourcebook on the subject of the cattle industry, this book contains a wealth of information and presents to the reader a vivid recreation of the achievements and conflicts of the Western American rancher.

Sharp, Robert, *Big Outfit: Ranching on the Baca Float* (University of Arizona Press, 1974).

As Edmund Randolph (see above), Sharp was concerned with large-scale cattle ranching in the Twentieth century. From 1937 through 1952, he served as general manager of the Baca Float ranch in Northern Arizona, a holding of the Cananea Cattle Company. In this first-hand account the author paid tribute to all the men he admired while describing how the Baca Float grew from a cow and calf operation to a profitable yearling operation.

Siringo, Charles A., *A Texas Cowboy: or Fifteen Years on the Hurricane Deck of a Spanish Pony* (1885) O.P.; reprinted by the University of Nebraska Press.

The first of six Siringo autobiographies, this book was the first authentic cowboy account published. Called the "cowboy's Bible," it is primarily concerned with two of Siringo's favorite subjects — life on the open range and tall tales about his contacts with Billy the Kid — although he also told of his boyhood years in Texas, Illinois, Missouri, and Louisiana. He became a cowboy in 1871 and spent the next fifteen years drifting, working the trails, and hiring on at various ranches. Siringo was an unreliable fabulist whose fast-paced, action-packed books are of historical interest today primarily because of their overwhelming popularity in the Nineteenth century and they do make for amusing reading.

Smith, Helena Huntington, *The War on Powder River: The History of an Insurrection* (McGraw-Hill, 1966) O.P.; reprinted by the University of Nebraska Press.

This is a well researched, thorough study of Wyoming's Johnson County War. Smith traced in great detail the history of the region beginning with the cattle boom in 1879 through the Johnson County War in 1892 and its aftermath. Of particular interest is Smith's well documented report of the hangings of Ella Watson and James Averell. By far the best book on the subject, this work fills in many of the voids left by Asa Shinn Mercer's anti-cattleman chronicle of the war, *Banditti of the Plains; or the Cattlemen's Invasion of Wyoming in 1892* (1894; University of Oklahoma Press, 1954).

Vestal, Stanley, *Queen of Cowtowns, Dodge City* (Harper's, 1952) O.P.; reprinted by the University of Nebraska Press.

Subtitled "The Wickedest Little City in America," this book serves well to perpetuate the myth of the lawlessness of the frontier cattle towns. Vestal focused on tales of violence, gunplay, and murder and the tone of the book is aptly described by its chapter titles which include "Pistol Practice," "The Bloody Woman," and "Marshals for Breakfast." The unreliability of many of Vestal's sources — Stuart N. Lake's *Wyatt Earp, Frontier Marshal* (Houghton Mifflin, 1931) and William MacLeod Raine's *Famous Sheriffs and Western Outlaws* (Doubleday, 1929) — contributed to the many factual errors contained in the narrative. However, research materials cannot be blamed for the seeming indifference to violence on the part of the author. The volume, which relies too much on hyperbolic legends, is best supplemented, if read at all, by Robert R. Dykstra's book (see above) on the Kansas cattle towns.

Suggested Fiction

Abbey, Edward, *The Brave Cowboy* (Dodd, Mead, 1956)
Adams, Andy, *The Log of a Cowboy* (Houghton Mifflin, 1903)
Bean, Amelia, *The Feud* (Doubleday, 1960)
Capps, Benjamin, *Sam Chance* (Duell, Sloan, 1965)
Eastlake, William, *The Bronc People* (1958; University of New Mexico Press, 1975)
Easton, Robert, *The Happy Man* (1943; University of New Mexico Press, 1977)
Evans, Max, *The Hi Lo Country* (Macmillan, 1961)
Guthrie, A.B., Jr., *These Thousand Hills* (1961; Gregg Press, 1980)
Kelton, Elmer, *The Day the Cowboys Quit* (Doubleday, 1971)
_____, *The Time It Never Rained* (Doubleday, 1973)
Manfred, Frederick, *Riders of Judgment* (1957; Gregg Press, 1980)
Mulford, Clarence, *Buck Peters, Ranchman* (A.C. McClurg, 1912)
Rhodes, Eugene Manlove, *Bransford in Arcadia* (1914; University of Oklahoma Press, 1975)
Richter, Conrad, *The Sea of Grass* (Knopf, 1937)
Santee, Ross, *Men and Horses* (1926; University of Nebraska Press, 1977)

Suggested Films

The Big Country (United Artists, 1958) directed by William Wyler.
Cowboy (Columbia, 1958) directed by Delmer Daves.
The Cowboys (Warner's, 1972) directed by Mark Rydell.
The Culpepper Cattle Company (20th-Fox, 1972) directed by Dick Richards.
The Lone Cowboy (Paramount, 1934) directed by Paul Sloane.
Man in the Saddle (Columbia, 1951) directed by André de Toth.
Monte Walsh (National General, 1970) directed by William A. Fraker.
Ramrod (United Artists, 1947) directed by André de Toth.
The Sea of Grass (M-G-M, 1947) directed by Elia Kazan.
The Virginian (Paramount, 1929) directed by Victor Fleming.
Will Penny (Paramount, 1968) directed by Tom Gries.

Frontier Professionals

by Claudia A. Krueger

I

i

Professional people made a unique contribution to the settling of the West and the shaping of its destiny. Professionals were not abundant in the 1800s and, consequently, the need for their services and skills was great. They were often called upon to serve a variety of functions as they were frequently the only educated people in the area. Some of the early explorers of the West were professionally trained people and, in fact, the practice of including doctors with expeditions into the wilderness was quite general. Others came West as towns were established and need of their services became more urgent. There were still others who became "professionals" as needs arose or opportunities presented themselves. Many learned through apprenticeship systems, without formal schooling, and some simply lied about their training, taking advantage of desperate and often unknowing people.

As towns emerged and communities formed, professional people quickly found their niche, often fulfilling many leadership roles, and were looked to as a source of both knowledge and security. The need for a medical doctor was often one of the first professional needs a rough and tumble pioneer town recognized.

The frontier doctor was usually the most prominent and easily recognizable professional in the developing West. They could be found in many settings, some devoting their practice to the unique needs of people in wagon trains, mining camps, railroads, or riverboats. Not that the pioneer doctor could afford the luxury of "specializing." They needed to be as comfortable delivering babies as amputating limbs, for they were looked to as the only available person to attend to a myriad of ills, accidents, and hardships.

Medical science in the 1800s was at best imprecise and considered by some to be a tragic failure. There was a vast array of terrifying diseases ready to confront settlers of this new land, with doctors able to offer few dependable protections or reliefs, let alone cures. As little was known of the etiology of disease, dependence on false premises left doctors with an imperfect understanding of causal factors and effective remedies. Coupled with fear and ignorance on the part of the general populace, one can see the additional "unknown frontier" which faced the frontier doctor.

In spite of these unknown territories, many courageous individuals met the challenge and made significant medical discoveries without the assistance of laboratories, instruments, or sometimes even any formal training. One such contributor was Ephriam McDowell who in 1809 in backwoods Kentucky made surgical history by successfully opening the abdominal cavity to remove an ovarian tumor. This revolutionary procedure was performed without benefit of modern anaesthesia and to a chorus of the angry mob outside his window, ready to lynch him for his "butchery." Another medical pioneer was William Beaumont who studied the human digestive process through a hole torn by a shotgun blast in the stomach of a young voyager, Alexis St. Martin. There were many frontier doctors whose contributions were significant, both to medicine, and to the shaping of the West.

Medical schools at this time in history were all located in the East and most awarded a diploma in one year; some offered a two-year course. Diploma mills were numerous, but a degree did not necessarily guarantee competence. On the frontier any man claiming to be a doctor or surgeon was allowed to practice (a courtesy rarely extended to "she" doctors). Most frontier doctors were not, in fact, formally educated, but learned through an apprenticeship system. The existence of a degree or license was not foremost in the mind of most pioneers who based their trust on demonstrated cures.

"Yarb and root" doctors, also known as "irregulars," provided a unique contribution with their array of herbs, oils, and powders — many recognizable today by the student of pharmacology. Much of this "science" was learned from various Indian tribes and their medicine men with their unique understanding of the natural healing properties found on the land.

The science of "climatology" also flourished in the late 1800s, as those interested in healing and land development teamed up to lure people West for "climate cure." Students of this movement claim that significant numbers of settlers in the West, particularly in the Southwest, came there for their health or that of their families. Given the failure of traditional medical science to provide cures for diseases which had reached epidemic proportions, this grasping at new and attractive "cures" seems rather understandable.

The West also had its share of bona-fide quacks who never failed to take advantage of those looking for an easy cure or magic solution. The claims made by these charlatans look humorous and absolutely outrageous now, but simply underline the sad fact that very little was known about disease and its prevention or amelioration. Prior to the enactment of the Pure Food and Drug Act of 1906, there were no restrictions on patent medicines and quacks took full advantage of the situation.

Although the medical profession was overwhelmingly male-dominated, the contributions of women in the field must not be overlooked. Because admission to medical schools was for many years denied to women, many went on to practice without a diploma. At first they tended to specialize in the treatment of women and children, some as so-called "irregulars"—homeopaths, hydropaths, eclectics, etc. Women of medicine found themselves the target of prejudice, jealousy, and scorn despite the success of women such as Florence Nightingale and the fledgling women's suffrage movement. Professional women had this additional frontier to face, but did so and went on to fill every imaginable role in their profession.

During the Nineteenth century thousands of doctors practiced in the West. Some made historic contributions and others practiced their profession in relative obscurity. There were bad doctors, but most were honorable and hard-working, with varying degrees of skill and ambition. But good, bad, or average, the doctors of the old West contributed immeasurably to the development of the frontier.

I

ii

The study of the legal profession in the Western frontier is not as clearly defined as is that of the medical profession. When looking at the subject of "the law," one is naturally steered toward books dealing with "Law and Order" which usually have little direct bearing on the legal profession as we know it. The earliest vestiges of "justice" were carried out by frontier settlers themselves—"tomahawk justice" or a scalp for a scalp, usually. Later, volunteers formed Committees of Vigilance—"vigilantes"— in the absence of formal institutions, or occasionally in addition to them when they were ineffective. "Lawmakers," the sheriffs and marshals of the West, made names for themselves and their towns, James B. ("Wild Bill") Hickok, Commodore P. Owens, and Pat Garrett among them (see the section on Gunfighters, Lawmen, and Outlaws). But none of these individuals or groups fit for purposes of this discussion within the framework of the "professional." The focus, and consequently a narrow one, will be on the lawyers and development of the legal profession in the West.

In his book *The Sod-House Frontier* (D. Appleton-Century, 1937), Everett Dick contended that lawyers were more numerous on the frontier than members of any other profession and were also more versatile than any other. As was the case with many professionals, they could be found in an assortment of livelihoods, but almost always taking some active role in the development of the frontier. Requirements for entry into the profession were low (e.g., twenty-one years of age, satisfactory evidence of "good moral character," and completion of an "examination" before a judge) and, as with doctors, the profession was customarily learned through apprenticeship. There is the implication in Western fiction that many lawyers who went West did so after being discredited in the East. This generality could, however, be applied to countless individuals who went West.

The first lucrative cases for the frontier lawyer were those dealing with land claims. This was known as land office practice which grew tremendously with the advent of the homestead laws and the "boom" years which followed. This kind of practice required no real legal skill but consisted primarily of helping claimants "prove up" and settle claim disputes. In connection with this public land business there was a branch of practice known as professional claim jumping. In this business a claim jumper watched for any delinquency on the part of the settler and, for a given sum, pointed out the opportunities to "contest" or "jump" a claim. The lawyer's close connection with consummation of the settler's homestead right placed him in a ready position to act as a loan broker, which many did. Given these early beginnings, one can perhaps appreciate the intense antagonism engendered in early settlers by the frontier legal profession.

Criminal lawyers generally practiced only in the larger cities, occasionally being called out to more remote areas, i.e., circuit riding. Frontier courtrooms (which frequently were not in courts) were seldom the scene of any formality. In contrast, they were looked to by many as one of the rare forms of entertainment available on the frontier. People came from miles around to hear a court case, expecting, and sometimes even demanding, a little excitement along with the verdict. Lawyers and judges were expected to deal in truth and justice, but public opinion was a powerful element to contend with. It was often impossible to convict a prisoner of a misdemeanor, no matter what the law, if public opinion was against it.

I

iii

Instrumental in shaping and amplifying public opinion were those involved in the founding, editing, and printing of frontier newspapers. These people came from various backgrounds, but had all followed the heeding of Horace Greeley to "go West, young man." Doing that, these new settlers developed their own brand of journalism — bold and aggressive, not unlike their environment.

Journalistic style in the late 1800s was far different from that of today. The "opinions" expressed through many of these early newspapers would, by today's standards, probably be unpublishable for fear of lawsuits, not to mention contemporary professional ethics. Many small town newspapers carried on long-running feuds, lambasting one another from editorial pages — much to the delight of readers, advertisers, and publishers.

Newspaper people appear to have changed locales frequently, usually surfacing with another paper in a new city. An historic example of this was the *Frontier Index*, often referred to as the Press on Wheels. This publication of Frederick and Legh Freeman followed the expansion of the railroads West, publishing in some sixteen sites as new boom towns developed, only to move on to the next promising site West. Newspapers were frequently subsidized by a local company which stood to make considerable gains in the development of new territories. The newspaper often preceded any other business in a developing frontier town and was frequently the vehicle designed to attract new settlers. The publisher of the newspaper was, therefore, often a person who was journalist, businessman, and politician in one. The spirit of optimism was a pervasive sentiment among this lot, most of whom were intent upon building their town into a great city. This spirit of optimism, combined with the drive for success, made newspaper people among the more colorful professionals to be found on the frontier.

II

i

There are many books available to the person interested in professionals on the Western frontier particularly regarding the medical profession. Many are suitable for a wide age range and others are highly specific to a particular topic. The books fall roughly into four categories.

There are an abundance of biographies, autobiographies, and personal accounts written by the professional or a family member. Many of these books would be suitable for a younger audience, providing many intriguing stories. Typically, books in this category describe the day-to-day practice of the professional, with varying degrees of detail and personal editorializing. Several are life-long accounts which include tales of growing up on the frontier and the struggles to become educated and to establish a practice. There are many works entitled *"Frontier Doctor"* and some include the name of the doctor in the title, e.g., *Dr. J.B. Cranfill's Chronicle: A Story of Life in Texas, Written by Himself About Himself,* and others with titles such as *Portrait of a Pioneer Physician* or *Stories of a Country Doctor*.

A second group of books deals specifically with contributions made by select individuals to their profession. Among them are works which deal with these people collectively or individually. Some of them focus on the person and his motivation while others focus more on a particular accomplishment and its significance to a field of study. Some of the well-known names in this category are physicians Daniel Drake, Ephriam McDowell, John McLoughlin, William Beaumont, and Marcus Whitman, and newspaper publisher, Legh Freeman.

A third group of books chronicles professional developments in specific geographic areas. These may be found listed by state or area (e.g., Northwest, Southwest, Plains, etc.). Highly specific information can also be found by consulting state or regional periodicals, often listed in bibliographies. Examples would include books dealing with topics such as medicine in California during the gold rush era, early medical developments in Texas, health-seekers in the Southwest, prairie doctors of the 1880s, early journalism in Utah, and so on. In addition to books specializing in professionals by geographic location, there are many books which deal with practices in specific sites (e.g., doctors on steamboats, in mining camps, and for railroads).

Perhaps the best books for an introduction to the topic are those in the fourth group which provide a general overview of the professional in the West. There are sources devoted either entirely or in part to this, i.e., many general books on the West include chapters on doctors and other professionals. These books, while not a definitive source on the subject, provide a good starting point for someone interested in the subject without highly specific needs in mind and they generally have exhaustive bibliographies which can help direct the reader to additional books which perhaps can provide more focus.

What follows includes some of the best books in all four groups.

II

ii

Ashton, Wendall, J., *Voice in the West: Biography of a Pioneer Newspaper* (Duell, Sloan, 1950) O.P.

Ashton traced, in great detail, the rise and development of the *Deseret News*, a pioneer among newspapers in the American West. The *News* was the voice of the newly settled Mormon community, its first issue dating from 1850. It was to remain one of America's oldest newspapers, enduring through the struggle, faith, and tenacity of those who guided it. The individuals who particularly contributed to the newspaper's success are all mentioned in this book, providing by their examples a look at many facets of the life of a pioneer journalist. The history of the Mormon community parallels that of the *Deseret News* and it, too, is chronicled in considerable detail.

Blassingame, Wyatt, and Richard Glendinning, *Frontier Doctors* (Watts, 1963) O.P.

This book gives a cursory view of the careers of ten frontier doctors who gained some share of notoriety in their lives. Captains Meriwether Lewis and William Clark are included, even though medicine was not their chosen profession, for they ended up using many learned medical skills on their expedition. Both had studied medicine and surgery under prominent physicians prior to their exploration. The author even goes so far as to suggest that without their medical and surgical skills their expedition might have failed, changing the course of American history. Ephriam McDowell, known as the father of abdominal surgery, performed the first removal of an ovarian tumor in 1809. Prior to this, the abdominal cavity had never before been surgically opened. William Beaumont spent years studying human digestion through a wound in the stomach of a young trapper. Marcus Whitman conducted a sort of wayside hospital on the Oregon Trail, making it possible for many a pioneer to continue the journey West. Henry Perrine, a physician-botanist-horticulturist, studied healing herbs and plants in the Florida territory. Crawford Long pioneered the use of anaesthesia in frontier Georgia. John Griffin was a doctor in the Mexican War, serving under General Stephen Kearny. Bethenia Owens-Adair was a woman pioneering the practice of medicine in a male-dominated culture. Samuel Crumbine (see below) practiced medicine in Dodge City, Kansas, when it was still known as the wildest town in the wild West. The stories of these medical people are told in simple terms, focusing on dramatic or adventuresome incidents.

Coe, Urling C., M.D., *Frontier Doctor* (Macmillan, 1939) O.P.

This is the personal account of a physician settling in the pioneer "boom town" of Farewell Bend, Oregon, in 1905. The book spans the years 1905–1911, 1911 being the year that the railroad arrived, signalling the end of the old frontier. Coe vividly described the life and life-style of the frontier doctor, imparting to his reader the genuine caring and dedication which he brought to his profession. The observations and opinions which Coe expressed regarding social and environmental issues are insightful and years before their time.

Crumbine, Samuel J., M.D., *Frontier Doctor* (Dorrance, 1948) O.P.

Dr. Crumbine recounted here his experiences in the practice of medicine in and around Dodge City, Kansas. His practice was established in the 1880s and continued until his retirement in the 1930s. The 1880s and 1890s were years which saw the beginnings of the change from a cattle and cowboy culture to that of modern agriculture and commerce. The years which followed were filled with swift advancements in medical science as well. Dr. Crumbine pioneered the field of public health in Kansas, crusading against unsanitary practices which spread disease and working to educate the public. Crumbine originated the slogan "Swat the Fly" (which led to the invention of the first fly-swatter) as part of the campaign against typhoid and was instrumental in banning the use of common drinking cups and towels in public places. His book provides an interesting account of the beginnings of public health interests around the turn of the century as well as tales of the early days of Dodge City.

Curti, Merle, *The Making of an American Community: A Case Study of Democracy in a Frontier County* (Stanford University Press, 1959).
    In this scholarly work the author applied scientific research methodologies to examine frontier democracy. The thesis being tested was Frederick Jackson Turner's contention that the most important effect of the frontier was the promotion of American democracy. The area studied was Trempealeau County, Wisconsin, 1850–1880. One aspect of the study was the examination of occupations, with the category of "professional" consisting of doctors, lawyers, and preachers. This study of frontier professionals differs from most in that it is based entirely on data and contains analysis of such things as nativity, age breakdowns, and occupational trends. Also of interest to the student of the frontier professional are chapters examining choosing officials, deciding issues, educational and cultural opportunities, and leadership.

Dick, Everett, *The Sod-House Frontier* (D. Appleton-Century, 1937) O.P.; reprinted by the University of Nebraska Press.
    Three chapters in Dick's book are germane. "The Pioneer Doctor" describes various facets of life for the doctor on the plains. Dick concentrated on the role of the doctor in the development of the frontier, professionally and politically, and gave a well balanced discussion of practical aspects of the doctor's daily practice, the training and education which prepared doctors in the years 1854–1890, and the diseases, suspected causes, and remedies/treatments which were used. The dual role of the circuit riding doctor-dentist is also described.
    In the chapter "Lawyers and Legal Proceedings," Dick discussed the fact that lawyers were more numerous than any other frontier profession, and went on to suggest possible explanations. Lawyers' first lucrative cases involved land claims, which boomed with the advent of homestead laws. Dick also discussed claim-jumping practice, criminal law, law enforcement efforts and the early days of the courts.
    In "The Pioneer Newspaper" the establishment of various plains newspapers is discussed. The motivations and philosophy of the editors and publishers are also described, along with the persuasive power of the press. Dick declared that the newspapers were often the first "institution of civilized life" in a new frontier town and were often the trumpet for a town company, promoting the often "get-rich-quick" schemes of the proprietors.

Dunlop, Richard, *Doctors of the American Frontier* (Doubleday, 1965) O.P.

Dunlop's book covers virtually every aspect of the frontier doctor in at least a cursory fashion. There is discussion of the role of doctors by location (e.g., riverboat, wagon train, mining camp, railroad, ship), by "specialty" (e.g., surgery, obstetrics, quackery, pathology), and by population served (e.g., military surgeons, Spanish doctors, missionaries, cowboy docs, sodbuster doctors). There is also discussion and description of the drugs and instruments used on the frontier, as well as home remedies and cures referred to as "Granny Medicine." Landmark cases and key people in frontier medicine are mentioned along with their contributions. An extensive bibliography refers the reader to books, periodicals, manuscripts, letters, and other documents. This is a good introduction and overview of a broad subject and one of the few books of its kind.

Eastman, Charles A., *From the Deep Woods to Civilization: Chapters in the Autobiography of an Indian* (Little, Brown, 1936) O.P.; reprinted by the University of Nebraska Press.

In continuation of the narrative begun in *Indian Boyhood* (McClure, Phillips, 1902), Eastman recounted his initiation into the white world where he learned to read and write English, became a Christian, and obtained a medical degree. He then returned to his people in 1890 as a government physician at Pine Ridge Agency, South Dakota. This was the first of several positions he held as an employee of the Bureau of Indian Affairs. Although the book does not focus as much as it might on Eastman's medical profession, it does provide a first-hand account of the adult life of an extraordinary man.

Flexner, James Thomas, *Doctors on Horseback: Pioneers of American Medicine* (Dover Books, 1969).

These are the stories of seven pioneers of American medicine: John Morgan, Benjamin Rush, Ephriam McDowell, Daniel Drake, William Beaumont, Crawford W. Long, and William T.G. Morton. Of particular interest to students of the frontier are McDowell, the father of abdominal surgery, Daniel Drake ("Genius on the Ohio"), medical geographer, physician, and founder of the Medical College of Ohio who pioneered Caesarian births, and William Beaumont, a Great Lakes military outpost surgeon who studied human digestion. Flexner highlighted the fact that much of early medical practice was a blind stumbling through darkness in search of cause and cure, with the constant challenge of disease upon the shoulders of the doctor. Without laboratories, instruments of precision, or often even any formal training, many great discoveries were made which helped to usher in the age of modern medical science.

Hawkins, Cora Frear, *Buggies, Blizzards, and Babies* (Iowa State University Press, 1971).

Recollections by the daughter of Dr. Edwin Frear, an Iowa doctor of the late 1800s, with additional information from his diary and other personal and general sources, this is a thoughtful and informative account of the dramatic and humorous episodes in a pioneer doctor's life.

Hertzler, Arthur E., M.D., *The Horse and Buggy Doctor* (1938) O.P.; reprinted by the University of Nebraska Press.

This is the autobiography of a Kansas country doctor, practicing around the turn of the century. Hertzler provided the reader with non-stop anecdotes beginning in grade school and his boyhood. The book gives an in-depth look at the life of a country doctor, although the constant barrage of Hertzler's personal opinions and social commentary does become a bit tiresome. His comments on his female patients are, by today's standards, sexist and paternalistic, although they were the prevailing sentiments of the era. Hertzler's approach and writing style can be summed up in one of his chapter headings: "Me and My Patient." He stated in the Preface that he carefully avoided revealing his own personal philosophy, "though I may seem to have done so." He certainly does seem to have done so — on every imaginable subject.

Heuterman, Thomas H., *Movable Type: Biography of Legh R. Freeman* (Iowa State University Press, 1979).

This is the fascinating story of one of the most prominent frontier journalists whose career paralleled a rapidly changing time in the history of the American West. In addition to operating *The Frontier Index*, Freeman was an explorer and a frontiersman, always looking for new opportunities while dispatching adventurous stories back to his paper. Heuterman contended that Freeman's imagination was shaped by the frontier and that he was in turn all too willing to perpetuate its myths through his life and his columns. Freeman was flamboyant and aggressive and caused a stir wherever he published. This contributed to his eventual downfall and he died in relative obscurity in 1915. Heuterman, in addition to recounting Freeman's life, provided a thoughtful analysis of frontier journalism in general.

Howard, Robert West, *This is the West* (Rand, McNally, 1957) O.P.

A brief chapter entitled "The Lawmakers" by Wayne Gard in Howard's book about the West gives an overview of the people who made and kept the laws on the frontier. The discussion includes vigilantes, sheriffs, and marshals as well as early lawyers and judges. Several individuals are mentioned, not all of whom would fit the criteria of "professional"; but in spite of this, the chapter is recommended as, at least, a starting point for someone interested in the beginnings of the legal profession in the West.

Hoyt, Henry F., *A Frontier Doctor* (Houghton Mifflin, 1929) O.P.

This book is the result of the variety of Dr. Henry Hoyt's occupations in different localities of the country during his life, his capacity for registering what he saw and heard, and his ability to be a very good storyteller. Hoyt took up the practice of medicine in 1877 at Deadwood, Dakota territory. He later moved to the Panhandle district of Texas where, unable to sustain himself through his medical practice, he became a cowboy. Moving to various locales in Texas and New Mexico, Hoyt recounted adventures with Billy the Kid and other colorful characters of the frontier. In later years Hoyt held a variety of positions including Commissioner of Health in St. Paul, Minnesota, Chief Surgeon of the Great Northern and the Chicago and Burlington Railroads, and local surgeon for a number of others. His diversified life was replete with many and varied experiences that have supplied him with a wealth of reminiscences and anecdotes that cannot fail to interest and please a reader.

Jones, Billy M., *Health Seekers in the Southwest* 1817–1900 (University of Oklahoma Press, 1967).

This is a fascinating account of the marketing of the West as a "health frontier" and those who came in search of cures for which medical science had none. At a time when the West was being billed as "The World's Sanitarium," it is estimated that one-third of the population of Colorado went there for their health or that of their families and that one in four California settlers were invalids. "Climatotherapy" emerged and the study of "climate therapeutics" by a rather large group of consumptive physicians was a significant trend which added a professional touch to the development of the health frontier in 1870. The failure of medical science to determine cause or cure for tuberculosis, "the white plague," reinforced the health seekers and the developers of commercial resorts, mineral and hot springs, and those promoting the "ranch cure" for pulmonary patients or "tent therapy" for consumption. The heyday of the health frontier and of climatotherapy was over by 1900, as science discovered more about bacteria and contagion, but its impact on the developing West is now beginning to be recognized.

Karolevitz, Robert F., *Newspapering in the Old West: A Pictorial History of Journalism and Printing on the Frontier* (Superior, 1965) O.P.; *Doctors of the Old West: A Pictorial History of Medicine on the Frontier* (Superior, 1967).

In *Newspapering in the Old West* the author met his goal of recreating the flavor and atmosphere of newspapering on the frontier. Every page is filled with photographs, drawings, maps, and reproductions of frontier front pages. There are chapters focusing on frontier editors, who they were and how they came to be, the printers and their machines, a chronicle of the first newspapers in the old West, *The Frontier Index* or the "Press on Wheels" and its fiery editor, Legh Freeman, women in newspaper publishing, and the role of newsboys. In addition there are chapters which outline the development of newspapering in specific states: Montana-Idaho, Nebraska, Nevada, Oklahoma, Oregon, Texas-New Mexico, Utah, Washington, and Wyoming. These chapters cite the first newspapers established, prominent people in their development, and journalistic trends or characteristics of individual papers.

Doctors of the Old West provides an engaging look at medicine in the old West. It features country doctors, railroad and military surgeons, nurses and mid-wives, doctors of prominence as well as unsung heroes. Karolevitz traced the development of the healing art with such related facets as hospitals, apothecaries, medicines, equipment, nursing, and midwifery. Photographs, drawings, and other reproductions (some in grisly detail) enable the reader to get the true flavor of the times.

King, Willis P., M.D., *Stories of a Country Doctor* (Burton, 1907) O.P.

In his book, Dr. King described not only the life of a country doctor, but provided observations on the Missouri frontier, its settlers, and their ways of life. The book is rich with stories and anecdotes, delivered in a somewhat dry humor. This is one of the earlier "doctor books" published and, being representative of the time, is frequently derisive to women, blacks, and other minorities. One area where King dealt in depth was with regard to "the quacks and scoundrels who infest our communities and, by their falsehoods and frauds, bring disgrace on a noble calling...."

Long, Francis A., M.D., *A Prairie Doctor of the Eighties* (Huse, 1937) O.P.

Dr. Long's book focuses on his career and on medical developments in the state of Nebraska where, later in his career, he served as President of the State Medical Society and founded its first medical journal. The book gives a clear and interesting account of the life of a pioneer doctor with anecdotes rich in detail without being verbose. Two chapters were contributed by Maggie E. Long on "The Prairie Doctor's Wife" which add an interesting dimension to the book. There is also a chapter on "The Practice of Medicine Among the Prairie Indians." Although the contemporary reader may discern racist undertones in this chapter, its very inclusion is significant.

Miller, Helen Markley, *Woman Doctor of the West: Bethenia Owens-Adair* (Julian Messner, 1960) O.P.

This is the inspiring story of Bethenia Owens-Adair who, in 1872, was one of the few women doctors on the West Coast. The story traces her life, growing up in Oregon, and the courage and determination which went into the establishment of a highly successful medical career. While in medical school for graduate studies, Owens-Adair wrote, "We believe woman should have a knowledge of the science of medicine. She is the natural nurse and physician of the family and is endowed with a desire to know more and more of those principles which are essential to the happiness and usefulness of her sex.... But the moment a women seeks advancement ... she is made the mark of poisoned arrows. It is by her own intrinsic worth and persistent perseverance that she secures a position in any profession." She was an example of someone who pioneered several frontiers and whose accomplishments were an inspiration, then and now.

Moorman, Lewis J., M.D., *Pioneer Doctor* (University of Oklahoma Press, 1951) O.P.

Dr. Moorman practiced in country, small town, and metropolitan settings in a time when medicine was making great advancements and becoming more complex. Moorman's eventual area of specialization was in the study and treatment of tuberculosis where he won far-reaching recognition. The first half of the book deals with Moorman's life as a pioneer doctor in Oklahoma, while the latter half focuses on his postgraduate studies and his work with tuberculosis.

Rehwinkel, Alfred M., *Dr. Bessie (The Life Story and Romance of a Pioneer Lady Doctor on our Western and the Canadian Frontier as Told by Herself and Here Presented in a Running Narrative by Her Husband)* (Concordia, 1963) O.P.

The title of this book pretty much tells it all. Dr. Bessie, who bucked tradition by becoming a (woman) doctor in 1900, practiced in two small Iowa towns. She moved her practice West in 1907 to the small town of Carpenter, Wyoming, where she met her soon-to-be husband, a young preacher. *Not* bucking tradition, she gave up her practice in 1912 to become a preacher's wife in rural Canada. She wrote, "I had loved my practice and never believed that anything could persuade me to give it up, but I discovered that there are greater things in the life of a woman than a professional success. A woman may succeed in a man's profession and enjoy the independence of a career, but she remains a woman still. And I learned that to be the wife of a good man and devoted husband and a mother of loving children is infinitely greater than the success in a profession." This book provides a perspective on the conflicts faced by women professionals and the pressures, both internal and external, which their careers brought about.

Tetlow, Roger, *The Astorian* (Binford and Mort, 1975).

This book is the personal history of DeWitt Clinton Ireland, pioneer newspaperman, printer, and publisher. Ireland gained recognition as editor of *The Astorian* (Astoria, Oregon), although his newspaper career took him to many areas of Oregon. In this book, Tetlow attempted to re-create Ireland's style of writing—over-punctuated, over-capitalized, long and rambling sentences, and flowery and repetitious working. Although this is at first disconcerting, it does capture the mood of the time, with the many excerpts from Ireland's editorials blending well with his life story.

Wright, Elizabeth, *Independence in All Things, Neutrality in Nothing: The Story of a Pioneer Journalist of the American West* (Miller Freeman Publications, 1973).

Wright is the granddaughter-in-law of Legh Richmond Freeman, pioneer journalist. She provided the reader with a thoughtful and compassionate look at Freeman and his family, using excerpts from his publications, drawings, and photographs from the period.

Suggested Fiction

Ferber, Edna, *Cimarron* (Doubleday, 1930)
Fox, Norman A., *Reckoning at Rimbow* (Dodd, Mead, 1959)
Sandoz, Mari, *Miss Morissa, Doctor of the Gold Trail* (1955; University of Nebraska Press, 1981)
Steelman, Robert J., *Surgeon to the Sioux* (Doubleday, 1979)

Suggested Films

Another Man, Another Chance (United Artists, 1977) directed by Claude LeLouche.
Law of the Lawless (Paramount, 1964) directed by William F. Claxton.
The Man Who Shot Liberty Valance (Paramount, 1962) directed by John Ford.
Strange Lady in Town (Warner's, 1958) directed by Mervyn LeRoy.

Pioneer Life

by Jimi A. Barry

I

Pioneer life was not glamorous. It was not the life portrayed on television or in movies. At best, life for the pioneer in the American West was one filled with difficulty, monotony, and deprivation. It could lead to a mental institution or an early death.

The American prairie — the Great Plains — was the last region in the West to be settled. For decades pioneers bound for Oregon or California passed over it, but few stayed. In the early part of the Nineteenth century, the prevailing opinion of this area was that it was totally unsuited for agriculture due to the lack of rainfall. This idea of a Great American Desert was supported by early explorers and writers. Washington Irving had written that the area was not suitable for civilized living and that it would breed brigands and robbers. It was generally believed that the arid region would impose a life-style similar to that of Native Americans upon the white man — that is, "uncivilized." Slowly this belief began to change.

The vision of early frontiersmen of transforming the desert into a garden was put down on paper by Josiah Gregg in 1844. Extensive cultivation and the expansion of shady groves would "contribute to the multiplication of showers" and have some effect upon the seasons. Then, in 1862, the Homestead Act was passed which gave any person, who was twenty-one years of age or the head of a household, 160 acres of land for a nominal

156

filing fee and other small charges. In the postbellum years the notion that rainfall was on the increase in the plains region was supported by well-known men as Horace Greeley. The passage of the Homestead Act and the idea that the arid climate could be altered by man helped create the rush to the prairie lands in the 1870s and 1880s. What the pioneer found upon his arrival was not exactly a garden.

The pioneer's first task was to select a site and build a temporary first home. For the majority this meant either a dugout—a cave carved out of the side of a hill—or a sod-house. Both were inexpensive and quickly built forms of shelter. These earthen homes had the advantage of providing excellent insulation against extremes in temperature but were problematic, during rain storms, for both inhabitants and their meagre belongings. The make-shift homes were located as close to a water supply as possible. Above ground water was the best, but wells of up to two hundred feet in depth often had to be dug.

Sanitation was a major problem for the pioneer. Cramped living quarters, dirt floors, fleas, bed bugs, a common drinking cup, improper nutrition, and a lack of adequate toilet facilities were suffered by all. These primitive living conditions, according to frontier doctor Cass Barns, gave rise to the numerous epidemics which swept the prairie communities, killing hundreds.

Corn or wheat was a staple food stuff. Protein came from game such as buffalo in the early years and smaller animals with the disappearance of the shaggy bison. Variety was added to the monotonous diet by gathering indigenous fruits and nuts. However, flapjacks or a lard gravy were more often the common sight on a frontier table. Foods were preserved in a salt brine or by a drying method since canning did not come into widespread use until the late 1800s. The pioneer diet was poor in nutrition because food sources were both highly localized and seasonal.

The clothing worn by the pioneer family was limited to what had been brought from the East. Women had to become creative when clothes wore out. Army blankets and feed sacks were found to have a second life by being made into trousers, jackets, or children's dresses. For the pioneer seamstress purchasing new yard goods was an unimagined luxury with miles separating her from the general store and money scarce. If wool or flax was available, women spun thread and wove cloth from which practical garments were made. In summer months feet went bare and when the cold months set in moccasins or cast-off Army boots were worn. When shoe soles wore out, they were replaced with carved wooden ones attached to the leather uppers. The pioneers' clothes, as their food and homes, were not stylish or elaborate, but served to meet minimal needs.

Frustration was shared by all members of a pioneer family. As Mari Sandoz wrote in *Hostiles and Friendlies* (University of Nebraska Press, 1959), "there was, of course, no training school for the pioneer. He went out and was or wasn't one." Farming on the prairie required methods and tools unlike those previously used in the East and the Trans-Allegheny region. Plows, with larger, sharper blades, pulled by oxen rather than horses were necessary to cut the virgin land. Cutting the prairie sod was an arduous and time-consuming job. It was thick and compact — perfect for sod-houses — but difficult to till into farm land. Once planted, crops were subject to extremes in weather and natural catastrophes. The years 1859 and 1860 were characterized by drought and then followed by severe winters in 1860 and 1861. Spring snow storms or hail destroyed the tender young plants. Dust and wind storms carried away the topsoil and sucked every bit of moisture out of the ground. Electrical storms caused prairie fires which swept unchecked for miles. Worst of all, as in 1874, hordes of grasshoppers would descend on an area destroying everything in sight as they fed off plants, clothing, and wooden implements. Contrary to what a number of writers had said about this agricultural utopia, Nature was uncooperative and untamable. All too often the result of the toil of the prairie farmer was not lush lands reaping bountiful crops.

The monotony of day-to-day life and the deprivations suffered by the pioneer were nothing compared to the loneliness which was experienced on the frontier. The lack of roadbeds made traveling for settlers almost non-existent. Towns or even groups of homes were a rare sight. While men and children were out in the fields, women were at home working on never-ending tasks without the benefit of human companionship or conversation. In O.E. Rölvaag's *Giants in the Earth* (Harper's, 1927) Per Hansa ventures across the prairie propelled by an inner desire to create a new path rather than follow an old one. His wife, Beret, feels exactly the opposite. Upon seeing the prairie for the first time, Beret says, "'Why there isn't even a thing that one can hide behind.'" Every experience was alien to Beret and caused, at times, immobilizing fear. Pioneer life in many ways was hardest on women and, in Nannie Alderson's words in *A Bride Goes West* (Farrar and Rinehart, 1942), "you *had* to keep up or go under."

Families on the prairie did without. When the staples and belongings brought from the East were gone or worn out, pioneers had to improvise and make use of what was available to them in the new land. Wheat or okra seeds made do for coffee, lard for butter. New clothes, reading material, furniture, trees, shrubbery, and flowers were merely memories from a different, earlier way of life. This primitive existence with its lack of trappings of a "civilized" life was a minor annoyance; but combined with a fear of the unknown, frustration, and loneliness, the spirit was beaten down in many a pioneer.

Those who survived the physical and mental tortures did so in an environment we cannot comprehend. As we look at the pioneer's life, we naturally tend to romanticize it. In truth, hard work and the ability to withstand the sparce living conditions, the new environment, and the loneliness were necessary ingredients in the pioneer's character. Mari Sandoz asserted that the pioneer was not a type of person but a mixed-bag of people who prevailed through stubbornness, tenacity, and "grim ruthfulness." Improvements in farming techniques and implements, weather prediction, and medicine eventually made life safer, easier, and more productive. More settlers arrived. Towns and cities grew from nothing and the pioneer was no longer alone.

II

i

Books about pioneer life fall into three general categories: histories, first-hand accounts, and second-hand accounts. In my research, I have found Everett Dick's *The Sod-House Frontier* 1854–1890 to be an invaluable and comprehensive history of the subject. It includes an exceptionally useful cross-referenced index and an extensive bibliography helpful to the reader interested in further research into various aspects of pioneer life and the Great Plains region. However, the most interesting and vivid reading experience for me came from first-hand accounts. Women have contributed significantly to our understanding of the vicissitudes of pioneer living. Reading of these primary sourcebooks gives depth and personality to the historical events of the period as they are recreations of the personal triumphs and defeats of the pioneers, for the most part rich in customs and manners.

Second-hand accounts rely heavily upon primary source materials. They reflect the author's own biases and prejudices. I highly recommend the works of Mari Sandoz — a lyrical writer and the daughter of a crusty Nebraska pioneer — and Joanna Stratton's book on pioneer women of Kansas (see below).

Perhaps the most vivid reconstructions we have of pioneer life are to be found in the fiction based on what was for the most part a glamorless and routine existence.

II

ii

Alderson, Nannie T., *A Bride Goes West* (Farrar and Rinehart, 1942) O.P.; reprinted by the University of Nebraska Press.

Alderson made the transition from urban East Coast life to being the wife of a small cattle rancher in Montana in the 1880s. She learned how to make something from nothing on her own and was the only woman in the area. She found that a positive mental attitude was most important in dealing with the wild, isolated lands of Montana. She wrote that "when you live so close to the bare bones of reality, there is very little room for sentiment," and her recollections are filled with humor about learning how to cope with the rigors of pioneer life, mostly through a trial-and-error process.

Barns, Cass G., *The Sod House* (1930; University of Nebraska Press, 1970).

An autobiography of sorts, this work pays tribute to the early home-steaders of the Kansas-Nebraska region. Barns, who worked as a profes-sional in the area where he immigrated in 1878, described in anecdotal fashion various aspects of prairie life and the people involved in settling the region. He discussed at length homestead laws and his description of the construction of a sod-house is one of the best accounts we have. His own experiences as a newspaper editor, physician, and dentist prompted him to report on the development of prairie newspapers and the medical aspects and health conditions of pioneer life. A subscriber to the idea of Manifest Destiny, Barns predictably viewed the Indians as "warring savages" and the disappearance of the buffalo and other wild animals as necessary to develop a "high class of farm animals."

Dale, Edward Everett, *Frontier Ways: Sketches of Life in the Old West* (University of Texas Press, 1959) O.P.

This book of essays on the social conditions of The Agricultural Frontier takes a positive and light-hearted view of pioneering. The term pioneer, in Dale's sense, takes in anyone who settled a new land. Among the topics touched on by Dale are food, culture, living conditions, how to build a sod-house, choosing a home site, and health. Dale stated that while the journey West was long it was as a rule "happy," which contradicts many of the first-hand accounts about the trek to the Trans-Mississippi West. He also contended that for women the frontier experience was ad-vantageous because it did away with a sexual division of labor. The book in these terms appears to be somewhat a reaction to the many books which stress the hardships and violence of pioneer life.

Dick, Everett, *The Sod-House Frontier* 1854-1890 (D. Appleton-Century, 1937) O.P.; reprinted by the University of Nebraska Press.

Dick's work is a comprehensive social history of the plains states of Kansas, Nebraska, North and South Dakota. It is based on extensive re-search into autobiographies, biographies, newspapers, diaries, interviews, monographs, and secondary sourcebooks. The entertainingly written nar-rative describes where the settlers came from, how they built homes and founded towns, how they lived, worked, and relaxed. Of particular interest are the chapters which deal with the day-to-day life of the pioneer — "Log Cabin Days" "The Sod-House," "Homesteading," "Women and Children on the Frontier," "Homesteader Days and Ways," "Fuel and Water," and "Food and Clothes." A chronological as well as topical treat-ment, Dick's book devotes a good deal of space to the problems and ob-stacles met by the pioneer and to the economic, social, and political con-ditions of the prairie country. The book's major deficiency is its failure to treat women other than in their roles as nameless mothers and wives.

Garland, Hamlin, *A Son of the Middle Border* (Macmillan, 1917) O.P.; various reprint editions are available.

This collection of autobiographical essays, in addition to being an evocative record of the Garland family's lives in Wisconsin, Iowa, and Dakota territory in the last forty years of the Nineteenth century, is also a social history of the "middle border." Garland described with an artist's touch the daily routines in a farming household, his education, the methods and tools of farming, the books and magazines that were read in the home, and he gave us telling portraits of the people he encountered. As with Mari Sandoz (see below), Garland's work is significant because of the fact that he grew up during the pioneering period which allowed him to note changes — social, economic, and political — as well as to describe pioneer life from a child's point of view.

Humphrey, Seth K., *Following the Prairie Frontier* (University of Minnesota Press, 1931) O.P.
 A second generation pioneer, Humphrey traveled from Wisconsin to the Cherokee Strip in the early 1890s. This book is a record of his journey which incorporates his observations, impressions, and reflections about the prairie country. A stop at a Dakota sod-house for a night's rest afforded him the opportunity to describe, although briefly, a pioneer family. Humphrey was more sensitive to the hard life facing pioneer women than were most. This work is of somewhat limited use in that it is primarily a travelogue.

Langford, J.O., with Fred Gipson, *Big Bend: A Homesteader's Story* (University of Texas Press, 1952).
 Set in West Texas in 1909, this book is about the trials of a homesteader from the man's point of view. Langford with his wife and daughter moved to the Big Bend area where, making use of the hot spring on their property, they developed a successful mineral bath business. In *Big Bend*, the reader finds out a great deal about this remote section of West Texas where the Langfords lived for four years as well as about the life and customs of the people. Of Langford we learn of his strong optimism and occasional concern for his wife's possible loneliness. (This land had been abandoned by other homesteaders because of its distance from civilization.) Few inner feelings are revealed by the author who emphasized instead the thrill of adventure and the beauty of Nature.

Sandoz, Mari, *Old Jules* (Little, Brown, 1935) O.P.; reprinted by University of Nebraska Press; *Sandhill Sundays* (University of Nebraska Press, 1970) O.P.
 Old Jules traces the life of the author's father, Jules Ami Sandoz, locator, community builder, and amateur horticulturist in Nebraska during the years 1884–1928. It presents a unique portrait of frontier life, depicting people struggling against the elements and against social conditions. Written in Sandoz' lyrical style, it shows the violence and joy of homestead life and embodies Sandoz' love and respect for the land and its settlers. Although it contains abrupt jumps in chronology, this remains one of the finest books written about the homesteaders of the Great Plains.

Sandhill Sundays is a collection of ten articles written between the years 1929–1965. Nine of the articles are set in the Sandhill country of Northwestern Nebraska and focus on friends and family from Sandoz' past. "Martha of the Yellow Braids" and "Marlizzie" are particularly of interest for their vivid and touching portraits of pioneer women. These well written pieces show how the Nebraska homesteaders lived, worked, and played. As Hamlin Garland (see above), Sandoz was a realist who did not shrink from showing the grim side of life but her books are also a celebration of the pioneering spirit.

Schmitt, Martin F., with Dee Brown, *The Settlers' West* (Scribner's, 1955); reprinted by Ballantine, both O.P.

Primarily a picture book, the text of this brief volume surveys the Westward movement of the Nineteenth century in very general terms. Topics such as town-building, cultural activities, farming, and weather are cursorily covered. Much time is spent on wild West shows, rodeos, and authors of Western fiction and this is where most of the factual textual errors creep in. A bibliography contains a potpourri of titles from books on farm machinery and motors to books on baseball! The most positive thing that could be said about it would be to cite its many valuable and unusual illustrative photographs.

Stewart, Elinore Pruitt, *Letters of a Woman Homesteader* (Houghton Mifflin, 1914) O.P.; reprinted by the University of Nebraska Press.

With this book, cast in the form of letters to a former employer, Stewart told of her homesteading days in Wyoming in the early 1900s. She left Denver, a widow with her daughter, to act as housekeeper for a Mr. Stewart, whom she eventually married. She took out a homestead claim, worked it herself, and viewed homesteading as the "solution to all poverty's problems," particularly for women.

Stratton, Joanna, *Pioneer Women: Voices from the Kansas Frontier* (Simon & Schuster, 1981).

This is an extraordinary and fascinating study of pioneer women who lived in Kansas in the last half of the Nineteenth century. Based on materials commissioned and collected by the author's great grandmother in the early 1920s, Stratton consulted these 800 pieces to present a "personal account of the pioneer experience described by those for whom 'history' was nothing more than daily life." Among the topics examined in the lives of pioneer women are their motivations for seeking new lands, their daily routines, their attitudes toward Indians, their battles against the elements, and their involvement in such social issues of the day as temperance and suffrage. This is strictly a study of literate white women who survived the frontier experience and excluded are minority women and women who returned East or ended up in mental institutions with their spirits and health broken. The obvious limitation of the book is that the women who contributed facts about their lives were writing long after the events took place and therefore time may have colored or distorted their memories. This well organized study presents a vivid portrait of life on the Kansas frontier from the woman's point of view and is significant for the new material it contains.

Suggested Fiction

Capps, Benjamin, *The Brothers of Uterica* (Meredith Press, 1967)
Cather, Willa, *O Pioneers!* (Houghton Mifflin, 1913)
Cooper, James Fenimore, *The Pioneers* (1823)
Davis, H.L., *Honey in the Horn* (Harper's, 1935)
Erdman, Loula Grace, *The Edge of Time* (Dodd, Mead, 1950)
Gardiner, Dorothy, *Snow-Water* (Doubleday, 1939)
Garland, Hamlin, *Main-Travelled Roads* (1891)
Guthrie, A.B., Jr., *Arfive* (Houghton Mifflin, 1970)
Haycox, Ernest, *The Earthbreakers* (1952; Gregg Press, 1979)
Lane, Rose Wilder, *Let the Hurricane Roar* (Longmans, Green, 1933)
Richter, Conrad, *The Trees* (Knopf, 1940)
_____, *The Fields* (Knopf, 1946)
_____, *The Town* (Knopf, 1950)
Rölvaag, O.E., *Giants in the Earth* (Harper's, 1927)
Rushing, Jane Gilmore, *Tamzen* (Doubleday, 1972)
Schaefer, Jack, *The Kean Land* (Houghton Mifflin, 1959)
Wilder, Laura Ingalls, *The First Four Years* (Harper's, 1971)

Suggested Films

All Mine to Give (RKO, 1958) directed by Allen Reisner.
The Emigrants (Warner's, 1971) directed by Jan Troell.
Heartland (Levitt Pickman, 1981) directed by Richard Pearce.
The Hired Hand (Universal, 1971) directed by Peter Fonda.
The New Land (Warner's, 1973) directed by Jan Troell.

First-Hand Accounts
and *Belles Lettres*

by Jon Tuska

I

"I thought of the anecdote (a very, very old one, even at that day),"
Mark Twain wrote in *Roughing It* (1872), "of the traveler who sat down to
a table which had nothing on it but a mackerel and a pot of mustard. He
asked the landlord if this was all. The landlord said:

"'*All!* Why, thunder and lightning, I should think there was
mackerel enough there for six.'

"'But I don't like mackerel.'

"'Oh—then help yourself to the mustard.'"

Robert Edson Lee in his book *From West to East: Studies in the
Literature of the American West* (University of Illinois Press, 1966) accused
Twain of pandering to his Eastern audience in *Roughing It* and, in the
course of his critique, enlarged this indictment to include so many others
that finally he had to lament that "since the experience [of the frontier] is
past, I conclude that it has been lost for all time." I am unable to accept
such a pessimistic view when it comes to Western fiction and, in terms of
the wealth of first-person narratives which are available, both in print and
in archives, it can scarcely be held *a priori* with regard to frontier memoirs.

What I would urge when approaching a first-hand account is caution.

164

There can be no substitute for a concept of historical reality when dealing with the period in which a Western film or story is set and the same principle must apply to first-hand accounts. When a first-hand account is indeed genuine, it can increase and deepen our understanding of historical reality in a way that is truly unique. However, the need for a concept of historical reality as a principle of evaluation is nowhere demonstrated so profoundly as when confronted by an account that purports to be true but which consists almost entirely of fiction. A prime example would be Nelson Lee's *Three Years Among the Comanches* (1859) which, but for its date of publication, might well have been a dime novel — that is, but for its date of publication and the fact that for decades it was accepted as fact rather than fiction. Walter Prescott Webb wrote an Introduction to the Western Frontier Library edition of Lee's narrative published in 1957 by the University of Oklahoma Press and made the claim that Lee could be trusted for his portrait of "how the Comanches lived before they were affected by the white man" and termed the account "invaluable."

I cannot say whether Lee ever so much as ventured into the West — nothing is known about him but what is presumably told in the text of his memoir — but in structure Lee's book follows the conventional form of the captivity novel. Although he was made a captive of the Comanches, Lee's mind was incessantly on his escape; his view of his captors was that they were savages and he related incident after incident to reinforce this conviction. Lack of humane feeling, indeed, is justified because Indians are not really human beings. "The next step," he wrote when describing how he chose a wife, "was to make a selection from the dusky daughters of the tribe, a matter about which I felt disposed to be somewhat fastidious. The chief sent for some half-dozen, submitting them to my inspection, before a choice was made. Some of them were hideous, either lank and cadaverous, or fat and flabby, having a fiery red new moon painted over each eye, and the full moon in the center of the forehead. These were rejected without hesitation or ceremony. At length one was brought that was pronounced entirely satisfactory. She was small and slender, very young and very agile. There was the grace of nature in her carriage, and, besides, she was not quite as filthy as her companions."

One wonders how clean Lee was at the time, or at any time during his *soi-disant* rugged life on the Texas frontier. At any rate, the Sleek Otter, as she was called, made him "a faithful and affectionate wife, skinned the deer, cooked the venison, pounded the corn, mended my moccasins, and in all respects [performed] her conjugal duties with cheerfulness and alacrity." Whatever their ostensible compatibility, there is no affection in the tone Lee used when describing the journey he was to undertake with the Comanche chief, Rolling Thunder. "Saluting the Sleek Otter, who little thought it was the last nod she would ever receive from her long-haired spouse ..., we trotted away from the village, myself in advance, neither of us destined ever to return." Although Rolling Thunder had treated Lee with great kindness, when he bent down for a drink of water, "standing by the horse's side," Lee wrote, "I observed the hatchet hanging from the pommel of the saddle. [It was indeed unusual for an Indian to use a white man's saddle, but Lee ignored this.] The thought flashed through my mind quick as the fierce lightning that the hour of my deliverance had come at last, and snatching it, in that instant, from its place, I leaped towards him, burying the dull edge a broad hand's breadth in his brain."

As in the romantic historical reconstruction in Western fiction, in fictional first-hand accounts such as Lee's there is always an *ideological* purpose behind the events narrated. For Lee, the message to his readers was two-fold. First, although he showed the Comanches and Apaches fighting each other, "that same season ... they buried the tomahawk and danced the pipe dance, and henceforward were at peace" — an incident, as stated, completely at variance with the customs of these peoples (i.e., "the pipe dance," etc.), but one which prepared the reader for Lee's warning that all Indians from all tribes and all nations were about "to enter into an alliance with the view of waging an exterminating and implacable war upon every train of emigrants or other party moving towards California, Oregon, the Great Salt Lake, or other points in either of those directions." Second, and very closely related to the first point, was the situation of "white prisoners, principally women" which prompted Lee to "turn with disgust from the contemplation of the cruelty to which these captive women were subjected by the lustful hellhounds as they bore them off in triumph to their camps." Taken together these two points admit to only one solution which Lee advanced negatively by citing the "hundreds of people, in the pursuit of their lawful business, [who] are captured yearly, enslaved, and barbarously put to death, without attracting the attention of government, whereas if the hundredth part of the same outrages were committed by any enlightened nation, it would call upon the people to fly to arms." The ultimate design behind *Three Years Among the Comanches* was therefore a clarion call to arms to exterminate Indians; it is an unsubtle variety of war propaganda.

Once a reader has become familiar with the period, the place, and the people, it will be readily evident which aspects of first-hand accounts, being fictional, are obviously classifiable as formulary or romantic, depending on their content and the interpretations illustrated by, or the conclusions drawn from, that content. This is not to say, much less imply, that all first-hand accounts are necessarily fictional in part or in their entirety; only that some of them are, and that the fictional content is customarily presented according to the same narrative structures operative generally for Western fiction.

Closely related to first-hand accounts, often cast in the form of a first-hand account, yet differing in many subtle ways are what the French have called *belles lettres*. Traditionally, *belles lettres* have been writings of an aesthetic rather than an informational or didactic character. In their way, *belles lettres* frequently constitute the finest literary flowering of any period and just as frequently they can bring a reader closer to the way people lived and thought in a given period than could either an historical or a fictional narrative.

II

i

Speaking only for myself, I prefer first-hand accounts and *belles lettres* to almost any other kind of literary endeavor. There is nothing else Mark Twain ever wrote which held me enraptured as did the first hundred-odd pages of *Roughing It* in which he recreated his first impressions of an overland stagecoach journey into the Far West. This being the case I have had to exercise more than usual restraint on myself in the number of such books I would recommend; and another consideration, no less important, is that I have tried to avoid reference to any first-hand account where the fictional content interferes too greatly with one's reading pleasure, where the distortions are such as to come into open conflict with what we know legitimately to have been true of a particular past reality.

I have also placed other limitations on my selections. Narratives by women, with the exception of the entry for Mary Austin, can be found in the section on Women; narratives by Native Americans can be found in the section on Native Americans. I do not distinguish between a first-hand account and *belles lettres* in the annotations because to do so with books being included such as Ross Santee's *Lost Pony Tracks* (1953; University of Nebraska Press, 1972) which is partly fiction, partly autobiography, and partly *belles lettres* would be imprudent. In actual practice, these categories have never been mutually exclusive. Santee is also a special case insofar as the other recommended first-hand accounts dealing with the cattle industry can be found in the section on Cowboys, Cattlemen, and the Cattle Industry. Indeed, virtually every section in Part I and Part II has one or more books included in the recommended reading that can be classified as first-hand accounts. What sets off the twenty-eight books by twenty-four authors which I have especially singled out for inclusion below is that they have in some cases an expanded scope, in others are possessed of such literary excellence as to constitute a very special variety of artistic expression, and in all cases are uniquely *des voyages spirituels*.

ii

Abbey, Edward, *Desert Solitaire* (McGraw-Hill, 1968) O.P.; reprinted by Ballantine.

Both a travel narrative about experiences in the Southwest — hence the subtitle "A Season in the Wilderness" — and a spiritual exercise contrasting the natural order with the technological chaos modern man would impose, Abbey in this book achieved a truly effective literary *tour de force*. You may not agree with all aspects of Abbey's philosophy — who can wholly agree with another? — but there is no denying that his is a refreshing and vibrant perspective and your first inclination, upon finishing this book, will be to do something to stem the current reckless course of events.

Austin, Mary, *The Land of Little Rain* (Houghton Mifflin, 1903) O.P.; reprinted by Peter Smith.

For Theodore Roosevelt, California was "West of the West," but for Mary Austin the climate, the people, the flora, and the fauna of California as it was once were the very essence of the West. Less concerned with pointed criticism of the Anglo-American socio-economic system than Abbey, Austin was just as conscious of the natural order and characterized vividly the locales she encountered and the people who inhabited those locales in a narrative that might be called *belles lettres*, except that Austin—and here is another common bond with Abbey—tended much of the time to be more didactic than aesthetic in her varied reflections.

Boller, Henry, A., *Among the Indians: Four Years on the Upper Missouri 1858-1862* (1867) O.P.; reprinted by the University of Nebraska Press, edited by Milo Milton Quaife.

This reprint edition includes the text and footnotes of the first thirty-three chapters of Boller's memoir, with the final ten chapters deleted which deal with Boller's experiences other than with the fur trade. "At the present time," Boller wrote in his original Preface, "when the Indian is being held up before the world as an incarnate fiend, it is but fair that his redeeming qualities should likewise be recorded. I shall ever look back upon the years spent in the Indian country as among the pleasantest of my life...." It is a touching and moving portrait of Indian life, as indeed its author intended.

Brady, Cyrus Townsend, *Indian Fights and Fighters* (McClure, 1904) O.P.; reprinted by the University of Nebraska Press with an Introduction by James T. King.

"With some notable exceptions, frontier officers as a rule were intelligent, well educated, and well trained," James T. King commented in his Introduction to the reissue. "A surprisingly large number were voracious readers, and in many campaign saddlebags, volumes of Shakespeare, Sir Walter Scott, or Thucydides (in the original Greek) might share space with hardtack and coffee." One cannot look to Brady for any clearer picture of the Indian response to the white man's invasion than one can look to Julius Caesar in *De Bello Gallico* for an honest report of Gaulic response to Roman conquest; in fact, Professor King cited George Bird Grinnell's *The Fighting Cheyennes* (1915; University of Oklahoma Press, 1956) as a viable companion volume, a view I would endorse. Where Brady *is* informative, as is Julius Caesar, is in his extraordinarily sympathetic, albeit at times apocryphal, reconstruction of Anglo-American military operations on the Western frontier and his portraits of frontier officers and soldiers.

Browne, J. Ross, *Adventures in the Apache Country: A Tour Through Arizona and Sonora, 1864* (1869) O.P.; reprinted by the University of Arizona Press, edited and annotated by Donald M. Powell.

The original edition of this memoir had some extraneous matter on the silver regions of Nevada which for the reissue was excised by the editor so that the account could be focused strictly on Browne's experiences in Arizona and Sonora. Lawrence Clark Powell in his book, *Southwest Classics* (Ward Ritchie 1974), claimed that "after following Browne's trail from Yuma to Nogales, I can report that except for the main highways and the few urban centers, Southern Arizona is unchanged from Browne's time of a century ago, the vast Papago Reservation least of all." What, of course, is absent is the eerie horror which Browne felt when he encountered Apaches crucified by the Pimas; and, being a graphic artist of competent skill, he managed to illustrate in both words and drawings the way humankind lived in this region more than a century ago.

Canton, Frank M., *Frontier Trails: The Autobiography of Frank M. Canton* (Houghton Mifflin, 1930), edited by Edward Everett Dale, O.P.; reprinted by the University of Oklahoma Press.

Stendahl once remarked that the books one writes are all part of a gigantic lottery the results of which are not known until a hundred years after an author's death. Wyatt Earp collaborated on a biography, but no one would publish it. Frank M. Canton, who in his later years was a frontier lawman and was involved in colorful episodes as the Johnson county cattle war and the pursuit of both the Wild Bunch and Bill Doolin and his gang, left behind at his death in 1927 the story of his life in law enforcement and Dale helped prepare it for publication. In this case, the lottery is a benefit because Canton was a more dedicated professional lawman than ever was Wyatt Earp and his personal account is free of so much of the hyperbole usually associated with this subject.

Cook, General D.J., *Hands Up; or, Twenty Years of Detective Life in the Mountains and on the Plains* (1882) O.P.; reprinted by the University of Oklahoma Press.

General Cook's account provides an ideal companion for Canton's portrayal of frontier lawlessness and the way in which it was really dealt with. Cook created the Rocky Mountain Detective Association, a semisecret and unofficial organization of sheriffs, police chiefs, and marshals which worked as an interstate network of law enforcement in those areas where there was little or no law otherwise to be had. In particular, Cook can be commended for his forthright approach to frontier violence, including the "hanging sprees," and his picture is not stylized after the fashion rampant in so much subsequent formulary Western fiction and Western films.

Cook, James H., *Fifty Years on the Frontier* (Yale University Press, 1923) O.P.; reprinted by the University of Oklahoma Press.

In the new edition there is both a Foreword by J. Frank Dobie and an Introduction by the late General Charles King praising this book. There is some nonsense in it. Cook described Billy the Kid as a New York tough (whereas even those who believe the Kid was born in New York City agree he left the city at a very early age); and he attributed the Kid's criminal behavior to the influence of sensational fiction! On the other hand, Cook's portrait of the Sioux Chief, Red Cloud, is perhaps the most authentic we have. Cook was involved in big game hunting, mustanging, ranching, became friends with the Sioux and Cheyennes, and even participated in the pursuit of Geronimo in the Southwest; yet, for me, among the most intensely interesting aspects of the book is the section on the fossil quarries at Agate Springs and, among the illustrations, is the assembled skeleton of the *Moropus cooki* which stood six feet high at the shoulders, a distant but distinct relative of the horse and the rhinoceros.

Fletcher, Baylis John, *Up the Trail in '79* (University of Oklahoma Press, 1968), edited by Wayne Gard.

Technically speaking, the section of this book, "Up the Trail in '79," while it was not published for the first time until 1966 and had been found in manuscript form at the time of Fletcher's death in 1912, would qualify as a trail drive narrative and thus would not have been included but for four additional and just as interesting frontier writings by Fletcher collected by Gard for inclusion in this book. These writings pertain to reminiscences concerning an attempted lynching, pursuit of some Comanche raiders, a religious camp meeting, and a train robbery in Nebraska. Taken as a whole, Fletcher's commentaries are competently crafted and filled with close and detailed observations.

Frémont, John Charles, *The Expeditions of John Charles Frémont, Volume 1: Travels from 1838 to 1844, Volume 2: The Bear Flag Revolt and the Court-Martial* (University of Illinois Press, 1970), edited by Donald Jackson and Mary Lee Spence.

This was certainly one of the most monumental accomplishments of American scholarship in our time and the University of Illinois Press is to be commended for its role in this project. The first volume combines Frémont's published reports of his first two transcontinental expeditions and selections from his *Memoirs* with unpublished manuscript materials and enlightening annotations often based on hitherto unpublished letters and other documents uncovered by the editors during the investigative research. The second volume includes a similar presentation of Frémont's 1845 expedition and the clash with the Californians, as well as extensive correspondence including that pertaining to Frémont's arrest and court-martial. The proceedings of the actual court-martial have been made available in a third, ancillary supplement, and a third volume is in preparation devoted to Frémont's fourth and fifth Western expeditions. A number of biographical and historical studies have, of course, appeared about Frémont, but in my opinion none of them can equal the immediacy of his own first-hand accounts (with Jessie Benton Frémont's help), especially in view of the support documents and informed annotations.

Garrard, Lewis H., *Wah-To-Yah and the Taos Trail* (1855) O.P.; reprinted by the University of Oklahoma Press with an Introduction by A.B. Guthrie, Jr.

In his Introduction to the reissue edition, A.B. Guthrie, Jr., was puzzled over why Francis Parkman's *The Oregon Trail* (1849) should have received so much literary recognition while Garrard's account came to be obscured; and how only in Parkman's original notes, which have recently been published, is there so much as a spark of the immediacy and vigor of his experience, whereas these are the qualities which mark every page of Garrard's narrative. I could not be more in accord. Parkman quite deliberately, it seems to me, translated his experiences into a literary format likely to please his Eastern readers — an exemplar of the tendency Robert Edson Lee noted in *From West to East* — while Garrard really never did. It is for this reason that Garrard deserves a much wider readership. Garrard was part of a caravan led by Ceran St. Vrain, journeying to Bent's Old Fort, and he was one of the volunteers to join William Bent in avenging the Taos rebellion. In my view, as George Frederick Ruxton (see below), Garrard was very adept at combining a subtle sense of characterization with a distinct and vital ability to invoke physical topography.

Irving, Washington, *A Tour of the Prairies* (1835) O.P.; reprinted by the University of Oklahoma Press.

In 1832 Irving embarked on an expedition onto the Great Plains and this book was his memoir. Irving wrote to his brother, Peter, that he expected on the trip to "have an opportunity of seeing the remnants of those great Indian tribes, which are now about to disappear as independent nations, or to be amalgamated under some new form of government. I should see those fine countries of the Far West, while still in a state of pristine wildness, and behold herds of buffaloes scouring their native prairies, before they are driven beyond the reach of the civilized tourist." The important words here are "civilized" and "tourist." It did not occur to Irving that the Indian nations might have any rights whatsoever to their lands; that they were in fact sovereign peoples not really in need of the invaders' government. Pierre Beatte, the mixed-blood hunter who had joined the expedition, inspired Irving to observe that he "had altogether more of the red than the white man in his composition; and as I had been taught to look upon all half-breeds with distrust, as an uncertain and faithless race, I would gladly have dispensed with [his] services...." But as the journey progressed, Irving modified his opinion of Beatte and discovered that "an Indian hunter on a prairie is like a cruiser on the ocean, perfectly independent of the world, and competent to self-protection and self-maintenance." Irving never stopped being a tourist; but he was notwithstanding a fine stylist and his memoir is not without its share of charm.

King, Clarence, *Mountaineering in the Sierra Nevada* (1872) O.P.; reprinted by the University of Nebraska Press.

King was a geologist and a mining engineer who conducted a

geological survey for the government of the fortieth parallel in 1867–1872 and became the organizer of the United States Geological Survey 1879–1881. His series of sketches brought together in this book comprises the first real literature of the Sierras and, as Mark Twain in *Roughing It* (see below), King was possessed of a keen sense of social perception which he incorporated into this narrative of his adventures, whereas his scientific training made him an acute naturalist. This is not to say, however, that King was not at the same time more a romantic than a realist and, in the optative tradition of his time, he believed that "what a man *is*, is of far less consequence than what he is becoming." The Far West for him, despite all its natural grandeur, was raw material for an even grander idea of empire.

Lewis, Meriwether, and William Clark, *The History of the Lewis and Clark Expedition* (1893) O.P.; reprinted by Dover Books, edited by Elliott Coues.

    I have conducted classes for some years now at Lewis & Clark College and it tends to prompt in me a special attachment for these journals. The Dover edition in three volumes is a reprint of the 1893 edition of Francis P. Harper in four volumes. Occasionally at Lewis & Clark College field expeditions are organized which follow as exactly as possible the course of the original expedition. There are those who are of the belief that the journals are dull and filled with needless information. Coues, thanks to his numerous and enlightening annotations, alleviated much of the substance behind such an objection and hence it is this edition which is recommended.

Lummis, Charles F., *The Land of Poco Tiempo* (1893) O.P.; reprinted by the University of New Mexico Press.

    Turbesé Lummis Fiske and Keith Lummis in their *Charles F. Lummis: The Man and His West* (University of Oklahoma Press, 1975) quoted a number of reviews of this book when it first appeared and, among them, a long article in the *London Spectator* which complained about Lummis' English which "sometimes ... is picturesque and forgiveness is easy; more often it is the reverse...." This was the most unfair remark of all about Lummis who actually wrote in a simple, direct, at times colloquial, but always clear style that illumines his text with a vivid immediacy. "So the day wears off," Lummis wrote at one point. "The breathless but more merciful night comes down and brings brief respite. ...How log-like that rest is, despite the stifling heat and the roughness of the couch, and unrefreshing as log-like. One arises from it still soaked in lethargy, and for hours afterward trudges on as in a trance." The reader is not so concerned with how Lummis stylized reality as with the reality itself! Fabulists such as Harvey Fergusson and Eugene Manlove Rhodes could equal but not surpass Lummis' descriptions of New Mexico, in Lummis' words "the United States which is *not* United States."

Nelson, John Young, *Fifty Years on the Trail* (1889) O.P.; reprinted by the University of Oklahoma Press with an Introduction by Donald E. Worcester.

The subtitle to this book reads "The Adventures of John Young Nelson as described to Harrington O'Reilly," and so it is a first-hand account through an amanuensis. Donald E. Worcester, author of *The Apaches: Eagles of the Southwest* (University of Oklahoma Press, 1975), one of the best books on these often misrepresented people, wrote the Introduction to the reissue and I can only agree with him that "Nelson might well be classed as the first and foremost expert on Sioux marriage and divorce customs, having had at least nine Sioux wives, including three at one time. It has been commonly believed, since a prospective groom made a gift of ponies to his intended's family, that the Sioux fathers sold their daughters into marriage. After proceeding through Sioux courtship customs on numerous occasions, Nelson [made] it clear that the girl had to be persuaded first and that the ponies were merely an earnest of the young warrior's intentions, given to convince the girl's parents of his ability to provide and of his generosity." In the half century Nelson narrated to O'Reilly, he rendered a detailed and for the most part accurate portrait of the frontier while, simultaneously, he revealed in his own personal life the useful and important role that could be played by someone who at any other time would have been considered a misfit and an outcast.

Olmstead, Frederick Law, *A Journey Through Texas: or, A Saddle-Trip on the Southwestern Frontier* (1857) O.P.; reprinted by the University of Texas Press.

This is one of three first-person narratives Olmstead wrote and commonly conceded to be his best. Olmstead was an Easterner and when he came to describe the life-style among Mexican-Americans and others on the frontier he shared to a degree Washington Irving's aloofness. Yet he had a passionate hatred for slavery and his portrait of Anglo-American slaveholders in Texas is discerning, finding that "there seemed to be the consciousness of a wrong relation and a determination to face conscience down, and continue it; to work up the 'damned niggers,' with a sole eye to selfish profit, cash down, in this world." I do not think I am in much danger when I warrant that the picture Olmstead has given us of the state of Texas in the early 1850s is quite the finest we have from that period and that it is a contrasting and necessary complement to the somewhat bucolic image engendered by the very different society of the Austin colony.

Parkman, Francis, *The Oregon Trail* (1849) O.P.; reprinted by New American Library with an Introduction by A.B. Guthrie, Jr.

The most unfortunate aspect of this book is its title insofar as it is not about the Oregon Trail at all, but rather a first-hand account of a journey overland which Parkman made in 1846 in the company of Quincey Adams Shaw. The journey took him first to Fort Laramie and then down to Bent's Fort, and finally back to St. Louis. Parkman's tone and attitudes were those of a Boston Brahmin. His style often lacks grace. By far, the most absorbing chapters are those which detail the time he spent living with Oglala Sioux. His knowledge of them and their customs remained superficial:

"Nay, so alien ... do they appear, that, after breathing the air of the prairie for a few months or weeks, [one] begins to look upon them as a troublesome and dangerous species of wild beasts." A reader must, at all times, attempt to see beyond Parkman's personal limitations to evaluate more fully what he witnessed; such an effort being made, his book does have value. He wrote as a man of letters, and not as the historian he later became, and he did not perceive the historical importance of most things he saw: he dismissed overland immigration and summed up Mormons as "blind and desperate fanatics." Yet he *did describe* what he saw, often in great detail, and it is this quality which still provides his account with its significance.

Pike, Zebulon Montgomery, *The Journals of Zebulon Montgomery Pike [1895] with Letters and Related Documents* (University of Oklahoma Press, 1966) in two volumes, edited and annotated by Donald Jackson.

Along with the Lewis & Clark journals and the Frémont records, Pike's memoirs of his expeditions are among the most valuable documents of American exploration. Indeed, Pike and his men were the first Anglo-Americans to venture into the region now embracing the states of Kansas, Colorado, and New Mexico. Pike, however, was not an accomplished stylist and in his case Professor Jackson performed a capital service by including in this edition the published accounts of Pike's two expeditions, the original manuscripts hitherto unpublished, and the support correspondence and related documents, both published and unpublished. Taken as an ensemble, all of these materials together contribute in a way impossible for any selection of them alone to recreate the conditions and experiences and especially the adversities of hunger and cold encountered on the journey into the West. The University of Oklahoma Press is to be especially congratulated for sponsoring this project.

Ruxton, George Frederick, *Adventures in Mexico and the Rocky Mountains 1846–1847* (1847) O.P.; reprinted by The Rio Grande Press; *Ruxton of the Rockies* (University of Oklahoma Press, 1950), collected by Clyde and Mae Reed Porter and edited by LeRoy R. Hafen.

Ruxton's grand journey which took him from the Southern coasts of Mexico through the Rocky Mountains and the plains of the American West — some 2,000 miles — has rightfully become a classic among travel narratives. He wintered with mountain men and while hunting and exploring he had experiences and heard stories and legends about the ways of men in that difficult clime. Ruxton came to accept the Native American belief in the balance of Nature and embraced a number of other Indian notions which seemed natural to him because he had been witness to the raw power of Nature and the littleness of man as few had been among his European readers, with their carefully tended gardens and Nature poetry. The sense of spiritual liberation which Ruxton felt in the wilderness was, in fact, the most singular moment in his relatively short life — he died unexpectedly of dysentery in St. Louis — and, fortunately for us, he left behind his wonderful memoir and his novel, *Life in the Far West* (1849). It was long thought that everything Ruxton had written had been published during his lifetime. Then, in the summer of 1947, Clyde and Mae Reed Porter were able to track down Ruxton's surviving notebooks and they organized this material, with the assistance of LeRoy R. Hafen, into a more complete record of Ruxton's travels in *Ruxton of the Rockies*. A good part of this latter book is drawn from *Adventures*, but both books have to be read in order to have a composite view; and I, for one, think Ruxton's adventures as a *voyageur* with Peshwego, his Indian guide, in the winter of 1843–1844, trekking through the frozen wastes of Ontario and Northern New York, reclaimed for *Ruxton of the Rockies*, is the best narrative he ever wrote.

Santee, Ross, *Lost Pony Tracks* (Scribner's, 1953) O.P.; reprinted by the University of Nebraska Press.
     I have found that unless you happen to be particularly interested in the cattle industry, range life, or cowboying, the majority of first-hand accounts available in this area will not sustain your attention. *Lost Pony Tracks* would seem, however, to be the exception. Santee wrote it when he was in his sixties, looking back over his life and the years, since early in 1915, that he had spent working as a ranch hand, his thoughts as an artist devoted to Western subjects, and, most of all, the people he had known who had made the strongest or most lasting impressions on him. The stories, shared adventures, the work with horses, the rodeos, a whole way of life are imperishably captured in his book.

Tibbles, Thomas Henry, *Buckskin and Blanket Days* (Doubleday, 1957) O.P.; reprinted by the University of Nebraska Press.
     Tibbles wrote this reminiscence in 1905 but it was more than fifty years later that it was first published. He was an admirable journalist and his experiences among several of the Plains tribes and his portrait of Indian territory as it once was and the aftermath of the battle of Wounded Knee have an intrinsic interest. He married the mixed-blood spokesperson, Bright Eyes, and as many another well meaning soul — including Helen Hunt Jackson — he supported the Dawes Act until its detrimental effects became painfully obvious. This is a fascinating account, encompassing many years, and Tibbles met and was involved at various times with Sitting Bull, General George Crook, and John Brown as well as being nominated for Vice President on the People's Party ticket with Thomas E. Watson in 1904. Tibbles came about as close as a white man could come to understanding both sides of the Nineteenth-century conflict between the Native Americans and the Anglo-Americans.

Townsend, John Kirk, *Narrative of a Journey Across the Rocky Mountains to the Columbia River* (1839) O.P.; reprinted by the University of Nebraska Press with an Introduction by Donald Jackson.
     Donald Jackson, the historian who performed such a fine service

with his work on the composite editions of the expeditions of both Frémont and Pike (see above), has written a fine Introduction to the reissue of this memoir by the University of Nebraska Press. Townsend was the first trained zoologist to cross the continent into the Far West, which he did as part of Nathaniel J. Wyeth's escort of a company of settlers bound for Oregon. Osborne Russell was also with the group and his *Journal of a Trapper* (1914; University of Nebraska Press, 1965) is cited in the mountain man section. Townsend's narrative was not limited, however, by his professional interests, and he was at his most instructive in his descriptions of his experiences among the mountain men of that period — 1834 — and among the various Indian tribes that he visited.

Townshend, R(ichard) B(axter), *A Tenderfoot in Colorado* (Dodd, Mead, 1923) O.P.; reprinted by the University of Oklahoma Press.

Townshend arrived in the American West in 1869, from his native England, where he had been schooled in Latin, French, and Cambridge English. He was taken with the Western vernacular, as he heard it spoken, and as Mark Twain (see below) he tried his best to reproduce it in his memoir. Townshend was involved with the effort to deprive the Ute Indians of their lands — gold had been discovered and Townshend accompanied the federal commission appointed to preserve the peace — and, eventually, he bought a cattle ranch twenty-five miles East of Colorado Springs which he sold out in 1874. This is the period covered in his book. Townshend had numerous other experiences subsequently, not recorded here, and, at thirty-three years of age, he returned to England, married, entered academic life, and, among other activities, translated Tacitus. Townshend's reminiscences are among the most articulate of any we have, and they recreate inimitably the experience of the free range era.

Twain, Mark (pseud. Samuel Clemens), *Roughing It* (1872); *Life on the Mississippi* (1883).

It is possible to complain about these books that there is no doubt more fiction in them than true reporting, that the style and tone are such as to appeal to an Eastern audience, that "reality" is altered or downright distorted for the sake of a humorous anecdote, that they have no real structure, and that the author is frequently distracted into extraneous, albeit amusing, irrelevancies — and be right on every count while missing their most essential quality: they are an unending delight to read and re-read. If one is concerned about any or all of the above-stated objections, then Mark Twain would not be an author to seek out; but he was an observer of the human condition and he perceived better than most of his generation the variety, absurdity, contradictoriness, greed, violence, cunning, hypocrisy, and energy of the American national character.

Part II

The Land

The Fur Trade

by Paul J. Blanding

I

Unlike the cry "Gold!," the cry "Furs!" could not empty a frontier town in a few days. Yet the fur trade was more important as a motive force in early exploration of the North American continent than was the search for precious metals. Large fortunes were made in that, according to one observer, the fur resources were "not surpassed by the mines of Peru." One such fortune was accumulated by John Jacob Astor, a butcher's son from Waldorf in Germany who landed on American shores in 1784 with a handful of change and seven flutes. In fifteen years Astor was the equivalent of a multimillionaire and by the time he died in 1848 he was the richest man in America. The "secret" of his success was the fur trade. Of course, the fur trade as a path to wealth was not really a secret by Astor's time. Europeans had begun trading with Native Americans for animal skins almost from the day they "discovered" North America.

The fur of small mammals such as beaver, muskrat, fox, and lynx were easily transportable by water and valuable in European markets and Sixteenth-century fishermen from many nations traded metal tools and utensils with coastal Indians in the new lands, not for gold, but for these furs. As the mercantile powers in Europe discovered this lucrative trade, greater manpower and organization were brought to bear in its exploitation. The French colonized the St. Lawrence, the Dutch New York, and the

English established a great trading company in the region around Hudson Bay. One by one the English overcame their rivals for control of the fur lands, final victory coming over the French in the French and Indian War (Seven Years War) in 1759. Although British interests would control the fur trade for the next half century and the Anglo-Americans would wrest control from them as they came to dominate the continent, the trade would always retain the flavor, the techniques, and language of its early French participants. Trading post/forts, the use of alcohol to turn Native Americans into pliant consumer-laborers, and a developed European market for furs, are elements of the trade that pre-dated and persisted throughout the Anglo-American take-over.

The whole story of the American fur trade cannot be reduced to focus on the individual or even a single fur company, but the reader, faced with a maze of names, dates, fur companies and their forts, might find it helpful to use the story of the American Fur Company (or "the Company") and its founder, John Jacob Astor, as a sort of lodestone, always guiding one towards the central events in the fur trade from 1806–1840. Such use would not be arbitrary, for Astor himself attempted to centralize the American fur trade under his own leadership and to monopolize its profits. He came close to succeeding.

It was the Lewis and Clark expedition that opened the eyes of the young American nation to the riches in the lands beyond the Mississippi whose fur resources were then being exploited by British companies based in Canada. Astor's first bold move, after incorporation of the American Fur Company in 1808, was to end-run these British concerns by establishing a post at the mouth of the Columbia River, a post that would act both as a collection point for furs from the interior and as a shipping depot for the lucrative China trade. Fort Astoria was founded in 1811, but Astor's plans collapsed with the outbreak of the War of 1812 and his post was sold to British interests in 1813. This episode ended the American attempt to dominate the fur trade from the Pacific shore. That domination would come, though more slowly, through control of the interior of the continent, especially control of that great water highway, the Missouri River.

A French, then a Spanish, then again a French, and finally an American city, St. Louis was the key to the Missouri. Led by Manuel Lisa, its small but vital community of merchant/traders ventured up river even before the return of Lewis and Clark and established trade with some tribes. Under the name The Missouri Fur Company, Lisa and his partners made a brave attempt to expand the trade farther, but the unremitting hostility of the Blackfoot Indians and certain other tribes blocked many of these efforts at a great cost of lives. The War of 1812 disrupted the Missouri trade just as it destroyed Astor's plans for Astoria, but the trailblazing efforts of the Missouri Fur Company continued through 1820 (the year of Lisa's death) and beyond. Astor, who had consolidated his hold on the cis-Mississippi trade after the war, made overtures to the St. Louis traders but was generally during this period rebuffed by them.

Our standard image of the fur trade revolves around the romantic image of the free trapper or mountain man, a hardy individualist, living alone (or perhaps with an Indian wife) in the mountains, tending trap lines in the fall and spring, "holed up" in some rude shelter during the bitter cold of winter, drinking and gambling away his profits in a brief orgy at the summer rendezvous. While this picture is not an entirely false one, especially of the Rocky Mountain trade that thrived in the period after 1820, it ignores many essential components of the earlier trade and exaggerates the importance of purely individual efforts. The fur trade in North America was big business. The collection and transportation of large numbers of furs was a job that required many hours of tedious labor, much of which was done by French-Canadian and French-American laborers working for the various trading companies. Wages were low for the average worker and a sort of "company store" system often kept him in debt to his employer for life. The trapping of beaver and the hunting of larger animals, while a pursuit of both free trappers and the Euro-American employees of the fur companies, was often accomplished through the labor of Native Americans. The Indians came to desire the metal tools, bright clothing, colorful adornments, and alcohol that trade with the whites could provide. They paid a huge price for such items, both culturally and materially, for European notions of property, credit, and labor disrupted traditional patterns of existence, the introduction of alcohol and epidemic diseases destroyed the health of whole tribes, and the obscene markup on trade goods by traders robbed them of the just fruits of their labor.

The period between 1820 and 1840 was the heyday of the American fur trade. A vanguard of trappers broke a trail Westward, exploring the interior of the continent and discovering rich trapping grounds. General William Ashley's expeditions out of St. Louis in the early 1820s created the Rocky Mountain fur trade, a trade characterized by the use of brigades of American trappers who lived in the mountains and worked for the Rocky Mountain Fur Company (the powerful company created by Ashley's successors) or one of its competitors. Such famous mountain men as Jedediah Smith, William Sublette, Thomas Fitzpatrick, Jim Bridger, and Joe Meek formed the backbone of the Rocky Mountain Fur Company during this period of high profits and high risks. While these intrepid mountain men were opening up the Rockies to the fur trade, John Jacob Astor was a step behind, buying up the Missouri River trade. With a foot in the St. Louis door by 1823, Astor went about forming partnerships with many of the leading traders of that city. In 1827 he bought out the Columbia Fur Company, the leading outfit on the upper Missouri, and his monopoly of that river's trade was virtually complete.

It was only after the consolidation of the Missouri trade that Astor set his sights on the Rocky Mountains. The period from 1830 to 1834 was a rough-and-tumble one in which the Rocky Mountain Fur Company fought off the attempts of Astor's American Fur Company (and several smaller competitors such as Captain Benjamin Bonneville and the ill-used Nathaniel Wyeth) to retain control of the mountain trade. The American Fur Company won out in the end, but the victory came late in the game. The mountain streams that had once been home to so many beaver were becoming trapped out. The European market for beaver fur was on the wane as hatters substituted other fur in the felting process and styles swung toward silk hats. Astor saw the proverbial handwriting and sold the American Fur Company in 1834. "The Company" kept the rendezvous system alive for another five years, but the Rocky Mountain trade slowly lost its vitality. This was not the end of the American fur trade, however, since an important trade in buffalo robes and other furs continued on the upper Missouri through the Civil War period and individual trappers remained in the mountains often trading their furs at the trading post/forts that ringed the Rockies (especially Bent's Fort, Fort Hall, and Fort Laramie); but the legendary era when furs were gold had come to an end. John Jacob Astor retired to tend his New York real estate investments. The men who worked for him and the other traders became lawmen or Army scouts or farmers or drunks (few could retire on their earnings). Native Americans played "host" to wave after wave of new immigrants, then became unwanted "guests" in their own land. Eventually the beaver came back in more remote streams, but by then the land was changed, the era gone.

II

i

The American fur trade is a topic well covered by historians and writers on the West. Presently, most of the major academic squabbles around the subject have been put to rest, except, perhaps, the question of the relationship between Native Americans and the trade, a question which is still of lively interest to contemporary historians. The evidential foundation for fur trade history is (relatively) broad, based as it is on copious written material (journals, letters, fur company records, etc.). The problem, then, for the general reader is one of an abundance rather than of a dearth of resources. Moreover, some of the general histories of the trade are written in the best literary tradition.

In the present book the American fur trade has been divided into two parts: general histories of the fur trade and fur companies which are annotated below in this section; and biographies and books dealing specifically with the personnel of the trade which are to be found in the section on Traders, Trappers, and Mountain Men.

The reader who wants a brief general introduction to the subject of the American fur trade is directed to either Ray Allen Billington's *The Far Western Frontier: 1830–1860* (Harper's, 1956) or Robert V. Hine's *The American West: An Interpretive History* (Little, Brown, 1973), both which contain overview chapters on the subject.

Finally, a note about the British fur companies based in Canada, the Hudson's Bay Company and the North West Company. A whole literature exists on these great British fur companies. No attempt is made here to introduce the reader to this literature, yet some elements of the American fur trade are inextricably linked with these British firms. The reader who is interested in this subject beyond its mention in the general histories annotated below is directed to John S. Galbraith's *The Hudson's Bay Company as an Imperial Factor* (University of California Press, 1957).

II

ii

Berry, Don, *A Majority of Scoundrels: An Informal History of the Rocky Mountain Fur Company* (Harper's, 1961) O.P.

Don Berry claimed to be an "amateur of history," but he was every bit the professional writer. This book combines accurate scholarship with entertaining narrative and is recommended as one of the reading joys of fur trade history. Beginning with General Ashley's first venture into the fur trade in 1822, Berry followed the various permutations of the trading company that would become the Rocky Mountain Fur Company and ended with its demise at the rendezvous of 1834. Berry never lost sight of his source material and was always above board concerning gaps in the historical record or instances where his interpretation of events differed from that of others. His appendices, covering the government factory system, the expeditions of Captain Benjamin Bonneville and Nathaniel Wyeth, and his reading of the sources are all valuable additions to the general narrative.

Chittenden, Hiram M., *The American Fur Trade of the Far West* (F.P. Harper, 1902) O.P.; reprinted by Stanford University Press in two volumes.

This work has long been considered the standard history of the American fur trade, but the appellation "old classic" should not put the reader off in this case. Chittenden's work is a model of good historical writing. He divided the subject into cogent sub-topics; the nature and character of the trade, the historical narrative, important background events to the fur trade era, notable characters and incidents of the trade, and the natural and human environment for the events; and he also included important documents, a list of trading posts (with short descriptions of each), and miscellaneous data in the appendices of the work. While the date of composition makes it inevitable that some events or their interpretations have been revised through the work of more recent historical studies, Chittenden's overall outline of the trade remains sound. If you can read only one book on the American fur trade, this should be the one.

Cleland, Robert Glass, *This Reckless Breed of Men: The Trappers and Fur Traders of the Southwest* (Knopf, 1950) O.P.; reprinted by the University of New Mexico Press.

The first half of this book, which deals with the mountain fur trade in general and with Jedediah Smith's exploratory expeditions, has little to recommend it over other works on the subject. Where this book is useful is in its treatment of the Taos trappers, that is, American trappers who worked the Southwestern Rocky Mountain region using Taos (then Mexican territory) as their base. James Ohio Pattie, Ewing Young, "Old" Bill Williams, and Joseph R. Walker are all portrayed, and Cleland gave an overview of the conditions of the Southwestern fur trade as well. Although superseded to some degree by Weber's more recent work (see below), this book can still serve as an introduction to the fur trade in this region.

De Voto, Bernard, *Across the Wide Missouri* (Houghton Mifflin, 1947).
A history of the Rocky Mountain fur trade, this book is a mixture of strengths and weaknesses which makes its overall characterization problematic. De Voto covered material not presented by Dale L. Morgan (see below) and provided useful perspectives on the fur trade, especially his presentation of Eastern American and European visions of the West during this period. De Voto's overall scholarship cannot be faulted, and yet his treatment leaves something to be desired. His narrative lacks the clarity one desires in a history and his treatment often lacks structure.

Gowans, Fred R., *Rocky Mountain Rendezvous: A History of the Fur Trade Rendezvous* 1825–1840 (Brigham Young University Press, 1975).
This work is not a real page turner, and I cannot imagine most people reading it cover to cover. However, it is useful as a reference tool since it is a chronological sketch of each of the rendezvous, using excerpts from eyewitness accounts. A black and white photograph and a simple map of each rendezvous site give some indication of the geography of this institution, and the bibliography (specifically rendezvous-oriented) is a jumping-off point for the reader with some deep interest in the subject.

Irving, Washington, *Adventures of Captain Bonneville* (1850) O.P.; reprinted by the University of Oklahoma Press, edited by Edgeley Todd; *Astoria; or Anecdotes of an Enterprise Beyond the Rocky Mountains* (1836) O.P.; reprinted by the University of Oklahoma Press, edited by Edgeley Todd.
Hubert Howe Bancroft accused Irving of fictionalizing much of this material; consequently these two works have had a poor reputation as accurate history. However, no less an authority than Hiram Chittenden helped vindicate Irving of Bancroft's charge, and as Edgeley Todd stated in his Introduction to *Astoria*, "Not only is *Astoria* generally dependable as history, but it also has literary merit." It is a statement that also holds true for the companion book.
Adventures of Captain Bonneville deals with Bonneville's exploits. He took leave from the Army and in 1832 led a party of trappers into the Rockies to seek their fortune. Bonneville turned out to be only a minor figure in the Rocky Mountain trade, but Irving's work gives the reader a

good picture of mountain life during this period. *Astoria* is perhaps more important to overall fur trade history, being a history of Astor's quest for empire on the Columbia River. Irving had access to Astor (a personal friend) and to his company's papers, as well as to many eyewitnesses to the events at Fort Astoria, and this remains one of the important histories of the venture.

Lavender, David, *Bent's Fort* (Doubleday, 1954) O.P.; reprinted by the University of Nebraska Press; *The Fist in the Wilderness* (Doubleday, 1965) O.P.; reprinted by the University of New Mexico Press.
    The partners, William and Charles Bent and Ceran St. Vrain, established one of the most important trading post/forts in fur trade history in 1833 in the Southeast corner of what is now Colorado. Lavender's narrative follows the partners' early lives (they were trappers, then traders in the Santa Fe trade), covers the building of the fort and the halcyon days of the partnership (1833–1848), and ends with the decline of Bent family fortunes and William Bent's death in 1869. The scope of *Bent's Fort* also extends far beyond the individual lives of the partners to encompass not only much fur trade history, but also much material on the Santa Fe trade and the Plains Indians (especially the Cheyennes). *The Fist in the Wilderness* is the story of the American Fur Company, focusing on the life of Ramsay Crooks (Astor's second in command). Lavender contended that Crooks was the "true fist in the wilderness," and that it was Astor who had to leash Crooks' daring and expansionist temperament. Whoever was truly the "fist," this work serves as a history of John Jacob Astor's American Fur Company, and, as all of Lavender's work, is dense with fact and anecdote, requiring attention (and perhaps a little background) from the reader. Your attention will be well rewarded.

Morgan, Dale L., *Jedediah Smith and the Opening of the West* (Bobbs-Merrill, 1953) O.P.; reprinted by the University of Nebraska Press.
    Though its title would indicate that this book is a biography, it is, as Don Berry once stated, "a meticulous chronicle of the trade during the years 1822–1831" and uses Jedediah Smith only as a focal point. Smith was a trapper, fur company partner, and perhaps the most important of the Trans-Mississippi American explorers other than Lewis and Clark. Morgan began his narrative at St. Louis in 1822 and followed Smith into the mountains, through his adventures on the Pacific Coast, to his death at the hands of the Comanches on a trading expedition to Santa Fe. Two appendices include the letters Smith wrote concerning his explorations and the bibliographic footnotes are among the best on the period.

Oglesby, Richard E., *Manuel Lisa and the Opening of the Missouri Fur Trade* (University of Oklahoma Press, 1963) O.P.
    The era between the Lewis and Clark expedition and Ashley's expeditions of the 1820s has not been focused on by fur trade historians as has the post-Ashley period, yet this earlier phase of the trade abounds in colorful

characters, intrigue (both commercial and international), and harrowing adventures to equal anything in the later heyday of the Rocky Mountain trade. Oglesby, while concentrating on the shadowy figure of Lisa, explored the whole realm of the early Missouri trade: early St. Louis, its trading families, the Osage trade, the War of 1812, and the Missouri Fur Company in all its incarnations. This is the best book on an important era.

Phillips, Paul C., *The Fur Trade* (University of Oklahoma Press, 1961) in two volumes with concluding chapters by J.W. Smurr.

This survey is the closest that the reader will come to a comprehensive history of the North American fur trade. Volume one deals with the European and colonial phases of the trade, beginning in the Sixteenth century and concluding with the American Revolution. Volume two surveys fur trade history from the Revolutionary period through the Nineteenth century. The reader should come to this work armed with a fanatical interest in the fur trade and plenty of time. The work contains a bibliography of over seventy-five pages.

Sandoz, Mari, *The Beaver Men: Spearheads of Empire* (Hastings House, 1964); reprinted by the University of Nebraska Press.

This book is inferior to much of the rest of Sandoz' work. The history can be described as less than reliable, and the lyrical conjuring up of places and events, long past, is missing, perhaps because Sandoz tried to illuminate such a vast period of time (1623–1834). It cannot really be recommended.

Saum, Lewis O., *The Fur Trader and the Indian* (University of Washington Press, 1965).

The reader interested in the perspectives of Native Americans on the American fur trade will be hard pressed to find a general work on the subject. Oscar Lewis' *The Effects of White Contact Upon Blackfoot Culture with Special Reference to the Role of the Fur Trade* (Columbia University Press, 1942), while excellent, is a specialized anthropological work; and Calvin Martin's provocative *Keepers of the Game* (University of California Press, 1978) deals largely with Canadian tribes. That leaves Saum's book. Although it would be better sub-titled "The Fur Trader's View of the Indian," this book's strength lies in its fairly comprehensive review of what fur traders (not trappers) wrote about the Indian. However, Saum made little attempt to compare the fur traders' views with that of the Indians themselves or to explain Native American cultures from other than the traders' perspective. This treatment leaves the reader with a lopsided view of Indian cultures, or perhaps more accurately, with a view of white (middle-class) culture and no reliable view of Native American cultures at all. Let us hope that a more balanced work is in the offing.

Sunder, John E., *The Fur Trade on the Upper Missouri*, 1840–1865 (University of Oklahoma Press, 1965).

The period covered by this book (1840–1865) is neglected by many of the writers of the fur trade, perhaps because it was a period of transition and decline for the American trade. The American Fur Company was splintered, the Rocky Mountain rendezvous were discontinued, and frontier economic activity, fueled by the overland migration of settlers and miners, shifted from fur gathering toward other endeavors. Yet the fur trade was far from dead and the various reorganizations of the American Fur Company still held sway in large portions of the upper Missouri country. As such, this is the best work on the period.

Weber, David J., *The Taos Trappers: The Fur Trade in the Far Southwest*, 1540–1846 (University of Oklahoma Press, 1971).

This book enlarges upon and, in many ways, supersedes the work of Robert Cleland (see above) although that earlier work still holds some merit as an introduction to the area. Weber went to Mexican archival sources to produce the other side of the Taos story, balancing the American side of the tale with the reactions of the Mexican authorities and the people of Taos to the invasion of their territory by a wild and "reckless" group of American free trappers. Weber also covered the early history of fur trading in Taos, including the Spanish colonial and the Comanche trade.

Wishart, David J., *The Fur Trade of the American West 1807–1840: A Geographical Synthesis* (University of Nebraska Press, 1979).

This analysis is not a history of the personalities or events of the American fur trade; rather it is an attempt to synthesize "the general characteristics of the whole," as the author stated, by studying "the interrelationships between the biological, physical, and cultural environments of the fur trade." The reader should not be put off by the occasional social-scientific jargon, for this little book really does help one understand the physical realities behind the history. Wishart described the geographic boundaries of the fur trade, explained the pertinent biological characteristics of the beaver, the buffalo, and other fur bearers, and explained the difference in strategies used in the upper Missouri trade as opposed to those in the Rocky Mountain trade. Further his concerns about our romanticization of what was an essentially environmentally destructive past are to the point. An added plus is the short, but up-to-date, bibliography.

Suggested Fiction

Fisher, Vardis, *Pemmican: A Novel of the Old Hudson Bay Territory* (Doubleday, 1956)

Suggested Film

Hudson's Bay (20th- Fox, 1941) directed by Irving Pichel.

The Mining Frontier

by Vicki Piekarski

I

A conversation about rainbows and their supposed riches both charming and fitting to the subject at hand was related by Marian Russell in her book, *Land of Enchantment* (1954; University of New Mexico Press, 1981).

"'Mother, is it really true about the pot of gold?' I asked, awed by Will's [Marian's brother] knowledge. She sat perched on the end gate of the great wagon, her eyes on the red splendor. 'They say so, child,' was her only answer.

"'Why the end of the rainbow is just beyond the little green hill before us. If Will will come with me, we will bring the pot of gold to you.' I was delighted.

"Mother's eyes came to rest on her small daughter. She smiled as she answered. 'The end of the rainbow is always much farther away than it seems, dear. If you climb the green hill the rainbow will still be before you. I think, perhaps, that it rests in California at a place called Sutter's Fort. We can only follow the rainbow and hope that it leads to fame and fortune.'

"For years I thought that the end of the rainbow was in California."

Indeed, so did many others, particularly in 1848 and 1849 when California was rich in placer deposits — loose gold easily mined from sandbars, gravel banks, or potholes in streambeds — and considered a poor

187

man's paradise. At the time of Russell's conversation with her mother—
1852—the rush to California had subsided. Nevertheless the discovery of
gold in January, 1848 on the South Fork of the American River had changed drastically the settlement pattern and the economy of both California
and the Far West. Subsequent discoveries of precious and base metals and
the development of a mining industry in California and twelve other
Western states in the last half of the Nineteenth century opened unattrac-
tive and remote lands which might have remained untouched but for the
echoing call of "gold" heard around the globe to both widespread invasion and grand-scale exploitation.

The Mining Frontier was never a static or stable one. It shifted from
region to region and each went through periods of "bonanza"—a Spanish
term meaning fine weather—and "borrasca"—a Spanish term meaning
foul weather. California produced the first, the most spectacular, and the
largest rush of men ever experienced West of the Big Drink (the Mississippi
River) and many of these men came to gamble their lives and their livelihoods in numerous subsequent "strikes" throughout the West. In 1858 an
estimated thirty thousand miners left California for the Fraser River in
British Columbia, only to find that the stories of gold had been greatly exaggerated. That same year rumors of placer color in Colorado were cir-
culated. The second largest gold rush resulted in 1859 when wagons pri-
marily from the Midwest and South, bearing the words "Pike's Peak or
Bust," blanketed the trails into Colorado, then part of Kansas territory.
The pattern of Western settlement was reversed in an Eastward direction
in 1859–1860 when 10,000 California miners headed for the silver mines of
Nevada's Comstock Lode—the region that was immortalized in Mark
Twain's Roughing It (1872). The decade of the 1860s saw discoveries in the
Pacific Northwest, Utah, Idaho, and Montana, the latter two offering rich
placer deposits, again, to the self-employed miner with limited capital. In
the 1870s silver was discovered in Arizona and New Mexico; and the Black
Hills of Dakota territory beckoned gold-seekers to its riches in spite of Sioux
and military opposition. The last strike of the century was in Nome,
Alaska, where placer gold was found in the beach sands in 1899. Fifty years
of discoveries on the ever-shifting Mining Frontier kept get-rich-quick
dreams alive, creating a restless population inflicted with a disease called
"gold fever."

Each mining frontier went through a similar "life cycle" with slight
variations due to the topography and climate of the region as well as the
type and amount of mineral yield. It began with the individual and the
discovery. Most discoveries were not accidental, but instead, based on an
extensive, demanding, prolonged search by a prospector, a man who
according to historian Otis E. Young possessed "a soldier's eye for terrain,
an artist's sensitivity for color, and a gopher's ability to dig." The prospector, differing from the miner in that he was generally the first to penetrate a
new mining district, usually did not work alone, but in partnership or in
small bands—as did the miner—since working in numbers was safer for
obvious reasons. Once the discovery was made, the local miners moved in.

A rush period followed lasting anywhere from months to years, or as long as optimism and individual earnings of the self-employed miners ran high. A rush reduced drastically, however, the take of gold per miner and drove up the cost of living as the availability of supplies, housing, and food decreased as the population increased. The ideal foundation for a rush was placer mining, but lode or vein deposits, as in the cases of Colorado and Nevada, could attract numbers sufficient to constitute a rush.

Once the easy, surface ore was exhausted by the pocket miner and his simple tools—pan, shovel, pick, rocker, cradle, long tom, and sluice box—a mining frontier was ready to make the transition to underground hardrock mining which was dependent upon capital investment, trained mining expertise, and expensive, sophisticated machinery. (Prior to the decade of the 1870s—a period in which a sort of technological revolution hit the American mining industry—the mining methods and materials in use were borrowed and adapted, although on a larger scale, from classical and medieval times and introduced in California by Europeans, Mexican-Americans, and, from the United States, Georgians, who had learned the age-old methods when gold was discovered in the Southeastern United States nine years after Benjamin Franklin had said in 1790 that "gold and silver are not the produce of North America which has no mines.") In the last stage of the cycle, a mining district witnessed a corporate takeover capable of absorbing the costly operation of vein mining, and, the self-employed miner, if he chose to stay, became a wage-earner. The combination of extremely hazardous working conditions, long hours, and nominal wages ultimately led to the Western labor movement and, beginning in the 1890s, fierce and sometimes bloody labor disputes and strikes.

One of the more interesting aspects of The Mining Frontier was the mining camp. These mud-ridden, disorderly settlements planted in gulches and along mountain slopes in danger of being swept off the map by a flash flood, a fire, or an epidemic, were make-shift in appearance and made more so by the names they were given—Hangtown, Bedbug, Hoodoo Bar, Cutthroat, Bladderville, and Gouge Eye. In the first study about the significance of mining camps, *Mining Camps: A Study in American Frontier Government* (1884), the author, Charles Howard Shinn, paraphrasing and very nearly plagiarizing the words of Prentice Mulford's article in an 1871 issue of *Overland Monthly*, described a typical mining camp of 1849. They were "flush, lively, reckless, flourishing, and vigorous. Saloons and gambling-houses abounded; buildings and whole streets grew up like mushrooms, almost in a night. Every man carried a buckskin bag of gold-dust, and it was received as currency at a dollar a pinch. Every one went armed, and felt fully able to protect himself. A stormy life ebbed and flowed through the town. In the camp, gathered as of one household, under no law but that of their own making, were men from North, South, East, and West, and from nearly every country.... They mined, traded, gambled, fought, discussed camp affairs; they paid fifty cents a drink for their whiskey, and fifty dollars a barrel for the flour, and thirty dollars apiece for butcher knives with which to pick gold...."

The mining camp was a distinctly masculine environment where few restraints were imposed and fewer questions asked. In all things behavior was prone to excess for the stakes were high and mining was difficult and monotonous work. In a lighter moment it was once said that only two types of men drank in the mining camps, the one fifth who were lucky and the four-fifths who were not. Prostitution, a topic left unessayed by the shy Shinn, provided the inhabitants with female companionship of which there was otherwise very little. The point is often made that on The Mining Frontier women were held in high esteem — which they were — but ignored is the fact that mining frontier prostitutes often suffered horrible lives and worse deaths, many of which were self-induced.

A great many mining camps never outgrew the frontier stage, created by a boom period; they just withered away and died a ghost town's death. Others, having outlived the slump following a boom, experienced a sort of *renaissance* during which time brick buildings replaced rows of tents and slat shacks, symbolizing a determination on the part of the citizenry to remain permanent. Within a brief span of time these urbanized mining towns boasted newspapers with some of the saltiest journalism in the West as well as theatres in which lecturers, musicians, singers, and actors entertained and informed the enthusiastic patrons. There were, of course, gutsier exhibitions for those who preferred them. Some of these seemingly incongruent cultural meccas developed into permanent Western cities as San Francisco, Denver, Butte, and Helena. Others struggled and suffered more through the boom or bust process.

In spite of the cosmopolitan flavor of the mining community, within a mining district's borders open racial discrimination of the worst kind was practiced. Monthly taxes were imposed upon the minority miners with the intention of driving them out if they were not in fact driven out by force. The Chinese received particularly harsh treatment since they undercut the wages charged by whites both in the mines and in business pursuits. Newspapers railed against "the almond-eyed Mongolian with his pigtail, his heathenism, his filthy habits," a "devourer of soup made from the fragrant juice of the rat," reinforcing the bigotry of the community. The Chinese immigrant was often the victim of violence on The Mining Frontier as were Mexicans, blacks, and Indians.

Native Americans, of course, were the original keepers of much of the land off which Anglo-Americans and Europeans fed their hunger for wealth. But the role of Indians in histories about mining has been limited to that of a nuisance. Wars, if they interfered with mining development and mineral exploitation, are touched upon briefly with the Indian taking the villainous part. For the white man The Mining Frontier meant a tremendous boost in the economy, the development of a new industry, swift Westward expansion, and booms creating jobs and money in the areas of transportation, trading, and agriculture. But what did it do to the native cultures when their land was wrenched from them for exploitation purposes to the point of exhaustion? Until studies examining what effects specifically were felt by the numerous Indian tribes involved, we will have to rely on scattered statements by Native Americans themselves. "We have sat and watched them pass here to get gold out," said Mawatani Hanska, a Mandan, "and have said nothing. My friends, when I went to Washington I went into your money-house and I had some young men with me, but none of them took any money out of the house while I was with them. At the same time, when your Great Father's people come into my country, they go into my money-house and take money out."

And so the white man still is making withdrawals from the money-house of the Native American. The dream of finding the Seven Cities of Cibola is never-ending.

II

i

The area of study falling under the heading "mining" is both broad and complex requiring, in addition to a knowledge of history, a familiarity with metallurgy, geology, chemistry, mechanics, and economics. The selections in the following annotated bibliography are limited to the standard books intended for the non-professional. Some highly technical and specialized books, reports, and journals can be found listed in the excellent bibliographies appended to Otis E. Young's *Western Mining* (University of Oklahoma, 1970) and Rodman W. Paul's *Mining Frontiers of the Far West 1848–1880* (Holt, Rinehart, 1963).

Considering the vast literature written on the various aspects of mining and Western mining frontiers, surprisingly few satisfactory general surveys have appeared. As yet no extensive history of all the mining frontiers of the Nineteenth century has been essayed. The Western mining histories extant are cursory, anecdotal surveys or are limited by the period covered — Rodman W. Paul's *Mining Frontiers of the Far West* covers a period from 1848–1880 — or by other arbitrary limitations — William Greever's *The Bonanza West* (University of Oklahoma Press, 1963) deals with "great" rushes and excludes coverage of the Southwest and Northwest. However, if read in tandem Greever's and Paul's books will provide an essential framework for an understanding of the Western mining frontiers.

A reader interested only in a brief introduction to mining is directed to *The Reader's Encyclopedia of the American West* (Crowell, 1977) edited by Howard R. Lamar. The entries contributed by historians Otis E. Young and Rodman Paul, among others, under the headings "Gold and Silver Rushes," "Mining, metal," "Mining, engineer," "Mining Law," "Mining Towns," and "Prospector" are well written and include basic information.

Good books examining mining in individual states and regions, with the exception of California, are hard to come by. Although they are filled with material not germane to mining, state histories are often the best sourcebook for this area of study. Some specialty studies are useful and noteworthy contributions. William J. Trimble's *The Mining Advance into the Inland Empire: A Comparative Study of the Beginnings of the Mining Industry in Idaho and Montana, Eastern Washington and Oregon, and the Southern Interior of British Columbia; and of Institutions and Laws Based Upon the Industry* (University of Wisconsin, "Bulletin," III, No. 2, 1914) and *A Reconsideration of the Gold Discoveries in the Northwest* (Mississippi Valley Historical Association, V, June, 1918) are highly recommended for the study of Northwest mining, an area terribly neglected. No study of the Comstock Lode should be made without reading Grant H. Smith's *The History of the Comstock Lode* 1850–1920 (University of Nevada, "Bulletin," XXXVII, No. 3, 1943) which corrects many of the errors in popular contemporary accounts. The best regional mining history is Watson Parker's *Gold in the Black Hills* (University of Oklahoma Press, 1966), a well organized, meticulously detailed study that should serve as an inspiration to and model for historians contemplating the writing of an in-depth examination of mining in a select region or state.

Because no comprehensive bibliographic sourcebook on mining exists currently, a reader curious about biographies, autobiographies, diaries, first-hand accounts, and reminiscences about The Mining Frontier will have to rely on the bibliographies contained in various mining histories. (*Roughing It* [1872] by Mark Twain is a must—and in a class by itself.) Fourteen accessible and interesting sources, excluded from the annotations below which stress the land and not the people, are listed here.

Adney, Tappan, *The Klondike Stampede* (1899)
Bennett, Estelline, *Old Deadwood Days* (J.H. Sears, 1928)
Chisholm, James, *South Pass: James Chisholm's Journal of the Wyoming Gold Rush* (University of Nebraska Press, 1960), edited by Lola M. Homsher
Clappe, Louise Amelia Knapp, *The Shirley Letters from the California Mines* 1851–1852 (Knopf, 1949), edited by Carl I. Wheat
Conner, Daniel E., *A Confederate in the Colorado Gold Fields* (University of Oklahoma Press, 1970)
Donaldson, Thomas, *Idaho of Yesterday* (Caxton Printers, 1941)
Ellis, Anne, *The Life of an Ordinary Woman* (1929; University of Nebraska Press, 1980)
Hafen, LeRoy R., (ed.), *Colorado Gold Rush, Contemporary Letters and Reports* 1858–1859 (Arthur H. Clark, 1941)
Hughes, Richard, *Pioneer Years in the Black Hills* (Arthur H. Clark, 1957), edited by Agnes W. Spring
Lockwood, Frank, *Pioneer Days in Arizona* (Macmillan, 1932)
Miller, James Knox Polk, *The Road to Virginia City: The Diary of James Knox Polk Miller* (University of Oklahoma Press, 1960), edited by Andrew F. Rolle
Parker, Morris B., *White Oaks: Life in a New Mexico Gold Camp* 1880–1900 (University of Arizona Press, 1971), edited by C.L. Sonnichsen

Reinhart, Herman Francis, *The Golden Frontier: The Recollections of Herman Francis Reinhart* (University of Texas, 1962), edited by Doyce B. Nunis

Stuart, Granville, *Prospecting for Gold: From Dogtown to Virginia City 1852-1864* (University of Nebraska Press, 1977)

ii

Dobie, J. Frank, *Coronado's Children* (The Southwest Press, 1930); *Apache Gold and Yaqui Silver* (Little, Brown, 1939), both O.P.; both reprinted by the University of Texas Press.

These two books are the best examples of the "lost mine and buried treasure" genre. Dobie collected and recorded centuries of fabulous tales about Southwestern lost Indian diggings, haunted mines, hidden Spanish caches, and concealed deposits of ore so rich in color that they could blind the eyes of the uncoverer. Although strictly books of folklore and utterly worthless in the study of mining and its history, it must be said that the legends contained in both books make for fascinating and compelling reading and remain a continuing source of material for writers of fiction.

Fisher, Vardis, and Opal Laurel Holmes, *Gold Rushes and Mining Camps of the Early American West* (Caxton Printers, 1968).

For her many hours of research over the years on this and other Fisher projects, Opal Holmes (Fisher's wife) was credited as co-author of this impressive volume which was published in the last year of Fisher's life. Essentially it is a social history of The Mining Frontier attempting to encompass everything that is pertinent (and sometimes not) to the subject. Because its base is so broad, it lacks any real cohesive structure and is thus not as good a book as it might have been. However, it is a constantly interesting work replete with stories of humor, tragedy, violence, and humanity and contains well selected and rare photographs, including four of Calamity Jane. An iconoclast whose literary output was immense, Fisher recognized that "when we enter books about the West we are in the realm of legend," and the book opens with a chapter condemning historians for their near canonization of such frontier personalities as Billy the Kid. Nonetheless, Fisher, too, often stressed the legendary aspects of the West and its people and he relied heavily upon questionable sources without apparently doubting their veracity. The book is divided into four major sections: "Gold Rushes" which focuses primarily on California mining and includes material on fables, metallurgy, and overland travel; "Life in the Camps" which covers cursorily a great many topics, among them camplife, camp inhabitants, food, culture, entertainment, prostitution, and sports; "Crime and Justice" in which too much time is spent on badmen and the Montana vigilantes but which contains some excellent material on lawyers, judges, jails, and juries; and finally, "Special Characters and Situations" in which biographical sketches of mining successes, failures, and adventuresses are recounted as well as accounts of duels, journalistic feuds, and tall tales. Fisher should be commended on the amount of space he devoted to women, which is substantial, albeit preoccupied with the famous and infamous. His personal preferences and prejudices are reflected throughout the work especially on the subject of Native Americans whom he regarded as being a basically lazy and dirty lot. In approaching this volume one is best advised to heed Fisher's own warning about Western books—"we must be alert on every page"—but it is well worth reading for Fisher's charming style and its vast store of information, including copious quotations from numerous primary sources.

Greever, William S., *The Bonanza West: The Story of the Western Mining Rushes*, 1848–1900 (University of Oklahoma Press, 1963).
	The general consensus among both historians and critics is that this book is a prime source on the American mining frontiers. I would have to agree, although I found that what kept me reading Greever's work was the informative material and not the author's narrative writing style which is excessively unimaginative. The author concentrated on what he called the "great" and "significant" rushes in the West and on this basis he excluded coverage of mining in the Pacific Northwest and the Southwest. However, the regions covered—California, Nevada, Colorado, Idaho, Montana, South Dakota, and Alaska—are covered extensively. The history of each mining frontier from the time of discovery is chronologically traced with especial emphasis placed on social and economic developments. Greever also characterized many of the key figures of each region, including literary figures and entertainers. Particularly helpful are Greever's brief chapter end summations in which he described the similarities and differences between the various mining frontiers. Containing a wealth of information, this book written with the general reader in mind is also useful for the scholar.

Lewis, Marvin, (ed.), *The Mining Frontier: Contemporary Accounts from the American West in the Nineteenth Century* (University of Oklahoma Press, 1967) O.P.
	Lewis edited and introduced this enjoyable collection of journalistic writings from the mining frontiers of California, Colorado, Nevada, Utah, Idaho, and Arizona. The selections demonstrate the broad scope of mining camp and boom town newssheets and papers while they present to the reader the life-styles, work habits, and concerns of the Nineteenth-century placer and hard-rock miner. A wide array of writers of varying talent are represented including the well known, e.g., Bret Harte, Mark Twain, and Joaquín Miller, and the pieces encompass the humorous and tragic sides of mining life. The book's weakness is its organization which is perhaps excusable due to the wide variety of topics covered in the pieces.

Paul, Rodman Wilson, *California Gold: The Beginning of Mining in the Far West* (Harvard University Press, 1947) O.P.; reprinted by the

University of Nebraska Press; *Mining Frontiers of the Far West:* 1848–1880 (Holt, Rinehart, 1963) O.P.; reprinted by the University of New Mexico Press; *The California Gold Discovery: Sources, Accounts, and Memoirs Relating to the Discovery of Gold at Sutter's Mill* (The Talisman Press, 1966) O.P.

Paul was the acknowledged authority on Western American mining frontiers. His infinitely readable but scholarly works on the subject are invaluable to both the non-professional and the savant. Two of his books have dealt specifically with mining in California. A standard work spanning a twenty-five year period (1848–1873), *California Gold* is the best detailed treatment of the evolution of mining in the state. In addition to tracing the development of California mining through three stages—flush period (1848–1851), transition period (1851–1860), and mature period (1860–1873)—Paul described the life-styles and work habits of the miner and addressed topics such as migration, wages, mining laws, and methods. He distinguished the California gold rush as an "international movement" in "which the whole world shared" since experienced Old World miners brought to California "the ideas, methods, and men without which the gold deposits of the Sierras would have long remained little more than a local curiosity."

The California Gold Discovery is a fascinating volume in which Paul assembled all the important documents, letters, oral testimonies, and reminiscences relating to the controversy over the specifics of the discovery of gold in 1848. Paul's commentary introduced each chapter and the final chapter contains the interpretations and conclusions of historians as Hubert Howe Bancroft and John S. Hittell about the contradictory evidence. This is an important book because it demonstrates perhaps better than any other single work the uncertainties involved in the process of historical inquiry.

A study not limited to California alone, *Mining Frontiers of the Far West*, is, to my mind, the best book written to date on mining between 1848–1880. Originally published as part of the "Histories of the American Frontier" series edited by Ray Allen Billington, it is a concise, comprehensive survey of mining in California, Nevada, Colorado, Idaho, Montana, New Mexico, Arizona, and South Dakota—with emphasis on the first two—and of the men who played significant roles in the organizing and development of a mining industry. It was the first mining history to show both the commercial and technological relationships between the various mining communities. This was accomplished by Paul's emphasis on the permanent features and phases of mining such as technical problems and advances and the importance of transportation routes and trade centers as San Francisco and St. Louis to the vitality of a mining frontier. In comparison to William Greever's book (see above), Paul's coverage of the social aspects of mining communities was cursory and, to avoid repetition, focussed on selected mining towns which illustrate best the stories of the mining centers. Particular attention was paid to the self-governing system of mining communities which is outlined in a separate chapter. This authoritative book exhibits Paul's masterful skill at synthesis and analysis and is highly recommended. It contains an excellent bibliographical essay limited to books published prior to 1963.

Shinn, Charles Howard, *Mining Camps: A Study in American Frontier Government* (1885); reprinted by Harper's, edited by Rodman Wilson Paul, both O.P.

Although the title of this ground-breaking book indicates extensive coverage of American mining camps, it deals, in fact, only with those of California. It is, however, an often-cited classic study of frontier law and the evolution of self-government in the California mining camps and is significant because Shinn recognized the historical significance of mining camps in the development of the West. The book's weakness, to a contemporary reader, is Shinn's attempt in the first third of the book to trace the origins of mining codes, to depict the Western mining era as a "stanza in the political epic of the Germanic race" — reflecting his training in the "scientific" study of history and politics at Johns Hopkins University. Nonetheless, the remaining two-thirds of the book is useful to the serious student because of Shinn's absorbing and well written examination and analysis of the California miners' behavior and customs with special emphasis on their self-government. The reader is directed to the Harper & Row edition which contains Paul's helpful Introduction on Shinn's background as well as his purpose and method of historical research.

Smith, Duane A., *Rocky Mountain Mining Camps: The Urban Frontier* (University of Indiana Press, 1967); reprinted by the University of Nebraska Press.

Smith's book is a fascinating study in which the role of the mining camp as the "urban center of the urbanized frontier" is examined. Spanning a period of time from 1859–1890, it is limited in its coverage to selected mining camps of the Rocky Mountain region (Utah, Wyoming, Idaho, Montana, and Colorado) and to South Dakota, Arizona, and New Mexico. Based on research into primary and secondary sourcebooks, newspapers, magazines, published and unpublished articles, approximately one half of the narrative is devoted to tracing the development and changing character of the mining camp from its embryonic stage when a discovery was first made through the mature mining community. The remaining portion is concerned with topics such as leadership, entertainment, racial prejudice, living expenses, wages, health, and prostitution. This is a valuable, serious treatment of the subject in which the dangerous, exciting, and glamorous aspects of life in a mining camp are de-emphasized.

Watkins, T.H., *Gold and Silver in the West: An Illustrated History of an American Dream* (American West Publishing Company, 1971) O.P.

Although at first glance this book might appear to be a typical "coffee-table" volume, it is not in that, in addition to its two hundred and forty plus well chosen photographs and maps, it contains an insightful narrative survey of the mining frontiers of the American West. Maintaining as its central motif humankind's age-old quest for treasure and "the power of the dream and its ability to shape the lives of those who followed," the first of the book's two parts chronologically outlines the key events and characters involved in the major mineral strikes of California, Colorado, Nevada, Idaho, Montana, South Dakota, Arizona, New Mexico, and Alaska. In the second part, Watkins assessed by topic and in fairly general terms, the geological, technological, economic, and social aspects of The Mining Frontier. Particularly useful as an introduction to the subject, a glossary of mining terms and chronology is appended to the work.

Wyman, Mark, *Hard Rock Epic: Western Miners and the Industrial Revolution 1860–1910* (University of California Press, 1979).

The focus of this concentrated study is the impact of the industrial revolution on the Western hard-rock mining industry and what effect it had on the social, cultural, and political life of the miner. Viewing technological advances as both "a godsend and a curse," Wyman showed how technical and economic gains for the mine owners frequently meant disaster and calamity in the working and personal lives of the mine laborers. The rise of the Western labor movement is traced through its various stages and detailed are the miners' struggles for wages, workman's compensation, industrial safety legislation, and corporate liability in the case of an accident. Containing some unusual photographs, this is a specialized book about an aspect of mining not necessarily of general interest.

Young, Otis E., Jr., *Western Mining: An Informal Account of Precious-Metals Prospecting, Placering, Lode Mining, and Milling on the American Frontier from Spanish Times to 1893* (University of Oklahoma Press, 1970).

Written with the assistance of Robert Lenon, a consulting mining engineer, this book is the best single source volume on the technical aspects of mining. It is a detailed and fairly specialized study in which are outlined the techniques of prospecting, assaying, salting, placering, lode mining, and milling employed by Spanish, Indian, Cornish, and, most especially, Anglo-American miners. Young devoted most of the text's narrative to how mining methods were adapted and improved over the years, particularly on the mining frontiers of California, Colorado, Nevada, South Dakota, and Arizona. This work dispels many of the mining myths — "the deeper the richer" theory — and presents better than any other secondary mining study a detailed account of the work environment of the Nineteenth-century miner. Containing many informative illustrations, an extensive glossary of Spanish and Cornish mining vocabulary, and a briefly annotated bibliography, Young's book is an excellent reference tool for the serious student and, despite its complex subject matter, eminently readable.

Suggested Fiction

Barry, Jane, *Maximilian's Gold* (Doubleday, 1966)

Bristow, Gwen, *Calico Palace* (Crowell, 1970)
Coolidge, Dane, *The Trail of Gold* (Dutton, 1937)
Fisher, Vardis, *City of Illusion* (Harper's, 1941)
Gardiner, Dorothy, *The Golden Lady* (Doubleday, 1936)
Harte, Bret, *Three Partners* (1897)
Haycox, Ernest, *Alder Gulch* (Little, Brown, 1941)
Hendryx, James B., *Gold and Guns on Halfaday Creek* (Doubleday, 1942)
London, Jack, "All Gold Canyon" from *Moon-Face and Other Stories* (Macmillan, 1906)
Waters, Frank, *Pike's Peak* (Swallow, 1971)

Suggested Films

Call of the Wild (United Artists, 1935) directed by William Wellman.
Copper Canyon (Paramount, 1950) directed by John Farrow.
The Far Country (Universal, 1955) directed by Anthony Mann.
Gold Is Where You Find It (Warner's, 1938) directed by Michael Curtiz.
MacKenna's Gold (Columbia, 1969) directed by J. Lee Thompson.
Silver City (Paramount, 1951) directed by Byron Haskin.
Silver Dollar (Warner's, 1932) directed by Alfred E. Green.
The Spoilers (Universal, 1942) directed by Ray Enright.
Sutter's Gold (Universal, 1936) directed by James Cruze.
The Treasure of Sierra Madre (Warner's, 1948) directed by John Huston.
The Walking Hills (Columbia, 1949) directed by John Sturges.

Buffalo

by Paul J. Blanding

I

General Phil Sheridan is reported to have testified to the Texas legislature in the 1870s that pending legislation to protect the buffalo from extermination was wrongly directed by 180 degrees. Rather than prohibit the slaughter, the legislators should strike bronze medals, with a dead buffalo on one side and a discouraged Indian on the other, to commemorate it. There is no record of such a medal having been struck, but neither was the legislation to protect the buffalo passed. Yet in an ironic echo, the United States Treasury Department in 1912 authorized that a "truly American coin" be struck. James Fraser's design with an American Indian on the obverse and an American buffalo on the reverse was chosen and the "buffalo" nickel came into being. In 1913 general circulation of this nickel began, in contrast to its subjects both of whose reduced numbers were by then penned in: the Indians on reservations, the few buffalo on reserves. The "truly American coin" was a token, if not a reminder, of the relationship that had lasted some four thousand years or more between Native Americans and the buffalo.

The forerunners of the North American bison came from Asia. During the Pleistocene (Ice Age) epoch, *bison prisus*, the steppe wisent, wandered across the Bering land bridge into Alaska. Brief warming periods allowed herds to escape the icebound Alaskan peninsula and move South

199

into the heartland of the continent. First evolving into the wide racked, giant *bison latifrons*, and then into the somewhat smaller *bison antiquus figginsi*, the bison competed well for grazing space, perhaps hastening the extinction of other grazing mammals, especially the horse.

The first direct evidence that early man hunted the buffalo is found in connection with *bison antiquus*. These early hunters may have been responsible for the extinction of *bison antiquus* since its smaller cousin, *bison bison occidentalis*, moved out of Alaska and replaced it on the Great Plains. Much evidence connects early hunters with the *bison bison occidentalis* including a large kill site near the Arkansas River. Such sites establish the fact of a remarkable continuity of hunting culture for over a period of 8,500 years.

Native American hunters used several methods to kill buffalo. The surround, in which the hunters circled a herd killing as many buffaloes as possible before a herd broke the circle, was an efficient method for group hunting. Large numbers could also be killed by driving a herd over a precipice, into a blind canyon, or into snow drifts. Later this method was refined by some tribes into a system of impounding in which pits or corrals were created into which a herd could be driven or decoyed.

Sometime in the Seventeenth century, Indians in the Southwest began acquiring horse culture (most probably from Spanish colonies in New Mexico). Horse culture spread rapidly and allowed the plains culture to blossom. At the heart of it was the increased efficiency at buffalo hunting that horses permitted. The surround on horseback was even deadlier than the surround on foot, and individual hunters (or groups) could "run" buffaloes from good horses, supplying meat for a family or the whole tribe. But the Plains Indians' dependence on the buffalo was the nexus of the entire culture of these Native Americans. Their sense of time and the seasons, their religious concepts and mythology, and their social status and relations were all connected to the buffalo in a direct way. Thus the cruel irony of General Sheridan's "discouraged Indian" remark. With the virtual extinction of the buffalo, Native Americans on the plains were not just "discouraged" but violently and utterly transformed. Thousands of years of tribal practices and perceptions were swept aside in less than a century.

When Europeans first traveled to North America, millions of buffalo blanketed the interior of the continent. Smaller, fringe herds were to be found as far East as Virginia and as far West as Oregon. It seems requisite that each writer on the buffalo take a stab at estimating their number at its zenith, but with "reliable" estimates running from 32,000,000 to over 600,000,000, the only certainty is that no one knows for sure how many there were.

It took the Europeans in the East a little over 200 years to exterminate all of the buffalo East of the Mississippi River. Most were killed by new settlers as they cleared the way West. Buffalo and other game were cheap food and subsidized settlers during the first struggling years before new farms yielded returns, nor did the freewheeling buffalo fit in with the European's concept of inviolable private property.

Some buffalo were killed for their robes in the Seventeenth and Eighteenth centuries, but it was the opening of the fur trade on the Missouri River at the beginning of the Nineteenth century that brought the buffalo into commercial prominence. This trade was in tanned robes rather than in raw hides. Robes had to be traded for since only buffalo killed in the late fall or in winter had the pelage to make a robe, and a long and tedious processing was necessary to cure a robe.

The robe trade, however, lucrative as it was, had certain natural limits, most especially the small amount of cheap, trained labor (Indian women) that could be exploited. But then came the railroads. The railroads brought destruction to the buffalo in several ways. Building across the plains with large gangs of men to feed, the railroad companies cut their food costs by hiring professional hunters to supply them with buffalo meat. The railroads also brought "sportsmen" to the buffalo. Several titled Europeans are now remembered exclusively for their wanton slaughtering of American game animals, though in fairness, their total takes could never equal the numbers killed by Army officers, Eastern businessmen, and just ordinary railroad passengers.

The hide trade started in earnest in 1871 because three elements came together; the railroads, the buffalo, and the tanneries to process raw buffalo hides. Previous to 1871 tanneries had no process for making buffalo hides into serviceable leather. But with the access to a large number of hides at low cost that the railroad offered, tanneries in Europe and the Eastern United States developed new processes. In the spring of 1871, J.N. Dubois, a Kansas City fur dealer, sent out circulars to meat hunters informing them that he could buy all the buffalo hides that they could supply. The trade in hides was on.

The first buffalo "boom" took place in Kansas. Leavenworth, Hays City, and Dodge City were all centers of the trade. As more tanneries began buying buffalo hides, the number of hunters jumped tremendously. Especially during the financial panic of 1873 when railroad workers were laid off and cattle prices were at rock bottom, the plains of Kansas were crowded with hunters and reeked of rotting buffalo carcasses.

The treaties signed at Medicine Lodge Creek, Kansas, in 1867 between the U.S. government and the Cheyennes, Arapahoes, Kiowas, Comanches, and Apaches, ostensibly restricted white hunters to North of the Arkansas River (this was agreed to orally but never in the texts of the treaties). While hunters were busy in Kansas, there was little problem in adhering to the agreement; but the buffalo began to play out in Kansas, even as early as 1873 in some areas, and many of the hide hunters looked South to the Panhandle as their next hunting grounds. The town of Fort Griffin in the Panhandle became the staging grounds for the Texas hunt. Rich with buffalo, the Texas plains kept the hunters busy through 1878. By the spring of 1879 the Texas slaughter was all but over. Many of the hunters retired from the business, the rest went North for the final round of slaughter.

Miles City, Montana, was a main staging ground for the last hunt.

The Northern herds had been thinned by Indian hunting for the robe trade, but large herds still existed in the North in 1878. The hide men ranged Montana, the Dakota territory, and parts of Wyoming for the last of the buffalo. Though never as large as the slaughter in the South, the Northern hunt reached its peak in the season of 1881–1882, when the Northern Pacific shipped 200,000 hides out of Bismarck, North Dakota, alone. By the fall of 1883 it was over. All the large herds were destroyed, and the frightened remnants were scattered.

The bone trade acted as a kind of mopping up after the slaughter. Buffalo bones were used in the refining of sugar and in the making of fertilizer, and their gathering became a lucrative, if short lived, trade. Many farmers in Kansas helped pay their mortgages with loads of buffalo bones, but more desperate were the Indians in the North who stooped to pick up the last remnants of their free and ancient existence.

The North American bison came within a hair of becoming extinct. In 1886 William Hornaday led an expedition for the Smithsonian to kill a few specimens for an exhibit. What he did not find shocked him. Except for a few bedraggled buffalo, the plains were bare. Hornaday spent the rest of his life trying to preserve the buffalo. In 1905 the American Bison Society was chartered and, through its lobbying efforts, several federal reserves were created to foster the growth of the buffalo population. "Preserved," the buffalo is a part of our "history" and now a zoological curiosity. After a minimum run of twenty-five years, the "buffalo" nickel was replaced by a coin with Thomas Jefferson's "pleasant smile" on the obverse and what reminds some of a Roman mausoleum on the reverse: out of pocket, out of mind?

II

i

As the great herds of the past themselves, references to the buffalo in frontier narratives and formal histories abound. Almost everyone venturing onto the Great Plains saw the buffalo, many mentioned them, but only a few took the time for systematic observation. Accounts by early Spanish explorers are the first European records of the buffalo, and subsequent references can be found scattered throughout the narratives of explorers and hunters of ensuing generations. Yet it was first in the Nineteenth century that readily accessible and detailed sources began to appear. *The Original Journals of the Lewis and Clark Expedition*, 1804–1806 (Dodd, Mead, 1904–1905) edited by Reuben Gold Thwaites contain many observations on the buffalo and the Plains Indian culture. George Catlin's descriptions of Indian buffalo hunts in *Letters and Notes on the Manners, Customs, and Conditions of the North American Indians* (1841; Dover Books, 1973) in two volumes are among the best and, combined with his paintings and drawings, comprise a cornerstone of our knowledge of Native American cultures on the buffalo plains. Another important source that devotes a chapter to the buffalo is Colonel Richard I. Dodge's *The Plains of the Great West and Their Inhabitants: Being a Description of the Plains, Game, Indians of the Great North American Desert* (1877). Dodge's zoological generalizations are not to be trusted, but his stories and verbal sketches remain of interest. John R. Cook's *The Border and the Buffalo; An Untold Story of the Southwest Plains* (Crane, 1907) is a rambling first-hand account, but it does contain some buffalo lore and a good description of the battle in 1876 at Yellow House Draw between buffalo hunters and the Comanches. Olive K. Dixon edited her husband's memoirs in *Life of "Billy" Dixon, Plainsman, Scout, and Pioneer: A Narrative in Which Are Described Many Things Relating to the Early Southwest, with an Account of the Fights Between Indians and Buffalo Hunters at Adobe Walls and at Buffalo Wallow, for Which Congress Voted the Medal of Honor to the Survivors* (Turner, 1914). Provided a reader is not put off by this imposing title, Dixon was an eyewitness and participant in many important frontier events, including the negotiation of the Treaty at Medicine Lodge in 1867, the buffalo hunter's fight at Adobe Walls in 1874, and Captain Nolan's lost scouting expedition of 1877, and his is one of the best narratives left by a buffalo hunter.

Many books dealing with the culture of the Plains Indians contain references to the buffalo, but particularly to be recommended are the appropriate chapters of George Bird Grinnell's *The Cheyenne Indians: Their History and Ways of Life* (1923; University of Nebraska Press, 1972) in two volumes which focus on Cheyenne hunting methods and their utilizations of buffalo. Grinnell also recorded the life of an Indian hunter before the coming of the white men in *When Buffalo Ran* (1920; University of Oklahoma Press, 1966). A somewhat related work is *Apauk, Caller of Buffalo* (Houghton Mifflin, 1916) by James Willard Schultz, a narrative of a Blackfoot who struggles to acquire the arcane art of buffalo calling.

Of more specialized interest are *Buffalo Bone Days* by Major Israel McCreight, a short work on the buffalo bone trade privately printed at Dubois, Pennsylvania, in 1939; *New Mexican Ciboleros of the Llano Estacado* (Hall-Poorbaugh Press, 1970) by James D. Shinkle, a brief book about early Spanish-American buffalo hunters; and, finally, *The Bison in Art: A Graphic Chronicle of the American Bison* (Northland Press, 1977), a well mounted picture book combining sketches, paintings, lithographs, advertising, and photographs.

II

ii

Allen, Joel A., *The American Bisons, Living and Extinct* (1876) O.P.; reprinted by the Arno Press.

This book by a zoologist is, along with Hornaday's work (see below), considered one of the Nineteenth-century classics on the buffalo. Part I deals with extinct forms of the genus Bison and bison behavior. In Part II Allen explored the historical evidence for the bison's existence in various regions of North America. Allen's detailed work is no longer definitive, but his treatment of the extent of the buffalo range remains useful.

Branch, E. Douglas, *The Hunting of the Buffalo* (D. Appleton-Century, 1929) O.P.; reprinted by the University of Nebraska Press with an Introduction by J. Frank Dobie.

This was Branch's re-annotated doctoral thesis. It covers the buffalo from their "discovery" by Europeans through their near extermination. The prose is humorous and moves swiftly. Unfortunately, Branch fell victim to both his sources and his own narrative pace and failed to cover important aspects with the thoroughness and accuracy they deserve, e.g., his generalizations on supposed buffalo migrations. Branch's chapter on Indian buffalo hunting is cursory. His strongest chapters treat of the robe and pemmican trade between Indians, mixed-bloods, and the various fur companies. Here he combined strong narrative with analysis and, though simplified, provided an adequate overview of the period prior to the hidemen. His final chapters on the extermination are inferior in scope to the works of Gard and Sandoz (see below), and his telling of the Adobe Walls affair contains several minor factual errors.

Gard, Wayne, *The Great Buffalo Hunt* (Knopf, 1959) O.P.; reprinted by the University of Nebraska Press.

This book is the most comprehensive history of the extermination of the buffalo by hidemen during the years 1868 to 1884. Gard introduced his subject with short chapters on the bison itself, Indian buffalo culture, and a survey of the early robe trade, but his main subject was the hide hunters. His treatment of such "heroes" as "Buffalo Bill" Cody is even-handed and factual, as he rightly saw the real story in the less famous, but important, hunters such as Wright Mooar, Charlie Rath, and Billy Dixon. Gard also presented the commercial and technological side of the story, explaining the roles played by the railroads, the Eastern tanneries, and improved firearms technology in the destruction. The fact that Gard's presentation is circumspect, his empathy with the Native American point of view muted, and some of his assertions debatable, e.g., "the hunters of the buffaloes were mighty men," his work, notwithstanding, can still be recommended as thorough and accurate and it contains a good bibliography.

Haines, Francis, *The Buffalo* (Crowell, 1970) O.P.

An historian, Haines mapped the contours of buffalo history, stretching back some 40,000 years. His account is especially focused on Native American cultures. Starting with prehistoric migrations from Asia, he broke the buffalo country down by geographic and tribal areas. Of great interest, his chapter on the horse and the Indian buffalo hunter recapitulates his theory as to the source of Native American horse culture (the Spanish colonies in New Mexico). Finally Haines divided the era of Indian-European confrontation into short periods, culminating with the modern attempt to save the buffalo from extinction.

Hornaday, William T., *The Extermination of the American Bison with a Sketch of its Discovery and Life History* (U.S. National Museum, 1887) O.P.; reprinted by the Shorey Book Store, Seattle, Washington.

Hornaday was the chief taxidermist for the Smithsonian whose hunt for specimens for the Museum in 1886 helped establish the fact of the near extinction of the buffalo and he was a central figure in their subsequent preservation. However his "classic" on the buffalo is a hodge-podge of material taken from other writers, and it contains some questionable assertions, e.g., his perpetuation of the myth of buffalo migrations ... something often repeated by later writers. A reader should consult this book cautiously, if at all.

Inman, Henry, *Buffalo Jones: Forty Years of Adventure* (1899) O.P.; reprinted as *Buffalo Jones' Adventures on the Plains* by the University of Nebraska Press.

Charles "Buffalo" Jones hunted buffalo when they were plentiful and preserved them when they were nearly extinct. In this somewhat meandering book, Inman pieced together various fragments of Jones' life, drawing on conversations with Jones himself, a journal Jones kept, and a short narrative by "E(merson) Hough" describing one of Jones' buffalo calf hunts. Skipping Jones' early years (he is portrayed as a budding John D. Rockefeller of the wild animal trade) and Inman's historical musings, the reader might find most interesting the narrative of Jones' expeditions to capture buffalo calves.

McHugh, Tom, *The Time of the Buffalo* (Knopf, 1972) O.P.; reprinted by the University of Nebraska Press.

This book is the best study of the relationship of buffalo to the Plains Indian culture yet written. While other works focus on a particular tribe, culture area, or span of years, McHugh, a zoologist, concentrated on the distinctive role the buffalo played in the dietary, technological, and religious life of these Indians. But the book's value does not end there, for it offers an updated natural history of the buffalo, as well as valuable generalizations on the true nature of buffalo behavior. McHugh spent considerable time observing herds in Yellowstone Park and Jackson Hole Wildlife Park, and his account is important both for its own sake and as a corrective to those authors who have uncritically passed on early generalizations on buffalo behavior.

Mayer, Frank H., and Charles B. Roth, *The Buffalo Harvest* (Sage Books, 1958) O.P.

Mayer was a professional buffalo hunter. *The Buffalo Harvest* is his recollection of the hide trade. Although written by Charles Roth, Mayer's words come through, exposing the character of the man and the buffalo hunter as a type. Mayer's basic contention was the buffalo hunters "harvested" the buffalo, much as a farmer might harvest crops. His most interesting historical claim was that the U.S. Army supplied many of the hunters with as much free ammunition as they could use. For the reader who is interested in the details of the destruction as told by one of the destroyers, *The Buffalo Harvest* may well be *the* book.

Roe, Frank Gilbert, *The North American Buffalo: A Critical Study of the Species in Its Wild State* (University of Toronto Press, 1951).

Frank Roe's immense discussion (the text alone is almost 700 pages) of the buffalo literature is a reference work of great importance. Roe examined the questions raised by earlier writers on the buffalo and analyzed their contradictions, prejudices, and unwarranted generalizations. The work is organized by questions, some of which are: what was the historical event of the buffalo range?, what is the case for or against buffalo migrations?, and what effects did Indian hunting practices have on the demise of the buffalo? Though copiously footnoted, this book is accessible (given a degree of interest in the subject); it has an extensive bibliography.

Sandoz, Mari, *The Buffalo Hunters* (Hastings House, 1954); reprinted by the University of Nebraska Press.

As many of Mari Sandoz' other historical works, this book is styled to read with the intimacy of a novel. Characters are pursued, conversations are overheard, tales are told, and always the sights and smells of the buffalo plains are conveyed as though sensed directly. The reader, now separated from this world by more than a century, is shuttled back in what seems direct contact with its inhabitants. However, Sandoz the literary stylist created a dilemma for Sandoz the historian. In her coverage of the period from 1867 to 1891, she was forced to focus on the colorful, the famous, the "characters" of the old West. "Wild Bill" Hickok, "Buffalo Bill" Cody, and General George A. Custer, and their kind, spend too much time upon her stage for the drama not to take on a theatrical rather than an historical tone, and, too often, the line between fact and imagination is left undrawn. Several stories related in the book under the guise of "someone said that ..." are fabrications from the dime novel West. Further, Sandoz perpetuated the buffalo migrations myth as though migrations were an established fact, despite her access to Frank Roe's (see above) excellent critique of the problem. These shortcomings are not fatal. For its lyrical recreation of the buffalo plains, *The Buffalo Hunters* will long remain an antidote for the dry, often lifeless histories of other writers.

Suggested Fiction

Grey, Zane, *The Thundering Herd* (Harper's, 1925)

Grove, Fred, *The Buffalo Runners* (Doubleday, 1968)
Kelton, Elmer, *Buffalo Wagons* (Ballantine, 1956)
Lott, Milton, *The Last Hunt* (1954; Gregg Press, 1979)
Williams, John, *Butcher's Crossing* (1961; Gregg Press, 1978)

Suggested Films

The Last Hunt (M-G-M, 1956) directed by Richard Brooks.
The Thundering Herd (Paramount, 1933) directed by Henry Hathaway.
The White Buffalo (United Artists, 1977) directed by J. Lee Thompson.

The Overland Trail

by Vicki Piekarski

I

Although it was headed toward the East, the last covered wagon to travel the Overland Trail was seen in 1910. The driver was seventy-nine year old Ezra Meeker, an overland immigrant himself in 1852 from Ohio. In 1906 Meeker had made a previous wagon trek East, ending up in Washington, D.C. to gain financial support to have markers placed along the Overland Trail to Oregon. President Theodore Roosevelt, upon viewing Meeker's outfit which had included an assistant or two, an old faithful dog, and one ox and one cow (a replacement for an ox that had died earlier in the trip), pledged governmental support to Meeker's mission. Meeker died in 1928 at the age of ninety-eight. Two years later the Oregon Trail Memorial Association, of which Meeker had at one time been president, celebrated the one hundredth anniversary of Meeker's birth. That same year President Herbert Hoover proclaimed April 10 to December 29, 1930 to be the Covered Wagon Centennial, commemorating the anniversary of the first wagon train Westward along the Platte route led by William L. Sublette, the fur trader.

The two thousand mile Overland Trail, over which at least a quarter of a million people traveled in its most widely used years (1840–1860), has provided historians and fictionalists with material that resounds with the romance and pathos associated with America's movement Westward.

208

This was not the adventure of the self-sufficient mountain man or the individualistic cowboy but, rather, it was a collective effort, a community of people on wheels. When Ezra Meeker began his Westward trek in 1852 from Kanesville (Council Bluffs), Iowa — the most commonly used "jumping off" point beginning in that year, having gained popularity over points in Missouri — travel on the Overland Trail had already changed significantly since the first overland immigrant train, known as the Bidwell-Bartleson party, had begun their journey to California in 1841.

During the 1840s in early May the overlanders would start from Independence which had been the main outfitting post for the Santa Fe traders, or a nearby settlement. By the gold rush years Independence was supplanted, first by St. Joseph, and then by Kanesville — the latter the Mormon "jumping off" point renamed Council Bluffs in 1853 when it had come to be predominantly used by Gentiles. It was at these launching points that immigrants made their final preparations for the trip — buying supplies, training animals for yoking or pack work, choosing leaders, and establishing trail rules. For the first forty miles the trail followed the same route as did the Santa Fe Trail before shifting Northwest toward Fort Kearny on the Platte River in central Nebraska. This first part of the trip was deceptively easy with its fairly simple river crossings and plentiful supplies of water, grass, and wood. Outside Fort Kearny, following the North Platte, the immigrants encountered natural rock formations like Courthouse Rock, Chimney Rock, and Scott's Bluff, before they reached Fort Laramie (Wyoming). After replenishing their supplies, making necessary repairs, washing clothes and bedding, and several days of rest for both people and animals at Fort Laramie, immigrants followed the trail along the North Platte across Wyoming, to the mouth of the Sweetwater, coming upon more natural phenomena — Independence Rock and Devil's Gate. The waterholes were increasingly tainted with alkali as the country became drier and rougher. Finally they reached the Continental Divide and passed over its eight thousand foot summit through South Pass. Leaving the South Pass, via the Southern route, the trail passed through Green River Valley and proceeded to Fort Bridger (Wyoming) and from there Northwest to Fort Hall (Idaho), a point usually reached by the middle of August. Several days out of Fort Hall, the Oregon-bound immigrants split from their California-destined companions.

Although the trip was at this point more than half completed, in either direction the trail ahead demanded even greater courage and stamina from its travelers. Those bound for California headed South to connect with the Humboldt River in Nevada. The terrain was extremely dry and hot but helped prepare the overlanders for what lay three hundred and seventy miles ahead at the Humboldt Sink: fifty-five miles of waterless, grassless desert. After crossing Humboldt Sink, where many animals had died and often both wagons and supplies had to be abandoned, time was of the essence for an early snowfall in the upcoming mountains could mean tragedy for all involved as it did for the Donner party in 1846. The trail led up the Eastern slope of the Sierra Nevadas and then twisted down

the Western slope to the Sacramento Valley, reached usually by October.
Immigrants bound for Oregon, who suffered great losses along the way due
to the many difficult river crossings along their route, followed the Snake
River past Fort Boise and then over the formidable Blue Mountains to the
Columbia River. The trail precariously followed the South bank of the
Columbia, which many ferried down at great expense to both humans and
property, to the mouth of the Willamette River, and headed South to the
Willamette Valley, the goal for the majority, arriving sometime in October.

Save for cut-offs and so-called shortcuts to ease the burden of wagon
travel, particularly on the Western end, the general route of the Overland
Trail remained the same over the years. However, the process of overland
travel between the years 1840–1860 did change significantly, particularly
with the proliferation and diversification of services and supportive
facilities available to the immigrant. "... [E]ach travel year evidenced
distinctive patterns, unique dramas of triumph and tragedy, new contributions to the mosaic of Western development," John D. Unruh, Jr. wrote
in *The Plains Across* (University of Illinois Press, 1979), a book that examines in detail the changes experienced by the overland immigrants and
contradicts much that has been written in the past by historians about the
supposedly "typical" years — 1843, 1846, and 1849 — of Westward migration.

Perhaps no other migration year contributed to trail changes as
much as did 1849, the first year of the gold rush to California. In the pre-
gold rush years migrations to the Far West consisted largely of Midwest
farming families most of whom were headed for Oregon in search of a
permanent home. From 1840 to 1848 approximately 14,000 people traveled the Overland Trail to Oregon and California and of these over 11,000
went to Oregon. The discovery of gold at Sutter's Mill and its promise of
wealth made California far more attractive to greater numbers of people
than Oregon had been. In 1849 over 25,000 immigrants undertook the
overland journey; less than 500 were destined for Oregon. No longer were
overlanders families of settlers; rather they were masses of plunderers who
generally intended to return East once they had accumulated their fortune.
The very size of the 1849 migration created problems that changed the
overland experience from what it had been prior to 1849. Trails became
congested to the point that, as one immigrant noted, wagons were lined up
twelve abreast at the "jumping off" points, campsites were extremely
crowded, grass areas desperately needed for animals were overgrazed. Due
to carelessly over-supplying themselves for the journey, the trail became
littered with discarded food, supplies, wagons, and equipment as well as
the rotting carcasses of thousands of animals that had died from lack of
food and water, abuse, or overwork — and in the case of the buffalo, sport.
These problems caused by the mass migration of 1849 — 1850 and 1852 saw
even larger migrations — also had to be dealt with by Native Americans, the
original inhabitants of the land over which the path of the Oregon and
California trails passed.

Although upon occasion a tribute might be extracted from immigrants by the Indians for crossing their land, generally relations between

Indians and Anglos, prior to 1849, were reasonably amicable. In fact, Indians provided important services to the early overlanders by acting as guides, directing them to water and grass supplies, potential alternate routes, and supplying assistance at numerous river crossings. But the accelerating numbers of immigrants encroaching on Indian land in the gold rush years, Indians, who had heard what had happened to their kinsmen in the East, began feeling more and more threatened. There was even talk among the Indians in 1849 that perhaps *they* should immigrate to the lands East of the Mississippi River, for they believed that few whites could remain in that part of the country with all those moving West. Thus during the 1850s encounters between the two races became more volatile. Notwithstanding, the number of deaths of overlanders attributed to Indians has been greatly exaggerated — disease, particularly cholera, drownings, and trail accidents claimed far more lives. However, editors discovered that mythical massacres sold newspapers. In 1855 an Illinois newspaper reported that all immigrants on the trail (approximately 2,000) had been killed by Indians! Based on his research, John D. Unruh found that Indians suffered far greater losses at the hands of the whites than did the whites by Indians. Unruh's statistics — "restricted to reasonable definite reports of deaths" which does not include disputed "massacres" as the Mountain Meadows Massacre for which the Indians were not responsible nor any other possible "white-Indian" attacks — show that three-hundred and sixty-two overlanders were killed by Indians compared to four-hundred and twenty-six Indians killed by whites.

There was an expression in use by the overlanders about "seeing the elephant" which meant experiencing some hardship or unpleasantness on the trail and somehow surviving it. What is commonly forgotten is that although many saw the elephant and some indeed forfeited their lives, the majority of immigrants successfully made the overland trip which was for each man, woman, and child a unique experience. Those thousands who traveled the Overland Trail, therefore, contributed to one of the epic periods in the annals of frontier history.

II

i

The following annotated bibliography is concerned primarily with general histories on the Overland Trail. There are, however, literally hundreds of first-hand narratives about Overland travel. Some of these accounts have been published in book form, others have only been excerpted in Overland Trail collections. The reader is directed to Merrill Mattes' *The Great Platte River Road* (Nebraska State Historical Society Publications, 1969) which contains an invaluable bibliography listing approximately seven-hundred overland narratives and their location in archival libraries. Irene D. Paden (see below) also included this kind of information in her books, albeit on a much smaller scale. The bibliography in *The Plains Across* (University of Illinois Press, 1979) by John D. Unruh, Jr. is likewise helpful.

II

ii

Faragher, John Mack, *Women and Men on the Overland Trail* (Yale University Press, 1979).

The relationship between men and women in mid Nineteenth-century Midwestern America is the focus of this book which has a somewhat misleading title. However, there are several chapters concerned specifically with the overland journey — the route followed, background on the people who attempted the trip (Faragher's primary focus is the Midwest family of the 1840s and 1850s who planned to settle permanently at the end of their trek), the vicissitudes of overland travel, and the divergent duties and concerns of the two sexes during the course of the trip. Almost half of the book is devoted to the familial and social roles, duties, and attitudes of the sexes in the Midwestern environment. It is a noteworthy contribution to Overland Trail history in that it explores the role of women — an area all too often neglected by historians — although readers may disagree with some of the conclusions drawn by Faragher in his final assessments.

Lavender, David *Westward Vision: The Story of the Oregon Trail* (McGraw-Hill, 1963).

This book was an early entry in McGraw-Hill's American Trails Series. Although generally praised by historians, it is far from a definitive history of the Oregon Trail. Lavender stressed the early explorers and travelers and cursorily covered the immigrants on the trail in the early 1840s. The narrative ends with a brief mention of the immigration of 1847. It is, however, entertainingly written.

Mattes, Merrill, *The Great Platte River Road: The Covered Wagon Mainline Via Fort Kearny to Fort Laramie* (Nebraska State Historical Society Publications, 1969).

The primary focus of this book is that portion of the Overland Trail spanning the distance between Fort Kearny and Fort Laramie. Mattes proposed that this part of the trail be distinguished from the whole of the trail — perhaps as the Great Platte River Road — since it was a natural roadway virtually free from cut-offs and was used by nearly everyone traveling the Oregon and California trails. This encyclopedic work starts off with an overview of the route followed and trail problems, occurrences and developments. A major part of the text reconstructs in intricate detail the Westward course of the immigrants between Mattes' two points of focus by quoting extensively from letters, journals, and reminiscences left by overlanders. However, Mattes' profuse use of quotations inhibited the flow of his prose, especially where he quoted from numerous sources on a single point or subject. Nonetheless, his knowledge of first-hand narratives was impressive and his exhaustive bibliography is invaluable. In addition, there are detailed maps and statistical information on the estimated number of overlanders on the trail between 1841–1866.

Monaghan, Jay, *The Overland Trail* (Bobbs-Merrill, 1947) O.P.; reprinted by the Arno Press.

Monaghan's narrative history is generally considered a standard work on the Oregon and California trails. Opening with the discovery of the Columbia River, the author chose a person or group of persons to represent what he called "changing epochs" in the history of the trail. Approximately half of the book's pages are devoted to the pre-1840 years. People generally overlooked in Overland Trail studies as Narcissa Whitman, the first white woman to cross the Rocky Mountains, emerge as significant historical personalities in Monaghan's treatment of the subject. However, coverage of the post-1840 period contains one large gap: the decade of the 1850s and all of the immigrants who traveled the trail during the period. Curiously Monaghan discussed the mass migration of 1843, the Donner Party of 1846, the Mormon migration of 1847, and the Forty-niners bound for California and then jumped ahead to the subject of the Pony Express. The book is best supplemented with a study as John D. Unruh's (see below) which discusses in depth the overlanders of the 1840s and 1850s.

Paden, Irene D., *The Wake of the Prairie Schooner* (Macmillan, 1943); *Prairie Schooner Detours* (Macmillan, 1949), both O.P.

Paden's two books are perhaps the best of those that fall into the category of "trail books"—present-day accounts of people locating and following the old trails. Her first book is concerned with the main route of the Overland Trail to Oregon and California and was followed by a companion volume about the Lassen and the Hastings cut-offs, the latter cut-off made famous by the Donner party. Paden, accompanied by her geographer husband, invested a great deal of time over the years doing fieldwork. She adeptly wove together material on the history of the trail based largely on first-hand diaries and letters written by overlanders, a personal reconstruction of the trails, as well as information she gleaned from present-day residents living in the areas she explored. These books are highly personal and readable accounts of the trails of yesterday and a look at them as they appeared almost one hundred years later.

Parkman, Francis, *The Oregon Trail* (1849) O.P.; available in numerous subsequent editions.

In 1846 Parkman embarked on his famous overland trip of which this is the record. Long on description and short on analysis, this book, thanks to classroom adoption, has become a Western classic. Unfortunately Parkman never ventured more than one hundred miles West of Fort Laramie and he failed to recognize the significance of the overland immigrants whom he encountered. What it comes to is that his book has very little to do with the Oregon Trail.

Rucker, Maude A., *The Oregon Trail and Some of Its Early Blazers* (W. Neale, 1930) O.P.
    Rucker edited this volume which contains some of the better known first-hand accounts of the Oregon Trail. It includes the often mentioned "A Day with the Cow Column" by Jess Applegate.

Stewart, George R., *The California Trail: An Epic with Many Heroes* (McGraw-Hill, 1962); *Ordeal by Hunger* (Henry Holt, 1936) O.P.; revised edition Houghton Mifflin, 1960; reprinted by Pocket Books.
    The California Trail is an excellent general study on the subject of overland migration in spite of the fact that Stewart confined himself to those immigrants bound for California between 1841–1859. With the exception of the Donner party, which is dealt with in *Ordeal by Hunger*, Stewart's coverage of immigrants on the trail between 1841–1849 is comprehensive—he devoted a chapter to each year and often drew parallels between them. Unfortunately the entire decade of the 1850s is capsulized in a twenty-three page section. Following the chapter on 1845 migrations—the year Stewart contended the story of overland travel was altered in that the competitive struggles of man would henceforth be against man whereas pre-1845 immigrants' main struggle had been against Nature—, Stewart interrupted his chronological narrative to discuss the "hows" of overland travel, including descriptions and illustrations of the mechanics of fording a river, maneuvering through a mountain pass, and a breakdown of the route followed. The subject of Indian-white relations is explored more deeply in this book than in most and Stewart believed that the blame for conflicts erupting between the two races must be shared by each.
    Ordeal by Hunger has been cited as the best modern historical and critical account of the Donner party—and it is. Stewart made use of the available records and he stuck to the facts in reconstructing the events that befell the eighty-seven members of the Donner caravan. The story itself is followed by a short section examining the possible causes of the disaster, what happened to some of the survivors after the rescue, and the taboo subject of cannabilism. The revised edition, which faithfully reproduced the 1936 book sans alteration, is supplemented by a survey of post-1936 scholarship on "Donnerana," a reconsideration of some controversial matters regarding the party's itinerary, and three first-hand accounts written by members of the Donner party—the diaries of Patrick Breen and James F. Reed and a letter written by Virginia Reed. Stewart's treatment of the Donner tragedy is free from the sensationalism often associated with the subject and becomes instead the story of a group's will to live.

Unruh, John D., Jr., *The Plains Across: The Overland Emigrants and the Trans-Mississippi West* 1840–1860 (University of Illinois Press, 1979).

This encyclopedic book (Unruh's doctoral dissertation published in book form subsequent to his premature death from a brain tumor) is American scholarship at its finest and should become a classic in Western American history. The subject is limited to an examination of overland immigration between the years 1840–1860, yet it encompasses so much more because of Unruh's extensive research. Combining strong narrative and insightful analysis, *The Plains Across* hypothesizes that there is not, contrary to popular and scholarly opinion, any such thing as a "typical" year of immigration. Unruh presented material by topic, demonstrating that antebellum overland travel was an ever-changing experience. The chapters on the roles of the federal government, private entrepreneurs, and the Mormon "Halfway House" — all of which contributed in various ways to the changes encountered by the overlander — are especially informative since they contain material generally not found elsewhere. Also noteworthy are Unruh's findings on the controversial issue of "Emigrant-Indian Interactions" in which he showed that whites claimed the lives of far more Indians than Indians did whites. In fact, without the help of Indians, especially in the early 1840s, travel would have been much more difficult. The flora and fauna of the region are also shown as not having been a totally negative force.

In his Introduction, Unruh surveyed and critiqued the major Overland Trail histories and a number of significant novels and found them generally lacking in focus or distorting the truth. Included in the narrative is information on outfitting, costs, equipment, disease, accidents, Eastbound traffic, relief expeditions, and the route itself — all based on sound research into original documents: diaries, letters, newspapers, and periodicals. Unruh also recorded new statistical data, by year, on the estimated number of overlanders, the average amount of time needed to make the journey, and costs of supplies at trading posts. Regrettably, this study does not examine the role of women although their journals and letters are occasionally quoted.

The Plains Across is an excellent starting point for anyone interested in the study of overland immigration and it will serve as a useful tool in evaluating other books on the subject for both the general reader and the scholar. It contains an extensive bibliography, maps, and illustrations.

Other Western Trails

III

i

There were a number of other trails that figured prominently in the history of the American Western frontier. These trails with their varying private and commercial uses will be dealt with or at least touched upon in other sections of this book, e.g., the Chisholm Trail in Cowboys, Cattlemen, and the Cattle Industry. The reader is also referred to McGraw-Hill's American Trails Series, General Editor, A.B. Guthrie, Jr. This series, which is highly readable and fairly reliable although not always consistent, includes among its titles, *Doomed Road of Empire: The Spanish Trail of Conquest* (1963) by Hodding Carter, *The Gathering of Zion: The Story of the Mormon Trail* (1964) by Wallace Stegner, *The Great North Trail: America's Route of the Ages* (1966) by Dan Cushman, *The El Dorado Trail: The Story of the Gold Rush Routes Across Mexico* (1970) by Ferol Egan, and *The Bloody Bozeman: The Perilous Trail to Montana's Gold* (1971) by Dorothy M. Johnson.

Included below are only some standard works—other than in the American Trails Series—on the more familiar Western trails.

III

ii

Duffus, R.L., *The Santa Fe Trail* (Longmans, Green, 1930) O.P.; reprinted by the University of New Mexico Press.

Although a number of books have appeared on this subject since its original publication, Duffus' history remains a standard work on the Santa Fe Trail along with Stanley Vestal's volume (see below). Relying heavily upon the first-hand accounts written by the trail's more well-known travelers, Duffus vividly recreated the important events in the history of the trail from its beginnings in the Sixteenth century up to its gradual disuse more than three centuries later with the coming of the railroad. Written with a general reader in mind, it is reasonably accurate in the information it presents, although Indians are viewed primarily as a heathen and savage menace.

Dunlop, Richard, *Great Trails of the West* (Abingdon Press, 1971) O.P.

An anecdotal quality is incorporated thoughout this book which is a combination of historical commentary taken from numerous first-hand narratives and the author's own Western travels with his family. It can be recommended only on the basis of its inclusiveness—it covers a great number of Western trails and cut-offs from the familiar, the Oregon Trail, to the more obscure, the Chilkoot Trail. This same material is handled better elsewhere, although this book might serve as a sort of general introduction.

Gard, Wayne, *The Chisholm Trail* (University of Oklahoma Press, 1954).

Gard's book is the best Chisholm Trail history (1867–1884) extant.

He sought out survivors familiar with the trail, manuscripts, public records, newspapers, and archival materials in order to clear up some of the confusion surrounding the trail, including its exact route. In addition to his comprehensive treatment of the commercial use of the Chisholm Trail, Gard devoted chapters to the origins of the Longhorn breed, the cattle drive, and the cattle industry of Texas. Cowmen are significant figures in this story and included are chapters on their roles in a cattle drive, their experiences on the trail, their sojourns in the Kansas cowtowns, and their songs. The book is a dependable, straight-forward historical account and contains an extensive bibliography.

Gregg, Jacob R., *History of the Oregon Trail, Santa Fe Trail, and Other Trails* (Binford & Mort, 1955) O.P.

The title of this book is ill-suited to the author's apparent purpose. Gregg's coverage of the history of the trails chosen is sporadic — as in the case of the Oregon Trail in which the thousands of immigrants who traversed its path in the 1850s are almost completely neglected. Conversely, there are a number of chapters devoted entirely to the misfortunes and tragedies encountered by the immigrants, an aspect of trail travel Gregg stressed throughout the book. An oddly organized and unbalanced history, it would best serve as a very general introduction for a non-specialist.

Gregg, Josiah, *Commerce of the Prairies* (1844) O.P.; various subsequent editions with the best being that reprinted by the University of Oklahoma Press, 1954, edited and introduced by Max L. Moorhead.

Although Gregg's memoirs have been criticized for their serious tone, they remain the primary historical sourcebook on the Santa Fe Trail and trade. Gregg recorded everything he encountered and all the facts he could collect, including information on wagon trains, packing, trail accidents, mileage, trading supplies, buffalo, Indians, Mexican culture and customs. His book contains a wealth of history, both natural and human, and will continue to be of interest for years to come.

Lee, Wayne C., and Howard C. Raynesford, *Trails of the Smoky Hill* (Caxton Printers, 1980).

Raynesford (1876–1967) made a forty-year study of the Butterfield Overland Despatch and Lee, who made use of this invaluable research in writing this book, credited Raynesford as the book's co-author. The book's focus is the historical role of the Smoky Hill River in the settlement of the plains region between the Missouri River and the Rocky Mountains and the trails that followed or crossed over its banks. Four major sections in the book trace generally the histories of the Leavenworth and Pike's Peak Express, the Butterfield Overland Despatch, the Kansas Pacific Railway, and the Chisholm Trail and present the characters involved, including colorful personalities as George Armstrong Custer, "Wild Bill" Hickok, William F. Cody, and John Wesley Hardin. Lee was least reliable in his depiction of Indians who are repeatedly referred to as "Indians" without mentioning any tribal affiliation and who are viewed merely as obstacles. The book is well illustrated with maps and photographs.

Madsen, Betty M., and Brigham D. Madsen, *North to Montana: Jehus, Bullwhackers, and Mule Skinners on the Montana Trail* (University of Utah Press, 1980).

This is a well organized history of the much neglected Montana Trail, the North-South thoroughfare extending from Salt Lake City through Eastern Idaho up to the gold fields of Western Montana. Concerned primarily with the years 1863–1884, this study includes material on the commerical and private traffic on the Montana Trail (with more emphasis on the former), modes of transportation, changes and problems encountered on the trail, as well as general historical facts about the region. Some unusual photographs are reprinted.

Magoffin, Susan Shelby, *Down the Santa Fe Trail and Into Mexico: The Diary of Susan Shelby Magoffin*, 1846–1847, (Yale University Press, 1926), edited by Stella M. Drumm; reprinted as a Yale University Press paperback, 1962, with a Foreward by Howard R. Lamar; both O.P.; reprinted by William Gannon and the University of Nebraska Press.

A highly cultured woman from a distinguished Kentucky family, Magoffin was probably the first white woman ever to travel the Santa Fe Trail. Discovered in 1926, the Magoffin diary relates Susan's experiences both on the trail and in Santa Fe as well as her brother-in-law's (James Magoffin) involvement in overthrowing the Mexican government in Santa Fe and has gained the reputation of being a Southwest classic. With its perceptive and at times almost sensuous descriptions, Magoffin's book, together with Marian Russell's memoirs (see below), constitutes rare glimpses of the Santa Fe Trail from a female point of view.

Moody, Ralph, *The Old Trails West* (Crowell, 1963) O.P.

Admittedly not a comprehensive study of trails, the author of this book set out to tell the story of seven Western trails — the Gila Trail, *El Camino Real*, the Old Spanish Trail, the Santa Fe Trail, the Big Medicine Trail, the Oregon Trail, and the California Trail — from their "origin to obliteration." Unfortunately Moody fell short of his goal and devoted the majority of his pages to the "origin" of the trails while the "obliteration" was usually covered in a paragraph or two. The book begins with a very brief overview of prehistoric Western America and the role of the Indian as the "original pathfinder," followed by seven chapters, each focusing on a single trail. A surprising number of errors appear in the book in spite of the fact that, in his research, Moody used a great many reliable secondary sources. To give but one example, the Stevens-Murphy party that successfully crossed the Sierra Nevadas into California via the Truckee Pass in 1844 are placed in the emigrating year of 1843. Moody's effort, as all too many books attempting to cover a variety of trails, is best approached with caution.

Russell, Marian, *Land of Enchantment: Memoirs of Marian Russell Along the Santa Fe Trail* (Branding Iron Press, 1954) O.P.; reprinted by the University of New Mexico Press.

Between 1852–1862 Russell (who grew from childhood to young womanhood in these years) traveled the Santa Fe Trail five times. There is a marvelous, lyrical, dream-like quality to Russell's prose — dictated to her daughter-in-law in the 1930s — in which she recalled her childhood days on and off the trail. Raised by an unconventional mother driven by wanderlust, this book is an interesting contrast to the diary of Susan Magoffin (see above) who was strongly influenced by the beliefs of her day about the proper behavior of a lady. Russell, whose husband was killed in the conflict over the Maxwell land grant, wrote that there are certain periods in her life in which "the big things seem little and the little things seem big." Her ability to recall details about things she saw, stories she heard, people she met and knew, as Kit Carson, and experiences she had make this book an unusual and invaluable first-hand narrative.

Vestal, Stanley, *The Old Santa Fe Trail* (Houghton Mifflin, 1939); reprinted by Bantam Books, both O.P.

Vestal's book is considered a prime work on the Santa Fe Trail. He felt that in order to know the Santa Fe Trail, one must know it as it was in the Nineteenth century. His book takes the reader "on the trail," so to speak, by reconstructing the Westward journey from Council Grove, Kansas, to Santa Fe, New Mexico, beginning with preparing a proper outfit in Missouri. Each chapter is devoted to an important trail point, or landmark, or to a familiar sight along the trail — as buffalo. Vestal described in colorful, swiftly-paced prose not only the sights, sounds, and smells of the trail but also the people who made the journey and, in his words, "typical historic events." Some of these "typical" events read more as other legends and tall tales woven into the narrative! The role of the Indian is treated substantially and fairly by Vestal and his material on Indian customs and culture was drawn from generally reliable sources.

His approach was obviously anecdotal and perhaps a bit too dependent upon generalizations that, taken wrong, could be misleading; yet it has to be said that a reader will come away with a sense of the Santa Fe Trail and the period. The book lacks an index but contains in its appendix a chronology of the trail, Josiah Gregg's mileage and cost tables, and an adequate bibliography.

Suggested Fiction

Bean, Amelia, *The Fancher Train* (Doubleday, 1958)
Binns, Archie, *The Land is Bright* (Scribner's, 1939)
Fisher, Vardis, *The Mothers: An American Saga of Courage* (Vanguard, 1943)
Guthrie, A.B., Jr., *The Way West* (Sloane, 1949)
Hough, Emerson, *The Covered Wagon* (Appleton, 1922)

Moore, Lucia, *The Wheel & the Hearth* (Ballantine, 1953)
Morrow, Honoré Willsie, *On to Oregon* (William Morrow, 1926)

Suggested Films

The Big Trail (Fox, 1930) directed by Raoul Walsh.
The Covered Wagon (Paramount, 1923) directed by James Cruze.
Thunder in the Sun (Paramount, 1959) directed by Russell Rouse.
Wagonmaster (RKO, 1950) directed by John Ford.
The Way West (United Artist, 1967) directed by Andrew McLaglen.
Wheels of Destiny (Universal, 1934) directed by Alan James.

Transportation
and Communication

by Vicki Piekarski

I

In the decade between 1850–1860 the Westward advance of settlement pressed onward and outward. Scattered outposts grew up along Lake Superior's shores and in Minnesota's Red River Valley while the established settlements of Minnesota expanded and merged with the populated areas of Wisconsin and Iowa. Settlers spread out across Iowa into Nebraska and Kansas and the concentrated population of East Texas crept Westward and Northward. The populated areas of Oregon, Washington, and California grew in both size and number as did those in the Salt Lake and Upper Rio Grande areas. Along the Eastern Rockies new communities sprang up. By 1860 the population of the two million square miles of the Western territory was 3,316,879 — not including Louisiana. The majority of new land offices were opening in the West where settlement was most intense.

In the mid-1840s the idea for a transcontinental railroad was initiated by New York businessman, Asa Whitney, who called for a link with the China trade. Ongoing discussions about a railway spanning the breath of the nation continued for another twenty years plagued by indeterminate delays. In the meantime the West, with its unique settlement pattern which jumped half a nation with the discovery of gold in 1848, was faced with the problem of how to connect the Western settlers not only with each other but with Eastern markets. Western inhabitants were clamoring for letters, newspapers, and precious goods that make life not only bearable but possible. It was unanimously agreed upon that private enterprise would have to build a Western transportation and communication network, a network based on animal, not elusive steam, power. Financing the herculean endeavor was the first item on the agenda. The problem was solved in time by the liberal policy of the federal government which supplied generous subsidies in the form of mail contracts to stagecoach operators and military contracts to freighters.

The first military contract to supply Southwestern army outposts was awarded to James Brown of Independence in 1848 after the government's own unsuccessful attempt to provide supplies to General Stephen Kearny during the war with Mexico. It was generally believed that if federal subsidies could cover the freighter's expenses, the freighter could make additional profits supplying non-military settlements and thus somewhat appease the demands of Western civilians. Brown's efficient handling of the job won him two additional annual contracts which were taken over upon his death in 1850 by his newly acquired partner, William H. Russell. Russell, an impeccable New Englander with a gambler's nature in business matters, formed a partnership with William B. Waddell, a Virginian with a conservative approach to business, and for the next three years they ran a thriving business. In late 1854 in order to gain control of freighting on the central plains, the partners joined forces with a rival freighter, Alexander Majors, a plainsman as comfortable roasting meat over a fire built of *bois de vaca* as he was running a company. This unlikely alignment of personalities operating out of Leavenworth, Kansas, grew from a 300 wagon operation to a 3,500 wagon operation and they essentially controlled the overland plains freighting of food and industrial produce to both military outposts and mining communities until the Civil War.

A relatively obscure frontier type, freighters, who pushed the wagons through for thirty-five dollars a month, were known as "bull-whackers" or "muleskinners" depending on what kind of quaduped pulled the weight of their lumbering wagons, although oxen were preferred. They were considered the low man on the transportation totem pole following riverboat captains and stagecoach drivers. Notwithstanding, the enormous importance of freighters and their precious loads can really only be understood when one is confronted by the staggering statistics of their trade. In *The Transportation Frontier: Trans-Mississippi West* 1865–1890 (Holt, Rinehart, 1964) Oscar Osburn Winther arrived at these figures for freighting in 1865 which also illustrate the financial significance of military contracts. "...[A]n excess of one hundred million pounds of freight valued at more than seven million dollars was shipped from these Missouri River ports ... [Atchison, Nebraska City, St. Joseph, Plattsmouth, Kansas City, and Omaha]; and by combining all points on the Great Plains from which goods were either shipped or reshipped by wagon, the aggregate figures reach an estimated two hundred and twenty-four million pounds. Roughly about one half of these goods were shipped by the United States government, mainly to military establishments, and the balance was forwarded to civilians, especially merchants...."

For more than half a century freighters contributed greatly to the development of the West by keeping the life-sustaining goods moving throughout the West. (The unregulated cost was generally one dollar per hundred pounds for each hundred miles traveled and these charges were passed on to the customer.) They transferred merchandise from railroad terminals and riverboat ports to military outposts and mining and agricultural settlements. After the coming of the railroad, which freighters helped to build by carrying construction materials, freight wagons augmented the modern service by providing feeder line service to outlying communities where the railroad did not run. Their impressive record of service continued briefly into the Twentieth century before they completely vanished from the Western scene.

Freighters bridged the goods and merchandise gap created by the spacious and weary miles between frontier settlements, but it was not an efficient means of communication. The success of local stagecoach services and express services in California and in the tier of states West of the Mississippi River convinced Western folks that the stagecoach was an adaptable means of conveyence for both mail and news as well as passengers. What was needed, they said, was a transregional overland service for which the federal government should supply mail contracts.

Prior to the rush of 1849, mail was transferred to the Far West by willing individuals who picked up letters that were left in either St. Louis or Independence. Beginning in 1849 the government tried a number of experimental subsidy programs. They established a mail service by water through the Isthmus of Panama from New York via the U.S. Mail Steamship Company and from Panama to San Francisco via the Pacific Steamship Company. It was both a slow and costly service and unsatisfactory to Westerners. At the same time two overland services were subsidized: one to Salt Lake undertaken by Almond W. Babbitt who resigned after his first attempt, having decided there were better ways to end up in a poor house, and a second to Santa Fe over which mail was irregularly carried by pack animals accompanying traders. These unsuccessful snail's pace attempts at transferring mails merely served to whet the appetites of Westerners since the mail was often months *en route*.

For the next six years few improvements were forthcoming. Small operators given paltry subsidies battled harsh winter conditions in the Sierras and Indian attacks and consistently lost money. It became obvious to the Trans-Mississippi inhabitants that what was needed was a subsidy large enough to allow stagecoach service along a 2,000 mile overland route with way stations where teams and drivers could be rotated so that coaches could continue moving without lengthy interruptions. A petition with 75,000 signatures demanding this kind of service arrived in Washington, D.C., in 1856.

Almost immediately the sectional issue raised its ugly head.

Southerners wanted an overland mail route through the South and North-
erners proposed a central and shorter route through South Pass. The
squabble became extremely heated because it was believed that the route
developed for the overland mail would determine the location of the ever-
promised transcontinental railroad. The issue was avoided by an astute
Congress when their 1857 Post Office Appropriation bill proposed that the
postmaster general, then Aaron V. Brown from Tennessee, accept bids
from private individuals who could choose whatever route they liked
provided they met the provisions of a twenty-five day or less semi-monthly,
weekly, or semi-weekly service carried in coaches which would incidently
carry passengers. After receiving nine bids, Brown, a loyal Southerner,
awarded the annual $600,000 contract to a New York businessman, John
Butterfield, who proposed a Southern route through Texas and Albuquerque along the 35th parallel. Known by its opponents as the "ox-bow" route,
Butterfield spent $1,000,000 during 1857 in preparing the route—fashioning
roads, setting up way stations at twenty to eighty mile intervals, purchasing 1,800 horses and mules as well as "celerity" wagons, coaches built low
to the ground for travel in unsettled country, and 250 Concord coaches for
travel at both ends of the route. Approximately 2,800 miles in length, the
ox-bow trail began in Tilton, Missouri, the Western terminal of the railroad from St. Louis, and ended in San Francisco. In September, 1858
stagecoaches left from the Eastern and Western termini and both arrived at
their destination in less than the allotted time of twenty-five days. The
overland mail service soon surpassed the sea mail route in business and
Butterfield settled down to the everyday worries of running a stagecoach
operation.

Stagecoach travel was tedious but the Butterfield service did not
want for passengers who paid $200 for a trip overland. It was a monotonous
trip in which sleep and comfort were difficult to come by. The food served
at the cramped, dusty way stations was a major complaint expressed by
passengers who did not relish fried pork fat, half-baked biscuits, and a
liquid concoction that was passed off as coffee. Nonetheless, potential overlanders were not deterred by the lack of amenities and often waited ten
days for a seat on the Butterfield Overland Mail, as it was known in deference to its president. However, if Butterfield's service lacked critics, his
ox-bow route did not. The sectional issue still managed to elicit heated
debate and was finally resolved when the Southern states withdrew from
the Union and the Southern route was abandoned in favor of that of a
central route.

At almost the same time, in 1859 Brown's successor as postmaster
general, Judge Joseph Holt, cut back or cancelled small overland mail
subsidies. Russell of Russell, Majors, and Waddell made an effort to gain a
substantial mail contract by trying to prove the superiority of a central
route. Attempting to cash in on the rush to the gold fields of Colorado,
Russell in partnership with John S. Jones formed the Leavenworth & Pike's
Peak Express Company to transport passengers and express from the
Mississippi Valley to Denver without the blessing or help of his freighting

partners. The operation's mounting expenses of $1,000 a day brought the company near bankruptcy two seasons after it made its first run in April, 1858. Fearing their freighting business profits threatened, Waddell and Majors bailed Russell out and purchased the Leavenworth & Pike's Peak Express Company (which now included a semi-monthly mail service between Independence and Salt Lake purchased by Russell from John M. Hockaday in a last effort to save his floundering business by extending his route). The firm which also secured the mail contract into Placerville, California, became the Central Overland, California, & Pike's Peak Express, but Russell was not through yet. His proposal to run a ten day "horse express" between Missouri and California was well received in Washington, D.C.; so well, in fact, that Waddell and Majors could not say no to the new project, though instinctively they were against it. The 1,866 mile Pony Express route, as it came to be called, was established in a relatively short period of time and began operation from St. Joseph, Missouri, on 3 April 1860. Its 120 riders and 500 horses delivered in its eighteen-month life-span 34,753 pieces of mail. The cost, to the customer, was between two and ten dollars an ounce, and to its operators approximately thirty-eight dollars, forcing the business to run at a great loss. The venture's fate was sealed with the completion of the transcontinental telegraph line on 24 October 1861. Two days later the Pony Express made its last run. Russell, Majors, and Waddell did not survive despite Russell's desperate and illegal attempts to gain money; the firm slid into bankruptcy. Yet, in the process, Russell, Majors, and Waddell had done their share to prove the superiority of the central route and had supplied the West with an historical era filled with romance and drama.

The Central Overland, California & Pike's Peak Express Company was purchased by Ben Holladay. Described often as a coarse businessman, he was unquestionably a shrewd and bold entrepreneur. Indeed, Holladay became known as the "Napoleon of the Plains" once he gained control of the transportation routes of the central plains. The Holladay Overland Mail and Express Company monopolized over 3,000 miles of transportation lines which he gained through efficient and improved service on established routes and the opening of new runs into the inland regions. He wisely sold out to Wells, Fargo in 1866, having had the foresight to realize what the completion of the transcontinental railroad would mean. Over the years stagecoach operations made possible the conveyance of people, mail, and parcels to and from practically all settled areas of the West and continued its inestimable services in many areas beyond 1900.

The steamboat, invented in its most successful form by Robert Fulton, was an important means of transportation of goods and people in the areas of the West that contained navigable waterways. It superseded such traditional Western river crafts as the flatboat, keelboat, mackinaw, pirogue, and one-way sailboat. Trade and travel via waterways in the West, however, had its limitations because rivers were often unpredictable. The Missouri River (the Big Muddy), the longest and most important Western river of the Mississippi system measuring 3,100 miles in length, for example, generally alternated between flood stage and low waters. Yet, Western riverboat transportation was a great advance over wagon freighting and stagecoach operations. It served an important role in the Rocky Mountain fur trade and in the development of mining camps.

The uniting of the country by the completion of the transcontinental railroad on 10 May 1869 at Promontory Point, Utah — situated in Jim Bridger's old hunting grounds — was a great cause for celebration all over the country. It came within the first decade of the postbellum railroad boom. In 1865 there were 35,085 miles of track in the United States, only 3,272 of which were laid West of the Mississippi River. In 1890 there were 72,473 miles of track in the West; and, three years later, five lines connected the Pacific coast with major Eastern railway networks. Asa Whitney's dream had come true, but the dream of a railroad spanning the nation held precious by Westerners, especially farmers, remained for the most part unfulfilled. Prices for shipping via the steel tracks were exorbitant and unaffordable for the average Western settler. The metropolises that were to appear with the arrival of the tracks never materialized. Many settlers were bypassed entirely. Railroads were monopolistic, capitalistic, discriminatory, showed favoritism, and charged excessive rates far above actual costs — said Westerners. To a certain extent they were right, but the business maneuverings, stock manipulations, subcontracting scandals of the railroad magnates are a complex subject and cannot by explained in a few paragraphs. Suffice it to say that fortunes were made by the architects of the Western railroads far in excess of those made by such men as Ben Holladay, fortunes made in the *building* of railroads, not in their operation.

Already in the mid 1850s it was acknowledged by many Americans that a transcontinental railroad was of paramount importance to the stability and development of the West. The sectional question which arose in the antebellum period led in 1853 to an Army expedition crew being sent out to survey the possible routes based on Nature's sculpting of the terrain. It produced thirteen illustrated and detailed tomes of findings and four potential routes — two in the South and two in the North! The South's secession determined the central route as preferable. The years spent in meetings, debates, and planning had, however, if nothing else, convinced Congress that land grants and direct loans would be needed before private capitalists would undertake the project. In 1862 two corporations were empowered to begin work on the railroad — the Central Pacific Railroad to bridge the Sierras in California which broke ground at Sacramento's levee on 8 January 1863 and the Union Pacific, which broke ground in Omaha on 2 December 1863 to build Westward from the 100th Meridian to meet the Central Pacific at the California-Nevada line. The generous subsidies in the form of rights of way, land grants, and loans made the construction a lucrative enterprise. In fact, in the heat of excitement both railroad companies laid 200 miles of parallel track until the government stepped in and made Promontory Point the meeting juncture. The government paid most dearly in land grants, giving the Union and Central Pacific Railroads 45,000,000 million acres. In the aggregate, in excess of seventy-five railroad companies received approximately 130,000,000 acres of Western land during the boom years.

Although a direct threat to the Native Americans who were wary of both the white man's "talking wire" and "iron snake" or "horse," the building of Western American railroads was a spectacular accomplishment. Labor problems were solved by the hiring of veterans and Irish emigrants by the Union Pacific and by the hiring of San Francisco's Chinese population and other Orientals imported for the job by the Central Pacific. Portable villages, referred to as "Hell on Wheels," accompanied the crews to each halting area at the end of the tracks, carrying bartenders, gamblers, prostitutes, speculators, outlaws, and outcasts. The most difficult part of construction was the actual laying of the tracks. When building commenced, an average day produced one mile of track, whereas at the height of building (1868–1869), the Union Pacific could lay as many as six to seven miles a day. Upon the railroad's completion, the West could be traveled in five days, although it took up to ten days in an immigrant car which gave right of way to all other trains and which resembled a cattlecar in both decor and the ways the passengers were treated. Before the completion of the transcontinental railroad, feeder lines were under construction across the West. Within a relatively short period of time the railroads acquired great influence and control over the economic and political development of the West.

The first transcontinental railroad and the others that followed in the next several decades displaced the intricate animal-powered network created by transportation and communication pioneers. The West had stepped into the "modern age," but the railroads failed then, as they do now, to serve as a truly public utility, to run for the public's benefit. The words of Henry David Thoreau perhaps most eloquently expressed the feelings of the railroad's critics: "We had constructed a fate. We do not ride on the railroad; it rides upon us. Did you ever think what those sleepers are that underlie the railroad? Each one is a man, an Irishman, or a Yankeeman. The rails are laid on them, and they are covered with sand, and the cars run smoothly over them. They are sound sleepers, I assure you. And every few years a new lot is laid down and run over; so that, if some have the pleasure of riding on a rail, others have the misfortune to be ridden upon."

The West became symbolically fused to the East through a ceremonial laurel tie into which were placed two gold spikes from California, one gold and silver spike from Arizona, and one golden spike from Nevada. The West was tied to the East by steel rails, but not by public concerns, ideologies, politics, or ways of life. Momentarily the West was received into the bosom of the East as the long lost prodigal. Celebrations lasted for days all across the nation. The celebrations ended and the Eastern industrialists and the capitalists began their exploitation of the West. Yet a symbolic joining of hands always is a good reason for merry-making, makes for good news copy, and encourages the idea of a "national" history.

II

i

Transportation and communication encompass a large area of study from trails and roads, to freighters and traders, to stagecoaches and steamboats, to railroads which by the turn of the century just about supplanted completely animal-powered vehicles. It is an area of Western study much neglected by historians. Many of the standard works on various aspects were written decades ago, some more than half a century ago. The books contained in the following bibliography are restricted to those generally cited by historians and considered standard works in their field. Two books about early Western water travel excluded from the bibliography, because somewhat specialized, are, however, worthy of mention here: Hiram M. Chittenden's *History of Early Steamboat Navigation on the Missouri River* in two volumes (Harper's, 1903) and William E. Lass' *A History of Steamboating on the Upper Missouri* (University of Nebraska Press, 1962).

A number of railroad histories dealing with individual state or regional lines are recommended for those interested in an extensive study of railroads of the West. V.V. Masterson's *The Katy Railroad and the Last Frontier* (University of Oklahoma Press, 1952) chronicles the history of the first railroad to enter Indian territory and is reliable save on the subject of Belle Starr. Based on company records, L.L. Waters' *Steel Trails to Santa Fe* (University of Kansas Press, 1950) is a history of the Atchison, Topeka, and Santa Fe Railroad. Railroad building in the Northwest is adequately covered in James B. Hedges' *Henry Villard and the Railways of the Northwest* (Yale University Press, 1930). The works of Richard C. Overton have been highly praised by historians and critics alike. Two of his works are *Burlington Route: A History of the Burlington Lines* (Knopf, 1965) and *Gulf to Rockies: The Heritage of the Fort Worth and Denver-Colorado and Southern Railways, 1861–1898* (University of Texas, 1953). *Then Came the Railroad: A Century from Steam to Diesel in the Southwest* (University of Oklahoma Press, 1958) by Ira G. Clark should be read in conjunction with Robert Riegel's book (see below) since it updates much of Riegel's work while more restricted in scope.

Pertinent chapters on transportation and communication in *Vanguards of the Frontier* (D. Appleton-Century, 1941) by Everett Dick and the chapter on transportation in Ray Allen Billington's *Westward Expansion* (Macmillan, 1974) both provide background material and either can be used as a general introduction to the subject.

A word about first-hand accounts is in order since they have been excluded from this annotated bibliography. *Seventy Years on the Frontier* (Rand, McNally, 1893), the memoirs of Alexander Majors, though highly readable and sometimes cited as a first-hand account on freighting, is in actuality an autobiography which contains little information on Majors' years in freighting or on his partnership with Russell and Waddell. The bibliographical essay in Oscar Winther's *The Transportation Frontier*

(Holt, Rinehart, 1964) lists first-hand accounts in each area of transportation and may be useful to the reader.

II

ii

Athearn, Robert G., *Union Pacific Country* (Rand, McNally, 1971) O.P.

This intelligent, extensively researched work which takes a positive view of the role of the Union Pacific railroad is truly a pleasure to read. Spanning a period of time from the 1860s through the 1890s, Athearn traced the settlement and development of the "Union Pacific country," especially Nebraska, Kansas, Colorado, Montana, Wyoming, Idaho, and Utah. The book covers the building of the Union Pacific and its auxiliary and branch lines but is essentially a social history focusing on the railroad's impact on Westerners and the Western frontier. Athearn, who had access to company records and the cooperation of the Union Pacific Foundation, presented a surprisingly well balanced account of the story of the railroad's pioneering era and the story of those who awaited the arrival of the railroad as well as those, as the Mormons, who did not. Some unusual photographs are also contained in the volume and it might well serve as an antidote for the numerous turgid, fact-packed railroad histories so common in the treatment of the subject.

Brown, Dee, *Hear That Lonesome Whistle Blow — Railroads in the West* (Holt, Rinehart, 1977).

This railroad history which emphasizes the first transcontinental line is essentially an attack upon the men who used the railroad, either in its building or its operation, to make financial fortunes. In his inimitable style, Brown incorporated often bizarre but always fascinating human stories connected with the subject. It is filled with all manner of human interest material about planning, construction, operation, and travel on the Western railroads. Included are many accounts of syndicate formations, stock manipulations, and fund diversions manuevered by the railroad magnates and their hirelings. However, what makes this book worth reading are Brown's stories about the nameless thousands who were used by the railroad in its construction and as customers. Also, Brown, as an accepted white spokesperson for the Indians, presented the Indian point of view on railroad expansion, an aspect of the subject generally ignored by historians. Notwithstanding a number of factual errors. Brown's book provides the balance needed to offset the numerous books which have only praise for the railroad in the name of progress.

Frederick, J.V., *Ben Holladay, The Stagecoach King: A Chapter in the Development of Transcontinental Transportation* (Arthur H. Clark, 1940) O.P.

This biography, focusing mainly on the professional pursuits of Ben Holladay, has come to be regarded as a standard work on the stagecoach business of the 1860s. Based on available documentary material and interviews, Frederick traced the development of the transportation network of the West while describing Holladay's entrance and establishment in the freighting and coaching business. The routes, schedules, and operational difficulties—weather, highwaymen, and Indians—of the Overland Stage Line are the concern of the second half of the book which ends with a personal sketch of Holladay, the man, husband, and father. There are errors in this book, e.g., the story told in the wild West shows about "Buffalo Bill" Cody's experience on the line between Three Crossing and Split Rock is recounted. Yet, it is on the whole a well organized and well written study of stagecoaching on the central and inland routes prior to the advent of the railroad. Attached appendices include business forms, schedules, loss documents, and mail contracts.

Hafen, LeRoy R., *The Overland Mail* 1849–1869: *Promoter of Settlement, Precursor of Railroads* (Arthur H. Clark, 1926) O.P.

Hafen's standard, comprehensive history of the development of the Western stagecoach mail carrying services ought to be reprinted. Based upon research into government documents, newspapers, first-hand accounts, and interviews, this pioneering study examines the political, financial, and operational aspects of establishing and maintaining an overland mail service. A chronological treatment spanning a period from 1848–1869, Hafen devoted chapters to the beginnings of the American postal service in the Eastern United States, ocean mail service, pioneering mail services, the Butterfield Overland Mail, the Pony Express, central route services, and the last decade of stagecoach mail. Hafen's work presents clearly and concisely the fascinating story of the men and the business of getting the mail through and is still a highly readable account of the subject.

Hungerford, Edward, *Wells Fargo—Advancing the American Frontier* (Random House, 1949) O.P.

One of three books written attempting to tell the history of the Wells, Fargo express company, Hungerford's work is still considered the best. The author worked for the company in the capacity of advertising manager beginning in 1912 which gave him access to Wells, Fargo records in the course of his research. This apparent conflict of interest resulted in a highly laudatory history of Wells, Fargo without any regard for the "little people" that the monopolistic company left strewn in its path. Hungerford does cover, however, nearly a century of the company's activities and he sought out employees who remembered the old days and ways of Wells, Fargo express service. If approached with caution, this book provides information on Wells, Fargo's founders, employees, operations, equipment, mergers, and consolidations.

Hunter, Louis C., with the assistance of Beatrice Jones Hunter, *Steamboats on the Western Rivers: An Economic and Technological History* (Harvard University Press, 1949) O.P.

The focus of this well researched, scholarly book is steamboating in the Trans-Appalachian West and not the Trans-Mississippi West, although steamboat operations on the Missouri River are cursorily covered. Three major sections trace the economic and technological development of the Trans-Appalachian steamboating industry in the Nineteenth century from the introduction of steam navigation through its peak and decline with the triumph of the railroads. Hunter's chapters devoted to the structural and mechanical development of Western steamboats, the techniques and hazards of steamboat operation, as well as those containing descriptions of steamboat cabin and deck travel and the duties of steamboat workers might serve as a background source for the reader interested in river transportation.

Jackson, W. Turrentine, *Wagon Roads West* (University of California Press 1952) O.P.

Subtitled "A Study of Federal Road Surveys and Construction in the Trans-Mississippi West, 1846–1869," this geographic-chronological treatment of selected regional and trans-regional Western road projects is a significant contribution to a neglected phase of transportation. It was Jackson's belief that over the years historians, in attempting to glorify the Western frontiersman, "conveyed the impression that private citizens, endowed with a pioneering or entrepreneurial spirit, were primarily responsible for building the transportation pattern of Western America..." and in the process sight was lost of the significant role of the federal government in creating avenues of migration, commerce, and communication. This work, acknowledging the cooperative efforts between the federal government and private enterprise, both describes and assesses the federal government's program of reconnaissance, exploration, surveys, and improvements of Western trails and roads prior to the advent of the railroad. In addition to manuscripts, newspapers, and secondary sourcebooks, Jackson utilized the reports of the Corps of Topographical Engineers, the Office of Explorations and Surveys of the War Department, and the Pacific Wagon Road Office of the Interior Department — agencies upon which he focused. Examining a fairly specialized area, Jackson's book is a well documented, detailed analysis of the development of Western roads.

Moody, Ralph, *Stagecoach West* (Promontory Press, 1967) O.P.

Transportation as the "key factor in expanding the limits of the known world, spreading civilization, developing natural resources, and promoting commerce," is traced from stone age man, through the Romans, then the British, and on into the United States until we arrive in the West, which is the key focus of Moody's study. In a rambling fashion Moody outlined the development of Western coaching—regional and trans-regional—between 1849 and the early 1880s. Included are descriptions of coaches, drivers, driving techniques, equipment, way stations, and the lay of the land along the routes. The book is weakened by textual incongruities and the seeming detachment by the author from the material, masquerading in this case as objectivity. It is, however, the only attempt at a comprehensive study of the subject, so, to that extent, it is valuable, although it is best approached with great caution.

Riegel, Robert Edgar, *The Story of the Western Railroads—From 1852 Through the Reign of the Giants* (Macmillan, 1926) O.P.; reprinted by the University of Nebraska Press.

Riegel's straight-forward history, published over half a century ago, of the Western railroads from 1852 through the completion of the "railroad net" is still the standard work on the subject. With emphasis on the first Pacific railroad, this book focuses on the financial, engineering, and industrial aspects of railroad building in the West. Riegel wrote that "the influence of the railroads in encouraging settlement in the new West can hardly be overestimated" and throughout the book he demonstrated how construction and settlement progressed together once the physical, capital, and labor obstacles of the Trans-Mississippi West were overcome. The influential figures in the railroad business are highlighted and a separate chapter is devoted to what the author called "The Gould System," a monopolistic system that "must be deplored." The final chapters treat briefly the regulatory movement and the reorganization of the railroad business subsequent to the Panic of 1893, As history, the book's weakness is Riegel's attempt to view Westerners as a specific type with common traits. Containing a wealth of information on the development of Western railroads, this is a generally reliable background history.

Settle, Raymond W., and Mary L. Settle, *Empire on Wheels* (Stanford University Press, 1949) O.P.; *Saddles and Spurs: The Pony Express Saga* (Stackpole, 1955) O.P.; reprinted by the University of Nebraska Press; *War Drums and Wagon Wheels: The Story of Russell, Majors, and Waddell* (University of Nebraska Press, 1966) O.P.

The Settles' work in the area of Western transportation and communication has been a significant contribution. *Empire on Wheels*, a well documented history, as are all their works, is still generally considered the standard work on freighting in the West. Essentially, it is a history of the Russell, Majors, and Waddell freighting firm. These three men and their pioneering work in the freighting business are also the focus of *War Drums and Wagon Wheels* which carries their story through 1861. In spite of the fact that small freighting firms are neglected by the Settles, these two highly readable books deserve to be reprinted for the invaluable information they do contain.

Saddles and Spurs is the most scholarly study extant on the Pony Express. Russell, Majors, and Waddell and the overland mail issue provide the background material on the Pony Express in the early chapters. The major portion of the book, however, is devoted to the operation of the Pony Express and separate chapters detail the available information on the individual riders, station keepers, stations, and the routes and equipment used. The final chapters are concerned with the difficulties encountered during the Paiute War and, finally, the demise of the Pony Express service. The information presented is generally dependable and the authors examined available documents in controversial matters, such as who the first pony express rider was. All three of these concise, well written books are recommended.

Thompson, Robert Luther, *Wiring a Continent: The History of the Telegraph Industry in the United States* 1832–1866 (Princeton University Press, 1947) O.P.

The story of the telegraph as a means of Western communication is told in this book which is a history of the American telegraph system from the time its inventor, Samuel F.B. Morse, an artist, returned to the United States in 1832 through 1866 when the telegraph industry had undergone a revolutionary development and emerged as the "first great [American] industrial monopoly." Thompson's work is considered a prime work on the subject and is generally reliable albeit much of the information contained here is irrelevant to the study of the American West.

Walker, Henry Pickering, *The Wagonmasters* (University of Oklahoma Press, 1966).

This book surveys the subject of freighting in the High Plains region "from the earliest days of the Santa Fe Trail to 1880" in a loosely chronological topical fashion. In it, Walker attempted to show how freighting contributed to the development of the West by helping the economy of the Missouri Valley; by bringing a high standard of living to the Southwest; by helping in the colonization of the Great Salt Lake basin; and by supporting and sustaining the Civil War by transporting gold out of Montana and Colorado. The book includes detailed information on trails, trading centers, types of people involved in the freighting business, equipment, animals, trail routines, and merchandise costs. Freighting into the High Plains states — Utah, Colorado, New Mexico, and Montana — are covered in individual chapters as is the role of the U.S. government as a customer. The book is flawed by a number of shortcomings: the author insisted on introducing topics which he took nowhere or dropped suddenly and without explanation and he over-simplified or generalized matters of history and supported his statements by stories that often sound fanciful or apocryphal. His treatment of Indians is biased and they come across as a race undisciplined, unorganized, savage, and only able to win in battle by luck. Until a thorough, more developed, and better organized study of Western freighting is essayed, this book, if read in conjunction with one of the Settles' books (see above) on freighting, would give a reader an adequate perspective on the subject.

Winther, Oscar Osburn, *Express and Stagecoach Days in California* (Stanford University Press, 1936) O.P.; *Via Western Express and Stagecoach*

(Stanford University Press, 1945) O.P.; *The Transportation Frontier: Trans-Mississippi West* 1865–1890 (Holt, Rinehart, 1964) O.P.; reprinted by the University of New Mexico Press.

　　Both *Express and Stagecoach Days in California* and *Via Western Express and Stagecoach* deal with the transportation and communication network established in California during the pre-railroad period. *Express and Stagecoach Days in California* is a more scholarly work, emphasizing the economic trends connected with the business of transportation and concentrates upon statistical information. *Via Western Express and Stagecoach* focuses on the human side of the business. Winther described the delights and dangers of stagecoach travel, the environment and offerings of wayside stations, stage and express men and drivers as well as highwaymen. Many first-hand accounts are extensively quoted. The work concludes with the stories of the Butterfield Overland Mail, and the Wells, Fargo Company. These two books deserve to be reissued in that they provide an understanding of the establishment and development of the West Coast's animal-powered transportation and communication services. *Via Western Express and Stagecoach* is an especially good introduction to the subject.

　　The Transportation Frontier is an invaluable and indispensible work which provides an overview of the transportation systems of the West between 1865–1890. After a brief introductory chapter on the 1865 status of Western towns and cities, Western routes open to travel and commerce, and demographical statistics, Winther surveyed, by topic, the various means of transporting people and goods that developed in the West. The areas covered are overland wagon trains, freighting services, overland stage services, steamboats, railroads, and finally a chapter on the movement to create better roads. Winther described where and how each network was set up, by whom, and the dangers, advantages, and disadvantages of each type of service. Both primary and secondary sources were utilized in the writing of the book and it contains important statistical information. The weakest chapter, entitled "Indians, Outlaws, and Wayfarers," emphasizes the sensational aspects of frontier transportation and, based upon questionable sources, Indians are presented as little more than savages comprising a grave hardship and peril to Western travelers. This book is an excellent starting point for anyone interested in the subject of transportation and it contains a helpful bibliographical essay.

Suggested Fiction

Binns, Archie, *You Rolling River* (Scribner's, 1947)
Bristow, Gwen, *Jubilee Trail* (Crowell, 1950)
Fergusson, Harvey, *In Those Days* (Knopf, 1929)
Flynn, T.T., *The Man from Laramie* (Dell, 1954)
Fox, Norman A., *Night Passage* (Dodd, Mead, 1956)
Giles, Janice Holt, *Six Horse Hitch* (Houghton Mifflin, 1969)

Grey, Zane, *The U.P. Trail* (Harper's, 1918)
Haycox, Ernest, *Trouble Shooter* (Doubleday, 1937)
Norris, Frank, *The Octopus* (Doubleday, 1901)
Schaefer, Jack, *First Blood* (Houghton Mifflin, 1953)
Spearman, Frank, *Whispering Smith* (Scribner's, 1906)
Twain, Mark, *Life on the Mississippi* (1883)
Wellman, Paul I., *The Iron Mistress* (Doubleday, 1954)

Suggested Films

Arizona (Columbia, 1940) directed by Wesley Ruggles.
Apache Uprising (Paramount, 1966) directed by R.G. Springsteen.
Denver & Rio Grande (Paramount, 1952) directed by Byron Haskin.
The Iron Horse (Fox, 1924) directed by John Ford.
The Mississippi Gambler (Universal, 1953) directed by Rudolph Maté.
Pony Express (Paramount, 1953) directed by Jerry Hopper.
Rails into Laramie (Universal, 1954) directed by Jesse Hibbs.
Stagecoach (United Artists, 1939) directed by John Ford.
Steamboat 'Round the Bend (20th-Fox, 1935) directed by John Ford.
Union Pacific (Paramount, 1939) directed by Cecil B. DeMille.
Wells Fargo (Paramount, 1937) directed by Frank Lloyd.
Whispering Smith (Paramount, 1949) directed by Leslie Fenton.

The Literature

Being conversant in things held true by the herd is not to possess understanding. — Herakleitos.

Much of our criticism, obsessed with pleasure-values and blind to influence-values, seems to me frivolously irresponsible (with eccentric exceptions like Tolstoy) towards the vital effect of books in making their readers saner or sillier, more balanced or more unbalanced, more civilized or more barbarian. — F.L. Lucas.

Western Fiction

by Jon Tuska and Vicki Piekarski

I

i

Before providing a brief literary history of the development and permutations of Western fiction in the Nineteenth and Twentieth centuries, some formal distinctions should be made, in keeping with the theory of modes. We have employed historical reality as the basic standard for determining the mode in which a particular fiction is written and on this basis there are three such modes: the historical reconstruction, the romantic historical reconstruction, and the formulary Western. The difference between what is termed an historical construction in Western history and what we term an historical reconstruction in Western fiction consists in this: An historical construction, ideally, should contain no statement not necessitated or supported by the factual evidence whereas an historical reconstruction, because it is fiction and not history, can embellish the details based on the evidence *while it cannot at any point contradict the factual evidence*. An author of Western fiction cannot write an historical reconstruction in which the known facts of Western American history are deliberately distorted or violated. Yet this is what invariably happens in the other two modes, the romantic historical reconstruction and the formulary Western.

There are, in fact, *two* very powerful links between these two alternate modes. They both distort factual history, as was mentioned, and they both share a reliance on the structure of romance. Romance, as it was first developed by the Greeks, consists of an *agon*, or conflict, followed by *pathos*, in which the conflict is brought to its conclusion, and ends with an *anagnorisis*, or a recognition. There is an optional middle term, a *sparagmos*, or a mangling. In the basic Perseus myth, the typical romance structure reveals a helpless community ruled by an old and ineffectual king. The community is threatened by a devouring sea-monster and, in order to propitiate the sea-monster, the community regularly offers up a human sacrifice. Perseus, the hero, comes upon the scene just as the king's beautiful daughter is about to be made the next sacrificial victim. Perseus defeats and slays the sea-monster in combat, winning, as his reward, both the princess and the kingdom. A *sparagmos* episode may be included, in which Perseus is mangled in the course of the combat. The *anagnorisis* in the Perseus myth, as is also the case invariably in the formulary Western, is that it requires a hero to vanquish the villain or villains. The romantic historical reconstruction also possesses this structure of romance, but in addition, in the *anagnorisis*, offers an *ideological* interpretation of human history. Whatever occurs in a romantic historical reconstruction occurs for ideological reasons and is never merely the result of interaction with the land or between peoples, as these phenomena have happened in history.

The theory of the modes of Western fiction amounts to a poetics of the Western and it is a subject addressed at length in Jon Tuska's *Four Studies in Western Fiction*, cited below in the bibliography section. However, these three modes are convenient distinctions to keep in mind when surveying the narrative structures within the wide body of Western fiction.

ii

The opening of the American West was heralded in two pseudo-epic poems, *The Mountain Muse* (1813) by Daniel Bryan and *The Backwoodsman* (1818) by James Kirk Paulding. These were followed by the first three novels in James Fenimore Cooper's Leatherstocking saga, *The Pioneers* (1823), *The Last of the Mohicans* (1826), and *The Prairie* (1827) as well as by Timothy Flint's Southwestern novel, *Francis Berrian* (1826). Originally Cooper intended *The Pioneers* to tell the story of his father and the founding of Cooperstown, but its ultimate literary significance rests in his creation in it of his most memorable character, Natty Bumppo, who would henceforth be known by the names given him by the peoples of the forest, Hawk-eye, Deerslayer, and Pathfinder. In *The Pioneers* Bumppo is a man no longer young and he is alone save for his friend, the Indian known as John Mohegan, who is a drunk.

The Last of the Mohicans was in many ways a literary landmark. It moved back in time, to the period of the French and Indian War, and featured Bumppo, called Hawk-eye, and Mohegan, referred to by his

Indian name, Chingachgook, in the full bloom of their manhood, roaming freely, if at their peril, through the wilderness of the New World—which was really a wilderness only to the white man and never to the Native American. As all of Cooper's frontier novels, it is a romantic historical reconstruction, putting forth an ideology in which Indians are divided into two groups, those who as Chingachgook and his son, Uncas, are allies of the white man and fight to further Anglo-American imperialism and those, as Magua, who are vicious savages identified with Satan and every kind of Hellishness. Cooper personally knew nothing of Native American tribal customs or history and he was so hopelessly befuddled by the Indians that he treated as interchangeable Maquas, Hurons, Iroquois, indeed the five nations (later six) of the Iroquois Confederacy. He could see none of their civilization nor the fact that the American form of government—as concerns initiative, referendum, recall, and the notion of leaders as public servants—was derived in large measure from the Iroquois constitution. At his most benevolent he lamented that "in a short time there will be no remains of these extraordinary people." Colonel Munro's daughters in *The Last of the Mohicans* reinforced another stereotype. The elder, Cora Munro, the dark hair, with her dusky complexion, a result of Negro blood in her heritage, is passionate and vibrant; both Uncas, among the noble savages, and Magua, among the infernal savages, covet her, although neither can possess her because Cooper himself had a horror of miscegenation. Given this fact, it can end only one way for Cora and Uncas: they are united in death. It is the younger one, Alice Munro, the yellow hair, with her light complexion and trembling ways who is found fit for civilized life and a legitimate marriage to Major Duncan Heyward, an American Colonial in service with the Royal Army. The image of Alice Munro would prosper in American fiction generally for nearly a century and a half, "the girl" who needs saving and male protection in literally thousands of melodramas, adventure stories, and ranch romances.

D.H. Lawrence in his *Studies in Classic American Literature* (Thomas Seltzer, 1923) called Natty Bumppo "a saint with a gun." Here, truly, was an image of a hero at the very advent of American frontier fiction who resolves human predicaments through the violent use of firearms—epitomized in *The Last of the Mohicans* in the scene where Hawkeye shoots and kills Magua—and it was in this guise that Bumppo became a heroic prototype. Timothy Flint based his characterization of Daniel Boone on Bumppo in his largely fictional *The Life and Adventures of Daniel Boone, the First Settler of Kentucky, Interspersed with Incidents in the Early Annals of the Country*.

Cooper was living in Paris when he wrote *The Prairie* which tells of the death of Natty Bumppo. In terms of internal chronology, it ends the Leatherstocking saga. *The Pathfinder* (1840) which appeared after Cooper had returned to the United States shows Bumppo middle-aged and tells of his one serious flirtation with love which ends with his rejecting it. By this time Cooper felt out of touch with the United States and what he could perceive as the overwhelming greed of its citizens and their obsession with raping the wilderness. His disenchantment forced him to muse even farther back in time, as he did in *The Deerslayer* (1841) set in the very area where he was then living, but long before, of course, there ever was a Cooperstown. It was this book which was Cooper's own personal favorite and while Hawk-eye is insistent throughout the saga that he is completely without Indian blood we are told of him that "he had caught the stoicism of the Indians, well knowing that there was no more certain mode of securing their respect than by imitating their self-command." But Cooper was still ambivalent. In *The Oak Openings* (1848), one of his very last books, he not only succeeded in writing a novel without a romance, but he chose for his hero a man who subdues Indians and the wilderness, rising to a position of influence in his community and even being elected a state senator. Cooper had made his peace at long last, but with it he confirmed for himself and his work a diminished stature as a creative moral force. Without Cooper's many ambivalences, waverings, biases, contradictions, and limitations, the Leatherstocking saga might have become a major work of art; but it did not.

Timothy Flint's first novel tells of the title character, Francis Berrian, who leaves his theological studies at Harvard to search for adventure in the West. He winds up falling in love with a Spanish señorita and subsequently rescues her from a hostile Indian named Menko with the help of an Indian maiden named "The Red Heifer." Berrian also manages to join the ranks of a Mexican revolutionary, eventually saving his Spanish fiancée's parents and their priest from death. The novel remains important because, however tritely written, it puts forth several popular stereotypes which were predominant in Southwestern literature in the Nineteenth century and in the Twentieth: the manly, courageous Anglo-American, the beautiful but helpless Spanish señorita, the treacherously vindictive Spanish rival, the menacing, lustful Indian, and the sweet, self-sacrificing Indian maiden. Incidentally, there is a direct line from the romanticized image of Pocahontas in history through "The Red Heifer" in this novel to Natzie in General Charles King's *An Apache Princess* (Hobart, 1903), to Redwing in Edwin Milton Royle's stage play, *The Squaw Man* (1905), to Annie-Many-Ponies in B.M. Bower's *The Heritage of the Sioux* (Little, Brown, 1916), to North Star in Will Henry's *No Survivors* (Random House, 1950), to Lotus in Vardis Fisher's *Mountain Man* (Morrow, 1965), to how many other Indian maidens in how many novels! The only stereotype mostly confined, it would seem, to the Nineteenth century is that of the scheming Roman Catholic priest.

George Frederick Ruxton, in addition to his personal journal, *Adventures in Mexico and the Rocky Mountains 1846–1847* (1847), wrote a novel about mountain men titled *Life in the Far West* (1849). Prompted to explore in the New World by Cooper's forest romances, Ruxton subsequently created two mountain men — based on personal experience — far more realistic than is Natty Bumppo. Ruxton's novel has exerted a continuous influence on other authors who have similarly written of this period and used mountain men as characters, from Mayne Reid in *The Scalp Hunters*

(1851) in the Nineteenth century to, in the Twentieth, Harvey Fergusson in *Wolf Song* (Knopf, 1927), Stewart Edward White in *The Long Rifle* (Doubleday, 1932), A.B. Guthrie, Jr., in *The Big Sky* (Sloane, 1947), Frederick Manfred in *Lord Grizzly* (McGraw-Hill, 1954), and Vardis Fisher in *Mountain Man*. Indeed, in several of these novels whole episodes are lifted directly from Ruxton's text with only minor alterations.

The Scalp Hunters was Mayne Reid's second novel and, despite his prolificacy, is perhaps his most memorable fictional work. Narrated in the first person singular by M. Henry Haller, the novel is set in the West from St. Louis to Santa Fe and extending South from El Paso into Chihuahua. Among its other characters is St. Vrain, who was a real-life Santa Fe trader. Haller earns his heroic reputation by riding a buffalo and is later saved from a death in quicksand by his horse, Moro, thus anticipating by more than half a century the glamorous stature accorded a hero's horse by both formulary Western fiction and "B" Western films in the Twentieth century. The latter part of the novel is a captivity story. This was, and to an extent remains, a popular sub-genre in Western fiction which had its beginnings in Colonial times with such tales as "A Narrative of the Captivity and Restauration of Mrs. Mary Rowlandson" (1862); in fact the central plot ingredient of both Cooper's *The Last of the Mohicans* and *The Deerslayer* is white women captured by the Hurons. The novel ends with Haller marrying and, unlike Cooper's novels, it became a convention in Reid's fiction to marry off all the available characters at the conclusion.

Reid made frequent use of the theme of the heroine's weak brother caught in the clutches of a lecherous villain with designs on the heroine. All of Reid's dramatic stress in his fifty-odd frontier sagas was on action and, hence, most of his characters, however unconvincingly drawn, are purely functional: they move along the plot. He also indulged excessively in the convention of having many of his characters speak in dialect to the point where at times what they are saying is incomprehensible to a contemporary reader. Reid almost invariably characterized Indians as "the enemy" and he believed the most outlandish notions about them, such as seconding Ruxton in the specious idea that the Pueblos and Navajos were descended from the Aztecs. Reid attributed what he felt was the "inferiority" of the Indians to cultural, rather than racial, deficiencies and he was, if anything, even harsher toward the Mexicans whom he portrayed as vicious and debased. His dislike for the Roman Catholic church prompted him to continue the stereotype of the culprit priest articulated by Timothy Flint and in *The White Chief: A Legend of Northern Mexico* (1855) the priests are shown to be behind all the trouble. Reid celebrated the spirit of Yankee imperialism which he firmly believed would alone be able to save the Southwest from the barbarism and low-life savagery into which it had fallen as a result of the malignant combination of Mexicans, Indians, and Roman Catholic priests. As Ruxton before him, Francis Parkman who was his contemporary, and Zane Grey after him, Reid condemned the Mormons for their polygamy. When *The Scalp Hunters* appeared, Reid was *en route* to London and there he remained for the rest of his life, anticipating by his example that large number of writers who lived in the Eastern United States or in Europe and who contributed greatly to the growing body of fantasy and delusion about what life was on the Western American frontier.

Bret Harte, hailed during his lifetime as the *doyen* of writers on the American West, went to California from the East when he was seventeen. He worked at various jobs, began writing, and an early version of *M'Liss; An Idyll of Red Mountain* (1863) was based on his experiences as a school-teacher in a mining district. By 1868 Harte had achieved sufficient local fame as a writer to be made editor of a new magazine, *The Overland Monthly.* It was in the pages of this magazine that Harte's most famous short stories first appeared, "The Outcasts of Poker Flat," "The Luck of Roaring Camp," and "Tennessee's Partner." Because of the national readership of *The Overland Monthly*, Harte's tales, so filled with new characters, new experiences, and new ways of looking at things, caused a sensation in the East and his reputation became such that his poem, "The Heathen Chinee" (1870), was a national bestseller and on everybody's lips.

In his short fiction over the next three decades, Harte introduced a number of original characters in his stories who were to become stereotypical in the hands of his many imitators. Among them, certainly, are his stage driver, Yuba Bill, the gamblers, John Oakhurst in four stories and Jack Hamlin in nineteen stories and Harte's long novel, *Gabriel Conroy* (1876), the garrulous Spanish-American Enrique Saltello, the lawyer and gentleman, Colonel Culpepper Starbottle, the intelligent backwoods practitioner, Dr. Duchesne, along with one-time appearances by Salomy Jane who saves an outlaw and makes a new life for them, Cherokee Sal, the prostitute in "The Luck of Roaring Camp," Uncle Jim and Uncle Billy whose friendship envisions an alternative life-style, and notable Chinese characters such as See Yup and Wan Lee. Harte wrote sympathetically of animals, especially of dogs and horses, and he was ever a champion of the oppressed. Not only did he object to the way in which Chinese and blacks were made victims of racial intolerance, but when the citizens of a town where he was the editor of a local newspaper massacred a village of Indians, the diatribe he printed led to his having to leave for San Francisco. Harte's literary West was not the black and white stereotype of virtue versus vice typical of so many later formulary writers; rather it embodied an image of a harsh, hostile world where, quite literally, luck or even a change in the weather could mean the difference between life and death. In romantic fashion, his bad men were occasionally good-hearted and his good men were frequently unjust and tyrannical; so much so that these ideological distinctions, in the ideology of his fiction, become ultimately nearly meaningless. His portraits of female characters were far in advance of his time in terms of Western fiction and in short novels such as *A Phyllis of the Sierras* (1891) and *Three Partners* (1893) they are drawn with a delicate understanding uncommon in a male author.

Because of his literary success, Harte was able to help Mark Twain's early literary career and that of several others. In 1877, having fallen into financial difficulties and having been unsuccessful as a lecturer, Harte collaborated with Twain on a play titled *Ah Sin* based on some Harte short stories and his poem, "The Heathen Chinee." The experience, viewed from Twain's side who was vociferous in his denunciations of Harte, was such as to make Twain permanently embittered.

In his own right, Twain is probably the most controversial literary figure in American letters in all of the Nineteenth century, beloved as much today for what he wrote and did not publish as he was once praised for what he did write and publish. He succeeded, where Harte failed, at making himself into a legendary personality, and his image, especially in his later years, became the incarnation of an American folk hero, kept alive into the present by various actors who continue to portray him in touring stage shows and in television docu-dramas. Twain's contribution to Western American literature is various, but a substantial part of it is to be found in his first-hand accounts. *Roughing It* (1872), devoted to his experiences in the Far West, and *Life on the Mississippi* (1883), both of which are sufficiently dependent on tall tales to qualify as fiction. Twain struck a compromise with his Tom Sawyer character; but in the conclusion to *The Adventures of Huckleberry Finn* (1884), when he showed Huck contemplating heading out for the Territory, he was giving voice to the other side of his soul, that side which, very much as Bret Hart in his fiction, identified the Far West with unconventionality, personal freedom, and individuality in the face of Eastern conformity.

While all this was happening, the tradition of the formulary Western was born in the dime novel. The notion of the dime novel emerged as a consequence of Erastus and Irwin Beadle in 1858, after the success of *The Dime Song Book*, engaging Robert Adams as a partner and starting a firm called the House of Beadle and Adams. The first complete novel under one cover, sold for a dime, was Ann S. Stephen's *Malaeska: The Indian Wife of the White Hunter* (1860). It sold 65,000 copies within the first few months. Edward S. Ellis' *Seth Jones: or, The Captives of the Frontier* (1860) soon followed and it sold 60,000 copies almost immediately, was translated into half a dozen languages, and, in time, sold an awesome 600,000 copies.

Orville J. Victor, formerly a journalist from Sandusky, Ohio, was hired as editor-in-chief for Beadle and Adams, a position he held for thirty years. Once rival publishers began to spring up, Victor had a ready solution: he advised Beadle writers to "kill more Indians." Although the formats might vary, the stories were nearly all the same. They ran between 30,000 and 50,000 words with the main emphasis on continuous action and inflated descriptions. Not all dime novels were Westerns, but a good many of them were. Unlike Cooper who at least mincingly attempted to face the tragic consequences of America's blind commitment to *material* progress, the dime novelists avoided the darker issues and instead celebrated the doctrine of Manifest Destiny. To take but one example, Percy St. John wrote of the pioneers in *Queen of the Woods: or, The Shawnee Captive* (1868): "Never weary, never conquered, they advanced still onward toward the setting sun, laying first the foundations of home and then of empire." It was this spirit that was infused into paintings such as Albert Bierstadt's "Sunset on the Oregon Trail" (1867) and John Gast's more familiar "Manifest Destiny" (1872); and it was this same sentiment that was still being celebrated in many Western films in the Twentieth century.

The heroes in the earliest dime novels were based on Natty Bumppo. They were also backwoodsmen, but, from the very beginning, they fell into two distinct types: the violent ugly white man who was invariably an Indian-hater and the saintly forest guide. Lew Wetzel, a well-known Kentucky scout, was a model for the violent ugly white man in adventures such as Emerson Radman's *Lew Wetzel, the Scout: or, The Captives of the Frontier* (1866). After 1870, however, this type was more and more relegated to a secondary role, usually in support of a virtuous backwoodsman hero; and, before long, the violent ugly white man was transformed completely into a comic sidekick, another innovation which was inherited by Western films.

Mayne Reid increasingly wrote for the dime novel market. Emerson Bennett in his best-selling novel, *The Prairie Flower* (1849), however much it might owe to borrowings from Ruxton, introduced Kit Carson by name as a frontier scout and thus contributed to the precedent set by Daniel Bryan's *The Mountain Muse* which featured Daniel Boone of using actual frontier personalities as protagonists in fictional adventures. In the decades from 1860 to 1890 Carson was featured in more than seventy original tales and reprints. As a character, Carson represented a transition from the backwoodsman hero, be it Daniel Boone or Davy Crockett, to the plainsman; yet, historically, Carson was perhaps more a mountain man than a plainsman. The prototype *par excellence* of the plainsman had to wait for Edward Z.C. Judson, who wrote under the pseudonym Ned Buntline, to glamorize an obscure frontier scout he had met at Fort McPherson, Nebraska. William F. Cody made his fictional debut in *Buffalo Bill, the King of the Border Men* (1869). This novel was made into a successful stage play and, before long, Cody embarked on his own show business career. When Prentiss Ingraham, Cody's publicity director, took over the Buffalo Bill stories, writing some 121 of the total 557 published, he exaggerated Cody's exploits to an even more incredible degree than had formerly been the case. Because of Cody's theatricalism, he was dressed as garishly in the novels as in person.

Two less prominent types of heroes in dime novels were outlaws and — chronologically last of all — cowboys. Edward L. Wheeler wrote *Deadwood Dick, the Prince of the Road: or, The Black Rider of the Black Hills* (1877) for Beadle and Adams, and it inaugurated a whole series of Deadwood Dick stories. Other firms seeking to compete did not bother with fictional outlaws (although as many as seven different road agents insisted they had been the model for Deadwood Dick) but chose actual criminals by name to idealize as heroes, men such as Jesse and Frank James, the Younger brothers, the Daltons, Butch Cassidy, and the Sundance Kid. Already in the Nineteenth century Americans were concerned about widespread political corruption, monopolistic power, and legal banditry, so it was perhaps inevitable that, feeling impotent to do anything about this situation or simply disinclined, they should willingly engage in a fantasy about being saved by these actual frontier thieves and murderers who were transformed into honest, heroic anti-establishment outsiders. Billy the Kid alone seems to have escaped this idealization process, probably because Pat Garrett, who shot him, wrote the prototypical dime novel about him and if Garrett was a hero the Kid could only be classed as a villain. Yet even the Kid began to live a dual life after the turn of the century, variously conceived as a vicious killer or a much-maligned hero.

Frederick Whittaker wrote *Parson Jim, King of the Cowboys: or The Gentle Shepherd's Big "Clean Out"* (1882) which is, technically, the first appearance in a dime novel of a cowboy hero. Prentiss Ingraham followed in 1887 writing about the supposed exploits of Buck Taylor, a star in Buffalo Bill's Wild West Show, but in a way these books were ahead of their time and failed to attract a wide number of readers. It was not until Owen Wister's stories about Lin McLean and the Virginian began appearing in *Harper's Magazine* that the cowboy hero emerged as a popular type. Wister's stories, "Hank's Woman" and "How Lin McLean Went East," the former featuring both Lin and the Virginian, appeared in 1892 and were so well received by readers that Henry Alden, the editor of *Harper's*, worked out a contract with Wister, who had been traveling to Wyoming for reasons of health since 1885, to journey throughout the West to search for further story material.

Wister was essentially an Eastern snob. In his first book collection of stories, *Red Men and White* (1896), he showed a condescending attitude toward Native Americans coupled with a disproportionate admiration for veteran Indian fighters such as General Crook who, in Wister's opinion, knew better how to deal with Indians than those Easterners who were "rancid with philanthropy and ignorance." The previous year Wister published his essay, "The Evolution of the Cow-Puncher" (1895), in which he set down his vision of the cowboy as a modern incarnation of the medieval knight of romance. "Destiny tried her latest experiment upon the Saxon," he wrote, "and plucking him from the library, the haystack, and the gutter, set him upon his horse; then it was that, face to face with the eternal simplicity of death, his modern guise fell away and showed once again the medieval man. It was no new type, no product of the frontier, but just the original kernal of the nut with the shell broken." There was no legitimate basis for such a notion in reality. It was an *idée fixe* Wister took with him into the West and projected onto the cow-punchers he found there; but it was also a notion which struck the fancy of the East.

Wister's first Western novel was *Lin McLean* (1897) which consists actually of six short stories strung together with the same central character. Lin falls in love twice in this novel, the first time with Katie Lusk, a hash-slinger from Sidney, Nebraska, who has a husband still living from whom she has never been divorced and to whom she returns once he has money again and Lin has lost what money he had; the second romance is with the wooden, lifeless, perverse Jessamine Buckner, a woman from Kentucky who is characterized from the outset by her unrealism. It would seem that Wister's personal values constantly interfered with his objective to describe the West and its people as they really were. Romance and marriage in his two novels, as in some of his stories, serve only to emasculate his cowboys, to make them seem more docile Easterners concerned mostly with personal ambition, accumulation of wealth, and achieving what by Eastern standards could only be considered social standing, rather than luxuriating in their freedom, the openness and emptiness of the land, and the spontaneity of its inhabitants combined with the West's utter disregard for family background or education. To make his cowboys more acceptable heroes *to himself*, Wister felt compelled, perhaps unconsciously, to provide them with what he felt were proper values and it is for this reason that his stories always fail to depict accurately the real nature of the clash between East and West.

The *Jimmyjohn Boss and Other Stories* (Harper's, 1900) contains Wister's short novel, "Padre Ignazio," the story of a European priest working in a California mission. He reversed the trend of the Nineteenth century which regarded Roman Catholic priests with suspicion and, instead, reinforced a new trend, romanticizing them.

In his political and social philosophy Wister was a Progressive and what has come to be termed a social Darwinist, meaning that he believed in a natural aristocracy, a survival of the fittest — the fittest being those who measured up best to his personal values. In *The Virginian* (Macmillan, 1902), which became a bestseller the month it was published and which has never been out of print since, Wister put his philosophy into the mouth of the Virginian when he remarks, "'Now back East you can be middling and get along. But if you go to try a thing in this Western country, you've got to do it *well*.'" Yet at the same time in his notebooks, which were subsequently published as *Owen Wister Out West: His Journals and Letters* (University of Chicago Press, 1958), Wister lamented the sloth which he felt the West induced in people and it was this lamentation which anticipated his disillusionment with the real West and his refusal, after 1911, ever to return there. Wister's basic defense against this was to exalt his heroes; but as the late Mody Boatright observed in "The American Myth Rides the Range: Owen Wister's Man on Horseback" in the *Southwest Review* (Summer, 1951) "Wister's pathetic search for a leader brought him to the conclusion that Theodore Roosevelt was 'the greatest benefactor we people have known since Lincoln.'"

Wister's heroine in *The Virginian* is Molly Wood. When Molly Wood made her first appearance in "The Winning of the Biscuit-Shooter," a Lin McLean story which ran in *Harper's* in 1893, McLean remarks, "'I'm glad I was not raised good enough to appreciate the Miss Woods of this world ... except at long range.'" As an indication of how much Wister had changed in the intervening years, in the final version of *The Virginian* McLean is one of Molly Wood's rejected suitors! Westerners such as McLean once was in Wister's earlier fiction might have been disgusted by Molly Wood, but Eastern women could easily identify with her and her romance with a shining Wyoming cowboy who spoke with a gentle Southern drawl. *The Virginian* was adapted for the stage; it was filmed four times; and it served as the basis for a television series. As early as *The Light of Western Stars* (Harper's, 1914), Zane Grey could use the new stereotype in place of characterization when he introduced his own hero as "a cowboy, and his entrance recalled vividly ... that of Dustin Farnum in the first act of *The Virginian*." Moreover, Wister's melodrama of a conflict between a hero and a villain which ends with the death of the villain and the marriage of the hero to the heroine gave new literary stature to a long-established pattern in the formulary Western as it had come of age in the dime novels.

Wister's last collection of short stories, *When West Was West* (Macmillan, 1928), conveys by the title itself how he felt that the West he had created had vanished and the tone is uniformly one of nostalgia and disillusionment. Most of these stories had been published in *Cosmopolitan* and reflect the kind of cynicism which typified short stories in that publication. For example, Wister's "Skip to My Loo" tells of a man returning home who decides to spend the night with a whore before seeing his wife only to discover that his wife is the whore. The last story in the collection is fitting. Titled "At the Sign of the Last Chance," Wister described how one night a group of cowboys in a poker game come to the realization that their time is over and they take down the sign of the saloon and bury it in remembrance of a West that was once but is no more.

Helen Hunt Jackson in 1879 in Boston heard Standing Bear, chief of the Ponca Indians, and Bright Eyes, a mixed-blood spokesperson for Indian rights, talk on tribal wrongs. She became concerned over the white man's treatment of the Indians and, after extensive research, published at her own expense *A Century of Dishonor* (1881), a bitter arraignment of the federal government for its handling of Indian affairs. The following year she was commissioned, along with Abbot Kinney, to review the living conditions of the mission Indians in California. No governmental action was taken on the commission's report, so Jackson decided to use the information she had collected for a novel intended to aid the Indian cause and which she titled *Ramona* (1884). Jackson claimed that *Ramona* might do for the Indians what her friend, Harriet Beecher Stowe, had done for blacks with her novel, *Uncle Tom's Cabin* (1852); but the readers of *Ramona* were more impressed by the romantic images of the California missions and the Spanish dons than with the problems of the Indians, and doubtless it was for this audience that Wister later intended his own treatment of the subject in "Padre Ignazio."

Timothy Flint and Mayne Reid, in dealing with the influence of the Roman church, put forth one kind of ideology, Jackson and Wister, as subsequently Willa Cather and Paul Horgan, another; neither view came close to the historical reality. "More important than the pueblos or presidial towns in early California were the mission stations," Ray Allen Billington wrote in *The Far Western Frontier: 1830–1860* (Harper's, 1956), "for here life and economic activity were centered. A chain of twenty-one of these imposing structures, located fourteen leagues apart (that being a day's travel), stretched from San Diego to the San Francisco peninsula. Their holdings were astronomical, for at the height of their power they technically possessed all settled land in California.... On these mission lands lived thirty thousand Indians in 1830, all not only converted but transformed into industrious farmers and herdsmen by the zealous Franciscan fathers.... At the San Gabriel Mission, the Indians cared for 150,000 cattle, 20,000 horses, and 40,000 sheep; while the holdings of all missions combined in 1834 amounted to 400,000 cattle, 60,000 horses, and 300,000 sheep and swine."

Frederic Remington's experience of the West, no less than that of Wister, resulted in disillusionment. In the summer of 1885, while prospecting in the Arizona territory, Remington learned that Geronimo had broken loose from his reservation captivity. Remington used the situation to his advantage, sketching several Apache Indians on the San Carlos reserve and three renegades who paid a hungry visit one night to his campsite. He never came within two hundred miles of Geronimo, but this did not faze Easterners who made his reputation almost overnight when his sketches began to be published. No less a one than Theodore Roosevelt who in *Century* magazine had just begun to publish early pieces from what would become his book, *Ranch Life and the Hunting Trail* (1888), asked for Remington to be his illustrator. Remington also illustrated Wister's stories. After these commissions, Remington himself turned to writing, often illustrating his own materials which appeared first in magazines and then in book form, comprising a brace of volumes, *Pony Tracks* (1895) and *Crooked Trails* (1898).

For Remington, as for Stephen Crane who also took a tour of the West and wrote several stories and sketches with a Western setting, the meaning of the Western experience was the confrontation between man and a hostile environment, be it physical or human. Remington was not romantic in the way Wister was, and his stories are not obsessed with the courtship of contrary women; nor was he a believer, as was Roosevelt, in the strenuous life for its own sake; albeit he was as much a racial elitist as they were. Remington might rail at wilderness conditions, but he felt inexorably drawn to them; and, as the years passed, his hatred for the industrial civilization of the East, where he continued to live, mounted in intensity. Toward the end of the century, Remington published four stories collected in *Sundown Leflare* (1899) in which Sundown complains that the "'white man mak de wagon, un de seelver dollar, un de railroad, un he tink dat ees all dair ees een de country.'"

Remington, also as Stephen Crane, became a correspondent during the Spanish-American War, covering the Cuban campaign. He went in enthusiastic and came out despondent. He was commercially cynical enough to paint, on a commission from Theodore Roosevelt, the fantasy portrait of Roosevelt leading the "Rough Riders" in a charge up San Juan Hill which had no basis whatsoever in fact, but to himself he hoped that the entire debacle would be sufficient to discourage Americans from ever engaging

in other such patriotic missions abroad. In what may well be his finest
fictional work and his only novel, *John Ermine of the Yellowstone*
(Macmillan, 1902), Remington narrated the story of a white child raised by
Indians who eventually joins the U.S. Army as a scout. Through Ermine's
eyes the reader contrasts the Indian way of life with the "senseless mass of
white humanity" always pressing further Westward. Ermine is popular
with the soldiers until he has the audacity to fall in love with a white
woman, the major's daughter, after which he is ostracized and, seeking
vengeance against her fiancé, is killed by a Crow scout seeking recognition
from the heroine. It was a powerful idea, but definitely out of keeping with
its time.

In 1899 *The Atlantic Monthly* published Jack London's story, "An
Odyssey of the North," which as a breath of fresh air introduced readers to
the Northland as London had experienced it while he was there prospecting
for gold during the Klondike rush of 1896. It was the first of London's
series of truly remarkable stories in which men and animals are pitted
against Nature, or men against animals, or men against men. Virtually all
of his Northland fiction deals with one aspect or another of the struggle for
survival, a unifying ideological metaphor. "To Build a Fire" which was
collected in *Lost Face* (Macmillan, 1910) demonstrates the difficulty of surviving amid the great cold; "In a Far Country" which was collected in *The
Son of the Wolf* (Houghton Mifflin, 1900) shows the devastating effect of
cabin fever on two men during a long winter; "The Law of Life" which was
collected in *Children of the Frost* (Macmillan, 1902) tells of an old Indian
left to starve by his tribe because of their mutual poverty and hunger. The
spirit of these stories culminated in what has come to be regarded as
London's lasting contribution to world literature, *Call of the Wild*
(Macmillan, 1903), a dog story which is also an allegory about modern
man's struggle to dominate Nature in which Nature and the wilderness
triumph as Buck, a domesticated dog, follows a wolf pack into the waste-
lands and becomes the pack's leader. London reversed this ideology in
White Fang (Macmillan, 1906) in which a wild dog becomes domesticated
by the end. In the short story, "Bâtard," which was collected in *The Faith
of Men and Other Stories* (Macmillan, 1904) London told of a dog and a
man held together by hate until at last, whipped and tormented beyond
endurance by the man, the dog kills him. In "All Gold Canyon" which was
collected in *Moon-Face and Other Stories* (Macmillan, 1906) London
illustrated the white man's dreadful plunder and rape of the earth. London
went on to write novels and stories with many different settings, but it was
his Northland adventures — often so much more than just
adventures — which inspired an entire group of writers in the early Twentieth century, among them Rex Beach, James Oliver Curwood, James B.
Hendryx, and the early Max Brand.

Alfred Henry Lewis' interest and travels in the American West
prompted him to create a character he named the "Old Cattleman" who
narrates what Lewis called the Wolfville stories, the first of which
appeared in the *Kansas City Star* in 1890. As Bret Harte and Owen Wister,

Lewis stressed local color, but unlike Harte he did so at the expense of a
well-made plot; and unlike either Harte or Wister he was hampered by his
narrator who has a penchant, as have many of Mayne Reid's characters, of
talking so exclusively in the vernacular as to make most of his stories somewhat inaccessible to a contemporary reader. In addition to these collections
of short stories, Lewis wrote a Western novel, *The Sunset Trail* (A.S.
Barnes, 1905), which was a fictional biography of Bat Masterson whom
Lewis knew and to whom he dedicated the book. *The Sunset Trail* is
largely fantasy, but it anticipated a legion of similar hero-worshipping
fictional biographies in the Twentieth century.

Two authors who were more or less ambivalent to the trends dominating Western fiction at the close of the Nineteenth century were Marah
Ellis Ryan and Hamlin Garland. In much of Ryan's fiction her love of
Nature and admiration for people living on the frontier was contrasted
with critical portraits of Eastern snobs. In *Told in the Hills* (1890) after
numerous wilderness adventures a woman from Kentucky rejects "civilized
life" forever and settles in Montana. In *That Girl Montana* (Rand, McNally,
1901) a woman raised in the West, having gone East to live in New York
City only to find the restrictions placed on her intolerable, returns to the
West. In books such as *Told in the Hills* and *Squaw Eloise* (1892), Ryan
perceived Native Americans as essentially noble savages and children of
Nature. In *Indian Love Letters* (A.C. McClurg, 1907), she structured her
book as a series of love letters written by a young Hopi Indian to a white
woman; while decidedly sentimental, it does nonetheless attain a lyrical
poetry at times which is sufficient to recommend it. *The Flute of the Gods*
(Stokes, 1909) followed and was hailed as a classic of Indian lore. Interestingly, it was not until after she had written *The Flute of the Gods* that
Ryan came to meet a Native American; it was then that she went to
Arizona to live with the Navajos and became the first white woman ever
admitted to their inner councils.

Hamlin Garland's Western writings seem to fall into three recognizable phases. In his earliest works, such as *Main-Travelled Roads* (1891), he
sought to dispel the myth of the West as a land of plenty and the home of
the "good life" by portraying the hard work and grim realities of actual
Western living. These stories are populated with men on the edge of
despair and women grown old before their time. "Under the Lion's Paw" is
perhaps the best-known story in *Main-Travelled Roads* and depicts what
happens to small farmers in the clutches of a land speculator. Frank Norris'
The Octopus (Doubleday, 1901) similarly narrates the tragic human consequences of monopolistic business practices.

In Garland's middle phase, work done primarily during the years
1895-1917, he appeared to be trying to perpetuate the myth of the glorious
West, especially in his Rocky Mountain romances. These novels usually
involve Easterners transplanted to the West or Westerners journeying East
for a comparison of life-styles. "For forty years," Garland once reflected,
"an infinite drama has been going on in those wide spaces of the West—a
drama that is as thrilling, as full of heart and hope and battle, as any that

ever surrounded any man—a life that was unlike any ever seen on earth, and which should have produced its characteristic literature, its native art chronicle." In this optative mood, Garland could not really do justice to the subject, but he wanted success. What continued to gnaw at him was what he perceived as the dreadful truth. He was present in 1905 when the Creek nation, one of the Five Civilized Tribes denied self-government after centuries of governing themselves, held their final council. "Nothing that I have seen in the Creek Nation has been so revealing, so significant of the changes in progress," Garland wrote in an essay finally published long after his death in *Hamlin Garland's Observations on the American Indian*: 1895–1905 (University of Arizona Press, 1976), "as this quaint and curious legislature, sitting in their decaying building while to the ring of the trowel and the tap of the carpenter's hammer white men are building a new, alien, and inexorable civilization around them."

Garland's final phase was mostly autobiographical. In books such as *A Son of the Middle Border* (Macmillan, 1917), *A Daughter of the Middle Border* (Macmillan, 1921), and *Back-Trailers from the Middle Border* (Macmillan, 1928), he told of the moving West of his family from Wisconsin to Iowa to Dakota territory and in recounting the hardships he hoped once more to demythologize the West. Garland is not to be censured for his indecision; at the very beginning of his writing career the American frontier was declared closed. In the new century the American frontier experience came to mean something different to virtually every person who had undergone it and certainly not just to Garland; as, indeed, the experience has come to mean something different for virtually everyone who has since come to write about it.

iii

Western fiction in the Twentieth century is perhaps dealt with best when divided according to its mode. Owen Wister's *The Virginian*, coming at the beginning of the new century, more or less set the basic pattern for the ranch romance variety of the formulary Western. In order for Molly Stark Wood to accept the Virginian as a hero, she must condone his placing property before friendship through his participation in the execution of his friend, Steve, and the necessity of the Virginian's having to shoot and kill Trampas.

Zane Grey was a New York City dentist who made his first trip West to Arizona in 1907 and his experiences there, combined with his romantic imagination, prompted him to write *The Heritage of the Desert* (Harper's, 1910). The story concerns a young man who comes to the West from the East. He is sickly and finds that the land and air and rugged terrain restore his vitality. The young man, Jack Hare, falls in love with Mescal, the half-blood grandaughter of Eschtah, a Navajo chieftain, who is being raised by a Mormon, August Naab. Mescal is frequently seen riding atop her mare, Black Bolly, accompanied by her dog, Wolf, thus providing the impetus which inspired Max Brand to use a triad hero (human/horse/dog) in his first Western novel, *The Untamed*, published in *All-Story Magazine* in 1918, and henceforth an oft-imitated story ingredient in formulary Westerns. As other Grey heroines—Jane Withersteen in *Riders of the Purple Sage* (Harper's, 1912), Madeline Hammond in *The Light of Western Stars*, Joan Randle in *The Border Legion* (Harper's, 1916), and even as late as Majesty Stewart in the posthumously published *Majesty's Rancho* (Harper's, 1942)—, Mescal takes a considerable time to realize that she really loves the hero. Typical of Grey's view, Snap, August Naab's son, is also in love with Mescal and, when she rejects his suit, he is condemned to a life of drunkenness. As other Grey villains in other novels—Jack Kells in *The Border Legion* or Honey Bee Uhls in *Majesty's Rancho*, to keep within the same group—, being denied the heroine's love compels Snap to take by abduction what is denied to him by consent and he pays the price: death. The principal villain in *The Heritage of the Desert*—a type not frequently encountered in Grey's fiction, with notable exceptions such as *Desert Gold* (Harper's, 1913)—embodies the Yankee business spirit that will stop at nothing to exploit both land and people for the sake of profit. He is killed by Jack Hare, but then, too, Hare is capable, as are so many of Max Brand's heroes and so many other heroes in formulary Westerns of this vintage, of letting off bad men if there is a chance of their rehabilitation.

Grey's next novel, *Riders of the Purple Sage*, became his all-time bestseller. It is usually cited as Grey's best work, but an equally strong argument could be made for its sequel, *The Rainbow Trail* (Harper's, 1915). *Riders of the Purple Sage* is dominated by dream imagery and nearly all of the characters, at one time or another, are preoccupied with their dreams. In its hero, the gunman Lassiter, Grey created another of his influential prototypes, the experienced Westerner to be contrasted with the neophyte Easterner, Lassiter with his "leanness, the red burn of the sun, and the set changelessness that came from years of silence and solitude ... the intensity of his gaze, a strained weariness, a piercing wistfulness of keen, gray sight, as if the man was forever looking for that which he never found." In this, too, Lassiter is the prototype of all those searchers and wanderers who are to be found in Grey's fiction, John Shefford in *The Rainbow Trail*, Adam Larey in *Wanderer of the Wasteland* (Harper's, 1923) and its sequel, published posthumously, *Stairs of Sand* (Harper's, 1943), and, to an extent, Buck Duane in *The Lone Star Ranger* (Harper's, 1915) and Rich Ames in *Arizona Ames* (Harper's, 1932). What Grey succeeded in doing was to write Western fiction with the moral perspective of a juvenile novel and for a number of years it was this spirit of supposedly adolescent innocence which dominated the vast majority of formulary Western novels. Throughout the Teens and the Twenties Grey's popularity was sustained. He increased his output by writing four or five novels a year which were serialized in slick-paper magazines, although his publisher only could accomodate two or three books a year, leaving a considerable backlog when Grey died. However, by the mid Thirties Grey's stories had become so repetitious, the style so lacking in vitality, interest began to wane and, increasingly, because his simplistic view was beginning to seem old-fashioned, he appealed chiefly to a juvenile audience. It might well be said, though, in Grey's defense that few have ever equalled his ability, when he was at his best, to create exhilarating Western fantasies.

Occasionally Grey would set one of his novels in the contemporary West. *Call of the Canyon* (Harper's, 1924) and *Captives of the Desert* (Harper's, 1952) – the latter was published posthumously but appeared in magazine form in 1925 – are set immediately in the period after what was once called the Great War. But as the United States went through the shocks of the Great Depression, Grey found it more difficult than ever to set a story during the time in which he was living, although he did make one effort to do so in *Majesty's Rancho*, featuring now as parents of the heroine the couple he first brought together in *The Light of Western Stars*.

Grey might lament the passing of the buffalo, as he did in *The Thundering Herd* (Harper's, 1925), or the social effects of the coming of the railroad, as he did in *The U.P. Trail* (Harper's, 1918), or the "vanishing" of his romantic Indian – a theme which will be explored somewhat in the next sub-section – , but his plots contradict these feelings; the pleasure he made almost tactile when showing the thrill of the buffalo stand, the glib assurances he gave that the removal of the buffalo and the vanishing of the Indian and the coming of the railroad combined to make the West safe for settlers, the way during Grey's halcyon days Americans were being taught in school to believe that they had made the world safe for democracy. *Man of the Forest* (Harper's, 1920) is a pale work about a mountain man compared to novels by Harvey Fergusson, A.B. Guthrie, Jr., Frederick Manfred, and Vardis Fisher; yet it has its place in Grey's romance with the West, demonstrating that the heroine cannot become a "true" woman until she accepts the necessity for violence. There is little in subsequent formulary Western fiction to equal the exciting races of horses and men in *Riders of the Purple Sage* or Mescal's race in *The Heritage of the Desert*; although in *Wild Horse Mesa* (Harper's, 1928) Grey's social Darwinism caused him to betray wild horses as he had the buffalo. He could make gunmen attractive – Lassiter and Nevada in *Forlorn River* (Harper's, 1927) and *Nevada* (Harper's, 1928) – and it is perhaps this prototype which proved the most influential in the future course of formulary Western fiction.

Both Stewart Edward White and Charles Alden Seltzer were contemporaries of Zane Grey and both were affected by the Grey tradition. Seltzer, in fact, concentrated on the figure of the grim gunman/cowboy hero, thus embellishing the tradition carried forward by other writers, perhaps most significantly by Ernest Haycox, Luke Short, Norman A. Fox, T.T. Flynn, Allan Vaughan Elston, Wayne D. Overholser, and Louis L'Amour. Stewart Edward White, anticipating Clarence E. Mulford, tried to write fiction detailing every aspect of the Westward expansion, although always, with the exception of the story collection, *Arizona Nights* (McClure, 1907), strictly in the formulary mode of hero, heroine, and villain.

Frederick Faust, who adopted Max Brand as one of nineteen pen names under which to write, was repulsed by the actual physical West and avoided, whenever possible, even driving through it. He lived much of his life in Italy and preferred to make his heroes and locales wholly mytholog-ical, and, therefore, timeless, in the way Grey tended to do only some of the time. In his hundreds of Western novels and stories, Faust gravitated toward one basic plot structure — pursuit and capture — with one variation: delayed revelation. Within this structure he projected his two basic myths: the son in search of an illustrious father and a warrior who has an Achilles heel. Faust's advice to beginning writers was to read a story half way through and imagine how it comes out. Then come up with a new be-ginning for the new conclusion and you have a new story. Whistling Dan Barry, Faust's hero in *The Untamed*, and his two constant companions, Black Bart, a wolf dog, and Satan, a stallion, have two further adventures in *The Night Horseman* (Putnam's, 1920) and *The Seventh Man* (Putnam's, 1921) before Barry dies and — in imitation of Jack London's *Call of the Wild* — Black Bart and Satan return to a life in the wilderness. Then, in *The White Wolf* (Putnam's, 1926), which features as a hero a white bull terrier, Brand imitated London's *White Fang* and White Wolf comes to live a happy, domesticated life at the end.

Faust's speed in writing and his reliance on pulp magazine pub-lishers resulted in many of his formulary Westerns suffering from cardboard characterizations and casual plotting, more dependent on super-ficial action than on reasoned development. When he sought to overcome partially these deficiencies in the early Thirties and tried to write at least better prose, his agent warned him against trying to write too well for the audience he intended to entertain. The plot of *Destry Rides Again* (Dodd, Mead, 1930) is a revenge story based on Homer's *Odyssey*: a man is dis-honestly framed and sent to prison. When he gets out, he dissembles to put his enemies at ease before he kills all of them.

In 1932 the president of Harper's told Faust that Zane Grey's sales had dropped off to only 30,000 copies a year in the aggregate. Dodd, Mead, having taken over publishing Max Brand titles from Putnam's, was having success. Harper's wanted their own line of Faust Westerns, so the Evan Evans pseudonym was born. Faust could readily do this. He was writing the equivalent of six or seven novels a year for pulp publications, so many in fact that twenty-five years after his death in 1944 his pulp serials were still being issued for the first time in book form.

Sir Walter Scott pioneered the theme in his fiction where the hero by the end of the story is compelled to chose between two distinct heroines; Cooper made his own use of it. It found renewed literary life in formulary Western fiction and Dane Coolidge employed it in his first Western novel, *Hidden Water* (A.C. McClurg, 1910). Coolidge had been trained as a naturalist and so he was too well-versed in the flora and fauna of the Western regions to indulge ever — to give but one instance — in fantasies about rattlesnakes to be found in novels such as Seltzer's *The Two Gun Man* (Outing, 1911), or Mulford's *Hopalong Cassidy Returns* (Doubleday, 1924). Coolidge also employed a variety of heroes. They might be middle-aged ranchmen as Lorenzo de Vega in *Lorenzo the Magnificent* (Dutton, 1925) and Charley Barr in *Bear Paw* (Dutton, 1941), both based on the New Mexico trader, Lorenzo Hubbell; they might be prospectors as John Calhoun in *Wunpost* (Dutton, 1920) and John Ware in *The Trail of Gold* (Dutton, 1937), salesmen as Juan Fox in *Wolf's Candle* (Dutton, 1935), mustangers as Johnny Lightfoot in *Horse-Ketchum of Death Valley* (Dutton, 1930), or train robbers as Sycamore Brown in *The Fighting Fool* (Dutton, 1918). As B.M. Bower, who made her first book appearance as a Western writer with *Chip of the Flying U* (Dillingham, 1906), Coolidge generally eschewed violence in his heroes, in contradistinction to Zane Grey and Charles Alden Seltzer who definitely did not. His heroes usually win through cunning. There are occasional exceptions to this rule, as Bill Enright in *Gun-Smoke*; (Dutton, 1928); but even here it is a matter of degree and the hero kills three men only when absolutely driven to do so: which itself became an important convention, violence forced upon a hero following provocation after provocation.

Coolidge established a dress code for females in his fiction, which was widely imitated, especially after it was adopted by motion pictures. His heroines are generally strong only when they were wearing men's clothing and this strength is conceived as being masculine in character. However, as with B.M. Bower's novels, Coolidge's heroines tend to become petty or contrary shortly after they appear and thus are able to remain emotionally aloof from the hero until the inevitable reconciliation at the end. With Bower, the romance is usually central. This was true for Coolidge, as for Mulford, only about half the time. Coolidge could easily write a novel as *Sheriff Killer* (Dutton, 1932) where the romance is strictly secondary to his retelling a fictionalized account based on Captain Burton Mossman's organization of the Arizona Rangers and the capture of the Mexican bandit, Chacon. But this is not to say that with the exception of *Gringo Gold* (Dutton, 1939), a romantic historical reconstruction based on the life of Joaquín Murieta, Coolidge's novels do not end with an amorous embrace, because they surely do. Then, too, there is a heroine such as Salome Lockhardt in *Bear Paw* who, while still married to the villain, declares that for Mark Trumbell, the hero, "'all I dream of now is a little home, with him, and I'll work my fingers to the bone.'" Some of Coolidge's heroes — and Mark Trumbell is decidedly one of them — are not as Puritanical as most of the heroic male characters in formulary Westerns by Grey, Seltzer, or, later, by Ernest Haycox and Luke Short, being more atavistic to Wister's Virginian who is not beyond having sexual relations with a woman toward whom he has no matrimonial aspirations.

In the late Twenties, Ernest Haycox began making regular magazine appearances in *Short Stories* and *West*, the latter entirely devoted to Western fiction, and his first novel, *Free Grass* (Doubleday, 1929), ran serially in *West* prior to book publication. As Zane Grey before him, Haycox followed this marketing procedure with all of his fiction during the Thirties and Forties, simply because the pay from magazines was so much more lucrative than from book sales. Hugh Vane, the hero in Haycox' short story, "Man with a Past" (1937), collected in *Outlaw* (Little, Brown, 1953), walks into a saloon. "Above the back bar hung an enormous painting of a coal-black racing horse; and beside it was another painting of a woman, both pictures, Hugh Vane thought idly, representing the deepest hungers of men — action and beauty." In Haycox' fiction, his heroes genuinely hunger for the heroines, and frequently the heroines for the heroes, albeit always in a chaste fashion. *Free Grass* employs the theme of the two heroines, and Haycox came to use this convention repeatedly in novels ranging from *Whispering Range* (Doubleday, 1931) through *Saddle and Ride* (Little, Brown, 1940) and *Canyon Passage* (Little, Brown, 1945) to a late romantic historical reconstruction, *Long Storm* (Little, Brown, 1946).

Throughout his formulary fiction, Haycox strove to provide added dimensions to all of his stereotypical characters. His heroes became increasingly reflective while never abandoning the commitment to action indigenous to the magazine serial; his villains became more complicated and morally more conscious. *Man in the Saddle* (Little, Brown, 1938), in a variation on the theme of the two heroines, has one of them marrying the villain and then regretting it, although the latter is scarcely typical of formulary villains thitherto, a man who, instead of being incarnated evil, is just flawed, given over to the disease of possession, envy, and the will to power. Sometimes, as in *Whispering Range* or in *Deep West* (Little, Brown, 1937), one of the rustlers turns out to be close to the hero and, by way of contrast, the spiritual agony which the Virginian did *not* feel for an errant friend was probed with insight and even compassion. Haycox' *Sundown Jim* (Little, Brown, 1938) is one of the very few novels in which Haycox silhouetted his fiction against the hostile background of a community in which he is everyone's enemy. It was at this kind of plot that Luke Short particularly excelled along with Peter Dawson in his early novels.

Haycox' formulary novels, followed later by his romantic historical reconstructions which begin with *Alder Gulch* (Little, Brown, 1941), and his short stories, which are often superior to any of his longer fictions because they are less stylized, embodied his philosophy of life. He believed that men and women fall victim frequently to basic compromises in life which make them forever prisoners of their own emotions. Although politically conservative, in his fiction he saw accumulated wealth as the fundamental source of social evil and, after 1935, his villains become villains because of a moral inferiority which compels them to make immoral compromises in order selfishly to accumulate wealth. In dealing with relationships between men and women, Haycox was intensely monogamous. The West symbolized for Haycox not only an alternative way of life, but a spiritual freedom, an antidote to disillusionment no matter how fraught it might be at times with hardship. More than any other formulary writer before him, Haycox attempted to lay bare the moral issues which, it seemed to him, were a vital part of Western fiction and, in this way, prepared the way for those who would further advance these notions in their fiction. In Haycox' best plots much of the discovery is self-discovery and much of the tension is psychological rather than physical.

With the exception of *And the Wind Blows Free* (Macmillan, 1945), Luke Short, unlike Ernest Haycox, never tried to transcend the conventions of the formulary Western, but rather satisfied himself with perfecting his formulary plot varieties. His ranch romances were written without conceit: he did not have Haycox' restlessness with the mode nor did he pretend, as Louis L'Amour would subsequently, that his formulary Westerns were somehow something else, exciting chapters directly from the pages of Western American history — although his paperback publishers might make this claim for him. Short himself knew what he was writing and he never felt it necessary to apologize for his fiction or to insist that it was other than what it was.

Beginning already in 1935 when he published his first novel, Short conceived of the old West as a volatile colloidal mixture of armed, unstable, and potentially violent Fascist camps needing only the proper catalyst before exploding into chaos. Haycox might have all of these ingredients in a novel such as *Sundown Jim*, but he could not generate the taut atmosphere of imminent disaster Short could using this narrative structure in novels such as *Savage Range* (Collins, 1939) or *Sunset Graze* (Doubleday, 1942). While Short's heroes might be as grim as Haycox', Haycox' heroes are also, unlike Short's, rather smug. You are never in doubt that, confronted by a brutal antagonist, the Haycox hero will readily be victorious. Short's heroes are shown to be somewhat more vulnerable; they are frequently duped; they will occasionally lose a fistfight and even be beaten nearly to death. Haycox' heroes are almost always in control; Short's very often are not, until the closing pages.

In style, Short owed more to the laconic economy of Ernest Hemingway's prose and that of Dashiell Hammett than he did to Haycox' somewhat florid imagery. As Hemingway's protagonists, Short's heroes must perform, for the heroines, for the society in which they live, most of all for themselves and their own sense of self-esteem. The story itself is the proving-grounds for Short's heroes. In *King Colt* (Collins, 1938) the heroine tells hero Johnny Hendry, "'Maybe I will marry you some day, Johnny — after you've proved you're worth it.'" While Johnny is in the process of proving his worth, the reader is supposed to accept and "understand Johnny's part of it" when he beats up a man later found to be innocent with "blows hard and savage, merciless, countless." In *High Vermilion* (Houghton Mifflin, 1948) the reader, similarly, is required to view with equanimity hero Larkin Moffat beating villain Bill Taff until "he was formless, inert, a sodden lump of flesh underneath the red muck that covered every part of him." In *The Stalkers* (Bantam, 1973) the reader follows hero Deputy U.S. Marshal Tim Sefton into a cell after a tough has called him a son-of-a-bitch and is supposed to approve Sefton's slapping the tough until his "nose and lips were bleeding." In this novel Short avoided the usual ranch romance ending with the heroine in the hero's arms; but the reason the heroine rejects Sefton is because his job as a lawman is very dangerous and he refuses to quit it for her sake. The reader is expected to admire Sefton for this sacrifice to his sense of duty. There is this surface veneer of pugnacity in virtually all of Short's heroes. What makes them different from Heming-way's protagonists who often share this quality is that Short's heroes have no insides whatsoever, no interiors; they are not even mildly introspective the way Haycox' are; they are instead bluff, virile, vigorous fighting machines. In this way the reader can be seduced into not asking questions about what motivates them because they never ask such questions of them-selves — they butt and push their way forward; they are stubborn, deter-mined, persistent, no matter how entrapped they may appear. And they always finally triumph.

Occasionally in one of his early novels such as *Bold Rider* (Collins, 1939) or *The Man on the Blue* (Collins, 1937), the Short hero might be an outlaw, or as in *Ramrod* (Macmillan, 1945) or *High Vermilion* a man initially on a lower social plane because of some difficulty in his past; but this notwithstanding he is definitely upwardly mobile. Later in his fiction, as Reese Branham in *Paper Sheriff* (Bantam, 1966), the Short hero is well established within the community; and, in all cases, after proving himself he is materially much better off than he was at the beginning of the story. The Short hero is a hero by virtue of divine grace; he may bring about the fall of the villains and their schemes, but in so doing he is only acting as an instrument for an immutable predestination unavoidable because ulti-mately Luke Short's West reflects the astringent moral rigor of Calvinism's inflexible God. "As God by the effectual working of his call to the elect perfects the salvation to which by his eternal plan he was destined them, so he has his judgments against the reprobate, by which he executes his plan for them," John Calvin wrote in Book III, Chapter XXIV of his *In-stitutes of the Christian Religion* (1536–1559). "What of those, then, whom he created for dishonor in life and destruction in death, to become the in-struments of his wrath and examples of his severity? ...The supreme Judge... makes way for his predestination when he leaves in blindness those whom he has once condemned and deprived of participation in his light. ...There-fore, we shall always be confused unless Paul's question comes to mind: Who distinguishes you? [I Corinthians 4:7] By this he [meant] that some excel others not by their own virtue but by God's grace alone."

Paper Sheriff readily illustrates the degree to which the tenets of predestination and distinction through grace were a part of Luke Short's world-view. The Hoad family in the novel is wicked beyond hope of recla-mation. Hero Reese Branham is married to Callie Hoad because of a youth-ful slip on the path of righteousness. Fortunately his sin had no issue; Callie lost the child through miscarriage. Branham's punishment is to live for a time as Callie's husband. Divine grace finally separates him from Callie and rewards him with the other heroine, Jen Truro, because, while Callie is a Hoad and therefore damned, Reese is predestined to be one of the elect.

Frequently in his novels Short would resort to the plot of what has been called the "inverted" detective story, merely placing it in a Western setting. R. Austin Freeman initiated this kind of backtelling in detective fiction where the reader sees the crime committed in the first half of the story and then follows Freeman's detective, Dr. Thorndyke, in the second half as he reconstructs the crime and lays bare the subterfuge used by the murderer to avoid discovery. Unquestionably a story told in this manner can generate as much excitement as Max Brand's use of delayed revelation. No less a personage than St. Thomas Aquinas once suggested that *"beati in regno coelesti, videbunt poenas damnatorum, ut beatitudo illis magis complaceat"* [the blessed in the kingdom of heaven will see the punishments of the damned so that the happiness of the former will be greatly increased]. Although their theology might differ, readers of a Calvinistic persuasion might feel no less an increase of happiness observing already in this life, in Calvin's words, "the wicked bringing upon themselves the just destruction to which they are destined." It is for this reason, perhaps, that one is never sympathetic to the fate of villains in formulary Western fiction. Moreover, there is no substantial difference between the social Darwinism of authors such as Owen Wister and Zane Grey and the Calvinist perspective of Luke Short and Ernest Haycox. "The laws of natural selection are merely God's regular methods of expressing his choice and approval," Thomas Nixon Carver wrote in *The Religion Worth Having* (Houghton Mifflin, 1912). "The naturally selected are the chosen of God." Harvey Wasserman put it another way. "The theory [social Darwinism]," he wrote in *Harvey Wasserman's History of the United States* (Harper's, 1972), "was seized in fashionable circles as a secular ally to the Calvinist belief in an aristocracy of the elect. It was used to 'prove' that man was 'superior' to all other animals, that the competitive system of economics was the only 'natural' one, and that the true state of man was constant struggle."

E. Douglas Branch in his book, *The Cowboy and His Interpreters* (Appleton, 1926), ranked William MacLeod Raine as one of the "aristocrats of cow country fiction" along with B.M. Bower, Charles Alden Seltzer, and Clarence E. Mulford. Raine's first formulary Western novel was *Wyoming* (Dillingham, 1908) and his last was *High Grass Valley* (Houghton Mifflin, 1955), completed posthumously for him by Wayne D. Overholser. Raine had little use for Indians, the Apaches in particular whom he characterized again and again as evil, callous, treacherous, and revengeful. His heroes all live by the code of the West, the most important and salient aspect of which, according to Raine, is a devotion to fair play. Such a hero must be game. He must be a man to tie to. He must always be chivalrous. He must be efficient. In contrast, Raine's heroines are consistently shown to be weak creatures whose virtue, above all else, must be protected. In *Oh, You Tex!* (Houghton Mifflin, 1920) even Raine's outlaws are chivalrous. When heroine Mona Wadley falls into outlaw Homer Dinsmore's hands, "she knew she was safe. This man had the respect for a good woman that is characteristic of the turbulent West in its most lawless days. He might be a miscreant and a murderer, but he would fight at the drop of a hat in response to the appeal of any woman who was 'straight.'"

In Raine's formulary fiction there is a total lack of atmosphere, any sense whatsoever of the land, and anything but the most superficial characterization. Raine kept himself removed from all of his characters, including his heroes. What alone usually propels a reader through his novels and what prevents them from being an ordeal is the constant stress on action: something is always happening. For Raine, his idea of the Western code and social Darwinism were manifestations of the same phenomenon. "'Might makes right,'" the hero, Waring Ridgway, of Raine's *Ridgway of Montana* (Dillingham, 1909), concludes. "'I'll win if I'm strong enough; I'll fail if I'm not.'" Raine carried this same attitude over when he wrote history. In *Famous Sheriffs and Western Outlaws* (Doubleday, 1929), a series of factually unreliable vignettes, Raine remarked of filibusterer Henry A. Crabbe that "by virtue of natural fitness, he was a born leader," just as he wrote of Billy the Kid that "by grace of natural fitness he was to become chief, because he was the worst bad man that ever strapped on a six-shooter in the West." However, because the code of the West is allied with social Darwinism, the morally superior must always win out against the moral reprobate. "The Anglo-Saxon has a passion for law and order," he declared. "It may come slowly, but come it does—the wiping out of the bad man."

The law of natural selection remains the operative principle in Louis L'Amour's formulary conception of the West. The man evolving in L'Amour's fiction is the Anglo-American and the values which his fiction demonstrates to be superior to all others are Anglo-American values. In *Guns of the Timberlands* (Jason Press, 1955) L'Amour made a distinction between two kinds of men, "them that come to build, and them that come to get rich and get out." L'Amour's villains are usually hybrids of the latter variety. In the same novel the reader is told of one of the sympathetic characters that he "was a disciple of the belief that evil always gets what it deserves, and he enjoyed seeing his philosophy borne out." For L'Amour the builders are the winners. This is the historical fantasy which informs his fiction. The naturally select, as the divinely elect, are those who work hard and make a better life for themselves. To bring this off, L'Amour had to restructure frontier history so that in his version the West is developed for the benefit of the Westerners, rather than the West being successfully exploited by the East for the benefit of the Easterners. This notwithstanding, it is to L'Amour's credit that in *Guns of the Timberlands* he introduced an ecological theme—loggers versus ranchers who stand to lose their ranches if their watershed is destroyed—before virtually any other formulary writer.

In L'Amour's *To Tame a Land* (Fawcett, 1955) L'Amour's hero, Rye Tyler, does not count either Indians or Mexicans in the running tab he keeps of the men he kills. The Indians in L'Amour's West are usually nonentities to be overcome through attrition or extermination. At one point Rye Tyler is told about the Indian that "'he's lived here a long time, lived well. Learn from him.'" But Rye learns nothing from the Indians, albeit he kills his share of them. However, because of this kind of dialogue, it is well not to attend to what L'Amour's characters say (or what is said to them), but to what they do.

L'Amour introduced a new action sequence every 800 words or so and, judging from his popularity, his readers apparently demand little more from a story than continuous action and perhaps would resent it if they found more. On numerous occasions L'Amour himself stated that it was not his practice to revise and the result of it can be seen in a novel such as *The Iron Marshal* (Bantam, 1979). On one page L'Amour called a character Bert and Hank a few pages later; another character is introduced as a "lean, wiry old man" and, some twenty pages later, his age is given as 29; another character acquires a Swedish accent for one bit of dialogue, although in the rest of the book he speaks colloquial English. In view of such carelessness, it cannot be action alone which distinguishes L'Amour's fiction in what is essentially an action mode of Western fiction; rather it is his celebration of the middle-class values of a one-settlement culture in the United States and his ability to make his readers believe that even the laws of natural selection endorse them.

There is so much killing in Dashiell Hammett's novel, *Red Harvest* (Knopf, 1929), that the characters, in Hammett's words, become "blood simple." Eugene Cunningham transposed Hammett's plot into a Western setting in his novel *Riders of the Night* (Houghton Mifflin, 1932) in which, in the course of the story, some seventy villains are killed. In *Buckaroo* (Houghton Mifflin, 1933) Cunningham expanded the number of villains who "needed" killing to 300!

While in *Riders of the Night* Cunningham, too, resorted to the theme of the two heroines, he did something else slightly more original: he introduced a trio of gunfighters named Sandrock Tom, Three Rivers, and Happy Jack to whom he gave the sobriquet the "Three Mesquiteers." Cunningham employed a different trio in *Buckaroo* so it was left to William Colt MacDonald to pick up on this idea and fashion a different trio which he also called the "Three Mesquiteers," beginning with *Law of the Forty-Fives* (Covici, Friede, 1933). MacDonald's trio of Tucson Smith, Stony Brooke, and Lullaby Joslin appeared in a series of novels in which the narrative pattern was identical to Cunningham's. Invariably this trio rides into a community intimidated by a master villain and his minions, a situation which, in Tucson Smith's words in *Law of the Forty-Fives*, calls upon the Mesquiteers to invoke "the only kind of law effective in this sort of case—gun law."

However indigenous violence may have been in formulary Westerns prior to Cunningham and MacDonald, never before had it been present in such abundance nor had the death of a human being been treated with quite their attitude of cavalier indifference. They did their work well; so well, in fact, that it would be extremely difficult to find a formulary writer after them who treats the death of a human being any other way, justified as such deaths are by both Calvinistic theology and social Darwinism. Even when the narrative structure of continuous blood-letting is not used, the moral posture embodied in it is all-pervasive. In Norman A. Fox' *Silent in the Saddle* (Dodd, Mead, 1945) Fox' hero, Brad Seldon, confesses after a shoot-out that he will never know "a moment's regret for that killing" and in Louis L'Amour's *The Tall Stranger* (Fawcett, 1957) L'Amour's hero, Rock Bannon, after shooting the villain, says "'he was born to fail ... he was too filled with hate to even accomplish a satisfactory killin'.'"

The idea of a formulary Western as an occasion for continuous killing and nothing more was carried forward by A. Leslie Scott under his Bradford Scott pseudonym in his 125 entries in his Walt Slade, Texas Ranger series in which Slade and two associates in novel after novel battle it out with a master villain and his minions, persistently blood-letting. It was also taken up in turn by several British writers, among them J.T. Edson, whose American publishers guaranteed the reader at least twelve major killings per book, and Terry Harknett. Harknett's career began with his novelization of Sergio Leone's *A Fistful of Dollars* (United Artists, 1966), after which under the pen name George G. Gilman he created the Edge series of *Blut und Boden* Western fiction as well as co-authoring the Apache series with Laurence James under the *nom de guerre* William M. James. Gordon D. Shirreffs pursued it among American formulary writers, especially in his Lee Kershaw saga in which the end of the book might well find Kershaw alone simply because everyone else has been killed. When in Shirreffs' *The Marauders* (Fawcett, 1977) the heroine is smashed in the face with a rifle butt by the master villain and her thigh ripped into by a shark, all she can think of is having sexual intercourse one last time with Kershaw. Kershaw accomodates her, after which she dies, this woman about whom earlier he had reflected "she was only a woman and a half breed Yaqui at that."

There is an inevitable progression from this kind of plot to the porno-Westerns which, since 1979, have proliferated. In the porno-Westerns — and nearly every major Western paperback publisher has one or is contemplating one — women are stripped of their dignity and their clothing; they are reduced to mere physical objects capable of producing detumescence in the heroes following the heroes' bouts of incredible carnage. These series are written by several different authors but published under such house names as Jake Logan and Tabor Evans. But there is nothing Western about any of these porno-Westerns save the manner of dress. All such series are pornography in a period setting and the logical consequence of all the lying about life in general and life in the American West in particular which has so long characterized the formulary Western.

The tradition of the formulary Western hero as a loner may have been given much of its initial impetus by Owen Wister, but so was the idea of the family Western. From the beginning Wister populated his West with characters who are bound together by common experiences and emotional ties; indeed, one of his story collections was actually titled *Members of the Family* (Macmillan, 1911). The same was true of B.M. Bower. Although her career as a Western writer spanned forty years, she would include regularly yet another adventure of Chip Bennett and other Flying U punchers whom she referred to collectively as "The Happy Family." Similarly Clarence E. Mulford began his saga about the Bar 20 punchers with Bar 20 (Outing, 1907), an outfit held together by ties of friendship and mutual commitment, including Hopalong Cassidy, Red Connors, Johnny Nelson, Buck Peters, Tex Ewalt, and, later, Mesquite Jenkins. The Bar 20 saga proved so popular that with *Corson of the JC* (Doubleday,

1927) Mulford launched a second saga with a different set of characters. The family notion even applied to the bandit in the Corson saga, El Toro. "'Now hees family weel get the money, and Pablo — hah!'" he says in *The Deputy Sheriff* (Doubleday, 1930). "'I have many such, and the tr-roubles of them ar-re my tr-roubles.... I am the father of a beeg family!'"

All of this provided the ground-work for Janice Hote Giles when she began her own saga with *The Kentuckians* (Houghton Mifflin, 1953), tracing the settlement of the American frontier through four generations of a Kentucky family that eventually moves West. Although scarcely in the same class, Louis L'Amour subsequently created three separate sagas of his own having to do with large families who migrate West. What Giles and L'Amour and a number of others have most in common is that they combined the quondam loose conclaves of individuals in Wister, Bower, and Mulford into actual families, bound by blood ties. For example, in *Bar 20 Three* (A.C. McClurg, 1921), Hopalong Cassidy and Red Connors come to the aid of Johnny Nelson when he is beset by villains; at the conclusion of *Mojave Crossing* (Bantam, 1964) L'Amour's hero, Tell Sackett, is saved from torture and death by Nolan Sackett, a distant relative and until that time a man in the employ of the villains. While there is a degree of individual initiative in the family Westerns, the fact remains that their major significance in the history of the formulary Western is the emphasis they place on collectivism as opposed to isolated individuals, their repudiation of individual freedom for cooperation within a community, their rejection of the Native American notion that each man must seek his own vision for which they substitute the American desire for social conformity, the search for that feeling of consensus which has so long both preoccupied and eluded white America.

Many individual authors of formulary Westerns have had to be overlooked without so much as a mention, albeit a number of their works can be found in subsection II ii of this section and in general all formulary works follow the same basic narrative formulae. The identification of the formulary Western, however, with Western fiction *per se* cannot be blamed on the reading public so much as on publishers and in particular the ways in which Western fiction has been marketed in the Twentieth century, very much a carry-over from the era of the dime novel. The distinctions "pulp" and "slick" which were sometimes applied to Western fiction in the heyday of periodical fiction were derived from the kinds of paper on which they were printed. Dime novels were pulp publications. They persisted into the 1920s. *Harper's*, on the other hand, was a slick. From the beginning of this century, the cowboy hero had a lively status in the slick, however much he might appear concurrently in pulp magazines. *The Saturday Evening Post* had a particularly aggressive editorial preference for Western stories by such authors as Emerson Hough, Alfred Henry Lewis, O. Henry, and Rex Beach. Many of Wister's stories in *Harper's* were long enough to be spread over two issues, but it was with *The Line of Least Resistance* by Eugene Manlove Rhodes in 1910 — the first Western serial in four parts to appear in a mass-circulation slick — that the

Post initiated its policy of featuring Western serials. Rhodes' novel has an additional distinction to its credit, that of being the first cowboy-and-the-lady romance to appear in a slick magazine, the romance in *The Virginian* never having been a central plot ingredient in any of the fragments of the novel Wister published prior to the book's appearance.

Street and Smith and other dime novel publishers began, after the turn of the century, to introduce new lines of pulp magazines which frequently featured Western serials and stories and, in due course, became devoted exclusively to Western fiction. In 1919 Street and Smith revamped the format of the *New Buffalo Bill Weekly* to become *Western Story Magazine*, a bi-weekly. The first issue, dated 5 September 1919, contained a story by William MacLeod Raine among others of lesser stature. Within a year *Western Story's* circulation hit three hundred thousand per issue and it was made a weekly which it remained for the next twenty-five years.

The late 1920s and the 1930s were the boom period for Western pulp magazines. Doubleday published *West* and *Frontier* as well as the somewhat more sophisticated *Short Stories* for which veteran Clarence E. Mulford frequently wrote. The firm also issued in book form Western stories which had been previously serialized in a series of *Four in One* volumes.

Doubleday's commitment to formulary Western fiction has continued into the 1980s when it is one of the few companies publishing a line of hardbound Western novels in its Double D series.

Clayton House published *Cowboy Stories*, *Ace-High*, *Ranch Romances*, and *Western Adventures*. Of these, *Ranch Romances* lasted into the 1960s. Fawcett published *Triple-X Western*, but made its greatest impact in the late 1940s and 1950s with its line of Western comic books which, at one time, included the adventures of movie cowboys Tom Mix, Hopalong Cassidy (William Boyd), Monte Hale, Ken Maynard, and Gabby Hayes. Similarly, the Whitman Publishing Company, which had begun during the 1930s to issue Big Little Books telling in words and pictures the storylines from films which starred Tom Mix, Ken Maynard, Buck Jones, and others, by the 1950s tried to repeat what Beadle and Adams had done with Buffalo Bill and issued a series of fictional adventures with Gene Autry, some of which were written by formulary Western novelist Lewis B. Patten, to compete with Doubleday's "new" Hopalong Cassidy series written by Louis L'Amour under the pen name Tex Burns because Mulford was no longer inclined to write more books and Fran Striker's series of Lone Ranger books for Grosset & Dunlop.

An ex-Clayton House editor, Harold Hersey, during the 1930s edited *Western Trails*, *Golden West*, *Riders of the Range*, and *Western Outlaws* which, as most of the pulps, established a house style and a group of house names for the stories which were customarily featured. Certainly one of the most ambitious publishers of Western pulps during the 1930s was Ned Pines who hired Leo Margulies to edit *Thrilling Western*, *Thrilling Ranch Stories*, *Popular Western*, and *Texas Rangers*. A. Leslie Scott, among others, contributed stories about Texas Ranger Jim Hatfield to

Texas Rangers under the house name Jackson Cole. *Dime Western*, from Popular Publications, was one of two pulps to which President Franklin D. Roosevelt subscribed.

In the 1930s Street and Smith added *Far West*, *Wild West Weekly*, and *Pete Rice Magazine*. However, the *old Far West* is not to be confused with the one published subsequently, as of the 1980s the sole surviving Western pulp magazine. The new *Far West* was only the latest evolution of Leo Margulies, who became a pulp publisher himself. As recently as 1969 Margulies tried to introduce a new Western pulp titled *Zane Grey Western Magazine* with Zane Grey's two sons as advisory editors and, in addition to reprinting some of Grey's original fiction, it contained a host of new stories and a new series of Buck Duane adventures written by Romer Zane Grey, Grey's eldest son, and based on the hero of Grey's novel, *The Lone Star Ranger*. While the venture was not entirely successful, it had to recommend it the fact that in the Teens and through the Twenties Zane Grey had been the most popular — and best paid — author of Western magazine serials, first in such periodicals as *Field & Stream* which serialized *Riders of the Purple Sage*, *Popular Magazine* which serialized *Desert Gold*, *Munsey's* which serialized *The Lone Star Ranger* and *The Border Legion*, and *Argosy* which serialized *The Rainbow Trail*; before Grey moved into the slick markets where he could command $50,000 for serial rights to a novel, usually selling to *Country Gentlemen* or *Ladies Home Journal*, both, as *The Saturday Evening Post*, periodicals of Curtis Publishing. Just how Grey changed editorial policy among the slicks will be mentioned in the next subsection.

All-Story was a weekly publication of the Munsey group edited by Robert H. Davis. After Grey moved on to the slicks, it was Davis who encouraged Frederick Faust to try and duplicate Grey's achievement. Faust soon became a heavy contributor to the pulps, appearing in *Western Story Magazine* alone a total of 834 times if each installment of a serial is counted as an appearance.

Adventure, *Argosy*, and *Blue Book*, in addition to *Short Stories*, were publications somewhere between the pulps for which Faust wrote and the slicks which were featuring Zane Grey. Often aspiring authors would begin in the most primitive of the pulps and work themselves up through these middling publications, if not all the way to *Collier's* and the *Post*. W.C. Tuttle, Harry Sinclair Drago, H.H. Knibbs, Dane Coolidge, Eugene Cunningham, Jackson Gregory, and, later, Borden Chase and Frank Gruber belonged to this group. Conversely, there were others who, it seemed, were born for the most rudimentary pulp writing, authors such as Walt Coburn and Nelson C. Nye who were utterly incapable of a well-made plot or even a thought-out story. Yet some readers preferred these writers for precisely those deficiencies which made them unacceptable to a more literate audience. At one time Coburn even had the distinction of having a pulp magazine named after him, so well established had he become among pulp *aficionadi*.

By the late 1920s Zane Grey's excessive romanticism was beginning to appear adolescent to slick magazine readers who seemed, increasingly, to desire greater "realism" in Western fiction which translated basically into more brutality. Grey was soon superseded by Ernest Haycox who began writing for *Western Story Magazine* in the mid 1920s and who, by the late 1920s, was a regular contributor to *Short Stories* and *West*. By 1931 he had broken into *Collier's* and his sober heroes, sensual romance, and grim situations comprised a wholly new tone which inspired a new group of imitators. In the mid 1930s, while Eugene Manlove Rhodes' last novels were being serialized in the *Post*, Conrad Richter, Stewart Edward White, MacKinlay Kantor, and S. Omar Barker were also writing concurrently for the *Post* or for *Ladies Home Journal*. By the mid 1940s Haycox himself was contributing regularly to the *Post*, followed presently by Luke Short and Louis L'Amour.

"*Nihil sub sole novum* [*est*]," St. Jerome translated Ecclesiastes, and so it was with formulary Western ficiction. With the demise of most of the pulps and slicks in the 1960s, the paperback original took over and replaced them; and, so, almost in a circle in the span of a century Western novels were again complete under one cover as they had been in the days of the dime novel — except that, with inflation, they now cost fifteen to twenty times as much.

The best marketing device publishers of dime novels devised was the continuing series and readers followed the adventures of the same heroes in one standardized book after another. The world of the paperback Western in the late Twentieth century is little different. There are action Westerns with only a moderate amount of explicit pornography such as Matt Braun's Luke Starbuck series, unrelieved violence in the Edge series with, more recently, pornographic overtones, porno-Westerns with varying amounts of bloody violence, and the "wholesome" family sagas. In the field of the formulary Western, obviously, the best marketing strategy remains the continuing series, but these newer extravagances may actually be indicative also of the exhaustion of the formulary mode. One observation, surely, can be made: having become brutally violent and openly pornographic, the formulary Western is unlikely to return to the more sedate pattern of the ranch romance which characterized it in previous decades.

iv

An example of a romantic historical reconstruction is Zane Grey's *The Vanishing American* (Harper's, 1925) which first appeared in 1922 in *The Ladies Home Journal*. The story tells of Nophaie, a full-blood Navajo, kidnapped when a child and educated by whites, returning to his reservation as a young man only to find it dominated by an unscrupulous Indian agent and, still worse, a vicious missionary who uses his dogmatic creed to get his way. As a social Darwinist, ideologically Grey believed that human existence and the survival of the races are guided by inflexible laws of an evolutionary scheme which endorses industrial progress and technology and which, therefore, endows white civilization with a self-evident and wholly natural superiority, provided, however, that what Grey meant by the "heritage of the desert"—the character developed as a result of subduing the elements of Nature and the need for everyone to develop such a character—be taken fully into account. In one of Grey's Indian stories, "Blue Feather," unpublished until long after his death when it appeared in *Blue Feather and Other Stories* (Harper's, 1961), Grey articulated his ideology of evolutionary social history, highest to lowest: "Human being, man, Indian, savage, primitive beast."

In *The Vanishing American*, Grey stripped Nophaie of his Nopah religion but also made him reject the missionary's Christianity, arriving instead at some nebulous pantheism in which the white Christ and Nature become dual manifestations of God. "Indians," Grey summed up his view of Native Americans, "were merely closer to the original animal progenitor of human beings." Nophaie falls in love with the blonde-haired, blue-eyed schoolteacher and, so inspired by his love does he become, he is prompted to enforce among his own people Grey's personal prejudice regarding the supreme importance of sexual virginity prior to marriage. Morgan, the missionary, likes to seduce young Indian maidens at his mission school. One of them Gekin Yasha, is taught by Nophaie that "when a white woman loves she holds herself sacred for the man who has won her." This moral exhortation does not do Gekin Yasha much good. She is seduced by Morgan, becomes pregnant, returns to the reservation, and marries an Indian, only to pay the price frequently paid in Zane Grey's West by those who indulge in sexual intercourse outside a monogamous relationship with only one person: she dies. When such a character is granted a reprieve, as is Magdaline, the Navajo girl impregnated by one of the villains in *Captives of the Desert*, admittedly a rare exception, she is permitted to lead a happy life only after she has killed the villain who misused her and has suffered a miscarriage.

"'Let the Indians marry white women and Indian girls marry white men,'" Nophaie comments in the magazine version, betraying the cultural integrity of his people. "'It would make for a more virile race ... absorbed by the race that has destroyed him. Red blood into white! It means the white race will gain and the Indian vanish....'" And so Grey advanced beyond James Fenimore Cooper in arriving at a final solution to Cooper's division of Native Americans into either villains or noble savages: Nophaie is a *romantic* Indian who wants to vanish for the betterment of the white race. The magazine version concluded with Nophaie and the yellow hair in each other's arms, about to achieve Grey's synthesis of "red blood into white," to achieve a century later the fulfillment denied Uncas and Cora in *The Last of the Mohicans*. But this ending, to say nothing of Grey's somewhat accurate portrayal of reservation missionaries, caused such a furor at the offices of *The Ladies Home Journal*, what with thousands upon thousands of angry letters of protest, Harper's refused flatly to publish the magazine serial as a book until Grey altered the ending. Assimilation had been suggested in the previous century as a solution to what the Anglo-

Americans termed the "Indian problem"; it was rejected in favor of a policy of extermination. In the book version, Grey had Nophaie shot fatally. While dying, he murmurs "'vanishing ... vanishing ... vanishing....'" Grey perhaps counted himself fortunate that, following an impassioned letter to Harper's, he was able to retain his damning portrait of a reservation missionary.

Nor did it end there. After the unhappy experience with *The Vanishing American*, all Curtis publications adopted an editorial policy prohibiting authors of Western stories and serials from characterizing Native Americans in their fiction. Indians might be present, but, if they were, they were renegades on the war path or minor characters. Moreover, it would be absurd to expect, when the Indian point of view was not characterized in the original stories, that it would somehow come to be characterized when films were made based on these stories.

Indeed, the best way in which to illustrate the difference between a romantic historical reconstruction and an historical reconstruction is to select a theme and contrast the varying ways in which it has been treated in the two modes. One such theme, for example, would be the captivity novel and, specifically, to focus on novels which deal with the captivity of whites by the Comanches — to take but one nation — during the middle of the Nineteenth century. Alan LeMay's *The Searchers* (Harper's, 1954) comes to mind as does Will Cook's *Comanche Captives* (Bantam, 1960), as well as Benjamin Capps' *A Woman of the People* (Duell, Sloan, and Pearce, 1966) and Matthew Braun's *Black Fox* (Fawcett, 1972). The first two are romantic historical reconstructions. It was a trend in the Fifties to introduce antihero elements into even formulary Westerns, but generically this trend was more apparent in romantic historical reconstructions. It was usually accomplished, as in *The Searchers* or in *Comanche Captives*, by splitting the traditional formulary Western hero into two distinct charcters. Alan LeMay did it by splitting his hero into Amos Edwards, a dark figure, and Mart Pauley, a young man adopted as a boy by the Edwards family; Will Cook did it by splitting his hero into Jim Gary, a lieutenant in the U.S. Cavalry, and Guthrie McCabe, sheriff of Oldham County, Texas. Cooper, of course, had done this kind of splitting with Indians in the previous century; in the 1950s the real novelty was the splitting of the leading *white* characters.

In *The Searchers*, Amos Edwards' two nieces are taken captive by the Comanches. One of them is raped and killed. The other, Debbie, is ostensibly still alive and for nearly six years Amos and Mart search for her. LeMay's Comanches are savages and it is their unredeemably savage spirit which comes to influence the conduct of both Amos and Mart in their quest. LeMay did not really find both sides in the conflict equally savage; he was totally unsympathetic with the Comanches, whatever lip-service he might grant their notion that they were fighting to protect their sacred lands. Amos and Mart become nearly superhuman during their ordeal. Amos, however, is clearly intent on killing Debbie because of the humiliation she has experienced by being made the wife of a Comanche war chief.

In this he is frustrated and, providentially, he dies at the hands of a Comanche squaw. Mart finds Debbie and, together, they find their once innocent love again — or, the reader is led to believe that they do.

Ernest Wallace and E. Adamson Hoebel in their book, *The Comanches: Lords of the South Plains* (University of Oklahoma Press, 1952), made the point that while "captive white children were generally initiated into the tribe by a series of terrifying experiences in which the Indians tried their courage by brutal treatment and threats of destruction," it was equally true that "some of the most hardened warriors are known to have wept because a captive of whom they had become fond returned to his own people." Such a perspective tends to humanize the Comanches. There is no such moderation in *The Searchers*. "Most of the village had emptied," LeMay wrote, describing the final battle when the Texas Rangers joined by a band of Tonkawas swoop down to massacre war chief Scar's Comanche village, "but at the far end a great number of Comanche people — squaws, children, and old folks mostly — ran like wind-driven leaves in a bobbing scatter. The Rangers were riding through to join the Tonkawas in the running fight that could be heard far up the Wild Dog; but they made it their business to stamp out the resistance as they went. The dreadful thing was that the fleeing people were armed, and fought as they ran, as dangerous as a torrent of rattlesnakes. Here and there lay the body of an old man, a squaw, or a half-grown boy, who had died rather than let an enemy pass unmolested; and sometimes there was a fallen Ranger."

The reader is perhaps supposed to be reassured that only "sometimes" there was a fallen Ranger, amid all those bodies of Comanche old men, squaws, and half-grown boys; and reassured also that the killing of old men, women, and half-grown boys was justified. Professor Richard W. Etulain in his Introduction to the 1978 reissue of the novel by the Gregg Press found that "another notable contribution of LeMay in *The Searchers* is his persuasive and penetrating pictures of Indians ... and thus his descriptions of the Indians are not gratuitous portraits of nameless and faceless savages." This kind of human and racial insensitivity is, happily, not as commonplace in literary criticism as it once was and therefore it probably does not warrant more than a passing mention: but if describing Indians — *any* Indians — "as dangerous as a torrent of rattlesnakes" is not a gratuitous portrait of nameless and faceless savages, it comes so close to it that it only causes one to wonder what about this picture is either persuasive or penetrating?

In *Comanche Captives*, Guthrie McCabe is hired by the U.S. Cavalry to bring back white captives from among the Comanches. He is accompanied on this mission by Jim Gary. All the white captives these two discover have been reduced to brutish animals as a result of their captivity and the one adolescent boy McCabe does bring back commits a vicious murder and is hanged by the morally outraged whites. Jim Gary rescues Janice Tremain, the niece of an U.S. Senator, who for five years has been the captive wife of Stone Calf. Gary kills Stone Calf, but he finds he must reject Janice because "he was a prudish man who wanted all women pure, until they were married at least." This was not so much a consideration for Mart Pauley, as for men generally on the real American frontier where there were very few single women to be found, virgins or otherwise. McCabe is saved from Amos Edwards' fate by being enslaved by the Comanches and only rescued by Jim Gary once he has learned the value of friendship and the virtue of community spirit.

Both of these novels were serialized in *The Saturday Evening Post* and so it is not to be expected that the Comanches would be characterized in any other way; but this deficiency alone does not make them romantic historical reconstructions. They may be termed this because in them history is being reconstructed for the purpose of proving something, because the characters behave as they do because of ideologies operative in the plots which they are supposed to illustrate and exemplify, and because these plots depend on heroes. A hero, as a faceless, savage Indian as a villain, is not human and can never be human.

What distinguishes the historical reconstruction, what sets it on an altogether different plane than either of the other two modes of Western fiction, is that in it the hero is replaced by a human being, a person of flesh and blood, while the structure is expanded to encompass historical reality free of ideological interpretation and bias. When they came to write their respective novels, Capps and Braun knew more about Comanches than had LeMay and Cook. This may be due to the circumstance that the history of the American West is being written more conscientiously today than it used to be, but it is also probably due to the fact that these authors cared enough about historical reality to discover what is was. In the historical reconstruction we come to recognize our solidarity with people from the past; we relive their lives, face the issues which confronted them, and, possibly, come to some deeper understanding of ourselves. The historical reconstruction, in its best instances, demonstrates that it is feasible to write fiction that is stirring and entertaining and notwithstanding historically accurate, truthful to the time, the place, and the people.

In *A Woman of the People*, Helen Morrison and her younger sister, Katy, are made captives of the Mutsani Comanches in 1854. The entire story is told from Helen Morrison's point of view and for all of it she remains living with the Comanches. We see her grow to womanhood among them, learn their customs and language, marry Burning Hand and bear him a child, and we see the touching relationship between these two. Because the Comanches are characterized, because there is an absence of heroes and villains, everyone can be and is humanized. *A Woman of the People* transcends mere fiction to become literature.

Capps was not concerned with arguing racial superiorities or cultural supremacy; instead, he showed the reader how and why the Comanches were different and in such a fashion that the Comanches can be respected for their differences. The same is true of Braun's *Black Fox*. The Black Fox of the title is Britt Johnson, a freed Black from the South. When the Comanches and the Kiowas stage a joint raid in 1860 to drive the white-eyes from their sacred lands and take captives, Black Fox, regarded by the whites as an uppity nigger, volunteers to negotiate to get the hostages back, not leastwise motivated because his own family is among the captives. Braun deftly characterized Running Dog and Santana among the Kiowas, Little Buffalo among the Comanches, showing the reader at the same time all the minute and quite distinct differences between these two Plains tribes, just as he characterized Black Fox and his relations within his own family and among the whites, the relations of the whites among themselves and with members of other races, and the multitude of ways in which various individuals perceive themselves and others. Britt's greatest inner conflict is induced by Running Dog, his friend among the Kiowas, who cannot understand why Black Fox prefers to live among the whites where he is subjected to the most demeaning treatment when he might live in freedom and dignity among the Kiowas. Each of the central characters is a fully rounded human being and so, from this perspective, the reader is better able to understand the suffering and personal travail in which each must live and yet somehow find his way within the human community and within himself.

Emerson Hough wrote his first novel, *The Girl at Halfway House* (Appleton, 1900), at the turn of the century; but it is for *The Covered Wagon* (Appleton, 1922) that he is best remembered. In its motion picture version, *The Covered Wagon* (Paramount, 1923) had a longer New York run than D.W. Griffith's *Birth of a Nation* (Epoch, 1915), while the novel remains an example *par excellence* of the romantic historical reconstruction. "Hough had his 1848 overland caravan literally hack its way through virtually all the Western Indian tribes massed at different points along the way for a 'final stand' against the plow-carrying home seekers," John D. Unruh, Jr., wrote in his excellent history, *The Plains Across* (University of Illinois, 1979). "Two major battles are fought, one with nearly 2,000 Sioux warriors, another with over 1,000 Crow and Bannock braves, and the sharpshooting overlanders kill in excess of 100 of these Indians. Four former mountain men — Bill Jackson, Jim Bridger, Kit Carson, and Caleb Greenwood — are prominently featured. Jim Bridger even ends up guiding part of the train nearly all the way to Oregon, free of charge! The romantic love story so central to Hough's plot even necessitated attention to California gold-mining in order for his hero to win the beautiful heroine."

This is romantic Western fiction on a grand scale. Eugene Manlove Rhodes fashioned his stories with no less romance, but the focus is more circumscribed, limited to New Mexico. When it came to women, Rhodes subscribed to an excessively chivalric code and he fully expected a reader to believe that Jeff Bransford in *Bransford in Arcadia, or the Little Eohippus* (Holt, 1914) and Johnny Dines in *Stepsons of Light* (Houghton Mifflin, 1921) would sooner face hanging than implicate a woman, no matter how innocently, in their respective plights. Many of Rhodes' stories appeared in *The Saturday Evening Post* and he never sought to undermine the *Post's* editorial prejudices: he never characterized Indians and he never questioned the Manifest Destiny of American expansionism. "While the incidents of Gene Rhodes' life were as vividly realistic as those of any modern novel," Henry Herbert Knibbs wrote of him in his Introduction to Rhodes' *The Proud Sheriff* (Houghton Mifflin, 1935), "intellectually and at heart he was a romantic." For his villains, however, Rhodes did choose the kinds of men who, historically, exploited the West, land speculators, bankers, mortgagers, monopolists, crooked politicians. Rhodes knew outlaws from personal experience and he was inclined to give them the benefit of the doubt. On the other hand, he could as easily side a lawman such as Pat Garrett, as he did when he made him a character in what is perhaps his finest short novel, *Pasó Por Aquí*, published in the *Post* in 1926 and obviously inspired by an apocryphal story told by Charles Siringo in *A Texas Cowboy* (1885) about how Billy the Kid once presumably paused in flight from the law to aid an ailing man. Indeed, it might be conceded that in *The Trusty Knaves* (Houghton Mifflin, 1934) Rhodes showed Bill Doolin to be less a bandit than the establishment which is planning a bank robbery. Although he would never have used these words, Rhodes portrayed outlawry, in whatever its form, as disorganized class struggle, men in their confusion trying to survive amid all the land-grabbers and Eastern capitalists preying upon them: this vision was at the heart of his fiction.

Henry Herbert Knibbs met Rhodes in the East, but he moved West to California before publishing his own first Western novel, *Lost Farm Camp* (Houghton Mifflin, 1912). As a Western writer, Knibbs was purely epigonal, but what Rhodes remembered of the West, its kindness and generosity, became equally strong themes for Knibbs. In *The Ridin' Kid from Powder River* (Houghton Mifflin, 1919), Knibbs based his outlaw leader, "The Spider," on Rhodes, and it almost disrupted their friendship when Rhodes claimed that Knibbs had taken unnecessary fictional liberties with the truth; Knibbs made up for it in *Partners of Chance* (Houghton Mifflin, 1921) in which he based his hero, Cheyenne Hastings, on Rhodes, making him a cheerful wanderer of the plains and deserts, a man always with a song on his breath, and a man who dislikes violence.

A romantic nostalgia for the past also preoccupied Western painter, sculptor, and, latterly, short story writer Charles M. Russell. Of the biographies and appreciations written about him, one of the best is *Recollections of Charley Russell* (University of Oklahoma Press, 1963) by Frank Bird Linderman. Linderman recalled in his memoir a time when both the Lindermans and the Russells were vacationing together in Santa Barbara, California, and how Russell held the guests at a local party captive with his stories. During the last years of his life, Russell began to feature these stories, tall tales, and anecdotes in a newspaper column and, eventually, they were collected in book form, *Rawhide Rawlins* (Montana Newspaper Alliance, 1921) and *More Rawhides* (Montana Newspaper Alliance, 1925). His last collection, published posthumously, was perhaps the best, *Trails Plowed Under* (Doubleday, 1927). As in so many of his paintings, which for light are set at dusk, twilight, or early dawn, and for feeling yearn after a bygone era, most of these short fictions are of the early Anglo-American West, of the people of that time, of the wild life, and of the animals. As Zane Grey, Russell felt the Indian half animal, half human being; but, unlike Grey, he was no social Darwinist: Russell celebrated the Indians' reverence for Nature and rejected the technology of the modern world.

As Eugene Manlove Rhodes, Harvey Fergusson left New Mexico territory to live in the East and returned only for brief visits. Of the fourteen books Fergusson wrote, critics have singled out five of them for special commendation. The first three, chronologically, are *Blood of the Conquerors* (Knopf, 1921), *Wolf Song* (Knopf, 1927), and *In Those Days* (Knopf, 1929) which Fergusson subsequently brought together in his *Followers of the Sun* (Knopf, 1936) trilogy. In terms of the internal chronology of the trilogy, *Wolf Song* comes first. It is a mountain man story and its hero, Sam Lash, was based loosely on Fergusson's impression of Kit Carson. The story concerns Sam Lash's impassioned love affair with Lola Salazar, a beautiful *rica* maiden, and his life and death battle with a savage Cheyenne warrior. As such, these might as easily be the ingredients of a novel by Mayne Reid and the plot is actually quite similar to that of Edwin L. Sabin's *The Rose of Santa Fe* (G.W. Jacobs, 1923). The Cheyenne is vanquished—of course!—and Lash is united with Lola at the end. But such a bald statement of Fergusson's plot does not convey the remarkable lyricism of his style nor his gift for vividly characterizing the land in its many moods. In his Foreword to *Followers of the Sun*, Fergusson insisted that "what ails the huge and infantile body of our conventional Western romance, from Beadle's dime novels on down, is not that its stories are melodramatic but that its heroes and heroines are lifeless." This is a significant statement. Fergusson tried to bring his heroes and heroines to life, but not in such a way that they cease to be types: they are still heroes and heroines.

Given this stereotypical tendency in characterization and the fact that, philosophically, Fergusson was a believer in white supremacy, Fergusson's critics have often appeared in the guise of apologists. William T. Pilkington commented in this Introduction to the reissue of *Grant of Kingdom* (1950; University of New Mexico Press, 1975) that "although readers today may see traces of racial or ethnic stereotyping in an occasional phrase or characterization, it must be remembered that such instances represent the feelings only of characters in the novel; in reprinting *Grant of Kingdom* the present publisher intends no endorsement of any such cultural prejudice, nor should prejudice be attributed to Harvey Fergusson, all of whose writings are marked by a deeply humanistic spirit." The key words in what Professor Pilkington wrote are "such instances represent the feelings only of characters in the novel...." "Arnold Blore," Fergusson observed in *Grant of Kingdom*, "learned from childhood how to be faultlessly polite to the men he dealt with and also how to despise them. Although he did not know it, he had toward these people the same attitude the Negroes had toward the whites—an attitude subtly compounded of hypocrisy, cunning, envy, and contempt." If Blore did not know it and Blore is the character being discussed, whose feelings then are being represented? At another point in the novel Fergusson reflected that "an Indian who had not been ruined by contact with dishonest white men was always a good friend in two ways. He would never forget you, any more than a dog or a horse will forget you, and he would keep his word." The generalizations are no less apparent about women. "Some of these Mexican girls took a powerful hold upon his flesh," the reader is told about the hero, Jean Ballard. "Many of them were pretty and they had a soft and voluptuous quality, a completeness of submission and response that made them wholly different from the shrill and nervous women, laborious and full of malaria, he had known in Indiana." Perhaps a reader might shrug his shoulders and say, well, all the Mexican women Ballard met were really this way, to say nothing of the "shrill and nervous" women back in Indiana. However, every character in this novel, and in Fergusson's Southwestern novels in general, seems to agree with Ballard's experience.

Fergusson's maternal grandfather, Franz Huning, arrived in Santa Fe in 1850 and in Albuquerque in the years after 1857 he became a successful merchant. Huning left behind him a memoir and Fergusson, to an extent, based *In Those Days* on it and the fifth, and best, novel of his Southwestern group, *The Conquest of Don Pedro* (Morrow, 1954). Robert Jayson, the hero of *In Those Days*, is a man who comes to New Mexico, becomes a prosperous merchant, only to wind up a victim of change. This is essentially the same plot as that of *The Conquest of Don Pedro* in which Leo Mendes, a Jewish peddler, comes to New Mexico, becomes a successful merchant, and, finally, loses everything, including his young and beautiful Hispanic wife who is attracted to and won by an Anglo-American; although for Leo "a man's destiny is a thing he discovers, a mystery that unfolds" and the end of the novel can be interpreted as a new beginning for him. Robert Jayson is a victim — as is almost every sympathetic male character in these five novels — to the encroaching Anglo-American invasion. He fails because ideologically he must fail because he is a victim; and he is a victim because the plot declares that he must be a victim in order to make poignantly evident the moral message concerning the spiritual emptiness of Anglo-American materialism. Leo Mendes, on the other hand, is not so completely a victim because he has an option: while Leo may be "wholly unable to deal with the world that was creeping up on him, a world in which men were always counting their dollars and their minutes," he can pull out and leave. The most compelling imagery in Fergusson's fiction is his whole-hearted questioning of Anglo-American values and the problem critics who like his fiction have with him is that they want to applaud this imagery and do not know what to conclude about the plot contrivances and stereotypical characterizations Fergusson employed in ideologically dramatizing it.

Conrad Richter, born at Pine Grove, Pennsylvania, was already a successful writer for the slick-magazine market when he moved to New Mexico in 1928. He published nine stories with Western settings in *The Ladies Home Journal* and *The Saturday Evening Post* between April, 1934 and January, 1936 before they were collected in *Early Americana and Other Stories* (Knopf, 1936). The heroes in these stories are the family unit and the community rather than the individualistic bias so common in formulary Westerns while the Indians — inevitably, given where the stories first appeared — are used only for dramatic purposes. *The Sea of Grass* (Knopf, 1937), anticipated in his earlier short story, "Smoke Over the Prairie" (1935), was serialized in *The Saturday Evening Post*, as were a number of Richter's later novels. It is a tale of cattlemen versus nesters. Colonel Brewton, the hero, personifies the pioneering spirit as Richter imagined it to have been; he represents the open range in New Mexico during the years 1885–1900, pitted against farmers who are obsessed with an impossible agrarian dream. Perhaps the most effective characterization in the novel is that of the Colonel's wife, Lutie, an Eastern woman incapable of adapting to frontier life. Jary Luckett, a character in Richter's next novel, *The Trees* (Knopf, 1940), and the first in his epic trilogy about the settling of the Ohio frontier between the years 1790–1860, is the exact opposite of Lutie Brewton. The heroine of the trilogy, which also includes *The Fields* (Knopf, 1946) and *The Town* (Knopf, 1950), is Sayward Luckett, anticipated by Sayward Hewett in Richter's short story, "The Rawhide Knot" (1938). *Tacey Cromwell* (Knopf, 1942) is set in Arizona territory and is a mining story about a brothel madam who, as her gambler lover, wishes to attain social respectability. Compared with other Richter novels, the plot seems forced and unduly melodramatic. *The Lady* (Knopf, 1957), Richter's third Southwestern novel, concerns a conflict between cattlemen and sheepmen, the heroine, Dona Ellen, a woman of Mexican and English ancestry, representing the latter group. Although in many ways the epitome of femininity, Dona Ellen was provided by Richter with many masculine traits so as to make credible her penchant for violence.

In *The Light in the Forest* (Knopf, 1953) and *A Country of Strangers* (Knopf, 1966) Richter attempted to show pioneer life more from the Indian point of view than he had in previous novels. Both are captivity stories; the former concentrates on a white boy raised by Delaware Indians, the latter on a white girl who conceived a child with an Indian. Richter claimed he found James Fenimore Cooper unreadable, but somehow he managed to carry over into these novels Cooper's distinction between noble savages and vicious savages; although, in all honesty, it must be admitted that the emphasis is primarily on the common term: savagery. As in Alan LeMay's novels, white civilization is pitted against Indian culture. The characters are confused for a time which to choose, but in the end white civilization is found superior. This outcome is consistent with Richter's view as to the function of historical fiction: ideally it should inspire Americans in difficult and troubled times. Ricther loathed formulary Westerns and dismissed them as mere escapism. He believed strongly that the glories of the American past, the winning out through hardships, held an answer for dislocations in the present. His ideology blunted all the edges. He could and did show abuses of Nature; he was ambivalent at times about the ultimate value of industrial society; but in the final analysis he felt compelled to cast his lot with the inevitability of Anglo-American progress. Yet, his prose is simple and often graceful and his female characters are seldom stereotypical.

Willa Cather is most often compared by critics with Conrad Richter and her novel, *A Lost Lady* (Knopf, 1923), the story of an aging beauty who, having survived the pioneer experience, dreams of the days when she entertained railroad workers, is frequently contrasted with Richter's *A Lady*. Certainly the structures of many of their novels have much in common and Cather, as Richter, had a tendency to use male narrators in her fiction. Cather was raised in Nebraska and, after her early work, heavily influenced by Henry James, *O Pioneers!* (Houghton Mifflin, 1913) heralded her literary transition, writing about pioneer days in Nebraska. *My Ántonia* (Houghton Mifflin, 1918) followed and the stories collected in *Obscure Destinies* (Knopf, 1932). These are her great works about the pioneering era, written in a nostalgic, elegaic tone, filled with warmth, humanity, and the richness of life. Authors such as A.B. Guthrie, Jr., have criticized Cather for dealing only with the positive aspects of pioneer life and omitting the brutality, the hardship, and the savagery. Of course, there is some justification in such a charge, but it was possibly never Cather's intention to present a complete portrait, but rather an impression, a mood, a moment of brightness in lives usually surrounded by shadows; most of all her Western fiction provided her with an opportunity to praise what she considered the primary human virtues and to stress values she herself treasured, felt absent in the modern world, and so projected back into a former time.

When Cather no longer had stories to write about Nebraska, she turned to the Southwest, an area that had fascinated her for many years and to which she had traveled regularly since 1912. As early as her short story, "The Enchanted Bluff" (1909), Cather had been interested in the ancient cliff dwellers of pre-Columbian Arizona. The literary consequences of her visits to Arizona and New Mexico resulted in the fourth part of *The Song of the Lark* (Houghton Mifflin, 1915) titled "The Ancient People"; "Tom Outland's Story," a story-within-a-story about the discovery of an ancient cliff dwelling city in *The Professor's House* (Knopf, 1925); and *Death Comes for the Archbishop* (Knopf, 1927). This last is a narrative, as Cather herself preferred to call it, about the organization of a vast diocese in mid Nineteenth-century New Mexico by Archbishop Lamy and his vicar, Joseph P. Macheboeuf, renamed Jean Marie Latour and Joseph Vaillant in the book. As is tyical of all of Cather's work, *Death Comes for the Archbishop* is written in an episodic and simple style in which lies its true beauty. For Cather the land of the Southwest and its inhabitants had been a tremendously moving experience and in writing this novel she attempted to celebrate, this time in the Southwest, the early pioneering spirit. It is a lasting book, as Cather told her publisher it would be, and deserves its reputation as one of the best American novels written in the first part of this century. Some have declared it to be an historical novel. This, however, it is not. It has rather the ingredients of the romantic historical reconstruction. It dramatizes an ideological interpretation of history.

Harvey Fergusson felt that Cather dealt with New Mexico as a tourist would and Mary Austin, in whose home Cather finished *Death Comes for the Archbishop*, was angered at Cather's use of a French protagonist which Austin felt was a betrayal of New Mexico's Spanish heritage.

Yet, this charge of being a tourist might as readily be lodged against Paul Horgan. His several novels have had various settings. *Far from Cibola* (Harper's, 1938), an early novel, deals with New Mexicans seeking government aid whereas *The Habit of Empire* (Rydal, 1938) focuses on Sixteenth-century New Mexico. Horgan's distinction as a regional novelist, it would seem, may rest on his most popular success, *A Distant Trumpet* (Farrar, Straus, 1960), and his short novel, "The Devil in the Desert" (1952). *A Distant Trumpet* is the story of Matthew and Laura Hazard, a young U.S. Cavalry couple who begin their married life at a remote outpost in Arizona territory during the final years of the Apache campaigns. It is in the tradition of Cavalry stories in the mode of the romantic historical reconstruction by Ernest Haycox and James Warner Bellah, but its portrait of the Apaches — albeit speaking only relatively — is somewhat more sympathetic than is the case in the majority of its precursors. Willa Cather was an Anglican. Paul Horgan was a Roman Catholic. He was unquestionably moved by her account of Archbishop Lamy to write his own biography of him, *Lamy of Santa Fe: His Life and Times* (Farrar, Straus, 1975), for which he won a Pulitzer Prize, as well as "The Devil in the Desert." In the latter he continued the convention of earlier writers such as Helen Hunt Jackson and Owen Wister of romanticizing the Roman clergy in the New World. However, in all justice to Horgan, as to Cather, religious bias is only one element in a more comprehensive ideology.

H.L. Davis sought in his first novel, *Honey in the Horn* (Harper's, 1935), to write a humorous yet scathingly satiric treatment of homesteading in Oregon during the first decade of the Twentieth century. Clay Calvert, the hero, falls into one adventure after another in a social landscape filled with rascals, scoundrels, romantic misfits, Indians, thieves, land exploiters, and assorted homesteaders, all searching for the metaphorical "honey in the horn." Clay seeks reality amid all the illusions which captivate the other characters. Davis' later novels, *Harp of a Thousand Strings* (Morrow, 1947), *Beulah Land* (Morrow, 1949), and *Winds of Morning* (Morrow, 1953), while making frequent contrasts between appearance and reality in the frontier experience, are more and more concerned with the growth of an inner spiritual reality that is not intrinsically related in a significant way to the Western setting.

A few pontiffs of academe have, somewhat quixotically, classified as Western writers three authors who are only peripherally that and who have virtually nothing in common. They are John Steinbeck, Wallace Stegner, and Larry McMurtry.

The reason usually given for viewing Steinbeck as a Western writer is that California, especially the Monterey region, is a central landscape in much of his fiction and that man in his environment is his most important theme. However, the truth of the matter is that Steinbeck novels such as *Tortilla Flat* (Covici, Friede, 1935) and *In Dubious Battle* (Covici, Friede, 1936) are more examples of what is called "main-stream" American fiction than they are especially regional. The major themes of *The Grapes of Wrath* (Covici, Friede, 1939) — the disenfranchisement of the homesteader and Western farmer by capitalist speculators, the economic exigency which compelled many farmers to depend on single-crop food production and how this combined with the effects of prolonged drought to produce the disaster of the Dust Bowl—these themes, on the other hand, might be regarded as belonging within the domain of Western fiction. Steinbeck's tone of social protest is often shrill, but it remains to his credit that he *could* take a regional theme and expand it to encompass a perspective in which man is perceived as part of a group and to survive must merge his identity with the group identity. Yet even this has nothing intrinsically to do with Western fiction or the Western regions. Nor does one novel qualify Steinbeck as a Western writer any more, really, than *The Big Rock Candy Mountain* (Duell, Sloan, and Pearce, 1943) would qualify Stegner as such or *Horseman, Pass By* (Harper's, 1961) McMurtry. If there is a common thread, however, in these three books—and it would be, admittedly, a very tenuous one—it might be a feeling of disillusionment with romanticism. Notwithstanding, this disillusionment does not lead to a sense of a greater reality. It is more self-indulgent than that: it is merely disillusionment.

The Big Rock Candy Mountain is clearly autobiographical. It can be regarded as an almost exact rendering of Wallace Stegner's view of his early years. Bo Mason impresses his son Bruce with his carelessness and his crudity; his mother impresses him with her gentleness and cultural refinement. Bruce is the survivor, "the only one left," in Stegner's words, "to fulfill that contract and try to justify the labor and the harshness and the mistakes of his parents' lives." *Recapitulation* (Doubleday, 1979) is a sequel of sorts. A much older Bruce Mason, looking back at his life, now blames his parents that he has not become more, while he is pleased with the degree of cultural refinement he has attained. A "Western view seems totally absent from Bruce's consciousness," John Milton wrote in *The Novel of the American West* (University of Nebraska Press, 1980), "and, along with his view on cultural deprivation, may identify his personal problem as an inability to see himself either as an intellectual Easterner or a spiritual Westerner." Stegner's *Angle of Repose* (Doubleday, 1971) is technically calculated, but it has no vitality. The issue with which it deals, while perhaps likely to appeal to an academic who has had to confront a sense of spiritual barrenness and personal defeat in his life, is scarcely to be associated with the American West. It is a story about a retired and physically disabled professor who has little use for the community in which he lives and who tries instead to find a greater meaning in the past by reconstructing the relationship between his grandparents.

Stegner anticipated his central theme in *Angle of Repose* in an essay titled "History, Myth, and the Western Writer" which he wrote for *Great Western Short Stories* (American West Publishing, 1967) edited by J. Golden Taylor. In this essay Stegner remarked that "the typical western writer loves the past of his native region, but despises the present." The reader should note the small "w" in Western. In this same essay Stegner made a distinction between the kinds of Western fiction—Western belonging to "the large, simple formulas of myth" and western (small "w") belonging to "fiction of a certain kind, a kind not so petrified as the Western, but related to it. It is almost by definition historical and rural, or at least limited to the life characteristic of the periods of raid and settlement." In this kind of western fiction, according to Stegner, the tone is one of nostalgic regret. "It is a tone that may seem odd in a new country, and yet it may express something quintessentially American: our sadness at what our civilization does to the natural, free, and beautiful, to the noble, the self-reliant, the brave. Many of the virtues of the typical western hero are virtues seen as defeated, or gone by, no longer honored." Therefore, as Stegner used the word, Western applies to formulary Western fiction and western is the romantic historical reconstruction. There was, for him, no third mode. Authors of westerns, he insisted, "do not ever question the validity of heroism," and insofar as they do not, whatever else they do, the "validity of heroism" as a first premise must make their fiction romantic as that term is here being used.

Setting in Larry McMurtry's fiction is no less irrelevant than it is in Stegner's. *Horseman, Pass By* was McMurtry's novel and, while it sold very few copies, it was made into a motion picture titled *Hud* (Paramount, 1963). It is concerned with an adolescent boy coming of age in rural Texas in the post World War II era. In it are established all the themes and the structure of McMurtry's later fiction. That structure seems to be a projection of Edgar Allan Poe's "The Fall of the House of Usher" (1839) into the modern West. The family we meet at the beginning is devastated by the end. McMurtry's central theme is the urgent obsession with sexuality, which must be broadened to include sexual intercourse with animals, a recurring motif. "Nobody I knew, and many of us were country boys, engaged in such practices," C.L. Sonnichsen commented in *From Hopalong to Hud: Thoughts on Western Fiction* (Texas A&M University Press, 1978). "Yet McMurtry makes a sort of speciality of zoophily and implies that when you say 'Boys will be boys,' this is one of the things you mean." In *Leaving Cheyenne* (Harper's 1963) the plot concerns a relationship so improbable that even McMurtry himself, in his collection of autobiographical literary essays, *In a Narrow Grave* (Encino Press, 1968), admitted it was a "male journalist's fantasy." The plot, simply put, is about a woman who prefers for forty years to sleep with two men who are best friends without any effort being made to probe into the obvious psychological complexity such a *ménage à trois* would require to exist, much less remain stable. In *The Last Picture Show* (Dial, 1966) McMurtry was again concerned with adolescent sexuality and the boredom come of living in a small rural town. Unfortunately, the subject of sexuality among dull and uninteresting people is not made less dull and uninteresting because it is sexuality. *The Last Picture Show* at least has some interesting characters. The same cannot be said about *Moving On* (Simon & Schuster, 1970) which is a tediously long novel about a married woman's abortive love affair with a male graduate student. *All My Friends Are Going to Be Strangers* (Simon & Schuster, 1972) is a semi-autobiographical novel about a Texas writer whose first novel is sold to motion pictures and who proceeds, through the course of the story, to have sexual intercourse with every female he meets until, since many of them are married and others merely neurotic, they have become "strangers" to him. *Terms of Endearment* (Simon & Schuster, 1975) is but a variation on this theme, only instead of a promiscuous male who is left on the brink of suicide at the end, it is a promiscuous female, sort of a throw-back to the promiscuous heroine of *Leaving Cheyenne*. *Somebody's Darling* (Simon & Schuster, 1978) is another variation on this theme, set in Hollywood and not in Texas, with a heroine who does not want to be seduced in order to be in motion pictures but who is, and is repeatedly.

The most notable characteristic of the romantic historical reconstruction is its ability to accomodate widespread diversity and variety. At one end of the spectrum in this mode is a novel such as Matthew Braun's *Jury of Six* (Pocket Books, 1980), very nearly a formulary porno-Western but for its inclusion of actual historial characters and historical events: it is concerned with the Lincoln County War. At the other end is a novel such as Willa Cather's *Death Comes for the Archbishop* where the ideological message is that each human being is searching for permanence in a world of perpetual change and that true permanence can best be found in the mystical tenets of orthodox Christian eschatology.

Whereas the events in a formulary Western exist to demonstrate the hero's mastery of a given situation, the hero in a romantic historical reconstruction *may* master events but he does not have to master them: just as he may be a manhunter or a saint, depending on the ideology being illustrated. There is thus room in this mode for the "failed" hero, a hero defeated, overwhelmed, even destroyed by events, but who is nonetheless a hero. Indeed, the fate of such a "failed" hero becomes the embodiment of the ideology of the story which prescribes his behavior in the face of the very events which destroy him, demonstrating by this means the historical view of life and events the author wants to prove.

In the historical reconstruction there are no heroes, although at times men and women can commit heroic deeds. It is a closer, finer approximation to a past reality than is true of either of the other two modes. However, this distinction does not imply a literary judgment. Several of the authors of romantic historical reconstructions are finer literary artists than some of those who have written historical reconstructions. Depending on a reader's taste, a story with an ideology may even be preferred to one that has none. The need for certainty is such that when knowledge is insufficient it can indeed be comforting to have an ideological view of the world, be it the cult of the hero, social Darwinism, a variety of Christian theology, or economic determinism; anything just so long as it is something which purports to explain and justify everything. The historical reconstruction, as history itself, is unable to provide such reassurance. This is not so in the mode of the romantic historical reconstruction because in this mode there is no immutable historical reality. The past is whatever we today wish it to have been and the only meaning the historical past has is that meaning which we wish to prove by means of it.

V

"*Felix qui potuit rerum cognoscere causas*" [happy is he who has been able to know the cause of things], Virgil once said, and happy, too, is he who knows what has happened as well as it can be known in the history of his own culture. We must finally learn enough history, and specifically enough Western American history, to distinguish between what is romance and what is not. It was, for example, a social and economic reality in 1890 that, three years before Frederick Jackson Turner proclaimed the frontier officially closed, there were more mortgages than families in Minnesota, the Dakotas, Kansas, and Nebraska, that after the drought of 1887 at least 11,000 families were evicted from Kansas farms, that in the 1890s nine million farm mortgages held what had once been free land for a ransom of nearly four billion dollars! It was an indelible part of the frontier experience to have been one of those who came to the open land, fought against the elements, trying to build a new life, only for the land to be seized and taken away by grasping speculators. Much of the real drama of the Westward expansion came about through the fact that the nature of a capitalistic system is not to distribute purchasing power, for this it can never do, but rather for capital to multiply itself for those who possess it to begin with. The drama of the American West must include the fact that the profit system prefers to lay waste and destroy rather than to conserve and reuse. The drama of the open land must accompany the fact that industrial and financial greed have forever destroyed natural resources, laid barren a once beautiful countryside, ravaged the earth for coal and iron and gold and oil, stripped the forests, ruined the beaches, polluted air and water everywhere, turned the Great Lakes through unprocessed sewerage into dead seas, while sucking the energy, the health, the meaning of life out of generations of working people, and always with the promise of a constantly better standard of living.

Due to the tremendous success of the anonymous publication of Homer Croy's *West of the Water Tower* (Harper's, 1923), Dorothy Scarborough's publisher wanted her novel, *The Wind* (Harper's, 1925), to be published anonymously as part of a publicity effort. By the end of 1925, when the book's sales had not reached Scarborough's expectations, she requested that her name be placed on all future printings, The appearance of the novel with her name on it brought hostile reactions from various groups in West Texas — it is set in Sweetwater, Texas, where Scarborough's parents homesteaded — including the West Texas Chamber of Commerce which felt that Scarborough had deliberately maligned and exaggerated the arid climate. Scarborough responded that, while a loyal Texan, she was a novelist, "convicted of realism in the first degree," and did not feel it her duty to promote the climate of West Texas. *The Wind* is told from the point of view of Letty, an orphaned eighteen-year-old girl from Virginia who comes to Sweetwater to live with her cousin and his wife. Letty finds all aspects of pioneer life alien, the isolated environment of her lonely shack after she is driven into a marriage, the other people she meets, and above all the wind which takes on an almost human dimension: each factor contributes in its way to Letty's emotional disintegration and final madness, ending in her suicide. Earlier writers such as Hamlin Garland and Frank Norris had never so completely permitted themselves the pessimistic interpretation of frontier hardships as did Scarborough. However, this novel, as well as O.E. Rölvaag's *Giants in the Earth* (Harper's, 1927) and Willa Cather's *My Ántonia*, focuses notably on the feminine component of pioneering rather than concentrating on male characters and their struggles.

Rölvaag was an immigrant from Norway and *Giants in the Earth* was the first novel in a trilogy about an immigrant family. In it Rölvaag described not the epic heroism of pioneer life but the terror and loneliness of the immigrants who had to endure storms, frosts, prairie fires, and droughts as well as conflicts with their neighbors. Beret Hansa is a lonely farmer's wife who goes insane in her estrangement from the land and becomes a religious fanatic. After the death of her husband in a blizzard, Beret's life story is continued in the second volume of the trilogy, *Peder Victorious* (Harper's, 1929), in which she regains her energy and her life spirit. The narrative also tells of the Americanization of Beret's son while the small Norwegian settlement is seen to grow into a Midwestern town. *Their Father's God* (Harper's, 1931) completed the trilogy, telling of the unhappy marriage of Peder and his Roman Catholic wife, Susie.

The male bias of many critics and academics writing about Western fiction has been such that Mari Sandoz and a number of other women writers have been undeservedly overlooked. Sandoz's finest novel, *Miss Morissa: Doctor of the Gold Trail* (McGraw–Hill, 1955), may have an uninspired title, but it is a gripping story. Set in the North Platte River Valley during the 1870s, it shows a young woman doctor's efforts to become part of a small homesteading community situated in the heart of the cattle country, one of all too few instances in Western fiction to treat with depth and insight the role of the professional woman on the frontier. Sandoz had published previously three novels which can be grouped together on the basis of their being more allegorical than realistic, the first of which was *Slogum House* (Little, Brown, 1937), a brutal story about a woman who destroys a number of people, including members of her own family, through her will to power. Horrified as was Willa Cather with the irrevocable changes taking place in modern technological society and the materialism and parasitism of people, Sandoz addressed this issue forcefully in *Capital City* (Little, Brown, 1939). In *The Tom-Walker* (Dial, 1947) Sandoz traced the changes taking place in the country through three generations of the Stone clan who move West after the Civil War. What is characteristic of Sandoz in these four novels, and what makes her different from Willa Cather, is that she did not permit herself Cather's romanticism and sense of nostalgia. Of lesser literary importance, but certainly not of less interest, is Sandoz' novel, *Son of the Gamblin' Man* (Clarkson N. Potter, 1960), a fictionalized account of John Cozad, a gambler and founder of Cozad, Nebraska, and his son, Robert Henry Cozad who, as

Robert Henri, became a world-famous artist and teacher. "The Vine" in *Hostiles and Friendlies* (University of Nebraska Press, 1959), occasional writings and stories, is probably the most moving short fiction Sandoz wrote.

Dorothy M. Johnson's two collections of short stories, *Indian Country* (Ballantine, 1953) and *The Hanging Tree* (Ballantine, 1957), constitute a major achievement. Johnson succeeded in her short fiction in breaking away from all of the usual stereotypes and, as in the short fiction of Jack Schaefer and even more so of A.B. Guthrie, Jr., she wrote about ordinary people, some of whom certainly are not admirable but whose actions occasionally take on an added spiritual dimension in the face of frontier adversity. Johnson's deep knowledge of Western history tended to make her situations and characters particularly credible and especially notable are those stories narrated from a child's or a woman's point of view. In stories which focus on Native Americans, the Indian life-style is shown as a unique kind of culture with its own integrity. Many of these stories were first published in slick magazines where the editorial policy was that a white "belongs" with white culture, the non-white with non-white culture. Any alternative to such segregation was considered impermissible unless it was shown to lead to the direst consequences. Therefore it should come as no surprise that when a white character comes to live for a time among the Indians, in the end he prefers to return to his Anglo-American culture. But, at best, this is a minor criticism.

Jack Schaefer's Western fiction might be characterized as a response to romantic myths about the frontier experience, or, rather, as a series of responses. In Schaefer's first and most famous short novel, *Shane* (Houghton Mifflin, 1949), the hero helps the nesters to overcome the tyranny of the local cattle baron and his hired gun; but in history, more often than not, the nesters, instead of triumphing, ended up becoming tenants and finally being evicted. In *The Kean Land* in *The Kean Land and Other Stories* (Houghton Mifflin, 1959), Schaefer showed how the land speculators win every round, albeit the story does conclude with an affirmation of the human spirit even in defeat. In a way, the contrast between *Shane* and *The Kean Land* is indicative of Schaefer's own considerable development as a conscious historical novelist. *The Canyon* (Houghton Mifflin, 1953) tells the story of a Cheyenne warrior seeking his own vision. By the time he wrote it, Schaefer had come to believe that "the Amerinds in general (with some exceptions) were truly civilized and ... we whites, better or ahead or whatever you want to call it only in our deadly emphasis on technology, were the invading barbarians." Schaefer had studied closely the customs and culture patterns of the Cheyennes in order to write the short novel and perhaps the only real criticism which might be lodged against its outcome is that Little Bear, the protagonist, has a vision more comprehensible to a modern Anglo-American than it would have been to a Cheyenne in the Nineteenth century. Among Schaefer's later works, the most outstanding is *Monte Walsh* (Houghton Mifflin, 1963), a picaresque novel dealing with cowboy life as a passing, subsequently glamorized, but essentially unromantic way of earning a living.

The realities of Western American history increasingly pressed themselves on Schaefer. In *Mavericks* (Houghton Mifflin, 1967) he found himself coming full circle. Here he was dealing with the end of wild life in the West, following the earlier course of the buffalo. Jake, the protagonist, confronted by the dwindling herds of wild horses can only echo Cooper's Leatherstocking before him — although his lamentation has much more bite to it — when he remarks that "'we can remember 'em, I reckon that's all we've left ourselves able to do.'" Suddenly, Schaefer was totally incapable of romance. "Always," he reflected, "I was writing about people, about us featherless bipeds who sum ourselves by genus and species as *Homo sapiens*. Any other creatures who crept in were merely stage furniture for the human drama. And then, as a writer, I came to a full stop. I had lost my innocence. I had become ashamed of my species and myself. I understood at last in full consequence that despite whatever dodges of motive and intent and personal activities I might cite ... I was a contributing part of the human onrush that was ruining the land I loved and forcing toward extinction ever more of my fellow creatures whose companion right to continued existence ought to be respected."

Vardis Fisher's first novel was *Toilers of the Hills* (Houghton Mifflin, 1928). It is set in the Antelope Hills region of Fisher's childhood and was cited at the time as the first important fiction to come out of the Rocky Mountain area. It also led to Fisher's name being linked with those of Hamlin Garland and Willa Cather. He objected, however, to any comparison with Cather, insisting she was a hopelessly romantic writer who failed to deal with the realities of pioneer life. In *Toilers of the Hills* and such subsequent novels as *Dark Bridwell* (Houghton Mifflin, 1931) and *April: A Fable of Love* (Caxton Printers, 1937), Fisher sought to juxtapose the beauties with the harshnesses of the land. In contrast to so many other authors writing about the Arcadian dream, Fisher's novels are extremely complex and never sentimental. Throughout his regional fiction, including *In Tragic Life* (Caxton Printers, 1932), the first novel in his autobiographical tetralogy, Fisher displayed his ability to draw interesting and believable characters as he made use of authentic dialogue, accurate descriptions of topography, flora, fauna, as well as folklore of the Idaho region. *Children of God: An American Epic* (Harper's, 1939) won the Harper Prize of $10,000 the year it appeared and it remains Fisher's best-known novel. For many years he had been contemplating a novel on Mormonism and in his essay, "Creative Historical Research in Fiction" (1940), he stated that he had wanted "to be impartial, to see the whole matter in reasonably clear perspective, and to avoid all editorializing and moral implications." The general consensus would support this insofar as *Children of God* is widely regarded as one of the most impartial books written about the Latter-Day Saints.

City of Illusion (Harper's, 1941) was Fisher's next historical novel and it deals with the rise and fall of Virginia City, Nevada. Silver was discovered there in 1859 and Fisher's intention — at which he succeeded — was to examine all the illusions that went with sudden wealth and power. *The*

Mothers: An American Saga of Courage (Vanguard, 1943) is the story of the ill-fated Donner expedition across the Sierra Nevadas in 1846–1847 which Fisher narrated from the point of view of the mothers in the group, underplaying any sensationalism. That same year Fisher published the first book in his *Testament of Man* series which occupied him for the next twelve years and which proved a financial disaster. It was finally left without a publisher until Alan Swallow offered to resume publishing the series. So as to circulate his name again among the reading public, Fisher wrote *Pemmican* (Doubleday, 1956), a romance set during the Pemmican War of 1815–1821 between the Hudson Bay Company and the Northwest Company for control of the Western fur trade. In Fisher's previous historical novels, he had confined himself to historical characters; here, for the first time, he added fictional characters to an historical framework. *Tale of Valor* (Doubleday, 1958), which followed, is Fisher's rendering of the Lewis and Clark expedition and just about the best fictional treatment of it, differing from such novels as Emerson Hough's *The Magnificent Adventure* (Appleton, 1916) before it and Will Henry's *The Gates of the Mountains* (Random House, 1963) after it — to cite but two examples — in that Fisher penetrated with greater assiduity into the minds of his principal characters and dramatized their unique qualities of leadership. Fisher was not very adept at the short story form and his one collection of short fiction, *Love and Death* (Doubleday, 1959), is less than satisfying. *Mountain Man* (Morrow, 1965) was his last historical novel and it contains some of Fisher's most lyrical prose. As *Pemmican*, it is noteworthy for showing the barbarism of whites and Indians alike in the primitive fight for survival. Sam Menard, Fisher's mountain man of the title, although based on a real person, "Liver-Eating Johnson," is the closest Fisher came to introducing a hero into one of his novels and, accordingly, *Mountain Man* is more even than *Pemmican* a romantic historical reconstruction.

Fisher was an iconoclast who never stopped pursuing his insatiable need to understand human beings and their behavior. If he had a glaring fault, it was his occasional tendency toward excess. In personal culture, he was almost more a European than an American, whatever the regional concerns of much of his fiction. Indeed, in his historical fiction and his histories, he was that rare combination, a Westerner who is a man of letters. Unlike Wallace Stegner, who tried to use personal culture to prove himself something more than he seemed secretly to believe he was, Fisher was without conceit or ostentation. He knew that in choosing the West as his subject matter, he was running a risk of remaining in undeserved obscurity; but, as he remarked in "The Western Writer and the Eastern Establishment" (1966), "if young writers of the West were to ask me for advice I'd tell them to be faithful to their talent and skeptical of their judges."

Walter Van Tilburg Clark, although he had grown up in Nevada, was teaching and coaching at a high school in Cazenovia, New York, when his first novel, *The Ox-Bow Incident* (Random House, 1940), was published. It was highly praised and established Clark as a foremost Western author. The story probes the notion of frontier justice and tells of three men, encountered on the trail by a gang of vigilantes, hanged for being cattle thieves only for them afterwards to be proven innocent. Certainly few authors of Western fiction prior to Clark had approached their subject with both his profound sense of erudition – a quality he shared with Vardis Fisher – and his grasp of its mythic potential. Clark's next novel was *The City of Trembling Leaves* (Random House, 1945), an initiation story in which any sense of the land, as of setting in general, is of negligible importance in terms of what happens to the characters. In 1946 Clark went to live in Taos, New Mexico, and then, toward the end of the decade, returned to Nevada. *The Track of the Cat* (Random House, 1949), Clark's third novel, shows how two hunters are killed pursuing a panther – a symbol for the principle of evil – because they do not understand it and how two hunters, who do understand it, are able to kill the panther. *The Watchful Gods and Other Stories* (Random House, 1950), a collection of short fiction which merits a good deal more praise than it received from critics when it first appeared, proved to be Clark's last published book.

A.B. Guthrie, Jr.'s family moved to Choteau, Montana, when he was six months old. "It was a fine country to grow up in," Guthrie later wrote in his autobiography, *The Blue Hen's Chick* (McGraw-Hill, 1965). "To find riches, a boy had only to go outside." His first novel was *Murders at Moon Dance* (Dutton, 1943), a detective story with a Western setting, a mixture of genres to which he would again return. *The Big Sky* (Sloane, 1947), the first volume in what was to become Guthrie's frontier tetralogy, tells of Boone Caudill who leaves his home in Kentucky in 1830 to find adventure on the frontier and who eventually becomes a mountain man. "I wanted to show the mountain man ... for what he was," Guthrie recalled in an essay, "The Historical Novel" (1954), "or what he seemed honestly to me to have been – not the romantic character, the virtuous if unlettered Leatherstocking, but the engaging, uncouth, admirable, odious, thoughtless, resourceful, loyal, sinful, smart, stupid, courageous character that he was and had to be." Guthrie's next novel, *The Way West* (Sloane, 1949), continued the story of Dick Summers, the experienced mountain man from *The Big Sky*, who is hired as a scout and guide for a wagon train. By means of a number of well-drawn characters, each of whom has a different reason for moving to Oregon, Guthrie chronicled the physical and psychological hardships encountered along the trail, particularly by women, as well as the tediousness of a journey that required months. To manage this complex perspective, Guthrie employed a multiple point of view, as he did again in *These Thousand Hills* (Houghton Mifflin, 1956) which narrates the life of Lat Evans, grandson of Lije Evans from *The Way West*, who leaves Oregon in the 1880s to become a cattle rancher in Montana.

The title story of *The Big It and Other Stories* (Houghton Mifflin, 1960) appears in a somewhat altered form in *These Thousand Hills* as a comical yarn spun by one of Lat Evans' partners when they are out wolfing for bounty. All but two of the stories in this collection had been published previously in magazines, slick and literary, but all are set in the West and they range from the comic to the ironic to the morbidly pathetic. The model for *Arfive* (Houghton Mifflin, 1970) was the town of Choteau, Montana, and this is a novel depicting the building of a small Western community with a cast of interesting but ordinary people. In particular, Guthrie's portrayals of women—both prostitutes and struggling wives and mothers—are to be commended for their humanity and realism. *The Last Valley* (Houghton Mifflin, 1975) continues the story of Arfive, with the addition of significant political overtones. "It has to be more than history faintly inhabited by figures," Guthrie remarked about the kind of fiction he was writing. "It has to be people, it has to be personalities, set in a time and place subordinate to them. Perhaps the hardest lesson for historical novelists, as it is also the hardest lesson of any writer of fiction, is that it isn't event that is important: it is human and individual involvement in and response to event."

Frank Waters wrote two novels with a Western setting, *Fever Pitch* (Liveright, 1930) and *The Wild Earth's Nobility* (Liveright, 1935), before he determined in 1936 to write full time, living first in Colorado and then finally settling in Taos, New Mexico. Very early Waters was attracted to Jungian psychology and in his fiction he undertook to search for a new unity, a oneness and harmony with those primal sources which have been scorned by modern technological civilization. Yet Waters' novels do not sermonize. They tell good stories. He relied heavily on personal family experience in his Colorado mining trilogy, perhaps his finest novel, consisting of *The Wild Earth's Nobility, Below Grass Roots* (Liveright, 1937), and *The Dust Within the Rock* (Farrar and Rinehart, 1941) which he revised and reissued in one volume as *Pike's Peak* (Swallow, 1971); and he portrayed sensitively several ethnic groups in another trio of novels— Spanish-Americans in *People of the Valley* (Farrar and Rinehart, 1941), Pueblo Indians in *The Man Who Killed the Deer* (Farrar and Rinehart, 1942), and mixed-bloods in *The Yogi of Cockroach Court* (Rinehart, 1947). Maria del Valle of *People of the Valley*, although archetypal in significance and function, is one of Waters' more successful female creations and certainly one of Waters' special qualities as a novelist is his ability to draw believable characters, both male and female, albeit the fact that his female characters are usually confined to minor roles is indicative of his masculine orientation. A reliance on the eternal earth is Waters' sustaining image, reflected in Rogier's search into the heart of the mountain in *Pike's Peak*, in Maria's preoccupation with all that moves and grows upon the earth, and in the Pueblos' insistence on the holiness of their particular mountain and its Blue Lake. *The Man Who Killed the Deer* is, in fact, one of the finest novels about Native Americans written by a non-Indian and it was instrumental in the restoration to the Pueblos of their sacred lake which was finally achieved through an act of Congress in 1970.

An author who can best be classified as falling between Guthrie's concern with questions of personal morality and Waters' fascination with spiritual and mystical meaning is Frederick Manfred, His reputation as a major Western novelist rests on five novels loosely related under the collective title of The Buckskin Man Tales. Although not published consecutively, in terms of their internal chronology *Conquering Horse* (McDowell-Obolensky, 1959) comes first and portrays the vision quest of a young Yangton Sioux circa 1800 on the Great Plains, a novel in which there are no white characters. It is quite definitely one of the best books of its kind, written with an intimate knowledge of the life-style and customs of the Indian nations portrayed (with the possible exception of the Pawnees: they may not have practiced the sun dance ceremony in quite the same way as the Sioux). *Lord Grizzly* (McGraw-Hill, 1954), next in sequence, was based on the exploits of mountain man Hugh Glass whose crawl for survival in South Dakota in 1823 became a legend. Vardis Fisher also made use of the Glass legend in *Mountain Man* and Manfred's novel compares favorably with his. In *Scarlet Plume* (Trident, 1964) Manfred introduced a white/Indian love story into the aftermath of a Sioux uprising in Minnesota in 1862, a novel which as Benjamin Capps' *A Woman of the People* represents a reversal of the traditional white supremacy approach to a captivity story. *King of Spades* (Trident, 1966) is a novel concerned with frontier family life in the Black Hills in 1876 while *Riders of Judgment* (Random House, 1957), the concluding volume in sequence, employs the Johnson County War in Wyoming in 1892 in order to focus on the conflicts of the cattlemen. Bringing together in these five novels the American Indian heritage and the Anglo-American frontier experience, it was Manfred's intention to explore the national character of Americans in the Nineteenth century.

Benjamin Capps, unlike Manfred, has concentrated on the West in all of his fiction. His first novel, *Hanging at Comanche Wells* (Ballantine, 1962), is a formulary Western, the only one Capps wrote. His next novel, *The Trail to Ogallala* (Duell, Sloan, and Pearce, 1964), constitutes a definite departure, dealing with a cattle drive from Texas to Nebraska with far more realism than Andy Adams' *Log of a Cowboy* (Houghton Mifflin, 1903), the latter being realistic only on the surface but essentially romantic in the cowboy tradition of Will James and Charles M. Russell. In *Sam Chance* (Duell, Sloan, and Pearce, 1965), Capps probed the life and times of a man who, mustered out of the Confederate Army at the end of the Civil War, through diligence, obsessionalism, and stubbornness builds a cattle empire in Texas. On its highest level, *Sam Chance* reveals the implementation of an Anglo-American dream, a dream which, unlike an Indian's vision, does not indicate to the dreamer his relationship with Nature and his role in the natural order; rather the dream requires that the natural order be destroyed. *The White Man's Road* (Harper's, 1969) is after a fashion a spiritual sequel to *A Woman of the People* and it is powerful and chilling in its grim view of Comanche reservation life. *The True Memoirs of Charley Blankenship* (Lippincott, 1972) is the sheerest kind of initiation novel, a picaresque comedy of sorts, but without the dark side Mark Twain could evoke in this kind of fiction. As a novelist, Capps has not simulated the role of an apologist and his novels never constitute social criticism the way Steinbeck's novels do. His fiction cannot be reduced ever to a matter of ideology; indeed, he tried too many different forms and perspectives for that ever to be said of him.

Will Levington Comfort wrote only one novel that can be called remarkable, and that is *Apache* (Dutton, 1931). It was his last book and is a fictional biography of Dasoda-hae, He That Is Just Sitting There, known to the white invaders as Mangas Coloradas. The novel depicts Dasoda-hae's education as a Mimbreño Apache warrior, his eventual assumption of the leadership of his tribe, and his role in fighting for Indian survival in the Southwest. "The book is true and strong, an extraordinarily penetrating analysis of the real Indian," Oliver LaFarge wrote of it when it was first published. This view still holds good today, but LaFarge himself tried to create real Indians in his own fiction, as have a number of Native American authors, among them John Joseph Mathews, D'Arcy McNickle, N. Scott Momaday, Leslie Silko, and James Welch.

From the summer of 1921 when he first went on an expedition to Tsegi Canyon on the Navajo reserve, LaFarge found himself interested in Indians. His first novel, which won a Pulitzer Prize, *Laughing Boy* (Houghton Mifflin, 1929), deals with a Navajo youth and his love for Slim Girl, a Navajo woman trapped in the twilight between the Navajo and Anglo-American world. Especially the stories "Higher Education" and "All the Young Men" contained in LaFarge's short story collection, *All the Young Men* (Houghton Mifflin, 1935), also deserve a modern reader's attention, although his finest literary achievement may be *The Enemy Gods* (Houghton Mifflin, 1937) which is a perceptive and moving portrait of the difficulty — and, finally, maybe the impossibility — of the Native American ever to adapt to white culture. D'Arcy McNickle, who wrote a biography of LaFarge, felt that his "most significant contribution was that he brought Indians into the consciousness of Americans as something other than casual savages without tradition or style."

John G. Neihardt is another author whose work merits attention. Besides his poetry which is discussed in another section of this book, he is known for his short story collections, *The Lonesome Trail* (John Lane, 1907) and *Indian Tales and Others* (Macmillan, 1926), as well as his novel, *When the Tree Flowered: An Authentic Tale of the Old Sioux World* (Macmillan, 1951). In these books, and in the book for which he is most renowned although he served only as an amanuensis, *Black Elk Speaks* (Morrow, 1932), Neihardt recognized that the fulfillment of both the cultural and spiritual ideals of Americans could not be separated from the vision of man's role as part of Nature; that not until all subsequent Americans came to love and respect the land as much as Native Americans always have would a truly spiritual and epical period be possible.

Although he was only one-eighth a mixed-blood, John Joseph Mathews was listed on the tribal roles and served on the Osage Tribal Council. His principal work of fiction is *Sundown* (University of Oklahoma Press, 1934), the story of Challenge Windzer, son of a mixed-blood father and a full-blood Osage mother. Windzer's mother and father symbolize in themselves the conflicting Indian and white traditions with which Chal has to deal. His mother refuses to change from her old Osage ways. His father believes that the federal government will help the Osages who are becoming rich quickly from the discovery of oil on their lands. Betrayed and disillusioned finally, Windzer's father commits suicide but leaves his son with enough money to drink and drift.

D'Arcy McNickle also had a mixed-blood heritage, the son of a Pennsylvania farmer and a Chippewa-Cree-French mother. His first novel, *The Surrounded* (Dodd, Mead, 1936), is the story of a mixed-blood Indian whose mother is Flathead and whose father is Spanish. It captures poignantly the misery of indeterminate reservation life—set in the year 1935—and it treats the issue of imposing the white man's religion on the Indian more profoundly and more intelligently than virtually any other novel on the subject. His remaining two novels appeared at widely spaced intervals. *Runner in the Sun: The Story of Indian Maize* (Holt, 1954) is a narrative about the Mesa Verde Indians. But it is McNickle's last novel, *Wind from an Enemy Sky* (Harper's, 1978), published posthumously, which may be his finest work. It is a vigorous and gripping drama about the Little Elk Indians seen entirely from the Indian point of view. Both *The Surrounded* and *Wind from an Enemy Sky* provide an interesting contrast, not only with a novel such as Zane Grey's *The Vanishing American*, but even with Frank Waters' *The Man Who Killed the Deer*.

Navarre Scott Momaday's *House Made of Dawn* (Harper's, 1968), which won a Pulitzer Prize, centers on Abel, a Twentieth-century Indian who desires to retreat to the mysticism of Indian culture and who is plagued by the problems of urban, relocated Indians in Los Angeles. Momaday's focus throughout is on the Indian as a human being, not as a stereotype, not the idea of the Indian as a totally different kind of being from all other human beings but as a human being trying to cope with two cultures. "None but an Indian," Momaday once wrote, "...knows so much what it is to have existence in two worlds and security in neither." To bring these two worlds closer together seems to be the objective behind Momaday's second major work, *The Way to Rainy Mountain* (University of New Mexico Press, 1969). The book is steeped in Kiowa mythology and legend; each section is divided into three parts: a Kiowa legend, lore collected by white historians or anthropologists, and Momaday's own memories. The purpose is to teach non-Indians the degree to which they can learn about and share in the Indian experience.

In commenting on *The Surrounded* and *House Made of Dawn*, Charles R. Larson in *American Indian Fiction* (University of New Mexico Press, 1978) observed that these "novels by D'Arcy McNickle and N. Scott Momaday are the bleakest examples of cultural irreconcilability we will encounter.... In their darkest passages, each novel presents a picture of cultural annihilation: McNickle's people are literally surrounded by another universe which is slowly strangling them. Momaday's Indians are either the aged and dying on the reservation or the younger transplants in the urban ghettos, isolated (like fish out of water) in an environment incapable of nourishing them. ...Yet even in their despair, in their depiction of cultural entrapment and renunciation, McNickle and Momaday admit the possibility of something better, of cultural survival — though it may not be an existence currently understood. ...For both, there is the implication that time is the most important factor; the Native American may eventually win in this numbers game with the white world because his patience is the greater."

Frederick Manfred to an extent in *Conquering Horse* and *Scarlet Plume* but even more so in *The Manly-Hearted Woman* (Crown, 1975) stressed the sexuality of his Indian characters and the last-mentioned novel deals with a problem of psycho-sexual indentity in the old Sioux world. Viewed in strictly erotic terms, these novels are to be contrasted with Leslie Silko's short stories, "Lullaby" and "Yellow Woman." "Lullaby," which was first included by Martha Foley in *The Best Short Stories of 1975* (Houghton Mifflin, 1975), is told completely from the point of view of an old Navajo woman and "Yellow Woman," initially published in Foley's anthology, *Two Hundred Years of Great American Short Stories* (Houghton Mifflin, 1975), takes an ancient Keres myth and weaves it into a contemporary abduction story. In her first novel, *Ceremony* (Viking, 1977), Silko used the ritual power of story-telling for healing and communion. Tayo, the protagonist, is ill as a result of his interaction with the white world during World War II, but Silko placed some of the blame with Indian culture itself. The Japanese and the Laguna Indians become synonymous to Tayo as he hallucinates, and it is through purification and ceremony that he discovers at last the logic, and not the chaos, of all things.

"I was as distant from myself as a hawk from the moon," James Welch's unnamed thirty-two year old narrator remarks in *Winter in the Blood* (Harper's, 1974). He divides his time between laboring on the reservation farm which belongs to his mother, drinking and fighting aimlessly in small-town barrooms in Montana, and dreaming about the past, especially about his father and his brother. *Winter in the Blood* resembles *House Made of Dawn* insofar as it, too, is a story of an alienated Native American seeking meaning in his life by means of contemplation of his ancestral heritage. Where it differs from the Momaday book, as well as from similar works by McNickle and Silko, is that Welch's protagonist finds the regaining of the Indian heritage less dramatically regenerative. The past, it would appear, however preferable, encouraging, and glorious, can do very little to assuage the misery of the present.

To the extent that either of them wrote fiction, preoccupation with the past — albeit the white man's past — has characterized the fiction of Robert Easton and Edward Abbey. Easton's collection of short stories and sketches, *The Happy Man* (Viking, 1943), is a narrative given unity because it is about life on a great California cattle ranch as seen through the eyes of Dynamite, a cowhand — according to some critics at the time of the book's appearance — who steps right out of drawings by Frederic Remington. The real power of *The Happy Man*, however, lies in the deep feeling it has for the land, for Nature in its wholeness, and man's place in Nature.

It was perhaps inevitable that Easton should become a foremost conservationist. Edward Abbey also made a similar, although in his case even more violent, onslaught against pollution, exploitation, and waste in his fiction and non-fiction alike. His first novel, *Jonathan Troy* (Dodd, Mead, 1954), is about a young boy from Pennsylvania who is drawn to the West, which for him represents freedom from the repression and corruption of the East. This theme was varied and elaborated in Abbey's next novel, *The Brave Cowboy* (Dodd, Mead, 1956), subtitled "An Old Tale in a New Time." It is concerned with Jack Burns, an anachronistic cowboy who prefers the wilderness to the city and his horse to an automobile. Burns attempts to save his friend, Paul Bondi, who has been jailed for refusing to cooperate with the Selective Service. Although the plot is somewhat formulary in terms of its stock characters, it is notable for its use of a traditional Nineteenth-century hero living in the modern West, a theme which, however, Robert Easton and Max Evans have perhaps handled more adroitly and imaginatively. Another unusual variation on a traditional formulary theme is *Fire on the Mountain* (Dial, 1962) in which Abbey's protagonist is a grandfather fighting to hold on to his land, only the land-grabbers seeking to take it away from him are agents for the U.S. government. Grandfather dies in the struggle—making the plot teeter on the brink of romance—but the vision is clear: as long as such a one is around to fight, personal human freedom may not be a foregone dream. From this point onward, Abbey's fiction became increasingly focused on ideological, rather than historical or characterological matters (*Fire on the Mountain* is based on an actual incident). *The Monkey Wrench Gang* (Lippincott, 1975) is set in the Colorado River region of Northern Arizona and Southeastern Utah and deals with the adventures of four unlikely characters who go about sabotaging various governmental and industrial projects. For Abbey, anarchy in this novel is a viable form of protest in the war against Anglo-American efforts to subdue continually the natural order and to replace it with the exhaustion of all natural resources in the name of "development."

All of which brings one to Elmer Kelton. "As a fiction writer," he once said in an address to the Texas Folklore Society, "I have always tried to illuminate history, to illuminate truth, at least as I see the history and truth. A fiction writer can often fire a reader's interest to make him want to dig into the true story and make him search out the real history to find out for himself what happened." His first novel was *Hot Iron* (Ballantine, 1955), a story set in Texas dealing with the cattle business that humanizes what in less adept hands would be stock characters. His second novel, *Buffalo Wagons* (Ballantine, 1956), is about hide hunters in the Comanche territory in the early 1870s; it won for him the first of three Spur Awards from the Western Writers of America. These first efforts and several that followed have more or less a combination of formulary and romantic ingredients, but with a stronger sense of historical reality than is oftentimes the case in these modes of Western fiction. As he matured as a novelist, as he became increasingly more concerned with historical reality and less with proving something on the basis of history, Kelton's fiction changed commensurately in tone and substance. This new course was truly heralded with the appearance of *The Day the Cowboys Quit* (Doubleday, 1971). Subsequently, with each novel, he became better and better both as an historical novelist with a precise and intimate knowledge of Western history and topography and as a literary artist capable of creating vividly real characters confronted with the complexities of life and the web and mystery of the natural order. *The Time It Never Rained* (Doubleday, 1973) — one of his best novels — is set in contemporary Texas, during a seven-year drought, and its protagonist, the aged Charlie Flagg, embodies those qualities which Kelton came to admire most in human beings: determination, integrity, and endurance. Beyond this, Kelton's portrayal of Mexican-Americans, their culture and their relationships with each other and with Anglo-Americans, is insightful and humane.

"Whereas in Shakespeare the effect is due to the way in which the characters *act upon* each other," T.S. Eliot wrote in his essay, "Ben Jonson" (1919), "in Jonson it is given by the way in which the characters *fit in* with each other ... their combination into a whole." What Eliot said about Jonson might as readily be said about Kelton, since his vision is one that sees first the whole pattern of humanity and *then* its individual manifestations. This is perchance nowhere more evident than in *The Wolf and the Buffalo* (Doubleday, 1980) in which the events taking place on the West Texas frontier in the conflict between the U.S. Cavalry with its complement of black soldiers from the South under white commanders and the Comanches is characterized from all sides. The terror inspired by these moments of confrontation is an *ethical* terror and the historical reconstruction focuses often on truly ethical questions — the issue of slavery and freedom, attitudes toward the wilderness, the destruction of peoples, animals, ways of life, economic exploitation, but as these questions occurred in history, never with the intention of proving anything one way or the other in terms of the historical outcome. In this way, the historical reconstruction is among that art which is the finest that a society can produce. The authors of historical reconstructions recognize that the past does have something to teach us, if we are willing to learn from it; and for Americans the Western novel and story are the ideal forms through which the American past can be evoked graphically and painfully — painfully because it was mostly painful.

Most of the best fiction about the American West is about *man in Nature*, not the denatured, mechanical, sterile world that increasingly has come to serve as a backdrop for human activity in other kinds of fiction. If we can legitimately find good in the past, and much good is to be found in historical reconstructions, then we might well continue to entertain, but in a chastened fashion, some hope for the American future. In this light, the American West remains what the Native American always thought it to be: the land beyond the setting sun, the Spiritland. The Delphic "know thyself" takes on a new dimension in terms of the American frontier experience. Our collective idea of humanity is deepened and broadened through a more truthful understanding and assimilation of our historical past.

II

i

As a matter of convenience so the reader will know precisely what to expect, recommendations of Western fiction have been subdivided into formulary Westerns, romantic historical reconstructions, and historical reconstructions. Because of the detailed literary history provided above in this section, novels by particular authors which are recommended below as well as book-length collections of short stories by some of these same authors—treated below the same as novels by them—have not been annotated and, thus, only with anthologies of Western fiction has it been deemed necessary to have annotations at all.

It is our regret—and we wish to state it in the most emphatic terms—that no trade publisher, paperback house, nor library publisher, with the exception of the Gregg Press, and this last only for a brief time and with generally inferior titles, has made a concerted effort to reprint classic novels and story collections in any or all of the modes of Western fiction. It is to be hoped that this situation will not persist indefinitely.

Brandt, E.N., (ed.), *The Saturday Evening Post Reader of Western Stories* (Doubleday, 1960).

This is an uneven but basically well-chosen collection of Western short fiction—much of it romantic, some of it formulary—which, when read as an ensemble, provides a rather good notion of what the *Post* defined as a "Western" story.

Collier, Ned, (ed.), *Great Stories of the West* (Doubleday, 1971).

The stories in this anthology were all "culled," according to the editor's Introduction, from *West* magazine, but surely this cannot be true for Stewart Edward White's "A Corner in Horses" which is from White's *Arizona Nights* collection of 1907. More formulary than the stories in the *Post* anthology, several are nonetheless very entertaining and some are by authors whose names are no longer familiar to readers, if indeed they ever really were.

Knight, Damon, (ed.), *Westerns of the 40's: Classics from the Great Pulps* (Bobbs-Merrill, 1977).

The word "classics" is definitely misused to describe these stories, as "great" is in describing their source, but the stories are unquestionably of the "pulp" formulary variety and make a distinct contrast—in terms of formulary plot ingredients and structures—with the "slick" formulary stories in the *Post* collection and the intermediate ones in the *West* collection. Brandt's Preface is only one paragraph; Collier's Introduction is longer; Knight's collection, which certainly could have used an Introduction, has none.

Maule, Harry E. (ed.), *Great Tales of the American West* (Modern Library, 1945).

Maule was at one time editor of *West* magazine, along with other pulp publications, before he became a vice president at Random House where he oversaw all Western fiction published by the firm. In this anthology he included eighteen stories, all of them worth reading and some of them — those by William MacLeod Raine, Clarence E. Mulford, W.C. Tuttle, James B. Hendryx, H.H. Knibbs, and Luke Short — very difficult to find elsewhere.

Schaefer, Jack (ed.), *Out West: An Anthology of Stories* (Houghton Mifflin, 1955).

Although not organized by place of publication, e.g., Brandt and Collier, or by kind of story, e.g., Knight, or by chronology, e.g., Maule, in fact organized alphabetically by author, this collection is notwithstanding saved from being a total hotch-potch by virtue, first, of many of the stories being very good and, second, because of Schaefer's often interesting (although not always biographically or factually reliable) annotations.

Tuska, Jon (ed.), *The American West in Fiction* (Mentor Books, 1982).

With a lengthy General Introduction, a back section devoted to suggested further reading, and prefaces to twenty short stories (or excerpts from novels able to function as short stories), this anthology was designed to provide a comprehensive overview of the varieties of Western fiction and a sense of the development of Western fiction as a unique body of literature. It is most effective if read sequentially.

ii

Formulary Westerns

Adams, Clifton, *The Last Days of Wolf Garnett* (Doubleday, 1970).
Ahlswede, Ann, *Hunting Wolf* (Ballantine, 1960).
Arthur, Burt & Budd, *The Stranger* (Avon, 1966).
Athanas, Verne, *Maverick* (Dell, 1956).
Ballard, Todhunter, *Plunder Canyon* (Avon, 1967).
Bonham, Frank, *Lost Stage Valley* (1948; Berkley, 1978).
_____, *Last Stage West* (1959; Berkley, 1979).
Bouma, J.L., *Ride to Violence* (Leisure Books, 1978).
Bower, B.M., *Chip of the Flying U* (Dillingham, 1906).
_____, *The Lonesome Trail* (Dillingham, 1909) [short stories].
_____, *Lonesome Land* (Little, Brown, 1912).
_____, *The Whoop-Up Trail* (Little, Brown, 1933).
Brand, Max (pseud, Frederick Faust), *The Untamed* (Putnam's, 1919).
_____, *The Night Horseman* (Putnam's, 1920).
_____, *The Seventh Man* (Putnam's, 1921).

_____, *The White Wolf* (Putnam's, 1921).

_____, *Destry Rides Again* (Dodd, Mead, 1930).

_____, *Silvertip* (Dodd, Mead, 1942).

_____, *The Best Western Stories of Max Brand* (Dodd, Mead, 1981) edited by William F. Nolan.

Burchardt, Bill, *Medicine Man* (Doubleday, 1980).

Calkins, Frank, *The Tan-Faced Children* (Doubleday, 1978).

Capps, Benjamin, *Hanging at Comanche Wells* (Ballantine, 1962).

Chase, Borden, *Blazing Guns on the Chisholm Trail* (Random House, 1947).

Coburn, Walt, *Law Rides the Range* (1935; Lancer Books, 1963).

Coldsmith, Don, *Trail of the Spanish Bit* (Doubleday, 1980).

_____, *Buffalo Medicine* (Doubleday, 1981).

Cook, Will, *The Drifter* (Bantam, 1969).

_____, *Bandit's Trail* (Doubleday, 1974).

Coolidge, Dane, *Gun-Smoke* (Dutton, 1928).

_____, *Horse-Ketchum of Death Valley* (Dutton, 1930).

Cox, William R., *Navajo Blood* [original title: *The Outlawed*] (Signet, 1963).

Cunningham, Eugene, *Riders of the Night* (Houghton Mifflin, 1932).

_____, *Texas Triggers* (Houghton Mifflin, 1938).

_____, *Riding Gun* (Houghton Mifflin, 1938).

Curwood, James Oliver, *Steele of the Royal Mounted* (Cosmopolitan, 1911).

_____, *Kazan* (Cosmopolitan Book Company, 1914).

Daniels, John S. (pseud. Wayne D. Overholser), *Smoke of the Gun* (Signet, 1958).

Dawson, Peter (pseud. Jonathan Glidden), *The Stagline Feud* (Dodd, Mead, 1942).

_____, *Gunsmoke Graze* (Dodd, Mead, 1942).

_____, *High Country* (Dodd, Mead, 1947).

Drago, Harry Sinclair, *The Desert Hawk* (Macaulay, 1927).

Ehrlich, Jack, *The Fastest Gun in the Pulpit* (Pocket Books, 1972).

Elston, Allan Vaughan, *Roundup on the Picketwire* (Lippincott, 1952).

_____, *Gun Law at Laramie* (Lippincott, 1959).

Ermine, Will (pseud. Harry Sinclair Drago), *Rider of the Midnight Range* (Morrow, 1940).

_____, *Rustler's Bend* (Doubleday, 1949).

Evarts, Hal, Sr., *Tumbleweeds* (Little, Brown, 1923).

_____, *Short Grass* (Little, Brown, 1932).

Farrell, Cliff, *Return of the Longriders* (Doubleday, 1964).

Field, Peter (house name: Francis Thayer Hobson), *Outlaws Three* (Morrow, 1934).

_____ (house name: E.B. Mann), *Boss of the Lazy 9* (Morrow, 1936).

_____ (house name: Davis Dresser), *Midnight Round-Up* (Morrow, 1944).

Fisher, Clay (pseud. Henry Wilson Allen), *Apache Ransom* (Bantam, 1974).

_____, *Black Apache* (Bantam, 1976).

Flynn, T.T., *The Man from Laramie* (Dell, 1954).

_____, *The Angry Man* (Dell, 1956).

_____, *Riding High* (Dell, 1961).

Foreman, L.L., *The Road to San Jacinto* (Dutton, 1943).
_____, *Rogue's Legacy* (Doubleday, 1968).
Foster, Bennett, *Seven Slash Range* (Morrow, 1936).
Fox, Norman A., *Tall Man Riding* (Dodd, Mead, 1951).
_____, *Ghostly Hoofbeats* (Dodd, Mead, 1952).
_____, *Night Passage* (Dodd, Mead, 1956).
_____, *Reckoning at Rimbow* (Dodd, Mead, 1958).
Gregory, Jackson, *Sudden Bill Dorn* (Dodd, Mead, 1936).
_____, *Guardians of the Trail* (Dodd, Mead, 1941).
Grey, Zane, *The Heritage of the Desert* (Harper's, 1910).
_____, *Riders of the Purple Sage* (Harper's, 1912).
_____, *The Rainbow Trail* (Harper's, 1915).
_____, *Wanderer of the Wasteland* (Harper's, 1923).
_____, *Captives of the Desert* (Harper's, 1952).
Grove, Fred, *The Buffalo Runners* (Doubleday, 1968).
Gruber, Frank, *Fort Starvation* (Rinehart, 1953).
Halleran, E.E., *Double Cross Trail* (Macrae-Smith, 1946).
Haycox, Ernest, *A Rider of the High Mesa* (1927; Pocket Library, 1960).
_____, *Lone Rider* [original title: *The Black Clan*] (1931) and *Lin of Pistol Gap* (1930) (Popular Library, 1959) [short novels].
_____, *Trail Smoke* (Doubleday, 1936).
_____, *Sundown Jim* (Little, Brown, 1938).
_____, *Saddle and Ride* (Little, Brown, 1940).
_____, *Rim of the Desert* (Little, Brown, 1941).
Hendryx, James B., *Black John of Halfaday Creek* (Doubleday, 1936).
Henry, Will (pseud. Henry Wilson Allen), *MacKenna's Gold* (Random House, 1963).
Hoffman, Lee, *West of Cheyenne* (Doubleday, 1969).
_____, *Wild Riders* (Signet, 1969).
_____, *The Land Killer* (Doubleday, 1978).
Hogan, Ray, *Overkill at Saddlerock* (Signet, 1979).
Holmes, L.P., *Catch and Saddle* (Dodd, Mead, 1959).
Huffaker, Clair, *The War Wagon* [original title: *Badman*] (Fawcett, 1957).
Kelton, Elmer, *Buffalo Wagons* (Ballantine, 1956).
_____, *Barbed Wire* (Ballantine, 1957).
Ketchum, Philip, *Gun Code* (Signet, 1959).
_____, *Wyoming* (Ballantine, 1967).
_____, *The Cougar Basin War* (Ace, 1970).
L'Amour, Louis, *Hondo* (Fawcett, 1953).
_____, *Showdown at Yellow Butte* (1953; Gregg Press, 1980).
_____, *Guns of the Timberlands* (Jason Press, 1955).
_____, *Last Stand at Papago Wells* (1957; Gregg Press, 1980).
_____, *War Party* (Bantam, 1975) [short stories].
Leonard, Elmore, *Hombre* (Ballantine, 1961).
_____, *Valdez Is Coming* (Ballantine, 1970).
Lomax, Bliss (pseud. Harry Sinclair Drago), *The Leather Burners* (Doubleday, 1939).

_____, *Colt Comrades* (Doubleday, 1940).

_____, *Their Guns Were Fast* (Dodd, Mead, 1955) [short stories]

Lutz, Giles A., *The Honyocker* (Doubleday, 1961).

McCarthy, Gary, *The Derby Man* (Doubleday, 1976).

MacDonald, William Colt, *Riders of the Whistling Skull* (Covici, Friede, 1934).

_____, *The Mad Marshal* (Pyramid Books, 1958).

Mann, E.B., *The Valley of Wanted Men* (Morrow, 1932).

Mulford, Clarence E., *Buck Peters, Ranchman* (A.C. McClurg, 1912).

_____, *Hopalong Cassidy Returns* (Doubleday, 1924).

_____, *Corson of the JC* (Doubleday, 1926).

_____, *Hopalong Cassidy and the Eagle's Brood* (Doubleday, 1931).

Newton, Dwight Bennett (first published under the name Dwight Bennett), *The Big Land* (Doubleday, 1972).

Nye, Nelson C., *Riders By Night* (Dodd, Mead, 1950).

Ogden, George Washington, *The Guard of the Timberline* (Dodd, Mead, 1934).

Olsen, Theodore V., *Bitter Grass* (Doubleday, 1967).

_____, *Rattlesnake* (Doubleday, 1978).

O'Rourke, Frank, *Latigo* (Signet, 1953).

_____, *The Last Chance* (Dell, 1956).

_____, *Bandolier Crossing* (Signet, 1968).

Overholser, Wayne D., *Buckaroo's Code* (Macmillan, 1950).

_____, *Tough Hand* (Macmillan, 1954).

_____, *The Dry Gulcher* (Dell, 1977).

Patten, Lewis B., *The Angry Horseman* (Hillman Books, 1960).

_____, *Death of a Gunfighter* (Doubleday, 1968).

_____, *Track of the Hunter* (Signet, 1971).

_____, *The Gallows of Graneros* (Doubleday, 1975).

Purdum, Herbert, *My Brother John* (Doubleday, 1966).

Raine, William MacLeod, *Ridgway of Montana* (Dillingham, 1909).

_____, *Brand Blotters* (Dillingham, 1912).

_____, *The Big-Town Round-Up* (Houghton Mifflin, 1920).

Reese, John, *Angel Range* (Doubleday, 1973).

Robertson, Frank C., *Freewater Range* (1933; Belmont Books, 1966).

Roderus, Frank, *Journey to Utah* (Doubleday, 1976).

_____, *Hell Creek Cabin* (Doubleday, 1979).

Savage, Les, Jr., *Land of the Lawless* (Doubleday, 1951).

Schaefer, Jack, *Shane* (Houghton Mifflin, 1949).

Seltzer, Charles Alden, *The Boss of the Lazy Y* (A.C. McClurg, 1915).

_____, *The Trail Horde* (A.C. McClurg, 1920).

Shirreffs, Gordon D., *The Border Guidon* (Signet, 1963).

Short, Luke (pseud. Frederick Glidden), *Savage Range* (1939; Dell, 1952).

_____, *Sunset Graze* (Doubleday, 1942).

Spearman, Frank H., *Whispering Smith* (Scribner's, 1906).

Steelman, Robert J., *Surgeon to the Sioux* (Doubleday, 1979).

Stuart, Matt (pseud. L.P. Holmes), *Dusty Wagons* (Lippincott, 1949).

Thompson, Thomas, *Brand of a Man* (Doubleday, 1958).
Turner, William O., *Blood Dance* (Berkley, 1967).
Tuttle, W.C., *Thicker Than Water* (Houghton Mifflin, 1927).
_____, *The Red Head from Sun Dog* (Houghton Mifflin, 1930).
_____, *The Santa Dolores Stage* (Houghton Mifflin, 1934).
Wisler, G. Clifton, *My Brother, the Wind* (Doubleday, 1979).
_____, *A Cry of Angry Thunder* (Doubleday, 1980).

iii

Romantic Historical Reconstructions

Adams, Andy, *The Log of a Cowboy* (Houghton Mifflin, 1903).
_____, *Andy Adams' Campfire Tales* (1956; University of Nebraska Press 1976) edited by Wilson M. Hudson [short stories].
Arnold, Elliott, *Blood Brother* (1947; University of Nebraska Press, 1980).
Barker, S. Omar, *Born to Battle* (University of New Mexico Press, 1951) [short stories].
Barr, Amelia, *Remember the Alamo* (1888; Gregg Press, 1979).
Barry, Jane, *A Time in the Sun* (Doubleday, 1962).
_____, *Maximilian's Gold* (Doubleday, 1966).
Beach, Rex, *The Spoilers* (Harper's, 1905).
Bean, Amelia, *Time for Outrage* (Doubleday, 1967).
Bechdolt, Frederick, *Bold Raiders of the West* (Doubleday, 1940).
Bellah, James Warner, *The Apache* (Fawcett, 1951).
_____, *Ordeal at Blood River* (Ballantine, 1959).
_____, *Reveille* (Fawcett, 1962) [short stories].
Berger, Thomas, *Little Big Man* (Dial, 1964).
Bristow, Gwen, *Jubliee Trail* (Thomas J. Crowell, 1950).
Brown, Dee, *Creek Mary's Blood* (Holt, Rinehart, & Winston, 1980).
Burnett, W.R., *Saint Johnson* (Dial, 1930).
Burroughs, Edgar Rice, *The War Chief* (1927; Gregg Press, 1978).
_____, *Apache Devil* (1933; Gregg Press, 1978).
Capps, Benjamin, *The True Memoirs of Charley Blankenship* (Lippincott, 1972) [picaresque novel].
Carter, Forrest, *The Vengeance Trail of Josey Wales* (Delacorte, 1976).
Cather, Willa, *O Pioneers!* (Houghton Mifflin, 1913).
_____, *My Ántonia* (Houghton Mifflin, 1918).
_____, *Death Comes for the Archbishop* (Knopf, 1927).
_____, *Obscure Destinies* (Knopf, 1932) [short stories].
Cook, Will, *Two Rode Together* [original title: *Comanche Captives*] (Bantam, 1960).
_____, *The Peacemakers* (Bantam, 1961).
_____, *The Tough Texan* (Bantam, 1963).
_____, *The Outcasts* (Bantam, 1965).
Coolidge, Dane, *Wun-Post* (Dutton, 1920).
_____, *Wolf's Candle* (Dutton, 1935).

Cooper, James Fenimore, *The Pioneers* (1823).
———, *The Last of the Mohicans* (1826).
———, *The Prairie* (1827).
Corle, Edwin, *Fig Tree John* (Liveright, 1935).
Crane, Stephen, *The Western Writings of Stephen Crane* (Signet Classics, 1978) edited by Frank Bergon [short stories, etc.].
Croy, Homer, *West of the Water Tower* (Harper's, 1923).
Culp, John H., *The Bright Feathers* (Holt, Rinehart, & Winston, 1965).
Cushman, Dan, *Stay Away, Joe* (Viking, 1953).
Davis, H.L., *Honey in the Horn* (Harper's, 1935).
———, *Winds of Morning* (Morrow, 1952).
Eastlake, William, *Dancers in the Scalp House* (Viking, 1975).
Everett, Wade (pseud, Will Cook), *Fort Starke* (Ballantine, 1959).
Ferber, Edna, *Cimarron* (Doubleday, 1930).
Fergusson, Harvey, *Wolf Song* (1927; Gregg Press, 1978).
———, *The Conquest of Don Pedro* (1954; University of New Mexico Press, 1974).
Fisher, Clay (pseud. Henry Wilson Allen), *Red Blizzard* (Simon & Schuster, 1951).
Fisher, Vardis, *Mountain Man* (Morrow, 1965).
Flint, Timothy, *Francis Berrian* (1826).
Garfield, Brian, *Bugle & Spur* (Ballantine, 1966).
———, *Wild Times* (Simon & Schuster, 1979).
Giles, Janice Holt, *The Plum Thicket* (Houghton Mifflin, 1954).
Grey, Zane, *The U.P. Trail* (Harper's, 1918).
———, *The Thundering Herd* (Harper's, 1925).
Gulick, Bill, *Treasure in Hell's Canyon* (Doubleday, 1979).
Harte, Bret, *Bret Harte: Stories of the Early West* (Platt & Munk, 1964) edited by Walter Van Tilburg Clark [short stories].
———, *Three Partners* (Houghton Mifflin, 1900).
Haycox, Ernest, *Bugles in the Afternoon* (1944; Gregg Press, 1978).
———, *The Earthbreakers* (1952; Gregg Press, 1979).
———, *The Best Western Stories of Ernest Haycox* (Bantam, 1960) [short].
Henry, O. (pseud, William Sydney Porter), *Heart of the West* (Doubleday, 1904) [short stories].
Henry, Will (pseud. Henry Wilson Allen), *The Last Warpath* (Random House, 1966) [short stories].
———, *I, Tom Horn* (Lippincott, 1975).
Hillerman, Tony, *The Blessing Way* (Harper's, 1970).
Horgan, Paul, *A Distant Trumpet* (Farrar, Straus, 1960).
Hough, Emerson, *The Covered Wagon* (Appleton, 1922).
Jackson, Helen Hunt, *Ramona* (1884).
James, Will (pseud. Joseph Ernest Nephtali Dufault), *The Lone Cowboy* (Scribner's, 1930) [a fictional autobiography].
Kelton, Elmer, *Massacre at Goliad* (Ballantine, 1965).
King, General Charles, *Two Soldiers* (1888) and *Dunraven Ranch* (1890) published together (Lippincott, 1900) [short novels].

_____, *An Apache Princess* (Hobart, 1903).

Knibbs, Henry Herbert, *The Ridin' Kid from Powder River* (Houghton Mifflin, 1919).

_____, *Partners of Chance* (Houghton Mifflin, 1921).

LaFarge, Oliver, *All the Young Men* (Houghton Mifflin, 1935) [short stories].

Lea, Tom, *The Wonderful Country* (1952; Gregg Press, 1980).

LeMay, Alan, *Painted Ponies* (Doran, 1927).

_____, *The Unforgiven* (1957; Gregg Press, 1978).

Lewis, Alfred Henry, *Wolfville: Episodes of Cowboy Life* (1897) [short stories].

London, Jack, *Great Short Works of Jack London* (Harper's, 1965) edited by Earle Labor [short stories and short novels].

McMurtry, Larry, *Horseman, Pass By* (Harper's, 1961).

Pattullo, George, *The Untamed* (Fitzgerald, 1911) [short stories].

Phillips, Henry Wallace, *Red Saunders* (McClure's, 1902) [short stories and an interesting short novel].

Remington, Frederic, *Crooked Trails* (1898) [short stories].

_____, *John Ermine of the Yellowstone* (Macmillan, 1902).

Rhodes, Eugene Manlove, *Once in the Saddle* (Houghton Mifflin, 1927) [also contains *Pasó Por Aquí*].

_____, *The Trusty Knaves* (1933; University of Oklahoma Press, 1971).

_____, *The Rhodes Reader* (University of Oklahoma Press, 1957) edited by W.H. Hutchinson [short stories and essays].

Richter, Conrad, *The Sea of Grass* (Knopf, 1937).

_____, *The Trees* (Knopf, 1940).

_____, *The Fields* (Knopf, 1946).

_____, *The Town* (Knopf, 1950).

Russell, Charles M., *Trails Plowed Under* (Doubleday, 1927) [short stories].

Ryan, Marah Ellis, *Told in the Hills* (1890).

_____, *Indian Love Letters* (1907; Rio Grande Press, 1972).

Santee, Ross, *Men and Horses* (1926; University of Nebraska Press, 1977) [short stories].

_____, *Cowboy* (1928; University of Nebraska Press, 1977).

Schaefer, Jack, *The Canyon* (Houghton Mifflin, 1953).

_____, *Monte Walsh* (Houghton Mifflin, 1963).

_____, *The Collected Stories of Jack Schaefer* (Houghton Mifflin, 1966) [short stories].

Sorenson, Virginia, *The Proper Gods* (Harcourt, Brace, 1951).

Stegner, Wallace, *The Big Rock Candy Mountain* (Duell, Sloan, 1943).

Steinbeck, John, *The Grapes of Wrath* (Covici, Friede, 1939).

West, Jessamyn, *The Friendly Persuasion* (Harcourt, Brace, 1945) [short stories].

White, Stewart Edward, *Arizona Nights* (McClure's, 1907) [short stories].

Wister, Owen, *Lin McLean* (1897).

_____, *The Jimmyjohn Boss and Other Stories* (Harper's, 1900) [short stories].

_____, *The Virginian* (Macmillan, 1902).

iv

Historical Reconstructions

Abbey, Edward, *Fire on the Mountain* (1962; University of New Mexico Press, 1978).

Ahlswede, Ann, *The Savage Land* (Ballantine, 1962).

Austin, Mary, *Starry Adventure* (Houghton Mifflin, 1931).

Berry, Don, *Trask* (Viking, 1960).

————, *Moontrap* (Viking, 1962).

Braun, Matthew, *Black Fox* (Fawcett, 1972).

Capps, Benjamin, *A Woman of the People* (Duell, Sloan, 1966).

————, *The White Man's Road* (Duell, Sloan, 1969).

————, *Woman Chief* (Doubleday, 1980).

Clark, Walter Van Tilburg, *The Ox-Bow Incident* (Random House, 1940).

————, *The Track of the Cat* (Random House, 1949).

————, *The Watchful Gods and Other Stories* (Random House, 1950) [short stories].

Comfort, Will Levington, *Apache* (1931; Gregg Press, 1980).

Easton, Robert, *The Happy Man* (1943; University of New Mexico Press, 1977) [short stories with the same central character].

Evans, Max, *The Rounders* (1960; Gregg Press, 1980).

————, *The Hi-Lo Country* (1961; Gregg Press, 1980).

————, *The One-Eyed Sky* (Houghton Mifflin, 1963) [short novels].

Fisher, Vardis, *Children of God: An American Epic* (Harper's, 1939).

————, *City of Illusion* (Harper's, 1941).

————, *The Mothers* (Vanguard, 1943).

Garland, Hamlin, *Main-Travelled Roads* (1891) [short stories].

Guthrie, A.B., Jr., *The Big Sky* (Sloane, 1947).

————, *The Way West* (Sloane, 1949).

————, *These Thousand Hills* (1956; Gregg Press, 1979).

————, *Arfive* (Houghton Mifflin, 1970).

Henry, Will (pseud. Henry Wilson Allen), *From Where the Sun Now Stands* (1959; Gregg Press, 1978).

Hoffman, Lee, *The Valdez Horses* (Doubleday, 1967).

Johnson, Dorothy M., *Indian Country* (1953; Gregg Press, 1979) [short stories].

————, *The Hanging Tree* (1957; Gregg Press, 1980) [short stories].

Kelton, Elmer, *The Day the Cowboys Quit* (Doubleday, 1971).

————, *The Time It Never Rained* (Doubleday, 1973).

————, *The Wolf and the Buffalo* (Doubleday, 1980).

Kesey, Ken, *One Flew Over the Cuckoo's Nest* (Viking, 1962).

LaFarge, Oliver, *The Enemy Gods* (1937; University of New Mexico Press, 1975).

McNickle, D'Arcy, *The Surrounded* (1936; University of New Mexico Press, 1978).

————, *Wind from an Enemy Sky* (Harper's, 1978).

Manfred, Frederick, *Lord Grizzly* (1954; Gregg Press, 1980).

_____, *Riders of Judgment* (1957; Gregg Press, 1980).

_____, *Conquering Horse* (1959; Gregg Press, 1980).

_____, *Scarlet Plume* (1964; Gregg Press, 1980).

_____, *King of Spades* (1966; Gregg Press, 1980).

Mathews, John Joseph, *Sundown* (1934; Gregg Press, 1979).

Momaday, N. Scott, *House Made of Dawn* (Harper's, 1968).

Neihardt, John G., *The Lonesome Trail* (John Lane, 1907) [short stories].

_____, *When the Tree Flowered: An Authentic Tale of the Old Sioux World* (Macmillan, 1951).

Norris, Frank, *The Octopus* (Doubleday, 1901).

Richter, Conrad, *The Lady* (Knopf, 1957).

Rölvaag, O.E., *Giants in the Earth* (Harper's, 1927).

_____, *Peder Victorious* (Harper's, 1929).

_____, *Their Father's God* (Harper's, 1931).

Ruxton, George Frederick, *Life in the Far West* (1849; Rio Grande Press, 1972).

Sandoz, Mari, *Miss Morissa: Doctor of the Gold Trail* (1955; University of Nebraska Press, 1980).

_____, *Son of the Gamblin' Man* (1960; University of Nebraska Press, 1976).

Scarborough, Dorothy, *The Wind* (Harper's, 1925).

Schaefer, Jack, *The Kean Land and Other Stories* (Houghton Mifflin, 1959) [short novel but not the short stories].

Silko, Leslie, *Ceremony* (Viking, 1977).

Van Every, Dale, *The Shining Mountains* (Messner, 1948).

_____, *The Day the Sun Died* (Little, Brown, 1971).

Waters, Frank, *People of the Valley* (Farrar and Rinehart, 1941).

_____, *The Man Who Killed the Deer* (Farrar and Rinehart, 1942).

_____, *Pike's Peak: A Family Saga* (Swallow, 1971).

Welch, James, *Winter in the Blood* (Harper's, 1974).

Williams, John, *Butcher's Crossing* (1961; Gregg Press, 1978).

III

i

The most disappointing aspect about literary criticism of Western fiction is the inferior quality of much that has been written. James K. Folsom included Richard W. Etulain's essay, "The American Literary West and Its Interpreters: The Rise of a New Historiography," in his collection of critical essays (see the annotated entry below for this volume), *The Western* (Prentice-Hall, 1979), and called it "an admirable example of the art of bibliography...." In the course of this essay, Etulain surveyed much of the critical writing about Western fiction since 1900 and mentioned that "more recently Russel B. Nye has discussed the Western as one significant form of American popular culture. His treatment is the best brief study of the development of the Western." This reference is footnoted and the book cited is Nye's *The Unembarrassed Muse: The Popular Arts in America* (Dial, 1970). An examination of this "best brief study" will illustrate some of the shortcomings in literary criticism of Western fiction.

The chapter Nye devoted to Western fiction is titled "Six-shooter Country." It starts out with a brief survey of Western fiction in the Nineteenth century, dwelling on Cooper, Robert Montgomery Bird's *Nick of the Woods* (1837), and the dime novel tradition. When we get to Wister, the text reads: "*The Virginian* [Macmillan, 1902] mentioned Indians once or twice." Actually *The Virginian* more than mentions Indians; it is the Indians who track the Virginian and who wound him seriously enough so he has to be nursed back to health by the Bear Creek schoolmarm. It is this experience which brings their romance to its climax. The schoolmarm's name is Mary (Molly) Stark Wood. Nye shortened this to "Miss Mary Stark of Bennington, Vermont."

One of the problems of course among academic critics is they often do not read original sources, but only other academics. Most of the errors made by Nye in this chapter have been repeated again and again by academics, but for the purpose of demonstration perhaps one instance can be made to suffice. Donald L. Kaufmann in his essay "The Indian as Media Hand-Me-Down," originally published in *The Colorado Quarterly* (Spring, 1975) and now reprinted in *The Pretend Indians: Images of Native Americans in the Movies* (Iowa State University Press, 1980) edited by Gretchen M. Bataille and Charles L.P. Silet, brought up *The Virginian* and had this to say: "Wister's novel mentioned Indians once or twice."

Nye insisted that *The Saturday Evening Post* "unfortunately convinced" Eugene Manlove Rhodes "that he needed to insert a love interest and a noble social message into what was otherwise first-rate Western fiction." This is untrue, as any study of Rhodes' fiction — much of which was run in the *Post without* a love interest — would prove, and, in fact, the three novels Nye cited — *West Is West* (H.K. Fly, 1917), *Pasó Por Aquí* (1927), and *The Trusty Knaves* (Houghton Mifflin, 1934) — have neither love interest nor a noble social message.

Nye claimed that B.M. Bower "created one of the better known cowboys of the period, Chip of the Flying U, in 1906" whereas this novel first appeared in serial form in 1904. "The Flying U outfit provided Mrs. Sinclair [Bower] with a cross section of ranch characters whose fortunes she followed in novel after novel, marrying them off one by one, and finally Chip himself." Chip is married in *Chip of the Flying U*, the first novel of the series. Nye wrote that "Paramount Pictures put actor William Boyd into Hopalong Cassidy movies in 1934," whereas Harry Sherman, an independent producer, cast Boyd in the role of Hopalong first in 1935 with Paramount releasing but not producing. "Television later gave him [Hopalong] wavy gold hair, a white hat and boots, a gold saddle, and pretty girl friends...." Boyd remained in the role on television and had white hair, not "gold"; moreover, since even the television series was in black and white, how could Nye know his hair was gold as well as his saddle? Boyd preferred his "monkey suit" with its black hat except when disguised and never wore white boots; nor did he have a "girl friend" after the character played by Nora Lane in 1938. "For the real, unadorned Hopalong, the reader must return to *The Roundup* [Doubleday, 1933], *Trail Dust* [Doubleday, 1934], *Me 'N Shorty* [actually titled *Me An' Shorty* (Doubleday, 1929)], *Hopalong Sits In, or On the Trail of the Tumbling T* [Doubleday, 1935]." Unfortunately Hopalong is not in *The Roundup, Me An' Shorty,* or *On the Trail of the Tumbling T,* which Nye could have determined just by flipping through the pages of these novels; "Hopalong Sits In" is a short story from 1929, but at least Hopalong is in it and in *Trail Dust.*

Of "William McLeod (sic) Raine," Nye remarked that "he knew the West intimately and what he wrote was authentic." He had him completing his last novel "in 1953, a year before his death" — whereas the only factual part of this statement is ... well, Raine died in 1954. Nye's opinion that *"The Covered Wagon,* published in 1922, [is] a soundly-researched account of the Oregon Trail" should be contrasted with the comment regarding this novel by John D. Unruh, Jr., quoted above in the text. Nye felt Zane Grey "found the right formula with his fourth book, *Riders of the Purple Sage* [Harper's, 1912]" which was not Grey's fourth book and "any book he [Grey] wrote had a guaranteed sale of at least half a million" with which even the president of Harper & Brothers disagreed when, as mentioned above in the text, he asked Frederick Faust to write a new series of Westerns for Harper's. Nye asserted that Eugene Cunningham first "hit the market with *Riders of the Night* in 1932" whereas Cunningham's first Western novel was *The Trail to Apacaz* (Dodd, Mead, 1924), that "Harvey Fergusson's historical trilogy of the Southwest ... was the first attempt at the serious Western novel," that ... but perhaps this is enough.

The reader might well ask: if Etulain in his "admirable example of the art of bibliography" was correct and Nye's "treatment is the best brief study of the development of the Western," then why even have a section devoted to literary history and literary criticism of Western fiction? The answer to this question is that Etulain was not correct. All that has really been demonstrated is that Nye had read none of the books about which he was writing, that Etulain in writing about Nye had not read any of the books either; and that Folsom in praising Etulain who praised Nye had not read any of the books, or at least had not read Nye so as to question Etulain's opinion. There has been responsible criticism written about Western fiction, just as there has been responsible literary history about the growth and development of Western fiction. The annotations below are harsh when, as in the case of a Nye or an Etulain, they need to be; but they are commensurately more expansive and cordial when it comes to the really fine work which has been done with regard to Western fiction.

A final word should perhaps be said about three essays which have nothing to do *per se* with Western fiction, but which apply significantly to the formulary Western and the romantic historical reconstruction. The essays are by George Orwell and can be found in *The Collected Essays, Journalism, and Letters of George Orwell* (Harcourt, Brace, 1968) edited by Sonia Orwell and Ian Angus: "Boys' Weeklies" which has much of importance to say about popular heroes and the political meanings of much of what they do, "Raffles and Miss Blandish" which is a study, among other things, of institutionalized violence, and "The Secret Life of Salvador Dali" which has a commentary on pornography. Orwell's critical approach was to survey varieties of popular fiction for their anti-humanitarian values, a posture that too few have assumed.

Following the annotated bibliography of more or less general studies about various aspects of Western fiction, some attention is paid to biographies, critical studies, or monograph series on individual authors. However, this listing is scarcely exhaustive and so the reader interested in an individual author is advised to consult the *Encyclopedia of Frontier and Western Fiction* (McGraw-Hill, 1983) of which we were the co-editors-in-chief. Each entry consists of a chronological biography section, a discussion of the author's major works or his particular contribution, and concludes with a complete bibliography of the author's published books as well as (where it applies) films or television productions based on the entry's works. A final notation includes reference to notable book-length studies which have been written about that entry.

ii

Adams, Ramon F., *Burs Under the Saddle: A Second Look at Books and Histories of the West* (University of Oklahoma Press, 1964) O.P.; *More Burs Under the Saddle: Books & Histories of the West* (University of Oklahoma Press, 1979).

Technically speaking, these books have nothing to do with literary criticism of Western fiction, but they *are* concerned with the fictional and fantasy contents as well as misinformation in several hundred historical and biographical books, elements which have certainly been incorporated into quite a few romantic historical reconstructions. Adams limited himself to gunfighters, outlaws, and conflicts such as the Lincoln County War, but when concerned with one or another personality in this general area it is a good idea to consult these volumes.

Boatright, Mody, *Mody Boatright, Folklorist: A Collection of Essays* (University of Texas Press, 1973), edited by Ernest B. Speck.

At the time of his death Boatright had very nearly finished his study of the rise of the cowboy as an American folk hero. Only two of the articles which were intended to be included in the study are to be found in this collection, but they are important ones: "The American Myth Rides the Range: Owen Wister's Man on Horseback" (1951) and "Theodore Roosevelt,

Social Darwinism, and the Cowboy" (1964). There is a selected bibliography at the back so the reader will be able to locate the equally valuable essays "The Western Badman as Hero" (1957), "The Beginnings of Cowboy Fiction" (1966), "The Cowboy Enters the Movies" (1966), "The Morality Play on Horseback: Tom Mix" (1968), and "The Formula in Cowboy Fiction and Drama" (1969). It is indeed regrettable that all of these essays could not have been included in this collection simply because, in their way, they have more to offer by way of critical insight into the subject than the efforts by Branch, Frantz and Choate, and Savage mentioned below.

Perhaps in arriving at his notion of the cooperative spirit on the frontier, Boatright was greatly influenced by the experience of the Austin colony, but there is more than a little support for his point of view and three essays, also included in this collection, are of relevance to this subject as well as to Western fiction: "The Genius of Pecos Bill" (1929), "The Myth of Frontier Individualism" (1941), and "Frontier Humor: Despairing or Buoyant?" (1942). Typical of Boatright's entire approach is what he had to say in "On the Nature of Myth" (1954): "Ritualistic behavior is both repetitive and nonrational. It prescribes the pattern of behavior and relieves the individual of the responsibility of thought; the behavior springs from the attitudes fixed by the myth." This is the best possible frame of mind in which to begin an inquiry into the role of the cowboy as an American folk hero and the impact of the American frontier on the growth and development of Western American fiction.

Branch, E. Douglas, *The Cowboy and His Interpreters* (Appleton, 1926); reprinted by Cooper Square Publishers, both O.P.

Adams in *Burs Under the Saddle* corrected the errors Branch made with regard to his account of the life of Sam Bass in this book. Harry Sinclair Drago in an Introduction to the Cooper Square edition corrected several additional errors Branch made throughout the text. Branch dealt, albeit superficially, with several aspects of the cowboy in fiction, among them Owen Wister's fiction, a chapter on pulp Western publications and another on the transition from wild West shows to Western films, and in a chapter titled "The Aristocracy of Novelists" he selected for his pantheon B.M. Bower, William MacLeod Raine, Charles Alden Seltzer, and Clarence E. Mulford. In the same chapter he also discussed Max Brand, Zane Grey, Harold Bell Wright, and singled out for special praise Eugene Manlove Rhodes and H.H. Knibbs. Much of the information Branch supplied about these authors' lives and backgrounds is erroneous and was not corrected by Drago in the later edition. Branch's opinions are quirky and permit no argument; you either agree or disagree, as, for example, with his judgment that "a novel by Max Brand, for instance, is much better than a short story by Max Brand." Above all, there is an elemental confusion between realism of detail and realism in structure, i.e., because Rhodes "was himself a cowboy for twenty-five years" it does not necessarily follow, as it did for Branch, that the plots of his fiction are thereby more realistic than those of Zane Grey because Grey had been a dentist, although it is possible to see a number of realistic details in Rhodes' fiction that cannot always be found in Grey's fiction. In the end, Branch's book is largely of historical interest and definitely *not* a place at which to begin.

Cawelti, John G., *The Six-Gun Mystique* (Bowling Green University Popular Press, 1975); *Adventure, Mystery, and Romance: Formula Stories as Art and Popular Culture* (University of Chicago Press, 1976).

Both of these books suffer from excessive dilettantism. Cawelti based his rather sweeping generalizations on a very limited exposure to the varieties of Western fiction and on an equally limited number of Western films. If his speculations are confined to Western fiction, and discounted entirely as they concern Western films, they are still of little value. For the most part Cawelti combined a number of theoretical notions about the frontier — e.g., Frederick Jackson Turner's racist antinomy between savagery and civilization suggested to Cawelti the notion of the "epic moment" when forces representing these factions are supposed to clash and led him to postulate that such "epic moments" are to be found throughout Western fiction. From such amalgams he concocted his series of generalizations in which the conclusion is already stated in the major premise. To give another example: Cawelti paraphrased Leslie A. Fiedler (see below) paraphrasing Sigmund Freud in *Civilization and Its Discontents* and "induced" that the Western story concentrates on death and destruction because of sexual repression on the part of the hero. The superficiality of Cawelti's efforts notwithstanding, his objective to approach the Western in terms of a variety of repetitive and yet changing plotlines and stereotypical situations in more knowledgeable hands could prove potentially promising.

Dobie, J. Frank, *Guide to Life and Literature of the Southwest* (Southern Methodist University Press, 1952); *Prefaces* (Little, Brown, 1975).

There are comments strung throughout Dobie's *Guide* on various Western stories and novels and their authors. He is always worth reading, albeit an idiosyncratic as well as dedicated enthusiast of Western life and lore. More to the point is *Prefaces* with its fine collection of reprinted pieces, foremost among them the essay on Andy Adams, the appreciations of Eugene Manlove Rhodes, Charles M. Russell, Frederic Remington, Helen Hunt Jackson, and even the reflections on Charles Siringo, more a fabulist than a truthful memoirist as Dobie himself demonstrated. During his long and productive lifetime, Dobie was inclined to change his mind about various authors, sometimes more than once; in his case this is best interpreted as a sign of his open-mindedness and never as caprice.

Duckett, Margaret. *Mark Twain and Bret Harte* (University of Oklahoma Press, 1964) O.P.

Overall this is a paradigm of what literary history and biography can be, and it deserves to be reissued. Duckett succeeded admirably in demonstrating that Mark Twain totally misrepresented Bret Harte's character and personality, and how, nonetheless, it was this misrepresentation which became an accepted convention among American literary and critical opinion. Not only is the actual relationship between the two men reconstructed but the more delicate question of influence is explored with insight and supported by a wealth of convincing evidence. While in no way diminishing Mark Twain's achievement, Duckett, based on an examination of Harte's writings, was compelled to conclude that "in his attitude toward sex, mental and emotional health, marriage, and family relationships, Bret Harte was much closer to the Twentieth century than was Mark Twain." Twain's chief attribute, as a literary stylist, was his mastery of the colloquial idiom, whereas Harte, with far greater consistency than Twain, argued for more mercy for human beings. Regrettably, Harte's moral principles were all too often obscured by his literary mannerisms. Harte's basic literary formula — that there is good in the heart of the outcast — unquestionably became a fundamental pattern in subsequent Western fiction and film and perhaps there is more than a little truth in Henry Seidel Canby's observation that "the literary West may be said to have founded itself upon the imagination of Bret Harte." Finally, there is the warning Bret Harte once gave to Mark Twain, a warning which, although by each in his own way, was later examined by Van Wyck Brooks in *The Ordeal of Mark Twain* (Heinemann, 1922) and Justin Kaplan in *Mr. Clemens and Mark Twain* (Simon & Schuster, 1966): "It is possible ... that the 'showman' may become in time part of the show — may yield his individuality and his intellectual integrity to that necessity that drives and controls him."

Etulain, Richard W., *Western American Literature: A Bibliography of Books and Articles* (Dakota Press, 1972) O.P.; Etulain, Richard W., and Michael T. Marsden, (eds.), *The Popular Western* (Bowling Green University Popular Press, 1974).

There are eight essays in *The Popular Western*, a selective bibliography, a foreword by Etulain and an afterword by Marsden. Of the eight essays, perhaps only three are worth reading. Roy W. Meyer in "B.M. Bower: The Poor Man's Wister" provided an even better survey (i.e., plot synopses with minimal critical commentary) than did Orrin A. Engen in his *Writer of the Plains* (The Pontine Press, 1973), the only chap-book on Bower; Daryl E. Jones presented the essence of many of his findings as a result of studying the dime novel in "Clenched Teeth and Curses: Revenge and the Dime Novel Outlaw Hero," although this essay is not a substitute for reading Jones' book on the subject (see below); and Gary Topping had some intelligent observations to make in "Zane Grey's West."

In his Foreword Etulain commented: "Many of us are basing our broad generalizations about the nature of the Western on too little evidence. Few of us have read a hundred popular Westerns when thousands have been published." Curiously, in writing this Etulain put his finger right on what makes the essays on Will Henry/Clay Fisher, Luke Short, Jack Schaefer, and his own "The Historical Development of the Western" worthless: the critics had not read widely enough in the field (in three cases of the four even in the author's work which they were discussing) to come to any valid conclusions whatsoever. Etulain also commented in the Fore-word that Topping's essay "suggests that a full-length study of the writings of Zane Grey can tell us much about popular attitudes in America" and in his essay on the historical development of the Western — which is a stag-gering index of just how much Etulain *had not read* — he concluded that "hints of change are good signs for the Western, for they will make it even more valuable as an index of the changing dimensions of the American popular mind." Apparently Etulain based this notion on a reading of Henry Nash Smith's *Virgin Land* (see below), but it is a questionable premise based apparently on some sort of intuitive process and not on scientific method as it would apply to verification of data from a study of Western fiction plots correlated with public opinions, attitudes, and activities of the American populace during a specified period. Lastly, Don D. Walker in "Notes Toward a Literary Criticism of the Western" evi-dently felt such contempt for the novels he cited to support his arguments that he neglected in virtually every case even so much as to supply the names of the authors or the titles of the books, although he did manage to quote Russel Nye from *The Unembarrassed Muse* on Will Henry and for this citation footnoted title of book, city of publication, publisher, year, and page number. *Vanitas academicorum vanitatum.*

Western American Literature is a thin volume — some 137 pages — and it would have been thinner yet had Etulain not included authors such as Wallace Stegner, John Steinbeck, Thomas Berger, Ambrose Bierce, Leslie A. Fiedler, William Inge, Norman Mailer, Mark Schorer, Robert Louis Stevenson, Nathanael West, Yvor Winters, and Thomas Wolfe along with about two dozen more whose presence is questionable and another two dozen who are exceedingly obscure. It is, however, a com-petent bibliography; its principal drawbacks are that it is out of print and more than a decade old.

Fiedler, Leslie A., *Love and Death in the American Novel* (Stein & Day, 1960) O.P.; revised edition published in 1966, O.P; reprinted by Delta Books; *The Return of the Vanishing American* (Stein & Day, 1968).

Love and Death in the American Novel is Fiedler's most enduring effort at literary criticism and the general cultural issues he addressed there have a distinct relevance to the literary criticism of Western fiction. Fiedler's chapter "James Fenimore Cooper and the Historical Romance" offers many penetrating insights into Cooper's fiction and its impact, not the least of which is the concluding statement — derived from D.H. Lawrence (see below) — that "his [Cooper's] version of a love between males, more enduring and purer than any heterosexual passion, had become an undying myth as had Natty and Chingachgook," and this, of course, was an apt prologue for much of the adolescent psychology and masculine hero-worship true of the formulary mode and to an extent of the romantic historical reconstruction in Western fiction.

The Return of the Vanishing American is another story. Fiedler trashed people throughout while demonstrating the most superficial knowledge of American history and Western fiction. Along the way he included a bad translation of Seneca's Latin, misspelled Montaigne's French, erroneously claimed that Sacajawea's name meant "Canoe Launcher" instead of "Bird Woman," referred to Frederick Faust as Clarence Faust, concocted the notion of replacing the white man's whiskey culture with the Indian drug culture (a nasty generalization), and made up a new myth in which a New Paradise is to be inhabited by only man and the serpent and in which woman is the intruder. He declared that the archetypal Western is one in which a European meets an Indian in the wilderness and as a result of this confrontation one must vanish; and he insisted that the New Western—whatever it will be—must be written either in a state of insanity or under the influence of hallucinogenic drugs.

Fiedler, as he matured, became very much the embodiment of a certain kind of critic whom Daniel Bell so ably described in "The Sensibility of the 'Sixties,'" a chapter from his book *The Cultural Contradictions of Capitalism* (Basic Books, 1976): "Faced with a play, a book, or a film, their purpose seemed less to evaluate it in traditional aesthetic terms than to express themselves about it: the work served mainly as an occasion for a personal statement."

Folsom, James K., *The American Western Novel* (Yale University Press, 1966) O.P.; (ed.) *The Western: A Collection of Critical Essays* (Prentice-Hall, 1979).

It is indeed unfortunate that *The American Western Novel* is out of print, since it is at its worst entertaining and at its best provides a stimulating commentary on a wide assortment of issues raised by various Western novels. With the exception of "Doc" Sonnichsen's *From Hopalong to Hud* (see below), it is the most engagingly literate discussion of some of the more general aspects of Western fiction to have appeared so far. This is not to say, however, that a reader will necessarily always, or even most of the time, agree with Folsom. Jean-Louis Leutrat in *Le Western* (Librairie Armand Colin, 1973) had occasion to cite Folsom's remarks about romance—or rather, the Romance as opposed to the Novel—and how the Romance is, in Folsom's words, "relatively free from the necessity of presenting historical 'truth' in any particular factual sense, though it may well deal with ... history as myth, or as metaphor." It is this notion of the Western novel as Romance which characterizes Folsom's approach. To take but one example: "*The Searchers* [by Alan LeMay] is clearly intended as a parable, and the Indians in it partake of abstract quasi-allegorical qualities which are not intended to have more than a minimal similarity to the historic facts of Indian life" and for this reason LeMay made "no pretense at drawing true-to-life Indians...." This is certainly one way of explaining why LeMay's Indians are not true-to-life in *The Searchers*. Leutrat put it another way in *Le Western* when he concluded "*l'indien a été, bien évidemment, la principale victime de l'imagerie raciste*" [the Indian has been, quite obviously, the principal victim in the business of making racial images]. Where *The American Western Novel* is most inadequate is in its neglect of the historical and humanitarian perspectives which must be adopted with regard to Western fiction and, as William T. Pilkington (see below) by regarding history as a myth or a parable, Folsom was providing a critical justification whereby the actual meaning of an historical event or responsibility for an action can be safely side-stepped and even racial genocide can be enjoyed because, after all, it is only a parable.

The Western: A Collection of Critical Essays cannot be recommended. It is possible to respect Vardis Fisher as highly as Folsom apparently did without creating an imbalance by including two essays by Fisher among a critical hotch-potch. There is J. Frank Dobie's Preface to Andy Adams' The Log of a Cowboy from Dobie's Prefaces (see above), W.H. Hutchinson's Introduction to The Rhodes Reader (see below), and, added to these, a ridiculously convoluted essay on Owen Wister's cowboy heroes, the chapter on The Ox-Bow Incident from Max Westbrook's literary study of Walter Van Tilburg Clark (Twayne Publishers, 1969) (see below), as well as general essays of lesser merit (and much less factual accuracy). A reader will come away from The Western bored, uncomfortable, and (if one knows little or nothing about the subject) a trifle confused. Somehow Professor Etulain's essay, "The American Literary West and Its Interpreters" (see III i of this section), is a fitting coup de partance for a poorly edited enterprise done so obviously in haste and without perspective.

Frantz, Joe B., and Julian Ernest Choate, Jr., The American Cowboy: The Myth and the Reality (University of Oklahoma Press, 1955) O.P.

William W. Savage, Jr., in The Cowboy Hero (see below) perhaps best summed up this book in commenting that "their [Frantz and Choate's] point, that media portrayals of cowboys gilded history, was hardly debatable then, and certainly it is not now; but the cowboy hero possesses a bit more cultural, sociological, and economic significance—and a good deal less historical significance—than they were prepared to allow. Their book is but one example, and it is hardly the worst, of the critical scholarship produced in the cowboy heyday of the 1950s." Three chapters in this book pertain to Western fiction, "The Literature: Before 1900," "The Literature: After 1900," and "The Critics." All three are disappointing. The chapter dealing with Western fiction before 1900 is an extremely superficial sweep over dime novels, Emerson Hough, Alfred Henry Lewis, and Owen Wister. That which deals with Western fiction after 1900 is confined, again with a superficial sweep, to mere mentions of Andy Adams, O. Henry, Stewart Edward White, Zane Grey, Dane Coolidge, William MacLeod Raine, Charles Alden Seltzer, and others from their era, with a brief citation— limited to eight books—of titles of later novels. In short, there is nothing here that is new or informative. The chapter on criticism is even more cursory. The authors were of the opinion that "the fiction of frontier days won't be truly accepted as classic unless and until the archetypal myths are woven into the story," and they used as their model of an American literary classic Herman Melville's Moby-Dick (1851) whose "mysticism and symbolism have made it great." The latter assertion may or may not be true, but there is nothing about *Moby-Dick* that can be identified as *intrinsically* American and, thus, the authors' suggestion for a classic Western literature amounts to stripping it of its Western American qualities, whatever they may be, and in such a case at least the demand for archetypal myths constitutes an empty rhetoric.

Fussell, Edwin, *Frontier: American Literature and the American West* (Princeton University Press, 1965) O.P.

One might not think ordinarily of Edgar Allan Poe or Nathaniel Hawthorne as "Western" writers, and, in fact, this book does not purport to treat them in that fashion. However, the author's thesis is that not only Cooper, but Hawthorne, Poe, Thoreau, Melville, and Whitman were all influenced in their literary works by some notion of the frontier and that it functioned for them as a complex symbol. The enervating flaw with this thesis is that, despite the new way of looking at a number of Nineteenth-century American authors, Fussell found himself without a truly workable definition of what the American frontier was and, therefore, what it was precisely that affected each of these particular authors. Fussell was also a member of a group wanting to use the concept of a "closed frontier" as a unifying guide to American literature (see Lee and Simonson below).

Gaston, Edwin W., Jr., *The Early Novel of the Southwest: A Critical History of Southwestern Fiction 1819–1918 with Emphasis on Forty Major Novels from L'Heroine Du Texas to The Desire of the Moth* (University of New Mexico Press, 1961) O.P.

Gaston's book consists for the most part of a general survey of Southwestern fiction during the time frame designated and concentrates on an analysis of plot types and techniques, character portrayal, geographical impressions, and philosophical concepts to be found variously in the forty novels he chose for comparison. Two appendices on the forty novels are devoted, first to synopses of the novels, and then to brief biographies of their authors. The greatest number of errors occurs in the biographical section, although Gaston also erroneously rendered some of the plot synopses. He was very strongly opinionated and, without really showing why or how he came to many of his conclusions by presenting first a coherent critical method, he simply pontificated to the reader, e.g., "Eugene Manlove Rhodes ... whose stories perhaps stand alone at the head of all range fiction, possibly superior both in imaginative interpretation and in art ...," or "Stewart Edward White's *Arizona Nights* ... is an inconsequential work ...," or "a late and vastly inferior historical novel of the post-Civil War period is General Charles King's *An Apache Princess....*" However, notwithstanding the lack of a consistent evaluative principle and the dogmatic air, Gaston did manage to come up with some valid insights through his comparative approach and his study of plot types, techniques, and character portrayal is on the whole commendable. This book deserves to be revised and reissued.

Gurian, Jay, *Western American Writing: Tradition and Promise* (Everett/ Edwards, Inc., 1975) O.P.

There is no essential coherence to the various chapters of this book, lest it be Gurian's dedication "to a new kind of Western — and American — Hero. The seeker after a new American dream, the defender of a new moral frontier." To an extent Gurian was obviously influenced by aspects of Leslie A. Fiedler's thesis in *The Return of the Vanishing American* (see above) and so McMurphy in Ken Kesey's *One Flew Over the Cuckoo's Nest* (Viking, 1962) is "the Western hero in the modern world" who "cannot win any more than Indian hero Crazy Horse could win in the West of one hundred years ago." Gurian was somewhat uninformed of Western American history or he could never have asserted that Thomas Berger's *Little Big Man* (Dial, 1964) "is a significant novel because it portrays Western 'society' in the Nineteenth century as it really was"; and his definition of what constitutes a "Western" is so elastic as to include the film *Easy Rider* (Columbia, 1969) as an example of the "new Western." His discussion of the good bad man as a hero would have benefitted immensely from Mody Boatright's essay on this subject (see above). What Gurian's book comes to in the end is a very personal essay trying to find some kind of new mythology for the Western genre and his conclusion — a quotation of Dennis Hopper in *Easy Rider*, "'Don't be scared. Go and try to change America.'" — certainly should be weighed against how in 1981, flush with confidence from what he termed a popular mandate, President Ronald Reagan urged Americans to attend the feature film *The Legend of the Lone Ranger* (Universal, 1981) because of its evocation of traditional American values.

Haslam, Gerald W., (ed.), *Western Writing* (University of New Mexico Press, 1974).

The best critical writing contained in this anthology is that done by Western writers themselves — principally A.B. Guthrie, Jr., on "The Historical Novel" and Vardis Fisher on "The Novelist and His Background" — and this is as it should be. Guthrie made the point that "a knowledge of the past brings ... [us] oneness with all time ..." which, ultimately, is the objective of an historical reconstruction. Fisher made an equally significant point: "When hero worship, so strong in the Greeks, was combined with the sacrificial scapegoat, which also was commonplace in the folklore of the ancient world, mankind got its symbol of the savior — and in the process brought women to that degraded level which comprises the most repulsive character in human history." Some of the essays are dull — Wallace Stegner's "On the Writing of History" and George R. Stewart's "The Regional Approach to Literature" — and some are a muddle of metaphysics — Max Westbrook's "The Practical Spirit: Sacrality and the American West" (unlike Francis Fergusson who in his criticism of the drama and of Dante could very effectively make use of metaphysical concepts: Westbrook could not) — and some are disappointing — J. Golden Taylor's "The Western Short Story" which is basically about the short stories in his rather uneven collection, *Great Western Short Stories*

(American West Publishing, 1967), and John G. Cawelti's "Prolegomena to the Western." Cawelti advanced the notion, later echoed by Professor Etulain (see above) and attempted unsuccessfully by Cawelti (see above), that were we "able to classify the types of Western plots, we would find that certain plots have been particularly popular at different times." In contrast to a notion such as this and more germane is a remark once made by Budd Boetticher, the director of a number of notable Westerns (see Western Films), quoted by Laura Mulvey in her essay "Visual Pleasure and Narrative Cinema" and included in *Women and the Cinema: A Critical Anthology* (Dutton, 1977) edited by Karyn Kay and Gerald Peary: "What counts is what the heroine provokes, or rather what she represents. She is the one, or rather the love or fear she inspires in the hero, or else the concern he feels for her, who makes him act the way he does. In herself the woman has not the slightest importance." This image of the heroine is unchanged in Western films from William S. Hart's *The Return of Draw Egan* (Triangle, 1916) right down to Michael Cimino's *Heaven's Gate* (United Artists, 1980), and in Western fiction from Zane Grey to Louis L'Amour.

Other essays have more to offer: J. Frank Dobie's "The Writer and His Region," Bernard De Voto's "Birth of an Art" in which he noted that "it was inevitable for Wister, as it remained necessary for his genre, to romanticize the use of murder as a business method," and W.H. Hutchinson's "The 'Western Story' as Literature" in which Hutchinson undertook to praise four authors in particular, Stewart Edward White for the stories in *Arizona Nights*, George Pattullo, Owen Wister, and Eugene Manlove Rhodes. Taken together with the first two, these later essays make this collection uniquely of interest even to the casual reader of Western fiction.

Hazard, Lucy Lockwood, *The Frontier in American Literature* (Crowell, 1927) O.P.

This is a much earlier application than Fussell's (see above) of the notion of the frontier as a substantial and continuous influence on American literature from its beginnings until the 1920s. Hazard was more dependent than Fussell on Turner's frontier thesis, but in her case this was a virtue of sorts insofar as it provided her with a unity of perspective whether she was assessing the "Puritan Frontier," as she termed it, or the "Southern Frontier," or any of several designations she used for various Western frontiers. Of what value can be the tracing of a geographical thesis about the American frontier through decades of American literature? Perhaps it is of little value — as a thesis. But Hazard was a much better literary critic than Fussell and what she observed about Cooper, Washington Irving, John G. Neihardt (as a frontier poet), Bret Harte (whom she accused of exaggerating the part at the expense of the whole in drawing his characters), Mark Twain, Hamlin Garland, Frank Norris, and Willa Cather can still be said to have some value. Her notion of the "Psychic West" perhaps deserves to be explored at length with modern critical methods, whereas her celebration of what she called "spiritual pioneering" has proven to have had the direst of consequences (see I of Western History).

Hutchinson, W.H., *A Bar Cross Man: The Personal Writings of Eugene Manlove Rhodes* (University of Oklahoma Press, 1956) O.P.; "Virgins, Villains, and Varmints" in *The Rhodes Reader: Stories of Virgins, Villains, and Varmints by Eugene Manlove Rhodes* selected by W.H. Hutchinson (University of Oklahoma Press, 1957; second edition, 1975); and VIII "Putting the Cover on *The Covered Wagon*" in *The World, the Work, and the West of W.H.D. Koerner* (University of Oklahoma Press, 1978).

Rhodes' wife, May Davison Rhodes, wrote a very personal memoir, titled *The Hired Man on Horseback: My Story of Eugene Manlove Rhodes* (Houghton Mifflin, 1938), and B.F. Day in *Gene Rhodes, Cowboy* (Messner, 1954) wrote a biography of Rhodes intended for children, but, clearly, the most elaborate and impressive biographical study of Rhodes to appear so far is Hutchinson's *A Bar Cross Man*. He might, ideally, have engaged somewhat more in literary criticism of Rhodes' work than he did, but the book, rich with Rhodes' personal correspondence, does provide a distinct sense of the man and his times.

Both the introductory essay for *The Rhodes Reader* and the chapter from the appreciation of W.H.D. Koerner are confined to an historical and developmental study of Western fiction from the turn of the century through the 1920s, and, despite a few errors of fact, what is there is cogent and of sustaining interest. No doubt, too, Hutchinson was correct in his surmise in the Koerner book that "neo-isolationism and a passionate desire for a 'return to normalcy' that placed Warren G. Harding in the White House ... bespoke a deep national desire to escape the impact of accelerating change and its erosion of traditional values deeply felt and strongly held. As a bulwark against the inchoate present, the nation turned inward and homeward to the most American of all American experiences, the frontier, and the formula Western story burgeoned accordingly." Indeed, this phenomenon was equally apparent in the first decade or so after the second World War. Hutchinson's major efforts have been in the field of literary history and biography and not literary criticism and so, therefore, it would be a mistake to look to him for an extended critique of Western fiction.

Jones, Daryl, *The Dime Novel Western* (Bowling Green University Popular Press, 1978).

In terms of its exposition, this is a valuable study. Jones was familiar with more dime novels than anyone else might be inclined to read and his cataloguing of dime novels according to their plotlines and structures and his observations about them are generally reliable. Where the book fails is in its last section, that given over to interpretation. There is, however, an explanation for this. *The Dime Novel Western* was the first, and so far is the only, entry in "The Popular Western Series" under the editorship of Richard W. Etulain and Michael T. Marsden. Reportedly, the book as Jones wrote it was rejected and he was required to graft onto his research the sweeping generalizations of John G. Cawelti so as "properly" to interpret what he had read, whereas, having read more than Cawelti had, Jones would actually have been in a better position to provide a comprehensive critical and interpretive apparatus derived from his knowledge of dime novels and the formulary conventions which they followed. Because the expository part of Jones' book is unaffected by the popular culture fadists' "goodthink" (the apt word in George Orwell's guide to "newspeak" for orthodoxy), it can serve the reader as a concise introduction to dime novels with Western themes.

Larson, Charles R., *American Indian Fiction* (University of New Mexico Press, 1978).

This book is that ideal, but exceedingly rare, combination of literary history and penetrating literary appraisal which both illuminates the fiction with which it is concerned as it evaluates individual efforts. Larson perceived Native American literature as a distinct genre — which, perhaps, it is really and should not have been integrated in I v of this section with historical reconstructions generally — "a vigorous, young literature, in many ways still undergoing the pains of parturition, yet in its wisdom and sense of tradition, years ahead of the culture that has often tried to subdue it." These are strong words indeed, but Larson demonstrated their validity at the same time as he illustrated, through his cogent literary criticism, that the Native American indeed "is no longer an opaque shadow, hidden away in the great forest, but a figure now looming on its outer perimeters, singing proudly in his own distinct voice." Because of Larson's consistent use of a comparative method throughout his encounters with Indian fiction, his effort might well also function as an extraordinarily perceptive general survey of the entire field of modern Native American literature.

Lawrence, D.H., *Studies in Classic American Literature* (Thomas Seltzer, 1923) O.P.; reissued variously and continuously since.

Long hailed a classic in literary criticism, Lawrence's book remains controversial. "Poe has no truck with Indians or Nature. He makes no bones about Red Brothers and Wigwams. He is absolutely concerned with the disintegration-process of his own psyche." Lawrence would not have entertained for a moment the notion about a frontier influence on Poe, Melville, or Hawthorne which Fussell and Hazard did (see above). Instead, he saw Poe's Gothic tales as necessary "because the old white psyche has to be gradually broken down before anything else can come to pass," and what he felt came to pass was a totally new consciousness, the American consciousness. Lawrence's book may, in fact, have become so popular among American critics precisely because he was willing to take such authors as Poe and Cooper seriously, to treat their works as literature, to confirm Americans in their supposition that the fiction of Melville, Hawthorne, Poe, and Cooper really had something to say about a unique American national character. "The essential American soul is hard, isolate, stoic, and a killer," Lawrence wrote. But is this essentially *the* American soul? Or is it only an alter-ego? Is it simply flattering to the swagger of

American vanity and, therefore, the stuff of which heroes are so often made in formulary Westerns and romantic historical reconstructions? It is perhaps because of a lack of enchantment with such images that, in part, Charles R. Larson (see above) could declare the wisdom of American Indian fiction "years ahead of the culture that has often tried to subdue it," especially if the coming of wisdom can in this instance be conceived as a linear rather than a vertical process. What this does point up is how even at his most extreme — and he is very often extreme — Lawrence can provoke his reader to think: is there any finer attribute that a book of literary criticism can possess?

Lee, Lawrence L., and Merrill E. Lewis, (eds.), *Women, Women Writers, and the West* (Whitson Publishing, 1979).

In the Preface to this book, the editors remark that "if we are going to understand the woman writer and take a fair measure of her contributions to literature we must meet her on her own ground, and that means on the ground of her own experience and within the literature forms of her own choosing." This is what this book accomplishes, and perhaps even a bit more since the subject is certainly one of the most neglected areas of Western writing. Fifteen of the nineteen essays were written by women and the result is a refreshingly "feminine" perspective throughout. Divided into five parts, the book opens with a poem by Clarice Short which is followed by an essay by Susan H. Armitage contending that the frontier myth — wherein violence is justified at the expense of distorting Indians and women — must be reevaluated from the woman's point of view and instead attention paid to how women related to the wilderness and to Native Americans. The second part, besides including a much needed appreciation of the historical biographies of Mari Sandoz, examines some of the real women who lived on the frontier and the forms in which they wrote about their experiences. The third part deals with the images of women in Western fiction by authors such as Hamlin Garland, O.E. Rölvaag, and Conrad Richter. A number of these essays are of particular interest because of their new approaches to the subject of the Western heroine. In the fourth part Bernice Slote provided an insightful essay on Willa Cather and her work, putting forth her reasons for refuting the label of regional writer usually assigned to Cather. There is also an excellent study of Dorothy Scarborough's *The Wind* (Harper's, 1925) and the folk narrative writings of Caroline Gordon. The last part is devoted to women writers whose works are concerned with frontiers outside the borders of the United States. Although this book may not be for the general reader, it is definitely of value to the serious student of Western fiction or of women writers.

Lee, Robert Edson, *From West to East: Studies in the Literature of the American West* (University of Illinois Press, 1966) O.P.

In part this book was written in response to Edwin Fussell's study (see above). "...I brood about Fussell's next sentence," Lee wrote: "'Granted that Thoreau, and the other major figures of the mid-century, lacked firsthand knowledge of the West; at least they had the advantage of a long perspective, and that advantage they capitalized on for all it was worth and sometimes more.' *This* study concerns firsthand knowledge, its necessity, and the failure of Western writers to turn it to literary use." However, where Fussell lacked a coherent idea of the meaning of the frontier, Lee was not always clear about all the connotations and meanings of the idea of West in his title *From West to East*. Despite numerous Native American authors writing before and contemporary with his book, Lee dismissed them all: "A people who cannot write cannot survive. Artifacts, pictographs, and oral legends are but the ghosts, the symbols of man. One could almost say that it was permissible to destroy the American Indian because he had no literature — no past other than the animal. ...And though the Western Indian has been to school for a century, he has not written a memorable word."

Lee's book is divided roughly into two parts, the first devoted to an examination of the writings of some notable authors who went from the East into the West, e.g., Lewis and Clark, Timothy Flint, James Hall, Washington Irving, and Francis Parkman, and the second which treats of authors who went from the West to the East, e.g., Mark Twain, Willa Cather, and Bernard De Voto. Sometimes Lee's research was faulty. He accepted Bernard De Voto's anecdote of how Owen Wister deleted the eye-gouging scene from even the magazine version of "Balaam and Pedro" (1892) whereas, had either De Voto or Lee after him consulted the back issue of *Harper's* containing the story, he would have found the scene intact.

However, whatever Lee's limitations, his perspective remains an essentially fruitful one. It permitted him and the reader in turn to see just how Mark Twain pandered to his Eastern audience in writing *Roughing It* (1872) and that, however amusing the book is, it is also "just another tourist piece, so subjective, so exaggerated, so distorted, so jolly, that the West would have to continue to wait for a more honest interpreter...." Contrasting some quotations from Mari Sandoz' *Old Jules* (Little, Brown, 1935) with Willa Cather's view of pioneer life, Lee could not but conclude that Cather "chose the rosy tints of romanticism.... She chose to write an idyll or a pastorale. Beautiful as it may be, it hasn't the strength or the vigor or the reality of the history itself.... She had come, by 1913, to write from the point of view of the East, substituting artifice for truth." It is for precisely this reason that Willa Cather above is classified as an author of romantic historical reconstructions and Mari Sandoz as an author of historical reconstructions. Lee lacked this type of descriptive structural categories. Had he had them and had he read more widely in Western fiction, including more of what Mari Sandoz — to take only one example — wrote, he perhaps would have seen that he was correct only in part that "the metaphor of the West had to be adjusted to the dimensions, the tastes, the modes of the East in its transformation from the basic document of experience to the ordering of literature" and altogether wrong that "since the experience is past, I conclude that it has been lost for all time." As it stands, Lee's book is of

interest for its perspective but untrustworthy as to its conclusions because
of the author's very limited knowledge of either the first-hand accounts of
life in the American West or the fiction about that life.

Milton, John R., *Three West: Conversations with Vardis Fisher, Max
Evans, Michael Straight* (Dakota Press, 1970); *Conversations with Frank
Waters* (Swallow, 1971); and *The Novel of the American West* (University
of Nebraska Press, 1980).

In 1964 Milton began an ambitious series of video-taped interviews
of authors of Western fiction conducted in the studios of KUSD-TV on the
campus of the University of South Dakota. By 1968 over forty such programs had been put on video tape and audio tapes had been made of
Walter Van Tilburg Clark, Harvey Fergusson, and Wallace Stegner. *Three
West* and *Conversations with Frank Waters* are printed transcriptions of
the video interviews with four of the Western authors who cooperated in
the project (although in the sixth conversation with Frank Waters author
Frederick Manfred joins the discussion). Michael Straight, at the time he
was interviewed, had written two historical reconstructions set in the
American West; but he is probably of the least interest. Frank Waters —
because of the length and depth of the interviews — is the best documented
in this group, but it would be a mistake not to read Milton's interviews with
Vardis Fisher and Max Evans, both of whom along with Waters will
continue to attract new readers and whose reputations appear to be secure.

Milton's opinion as to what constitutes Western fiction worthy of
being considered literary art and what does not was set out very early in his
own writings — as early as the essay "The Novel in the American West"
(1964) contained in Haslam (see above) and Pilkington (see below) — and it
did not really change very much from the time of his first formulations
until the publication of *The Novel of the American West*, save that a few
authors such as Paul Horgan were dropped from Milton's very select
pantheon. His vision of Western fiction was much too narrow, therefore,
for an interested reader to look to him as any kind of general critical guide
to Western fiction, but, whatever his elitism, Milton's criticism is nonetheless singularly illuminating in connection with the authors whom he chose
to favor and whose works he studied carefully over the years. These authors
are Vardis Fisher, A.B. Guthrie, Jr., Frederick Manfred, Walter Van
Tilburg Clark, Harvey Fergusson, and Frank Waters. With the exception
of Harvey Fergusson, all of them have written historical reconstructions,
that is fiction true to the period, the place, and the people. In one of his
introductory chapters, Milton mentioned a number of formulary Westerns
and elsewhere he claimed to have read quite a few; however, the
experience apparently left little impression, since he did nothing more in
The Novel of the American West than to cite some titles and some authors'
names. Milton's remarks in the final chapter, particularly his assessments of
Wallace Stegner and John Steinbeck, are particularly cogent. However exclusive his view, Milton's stated objective was to prove that, given the
authors he discussed at length, it is indeed possible to assert that Western

American literature can stand on equal terms with any literature in the world. Such a thesis is a matter of personal opinion, but it is well argued.

Pilkington, William T., *My Blood's Country: Studies in Southwestern Literature* (Texas Christian University Press, 1973) O.P.; (ed.), *Critical Essays on the Western American Novel* (G.K. Hall, 1980).

Pilkington's book, *Harvey Fergusson* (Twayne Publishers, 1975), is dealt with later on in this subsection with all the relevant books in the Twayne United States Authors Series. The Twayne book is probably his best critical effort, but it must be approached with a high degree of cautious reserve because it is characterized by the same kind of ill-conceived extravagance with which Fergusson, as well as a number of other Southwestern writers, is dealt with in *My Blood's Country*. Pilkington's claim that Fergusson's "fictional world is essentially a masculine one" is an apt observation, and perhaps, too, Fergusson's "most successful vantage points are the minds of his male characters," but few sensitive female readers (and maybe more than a few male readers) would agree that "the women in his novels are presented realistically enough." Pilkington was aware that "in his portrayal of Spanish- and Mexican-Americans the writer [seemed] to accept a somewhat objectionable stereotype," but Pilkington's own bias, it would appear, prevented him from perceiving the same stereotyping process at work in Fergusson's treatment of Native Americans, blacks, and female characters generally. In dealing with Edwin Corle, Pilkington declared that *Fig Tree John* (Liveright, 1935) is "as objective and convincing a portrait of an Indian as any white man is likely ever to achieve." What apparently prompted Pilkington to this excess of praise was what he perceived as Corle's ideology in the novel; Corle, in Pilkington's paraphrase, "further [assumed] that skirmishes are inevitable and that the only practical solution to such conflicts is total capitulation by one side or the other (that is, as things now stand, the Indian must concede his traditional way of life or be destroyed). I realize, of course, that the 'clash of cultures' theme is a common one in literature about the Indian, but few writers have had the courage to express the bleak conclusion that this conflict suggests." Those novels Corle wrote in which the Indian does not capitulate were, accordingly, dismissed by Pilkington, as was Corle's *Billy the Kid* (Duell, Sloan, 1953), as "a bit of fluff" and "testimony to the deterioration of the author's talents"—an interesting judgment to contrast with Pilkington's defense of *Billy the Kid* in his Introduction to the 1979 reissue of the novel by the University of New Mexico Press.

The main problem with *Critical Essays on the Western American Novel* is who would be likely to find it of use or interest? Approximately one third of the collection is devoted to "General Criticism," which ranges from essays by John Milton and Mody Boatright which are worth reading to John G. Cawelti's "Prolegomena to the Western" (1970) and two essays by Richard W. Etulain which are not. Etulain, for example, in "Origins of the Western" (1972) which has footnotes almost as long as the text of his essay claimed that "Wister ... [produced] the first Western in *The Virginian*" and in a footnote commented that since this essay was written "Russell (sic) B. Nye's *The Unembarrassed Muse* ... has appeared" and that "the section in his book dealing with the rise of the Western agrees with several of my contentions...." (See III i of this section.)

The remainder of the book consists of essays on various individual authors, most of which are of inferior quality. Delbert E. Wylder in a study of "Emerson Hough and the Popular Novel" (1972) was able to abstract Hough's basic formula in writing his fiction, but it is misleading to describe any novel by Hough, as Wylder did, as "carefully researched." Donald E. Houghton in "Two Heroes in One: Reflections on the Popularity of [Owen Wister's] *The Virginian*" (1970) invoked the Henry Nash Smith thesis (see below), i.e., that by studying the "unique staying power" of this novel "we might understand a little more about Americans themselves and more specifically about American attitudes toward that frontier experience which is so central in American history and folklore." This does not happen, however; Houghton built his thesis of two Virginians in the novel on Wister's laziness at integrating parts of the novel from stories which appeared much earlier in magazines and it is a better index of Wister's slipshod technique than a guide to "American attitudes." Perhaps the best essays in this part of the book are John D. Nesbitt's "Change of Purpose in the Novels of Louis L'Amour" (1978), which is fine as far as it goes but which does not go far enough, and L.L. Lee's altogether commendable "Walter Van Tilburg Clark's Ambiguous American Dream" (1965) and John Milton's "The Primitive World of Vardis Fisher: The Idaho Novels" (1976).

Pilkington's essay "Edward Abbey: Western Philosopher" (1974) was unrevised for this inclusion and is as dissatisfying as his treatment of Abbey in *My Blood's Country*. Referring to a character in Abbey's novel *Black Sun* (Simon & Schuster, 1971), Pilkington concluded his appraisal of Abbey with this sentiment: "The task then—for Will Gatlin, for Edward Abbey, and for Americans generally—is, as Gatlin's Indian friend says, to learn how to be 'a happy Hopi hippie.'" Two essays by Max Westbrook, "The Themes of Western Fiction" (1958) which is excellent and "The Western Esthetic" (1969) which is the reverse, serve as an indication of Westbrook before and after he came up with his notion of "sacrality." Briefly defined, this "sacrality" is positing a primordial reality knowable, it would seem, only through unconscious intuition. It is a clumsy mystical pretense at best since Westbrook never really can define it—indeed, by definition it would be indefinable—and, therefore, it is of little help as a critical standard of value. Pilkington, however, in his Abbey essay felt that "Abbey ... has contributed significantly to that ongoing tradition of Western American literature that Professor Max Westbrook has called Western 'sacrality.'" By means of either a clever or inept—one cannot ultimately be sure which—juxtaposition of quotations, Pilkington managed to distort completely what Abbey had to say in *Desert Solitaire* (McGraw-Hill, 1968) and then proceeded to apply this distortion in order to interpret Abbey's fiction.

One example will have to suffice. Sandy, the major female character in *Black Sun*, according to Pilkington, "is torn between her intuitive, natural love for Will and her rational, socially acceptable love for her Air Force cadet. The more she thinks about her choice, the more her ability to choose is undermined. In *Desert Solitaire* Abbey [noted] 'reason is and ought to be, as Spinoza (sic) said, the slave of the passions.' Unfortunately this is a lesson Sandy never learns, and she pays dearly for her ignorance." The (sic) appears, first of all, because, as the reader may recall, in Part IV of *The Ethics* (1677) Spinoza wrote that "human infirmity in moderating and checking the emotions I name bondage" and concluded in the Appendix that "in life it is before all things useful to perfect the understanding, or reason, as far as we can, and in this alone man's highest happiness or blessedness consists...." It appears, second of all, because in *Desert Solitaire* Abbey wrote: "Today is my last day at the Arches; tonight I take a plane for Denver and from there a jet flight to New York. Of course I have my reasons which reason knows nothing about; reason is and ought to be, as Hume said, the slave of the passions. He foresaw the whole thing." What is it that Hume supposedly foresaw? It is a philosophical question, of course. In Part IV Section II of *A Treatise of Human Nature* (1739), Hume wrote that "the sceptic still continues to reason and believe, even though he asserts that he cannot defend his reason by reason; and by the same rule he must assent to the principle concerning the existence of body, though he cannot pretend, by any arguments of philosophy, to maintain its veracity." Abbey in *Desert Solitaire* would escape those potential terrors of skeptical reason which befell Hume. In the antinomy Abbey constructed, between civilization and culture, for Abbey "civilization is tolerance, detachment and humor, or passion, anger, revenge; culture is the entrance exam, the gas chamber, the doctoral dissertation and the electric chair...." Confronted with Hume's dilemma, Abbey opted for the solution advanced by George Santayana in *Skepticism and Animal Faith* (Scribner's, 1923) and this was why he could write near the conclusion of *Desert Solitaire*: "I have seen the place called Trinity, in New Mexico, where our wise men exploded the first atomic bomb and the heat of the blast fused sand into a greenish glass — already the grass has returned, and the cactus and the mesquite. On this bedrock of animal faith I take my stand, close by the old road that leads eventually out of the valley of paradox." The carelessness with which Pilkington could substitute Spinoza for Hume and his insensitivity to the basic philosophical issues under discussion made him peculiarly ill-equipped to discuss Abbey's philosophical reflections, no less so than to apply these reflections to an interpretation of Abbey's characters or what happens to them in Abbey's fiction.

It is this same kind of superficiality in approach allied with a seeming ignorance of history that must have prompted Pilkington in his Introduction to *Critical Essays on the Western American Novel* to describe Andy Adams' *Log of a Cowboy* (Houghton Mifflin, 1903) as "superbly realistic"; and, when this was combined with an insufficient knowledge of the structural characteristics of formulary Western fiction and a confused notion of just what can properly be termed "mythic," to assert that "since Western movies, like popular Western novels, are normally set in a mythic rather than a realistic West, Cawelti — as well as numerous other scholars working in this area — travels easily between print and film, an approach that seems not only justified but necessary." Nothing Cawelti wrote in his essay, and nothing in any other essay, would justify this myopia toward very real and demonstrable differences between Western fiction and film (as indeed between fiction and film generally), much less warrant for such myopia a word as compelling as "necessary." Pilkington ended his Introduction by quoting Etulain to the effect that "'Western literary studies are no longer in their adolescent stage....' The essays brought together here testify eloquently to the accuracy of that assessment." Sadly, a more impartial assessment of this collection would find both Etulain and Pilkington in error.

Powell, Lawrence Clark, *Southwest Classics: The Creative Literature of the Arid Lands. Essays on the Books and Their Writers* (Ward Ritchie, 1974).

By "creative literature" Powell did not mean merely fiction, since he chose to include a number of memoirists — Josiah Gregg, Lewis H. Garrard, Susan Shelby Magoffin, J. Ross Browne, Martha Summerhayes, John Wesley Powell, and Theodore Roosevelt among them — and books not readily classifiable as either fiction or reminiscences but what the French call *belles-lettres* by Charles F. Lummis, Mabel Dodge Luhan, Mary Austin, Erna Fergusson, Ross Santee (whose book *Lost Pony Tracks* [1953; University of Nebraska Press, 1972] is partly fiction, partly autobiography, and partly *belles-lettres*), Joseph Wood Krutch, and John C. Van Dyke. The reader might wonder what Theodore Roosevelt is doing among this group since he neither lived in nor wrote about the Southwest, but Powell made a sound case for him on the basis of Roosevelt's wild-life and conservation efforts in the Southwest during his presidency. When it comes to authors of fiction, Powell was perhaps unfair to Zane Grey and praised Harvey Fergusson too much. What he had to write about Willa Cather, Eugene Manlove Rhodes, Stewart Edward White, and Will Levington Comfort is extraordinarily apt; while what he wrote about Oliver LaFarge's novel *Laughing Boy* (Houghton Mifflin, 1929) would indicate an ignorance of the Navajo people and their customs. Powell used a common structure in approaching each subject: to narrate his responses to an author's works while recounting that author's life, the whole fabric interwoven with Powell's personal reminiscences where they illumine his subject. The methodology works rather well in this book and it is a genuine pleasure to read, written with grace and *élan*.

Savage, William W., Jr., *The Cowboy Hero: His Image in American History and Culture* (University of Oklahoma Press, 1979).

This is not really a work of literary criticism, but it is a necessary critique of the background against which much of Western fiction has been written and explores the notion of the cowboy hero in the popular media. It may be our fault, Savage suggested poignantly, that no distinction has been made between history and entertainment. Savage also rightly criticized both Western fiction and Western films for shaping male attitudes toward women. It is not demonstrable, as Savage asserted, that a masculine hero necessitates a heroine, but a hero *does* necessitate a villain, a concept that is at the very center of the middle-class American *Weltanschauung*. There are errors in this book. Hoot Gibson had only three wives, not four; William Boyd appeared in sixty-eight feature films as Hopalong Cassidy, not fifty-four, and Clarence E. Mulford's books were never rewritten. When Savage addressed the subject of women on the frontier contrasted with their roles in Western films, he did not know what he was writing about — to express it charitably. Some may also object to his belief that Stepin Fetchit was a better actor than Will Rogers. However, whatever its shortcomings, this is the best book so far to have appeared on the cowboy hero as a creation of the popular media to be mass-merchandised for profit and which, unfortunately, has had anything but a commendable social effect; although by terming this "the best book" no warranty is implied and a better book surely is possible, one that would be still more probing and unrelenting in its examination. *The Cowboy Hero* is, in these terms, just a beginning, but superior to the efforts of Branch and Frantz and Choate in the past (see above).

Simonson, Harold P., *The Closed Frontier: Studies in American Literary Tragedy* (Holt, Rinehart, 1970) O.P.

The thesis of this book was addressed in I of Western History. The tone, for the most part, tends to the hysterical (reminiscent of Leslie A. Fiedler at his worst). Simonson's thesis is that much of American literature is a response to a recognition that the frontier is closed, that this situation has created the atmosphere in which tragedy is possible, and that tragedy somehow conveys the most profound truth. "Americans had spent two centuries pushing back the wall [i.e., closing frontier] or denying its existence. But the wall still stands. Perhaps a man's only immortality is what he writes on it. Perhaps in some mysterious way it is through the tragedy he there records that he shall come to know the comedy that is divine." Apparently to Simonson these sentences were meaningful. He concentrated on Mark Twain, O.E. Rölvaag, and Nathanael West at some length to illustrate his thesis, but his pages are also filled with numerous other citations, many of them as this one: "The writer of tragedy denies the possibility of this breakthrough, concurring with Camus that Kierkegaard's 'leap of faith' is fallacious." Ultimately Simonson's book is an attempt — without his being aware of it — to wed post-war Existentialism with American fiction; the West as a place is really rather irrelevant to the enterprise.

Smith, Henry Nash, *Virgin Land: The American West as Symbol and Myth* (Harvard University Press, 1950); *Mark Twain: The Development of a Writer* (Harvard University Press, 1962).

The Virgin Land is frequently cited by popular culture fadists as a primary example of how to deduce the sentiments supposedly felt by a wide number of people by analyzing a sampling of their popular fiction. Yet this is precisely what Smith's book does *not* do. In his "Preface to the Twentieth Anniversary Printing" issued by Harvard University Press, Smith confessed that "on rereading the book now I am forced to the chastening realization that I was guilty of the same kind of oversimplification I ascribed to others. Although I had gained some theoretical perspective on the nature of fictions from [Henri] Bergson, [Lucien] Levy-Bruhl, and [Hans] Vaihinger, my attitude toward popular beliefs about the West was in practice often reductionistic. ...The vestiges of dualism in my assumptions [between what he meant by symbol and myth] made it difficult fo me to recognize that there was a continuous dialectic interplay between the mind and its environment, and that our perceptions of objects and events are no less a part of consciousness than are our fantasies."

Smith did spend two chapters analyzing the formulae of dime novels and he also tried to examine attitudes toward the American West to be found in fictional works by such authors as Timothy Flint, Emerson Bennett, and James Fenimore Cooper. His book was an experiment in perspective, an attempt to view the Westward movement through the propaganda and fictions inspired by it. However Smith's premise in approaching the dime novel, that "the individual writer abandons his own personality and identifies himself with the reveries of his readers," is far-fetched to say the least. The reading public may pick an author who comes closest to its collective reveries, or an author who, in C.G. Jung's sense, may try to compensate in his fiction for what he feels is lacking in the spiritual climate of his age; but ultimately the mood of the reading public is formed by such a confluence of factors as to be unknowable and incapable of measurement. Smith's methodology, while entertaining, cannot demonstrate by intuition any correlation between popular fiction and public sentiment that is meaningful, that can somehow be measured or even verified negatively, i.e., by some result that would prove to be inconsistent with it.

It is also interesting to note that Smith, in writing one of the better books on Mark Twain, not only abandoned his notion of popular literature as an index of public sentiment about the West but he even criticized earlier Twain biographers Van Wyck Brooks and Bernard De Voto for excesses in this regard. "...We must make a special effort to avoid seeing Mark Twain merely as a spokesman for the emergent energies of the frontier, the West, in opposition to established tradition," he wrote, and added that while "his [Twain's] work was shaped by two opposed forces, [it] cannot be neatly identified with different regions. The conflict was rather between the conventional assumptions he shared with most of his countrymen and an impulse to reject these assumptions, also widely shared, that found expression in humor." The historian can be of assistance to the literary critic, but not as Smith first suggested, not through oversimplification; indeed, the historian can even become a literary critic, provided he uses his knowledge of history of a particular period precisely to safeguard against oversimplification regarding a literary subject, a particular period, a people.

Sonnichsen, C.L., *From Hopalong to Hud: Thoughts on Western Fiction* (Texas A&M University Press, 1978).

This volume consists of nine essays purportedly focusing on various aspects of Western fiction—they do not, in every case—and a brief Prologue and an equally brief Epilogue. In the brief Prologue Sonnichsen noted as one of the reasons for studying Western novels the fact that "the social scientist finds them more and more significant ... for what they show about the country which produced them and the people who read, or did not read, any or all of them." What can a Western novel "show" about a person who did not read it? Fortunately, Sonnichsen made no attempt to pursue this line of thinking very far, albeit he did credit Henry Nash Smith (see above) with having originated it.

The real weakness of Sonnichsen's book is that he lacked any kind of functional critical apparatus with which to approach Western fiction. In the same Prologue he spoke of two roads extending from Owen Wister's *The Virginian* (Macmillan, 1902). These two roads for Sonnichsen were also the same as the dichotomy developed by Wallace Stegner between "Western" and "western" (see I iv of this section), except that Sonnichsen reversed Stegner's definitions and for him "western" applies to "'genre' or commerical westerns," i.e., the formulary Western, while "Western" is to designate fiction by authors such as Paul Horgan and Frank Waters. Notwithstanding, this dichotomy really did not work for Sonnichsen. On the "high road" he grouped "superior writers like Stewart Edward White, Eugene Manlove Rhodes, Emerson Hough, Conrad Richter, and Walter Van Tilburg Clark," authors who, in all justice, do not really belong grouped together; and on the "low road" Sonnichsen included authors such as Zane Grey, B.M. Bower, Luke Short, and William MacLeod Raine "while in between" there are authors such as Alan LeMay, Ernest Haycox, and Jack Schaefer. This is a poor excuse for a set of literary categories and despite spending two chapters on various aspects of the Wyatt Earp legend in fiction and history it never seems to have occurred to Sonnichsen to adopt historical reality as a standard of value in classifying the varieties of Western fiction. Aristotle demonstrated long ago in the *Poetics* that the most viable form of literary categories are those determined according to structure, then content, and finally style. As it stands, Sonnichsen's "in between" category has writers who wrote formulary Westerns (LeMay, Haycox, and Schaefer), who wanted to write better and so wrote romantic historical reconstructions (LeMay, Haycox, and Schaefer), and one who strove to go farther yet and who wrote, ultimately, historical reconstructions (Jack Schaefer). Sonnichsen's categories permit no means by which to measure the personal growth and development of the writers who are to be classified by means of them and assignment to a category seems, on the whole, to have been rather arbitrary.

Lacking a critical methodology or unity of focus are basic flaws, but there is something of value to be found in this book. The essay on "The Ambivalent Apache" surveys how Apaches have been treated in (formulary and romantic) Western fiction and they have been treated (although Sonnichsen did not use this term) with the grossest kind of political "double-think" (the term, according to George Orwell, used to mark the transition between "old-speak" and "newspeak") in which killing an Apache *means* bringing peace and prosperity. Sonnichsen's chapter "Sex on the Lone Prairie" begins with the sentence: "Western fiction has traditionally been clean." In this context "clean" can be taken as an equivalent for the "newspeak" word "goodsex" which means chastity. And Sonnichsen, because he lacked a functional critical methodology, loses his reader in the dichotomy between "goodsex" and the porno-Western because there is no middle term. The chapters on Miss Sue Pinckney and sharecroppers are peripheral to Western fiction. In his survey of the changing images of the Western hero in the title essay, Sonnichsen attached far too much significance to the fiction of Larry McMurtry, who is, in the final analysis, a minor author and one who has not really influenced Western fiction at all. As J. Frank Dobie and Mody Boatright before him, however, Sonnichsen can be said to have united compassion for the human predicament with whatever is the subject about which he chose to write and, also as they, his treatment of a subject is rarely dull.

Tuska, Jon, *Four Studies in Western Fiction* (work in progress).
    The first of these four studies is titled "The Concept of Historical Reality and Its Use as a Standard for Evaluation." It consists of a discussion of the role of logic in historical inquiry, the role of ethics, then defines the concept of historical reality, and finally demonstrates how the concept of historical reality can be used as a basic standard for evaluating Western fiction in terms of the mode of deviation from or agreement with this standard, along the lines described throughout the first subsection of this section. The second study is concerned with the basic narrative patterns in the formulary Western and illustrates variations through using a number of formulary writers as literary paradigms. The third study is concerned with basic narrative structures employed in romantic historical reconstructions and again a number of paradigms are used, analyzed in depth, to show the varieties and limitations of this mode. The last study is devoted to the idea of Western fiction as a reconstruction of historical reality and, again, various techniques and approaches are analyzed through the employment of paradigmatic studies of particular authors.
    However, in terms of aesthetic judgments, once formulary Westerns and romantic historical reconstructions have been identified, their composition, structure, style, and execution, as well as their relationship to historical reality, become factors in the process of critical evaluation. In the Epilogue it is stressed, all of this notwithstanding, that no critical and theoretical system for properly studying Western fiction can afford to be internally inconsistent; to the contrary, it must be as general as possible in its applicability and in all cases logically derived from the evidence in terms

of the conclusions which are reached. It is the objective of these four studies to put a reader in a position to determine the mode of *any* Western fiction, as well as to be better able to evaluate specific Western fictions; yet, when it comes to aesthetic evaluations, the myth of so-called "objective" criticism is debunked; the ranking of novels and stories is ultimately a form of *dialecta masturbata*. However logical and consistent the standards and assumptions of critical theory, including the poetics provided in this book for Western fiction, preferences remain personal and wholly idiosyncratic. There is no Platonic heaven in which the pure and ideal forms of the perfect Western fiction can be said to reside, while all that is written is to be regarded as only an inferior copy. In a society of free-thinking individuals, a person's own preference becomes that person's final *arbiter elegantiae*.

Walker, Franklin, *San Francisco's Literary Frontier* (Knopf, 1939) O.P.; *A Literary History of Southern California* (University of California Press, 1950) O.P.

Both of these books ought to be reissued. *San Francisco's Literary Frontier* is a fascinating account of the literary, social, economic, and political environment which produced what Walker, in one chapter, rightly called "The 'Golden Era.'" As Henry Nash Smith in his study of Mark Twain (see above), Walker combined the discipline of the historian with a unified theory of literary criticism which permitted him, in addition to narrating events and describing settings, to come to aesthetic evaluations, as when he wrote of Bret Harte: "One cannot make the charge that Harte missed the significance of the scene around him; rather, he was the first of the Western writers to sense its possibilities. What one does regret is that ever hampering sense of cautiousness, that overdeveloped critical attitude which put fetters on his feelings as well as his writing." Walker's portrait needs only to be balanced with Margaret Duckett's *Mark Twain and Bret Harte* (see above).

It is possible to quarrel with Walker for inclusion of Zane Grey who was an Eastern immigrant to Southern California in *A Literary History of Southern California* while completely ignoring Dane Coolidge who was a native of the state, lived in the Bay area most of his life, and wrote Western fiction often superior in verisimilitude if not romance to that of Grey; but what Walker did address, he addressed well, and his discussion of major literary figures in this region, such as Mary Austin and Charles F. Lummis, is made more vivid due to the detailed historical background against which they are set in relief. Before an objection be raised that the Bay area cannot properly be considered as Southern California, it should also be mentioned that the Grey novels cited are set in states other than California, whereas in novels such as *Horse-Ketchum of Death Valley* (Dutton, 1930) it is the California desert which Coolidge described and where his story is set.

In the general survey above little mention has been made of biographies and critical studies of individual Western authors, with such notable exceptions as Smith's study of Mark Twain (who was not exclusively a Western author) and Hutchinson's biography of Eugene Manlove Rhodes. There is quite an assortment of these, but only a few can be recommended on the basis of merit. In addition, to date there have been three separate monograph series, the Steck-Vaughn Company Pamphlets on Southwest Writers, now all out of print, the Western Writers Series published by Idaho State University at Boise, Idaho, which is still in print and still on-going, and various volumes on Western writers in the on-going Twayne United States Authors Series. To a not altogether surprising degree the format for each respective monograph series is formulary and the quality of individual entries varies widely, from adequate to mediocre in the Steck-Vaughn series, from good to poor in the Idaho State University series, and from indispensable to unreliable in the Twayne series.

In the Steck-Vaughn series, *Eugene Manlove Rhodes: Cowboy Chronicler* (#11) by Edwin W. Gaston has no conclusion that is not a paraphrase of some previous critic and some plot ingredients are in error, e.g., claiming that Krumm in *The Proud Sheriff* (Houghton Mifflin, 1935) is "shot" when instead he is clubbed to death — minor points, perhaps, except that this is a problem that also plagues Gaston's *The Early Novel of the Southwest*. More generally praiseworthy are *Conrad Richter* (#14) by Robert J. Barnes, *A.B. Guthrie, Jr.* (#15) by Thomas W. Ford, and *Mary Austin* (#16) by Jo W. Lyday. *Harvey Fergusson* (#20) by James K. Folsom is probably the best criticism so far to appear on Fergusson, but as with William T. Pilkington in *Harvey Fergusson* (Twayne Publishers, 1975) an entire dimension is lost because neither critic was aware of Fergusson's distortions of Western American history and his penchant to create stereotypes rather than characters — although Folsom came closest to such a recognition when he observed about Fergusson's earlier novels that "we do not feel involved in the plight of his fictional people because we sense uneasily that they are not people so much as philosophical viewpoints."

No royalites are paid to authors who write pamphlets for the Western Writers Series from Idaho State, but it would be misleading to take this to indicate that the authors are more concerned with having a writing credit for the purpose of academic advancement than for any other reason. For a few this was obviously the case, but there are, conversely, a number of very fine entries, more in fact on an-author-for-author basis than is true for the Steck-Vaughn series. Especially noteworthy are some of the entries written by female critics, in particular *N. Scott Momaday* (#9) by Martha Scott Trimble, *Plains Indian Autobiographies* (#10) by Lynne Woods O'Brien, *Zane Grey* (#17) — actually quite the best criticism on him — by Ann Ronald, *Stewart Edward White* (#18) by Judy Alter, and *John G. Neihardt* (#25) by Lucile F. Aly. Also of exceptional quality is *George Frederick Ruxton* (#15) by Neal Lambert, literally the best introduction to his works to be found, as is *Jack Schaefer* (#20) by Gerald Haslam for Jack Schaefer, although in the instance of the latter one could wish that more time had been spent on some of Schaefer's short stories and that a filmography had been included. *Walter Van Tilburg Clark* (#8) by

L.L. Lee is less cluttered by clumsy, and ultimately questionable, metaphysical concepts as "sacrality" which characterize *Walter Van Tilburg Clark* (Twayne Publishers, 1969) by Max Westbrook.

The foregoing, however, is not to be interpreted as a complete dismissal of Westbrook's study of Clark, only his methodology, notwithstanding that Westbrook was inevitably prompted in this direction because Clark, as Frank Waters, belongs to the metaphysical tradition among American authors. In Westbrook's case it would have been to his advantage had he been even more knowledgeable in the philosophy of history, Kantian metaphysics, Jungian psychology, English and German Romanticism, and the modern study of mythology than he was; as it stands, his book *is* worth reading, but with extreme critical caution. Similarly worth reading, albeit with equal caution, is William T. Pilkington's *Harvey Fergusson* in the Twayne series. The same, however, cannot be said for Carlton Jackson's *Zane Grey* (Twayne Publishers, 1973), the excessive plot synopses many of which are often in error and even at times have misspelled character names. Robert L. Gale's *Luke Short* (Twayne Publishers, 1981) is the only book available on Short at present.

On the other hand, and to the extent that it pertains to Jack London's Northland fiction, Earle Labor's *Jack London* (Twayne Publishers, 1974) is a necessary adjunct to Andrew Sinclair's altogether admirable biography of London, *Jack: A Biography of Jack London* (Harper's, 1977). Despite the equally broad dispersion in the quality of biographical and critical studies of Western authors published other than in a series, among the very best to be mentioned are *Max Brand: The Big "Westerner"* (University of Oklahoma Press, 1970) by Robert Easton, *My Dear Wister — The Frederic Remington-Owen Wister Letters* (American West Publishing, 1972) by Ben Merchant Vorpahl, now out of print, and Vorpahl's *Frederic Remington and the West: With the Eye of the Mind* (University of Texas Press, 1978). What flaws G. Edward White's now out-of-print *The Eastern Establishment and the Western Experience: The West of Frederic Remington, Theodore Roosevelt, and Owen Wister* (Yale University Press, 1968) is the author's covert endorsement of too many strictly "Eastern" values and rather biased, unsubstantiated judgments such as condemning Geronimo as a "thoroughly vicious, intractable, and treacherous" savage. Unfortunately Oliver LaFarge never really comes to life in *Indian Man: A Life of Oliver LaFarge* (Indiana University Press, 1971) by D'Arcy McNickle, but McNickle's literary evaluations are sound for the most part. Perhaps the most charitable remark that could be made about Frank Gruber's *Zane Grey: A Biography* (World, 1970) is that it is an example of how a biography should *not* be written; the reader really knows very little more about Grey or his work after finishing the book than before he started it and, after praising *Riders of the Purple Sage* as his favorite Grey novel, Gruber proceeded to render an inaccurate plot synopsis of it.

It would seem nearly self-evident by now that Western fiction has finally come of age and that it does indeed represent a significant tradition in American literary history. It should not be too long any more before acknowledgment of this tradition will be reflected in a growing body of reliable, and even philosophically and spiritually challenging, literary criticism, literary biography, and a continuation of the achievements in literary history pioneered by Franklin Walker, Mody Boatright, and Margaret Duckett. It should, however, also be stressed — in view of the onslaught by the popular culture fadists mentioned above — that, as Northrop Frye remarked in *The Critical Path: An Essay on the Social Context of Literary Criticism* (Indiana University Press, 1971), "criticism is the theory of literature" and that one, ideally, ought to avoid "the impulse to find the ultimate meaning of literature in something that is not literature...."

Poets of the American West

by Margaret Marsh Anderson

I

Literary historians and critics have long debated if there is a body of poetry that can be called "Western." One major identifying characteristic that has been proposed is that the poetry must in some way be influenced by the land. The land ought to have been the inspiration for the poetry, or it may have fostered certain attitudes and personality traits, such as determination, self-reliance, independence, that are reflected in the poetry.

The earliest poetry of the West was probably the songs and ballads that expressed the joys and sorrows of the pioneers, riverboat men, trappers, and others, passed on as an oral tradition. Certainly early life on the frontier was not conducive to the writing of poetry — or culture in general. Most time was taken with the exigencies of survival. John Lomax was a folk musicologist of the early part of the Twentieth century. He traveled extensively throughout the United States collecting Western ballads and other folk music. His earliest published volume was *Cowboy Songs* (Macmillan, 1910) in which both "Get Along Little Dogie" and "Home on the Range" first appeared in print.

Among the earliest of published poets was William Davis Gallagher (included among his admirers was Edgar Allan Poe) who, in the 1830s, wrote Nature poems of strong descriptive power. He sought to promote the growth of literature on the frontier and in 1841 published *Selections from the Poetical Literature of the West* in which he included thirty-eight Western writers of rather conventional verse, leaving out the tedious "epic" poets and barbed satirists who were writing at the time.

Of particular interest in considering poets of the West would be poetry that uses the West as its locale, written by poets who spent part or all of their creative lives in the region. Among the poets of the early West that might fit this description was Bret Harte. Though remembered primarily for his short stories of life in the mining camps of the 'Forty-niners, he also wrote poetry. He lived in California when he was a very young man and his first book was an anthology of poems by California poets called *Outcroppings* (1865), followed two years later by a volume of verse called *The Lost Galleon and Other Tales*. Many of Harte's poems showed the same comic flair as his stories.

Joaquín Miller was a colorful character on the early literary scene. His given name was Cinncinnatus Hiner Miller, but he later took the name Joaquín in honor of the legendary Mexican bandit, Joaquín Murieta. He claimed to have been born in a covered wagon "pointing West." As a young boy Miller moved to Oregon, working for a time in the local mining camps and later as a pony express rider between Walla Walla, Washington, and Idaho. After he had gained some fame as a poet he spent some time in Europe where he was adopted by the literary set as a romantic representative of the rough and ready American West. In 1886 he went back again to California. Miller's poetry tended to be florid, wordy, and conventional.

In 1884 Charles F. Lummis walked from Cincinnati to Los Angeles. A fascinating account of this journey is found in *Charles F. Lummis: The Man and His West* (University of Oklahoma Press, 1975) by Turbesé Lummis Fiske and Keith Lummis. The rest of his life was spent in Southern California, with many trips of exploration throughout the American continent. His greatest interest was in the American Southwest. He wrote verse all his life, though he is chiefly remembered for his non-fiction. His first set of poems was called *Birch Bark Poems* (1879) and was printed on birch bark, "the loveliest page that ever poetry was printed on." A representative collection of his verse, *A Bronco Pegasus* (Houghton Mifflin, 1928), was published the year he died. Contemporaries of Lummis, also poets, were Henry Herbert Knibbs and the active Eugene Manlove Rhodes; the latter better known for his fiction, wrote at least thirty-two known poems.

John G. Neihardt, the poet laureate of Nebraska, had read Tennyson and Browning as a young boy which greatly influenced his later writings. He worked as an assistant to the Indian agent at Omaha Indian Reservation for many years, familiarizing himself with Indian customs, language, and lore. In 1908 he began a study of the American West and started work on a cycle of epic poems about the West which was not completed until 1949. Neihardt saw figures such as Jim Bridger and Sitting Bull as the equal of Homer's heroes. In the preface to "Song of Three Friends," one of the songs of the epic cycle, he said, "the heroic spirit, as seen in heroic poetry, we are told, is the outcome of a society cut loose from its roots, of a time of migrations, of the shifting of population." *The Cycle of the West* (Macmillan, 1949) is as long as the *Iliad* and the *Odyssey* — 16,000 lines in heroic couplets. Neihardt's literary style has been criticized for being too self-consciously Victorian, though his writings are characterized by a profound knowledge of the American Indian. It was as a writer of prose that he later distinguished himself, particularly *Black Elk Speaks* (Morrow, 1932) for which he served as amanuensis.

Charles E.S. Wood graduated from the United States Military Academy in 1874 and was assigned to frontier duty. He explored Alaska in 1876, participated in the Nez Percé campaign, and recorded Chief Joseph's surrender speech in the Montana territory in 1877. By 1884 he was practicing law in Portland, Oregon. Most of Wood's poetry deals with the West. *Poet in the Desert* (F.W. Baltes, 1915), set in the high desert of Southeastern Oregon and which he considered his best work, contains passages that evoke the desert's stark beauty.

H.L. Davis was born in Oregon in 1896 and worked as a sheepherder, cowboy, surveyor, editor, and deputy sheriff. Though best remembered for his fiction he considered himself primarily a poet. He wrote realistic and sensitive poetry of the Pacific Northwest at the time of his youth, and of homesteading in early Oregon. He is considered one of the best recreators of the past of the American West, winning the Pulitzer Prize in 1936 for his novel of early life in Oregon, *Honey in the Horn* (Harper's, 1935). A collection of his poetry, *Proud Riders and Other Poems* (Harper's, 1942), was published in 1942.

Robinson Jeffers settled in Carmel, California, when it was still unspoiled, open country in the early part of the Twentieth century. He wrote brooding poetry of great beauty and power, strongly influenced by the landscape of the craggy Pacific Coast. His first two volumes of poetry were traditional in form and subject, but after the Twenties he wrote only in free verse. He was called the advocate of disillusion. His work went through surges of popularity — after being universally acclaimed in the Twenties it was almost universally vilified in the Forties. Now his popularity is again on the rise. His poetry not only provides us with insight into the human condition, but also into the glory of the natural world. He is considered by many to be one of the finest American poets.

In more recent times many poets, including Thomas Hornsby Ferril, Winfield Townley Scott, William Stafford, and Gary Snyder (who was awarded the Pulitzer Prize for Poetry in 1975 for *Turtle Island* [New Directions, 1974]), have written and are writing evocative poetry that captures the sense of place that has long been a feature of Western poetry.

II

i

General Books on Poets

Fife, Austin and Alta, (eds.), *Ballads of the Great West* (American West Publishing, 1970) O.P.

In this anthology of folk and primitive poetry of the American West, the editors note that it is meaningless to try to separate this verse from ballads and songs, as many such poems have had a "dual life" in this respect. The book has a very entertaining and informative Introduction.

Hobson, Geary, (ed.), *The Remembered Earth: An Anthology of Contemporary Native American Literature* (University of New Mexico Press, 1981).

This is an excellent anthology, listed here because of the significant amount of poetry it includes and the interesting and informative Introduction by Hobson detailing some of the history of Native American literature and a discussion of its recent renaissance.

Howard, Helen Addison, *American Indian Poetry* (Twayne Publishers, 1979).

This can serve as an introduction to Native American poetry. It includes samples and discussion of style, subject matter, form, and rhythm. There are interesting sections of biographical material on the major translators and interpreters, including leading Western writer, Mary Hunter Austin.

Lomax, John A., and Alan Lomax (eds.) *Cowboy Songs* (Macmillan, 1952) O.P.

This is a compilation of ballads of the range, many with music, with brief interesting introductions.

Rusk, Ralph Leslie, *The Literature of the Middle Western Frontier* (Columbia University Press, 1925) O.P.; reprinted by the Greenwood Press.

A detailed study (two volumes) of Western literature through 1840, the date the author chose to regard as the close of the frontier period in this area. The chapter on poetry is of particular interest, especially because of its emphasis on very early Western poetry, such as that written by William Gallagher and others.

Walker, Franklin, *San Francisco's Literary Frontier* (Knopf, 1939) O.P.

This is an entertaining account of the literary history of San Francisco from 1848 to 1875. The author combined a social history and a group biographical approach, "preferring an inclusive continuity to a series of more or less detached biographies." Two of the literary luminaries treated here in some detail are Bret Harte and Joaquín Miller. The author concentrated on San Francisco as he felt this city was the focal point and literary capital of the huge frontier territory and "almost all important writers West of the Rockies, from Oregon to Arizona, sooner or later became identified with its literature." Especially pertinent is the chapter entitled "A Rash of Poetry." The book is illustrated with photographs of the writers.

Zolla, Elemire, *The Writer and the Shaman: A Morphology of the American Indian* (Harcourt, Brace, 1969), translated by Raymond Rosenthal.
    This book has excellent synopses of literature, fiction, nonfiction, songs, and poetry, about and by the American Indian from the late 1500s to the present and a history of their literature with commentary and criticism.

II

ii

Books about and by Specific Poets

Beilke, Marlan, *Shining Clarity: God and Man in the Works of Robinson Jeffers* (Quintessence Publications, 1977).
    This is an intensive study of Jeffers' work, interwoven with the events of his life. It also includes the never-before-published poem, "The Last Conservative."

Bennett, Melba Berry, *The Stone Mason of Tor House: The Life and Works of Robinson Jeffers* (Ward Ritchie, 1966) O.P.
    This detailed and fascinating biography of Jeffers was written by the friend, author, and critic chosen by Jeffers and his wife Una to serve as his biographer. It is illustrated with many early photographs of Jeffers and Una, family members, and places of significance.

Brower, David (ed.), *Not Man Apart: Photographs of the Big Sur Coast, with Lines from Robinson Jeffers* (Sierra Club, 1965) O.P.
    This breathtaking book has photographs of the Big Sur Coast by various photographers including Ansel Adams, Morley Baer, and Wynn Bullock, accompanied by lines from the poetry of Jeffers (and in some cases entire poems). It also includes a Foreword by noted naturalist and writer, Loren Eiseley, in which he wrote: "I cannot imagine him [Jeffers] as having arisen unchanged in another countryside. The sea-beaten coast, the fierce freedom of its hunting hawks, possessed and spoke through him. It was one of the most uncanny and complete relationships between a man and his natural background that I know in literature. It tells us something of the power of the Western landscape here at the world's end where the last of the American dream turned inward on itself."

Bryant, Paul T., *H.L. Davis* (Twayne Publishers, 1978).
     An entry in the Twayne United States Authors Series, this book has a
brief biography of Davis, followed by a study of representative poems, the
best of his short prose, and all five of his novels.

Davis, H.L., *Proud Riders and Other Poems* (Harper's, 1942) O.P.
     This is a comprehensive collection of Davis' poems with a section
called "Far Western Pastorals" (which includes a favorite of mine, the
poignant "Baking Bread"), and a group of narrative poems.

Ferril, Thomas Hornsby, *New and Selected Poems* (Harper's, 1952) O.P.
     This collection includes selections from an earlier book of Ferril's
poetry. In H.L. Davis' Introduction to this collection, he commented on
the influence of the plateau country of the Rocky Mountains on Ferril's
poetry and on Ferril's extensive knowledge of Western history. Carl Sandburg said of Ferril: "Reading T.H. Ferril you will find him often pure
crystal. Or again he may haunt you with horizon blurs in yellow dust and
green mist."

Fiske, Turbesé Lummis, and Keith Lummis, *Charles F. Lummis: The Man
and His West* (University of Oklahoma Press, 1975).
     This is a competent biography of the many-faceted Lummis. Begun
by his daughter and finished by his son at her death, the book is rich with
photographs and illustrations and Lummis' own accounts of his adventures
and associations with, among many others, Charles M. Russell, Theodore
Roosevelt, Harold Lloyd, Will Rogers, Eugene Manlove Rhodes, Edward
Borein, and Maynard Dixon.

Frost, O.W., *Joaquín Miller* (Twayne Publishers, 1967).
     An entry in Twayne's United States Authors Series, this book follows
the usual format of a brief biography and study of Miller's work organized
chronologically with emphasis upon the main themes of each successive
period of his writing career. The works most admired by his contemporaries are particularly stressed.

Harte, Bret, *The Complete Poetical Works of Bret Harte, Vols. I and II*
(Houghton Mifflin, 1912) O.P.
     Although long out of print, these two volumes contain all the poetry
Bret Hart published. Fortunately, many copies were sold and the volumes
remain easily accessible in libraries.

Jeffers, Robinson, *The Selected Poetry of Robinson Jeffers* (Random House,
1978).
     This book has never been allowed to go out of print and, as of 1978,
it was in its fifteenth printing.

Knibbs, Henry Herbert, *Riders of the Stars, A Book of Western Verse*

(Houghton Mifflin, 1916); *Songs of the Trail* (Houghton Mifflin, 1920); *Songs of the Lost Frontier* (Houghton Mifflin, 1930), all O.P.

These volumes constitute the mass of ballads and narrative poems by this contemporary of Charles F. Lummis and Eugene Manlove Rhodes. Knibbs was, unfortunately, a second-rate poet and his work has not stood the test of time.

Lummis, Charles F., *A Bronco Pegasus* (Houghton Mifflin, 1928) O.P.

This is a collection of Lummis' poetry. In his Introduction Lummis said the collection was to "gratify a natural desire to save the least unpardonable of my verse in the last half-century by the apologetic format of a 'sort of human' book of verse, divided up into epochs, interrupted by pictures and footnotes, and otherwise avoiding the smugness of dress which becomes the more ridiculous the more splindling the body within."

Marberry, M.M., *Splendid Poseur: Joaquín Miller, American Poet* (Crowell, 1953) O.P.

This remains a highly entertaining and amusing biography of the flamboyant "Poet of the Sierra." In an Afterword is a brief and intensely interesting section which presents the attitudes and reactions of many of the people who knew Joaquín Miller, e.g., Walt Whitman who said: "Miller is big, wholesome, does things his own way, has lived in the open, stands alone—is a real critter: I rate him highly." Many may not agree.

Miller, Joaquín, *Songs of the Sierras* (1871) O.P.

Most critics who are partial to Miller cite this volume as his best work.

Neihardt, John G., *The Cycle of the West* (Macmillan, 1949).

This edition contains all five of the epic cycles Neihardt worked on for over forty years.

Nolte, William H., *Rock and Hawk: Robinson Jeffers and the Romantic Agony* (University of Georgia Press, 1978).

This is perhaps the best scholarly study of Jeffers' poetry to appear so far. The author's evocative yet informed style is a distinct reading pleasure.

Snyder, Gary, *Riprap and Cold Mountain Poems* (Four Seasons Foundation, 1965); *The Back Country* (New Directions, 1968); *Turtle Island* (New Directions, 1974).

Snyder was awarded the Pulitzer Prize for poetry in 1975 for *Turtle Island* and ranks as one of the most important contemporary poets of the American West.

Stafford, William, *Stories That Could Be True: New and Collected Poems* (Harper's, 1977).

As Snyder, Stafford has gained a considerable reputation for his Western poetry.

Wood, Charles Erskine Scott, *Collected Poems of Charles Erskine Scott Wood* (Vanguard Press, 1949) O.P.

Although out of print this collection includes *The Poet in the Desert* and *Poems from the Range* and a thoughtful Foreword by Wood's wife, Sara Bard Field. Since the original editions of Wood's poems were very limited, this edition is the most accessible.

Artists of the American West

by Margaret Marsh Anderson

I

The art of the old West is narrative in form, accurate in representation, and evokes a sense of the land. It tells the story of the changes brought about in the land and its inhabitants by the inexorable Westward movement of white settlement. Artists of the American West were chroniclers of this changing landscape.

There is in Western art a unique blend of realism — a feeling of factual, historical documentation — and romanticism, symbolizing the spirit of the West. Though objective observation and authenticity of detail have been the major thrust, the myth of the West as a land of heroic figures comes through in the work of each generation of painters.

Two characteristics that have been attributed to Western artists are a passion to record the world around them and a spirit of adventure. "Art flourishes where there is a sense of adventure," philosopher Alfred North Whitehead once said. Certainly this is the case with the art of the American West. The vistas of grandeur and color, of action and danger and mystery, that come to us from the Western artists clearly convey this sense.

In 1819–1820 Major Stephen Long conducted an expedition of exploration to the Rocky Mountains. Along with him were Samuel Seymour and Titian Famsey Peale. They were among the first artists to venture West of the Mississippi. Their chief function was to document the journey, but

343

the drama of the subject matter must have made its impact. From that time on most government expeditions and many private ones took along artists serving much as photographers do today. This practice continued until the time field photography became more practical, about the turn of the century, coinciding with the close of the frontier.

The real history of art in the West began in the 1830s when a significant number of artists were working along the Missouri and beyond. One of the most important was George Catlin. In Philadelphia in 1824 he had seen a group of Indians passing through on their way to Washington. Thinking that they were doomed by advancing civilization, Catlin felt he had found the purpose he had been seeking — to be the historian of the Indians. In 1832 he wandered 2,000 miles up the Missouri River to the heart of the Northern plains, painting as he went. Catlin promoted the idea of a national park along the edge of the Rockies, a permanent sanctuary for Indians and native game animals of the West. He was often accused of being a sentimentalist regarding the Indians and because of his crusade in their behalf; yet his 600 paintings are the most complete pictorial record we have of Plains Indians in their natural state.

In 1833 Karl Bodmer spent a year along the Missouri making highly accurate drawings and watercolors of Indians. Later, in the 1840s, John Mix Stanley painted an Indian gallery from sketches made on his travels to California and the Pacific Northwest and with the Isaac Stevens Pacific Railroad survey. During that time Seth Eastman, a military man, also documented the life of the Indians with great realism and accuracy.

In 1836 artist Alfred Jacob Miller traveled with Scotsman William Drummond Stewart to the Rockies. He was the first to paint the Indians and scenery along the Oregon Trail. With his technique of rapid execution that was well suited to capturing action, Miller was the only artist to have depicted the wild and lively fur trappers' rendezvous. Miller was unique among early painters of the West in his portrayal of highly romantic, idyllic scenes.

George Caleb Bingham was the only artist of real significance to have grown up on the frontier. His paintings of the lower Missouri and Mississippi, done between 1845–1855, were of simple everyday life on the frontier — portraits, historical subjects, and scenes relating to America's rural and political life.

Since the mid Nineteenth century Western American painters have celebrated the rich natural heritage of the West. The land inspired not only the artists, but also, through their art, a sense of national pride. In 1869 the completion of the transcontinental railroad made the West accessible to everyone. By that time artists were traveling West in growing numbers and many began to see the changes that were brought about by an increasing population. There was a large market for paintings of the West made from sketches done on the scene.

Albert Bierstadt traveled to the Rocky Mountains with an expedition in 1859. From this and later travels to California he produced many works that gained national attention. Though in his paintings the already magnificent scenery of the Rockies and of the natural wonders of California became almost theatrical, Bierstadt was one of the painters who captured the grandeur of the American West and made our nation aware of it and desirous of going there.

In 1871, Thomas Moran accompanied F.V. Hayden's geological survey to the Yellowstone with photographer William Henry Jackson. Color, not then possible in photography, was considered crucial to collectors of Western landscapes. Moran despaired of capturing the colors, convinced they were beyond the reach of art. Nonetheless, he succeeded in breathtaking fashion. From this trip came the beautiful watercolor studies that were the most important factor in Congress' decision to set aside that portion of the West as a national park in 1872. In the same year Moran won acclaim as *the* painter of the American West with a seven-by-twelve foot oil of the Grand Canyon. Moran was considered the primary artist of the final decades of exploration.

Among the artists of note during the 1870s and 1880s were Thomas Hill, William Keith, and Henry Farny. Hill and Keith produced scenes of the grandeur of California. Farny painted memorable quiet scenes of Indian daily life.

Near the close of the frontier era many artists tended toward illustration. A form of realism seemed to have emerged based on accuracy and imaginative storytelling. Frederic Remington and Charles Marion Russell were the most celebrated artists of this closing phase.

Charles Russell was a cowhand in his teens and young manhood and was considered by his comrades to be "a ragged jester and good fellow." He was a self-taught, unorthodox painter whose works have a direct, hand-hewn quality. Many of his paintings have a twilight and sunset quality that adds to the feeling of vistas. Russell, as Remington, lamented the loss of the old ways of the West.

Frederic Remington has been both criticized for being "just a storyteller" and for being a romanticist and praised for his storytelling power and for his accuracy. He used bright sun and luminous shadow to dramatic effect. His direct artistic style in later years became more subjective and impressionistic, as if he felt, with the passing of the old West, that there was nothing more to report, only to remember. Remington's concept had been of the old West as a stronghold of purity, America as it should be.

Remington has been considered by many to be one of our major American painters because of his power of selection and sense of the significant. He has also been considered one of our foremost interpreters of the myths of the old West. More than once he has even been credited with creating the wild West. Many of his paintings, as well as those of Russell and other Western artists, planted the seeds that later influenced the imagery of Western filmmakers. Remington and Russell were painting at the turn of the century as the frontier era of the West drew to a close.

During the Nineteenth century the West had been seen as the land of the future. By the Twentieth it was being extolled as the heroic land of the past. The frontier has always fascinated America and the world. It has played a significant role in the world's concept of America, and America's concept of herself. Much that is considered most typically American can be traced to some degree to the influence of the West. Paintings of the old West are not only valuable as a pictorial record of the American land and people, but also as a reflection of the changing ideals and beliefs of Americans. The recent resurgence of interest in the art of the American West may have come not only as a wish to preserve images of a West gone by, but also as one of the ways of rediscovering, and re-evaluating, our nation's past and its impact on the present and the future.

II

i

General Books about Art and Artists

Broder, Patricia Janis, 50 Great Paintings of the Old American West (Crown, 1979).
 This is an extra, large-sized paperback poster book covering the works in roughly chronological order of forty-two Western American artists. The prints are all in color with short biographical sketches on each artist and a thoughtful Introduction is included.

Curry, Larry, The American West: Painters from Catlin to Russell (Viking Press in association with the Los Angeles County Museum, 1972).
 This is a book that accompanied an exhibition of early Western American artists. It has one color plate for each artist represented; the rest of the prints are in black and white. There is an excellent introductory section on the American West outlining the history of early Western art. A chronology of each artist is also included.

Czestochowski, Joseph, The Pioneers: Images of the Frontier (Phaidon, 1977).
 This extra large paperback has 109 illustrations (most in color) of paintings and sculpture over a two hundred year period dealing with pioneers and frontier life. Also included are notes on each plate, giving background information on the artist and the painting (that the notes are all in one section necessitates some awkward flipping back and forth), and an introductory overview.

Ewers, John C., Artists of the Old West (Doubleday, 1973).
 A lavishly illustrated book, this volume provides extensive biographies of twenty-two of the more important Western artists. A great many of the illustrations are in full color, some of them two-page spreads.

Harmsen, Dorothy, *Harmsen's Western Americana* (Northland Press, 1971).

This is a collection of 100 Western paintings, covering a span of 150 years (1821–1971) with biographical profiles of the artists. All pictures are color plates, but many, though printed in a large-sized book, are photographed in the frame and small in size, some only one-third of the page. An interesting Introduction gives the history of the Harmsen collection, plus a brief history of Western art.

Hassrick, Peter, *The Way West: Art of Frontier America* (Harry M. Abrams, 1977).

This book is a carefully researched and documented collection of frontier art with an introductory section and biographical studies of outstanding painters and sculptors of the pioneer West. There are 103 color plates and 130 black and white illustrations.

Hassrick, Royal B., *Western Painting Today: Contemporary Painters of the American West* (Watson-Guptill Publications, 1975).

A survey of America's leading contemporary painters of the West, this book contains short biographical sketches of the seventy artists covered. An interesting introductory section is followed by eighty black and white illustrations and forty-eight full-color plates.

Hogarth, Paul, *Artists on Horseback: The Old West in Illustrated Journalism, 1857–1900* (Watson-Guptill Publications, 1972).

Published in cooperation with the Riveredge Foundation, Calgary, Canada, this book details the experiences of eight British artist-reporters, called Specials, in America and Canada. A full chapter is devoted to each Special Artist's adventures in the New World, with over 200 illustrations in all.

McCracken, Harold, *Portrait of the Old West with a Biographical Check List of Western Artists* (McGraw-Hill, 1952).

This is an enjoyable book of sketches and paintings by early Western artists with biographical notes on the artists. It has 135 illustrations, forty of them in full color.

Rossi, Paul A., and David C. Hunt, *The Art of the Old West* (Knopf, 1971) O.P.

From the Collection of the Gilcrease Institute of American History and Art, this beautiful volume includes highly interesting historical material documented with hundreds of illustrations from the art of the old West. Over one hundred of the illustrations are in full color and some biographical information on the artists is supplied.

Taft, Robert, *Artists and Illustrators of the Old West, 1850–1900* (Bonanza Books, 1953) O.P.

This is a thorough study of the subject and, following the text, is an extremely extensive section (130 pages) on sources, notes, background information, etc., and another section with examples of the works (ninety-one in all) of thirty-five of the artists, though in small-sized, black and white reproductions.

II

ii

Books about Specific Artists

Baigell, Matthew, *The Western Art of Frederic Remington* (Ballantine, 1976) O.P.

There are forty-six color plates and several black and white illustrations in this fine collection of Remington's work. The book has an extensive introduction.

Catlin, George, *Letters and Notes on the Manners, Customs, and Conditions of North American Indians Written During Eight Years' Travel (1832–1839) Amongst the Wildest Tribes of Indians in North America* (Dover Books, 1973).

This fascinating two-volume set of Catlin's works, with over 250 photographic reproductions of Catlin's paintings plus numerous sketches and six color plates, well deserves its imposing title. Earlier editions of these books are often found in the rare book section of university libraries, so it is a pleasure to see them as affordable paperbacks. Photographic reproductions of Catlin's paintings were, of course, not possible when the first edition came out (1844) and this makes this edition even more of a treasure. Marjorie Halpin provided an informative Introduction.

Christ-Janer, Albert, *George Caleb Bingham: Frontier Painter of Missouri* (Harry N. Abrams, 1975).

A sumptuous "picture-book" and biography designed to display Bingham's best paintings and drawings, this book contains a selection of Bingham's writings and biographical material. Many of the plates are in full color.

Clark, Carol, *Thomas Moran: Watercolors of the American West* (University of Texas Press, 1980).

A brief biography of this remarkable painter with extensive sections given to the history of the paintings, the book is illustrated with sixty of Moran's watercolors, ten in color. The book accompanied an exhibition in 1980 of these works by the Amon Carter Museum of Western Art.

Denver Art Museum, *Frederic Remington: The Late Years* (Denver Art Museum, 1981).

A superb paperback collection of the later works by this remarkable artist, the text discusses the paintings and the development of Remington as an artist from 1890 through 1909. These beautiful later paintings clearly show Remington's genius with light — flickering firelight, moonlight and its shadows, blazing sun — painted in a much more impressionistic style than his earlier paintings. The book has an Introduction by Peter Hassrick, director of the Buffalo Bill Historical Center, Cody, Wyoming.

Hendricks, Gordon, *Albert Bierstadt, Painter of the American West* (Harry N. Abrams, 1974).

Published in association with the Amon Carter Museum of Western Art, this handsome and interesting biography of Bierstadt is illustrated with photographs, sketches, early works, and sixty full-color plates.

Ladner, Mildred, *O.C. Seltzer: Painter of the Old West* (University of Oklahoma Press and Thomas Gilcrease Institute of American History and Art, 1979).

A detailed biography of this contemporary and friend of Charles Russell is to be found in this enjoyable book containing 115 black and white illustrations and thirty-eight color plates.

Linderman, Frank Bird, *Recollections of Charley Russell* (University of Oklahoma Press, 1963).

This is an entertaining account of Linderman's experiences with Charles Russell and remains one of the best portraits we have of Russell.

McCracken, Harold, *The Charles M. Russell Book* (Doubleday, 1957); *George Catlin and the Old Frontier* (Dial, 1959) O.P.

This extraordinary biographical portrait of the colorful life of the cowboy artist includes 180 of Russell's drawings and thirty-five full-color paintings. It is a beautiful book that is also a pleasure to read.

George Catlin and the Old Frontier is a highly interesting and detailed biography of one of the first documentary artists of the old West. Containing 165 illustrations (thirty-six in color), it is a good supplement to Catlin's own memoir (see above).

McDermott, John Francis, *George Caleb Bingham, River Portraitist* (University of Oklahoma Press, 1959) O.P.; *Seth Eastman: Pictorial Historian of the Indian* (University of Oklahoma Press, 1961) O.P.

George Caleb Bingham is a thorough and well written biography of Bingham divided into three sections that deal with the country where he spent his boyhood, a narrative of his career, and an evaluation of his work. It is illustrated with Bingham's works, though none are in color.

An interesting biography of the artistic career of this vigorous painter who gave us, in the author's words, "the homely truth of the Indian world," *Seth Eastman* is illustrated with 116 illustrations, eight of them color plates.

Renner, Frederic G., *Charles M. Russell: Paintings, Drawings, and Sculpture in the Amon G. Carter Collection* (University of Texas Press, 1966) O.P.

     A descriptive catalog of Russell's works can be found in this collection, many in color, with a biographical section on Russell and interesting and informative "biographies" of the sketches, paintings, and sculptures.

Vorpahl, Ben Merchant, *Frederic Remington and the West: With the Eye of the Mind* (University of Texas Press, 1978).

     This is the best biography and analysis of Remington's work so far to appear.

Wilkins, Thurman, *Thomas Moran: Artist of the Mountains* (University of Oklahoma Press, 1966) O.P.

     While this is a thorough and interesting biography of Moran, and although it contains some illustrations of his work, it is mounted on a small scale and has been superseded by Carol Clark's study (see above).

Western Films

by Jon Tuska

I

The Western film made its debut very early with the release of *The Great Train Robbery* (Edison, 1903) directed by Edwin S. Porter. This film was the first narrative Western, a reel in length lasting eight minutes. It established a basic plot structure that would be used frequently in subsequent Western films: crime, pursuit, retribution. In 1903, D.W. Griffith started directing one-reel Western films for Biograph release and G.M. Anderson, who had had four roles in *The Great Train Robbery*, went presently into production of one-reel Westerns. With the purchase from author Peter B. Kyne of screen rights to Kyne's fictional character Broncho Billy, Anderson initiated what were the first personality Westerns, films with an identifiable star which were regularly released according to a fixed annual schedule. It was this innovation which most significantly influenced Western film production for the next several decades and which gave birth to the notion of the movie cowboy, an actor identified exclusively with the Western roles he played in a series of films. Within time, these actors used their personal names on screen as well as off, implying that they were indeed much the characters they were portraying. It is impossible to be actually a one-dimensional movie cowboy hero and the contradiction of being known far and wide for supposedly being a fantasy that could never exist in the non-make-believe world brought nearly all of these performers

351

to personal ruin. On the other hand, it was easy for the public to believe that these movie cowboys were really what they appeared to be in their films because in nearly all cases the movie cowboys themselves believed it, even if they had to hide from the public as well as from themselves the terrible consequences of this collective pretense.

While "Broncho Billy" Anderson was starring in his film series, D.W. Griffith, joined by another producer/director, Thomas H. Ince, continued to produce *story* Westerns. The story Western, in contrast to the personality vehicle, put more emphasis on the events being dramatized than on the character of the hero. *The Battle at Elderbush Gulch* (Biograph, 1914), perhaps Griffith's best Western film, is concerned with settlers besieged by Indians only for them to be rescued at the last minute by the U.S. Cavalry. Griffith was generally indifferent to Native Americans whereas Ince in his productions often tended to be somewhat sympathetic. *The Invaders* (Bison, 1912), for example, which starred Francis Ford, elder brother of film director John Ford, remains one of Ince's more stirring Westerns in which Native Americans are shown to be largely victims of white American expansionism. It must be stressed, however, that if the story Western lacked the unifying identity of a recognizable movie cowboy, both kinds of Western films were subject to similar social and historical, in short *fantastical*, interpretations of just what was presumably the meaning of the American frontier experience. These fantasies not only did not change significantly in Western films from decade to decade, but, as in the preponderance of Western American fiction, the stories and plotlines most often fell into the categories of the formulary Western or the romantic historical reconstruction. Accurate historical reconstructions as to period, people, and place have been even more of a *rara avis* in Western films than, correspondingly, they have been in Western fiction.

The Squaw Man (Paramount, 1914) directed by Cecil B. DeMille was the first Western feature film. It was based on a successful New York stage play and starred Dustin Farnum, who had played the role on stage. The same year DeMille also produced and directed the first screen version of Owen Wister's novel *The Virginian* (Paramount, 1914), again with Dustin Farnum in the lead. The popular response to feature-length Westerns which these films occasioned brought about an inevitable change. While Westerns of one and two reels continued to be made, toward the end of the Teens the major thrust in Western film production was toward features.

William S. Hart, who began making films while under contract to Thomas H. Ince, was intent on portraying the American West differently on screen than had so far been the case, commencing with a brace of two-reelers and his first feature Western, *The Bargain* (Mutual, 1914). What this came to in practice was that Hart stressed melodrama, sentimentality, and an almost morbid righteousness in depicting his Western heroes. The same year that Hart made *Hell's Hinges* (Triangle, 1916), a morality play with a strong temperance theme, the first Western chapter play was released. *Liberty, A Daughter of the U.S.A.* (Universal,

1916), which starred Jack Holt. Harry Carey, whose career had begun at Biograph being directed by D.W. Griffith, also starred in a series of personality Westerns for Universal in the late Teens. Among Carey's directors was John Ford and Ford's first Western feature, *Straight Shooting* (Universal, 1917), starred Carey and had Hoot Gibson as a second lead. The Carey Westerns, as the Hart vehicles and to an extent the Broncho Billy Westerns, emphasized austerity and virtue, not glamor. It took Tom Mix to change all this.

Although Mix had started his career with the Selig Polyscope Company in 1910, it was not until he had signed with the Fox Film Corporation and after several two-reelers began appearing in Western features filled with dash and racy stunts that his popularity soared. It was also about this time that formulary Western fiction by such popular authors as Zane Grey and Max Brand began influencing Western film production. Fox Film Corporation bought film rights to several of Grey's novels and brought them to the screen, in the late Teens with William Farnum starring, in the mid Twenties in remakes with Tom Mix starring, and in the early Thirties in more remakes with George O'Brien starring. For a time Zane Grey himself headed his own film production company, finally selling out to Paramount in the early Twenties. Paramount customarily brought at least two, and sometimes more, of his stories to the screen in any given year, often with Jack Holt in the leading role. Max Brand's first Western novel was filmed as *The Untamed* (Fox, 1920) and starred Tom Mix. Yet, with fabulists such as Grey and Brand for inspiration, the cinematic Western became, if anything, even more formulary and romantic than it was before and further removed from the realities of Western history. Meanwhile, in a retrograde movement, Tom Mix and Paramount with its Zane Grey series stopped filming Westerns in Southern California, as had for so long been the standard procedure, and went on location throughout the Western states to scenic areas of breathtaking beauty. These locations tended to be lyrical and even epical of themselves, notwithstanding the plotlines which remained wholly predictable. Some fifty years later, viewing these films one is able to see what the American West once looked like, and, indeed, what it had looked like in the Nineteenth century, long before campers, urban sprawl, and sub-divisions drastically altered so much of the topography.

Perhaps the fundamental premise of all Western films during this period was the unequivocal belief that mankind could readily be divided into two groups, those who are among the elect through the grace of God and those who are reprobates and were doomed from the predestination of souls at the beginning of time. The dress code for Western films increasingly exemplified this ideology. It was also self-evident that no matter what might have happened in the rest of the world, in the United States it had become the destiny of virtue to be always triumphant—or, put more cynically, what was triumphant was to be universally regarded as virtue.

The strongest incentive toward increased Western production in the Twenties came about as a consequence of the box-office impact of Western "epics" such as *The Covered Wagon* (Paramount, 1923) directed by James

Cruze and *The Iron Horse* (Fox, 1924) directed by John Ford. The kind of Westerns Hart and Carey had been making fell quickly into disfavor and, if not a Western with epic numbers of players, the least to be expected was a film with a flashy personality or a light-hearted approach. Because Tom Mix was the most popular Western player of the decade, a wide assortment of imitators sprang up, running the whole gamut from the comic Westerns of Hoot Gibson, who became a star in his own right at Universal, to the spectacular essays in horsemanship starring Ken Maynard at First National and Tim McCoy at Metro-Goldwyn-Mayer, to the more pedestrian low-budget efforts with movie cowboys such as Jack Hoxie and Buck Jones. The same year that Tom Mix appeared in a remake of Zane Grey's *Riders of the Purple Sage* (Fox, 1925), William S. Hart made his farewell to the screen in his so-called "epic," *Tumbleweeds* (United Artists, 1925), a film which when compared with the Mix Westerns seems already old-fashioned and excessively sentimental.

    Wanderer of the Wasteland (Paramount, 1924), based on a Zane Grey novel and starring Jack Holt, introduced a novelty that was slow to win acceptance: it was the first Western feature filmed entirely in a two-color process. An innovation with more immediate repercussions was the coming of sound and many were convinced that this would bring about generally the demise of the outdoor drama. Even though *In Old Arizona* (Fox, 1929) directed by Raoul Walsh and starring Warner Baxter in the role of the Cisco Kid (for which Baxter won an Academy Award) was the first all-talking Western and enjoyed a good reception, producers were still reluctant to invest in the sound equipment necessary to film out of doors. King Vidor directed a total fantasy called *Billy the Kid* (M-G-M, 1930) which starred Johnny Mack Brown and which was also a success; but Raoul Walsh's effort at a sound Western "epic," *The Big Trail* (Fox, 1930), with new-comer John Wayne proved a flop. *Cimarron* (RKO, 1931) was directed by Wesley Ruggles and won an Academy Award for Best Picture. They were, however, ambiguous barometers. It was not until Tom Mix launched a new series of sound Westerns at Universal, beginning with *Destry Rides Again* (Universal, 1932) based on a Max Brand novel, that confidence was completely restored. Budgets were increased in the production of competing series, a number of new series were begun, and presently Ken Maynard, Hoot Gibson, Buck Jones, Tim McCoy, Bob Steele, Tom Tyler, and numerous other stars of silent series were to be found riding the celluloid plains portraying virtuous heroes protecting imperiled young ladies from clearly identifiable villains.

    There had always been a fantasy element in the personality Western, but in the Thirties this trend intensified in a new way that was only possible because of the addition of sound recording. It was a short but decisive step from the image of the Western hero, shy and bashful in the heroine's presence but more than a match for any challenge of gun, or rope, or horsemanship, or fists, to a cowboy figure who did not need gun, rope, horsemanship, or fists, who conquered instead with a song.

    Gene Autry made his screen debut in *In Old Santa Fe* (Mascot, 1934), a Ken Maynard Western. While Maynard had included songs in his Westerns as early as 1929 and Bob Steele had sung a number of songs in *Oklahoma Cyclone* (Tiffany, 1930), these were musical interludes in an action Western format. Autry was primarily a singer; in fact, he scarcely knew how to ride and, compared with other movie cowboys of that time, he had neither the stature nor the physical appearance associated with a Western hero. All of this to one side, with his emergence the screen found a new prototype. Autry in a film such as *Red River Valley* (Republic, 1936) could get day laborers to work for no pay by singing to them; in *Mexicali Rose* (Republic, 1939) he could prompt a bandit to reform by singing to him; and by the time he made *The Cowboy and the Indians* (Columbia, 1949) this "philosophy" was extended to deal with massive social problems and Autry is seen to solve the plight of reservation Indians by riding up to their shacks and hovels with wagons loaded with presents, singing "Here Comes Santa Claus."

What may now seem utter lunacy became standard fare in personality Westerns for more than two decades. A whole new breed of cowboy hero arose, singing cowboys such as Roy Rogers, Tex Ritter, Fred Scott, and, after World War II, Monte Hale, Rex Allen, and a dozen others. During the war, in the case of the Roy Rogers vehicles, the musical production numbers became so elaborate that these films can be regarded more as Western musicals than musical Westerns. Simultaneously, the budget, or "B," Western continued to promote new action stars who did not sing, such as Charles Starrett and Bill Elliott, although here, likely as not, the hero would be supported by a singing sidekick or by some sort of song-making ensemble, the Sons of the Pioneers in the case of Starrett's early films, or Tex Ritter who joined variously Bill Elliott and Johnny Mack Brown in a number of their series Westerns. Smiley Burnette, who began as Gene Autry's "stooge," branched out eventually on his own and was frequently teamed as the musical component with a straight action star, co-starring with Sunset Carson (whose career proved short-lived) in one series and Charles Starrett in dozens of Starrett's films in the late Forties.

There were series Westerns that were not dominated by music-making, most notably Harry Sherman's Hopalong Cassidy series starring William Boyd and based on characters created by Clarence E. Mulford, the Three Mesquiteer series based on characters created by William Colt Mac-Donald, and the long-lived Zane Grey series. But here, as often in major Western productions such as John Ford's *Stagecoach* (United Artists, 1939) which made John Wayne a star, a song or musical interlude because of the Autry phenomenon was almost obligatory. Budget Westerns continued to be produced throughout the Forties and into the Fifties before television took over (see the section on Television Westerns), but with lower and lower budgets, an increasing and, finally, almost total reliance on stock footage from previous productions, and the shoddiest production values. Nonetheless there remained a following for these films, particularly among children and in rural areas, and even actors who customarily played villains in them achieved a devoted following of sorts.

The aftermath of World War II proved to have a propitious effect on the production of major Westerns. To be sure, most of these films were still convenient, self-congratulatory, reassuring fantasies in which Americans (or any viewer from any country) through identifying with John Wayne, Randolph Scott, Joel McCrea, and others could dream about the grandeur of winning the West and continue to ignore the price that "winning" had exacted in the extermination of the Native American way of life, the racism rampant on the frontier, the greed which led to constant bloodshed, the decimation of the buffalo, the destruction of free land, the failure of the Homestead Act of 1862, the rape of natural resources, the pollution of so much natural beauty. These new major Westerns, no less than the low-budget variety, continued to foster the delusion that somewhere, if only in the imagination, there was a West that, while it might resemble the physical and historical American West, was fundamentally different; for here evil was always still clearly discernible; and even if the heroes might have too much self-doubt to be heroic in every case, right and virtue ultimately triumphed. The dress code was altered to permit women increasingly to wear tight pants — actress Peggy Stewart once told me that she resented having her backside to the camera in Westerns more often than her face — only for these same heroines to recognize finally that they were no match for the villains and they must switch to dresses before the heroes could save them, or right after they had been saved. The many attempts that were made to justify the genocide of the Indian nations were clumsy and unrealistic at best, such as going to the extreme of remaking the anti-Nazi film, *Sahara* (Columbia, 1943), as *Last of the Comanches* (Columbia, 1953) with the Indians playing the same roles the Germans had in the earlier film.

John Ford was foremost among those directors in the sound era who tried to raise the stature of the Western film from the level of fantasy to that of myth, without ever really succeeding. *Stagecoach* was in fact his first sound Western and it remains a classic of its kind, albeit in the Bret Harte tradition, i.e., there is good in the heart of an outcast. The same year Ford brought *Drums Along the Mohawk* (20th–Fox, 1939) to the screen, his first color film. He directed no more Westerns until *My Darling Clementine* (20th-Fox, 1946), a remake of *Frontier Marshal* (Fox, 1934; 20th-Fox, 1939) which, as its two previous screen incarnations, was based on Stuart N. Lake's specious biography of Wyatt Earp. Ford continued the trend of attempting to make the Earp brothers and Doc Holliday into men of heroic proportions. The gunfight at the O.K. corral was highly and inaccurately dramatized. The actual historical gunfight took approximately thirty seconds; Ford's version takes considerably longer on screen.

In the late Forties Ford began directing his remarkable series of Westerns combining his love for Roman Catholicism and heavy drinking with a nearly mystical treatment of Western fantasies, showing the West as John Ford would have wanted it to have been. The first of this new group, the first of Ford's essays in apologetics for the Indian campaigns, and the first of what has come to be known commonly as Ford's Cavalry trilogy was

Fort Apache (RKO, 1948). It was followed by *She Wore a Yellow Ribbon* (RKO, 1949) and *Rio Grande* (Republic, 1950); in the latter two Ford cast John Wayne as an aging, sympathetic Cavalry officer. André Bazin, among the French critics, cited this trilogy as supposedly marking Ford's political rehabilitation of the Native American, when, in fact, nothing could be further from the truth. Ford knew nothing about Native Americans and was basically contemptuous of them. He chose to locate his Westerns in Monument Valley, on the Navajo reservation, and had whatever tribe the script called for—Apaches, Kiowas, Comanches, Cheyennes—played by Navajos.

Ford's *Wagonmaster* (RKO, 1950) was a formulary Western rife with melodrama. It was followed by *The Searchers* (Warner's, 1956), a film which introduced a somber tone into his previously rather nostalgic view of the West. While *The Searchers* has come to be considered a cult film by many critics and even filmmakers who like its staginess and remarkable photography, in terms of its influence-value it was by far Ford's most vicious anti-Indian film. His idea of comedy had one of the white characters kick a squaw out of bed; white captives of the Comanches were depicted as having gone hopelessly insane as a result of their captivity. The view of the Comanches in Ford's *Two Rode Together* (Columbia, 1961) was, if anything, even more racist, with star James Stewart describing their life-style as brutish and their speech as "grunts Comanche." In *Two Rode Together* Ford showed more white captives of the Comanches, reduced to groveling animals, while many of his Comanches obviously preferred simulated Mohawk hairpieces to their traditional hair styles. Apologists for Ford's racism point to his films as being myths, not renderings of actual historical events, rather after the mode of one of the characters in *Two Rode Together* who comments, concerning his wife, "If I can give her comfort in a lie, God won't kick me out of heaven." What all of Ford's apologists seem to forget is that Native Americans are not mythical and that the lies told about them in these films could scarcely be expected to engender any greater social and cultural understanding.

Ford's enthusiasm for portraying his heroes as military men intensified in such films as *The Horse Soldiers* (United Artists, 1959), *Sergeant Rutledge* (Warner's, 1960), and the "Civil War" segment which he directed for *How the West Was Won* (M-G-M, 1962). In *Sergeant Rutledge* Ford went so far as to try to gain viewer sympathy for a black horse soldier accused of rape and murder—of which he is ultimately proven innocent—by showing how he would pause and help kill Indians while under military arrest rather than attempt to escape. Moreover, by way of an illustration of Ford's cavalier attitude, Woody Strode, the black actor he cast as Sergeant Rutledge, he later cast in the role of Stone Calf, the Comanche war chief in *Two Rode Together*. It did not matter, however, whether Strode was playing a black or an Indian; when on location for a John Ford picture, the outhouses were segregated without distinction: whites and non-whites.

Cheyenne Autumn (Warner's, 1964), Ford's last Western, was clearly a disappointment in which Ford felt compelled to have the Cheyennes prove immediately successful in their 1,500-mile trek to their homelands rather than to tell the truth which was certainly to be had in the Mari Sandoz book on which the film was based. The biggest absurdity in the picture was the characterization of Secretary of the Interior Carl Schurz, played by Edward G. Robinson. At one point, he stands before a framed portrait of Abraham Lincoln asking it, "Old friend, old friend, what would you do?" What he decides to do in the picture is to come out to the Black Hills and give the Cheyennes their reservation. What he did in history—according to *U.S. Congress* 46th. 2nd session. Senate Report 708—was to say, "the Indians should be taken back to their reservation," by which he meant taken back to Indian territory from whence they had fled.

Ford's weaknesses as a director of Western films were of two kinds. Ideologically he couched his racism behind a facade of apparent paternalism, something John Wayne began to imitate. Dramatically, his penchant for excessive sentimentality, low comedy, and stereotypical, brawling male characters tended to create films which now seem slow and at times rather dull. These defects are partially offset, however, by his masterful use of outdoor locations, pictorial splendor, and images of memorable composition and beauty. Perhaps the most rewarding aspect of many of his Westerns is the portrayal of human friendship, certainly of itself one of the most important social factors in the Westward expansion.

The tendency toward Western films with increased verisimilitude and somewhat subdued heroics characterized the contribution of Howard Hawks in his six cinematic efforts at filming frontier stories. "*Quand j'ai fait Red River* [United Artists, 1948]," he was once quoted in the film journal *Cahiers du Cinéma*, "*j'ai pensé que l'on pouvait faire un western adulte, pour grandes personnes, et non pas un de ces quelconques 'cowboys'....*" [when I made *Red River*, I though that it might be possible to make an adult Western, for mature people, and not one of those about mediocre cowboys]. Hawks' last three Westerns, *Rio Bravo* (Warner's, 1959), *El Dorado* (Paramount, 1967), and *Rio Lobo* (National General, 1970)—which, as *Red River*, starred John Wayne—resemble Ford's films in the stress placed on friendship and, in a sense, repudiate the despair concerning American society to be found in such Westerns as *High Noon* (United Artists, 1952) directed by Fred Zinnemann, *Silver Lode* (RKO, 1954) directed by veteran Allan Dwan, and *3:10 To Yuma* (Columbia, 1957) directed by Delmer Daves.

Daves, incidentally, represented a strong counter-thrust to John Ford's romanticism and his Westerns simulated (without really possessing) a documentary look. Daves' *Broken Arrow* (20th-Fox, 1950) which cast white Jeff Chandler as Cochise is still a memorable attempt to portray a friendship between an Anglo-American and a Native American based on mutual respect. Although it might be claimed with some justification that *Broken Arrow* was romanticized in a different way than the majority of Westerns, much of this vanished in Daves' subsequent *Drumbeat* (Warner's, 1954). In all of Daves' Westerns, his principal characters are interlocked segments of the economic community of the West—ranchers in *Jubal* (Columbia, 1956), cattle drovers in *Cowboy* (Columbia, 1958), and miners in *The Hanging Tree* (Warner's, 1959); and it is this quality which makes Daves' *The Last Wagon* (20th-Fox, 1956) a better treatment of a wagon train theme than Ford's effort in *Wagonmaster*.

Henry King continued the trend toward glamorization of frontier outlaws and killers which directors as King Vidor had begun in the early Thirties. King's *Jesse James* (20th-Fox, 1939), notable for its stunning photography, is a highly fanciful treatment of the James gang. The film proved so successful that Fritz Lang directed a sequel the next year titled *The Return of Frank James* (20th-Fox, 1940). Perhaps King's most memorable Western remains *The Gunfighter* (20th-Fox, 1950) which with its black and white photography harked back to the look cinematographer Gregg Toland achieved in *The Westerner* (United Artists, 1940) directed by William Wyler. In *The Gunfighter* Gregory Peck played a gunman weary of having to live with his reputation; the elements are the same as those in many a William S. Hart film, but King altered the tone to fit the sense of isolation and social paranoia of the post-war United States. William Wyler, on the other hand, who began his career directing "B" program Westerns at Universal and who made *Hell's Heroes* (Universal, 1930) early in the sound era, in such films as *Friendly Persuasion* (Allied Artists, 1956) and *The Big Country* (United Artists, 1958) tried unsuccessfully in every way but financially to amplify the formulary plot of good guys vs. bad guys to epic proportions.

Between such Western romances as *Robin Hood of El Dorado* (M-G-M, 1936), based on the life of fictional bandit Joaquín Murieta, and *Buffalo Bill* (20th-Fox, 1944) a film tainted by blind hero-worship (which he later regretted having made), William Wellman directed *The Ox-Bow Incident* (20th-Fox, 1943) based on the novel by Walter Van Tilburg Clark. Wellman, by pondering the motives behind human violence, accomplished in film what Clark accomplished in Western fiction, creating a morally ambiguous climate in which black and white morality vanishes to be replaced by the spectre of universal guilt. The only Western Wellman was to direct later which approached the raw power and psychological depth of *The Ox-Bow Incident* was the thoughtful and introspective *Yellow Sky* (20th-Fox, 1948).

Another veteran director who, as John Ford, did his best to romanticize the West was Raoul Walsh. Following films I have already mentioned such as *In Old Arizona* and *The Big Trail*, Walsh cast John Wayne in *The Dark Command* (Republic, 1940), a slick, formulary production with all the emphasis on action. In *They Died with Their Boots On* (Warner's, 1941), with Errol Flynn cast as General George Armstrong Custer, Walsh reinforced the trend to glorify Custer as a hero which continued to be a Western film convention. John Miljan is wholly admirable as Custer in Cecil B. DeMille's *The Plainsman* (Paramount, 1936) as is Ronald Reagan in Michael Curtiz' *Santa Fe Trail* (Warner's, 1940), and this image is more or less preserved intact in such films as Roy Rowlands' *Bugles in the Afternoon* (Warner's, 1952), Sidney Salkow's *Sitting Bull* (United Artists, 1954), Joseph H. Lewis' *7th Calvalry* (Columbia, 1956), and Robert Siodmak's *Custer of the West* (ABC, 1968), with only an occasional dissenting voice such as Arthur Penn's *Little Big Man* (National General, 1970) which attempts, perversely, to depict Custer as a vainglorious lunatic. Walsh directed *Pursued* (Warner's, 1947), a Western in the *film noir* style, and followed it with several interesting films such as the moody *Colorado Territory* (Warner's, 1949), *Distant Drums* (Warner's, 1951), and *The Tall Men* (20th-Fox, 1955), all of which embody an adept sense of pacing, breakneck action, and sharp characterization, although the plots are strictly formulary.

What Arthur Penn did to the image of Custer is more or less typical of his screen work. He was anti-historical in a reverse way to the self-congratulatory impulse of the majority of directors of Western films. Penn's first Western, *The Left-Handed Gun* (Warner's, 1958), perpetuates through its title the erroneous notion, originally caused by reversing a photo negative of a surviving full-figure photograph of Billy the Kid wearing a gunbelt, that the Kid was left-handed. Paul Newman portrayed the Kid as a sullen, silent, anguished, and haunted neurotic. A good many of the characters in Penn's Westerns, as a matter of fact, are mentally ill, or entire communities suffer from a mass psychosis. In Penn's *The Missouri Breaks* (United Artists, 1976) a bounty hunter is depicted as a transvestite psychotic while the protagonist, as the sheriff in Penn's *The Chase* (Columbia, 1966), recognizing his impotence to fight corruption turns his back on it instead and leaves.

"A Western," director John Sturges once said, "is a controlled,' disciplined, formal kind of entertainment. There's good and bad; clearly defined issues; there's a chase; there's a gunfight." In the instance of Sturges' *Gunfight at the O.K. Corral* (Paramount, 1957), the famed gunfight lasts five minutes on screen and required forty-four hours to film; beyond this, all of the events leading up to the confrontation, and during it, are inaccurately presented. Sturges' subsequent *Hour of the Gun* (United Artists, 1964) begins with the O.K. corral gunfight, staged somewhat differently but still inaccurately, and then goes on to falsify most of the events which took place after the shooting stopped. All of which raises an issue usually avoided in nearly all of the criticism written about Western films. Even granting Sturges' definition as to the ideal contents of a Western film, why choose actual historical characters and force their lives and times to fit into these romantic or formulary molds? By distorting or whitewashing or blackwashing, in a word in *lying* about the historical past is some constructive purpose achieved?

The answer generally offered is that every culture needs its national mythology, its gods and heroes. Julius Caesar claimed descent from Aeneas who, in turn, was supposedly descended from Anchises and Venus. It is therefore argued that Americans naturally have come to regard Jesse James as a Robin Hood figure in the old West and Billy the Kid as a protector of innocent women and children. Films with plots such as *The Searchers* are no different than films with plots such as *Jesse James Meets Frankenstein's Daughter* (Embassy, 1966) and *Billy the Kid vs. Dracula* (Embassy, 1966) save in the *quality* of the myth-making. If, as Count Joseph de Maistre once wrote, "...*le véritable vainqueur, comme le véritable vaincu, c'est celui qui croit l'être*" [the true victor, as the truly vanquished, is he who believes himself to be the victor], then it is the same with historical personalities; they are whatever we today wish them to have been: they have no historical reality because there is no historical reality. "Day by day and almost minute by minute the past was brought up to date," George Orwell wrote in *1984* (Harcourt, Brace, 1949). "In this way every prediction made by the Party could be shown by documentary evidence to have been correct; nor was any item of news, or any expression of opinion, which conflicted with the needs of the moment, ever allowed to remain on record. All history was a palimpsest, scraped clean and reinscribed exactly as often as was necessary." For Orwell, the constant rewriting of history served a political purpose; no doubt, in connection with the Western film, the falsification of the past is far more complex, but, perhaps, in the end, no less ominous in its psychological and social implications.

Sturges' *The Magnificent Seven* (United Artists, 1960), based on a Japanese samurai film, inspired a number of sequels, none of which was directed by Sturges; but, again, it proved that the formulary plot ideas from another culture could be easily translated into the American West. John Huston displayed an attitude no less audacious than that of Sturges when he directed *The Unforgiven* (United Artist, 1960) which rivals John Ford's *The Searchers* as an unusually vicious anti-Indian film; nor is it insignificant that both the Huston and Ford films were based on novels by Alan LeMay. However, it should be observed with reference to Huston that in his Westerns — including *The Treasure of Sierra Madre* (Warner's, 1948), *The Misfits* (United Artists, 1961), and *The Life and Times of Judge Roy Bean* (National General, 1973) — the main thrust is concerned primarily with the flawed, at times corrupted, natures of the characters and with the sources of corruption in society and, in these terms, the Western settings of his films are artistically irrelevant.

The Western films of Henry Hathaway and Anthony Mann are more difficult to assess. Hathaway began his directorial career in the early Thirties directing remakes of silent Zane Grey Westerns at Paramount, of which *Wild Horse Mesa* (Paramount, 1933) was the first. Although these films never quite equalled the original versions, entries such as *Man of the Forest* (Paramount, 1933) and *The Thundering Herd* (Paramount, 1934) have solid story values and impressive locations. To Hathaway must go the credit for directing the first outdoor sound Western to be filmed in color, *The Trail of the Lonesome Pine* (Paramount, 1936), and he went on to direct two of the most outrageously sentimental and romantic Westerns produced in the early Forties, *Brigham Young — Frontiersman* (20th-Fox, 1940) and *Shepherd of the Hills* (Paramount, 1941). It was not really until Hathaway directed films such as *Rawhide* (20th-Fox, 1951) and *From Hell to Texas* (20th-Fox, 1958) that it became fully apparent just how much attention he was paying to atmosphere and character, as well as to the creative use of authentic locations. *From Hell to Texas*, as *High Noon* and George Stevens' *Shane* (Paramount, 1953), employs a plot which is common to a number of Westerns over the years, namely the slow building up of a tense situation which finally compels the thitherto peace-loving hero to lash out in violence, killing the villains only after exhausting every other possible response to their evil and having been consistently frustrated. That violence, indeed, is sometimes the only solution to social problems is also affirmed in Hathaway's *The Sons of Katie Elder* (Paramount, 1965) and *True Grit* (Paramount, 1969), both films comprising John Wayne's best screen work other than the Westerns in which he appeared directed by Ford and Hawks.

Anthony Mann is another story. In the notable group of Westerns he directed during the Fifties, he explored more probingly and more intelligently than many of his contemporaries the problem of human evil. The context of the American frontier provided him, it would seem judging by his films, a unique opportunity to observe the motives and effects of violence. Mann's protagonists, as those of Hathaway, are often at war with their own pasts and are generally forced into renewed violence against their wills. But there is a difference. Mann's villains, unlike those in most Westerns, embody an evil that delights in savagery for its own sake and they are seldom motivated simply by greed or the will to power. Particularly noteworthy among Mann's Westerns are those with James Stewart as the protagonist, *Winchester '73* (Universal, 1950), *Bend of the River* (Universal, 1952), *The Naked Spur* (M-G-M, 1953), *The Far Country* (Universal, 1955), and *The Man from Laramie* (Columbia, 1955), although *Man of the West* (United Artists, 1958), starring Gary Cooper, is probably Mann's best Western film. Equally worth seeing are *The Last Frontier* (Columbia, 1955) which features Victor Mature as a semi-savage who wants to become a Cavalry soldier and *The Tin Star* (Paramount, 1957) with Henry Fonda which, more than any other Mann Western before it, deals with the folly of denying the reality of evil.

After a series of rather routine Westerns in the early Fifties, toward the end of the decade Budd Boetticher made a remarkable series of Westerns with Randolph Scott as the star. Produced by Harry Joe Brown, with scripts in many cases by Burt Kennedy, Boetticher's films feature Scott as an isolated hero, bleak as the landscape through which he rides and determined on a course of action through some outrage perpetrated against him in the past. The metaphor of life as a bullfight is a recurring theme and, through it, Boetticher who had once been a professional matador could make his flamboyant villains more violent and sympathetic; and, although the hero does eventually triumph, the victory is always anticlimactic to the ritual of the struggle. At times, indeed, the hero's behavior can border on the ludicrous, as it does in *Buchanan Rides Alone* (Columbia, 1958). In Boetticher's words, his characters "decide to do something because they want to do it. If they get killed on the way — and most of them do — it is because their desire cannot be accomplished without a struggle." While his framework would not have held up indefinitely without itself becoming formulary, it nonetheless produced several exceptional Western films that retain a peculiar power and appeal. If Boetticher is to be criticized for anything, it would be the frivolous way in which he treated Native Americans. In *Comanche Station* (Columbia, 1960), the Comanches wear Mohawk hair styles and inhabit the area around Lone Pine, California, where they never went; but in this film he was nowhere as severe as John Ford in dealing with the supposed consequences of Indian captivity.

Two directors whose names are not usually associated with Western films but each of whom has nevertheless directed important Westerns are Richard Brooks and Sydney Pollack. Brooks certainly deserves recognition for *The Last Hunt* (M-G-M, 1956) which, based on the novel of the same title by Milton Lott, remains the only film even to attempt to deal intelligently with the waste of the buffalo while both his *The Professionals* (Columbia, 1966) and *Bite the Bullet* (Columbia, 1975) were filmed at visually remarkable locations and are concerned with characters who have been as much shaped and formed by the land on which they live as by any other influence. Also, in the latter two films, Brooks stressed the fundamental interdependence of human beings, pulling together for the common good or pulling together to destroy, a theme with which Sydney Pollack dealt somewhat differently principally because in his Westerns the balance with Nature is a constant which all men must somehow maintain and which, when they violate it, can and generally does lead to their ruin. Nowhere is this more apparent than in *Jeremiah Johnson* (Warner's, 1972), but it was already anticipated in the earlier *The Scalphunters* (United Artists, 1969). Both of these films are to be further commended for the perceptiveness with which they portray Native Americans. Pollack obviously went to great lengths in his preproduction research and it shows on the screen.

The focus on villainous characters in Budd Boetticher's later Westerns was elaborated by Sam Peckinpah in films such as *The Deadly Companions* (Pathé-American, 1961), which has many other similarities with Boetticher's work, *Ride the High Country* (M-G-M, 1962), and *The Wild Bunch* (Warner's, 1969). However, this does not imply a more historically accurate portrayal of people or times, as is best illustrated by Peckinpah's fantasy about *Pat Garrett and Billy the Kid* (M-G-M, 1973). As Daves and Boetticher before him, Peckinpah determined to make Westerns that constituted a departure from the sentimental romanticism of John Ford, while laying an even heavier stress on the atmosphere of violence. All three can be said to have dealt with the theme of isolation to varying degrees, but for Peckinpah it became disorientation and, finally, rejection; his principal characters do not belong in the time in which they find themselves and, ultimately, can do nothing about it except die.

Burt Kennedy's first directorial effort at a Western was *The Canadians* (20th-Fox, 1961), a Northern with a standard Western plot. Kennedy's highly developed sense of humor was evident in his screenplays for Boetticher, but left unchecked, as it was in his own Westerns, it tended to weaken them. In such films as *Support Your Local Sheriff* (United Artists, 1969), the Western setting is irrelevant to the comedy, whereas *Dirty Dingus Magee* (M-G-M, 1970) is an outright disaster surpassed only by *Hannie Caulder* (Tigon British, 1971) with Raquel Welch cast improbably as a semi-nude bounty hunter.

Sexuality intruded into the prepubescent mentality of Western films in pictures such as Howard Hughes' *The Outlaw* (RKO, 1943), in terms of story another Billy the Kid fantasy, and was carried to further extremes by King Vidor in David O. Selznick's production of *Duel in the Sun* (Selznick, 1947), although both seem rather tame when compared to *Hannie Caulder* or a good many more recent Westerns. In this regard, Sam Peckinpah's *The Ballad of Cable Hogue* (Warner's, 1970), however inaccurate it may be and however fanciful, remains a touching love story in which the Western setting plays an intrinsic role.

In the Sixties, Clint Eastwood found himself a major box-office attraction as a result of appearing in a number of Westerns produced in Europe and directed by Sergio Leone. *A Fistful of Dollars* (United Artists, 1966), the first in the series, has almost no plot, but it is a mechanically contrived vehicle permitting Eastwood to shoot and maim his way through the picture (although he is badly beaten up himself by the heavies at one point) and, as its successors, seems to have as its *raison d'être* making a showcase of violence of every kind. These films completely dehumanize the protagonists and, it would appear, drew their popularity with audiences from this very circumstance. How else, indeed, would one explain the failure in the United States of *Once Upon a Time in the West* (Paramount, 1969), a Leone film which combines, in contrast, a muted violence with touchingly human scenes such as the first meeting between Claudia Cardinale and Jason Robards, Jr., and similar moments of poetic drama?

While the distinction for having directed the highest grossing Western in film history still goes to George Roy Hill for *Butch Cassidy and the Sundance Kid* (20th-Fox, 1969), a romantic view of theft and outlawry to say the least, on the more positive side there was also a laudable tendency in some recent Westerns to question the values of American society and Manifest Destiny, films such as Martin Ritt's *Hombre* (20th-Fox, 1967), Tom Gries' *Will Penny* (Paramount, 1969), Ralph Nelson's *Soldier Blue* (Avco-Embassy, 1970), William Fraker's *Monte Walsh* (National General, 1970), Richard Winner's *Lawmen* (United Artists, 1971), Peter Fonda's exceptional *The Hired Hand* (Universal, 1971), and Cliff Robertson's *J.W. Coop* (Columbia, 1972). *Buck and the Preacher* (Columbia, 1972), directed by its star, Sidney Poitier, is noteworthy for its compassionate treatment of blacks and Indians on the frontier, while Robert Altman made two exceedingly interesting forays into social criticism of American success myths in *McCabe and Mrs. Miller* (Warner's, 1971) and *Buffalo Bill and the Indians* (United Artists, 1976).

In summary, then, more Westerns have been produced by

American filmmakers than any other kind of generic film between 1903 and the present time. Any genre that has so dominated film production cannot help but engender heated argument, preferences, and critical disagreements. There are those who confessedly want Western fantasies and formulary Westerns instead of historical reconstructions despite the fact that fantasies and romances may indeed only further the already incredible American reliance on falsehood. In the Western, however, this tendency toward falsehood is uniquely dangerous because the subject matter of Western films is *not* the product of fantasy. It is lamentable that for so many the fantasies embodied in Western films — about Native Americans, about women, about old people, about young people who refuse to conform, about Mexicans and other "foreigners," about the supposed nature of heroism and villainy — have come to replace all cognizance of a greater social, psychological, and historical reality.

II

The following list of Western films is intended to be a representative selection, providing some sense of the growth and development of the Western as a form of entertainment, as the embodiment of an emerging national legendry, and — albeit only very, very rarely — as a commentary on the meaning and significance of the American historical past. This is not, however, a listing of my favorite Western films or of what, in my opinion, are the best Western films. It will prove most useful if these titles are viewed in chronological order.

1. *The Great Train Robbery* (Edison, 1903) directed by Edwin S. Porter.
   The first narrative Western.
2. *The Invaders* (KayBee-Bison, 1912) credited as having been directed by Thomas H. Ince.
   The conflict between white settlers, the Cavalry, and the Indians is depicted with more sympathy than was generally the case before it and for a long time after it.
3. *The Battle at Elderbush Gulch* (Biograph, 1914) directed by D.W. Griffith.
   A more typical view of the conflict between the Indians and the encroaching white men, with the Cavalry riding to the rescue at the last moment.
4. *The Squaw Man* (Famous Players-Lasky, 1914) directed by Cecil B. DeMille.
   The first feature-length Western film and the first feature film produced at Hollywood, California. The point is made that the white man's civilization is far superior to that of the Native American.
5. *Wagon Tracks* (Famous Players-Lasky, 1919) directed by Lambert Hillyer.
   This film has better production values than most of William S.

Hart's earlier Westerns and, unlike films such as *Hell's Hinges* (Triangle, 1916), it is not super-charged with distracting religious pretensions. The story-line involves an early use of the incident whereby an Indian is inopportunely killed by a member of a wagon train and the Indians demand a white life for his life, with Hart, although innocent, volunteering.

6. *The Covered Wagon* (Famous Players-Lasky, 1923) directed by James Cruze.

This was the screen's first attempt to film a Western "epic" which, in reality, means that there is *more* of everything and everything is shown on a vaster scale, even if the basic conflict is retained between hopelessly bad men and an unmistakably good man (unmistakably good, that is, to everyone but the heroine, who tends to be somewhat dim-witted by comparison).

7. *The Iron Horse* (Fox, 1924) directed by John Ford.

This second effort to film an "epic" relied on a different set of clichés. Ford emphasized Irish humor, Irish brawling, Irish drinking — as he did in nearly all of his films — but against a lavish background of building a railroad. The Indians, somewhat predictably, are raging savages and are led by Fred Kohler, cast as a white man. It has been a truism since the Declaration of Independence that Indians generally require white leadership.

8. *Tumbleweeds* (United Artist, 1925; Astor, 1939) directed by King Bagott.

William S. Hart's attempt to film an "epic" had fewer interesting characterizations than either Cruze's or Ford's effort, while possessing all the usual ingredients of Hart's sentimental screen style. The great land rush sequence, however, remains impressive and Hart's spoken introduction (for the reissue in 1939) is expressive of his emotional commitment to his kind of Western filmmaking.

9. *The Vanishing American* (Paramount, 1925) directed by George B. Seitz.

Zane Grey shocked readers when he ended the serialization of *The Vanishing American* with his Navajo marrying the blonde, blue-eyed schoolteacher, so he had to change it for the book edition and Nophaie dies at the end. He does the same in the film, which is further simplified to the point where the majority of problems between whites and Indians is reduced to the connivings of a crooked Indian agent. The film is well produced, however, and was exceedingly influential for many years.

10. *The Great K & A Train Robbery* (Fox, 1926) directed by Lewis Seiler.

Just how effective the combination was of Tom Mix' ebullience, continuous action with breathtaking stunts, and the backdrop of stunning natural beauty in terms of location can be seen in this film. It has a charm all its own, even if its plot is totally conventional, pitting a wholesome hero against greedy villains.

11. *The Virginian* (Paramount, 1929) directed by Victor Fleming.

This is the best screen version of Owen Wister's novel (which Wister also adapted for the stage), largely because of Gary Cooper's reserved performance in the leading role. Cooper removed some of the self-righteousness from the character of the Virginian; enough so, in fact, that it is even possible to like him.

12. *Billy the Kid* (M-G-M, 1930) directed by King Vidor.

This film marked the beginning of the effort to make heroes of both the Kid and the man who killed him, Pat Garrett. It manages it by having Garrett let the Kid and his girl slip across the border to happiness with Garrett ineffectually shooting at him. By contrast in *Billy the Kid* (M-G-M, 1941) directed by David Miller the Kid out of guilt wants to be shot down by a lawman. In *The Outlaw* (RKO, 1943) directed by Howard Hughes the Kid escapes with Jane Russell to a life of happiness in seclusion. In *The Left-Handed Gun* (Warner's, 1958) directed by Arthur Penn the Kid is profoundly neurotic and his death is a psychic martyrdom. In *Pat Garrett and Billy the Kid* (M-G-M, 1973) directed by Sam Peckinpah the Kid is a necessary sacrifice Garrett has to make in selling out to the Establishment. *Dirty Little Billy* (Columbia, 1972) directed by Stan Dragoti does not make a hero of the Kid in any way, but the film lacks a coherent story-line and adequate characterization. In addition to these more notable contributions to the Billy the Kid legend, both Bob Steele and Buster Crabbe appeared in "B" series about the Kid in which he is basically an altruistic do-gooder. From this it was only a short step to films such as *The Law vs. Billy the Kid* (Columbia, 1954) directed by William Castle in which Billy is forced to take the law into his own hands because the law is represented by evil and corrupt men, and on to *Billy the Kid vs. Dracula* (Embassy, 1966), and even beyond that to *Chisum* (Warner's, 1970) in which John Wayne, playing the title character, proves himself to be a better man than either Garrett or the Kid. Before watching any of these films, I urge reading Ramon F. Adams' *A Fitting Death for Billy the Kid* (University of Oklahoma Press, 1960) and Leon C. Metz' *Pat Garrett: The Story of a Western Lawman* (University of Oklahoma Press, 1974).

13. *Rider of Death Valley* (Universal, 1932) directed by Albert Rogell.

This is among the very best Tom Mix Westerns which survive from either the silent or the sound era, although it is somewhat lacking in the stunting for which Mix became so well known; instead, it is a film of remarkable imagery, effective use of locations, and well-etched characterizations.

14. *The Last Outlaw* (RKO, 1936) directed by Christy Cabanne.

Based on a story by John Ford which Ford himself directed at Universal in the Teens but not with the same stars as in this remake, Harry Carey and Hoot Gibson, the film is a singularly moving depiction of the variance in values between the old West and modern times (circa, 1936) as well as a strong evocation of male friendship. RKO had the negative to this film shredded in the Forties and I saved it by having a new negative struck from John Ford's personal 35mm. nitrate print.

15. *Stagecoach* (United Artists, 1939) directed by John Ford.

Ford's first sound Western and, at least in my opinion, the best Western he ever directed, although, in one sense, the plot owes more than a little to themes used by D.W. Griffith in *The Battle at Elderbush Gulch* and by Ford himself in his early rendering of *The Outcasts of Poker Flat* (Universal, 1919). Taken as a whole, *Stagecoach* is an apt embodiment of both Ford's attempt to mythologize the old West and of the values he liked to pretend were particularly Western in nature and which found their truest expression when in a Western setting.

16. *Jesse James* (20th-Fox, 1939) directed by Henry King.

When Fred Thomson made *Jesse James* (Paramount, 1927), its *apologia* for the James gang caused such a wave of protest that the film proved to be Thomson's finish at the box office. Yet twelve years later *Days of Jesse James* (Republic, 1939) was released without a murmur, starring Roy Rogers and featuring Donald Barry as a wronged Jesse. What made this latter picture possible, and so many which have followed since, was the appearance and the wide acceptance accorded Henry King's version. By casting then-popular Tyrone Power as Jesse and Henry Fonda as Frank James, King more than stacked the deck in favor of his whitewashing interpretation. King claimed to have thoroughly researched the lives of the James brothers; but, if he did, little of the historical reality made it to the screen. A necessary prerequisite before viewing any cinematic narrative concerning the James gang and its activities would be to read William A. Settle's *Jesse James Was His Name* (1966; University of Nebraska Press, 1977). The King version was still in vogue as recently as *The Long Riders* (United Artists, 1980) directed by Walter Hill. Perhaps all that this demonstrates may be that Carl Sandburg was right when he said "Jesse James is the only American bandit who is classical, who is to this country what Robin Hood or Dick Turpin is to England, whose exploits are so close to the mythical and apocryphal."

17. *Santa Fe Trail* (Warner's, 1940) directed by Michael Curtiz.

This was the third Western Errol Flynn made under Curtiz' direction—*Dodge City* (Warner's, 1939) and *Virginia City* (Warner's, 1940) preceded it. It is especially notable for its distortion of history with Flynn as J.E.B. Stuart and Ronald Reagan as George Armstrong Custer, raising again the question that *Billy the Kid* and *Jesse James* and so many other Westerns pose: why were (and are) these distortions of historical events deemed necessary and what psychological and political significance do they have?

18. *The Westerner* (United Artists, 1940) directed by William Wyler.

Niven Busch, who worked on the screenplay, related the story of how he would take new pages of the script and read them to star Gary Cooper, figuring Cooper knew more of Western lore, terrain, and

history than he did. Stuart N. Lake, who did so much to make a legend of Wyatt Earp (see entry 21 below), provided the original story
which is a gross romanticization of Judge Roy Bean. What makes
this Western interesting is its characterizations, particularly the relationship between Cooper and Walter Brennan as Bean; although it
would be prudent to read C.L. Sonnichsen's *Roy Bean: Law West of
the Pecos* (Devin-Adair, 1958) before viewing either this film or the
even more inaccurate *The Life and Times of Judge Roy Bean* (National General, 1972) directed by John Huston. To begin with, it is
not recorded that Bean, according to Hollywood "the hanging judge,"
ever hanged anybody.

19. *They Died with Their Boots On* (Warner's, 1942) directed by Raoul
Walsh.

Taking up, in a fictional sense, where *Santa Fe Trail* left off, in
this film Errol Flynn was cast as George Armstrong Custer, and it is the
most notorious of the cinematic efforts to make a hero and martyr of
the man who believed, in his words, that in the Native American we
find "the representative of a race ... between which and civilization
there seems to have existed from time immemorial a determined and
unceasing warfare" and "a *savage* in every sense of the word."

20. *The Ox-Bow Incident* (20th-Fox, 1943) directed by William Wellman.

This film is by no means a substitute for reading the fine novel
by Walter Van Tilburg Clark on which it was based, but it does make
an interesting contrast with it. The condemnation of the notion of
frontier justice — so long associated with Western films and which, if
anything, became more emphatic than ever in the Sixties and Seventies
in such films as *Hang 'em High* (United Artists, 1968) directed by Ted
Post — is still vitally contemporary in its social ramifications. The
stage-bound sets which can be so annoying when viewing *The Westerner* or John Ford's *The Man Who Shot Liberty Valance* (Paramount, 1962) in the instance of this film tend to amplify and complement the psychological atmosphere and allegorical nature of the story.

21. *My Darling Clementine* (20th-Fox, 1946) directed by John Ford.

Frontier Marshal (Fox, 1934) directed by Lewis Seiler was the
first film to be made based on Stuart N. Lake's *Wyatt Earp: Frontier
Marshal* (Houghton Mifflin, 1931); its star is George O'Brien, an actor
whom John Ford first cast in a leading role in *The Iron Horse*. It was
remade a second time under the same title, *Frontier Marshal* (20th-
Fox, 1939), directed by Allan Dwan and this time starring Randolph
Scott as Wyatt. Ford's film was the third make based on Lake's book.
I recall John Ford telling me how, in his early days as a director at
Universal, Wyatt Earp would frequently stop by the set and tell him
about events from his past life such as the gunfight at the O.K. corral
(it was actually some distance away from the corral). Ramon F.
Adams in *Burs Under the Saddle* (University of Oklahoma Press, 1964)
remarked rightly that Lake's "book leaves out all the shady incidents
of Earp's life and does everything possible to glorify him. One wonders

if such a man is human: a fabulous and invincible hero, a man who could do [no] wrong, a man who never lost a conflict, a man without fear or fault, a man who could make notorious gunmen quake with fright." Wyatt Earp himself was not entirely to blame; he tried to have published an accurate biography, but no publisher would contract for it. Ford, of course, would not have been impressed with the truth, even had he known it; he was unmoved by objections I raised regarding the manner in which he depicted the gunfight with the Clantons; he was, he felt, providing Americans with a tangible heritage of heroism in which to believe. "Did you like the film?" he asked, and when I said I did, *as a film*, he responded, "What more do you want?" By way of an answer to the reader, I would suggest reading *I Married Wyatt Earp: The Recollections of Josephine Sarah Marcus Earp* (University of Arizona Press, 1976) collected and edited by Glenn G. Boyer, paying special attention to Boyer's Epilogue. He had some of his facts wrong about the 1939 version of *Frontier Marshal*, but taken as a whole this book remains the best we have so far on Earp's *entire* life. For a somewhat negative view, there is Frank Waters' *The Earp Brothers of Tombstone: The Story of Mrs. Virgil Earp* (1960; University of Nebraska Press, 1976), necessarily augmented by Adams' corrections in *Burs Under the Saddle* for this book, Lake's biography, and for Walter Noble Burns' *Tombstone: An Iliad of the Southwest* (Doubleday, 1927). Finally, insofar as he was concerned, I would recommend Pat Jahns' *The Frontier World of Doc Holliday: Faro Dealer from Dallas to Deadwood* (1956; University of Nebraska Press, 1979). I do not doubt that Ford felt an historical personality was more credible as a hero. However, it does not have to be this way. Will Henry romanticized Wyatt Earp in his novel, *Who Rides with Wyatt* (Random House, 1955), and yet when it was adapted for the screen and filmed as *Young Billy Young* (United Artists, 1969) directed by Burt Kennedy, the screenplay, also by Kennedy, preserved many of the incidents and characters from the novel while making them wholly fictitious in name as well as in deed, and, consequently, somewhat more palatable. Over and above all of this, however, Ford's film is extremely well mounted, charming, and dramatically effective. It is an example of notable filmmaking, whatever reservations one must have about it as accurate history or biography, or its ideology.

22. *Red River* (United Artists, 1948) directed by Howard Hawks.

Hawks told me it was his intention in making this film to emphasize the conflict between generations and that he felt John Wayne was at his best playing an older man. So, evidently, have the film's viewers ever since, including first of all John Ford who remarked, after seeing *Red River*, that prior to this picture he had not thought "that big sonofabitch could act." Following *Red River*, Ford himself began casting Wayne as an older man, most notably in Westerns such as *She Wore a Yellow Ribbon* (RKO, 1949) and *Rio Grande* (Republic, 1950). *Red River*, after all this time, still remains one of the finest —

if not *the* finest — cattle-drive Westerns ever made and its characterizations, compositions, and *mise-en-scène*, its humor, pathos, and humanity constitute a remarkable achievement; critics, at any rate, appear to be unanimous in declaring it Howard Hawks' finest Western.

23. *The Gunfighter* (20th-Fox, 1950) directed by Henry King.

According to William MacLeod Raine in *Famous Sheriffs and Western Outlaws* (Doubleday, 1929) when President Theodore Roosevelt offered Bat Masterson the job of being United States Marshal of Arizona, Masterson declined. "'If I took it.'" Raine reported Masterson to have said, "'inside of a year I'd have to kill some fool boy who wanted to get a reputation by killing me.'" Although that has since been the plot of many a Western novel and film, no one perhaps has handled the subject as well as Henry King did in this film. Gregory Peck appears to have been aptly cast as the world-weary gunfighter and Richard Jaeckel turns in an admirable performance as the youthful gunslinger envious of the older man's reputation. Darryl F. Zanuck, the film's producer, once told me, and Henry King subsequently confirmed it, that it was Zanuck's idea for *The Gunfighter* to be filmed in black and white in order to create much the same atmosphere William Wellman generated in *The Ox-Bow Incident*. As an accompaniment, I would suggest reading Eugene Cunningham's *Triggernometry* (1934; Caxton Printers, 1941) along with Ramon F. Adams' notes on it in *Burs Under the Saddle*, as well as Joseph G. Rosa's *The Gunfighter: Man or Myth?* (University of Oklahoma Press, 1964).

24. *High Noon* (United Artists, 1952) directed by Fred Zinnemann.

In contrast with either *The Ox-Bow Incident* or *The Gunfighter*, *High Noon* is *not* a tragedy. Its basic story-line is to show how the sheriff played by Gary Cooper is able by stubbornly persisting, when the chips are down, to compel his Quaker wife, played by Grace Kelly, to join him in taking up arms and killing the bad guys. Gregory Peck was first offered the role, but turned it down due to its similarity with his previous role in Henry King's film. What still makes this Western worth viewing is the economy with which the story is told, the way dramatic tension is sustained, and the effective use of a ballad to carry a film which, quite frankly, without it would not have excited very much attention, either initially or subsequently. It certainly contributed to Gary Cooper's performance as a desperate, anxiety-ridden man to have been suffering, as he was, from a bleeding ulcer during the filming.

25. *Shane* (Paramount, 1953) directed by George Stevens.

"Of the serious Westerns of the Fifties," Ralph Brauer wrote in his essay "Who Are Those Guys? The Movie Western During the TV Era" reprinted in *Focus on the Western* (Prentice-Hall, 1974), "*Shane*, *The Gunfighter*, and *The Left-Handed Gun* are usually cited as among the best. Jon Tuska of *Views & Reviews* said on his *NET* documentary 'They Went Thataway' that he thought *Shane* ... was *the* best Western. Perhaps it is indicative of our respective generations that Tuska picked for his choice what I consider a nostalgic vision while I would pick the more violent *The Wild Bunch* [Warner's, 1969; see entry 40 below]." I dislike being heretical, but personally I find neither *Shane* nor *The Wild Bunch* to my taste. However, what I did say in the above-mentioned documentary was that if I were asked to choose from all the Westerns that had been made prior to 1969 one that was the most representative of the Western genre itself, it would be *Shane*. I have found no reason to alter that opinion, despite the passage of time. I also agree with Brauer that what *Shane* imparts, most of all, is a feeling of nostalgia, a romantic feeling of loss concerning an ideal period in time which, in reality, never existed at all, but filmed in such a realistic style—a brutal fistfight, the powerful impact of a bullet, the crudity of life in the West, and the rather terrifying spaciousness—that it is almost believable.

26. *Drumbeat* (Warner's, 1954) directed by Delmer Daves.

I opt for this film as opposed to Daves' earlier and critically more acclaimed *Broken Arrow* (20th-Fox, 1950) because Daves himself felt *Drumbeat* to be his best Western, because he wrote the screenplay, and because all of the distortions and misrepresentations of the Modoc War incorporated in it can and must be compared with historical accounts such as Keith A. Murray's *The Modocs and Their War* (University of Oklahoma Press, 1959) in order to assess the validity of Daves' claim at the beginning of the film that it is a true "historical" account. Dialogue that occurred between Hooker Jim and Albert B. Meacham is given to Captain Jack and General Canby; Jack is totally misrepresented, as are most of the other characters and events; and the film ends, instead of showing the removal of the Modocs to Indian Territory, with the sentiment, "among the Indian people, as among ours, the good in heart outnumber the bad."

27. *Johnny Guitar* (Republic, 1954) directed by Nicholas Ray.

It became fashionable in the Fifties for women to undergo something of a transformation in a number of Westerns, most notably Barbara Stanwyck's portrayals in *Cattle Queen of Montana* (RKO, 1954) directed by Allan Dwan, *Forty Guns* (20th-Fox, 1956) directed by Sam Fuller, and *The Maverick Queen* (Republic, 1957) directed by Joseph Kane, Marlene Dietrich's role in *Rancho Notorious* (RKO, 1952) directed by Fritz Lang, and Joan Crawford's portrayal in this film. Women in these Westerns dress more as men, although their clothes are so tight-fitting as to call more attention than ever to their figures; women in these films at the beginning usually behave as male stereotypes and dominate men, running successful ranches or saloons; but by the fade, invariably, they have to be saved by a man, or at least fall under the spell of a man and have to admit they are somehow still the weaker sex. This ideological transformation was never really that far removed from, say, the dress code established for women by films such as *The Desperadoes* (Columbia, 1943) directed by Charles

Vidor, but at least in *Johnny Guitar* Nicholas Ray managed to tell his story, for almost everyone who has seen it, with a powerful and haunting imagery.

28. *The Searchers* (Warner's, 1956) directed by John Ford.

John Wayne was cast as Ethan Edwards, a name change from the Amos Edwards character in the Alan LeMay novel and a change which denotes how the screenplay modified the original character to remain consistent with John Wayne's screen persona; Amos in the novel dies, whereas in the film, in the words of J.A. Place in her Master's thesis which was published under the title *The Western Films of John Ford* (Citadel Press, 1974), "Ethan Edwards is perhaps Ford's most ambiguous character. In him are all the qualities that make a Western hero—strength, individualism, self-sufficiency, leadership, authority." These are all more or less admirable qualities, especially when stated in this fashion. It is only when a viewer has become sensitive to the way the Comanches are misrepresented and exploited in this film that one might expect another series of words would come to be used to describe the Ethan Edwards' character, fanaticism, not strength, monomania not individualism, alienation not self-sufficiency, obsessionalism not leadership, dogmatism not authority. At any rate, a more enlightened view of the film can be had by reading LeMay's *The Searchers* (1954; Gregg Press, 1978) and then contrasting it with Benjamin Capps' *A Woman of the People* (Duell, Sloan, 1966) and Matthew Braun's *Black Fox* (Fawcett, 1972) and, added to this, *The Comanches: Lords of the South Plains* (University of Oklahoma Press, 1952) by Ernest Wallace and E. Adamson Hoebel. Given this kind of preparation it will become obvious how much Ford's film depends on the racial bias of his perspective and I think it is wrong to stress the mythic and dramatic aspects of *The Searchers* without at the same time understanding just how historical reality was stylized to make those aspects viable.

29. *The Last Hunt* (M-G-M, 1956) directed by Richard Brooks.

This film was based on *The Last Hunt* (1954; Gregg Press, 1979) by Milton Lott. While it is not as fine a novel on this subject—the wasteful slaughter of the buffalo—as is John Williams' *Butcher's Crossing* (1961; Gregg Press, 1978), it is a superior treatment to more popular fictional accounts such as Zane Grey's *The Thundering Herd* (Harper's, 1925). I would suggest prior to viewing *The Last Hunt* reading Tom McHugh's *The Time of the Buffalo* (1972; University of Nebraska Press, 1979), Mari Sandoz' *The Buffalo Hunters: The Story of the Hide Men* (1954; University of Nebraska Press, 1978) plus the corrections by Ramon F. Adams in *Burs Under the Saddle*, and Wayne Gard's *The Great Buffalo Hunt* (1959; University of Nebraska Press, 1968). This may seem an excessive amount of preparation, but nothing illustrates more the real meaning of the "opening" of the West than the destruction of the monarch of the plains. *The Last Hunt* is rather unique among Western films in that it deals somewhat realistically with what was an actual issue on the frontier and not the formula-rized version presented by most Western films. Robert Taylor played a character quite similar to John Wayne's Ethan Edwards and his attitude is similar when, unlike Stewart Granger, he still endorses the belief that "one less buffalo means one less Indian." Debra Paget por-trayed an Indian maiden in this film, much the same as she had in *Broken Arrow* and in *White Feather* (20th-Fox, 1955), the latter directed by Robert Webb, surely one of the more obvious examples of the white man's Pocahontas stereotype.

30. *Man of the West* (United Artists, 1958) directed by Anthony Mann.

Nearly all of Mann's Westerns are worth seeing once, but the performances in this film — particularly from the principals, Gary Cooper, Julie London, and Lee J. Cobb — are consistently impressive. The plot is such that it certainly could have occurred in the American West while the depiction of a wholly evil family comprises an inter-esting, if ironic, contrast with the idealized families so typical of both television and movies throughout this decade.

31. *Ride Lonesome* (Columbia, 1959) directed by Budd Boetticher.

Randolph Scott is a man frozen by his past, by the brutal murder of his wife. The brother of the man responsible for this murder has a price on his head and is captured by Scott. These two are joined by Pernell Roberts and James Coburn, who are outlaws, and by Karen Steele who has recently been widowed by marauding Indians. Boet-ticher managed admirably to evoke from this situation a unique, mounting tension as each character is brought face to face with his or her own soul, including that of the man who once, for revenge, killed Scott's wife by hanging her. This is no simple morality play, the way all too many Westerns continue to be; it is, instead, a probing of num-erous moral issues; and it is a film which comes to a resolution while ending neither happily nor tragically.

32. *Rio Bravo* (Warner's, 1959) directed by Howard Hawks.

Hawks once told me that this film was made as a response to *High Noon* and other Westerns of that ilk, rejecting the notion of a man who is justified having inevitably to stand alone when he is threatened by outside forces. And what makes it still worth viewing is precisely this sense of Americans pulling together when the chips are down, a phenomenon so common and so necessary on the frontier and so conspicuous by its absence since.

33. *Warlock* (20th-Fox, 1959) directed by Edward Dmytryk.

Oakley Hall based his novel *Warlock* (1958; University of Nebraska Press, 1980) on Tombstone in the 1880s and his Clay Blaisdell char-acter on the Wyatt Earp legend, but these sources are of little rele-vance in viewing the film. What is important is that the confrontation with human evil is carried over from the novel — indeed, carried over albeit softened because Dmytryk's liberal orientation prohibited him from entirely endorsing Hall's view that human evil is real and in-eradicable; for this reason, the novel, which is a highly literate Western in its own right, provides a telling contrast with the extraordinarily well-made film, showing how essentially the same story can be used to arrive at two radically different conclusions about frontier life and human nature.

34. *Lonely Are the Brave* (Universal, 1962) directed by David Miller.

As Edward Dmytryk, Dalton Trumbo, who wrote the screenplay for this film, was one of what has come to be known as the Hollywood Ten, which is to say that group of motion picture people held in contempt of Congress for refusing to give information to the House UnAmerican Activities Committee. Trumbo's rather rhetorical novel, *Johnny Got His Gun* (Lippincott, 1939), is still in print and is still, in its way, the most moving plea yet to appear on behalf of the common soldier, the millions of men picked by nations to die in wars declared by the leaders of those nations, and, when not to die, to be maimed, wounded, suffer amputation and loss of faculties. He was the ideal choice, it would appear, to adapt Edward Abbey's novel, *The Brave Cowboy* (1956; University of New Mexico Press, 1977), the story of a man with frontier values and sympathies confronted and ultimately destroyed by the mechanized indifference and callous selfishness of the modern technological world. Abbey's concerns have been always the individual human being and the rights of the wilderness to be wilderness; Trumbo's concern was with the individual human being; David Miller tried to make a tragedy out of *Billy the Kid* in 1941 and failed, but given this story and this adaptation he finally succeeded, and admirably, proving that art can replace romance in a Western.

35. *Per un Pugno di Dollari [A Fistful of Dollars]* (United Artists, 1966) directed by Sergio Leone.

There are those who believe that the European Westerns of the Sixties, of which this entry is readily a prototypical example, had something unique to offer the public. The emphasis was on aimless killing and extreme physical brutality, without any real story and certainly without any sympathetic characters. However, for a number of viewers such omissions must not have been important. Terry Harknett, a British hack writer, did a novelization of the screenplay which met with such success that he embarked on writing Western fiction filled with similar gore and a total lack of characterization, most notably in his Edge series under the pseudonym George G. Gilman. Violence had always, it would seem, been part of the movie Western just as it really had been part — albeit only *part* — of the American frontier; but this trend of stressing violence to the exclusion of everything else intensified the formulary need for violent excesses in Western films and Western fiction alike, a factor that in the present continues to exert an influence.

36. *The Professionals* (Columbia, 1966) directed by Richard Brooks.

To an extent this effectively directed and well acted film was the logical extension of story ideas such as the alliance of forces in *Rio*

Bravo, the traditional notion of rescuing a kidnapped heroine, and the emphasis on violence characteristic of the European Westerns of the time combined with the racial transition which Hollywood Westerns underwent whereby the enemy-by-definition-and-without-need-of-further-motivation-than-his-origin passed from the Native American to the Mexican. I think *Bite the Bullet* (see entry 48 below) is a better Western for Brooks and I believe its ethical perspective has more to offer than that of *The Professionals*, but there is no denying that this is a dramatically exhilarating film filled with uniformly fine performances from the cast, especially Burt Lancaster, Lee Marvin, Robert Ryan, and Woody Strode (quite possibly Strode's best Western film) as the professionals, and Jack Palance as their chief adversary.

37. *Will Penny* (Paramount, 1968) directed by Tom Gries.

I recall when I was at work on *The Filming of the West* (Doubleday, 1976) I happened to be in a Paramount executive's office in the Gulf & Western Building in New York and he asked me what I thought was a good Western. I told him I liked *Will Penny*. He flipped through his computer print-out of quarterly earnings reports and announced to me, somewhat disdainful of my opinion, that *Will Penny* had earned only $232 the previous quarter. Critics noted that it did not have "a happy ending," by which they meant that Charleton Heston, playing an aging cowboy during a time of range depression, did not marry the widow played by Joan Hackett; although, in truth, a marriage between two such disparate types might have been anything but happy. *Will Penny* comes closer to presenting the image of the cowboy as a hired man on horseback than most Westerns, a circumstance which is not completely diminished even by the conventional plot with its stereotypical villains led by Donald Pleasence.

38. *The Scalphunters* (United Artists, 1968) directed by Sydney Pollack.

Pollack's first effort at making a Western turned out rather well, an unconventional comedy rife with new ideas and perspectives. Burt Lancaster was cast as a trapper and a loner who has been hunting in lands claimed by the Kiowas. A band of Kiowas happen upon Lancaster and take his furs. The rest of the action involves Lancaster's attempt to get his furs back and the plot has him thrown together with a runaway slave played by Ossie Davis, and brings him into contact with Telly Savalas, cast as the head of a mercenary gang of scalphunters. Savalas is accompanied by a whore played by Shelley Winters. The performances of all the principals are particularly accomplished and the impression with which the film ends is that the Lancaster character realizes that he cannot make it alone; the Davis character realizes that he has a friend in Lancaster and that they both, as the Kiowas, must nurture a friendship with the land; while the Shelley Winters character, far from fearing the Kiowas when she falls into their hands, realizes that they are, after all, only men: indeed, it is interesting to contrast this scene with a similar scene from

Winchester '73 (Universal, 1950) directed by Anthony Mann where, during an Indian attack, James Stewart slips Shelley Winters a gun and she says, "I understand about the last one."

39. *Butch Cassidy and the Sundance Kid* (20th-Fox, 1969) directed by George Roy Hill.

The usual reasons advanced for citing this Western are the fact that it still ranks as the top-grossing Western film ever made and the consummate portrayals of its principals, Paul Newman as Cassidy, Robert Redford as Sundance, and Katharine Ross as Etta Place. I should not want to depart from these reasons. There is little factual accuracy in the film and Newman and Redford excel at playing charming and wholly admirable outlaws. Rather than to show their being shot down at the end, the film concludes with a freeze frame of Cassidy and Sundance making a dash for freedom while the soundtrack carries massive volleys of gunfire. Thus these two are welcomed to that pantheon of heroic and delightful miscreants reserved for the West's noted outlaws. A necessary complement to such nonsense is to read Larry Pointer's *In Search of Butch Cassidy* (University of Oklahoma Press, 1977).

40. *The Wild Bunch* (Warner's, 1969) directed by Sam Peckinpah.

There is no question but this was and remains a controversial film. Everyone in it is to an extent a villain and so, in a sense, it is a clear break with the traditional roles of the formulary Western. It has, as many of the European Westerns, more than the average amount of violence; some critics have gone so far as to applaud this aspect, calling it everything from catharsis to ballet. In Peckinpah's *Major Dundee* (Columbia, 1965), the emphasis is still on killing Indians. In *The Wild Bunch* the slaughtering of Mexicans rises to genocidal proportions, suggesting to some a parallel with the Vietnam War. Whatever the case, Peckinpah's view of society, on either side of the border, is one of pervasive corruption and savagery.

41. *True Grit* (Paramount, 1969) directed by Henry Hathaway.

John Wayne won his only Academy Award for his work in this film, in many ways a role which was the culmination of the aging Westerner he had played for the first time in *Red River*. The Rooster Cogburn character permitted Wayne to emphasize all of his personal idiosyncracies and yet embody on film the most deeply felt of his personal sentiments about life.

42. *The Ballad of Cable Hogue* (Warner's, 1970) directed by Sam Peckinpah.

This Western was as much Peckinpah's personal statement as *True Grit* was Wayne's. In a dozen ways, Peckinpah gave tribute to John Ford's West, in the love shown toward the American flag (recalling a similar moment in Ford's *Drums Along the Mohawk* [20th-Fox, 1939]), the yellow ribbon Susan O'Connell wears in her hair (reminiscent of Ford's *She Wore a Yellow Ribbon* [RKO, 1949]), the attitude of the townspeople toward the prostitute played by Stella Stevens (recalling the scene in Ford's *Stagecoach* when Claire Trevor's

Dallas is forced to leave town), and a reversal from nearly all Westerns, and especially Ford's, in showing a compassionate banker willing to take a chance and make a character loan. The film had the same cinematographer as did *True Grit*, Lucien Ballard, and the photography is as lyrical as the story-line. There is unquestionably an element of romance in *The Ballad of Cable Hogue*, as there is in *Will Penny* and *True Grit*, but it is not the nostalgic romance of *Shane*; rather it is the emotion one feels when confronted by sharply aggressive and self-willed men and women who regard as a personal virtue an unwavering sense of direction.

43. *Soldier Blue* (Avco-Embassy, 1970) directed by Ralph Nelson.

   After ridiculous, if well-intentioned, attempts to treat the Sand Creek massacre of 1864 in such films as *Massacre at Sand Creek* (Screen Gems, 1956) directed by Arthur Hiller and *The Guns of Fort Petticoat* (Columbia, 1957) directed by George Marshall, Ralph Nelson set out to put it on the screen truly, more or less as it happened or more or less as it would have appeared had the viewer been there to witness it. As *The Wild Bunch*, much of the notoriety surrounding this film upon its release may have come about as a result of parallels with atrocities committed during the Vietnam War; but, beyond this, and in a way in spite of it, and notwithstanding the effectiveness of some of the images, the participants as depicted in the film are *not* those involved in the historical battle itself and the military conflict is unfortunately framed by the routine formulary plot ingredients derived from the literary source, T.V. Olsen's *Arrow in the Sun* (Doubleday, 1969). Moreover, viewed from another perspective—that of visual violence—*Soldier Blue* outdoes nearly all of the European Westerns and rivals *The Wild Bunch*.

44. *Little Big Man* (National General, 1970) directed by Arthur Penn.

   The basis for this film was, of course, Thomas Berger's novel, *Little Big Man* (Dial, 1964). The novel was intended, presumably, as a satire; certainly its author had little genuine understanding of the Plains Indians and less knowledge of Western history. Prior to viewing the film, I would therefore suggest reading, for some background on the Sioux, John G. Neihardt's *Black Elk Speaks* (1932; reissued by Pocket Books first in 1972 and continuously since), Luther Standing Bear's *My People the Sioux* (1928; University of Nebraska Press, 1975), and Royal B. Hassrick's *The Sioux* (University of Oklahoma Press, 1964); for some background on the Pawnees George Bird Grinnell's *Pawnee Hero Stories and Folk-Tales* (1889; University of Nebraska Press, 1961); and for some background on the Cheyennes both Grinnell's *The Fighting Cheyennes* (1915; University of Oklahoma Press, 1956) and his invaluable two-volume study *The Cheyenne Indians: Their History and Ways of Life* (1923; University of Nebraska Press, 1972). Arthur Penn himself admitted that he had done little in this film to recreate the way of life of the Plains Indians and the better informed the viewer is the more apparent will this deficiency become.

The most comic element of the picture is derived from watching the protagonist, Jack Crabbe, played by Dustin Hoffman, become dissolute
among the white men and more or less sober and upstanding among
the Indians, as the story follows him back and forth. As *Soldier Blue*,
Little Big Man addressed the anti-war sentiments in the United States
at the time it was made, and unfortunately for all concerned did so at
the expense of distorting Western history in a way opposite from the
self-congratulatory fantasies of previous decades but with no more
real insight into the historical reality of the period in which it was set.

45. *McCabe and Mrs. Miller* (Warner's, 1971) directed by Robert Altman.

"The Western is like an ancient ballad," Altman said when he went
into production on this film. "We take advantage of the fact that
audiences know the standard plots. We tell the story behind the ballad." Altman once told me that he enjoyed debunking popular American myths and, to be sure, much of his cinematic activity has been a
thrust in this direction. Here his idea was to satirize the town-building,
church-going image of Westerns, particularly in the Fifties, and typical of many of the Western television series which were once popular and episodes of which Altman directed before he turned exclusively to theatrical films. Nearly the entire picture was shot through a
fog filter, giving the images the atmosphere of a dream, with a location rigged for rain, a rain which became snow before shooting was
completed. In a sense *McCabe and Mrs. Miller* is a love story; it is
also a commentary on the American spirit of commerical enterprise
which so often reduces in practice to exploitation of one kind or
another. If the traditional Western has been termed a morality play
by some, Altman in this film accepted such a definition, but with a
Nietzschean revaluation of values, and the last scene where McCabe,
played by Warren Beatty, bleeds and freezes to death in the snow
while the townspeople are preoccupied with a church fire remains a
high point in Altman's screen work.

46. *Buck and the Preacher* (Columbia, 1972) directed by Sidney Poitier.

In the instance of this film there are, again, a couple of books it
would be advisable to read beforehand, William H. Leckie's *The
Buffalo Soldiers: A Narrative of the Negro Cavalry in the West* (Uni-
versity of Oklahoma Press, 1967), Colonel Bailey C. Hanes' *Bill
Pickett, Bulldogger* (University of Oklahoma Press, 1977) and, possibly,
The Negro Cowboys (Dodd, Mead, 1965) by Philip Durham and
Everett L. Jones provided Ramon F. Adams' entry on their book in
More Burs Under the Saddle (University of Oklahoma Press, 1979) is
consulted. To this list of titles I would only add Matthew Braun's
Black Fox, cited above, and Elmer Kelton's fine novel, *The Wolf and
the Buffalo* (Doubleday, 1980). When I was working on *Images of
Indians* (PBS, 1980) the Native American co-producer singled out *Buck
and the Preacher* for its sympathetic view of the Indians, motivated, he
suggested, by the fact that racial prejudice toward blacks was so much a
theme. Whatever the case, he was right, and the Native Americans in

the film are responsible for rescuing a caravan of black homesteaders. However, this is a distortion of history in an opposite direction; it is a way to provide an optimistic, hopeful ending quite in keeping with so many of the endings of pictures dealing with whites moving West. In this film, a formulary view is broadened to encompass another race, but that does not prevent it from being notwithstanding a formulary view. Even so, the acting and direction are noteworthy and the characters engaging.

47.   *Jeremiah Johnson* (Warner's, 1972) directed by Sydney Pollack.

It was Robert Redford's desire to make this film, and his contribution is certainly as significant as Pollack's expert direction. The picture was adapted from Vardis Fisher's *Mountain Man* (Morrow, 1965) and *Crow Killer, the Saga of Liver-Eating Johnson* (Indiana University Press, 1958) by Raymond Thorp and Robert Bunker. Reading these books will enhance watching this film, but beyond them I would recommend George Frederick Ruxton's *Life in the Far West* (1849; The Rio Grande Press, 1972), the compilation of Ruxton's miscellaneous writings by Clyde and Mae Reed Porter edited by LeRoy R. Hafen and titled *Ruxton of the Rockies* (University of Oklahoma Press, 1950), Milo Milton Quaife's edition of Henry A. Boller's *Among the Indians: Four Years On the Upper Missouri, 1858–1862* (University of Nebraska Press, 1972), John Kirk Townsend's *Narrative of a Journey Across the Rocky Mountains to the Columbia River* (1839; University of Nebraska Press, 1978), Clarence King's *Mountaineering in the Sierra Nevada* (1872; University of Nebraska Press, 1970), and *A Majority of Scoundrels: The Western Frontier 1822–1834* (Comstock Books, 1977) by Don Berry. Viewing *Jeremiah Johnson* with this kind of preparation will enable a viewer to appreciate fully the magnitude of its achievement. The essential conflict in the film is Johnson's inability to accept the new values of the mountains, maintaining the balance with Nature true to the Indians. "I was striving for a sense of mysticism," Pollack remarked about this film. "There is a lot of dialogue in the film with innuendo and mysticism. The other mountain men survive because they do not get involved. Jeremiah's problem was his humaneness in an inhuman atmosphere. What destroyed Jeremiah was the set of values we uphold. He could not escape them." As Ralph Brauer put it in his essay "Who Are Those Guys? The Movie Western During the TV Era," Johnson is a tragic figure, "one whose soul is disputed over by two forces — the settlers and the Indians. The settlers symbolize progress, 'civilization,' taming the land as opposed to the Indians' preference for living with the land."

48.   *Bite the Bullet* (Columbia, 1975) directed by Richard Brooks.

In terms of the panoramic scenic locations, the propulsive action which never lets up throughout the duration of the film, the interesting and sometimes engaging characters, and the psychology of winning which is at the heart of so much American activity, *Bite the Bullet* is an extraordinary Western. But what seems even more

impressive is the varying attitudes toward horses reflected in the film
and the deep significance of a sense of personal loyalty, whether it be
to another person — as in the cases of Gene Hackman, James Coburn,
Candice Bergen, or Mario Arteaga in their complex interrelationships
with each other and with other characters — or whether it be to an
abstract ideal, such as that which motivates the character played by
Ben Johnson. At the same there is the cavalier male cohesiveness
which, to a degree, is the dominant fantasy underlying Brooks' earlier
effort in *The Professionals* and so many Westerns, from those directed
by John Ford and Howard Hawks to those directed by Sam Peckinpah;
Brooks, however, in his sympathies and in his treatment of this theme
was consciously much closer to Ford than he was to Peckinpah.

49. *Buffalo Bill and the Indians, or Sitting Bull's History Lesson* (United
Artists, 1976) directed by Robert Altman.

In the preproduction process, Altman had researchers put to
work to determine just what was fact and what was fiction in the
Buffalo Bill phenomenon. His film is by no means a substitute for
reading Don Russell's carefully documented study, *The Lives and
Legends of Buffalo Bill* (University of Oklahoma Press, 1960), but it
does make a very intriguing contrast with *Buffalo Bill* (20th-Fox,
1944) directed by William Wellman, a film which Wellman stated
repeatedly only succeeded in making him want to vomit but one
which, by contract, he had to direct. Altman's effort succeeds unquestionably in debunking the Buffalo Bill legend, and it did poorly
at the box office, which might mean any number of things, including
the often-expressed opinion that Americans do not want their legends
debunked. But what Altman's film does primarily, beyond exposé,
is show that the whole of American frontier culture — and by implication the whole of American culture today — constitutes little more
than hyped illusion, a self-perpetuating attempt to produce constantly the Greatest Show on Earth, an attempt that thrusts hollow
and spiritually barren men to the forefront, making heroes of them.

50. *One Flew Over the Cuckoo's Nest* (United Artists, 1975) directed by
Milos Foreman.

There are, of course, those who would say definitely that this
film is not a Western, and so in deference I have placed it last in this
listing and out of chronological sequence. It was based on Ken Kesey's
novel *One Flew Over the Cuckoo's Nest* (Viking, 1962), a book which
was cited by academic critic Leslie A. Fiedler in his study, *The
Return of the Vanishing American* (Stein and Day, 1969), as being in
support of his thesis that any story featuring a Native American is,
by definition, a Western. For me, this story is essentially that most
elusive of all types of fictional narrative, an allegory, in which it is
significant that the whites have imprisoned themselves in an insane
asylum from which there is no escape and from which, in the film as
in the novel, an Indian named Chief Bromden, played by Will Sampson in the film, breaks out and seemingly can alone gain freedom.

When I had occasion to work with Will Sampson on *Images of Indians*, I made it a point to ask him if he felt this ending was intended to be tragic. Not at all, he assured me. He interpreted the picture to mean that the white man is destined to live in a world of his own creation which must inevitably deny him his liberty, whereas the Native American lives in the world of Nature; he can only be destroyed if he remains in the white man's man-made world. It is a conflict which has been with Americans since the beginnings of frontier fiction in the novels of James Fenimore Cooper and, ultimately, I suppose is still at the heart of our complex and contradictory national character.

In having made this compilation, it may be judged as an oversight that I have included no "B" Westerns on the list. It has not been; it has been intentional. While it is a matter of personal taste to select which was the best example of a "B" Western in which Ken Maynard, Bob Steele, Tim McCoy, Buck Jones, Gene Autry, Roy Rogers, or Johnny Mack Brown, or any of the other stars of such vehicles appeared over the years, I recall the late Tim McCoy telling me, after we had screened *Bulldog Courage* (Puritan, 1935) together, a film in which I felt he had presented himself well, "I was paid to make them, Jon, not to watch them." Those for whom the "B" Western is still to be regarded as a source of enjoyment and enter- tainment have, I am sure, their own lists as to which of them they find more diverting and pleasant than others; while those for whom the "B" Western offers nothing would be bored watching any of them.

There may, however, be those who might like a brief listing of "B" Westerns that, if they are unfamiliar with the majority of these pictures, could be taken to serve as typical examples or, in a few cases, as unusual variations of the most formulary of all formulary Western plot structures. Again, these Westerns do not reflect so much my own preferences as they comprise a reasonably brief and selective group from the genre. I have purposely limited them to ten in number.

1. *Desert Vengeance* (Columbia, 1931) directed by Louis King and starring Buck Jones.

    Directed by Henry King's brother, this film is a good illustration of what Buck Jones could do when he combined his penchant for an off-beat story with an exotic location.

2. *End of the Trail* (Columbia, 1932) directed by D. Ross Lederman and starring Tim McCoy.

    Filmed for exteriors on the Arapaho reserve in Wyoming where McCoy once worked as a rancher and in service with the Bureau of Indian Affairs, despite its obvious paternalism and condescension, this was one of the small handful of "B" Westerns which attempted to portray the Native American in a somewhat sympathetic light. The ending which originally had McCoy dying trying to bring peace be- tween the U.S. Cavalry and, in the words of the script, "those Indian half-children out there," was changed prior to release to show McCoy instead, his commission restored, marrying an Indian maiden played by white Luana Walters. Many real Arapahoes and Cheyennes do appear in the picture, however, and the Powder River no longer looks as pristine and majestic as it once did when this film was made.

3. *The Strawberry Roan* (Universal, 1933) directed by Alan James and starring Ken Maynard.

This was Maynard's favorite among his films and the one he asked me to show him shortly before his death. It still demonstrates to good advantage the alluring use of a theme song within an action format which remained the hallmark of Maynard's better efforts.

4. *Hop-A-Long Cassidy* (Paramount, 1935) directed by Howard Bretherton and starring William Boyd.

Retitled *Hopalong Cassidy Enters* upon rerelease, this entry was the first in the series based on Clarence E. Mulford's characters and for this reason seems to be less cliché-ridden as to story and less stylized as to acting. It is also notable for the effectiveness of the chase music — in this case, the "Dance of the Furies" from Glück's *Orfeo ed Euridice* — used in the final reel.

5. *Frontier Justice* (Diversion, 1936) directed by Robert McGowan and starring Hoot Gibson.

Although all too few fine examples of Gibson's carefree humor and art of mimicry survive, this film does capture some of it, and features Gibson in several amusing scenes.

6. *Marshal of Mesa City* (RKO, 1939) directed by David Howard and starring George O'Brien.

David Howard was perhaps one of the best directors of low-budget Westerns in the Thirties, turning out slick, fast-paced product. The humor is well played by O'Brien and the story is not without dramatic interest with a strong supporting cast to assist in its realization.

7. *Mexicali Rose* (Republic, 1939) directed by George Sherman and starring Gene Autry and Smiley Burnette.

As Howard, George Sherman was an extremely competent low-budget director, only in his case he would go on to directing higher budget Westerns in the Fifties. Burnette was the perfect foil for Autry who in his Westerns raised to a major ingredient the role of the "stooge" opposite him. This is one of the best examples I can think of embodying the Autry fantasy, that incredible formula for make-believe so unique to his pictures.

8. *Texas Stagecoach* (Columbia, 1940) directed by Joseph H. Lewis and starring Charles Starrett.

Joseph H. Lewis subsequently directed several notable *films noirs* and currently has a vogue in Europe. What is most interesting to watch is how he employed unusual camera set-ups and angles to create visual variety that might incline a viewer almost, if never quite, to overlook the plot.

9. *Phantom of the Plains* (Republic, 1945) directed by Lesley Selander and starring Bill Elliott.

This was an entry in the Red Ryder series from Republic which cast Robert Blake as Little Beaver — to be contrasted, perhaps, with Blake's subsequent role as an Indian in *Tell Them Willie Boy Is Here* (Universal, 1970) — and Elliott in the title role. It is a good illustration of the rapid, assembly-line, slick production work of which this studio was capable in making its numerous "B" Western series.

10. *My Pal Trigger* (Republic, 1946) directed by Frank McDonald and starring Roy Rogers.

I was responsible for saving the original full-length version of this film from destruction. It was Roy Rogers' favorite among his Westerns and, although the plot and characters are strictly "B" grade, this is one of the few "A" budget films Rogers made. It features cast regulars Dale Evans and George "Gabby" Hayes and it is perhaps interesting to see how the Sons of the Pioneers — in support of Rogers here as they are in support of Starrett in *Texas Stagecoach* — and the musical format of singing Westerns varied (I could scarely say *matured*) over the years.

III

i

It is probably symptomatic of the generally low esteem in which Western films have been held for so long that the majority of books to have appeared have been ill-formed, poorly researched, or given over to the most flagrant distortions. Many of the writers who have addressed the subject of the Western film have known little or nothing about Western American history — except maybe what they have learned from movies — and, in their defense, insist that any knowledge beyond this would be irrelevant to appreciating a Western film. I would be more inclined to accept this position if, correspondingly, in their critical remarks these same writers made no comment about the historical accuracy of a particular film or laid no claim on behalf of one filmmaker being more "realistic" in depicting the American West than another. Unfortunately this has not been the case. In addition, most of these same critics ignore cinema history itself so that whatever has happened has happened ostensibly because of some aesthetic consideration, rather than, as was and as continues to be most often the case, because of some behind-the-scenes event in film production, corporate machinations, or marketing strategy. To make matters still worse, many of these same critics who have remarked on the historical accuracy of a film while knowing nothing of history and who have spoken authoritatively about production details without knowing anything about them have also critically praised films without ever having seen them.

One example should suffice. In "The Stereotyping of North American

Indians in Motion Pictures," an essay by John A. Price which first appeared in *Ethnohistory* (Spring, 1973) and which has been reprinted in *The Pretend Indians: Images of Native Americans in the Movies* edited by Gretchen M. Bataille and Charles L.P. Silet (see the entry for this book below), Professor Price asserted: "A few of the M-G-M silent Westerns that starred the Indian expert Tim McCoy, such as *The Covered Wagon* and *The Vanishing American*, were made on Indian reservations with Indian extras." There is only one accurate fact in the whole of this assertion. *The Covered Wagon* and *The Vanishing American* were both made by Paramount, not M-G-M. Tim McCoy appeared in neither film, much less starred; he worked with the Indian extras in *The Covered Wagon* and had nothing whatever to do with *The Vanishing American*. Although McCoy was able to organize Indian groups with the skill of a consummate showman, he was not an Indian "expert" in any meaningful sense of that word. McCoy had to help transport the Indians featured in *The Covered Wagon* *from* their reservations to the Snake Valley in Nevada. The truthful part of the statement is that scenes in *The Vanishing American* were photographed on the Navajo reservation and that Navajos were used as extras. Had Professor Price seen either of these films and assuming that he knew enough about the customs, dress, and beliefs of the Plains Indians featured in *The Covered Wagon* and the Navajos featured in *The Vanishing American*, he would have recognized at once that—in view of how both of these films treat the Indians in them—it is not a significant factor whether or not the films were made on Indian reservations using Indian extras. Furthermore, since neither the editor of *Ethnohistory* nor the editors of *The Pretend Indians* made any effort to correct the errors in Professor Price's text, it is at least probable that they did not know there were errors that required correction or perhaps the presence of such errors did not greatly matter to them.

There is an anecdote in C.L. Sonnichsen's book, *From Hopalong to Hud: Thoughts on Western Fiction* (Texas A&M University Press, 1978), about Mrs. Sophie Poe. She was the wife of John Poe, the latter having been present when Garrett shot the Kid. Mrs. Poe was invited to Hollywood to act as a consultant to King Vidor while he was filming *Billy the Kid*. Disgusted by what she was seeing, she remarked to Vidor, "Sir, I knew that little buck-toothed killer, and he wasn't the way you are making him at all." "Mrs. Poe," Vidor responded, "I understand your feelings, but this is what the people want." Presently she was removed from her consulting position and replaced by movie cowboy William S. Hart whose activity appears to have been confined to giving the star, Johnny Mack Brown, a pistol reputed to have belonged to the Kid, a gesture that was well publicized.

All too often film historians and critics seem equally intent on giving people what they suppose them to want at the expense of accuracy. What is most lacking in the majority of the books cited below is some conception of historical reality which can be used as a standard of value in judging the historical dimension of a Western film. Without it, these critics and historians are lost in a miasma of misinformation and are doomed to perpetuating each other's errors because not one of them seems willing to make the effort necessary to study enough history to know the difference between accuracy and falsehood. If some of the annotations below seem even more harshly critical than those in the area of Western fiction, this is because in the area of Western films the abuses have been commensurately that much more pronounced.

ii

Adams, Les, and Buck Rainey, *Shoot-Em-Ups: The Complete Reference Guide to Westerns of the Sound Era* (Arlington House, 1978).

The title of this book is unfortunate in two ways. The first part of it implies that the book's main function is nostalgia for the "B" Western, which is not entirely true—although more than a little time is spent in the textual parts of the book on various "B" Western series and their stars. The second part implies that the book is complete, which it is not, since a number of outstanding Western films escaped the authors' inclusion—to give but two examples: *Fort Apache* (RKO, 1948) directed by John Ford and based on a short story by James Warner Bellah and *Ambush* (M-G-M, 1949) directed by Sam Wood and based on a novel by Luke Short.

In favor of this book—and of absolutely overriding significance—is the fact that the cast and technical credit information, releasing company, release date, as well as running time for each film listed could not be assembled very easily and it cannot be found anywhere else in a single volume. Of course, the format followed is that of the *Film Daily Yearbook*, but in this volume it begins in 1929 and extends beyond the expiration of the *Film Daily Yearbook*. To purchase the out-of-print *Yearbooks* themselves would be, by comparison, abortively expensive, even if possible.

More thorough scholarship, of course, would have gone beyond the *Film Daily Yearbook* format, especially with regard to the literary sources of Western films, but what data are to be found here are of unquestionable utility. Most of the background sections on Western films are written in the spirit of sentimental nostalgia, and many will question the authors' designation of Buck Jones as a standard of value against which other Western players ought to be judged.

Although either prospect is unlikely given the present situation in American publishing, this volume might ideally be revised periodically and kept up to date, coupled with a similar volume covering the silent Western film. In view of the unlikelihood of the former, whatever its imperfections *Shoot-Em-Ups* remains the best book of its kind so far to become available.

Bataille, Gretchen M., and Charles L.P. Silet (eds.), *The Pretend Indians: Images of Native Americans in the Movies* (Iowa State University Press, 1980).

A book on this subject is desperately needed, but sadly this is not the book. The editors in assembling various critical essays and reviews on the topic of the way Native Americans are portrayed in Hollywood films made no effort to correct errors of fact in any of the pieces included (and there are many, many errors), nor even to call attention to the existence of errors in the prefatory matter. Above all, this book cries out for the editors to have established some conception of historical reality and maintained it throughout, since the essayists themselves lack any such conception and are constantly contradicting each other. Stephen Farber in a review of *A Man Called Horse* (National General, 1970) included in this book remarked about this picture that "the attention to carefully researched details of setting, costume, and ceremony produces some extraordinarily beautiful images, a tableau of Indian life more striking than anything seen on the screen before." In another essay Dan Georgakas summed up his view of *A Man Called Horse* as "a fantasy from start to finish."

Actually neither critic knew enough about Sioux Indians to substantiate his claim for this film. In trying to prove the picture a fantasy — which, incidentally, it is — Georgakas made mention that "an angry Sioux writing to the *Village Voice* ... noted that the Sioux never abandoned widows, orphans, and old people to starve and freeze as shown in the film." This must be tempered. "Some old people, unwanted or without relatives, had no place to go," Royal B. Hassrick noted in his generally reliable book, *The Sioux* (University of Oklahoma Press, 1964). "These were forced to live alone at the edge of the encampment. Here they were given food and supplies by the generous young men who thereby gained prestige ... but at best theirs was a tragic lot, too often filled with insecurity and despair." On the other hand, Farber's contentions about the film being a "painstaking reconstruction" and "almost an anthropological document" are made to appear absurd by somewhat more valid objections raised by Georgakas concerning the European methods of attack employed by the Shoshonis and the total misrepresentation of the Sun Dance ceremony (which Georgakas did not realize was, as presented in the film, not the Sioux version of this ceremony, but the *okipa* ceremony of the Mandans).

Professor Silet has informed me that the purpose of this book is to demonstrate the confusion of Anglo-American writings about images of Indians in motion pictures from the early days to the present. This function the book certainly fulfills. Moreover, the more you know about Native American cultures, about motion picture history, about individual motion pictures, the more about American history, the more errors will become apparent to you, not dozens, but literally hundreds, in the course of reading these essays. It would seem to me that I would rather believe Professor Silet's assertion that there is nothing but confusion in what has hitherto been written and hold in my hand a book that purported to set the record straight, than the book he and Professor Bataille produced.

Vine Deloria wrote a Foreword for this volume which, when coupled with his essay "The American Indian Image in North America," provides the most honest, truthful, and cogent writing in the entire book. I also agree with the editors that "Indian life on the screen has been and continues to be artificial and unreal, yet it is these visual images that have 'educated' a nation about its own history." I would add to this that it is these images which have "educated" the world about the role of the Native American in American history. But let the final reflection be Vine Deloria's. "Underneath all the conflicting images of the Indian one fundamental truth emerges — the white man *knows* that he is an alien and he *knows* that North America is Indian — and he will never let go of the Indian image because he thinks that by some clever manipulation he can achieve an authenticity that cannot ever be his."

Bazin, André, *Qu'est-ce Que le Cinéma?* Tome II. *Le Cinéma et les Autres Arts* (Éditions du Cerf, 1967); *What Is Cinema?* Volume II (University of California Press, 1971) translated from the French by Hugh Gray with a Foreword by François Truffaut.

This second volume of Bazin's four volume *Q'est-ce Que le Cinéma?* contains his essays "The Western, or the American Film *par excellence*" and "The Evolution of the Western" as well as his notes on *The Outlaw* (RKO, 1943). Bazin was ill-informed about Western American history, or he would not have asserted that the establishment of justice and respect for the law were the most vital issues in the United States in the Nineteenth century; he got his history by watching Western films. He knew as little about Western fiction, or he could not have dismissed it as a minor litera-ture. Nonetheless, Bazin's criticism became the cornerstone of the French approach. *"Le Western est né de la rencontre d'une mythologie avec un moyen d'expression"* [the Western is born of the encounter of a mythology with a means of expression] — for some reason a statement translated by Gray as if it were in the imperfect and not the passive voice of the present indicative. Exalting a commercial enterprise to the status of mythology seems preposterous, but unfortunately Bazin has had followers who have not thought so and who have written extensively from this point of view.

Brauer, Ralph, with Donna Brauer, *The Horse, the Gun, and the Piece of Property: Changing Images of the TV Western* (Bowling Green University Popular Press, 1975).

Quite the best and most searching study hitherto done on television Western series, addressing both the philosophy incorporated in individual series as well as the significance behind variations in formulary patterns. Also see Brauer's entry on Television Westerns which follows this section.

Brownlow, Kevin, *The Parade's Gone By ...* (Knopf, 1968); reprinted by Bonanza Books; *The War, the West, and the Wilderness* (Knopf, 1979).

The Parade's Gone By ... is an oral history of the silent film including much material on early Western films, their directors, interviews with players, and interesting production stills. Brownlow was one of the very first writers on the American cinema to bring to his work the critical rigor of the professional historian. Unhappily, his approach has not been widely imitated among cinema historians.

The War, the West, and the Wilderness is rather an unlikely collective subject for a unified history, and of course the book is not unified;
but the Western films discussed are treated with such depth, replete with
interviews with those involved in their production and this personal testimony scrutinized in terms of the facts which are known, that discursive-
ness almost becomes a virtue. Brownlow was again among the very small
minority of cinema historians who took pains to maintain historical
accuracy in production details and actually screened the films about which
he wrote.

Calder, Jenni, *There Must Be a Lone Ranger: The American West in Film
and Reality* (Taplinger, 1974); reprinted by McGraw-Hill Paperback.
      The basic premise of this book is one worthy of critical exploration,
but this is not achieved in Calder's effort. There is not only an error on
every page; there is some kind of error in practically every paragraph.
Calder obviously had only the most minimal exposure to Western films
and, therefore, much of her criticism is worthless. Beyond this her grasp of
the "reality" was exceedingly tenuous with more than a hundred
misstatements of historical fact, e.g., her assertion that Sitting Bull died at
Wounded Knee when he was not even there. A book definitely to be
avoided.

Cawelti, John G., *The Six-Gun Mystique* (Bowling Green University
Popular Press, 1975); *Adventure, Mystery, and Romance: Formula Stories
as Art and Popular Culture* (University of Chicago Press, 1976).
      The Six-Gun Mystique, as Cawelti's subsequent volume, suffers
from excessive dilettantism. Cawelti based his rather sweeping generalizations on a very limited exposure to the varieties of Western fiction and an
equally limited number of Western films — while obviously preferring the
latter. If his speculations are confined to Western films, and discounted
entirely as they concern Western fiction, they still represent an abuse of
deductive reasoning. Because of the scope of the Western film, a much
broader sampling would be necessary for conclusions such as Cawelti drew
to have any validity. To cite but one example, in *Adventure, Mystery, and
Romance*, Cawelti spent an entire section trying to prove that heroes in
Zane Grey's fiction and in William S. Hart's films were somehow significantly related. A number of passages from Grey's fiction are quoted and
then contrasted with Hart's *Hell's Hinges* (Triangle, 1916). Such a limited
sampling — one film — is not sufficient to verify this assertion, and what of
William Farnum, Tom Mix, and Jack Holt who portrayed Zane Grey
heroes repeatedly on screen whereas Hart, their contemporary, never did?
Had Cawelti seen more Hart films — most of them survive — and read Hart's
Western fiction, I believe he would have found a more apt comparison to
be that between Hart's view of the West and the view of Harold Bell
Wright's fiction. The superficiality of Cawelti's efforts notwithstanding, his
objective to approach the Western in terms of a variety of repetitive and yet
changing plotlines and stereotypical situations in more knowledgeable

hands could prove potentially promising. It might also be said, on Cawelti's behalf, that those sections in *Adventure, Mystery, and Romance* devoted to detective fiction show him to have been more passionately engaged by this subject and more imaginatively and critically equipped to approach it with genuine insight than was the case with the Western. Finally, his essay "*Chinatown* and Generic Transformation in Recent American Films," in the second edition of *Film Theory and Criticism: Introductory Readings* (Oxford University Press, 1979) edited by Gerald Mast and Marshall Cohen, is quite the best work he has done, and in it he did address some of the changes in Western films and other genres which demonstrate rather decisively the rightness of the structural approach he can be said to have pioneered.

Corneau, Ernest N., *The Hall of Fame of Western Film Stars* (Christopher Publishing, 1969) O.P.

A series of brief biographical vignettes of actors known primarily for playing screen cowboys, this book indiscriminately assembles more misinformation about its subjects than reliable facts. It does, however, include references to players too obscure or little known today to appear in any other readily available source and, in their cases at least, this might be regarded as a place at which cautiously to begin.

Eyles, Allen, *The Western: An Illustrated Guide* (A.S.Barnes, 1967) O.P.

This book deserves to be updated. The biographical data it does contain on actors, screenwriters, directors, cinematographers, and others associated with Western filmmaking are generally reliable. Eyles brought greater rigor and a desire for accuracy to his effort than have other British writers—Jenni Calder above, Philip French below—and, given the date of its publication, his guide is trustworthy.

Fenin, George N., and William K. Everson, *The Western: from Silents to Cinerama* (Orion Press, 1962); revised edition, *The Western: from Silents to the Seventies* (Grossman, 1973) both O.P.

This was the first book that attempted a comprehensive approach to the history of the Western film. The original version contained more than two hundred errors of fact, none of which was corrected for the revised version. Because it was the first, these errors have been perpetuated in a number of subsequent books by other authors. It you accept the proposition that no information is preferable to misinformation, this book might best be avoided, especially since this same ground has been covered better elsewhere. On his own between appearances of *The Western*, William K. Everson published *A Pictorial History of the Western Film* (Citadel, 1969), a book which repeated many of the errors of fact in the earlier book and added a few gratuitously on its own; its only real attraction is a number of interesting photo illustrations. A critical peculiarity common to both *The Western* and *A Pictorial History of the Western Film* is the adoption of the highly sentimental melodramas of William S. Hart as prime examples of "realism" in Western films and then to judge capriciously all subsequent Westerns against this rather eccentric standard.

French, Philip, *Westerns: Aspects of a Movie Genre* (Viking, 1973) O.P.; revised edition, *Westerns: Aspects of a Movie Genre* (Oxford University Press, 1977).

No matter which edition of this book you read, it relies on the dubious and even absurd premise that Hollywood Westerns were somehow significantly related to the foreign and domestic policies of American presidents. French was without any knowledge that is discernible of the history of Western film production or Western American history, and so his idle speculations with their political overtones — guided by no demonstrative logical or critical principle — remain a curiosity.

Hurst, Richard Maurice, *Republic Studios: Between Poverty Row and the Majors* (Scarecrow Press, 1979).

The appearance of this brief studio history is to be applauded; firstly, because it is surprisingly accurate as far as it goes; secondly, because it deals perceptively with the Western films and Western players manufactured by this studio; and thirdly, because the author employed a rather fruitful method — similar to my own and to that of Jean-Louis Leutrat among the French critics — of evaluating Western screen images and Western heroes in terms of the ethical qualities they are supposed to embody and which audiences are expected to find admirable. Nor is it incorrect to use the verb "manufactured" in connection with Western screen players; they were as much a manufactured and marketed product as were their films and the ideologies those films promulgate. Where this book does fall short is in living up to its title in terms of comprehensiveness; to do that the author would have had to view a great many more Republic Westerns and other Republic product than obviously he did and his book would have had to be much longer than it is.

Kitses, Jim, *Horizons West* (Indiana University Press, 1969) O.P.

This book concentrates on the screen work of three film directors and confines itself to their Western films, namely Anthony Mann, Budd Boetticher, and Sam Peckinpah. What a Western film may state about American history is adventitious as far as Kitses was concerned and, accordingly, is ignored. This limitation, however, leads to a multitude of contradictory problems. On Kitses' behalf, it should nevertheless be observed that he was more effective and articulate as a spokesperson for a structuralist approach to the Western film than have been a number of other critics who have attempted it.

Koszarski, Diane Kaiser, *The Complete Films of William S. Hart: A Pictorial Record* (Dover, 1980).

Here is a book that, had he had it, Cawelti (see above) could have used to advantage by contrasting the plots of Hart's films with the plot synopses of Zane Grey's Western novels, only it would have made insupportable his thesis that they were significantly related. Koszarski wrote a balanced and insightful introductory biographical essay on Hart and the development of his screen work. This is followed by a series of cinematographs—production credits, cast with character identifications, detailed *and accurate* plot synopses, and brief samples of reviews from the time of original release—covering every film in which Hart appeared. The photo illustrations are carefully and appropriately chosen and, for the most part, evoke the spirit of the films to which they pertain. An added plus is a notation as to where prints of a given title can be found for screening purposes—and, as stated above, most of Hart's films do survive and are available. However it should be mentioned that two of the characteristics which Koszarski stressed about Hart's films—i.e., that the West was morally superior to the East and that his heroines were invariably chaste women—were typical of most Western films during the years 1915—1923, the basic years of Hart's box office popularity, and Hart ought not be singled out for praise or blame because of the presence of these elements in his films.

Lahue, Kalton C., *Winners of the West: The Sagebrush Heroes of the Silent Screen* (A.S. Barnes, 1970) O.P.

Brief and generally inaccurate profiles of thirty-eight Western players are to be found here, the author's tone continually vacillating between condescension and nostalgic reverie. This is a book best left unopened. Reportedly, after a few efforts at writing cinema history in which he depended almost completely on secondary and wholly unreliable sources, Lahue turned with better success to preparing technical manuals.

Lenihan, John H., *Showdown: Confronting Modern America in the Western Film* (University of Illinois Press, 1980).

This is a sensitive, intelligent, and fairly comprehensive survey of the way in which Western films since 1945 have reflected distinct attitudes toward racism, individualism, social conformity, and international *Realpolitik*. It is a book which is better prepared than that of Philip French (see above) to view the Western film as American social self-criticism as well as self-congratulation and it does manage to demonstrate how Westerns embody a number of identifiable ideologies. Where it fails—where every such effort done from an intuitive rather than an empirical perspective *must* fail—is in trying to relate in a meaningful and verifiable way information gathered from screening Western films to attitudes presumed to exist in American society at large during some specific period. Andrew Tudor commented with profound wisdom in his book *Image and Influence: Studies in the Sociology of Film* (St. Martin's Press, 1974): "...Do not make premature assumptions about the direction and nature of the links between movies and society. The one thing we should have learned from the history of such studies is that we are dealing with interaction and not with simple cause and effect." Had Lenihan had such an open-minded premise as

Tudor suggested and had he availed himself of a valid empirical method, he might well have succeeded; as it turns out, he had neither.

Leutrat, Jean-Louis, *Le Western* (Librairie Armand Colin, 1973).
This is unquestionably the most thought-provoking and stimulating book so far to appear concerned with the social, psychological, and philosophical significance of Western films. Leutrat steeped himself in much of the French critical literature on the subject — and the number of quotations and the depth of insight contained in them astounds the reader, especially if one is accustomed only to the inferior quality of British and American criticism from authors such as Jenni Calder and William K. Everson. Leutrat also availed himself of several interviews with the directors of important cinematic Westerns; perhaps because these American filmmakers were being asked different kinds of questions by the French than they have been asked traditionally by American critics, their answers were commensurately more revealing about aspects of their films which, for the most part, have been overlooked by American critics. "*Notre propos n'est d'ailleurs pas d'établir un bilan de curiosa,*" Leutrat wrote in his Foreword, "*mais de présenter le Western et de poser à son propos un certain nombre de questions*" [our purpose, moreover, is not to establish a summary of details, but to present the Western film and to pose a certain number of questions as to its design]. Too often what has been written in English on Western films is nothing more than "*un bilan de curiosa,*" and when, rarely, questions have been posed, they have been almost invariably superficial. Leutrat divided his overall treatment of the Western into three sections, titled *le genre*, *le récit*, and *le discours*, a structure which of itself indicates the ultimate focus of his study and his basic approach. In *le discours* section of *Le Western*, Leutrat found himself equally at home appealing to Henry Nash Smith's remark in *Virgin Land* (Harvard University Press, 1950) about "*l'ambivalence liée au monde de l'Quest lorsqu'il étudie le myth créé autour de la personne de Daniel Boone*" [the ambivalence connected with the world of the American West when one studies the myth created around the person of Daniel Boone] and reasoning beyond this to the resume of antinomies between the wilderness and civilization which Jim Kitses developed in *Horizons West* and concluding that "*a l'intérieur d'une même période, dans l'oeuvre d'un seul auteur, ou dans le cadre d'un film unique, il est possible de voir l'oeuvre le systéme d'antinomies dont Jim Kitses a dressé la liste*" [in the interior of even one period, within the work of a single *auteur*, or within the framework of one unique film, it is possible to perceive in the work that system of antinomies of which Jim Kitses has composed a list]. Such a statement should be considered in the light of Andrew Tudor's warning in *Theories of Film* (Viking, 1973): "...There is no *a priori* reason for employing dichotomization, particularly when it is assumed — as it frequently is — that these dichotomically related themes are inherent in the films themselves independent of the observer. Dichotomization can be at best only an epistemological weapon. Its claim to ontological universality is deeply problematic."

All this notwithstanding, Leutrat's book, calling upon a totality of sources and techniques, should be definitely translated into English; it might serve readily as a paradigm for future criticism of the Western film; and, at the very least, one ought not write critically of the Western film henceforth without first having read it.

McClure, Arthur F., and Ken D. Jones, *Heroes, Heavies, and Sagebrush: A Pictorial History of the "B" Western Players* (A.S. Barnes, 1972).

To use Leutrat's phrase, this is *"un bilan de curiosa,"* a summary of details about the public biographies of the principal players in Hollywood budget Westerns during the era from 1929 through 1954, or a bit beyond. The word "public" must be stressed because the brief biographies of these men contain nothing very personal and certainly nothing compromising. The sections of the book are devoted to heroes, sidekicks, heavies, Indians, and assorted players. They reflect, by exclusion, the minimal role that women played in these films. For the most part, the *terminus a quo* and *terminus ad quem* dates (where a *terminus ad quem* date exists) are correct and the biographical information is generally (but *not always*) reliable, if sketchy. The *terminus ad quem* dates are, of course, valid only as of the publication date of this book.

Meyer, William R., *The Making of the Great Westerns* (Arlington House, 1979).

In terms of format and lay-out this book can be compared to *The Great Western Pictures* by James Robert Parish and Michael R. Pitts annotated below. Meyer, however, went into much more detail and his book contains only thirty entries. It might be argued that these thirty are not *the* great Westerns, but there is no question that the majority of them have been important events in the history of the Western film. Much of the background and production information Meyer provided is genuinely of interest, but he was an enthusiast of the genre and so you will not find any awareness of generic stereotypes. When, for example, the book deals with *Broken Arrow*, the text sounds more as a 20th-Fox publicity release than anything else: "As usual, the Fox research department thoroughly assembled information on the people and the period of *Broken Arrow*." The reader is told that Delmer Daves was inspired to do the picture when he read a novel titled *"Blood Brothers* [sic] by Elliott Arnold." Admittedly the latter is a minor error, but the inaccuracy of the former is more serious. To include a wrist-cutting blood ceremony practiced among European secret societies and to present it as a bona-fide religious ceremony among the Chiricahua Apaches is not a tribute to either the research department at 20th-Fox or to Daves. But this points up the major problem with Meyer's book. It gives you all the information and misinformation, the production data and the press book hype that Meyer could find on each of these thirty pictures, but never any critical insight into them and his book is wholly without cognizance of the historical reality purportedly being variously represented or distorted in these films (although Meyer devoutly quoted studio claims as to absolute authenticity). The cast listings are less complete than in the Parish/Pitts book. But, as in the case of the Parish/Pitts book, a reader must be specifically interested in one or more of the thirty films Meyer selected for his book to be of much use.

Miller, Don, *Hollywood Corral* (Popular Library, 1976) O.P.

The author of this book appears to have screened a large number of budget Westerns and this first-hand acquaintance is reflected in the text. Miller did not question any of the premises behind "B" Westerns, nor was he concerned with either the personal lives of the players or the history of Western film production. His focus was clearly nostalgic; he accepted the "B" Western as a definite kind of art form and evaluated and compared entries according to the standards implicit in this sub-genre of the Western film. While the book he wrote, therefore, remains another kind of *"bilan de curiosa,"* it is also, undoubtedly, the best informed and comprehensive survey of its kind. "The Western," Miller remarked in the Preface, "was an exhibition of bravery and cowardice, crime and punishment, adventure and romance. To the devotees, it was as familiar, and beloved, as the ancient Chinese plays were and are to their audiences." The analogy is perhaps somewhat strained. The "B" Western seems to hold very little attraction for contemporary audiences.

Nachbar, Jack (ed.), *Focus on the Western* (Prentice-Hall, 1974) O.P.

This volume was an entry in Prentice-Hall's abortive series of film books all of which began with the word *"Focus"* and hence the title. Actually, the book focuses neither on Western fiction nor on Western films. The essays collected by Nachbar were presumably intended to supply subjects for college theme papers and, as such, have for the most part rather limited interest. Robert Warshow's essay on "The Westerner" from his book *The Immediate Experience* (Doubleday, 1962) is included, but the sweeping generalizations Warshow drew from seeing only a handful of Western films are dubious in the extreme; at one point he criticized Gene Autry and Roy Rogers at the same time as he confessed to having never seen any of their films. Nachbar stated in his Introduction that the three final essays in the book all "agree that contemporary Westerns are groping for a new myth of the American experience, one which might include an admission of past sins and an acknowledgment that the end of the frontier has been reached." On the face of it this would seem an impossible objective and Ralph Brauer seemed to mirror this sentiment in his essay when he concluded that "in the work of Peckinpah, Hellman, and Altman the options are closing and those who believe them to be open or who fight to keep them open are those who suffer the most." It is also worth noting that those film directors who promoted this perspective in their films, particularly in the Seventies, were presenting an allegory of modern life in America and were projecting it backwards into American history. The sense of American destiny was already lost by the Sixties and these films did and could do nothing to restore it.

Parish, James Robert, and Michael R. Pitts, *The Great Western Pictures* (Scarecrow Press, 1976).

The major problem with this book is that of defining who would be likely to read it or find it of use. Most of the text is given over to approximately three hundred short entries, each one devoted to a Western film that the authors felt somehow of significance. The format is standardized so that each entry contains a listing of the principal credits, a short paragraph telling why the film was important or how it came to be made, a plot synopsis, concluding with quotations of critical assessments from various sources. I have no objection to this format. It was the format we devised for film retrospectives when I was editing and publishing *Views & Reviews* Magazine. However, to be of general reference use, this procedure would have had to be followed for *all* Western films; as it is, most of the films are treated adequately, provided the reader is interested in any, some, or all of the Westerns selected and, provided further, that no more detailed information than what is supplied is required.

Parkinson, Michael, and Clyde Jeavons, *A Pictorial History of Westerns* (Hamlyn, 1972) O.P.

The similarity between the title of this book and the one by Everson mentioned above is more than coincidental since both books are ostensibly on the same subject. Parkinson and Jeavons were somewhat less prone to flagrant error than Everson, but there is nonetheless an extraordinary amount of misinformation for such a brief text (and some of it, certainly, was cribbed outright from Everson's text). The only attraction of this book, as is also the case with Everson's, is the number of interesting photo illustrations, some of which have the added and unique advantage of being color reproductions.

Pilkington, William T., and Don Graham, (eds.), *Western Movies* (University of New Mexico Press, 1979).

This book is an even more unlikely proposition than *The Great Western Pictures*. It is limited to twelve essays on fourteen Western films. Unlike *The Great Western Pictures*, no credits are provided; the essays themselves seem all to have been written by college professors and, in any case, they treat a Western film as if it were a novel. The standard procedure here was to retell the plot, and, throughout the retelling, make observations on the characters involved in the action, look for potential symbolism, speculate as to what the director's intention may have been, and usually prove some thesis, i.e., some academic interpretation of what the film *really* means. The majority of the professors who contributed to this volume were English teachers and what the book tends best to illustrate is that traditional subjects for academic writing, such as Henry James, have either lost their fascination or have been exhausted and new subjects for the application of the same Modern Language Association style-sheet formulary writing with its cumbersome and often irritating footnotes had to be found. The eight critical approaches to the Western film outlined by the editors in their Introduction have been subjected to an exhaustive critique by me in my book, *The American West in Film* (see below).

Rainey, Buck, *Saddle Aces of the Cinema* (A.S. Barnes, 1980).

There are fifteen "saddle aces" included in this volume, from the familiar — Tom Mix, Buck Jones, Gene Autry — to the downright obscure — Reb Russell, Al Hoxie — and some in between. Each of the fifteen chapters is divided into a career survey and a filmography. The career surveys are factually quite reliable and may be considered definitive for the personalities included, as opposed to earlier efforts by Corneau, Lahue, and others. There is however, no critical or psychological insight provided — as McClure and Jones, Rainey confined himself to *"un bilan de curiosa"* about the public careers of his subjects — and the tone often becomes maudlin, such as summing up Buck Jones by saying, "time only magnifies his memory and popularity with those who remember yesterday's Saturdays and a childhood never outgrown," or writing, "Rex Bell's saddle is empty — but not his place in the hearts of Western film addicts." I would question, indeed, how many people today, even among those who like Westerns, have ever heard of Rex Bell. The best reference feature about the book is the detailed filmographies which are particularly important — because difficult to find — for films made during the early silent era.

Rieupeyrout, Jean Louis, *La Grande Aventure de Western*: 1894–1964 (Éditions du Cerf).

This book was an expansion and perpetuation of Rieupeyrout's earlier study of the Western film entitled *Le Western ou Le Cinéma Américain par excellence* (Éditions du Cerf, 1954) for which André Bazin wrote by way of an Introduction his essay known by the same title. In this later book Rieupeyrout addressed virtually every aspect of the Western film: literary sources and prototypes, the history of American film production and the early producing companies, the major events and personalities of Western American history, the screen images of the leading Western players including the matinee cowboy heroes, the cinematic styles and contributions of all the principal directors of Western films, and a critical evaluation of numerous individual Westerns. He was not, however, sensitively aware of the process of stereotyping or, unlike Leutrat, did he devise a coherent critical approach for treating these varying aspects of Western films.

The book is especially valuable for its bibliography and for the many references throughout the text to various articles appearing in French periodicals during the years with which Rieupeyrout was concerned. *"Sa réputation,"* Rieupeyrout wrote about movie cowboy Hoot Gibson — to give but one example — , *"de témérité alla de pair avec celle de ses capacitiés de comique dont on ne savait trop si elles relevaient d'un talent originel ou de l'application mise à le simuler"* [one does not know very well if his reputation for temerity which is on a par with that of his comic abilities is the result of an original talent or merely diligent shamming]. To which, quoting Albert Bonneau in *Cinémagazine* in 1926, he added, "'*le mimique embarrassée de Hoot Gibson, son air gauche ont le don de déchaîner inévitablement le rire. Il ne se contente pas d'être un cavalier de premier ordre, il soigne son jeu et tend à le rendre le plus vrai possible....*'" [the embarrassed mimicry of Hoot Gibson, his left-handed air have inevitably the tendency of inspiring laughter. He is not content to be just a cavalier of the first order; he has his fun in such a way as to reveal the most truth possible ...]. One will look without success for this kind of appreciation of Gibson's comic ability among American and British critics, if they so much as comment on him.

It would be difficult, if not impossible, to demonstrate that "*la Dallas de Ford*" (the prostitute in John Ford's *Stagecoach*) "*n'etait-elle pas conforme en tout point à la Élisabeth Rousset, fille légère chez Maupassant*" [does not she conform in all ways with Elisabeth Rousset, that woman of easy virtue in Maupassant's] famed short story "*Boule-de-suif*" ["Pot of Fat"], although, unquestionably, by his own admission Ford was influenced to a degree by the character in the story. Usually, however, Rieupeyrout's comments about a director of Western films are somewhat more cogent, such as his observation that "*John Ford y a créé* [in his Westerns] *un monde à part qui exige, pour être apprécié, une sympathie profonde avec ses personnages et leur époque, vus avec l'inévitable distorsion de la légende à la manière d'un Bret Harte et de tous les conteurs de noble lignée*" [John Ford has created (in his Westerns) a world apart which demands, in order to be appreciated, a profound sympathy with its personalities and their epoch, viewed through the inevitably distorting lens of legend, quite after the manner of a Bret Harte and all those storytellers of that noble line]. In this context it becomes easier to discern the links in Ford's career which connect his film version of *The Outcasts of Poker Flat* (Universal, 1919) with *Stagecoach* twenty years later. Rieupeyrout's book is filled with a richness of insight and it definitely deserves to be translated into English.

Rothel, David, *The Singing Cowboys* (A.S. Barnes, 1978).

Extreme caution must be exercised in making use of this book. There are chapters devoted to eight singing cowboys—that is, movie cowboys who sang in their films—and a chapter on "unsung singing cowboys." The major chapters of the book, accounting for almost half its contents, are devoted to Gene Autry and Roy Rogers and Rothel depended very much on personal interviews with these two for his facts—hence the reason to exercise caution. Autry, in particular, had many of his facts wrong, but there are problems with many of the other recorded interviews as well, those with Rogers, Eddie Dean, Jimmy Wakely, and Monte Hale. The discographies for these performers are not really of professional reference value. The strong points—perhaps the only strong points—of the book are the photo illustrations and the somewhat detailed filmographies, especially those of Autry's and Rogers' films since they have brief plot synopses; but here, again, one is confronted with the dilemma of so many books of this kind where there is almost as much misinformation as reliable factual history.

Tuska, Jon, *The Filming of the West* (Doubleday, 1976) O.P.; *The Vanishing Legion: A History of Mascot Pictures* 1927–1935 (McFarland, 1982); *The American West in Film* (Greenwood Press, 1985).

My earlier book, *The Filming of the West*, deals with the personal as well as the professional lives of those most intimately and significantly associated with Western film production from 1903 until the middle Seventies. It was a book which, because so many of the people included in it were still alive, had to settle quite often for a sort of compromised and suggestive portraiture. It was withdrawn in 1978 and now is in the process of extensive revision, ultimately to be published again under this title but with much more detail about production history and biographical portraits of principal players.

The Filming of the West is concerned with the history, development, and demise of production units and companies specializing in Westerns and with those who manufactured, packaged, and marketed Western heroes and heroism for mass consumption and personal profit. Playing movie cowboys very often had the effect of bringing about the psychological ruin of the men who were cast in these roles and this part of the story, to my way of thinking, is indelibly linked with the portrayal of heroes on the screen, pretending and becoming well known for being someone who could not exist in reality and who represents an idealized, dehumanized, impossible *modus vivendi*.

The American West in Film, as the title suggests, is not about the *filming* of the West, but rather about what was filmed, a comparison of the fantasies about the American West recorded on film with the historical and physical reality of the American West. This volume is intended as a comprehensive overview of Western films, grouped by decade, by theme, in terms of frontier legends, and, lastly, the ideological contents of Western films in terms of the many stereotypes, particularly about women and other minorities, among them and perhaps above all Native Americans.

The Vanishing Legion is somewhat more circumscribed in scope, focusing on the history of a single motion picture company, one that merged in 1935 to form Republic studios. The book is of relevance because of the contribution Mascot made to Western film production, including introducing the Gene Autry singing Westerns, and the intimate portraits of Tom Mix, Ken Maynard, and Autry, showing the effects of their public personae on their private lives.

Wright, Will, *Sixguns & Society: A Structural Study of the Western* (University of California Press, 1975) O.P.

While it would not be an exaggeration to say that there is little of value in the contents of this book, that is not to say that the idea of a structural approach to the Western film cannot be fruitful. Peter Wollen, for example, in his book, *Signs and Meaning in the Cinema* (Indiana University Press, 1973), applied a structural analysis to John Ford's films with some very interesting *and* some rather ridiculous results. One of the former would be tracing the "vagrancy versus home antinomy" through several of Ford's films; one of the latter would be concluding that Ford was a more versatile director than Howard Hawks. In contrast, Wright's prose is turgid and academic and his approach found him writing that "as a myth the Western consists of paradigmatic and syntagmatic structures — conceptual oppositions and narrative functions." Wright went over much the same ground that Christian Metz did in his *Film Language* (Oxford University Press, 1974) and *Language and Cinema* (Mouton, 1974) but without anything near Metz' success at explaining the operation of a film and understanding the experience of the medium in terms of structural paradigms and syntagms; nor had Wright, according to his text, read Metz' books. Compared with Metz' and Wollen's structural studies of film in general and Leutrat's, Rieupeyrout's, and Kitses' structural studies of the Western, Wright's study is abysmal. What is probably even more needed than a structural analysis of the Western film, however, would be the kind of study Siegfried Kracauer did of the German film industry in *From Caligari to Hitler* (Princeton University Press, 1947). French and Lenihan both failed at it, and I have no more than surveyed the terrain; but the potential is there.

It is evident, of course, that in the above listing no mention has been made of books by or about film directors notably associated with Western films, with the exception of Kitses' *Horizons West*. There is quite a wide assortment of these, but only a few can be said to have a special significance for the reader interested in the history and ideological orientations of the Western film.

Of those books which have appeared about John Ford and which can, in good conscience, be recommended, whatever their individual drawbacks, the foremost would be *John Ford* (University of California Press, 1978; revised edition) by Peter Bogdanovich simply because it contains the results of an extensive interview with Ford himself. One of the better critical appraisals of Ford's Western films in the context of his total screen work is *The Cinema of John Ford* (Tantivy/A.S. Barnes, 1971) by John Baxter. Both Andrew Sinclair in *John Ford: A Biography* (Dial, 1979) and Dan Ford, a grandson, in *Pappy: The Life of John Ford* (Prentice-Hall, 1979) have written biographical treatments of Ford, but neither is wholly satisfying. Sinclair's assertion that Yakima Canutt "was one of Ford's beloved stuntmen" should be contrasted with the interview with Canutt contained in my career study of him in *Close-Up: The Contract Director* (Scarecrow Press, 1976). Sinclair claimed that Tom Mix deserted the U.S. Army "to go and fight as a soldier of fortune in the Boer War" and cited in support *The Filming of the West*. Had he more closely read what I wrote about Mix, he would have realized that Mix deserted not to become a soldier of fortune anywhere but in order to get married because his fiancée refused to marry him while he was in the service. Quixotically, Sinclair admitted that Ford's version of the O.K. corral gunfight was inaccurately staged, but when he wanted to tell the reader the actual way it happened he did not find out for himself but quoted one of Ford's former film editors who got the facts (albeit differently) as wrong as Ford had them! Neither Ford nor Sinclair were aware, apparently, that Doc Holliday was a dentist and not a medical doctor. Dan Ford got into fewer problems of this kind because he was less intent on providing a commentary on Ford's films or their contents and concentrated more on the details of Ford's life. However, even here there were problems: Sinclair claimed that Harry Carey died of a heart attack induced by a black widow spider bite; Dan Ford insisted that Carey died of cancer. Only if you put the two of them together — Carey had cancer of the lungs when he was bit by a black widow spider, the poison inducing a myocardial infarction — would you have all the medical data; but this is not always the case and neither is even reasonably critical of Ford's films. Dan Ford in this respect, however, is somewhat superior since he can recognize in an author as James Warner Bellah a racist and Indian-hater whereas Sinclair confronted by the same phenomenon — the role of Indians in Ford's Westerns — became an apologist.

Howard Hawks, although ultimately a more capable film director than Ford, has been less than adequately represented in the secondary literature about his life and his screen work. An entire section of my career study on him contained in *Close-Up: The Contract Director* deals with Hawks' contribution to the Western as does a chapter from *The American West in Film* and a chapter from Donald C. Willis' book *The Films of Howard Hawks* (Scarecrow Press, 1975). Of more peripheral interest but by no means to be ignored are the pertinent sections in *Focus on Howard Hawks* (Prentice-Hall, 1972) edited by Joseph McBride, now out of print, the interview in *The Men Who Made the Movies* (Atheneum, 1975) by Richard Schickel, also out of print, as well as the critical essay "Howard Hawks" by John Belton in Volume 3 of *The Hollywood Professionals* (Tantivy/A.S. Barnes, 1974).

The Men Who Made the Movies also includes interviews with William Wellman and Raoul Walsh, but in each instance these should be augmented, in Wellman's case with his often hard-to-follow autobiography, *A Short Time for Insanity* (Hawthorn, 1974), now out of print, and "William Wellman," a career study by David Wilson in *Close-Up: The Hollywood Director* (Scarecrow Press, 1978), and in Walsh's case with his autobiography, *Each Man in His Time* (Farrar, Straus, 1974), also out of print. Another book of interviews with film directors is *The Director's Event* (Atheneum, 1970) by Eric Sherman and Martin Rubin; although out of print, it has interviews with Peter Bogdanovich, Sam Fuller, Arthur Penn, Abraham Polonsky, and Budd Boetticher. My one regret is that the interviews were not more searching.

Edward Dmytryk's autobiography, *It's a Hell of a Life But Not a Bad Living* (Times Books, 1978), is of interest regarding his reflections on his Western, *Warlock* (20th-Fox, 1958), based on Oakley Hall's novel of the same title, and *Shalako* (Cinerama, 1968), based on a formulary Western by Louis L'Amour. Also among Dmytryk's credits is *Broken Lance* (20th-Fox, 1954), an above average Western.

Paul Seydor's *Peckinpah: The Western Films* (University of Illinois Press, 1980) is an essay in apologetics, defending Peckinpah against his critics, and is as much a study of American literature as Peckinpah's Westerns, Seydor placing Peckinpah somewhere between Nathaniel Hawthorne and Norman Mailer. The book would have benefitted had its author known more about Western American history and Western films. I would cite as more reliable Max Evans' memoir of the filming of *The Ballad of Cable Hogue* in *Sam Peckinpah: Master of Violence* (University of South Dakota Press, 1972), Kitses' chapter on him, and my own career study "Sam Peckinpah" in *Close-Up: The Contemporary Director* (Scarecrow Press, 1981).

Beyond these, I would recommend among directors' studies Vicki Piekarski's career study of "Sydney Pollack" in *Close-Up: The Contemporary Director*, my career study "Henry King" in *Close-Up: The Hollywood Director*, and Clive Denton's chapter "Henry King" in Volume 2 of *The Hollywood Professionals* (Tantivy/A.S. Barnes, 1974).

The area of star biographies and autobiographies is, by comparison a virtual wasteland of misinformation and fantasy. Almost none of them are to be trusted. Three such books, however, are worth consulting, provided they are regarded with careful skepticism, William S. Hart's autobiography, *My Life East and West* (1929; Benjamin Blom, 1968), Tim McCoy's *Tim McCoy Remembers the West* (Doubleday, 1977) written with Ronald McCoy, now out of print as is Maurice Zolotow's *Shooting Star: A Biography of John Wayne* (Simon & Schuster, 1974).

The major problem that I perceive as rampant in the field of criticism of Western films seems to be caused, first of all, by the relative inaccessibility of the majority of these pictures for the purpose of protracted study and evaluation. When you come right down to it, the paucity of so much that has been written is the direct result of the various critics not being able to see the films about which they wish to write. The film industry, generally, has been uncooperative and the archives both in the United States and abroad do not have very comprehensive collections. There just is not funding available, even when an archive might gain control of negative materials, to have prints struck for purposes of research screenings. The emergence of video cassettes might contribute in a significant way to alleviating this difficulty, but until it does what is likely to continue is the present practice of relying on erroneous plot synopses from old reviews or from nostalgia books, which most often only serves to perpetuate errors and to distort accurate evaluations. The situation is so bad that over the years on numerous occasions film companies and the television networks have contacted me to furnish them with information about a particular Western film or to render a plot synopsis. In very many cases, when it comes to vintage films, the titles are sold and plot synopses have been provided by me for program listings before a print is struck. Almost as many times I have been consulted by archives when they have been offered a print or negative material on a title, asking if in my opinion it is worth storing and preserving. It took me ten years, screening on the average two Western films a day, to see virtually all that has survived. I do not believe it is possible to conduct a truly effective and valid media study without this kind of exposure, but I know that to do this is beyond the ability of most researchers, granted they had the inclination and dedication. I will, however, close these remarks with this observation. My basic response, after having undertaken this ordeal, was a profound sense of sorrow that with so much money and talent and time expended the results were consistently so mediocre. The Western film has yet to approach with even moderate success the artistry of much of the best in Western fiction.

Throughout its history, the Western film has, for the most part, remained a sentimental entertainment, and I am not at all certain if it can survive as a film genre in an artistic climate in which sentimentality and the American agrarian dream have increasingly less currency in the emotional lives of the viewers. Speaking only for myself, I would like to see Western films that — embodying well-made stories with beginnings, middles, and ends — depict events and people with historical accuracy and truthfulness because I am convinced there is more to be learned from the history of the American West as it happened than there can ever be profit in comforting fantasies about the American West as it never was and could never have been. However, Western films have been doing the latter for so long and so many of them have been made, their imagery, plots, and stereotypical characters all being so familiar, I do not know if such a transition as I have suggested would be feasible from a commerical point of view. Indeed, to tell of the history of the West as it happened is considered by many people to be inappropriate, definitely depressing, and, in any case, unAmerican; and, therefore, Robert Altman may have been correct: the best we can ever hope for is for the Greatest Show on Earth to go on and on and on. A Western film that is not a mandate to go forward proudly, a Western film that reveals the crimes and follies of the past rather than pretending to find only triumphs and righteousness in that past, a Western film with still enough sentimentality to show people pulling together in a common cause, be it only a drunken foray to exterminate Indians, where nearly everyone is consumed by some form of materialism and calling it the American dream? — I do not know, as I have said, if such a Western would be commercially feasible. The few attempts in this direction have not been especially successful and many of them have been dismal failures. Yet, unless some alteration along these lines is made, if there are any Westerns at all in the future, I imagine they will only be more of the same. It is indeed ironic that in telling about some of the most *unconventional* generations of human beings the world has even known, we should have become so hopelessly mired in these rigid, formulary conventions. Ironic, but I do not think it has been accidental. Freud perhaps stated it best when he remarked that *"ein Nichtverstehen ist oft ein Nichtverstehenwollen"* [not understanding is often not wanting to understand].

Television Westerns

by Ralph Brauer

The early days of the TV Western were days of transition as "B" Western stars as William Boyd playing Hopalong Cassidy, Gene Autry, and Roy Rogers moved from movies into television. Autry, who can be called the pioneer of the TV Western, made the move in 1947 and, after surviving suits by film distributors and producers who felt his TV films would draw audiences away from the theatres, he established himself as the leading producer of early TV Westerns, producing shows as *The Range Rider* (syndicated 1951–1953), *Annie Oakley* (ABC, 1953–1958), as well as his own show under the banner of Flying A Productions. Other stars as Rogers and Clayton Moore playing The Long Ranger followed Autry's lead and soon the screen was filled with half-hour Western films that were being produced solely for television, Ziv Productions beginning to film *Cisco Kid* episodes in color in 1951 anticipating the advent of color television.

All of these early Westerns were produced for children and featured formulary heroes (Autry, Rogers, The Lone Ranger) who rode highly intelligent, almost magical horses (Champion, Trigger, Silver) and were accompanied by sidekicks (Pat Buttram, Pat Brady, Tonto). More often than not the sidekick role was played for laughs (Buttram, Brady) or was an outsider (Tonto). Together the hero, his magical horse, and sidekick roamed the wide, open spaces as free individuals with no social ties, righting wrongs in terms of a strict moral code. By and large these early "horse" Westerns featured little violence and almost no killing.

In September, 1955, a new TV Western series, *The Life and Legend of Wyatt Earp* (ABC, 1955–1961), made its debut. Designed by its producers as an "adult" Western, *Wyatt Earp* began a new phase of the TV Western, a phase that featured more violence, gunplay, and "adult" relationships. *Earp* was followed by shows as *Have Gun, Will Travel* (CBS, 1957–1963), *Lawman* (ABC, 1958–1962), *Wanted: Dead or Alive* (CBS, 1958–1961), and, in 1955, *Gunsmoke* (CBS, 1955–1975), which became the longest running Western series of them all. In 1959, the peak year of the adult Western, there were twenty-eight Westerns on the air, producing 570 hours of new footage — far more than Hollywood produced during the peak years of the "B" Western craze.

In the "adult" Western the hero became an organization man, taking a job such as lawman or bounty hunter with the result that the code personified by Autry and Rogers became linked as much to the job as to the individual. Moreover, the code became not so much a series of moral values but a set of legal guarantees and procedures. The hero and the code became a part of society. Linked to the heroes were an array of outlandish weapons creating a TV "arms race" that paralleled the nuclear paranoia of the late Fifties. Wyatt Earp (Hugh O'Brien) carried the sixteen-inch Buntline Special, Josh Randal (Steve McQueen) of *Wanted: Dead or Alive* carried a custom chopped shotgun in his holster, Lucas McCain (Chuck Connors) of *The Rifleman* (ABC, 1958–1962) carried a modified rifle with the uncanny ability to outfire anything but a modern machine gun. The magical horse of the early Westerns disappeared and was replaced by nondescript horses. One hero, Paladin (Richard Boone) in *Have Gun, Will Travel*, was a bounty hunter who passed out business cards and rented his horses at the livery stable. The horse became only an ornament on Paladin's holster and business card.

Almost at the same time the gun Westerns were reaching their peak saturation point, two new Westerns, *Wagon Train* (NBC, ABC, 1957–1965) and *Rawhide* (CBS, 1958–1966), made their appearance. Establishing a formula of a free-roaming male group possessing both a social order and a moral order, these two Western series spawned several imitators, including *Iron Horse* (ABC, 1966–1968) and *Laredo* (NBC, 1965–1967). Starring Eric Fleming and Clint Eastwood, *Rawhide* was as an athletic team led by an autocratic coach who laid down rules of behavior that the crew must follow. As *Rawhide*, *Wagon Train* was run by a team with the wagonmaster (Ward Bond) as absolute boss (when Bond died, he was replaced by John McIntyre in the role). The emphasis, though, in *Wagon Train* was more on community than on the team idea of *Rawhide*. Virtually a microcosm of American society, the wagon train journeyed West, trying to hold itself together in the face of internal and external pressures.

In 1959, with the advent of *Bonanza* (NBC, 1959–1973), the TV cowboy settled down. Featuring the motherless family of father Ben Cartwright (Lorne Green) and sons Adam (Pernell Roberts), Hoss (Dan Blocker), and Little Joe (Michael Landon), *Bonanza* dealt with the adventures of the Cartwright family as they defended their large ranch, the Ponderosa. The property motif of *Bonanza* was followed by similar property shows as *The Big Valley* (ABC, 1965–1969) featuring Barbara Stanwyck and Lee Majors, *The Virginian* (NBC, 1962–1970) featuring Lee J. Cobb and James Drury, and *The High Chaparral* (NBC, 1967–1971) featuring Cameron Mitchell and Leif Erickson. In the late Sixties these property shows, which featured families defending large ranches, came to dominate TV Western programming. Paralleling the conservative "law and order" philosophy of the Nixon administration, the property shows emphasized legal procedures and social order. Gone was the moral code of the free, roaming hero of the early days of the TV Western, the free individual was regarded with suspicion and the open prairie was a place to be feared. Even other Westerns on the air, as *Gunsmoke*, tended to follow the property Western's fear of the prairie and its emphasis on law and order.

With the mid Seventies, the TV Westerns fell on hard times. *Bonanza* left the air in 1973, followed by *Gunsmoke* in 1975. Various types of Westerns were aired in the late Seventies, including *How the West Was Won* with former *Gunsmoke* star James Arness and *Little House on the Prairie* with former *Bonanza* star Michael Landon, but their success has been sporadic.

Name Index

407

Title Index

419